11·7·11   56878   35.05

Praise for the first edition of *An Introduction to the New Testament*

"C. B. Puskas is undoubtedly an authority on the New Testament. All readers interested in the New Testament will welcome this work."

—*Neotestamentica*

"Puskas has written a remarkable book. I have seldom found a New Testament text which does what I want to do—namely, introduce the student to text criticism, form, redaction, and literary criticism. Also there should be something about the Greek and Jewish backgrounds and introductory views of each of the gospels. The man does the job admirably. I am rather choosy in textbooks and I am just rejoicing in your textbook and hope I can use it for many years to come"

—W. R. Stegner

"The author of this work has undertaken a formidable task and accomplished it in a masterful and quite balanced fashion, with a firm stamp of scholarly integrity. This is truly an introduction to the New Testament, with emphasis on the kind of world in which it took shape . . . I recommend this book not only for textbook use by college or seminary students, but also to anyone who simply wishes to be better informed about the New Testament, its origins, its literary forms, its reading publics, and its history of transmission, including modern texts and translations."

—Frederick W. Danker

"Puskas has a thorough acquaintance with the significant secondary literature and makes a genuine effort to be non-sectarian. Teachers will delight in his imaginative presentation, which leads the reader, step by step, into a deeper appreciation of the nature and content of the individual message of each NT author."

—Robert F. O'Toole, SJ

"This book is designed for students beginning serious exegetical study and admirably meets their needs."

—*Revue Biblique*

"Geared for the student . . . a teacher-aided textbook."

—*Religious Studies Review*

"Provides a concise treatment of not only the New Testament literature, but also Judaism in the Greco-Roman world, New Testament Greek, textual criticism, the development of the New Testament canon, and English versions."

—M. A. SEIFRID

"A necessarily select, but well-written compendium of information that will serve the uninitiated . . . as a point of departure for further study. Puskas . . . helpfully signposts the pertinent primary and secondary material; and tackles a good number of the fundamental issues with an eminent reasonableness."

—EVANGELICAL QUARTERLY

"This book provides a very good service to students of theology and to the persons who try to approach the world of the NT and obtain information on the Christian origins."

—ESTUDIOS BÍBLICOS

AN INTRODUCTION TO THE NEW TESTAMENT

AN INTRODUCTION TO THE NEW TESTAMENT

Second Edition

Charles B. Puskas *and*
C. Michael Robbins

CASCADE *Books* · Eugene, Oregon

AN INTRODUCTION TO THE NEW TESTAMENT
Second Edition

Cascade Books
An Imprint of Wipf and Stock Publishers
199 W. 8th Ave. Suite 3
Eugene, OR 97401

www.wipfandstock.com

ISBN 13: 978-1-60608-785-5

Cataloging-in-Publication data:

Puskas, Charles B.

An introduction to the New Testament / Charles B. Puskas and C. Michael Robbins—second edition.

xx + 374 p.; 25.4 cm. Includes bibliographical references and indexes.

ISBN 13: 978-1-60608-785-5

1. Bible. N.T.—Introductions. 2. Bible. N.T.—Textbooks. I. Robbins, C. Michael, 1955–. II. Title.

BS2330.2 P87 2011

Manufactured in the U.S.A.

Acknowledgments

Unless otherwise noted, all Scripture quotations contained herein are from the New Revised Standard Version Bible, copyright © 1989 by the Division of Christian Education of the National Council of the Churches of Christ in the U.S.A., and are used with permission. All rights reserved.

The authors and publisher gratefully acknowledge the permission to use diagrams and photos from:

Codex Sinaiticus © British Library Board. All rights reserved.

R. E. Brown, "Not Jewish Christianity and Gentile Christianity, but Types of Jewish/Gentile Christianity." *Catholic Biblical Quarterly* 45 (1983) 74–79.

Raymond E. Brown and John P Meier, *Antioch and Rome*. Copyright © 1983 by Paulist Press.

W. G. Doty, *Letters in Primitive Christianity*. Copyright © 1973 by Fortress Press.

J. Harold Greenlee, *Introduction to New Testament Textual Criticism*, fig. 4, p. 23. Copyright © 1995 Hendrickson Publishers.

The Works of Josephus: Complete and Unabridged Edition, maps, pp. 927, 930. Copyright © 1987 Hendrickson Publishers.

H. W. Hoehner, *Chronological Aspects of the Life of Christ*. Copyright © 1978 by the Zondervan Corporation.

H. Wayne House, *Chronological and Background Charts of the New Testament*. Copyright © 2009 by the Zondervan Corporation.

Robert Jewett, *A Chronology of Paul's Life*. Copyright © 1979 Fortress Press.

Philip L. Shuler, *A Genre for the Gospels: the Biographical Character of Matthew*, pp. 91–106. Copyright ©1982 Fortress Press.

Charles B. Puskas and David Crump, *An Introduction to the Gospels and Acts*. Copyright © 2009 Wm. B. Eerdmans.

Arch of Titus and Herodian Temple © Charles B. Puskas. All rights reserved.

Statue of Apostle Paul © Ralph Harris. All rights reserved.

Cave 4 at Qumran © R. Hodge. All rights reserved.

Isis cult ceremony © National Archaeological Museum, Naples. All rights reserved.

Caesar Augustus and The Temple of Athena Parthenos © iStock Photo, Calgary, Alberta, Canada. All rights reserved.

Chester Beatty Papyris II (P46, third century) © Chester Beatty Museum. All rights reserved.

Contents

List of Figures, Charts, and Maps

Abbreviations

Abbreviations for journals, periodicals, major reference works, ancient works, and series follow those of *The SBL Handbook of Style: For Ancient Near Eastern, Biblical, and Early Christian Studies*, edited by Patrick H. Alexander et al., Peabody, MA: Hendrickson, 1999; and also *The Chicago Manual of Style*, 15th edition, Chicago: University of Chicago Press, 2003. Below are a selection of those regularly used in this book. Dates are included in some titles to distinguish them from earlier editions. Abbreviations (e.g., for journals, encyclopedias, and series) are used in the bibliography.

ANCIENT WORKS

Adv. Haer.	Irenaeus, *Against Heresies*
Ag. Ap.	Josephus, *Against Apion*
Anab.	*Anabasis Alexandri* (Arrian/Xenophon)
Ann.	Tacitus, *Annals*
Ant.	Josephus, *Antiquities of the Jews*
Apoc. Adam	*Apocalypse of Adam*
Apoc. Pet.	*Apocalypse of Peter*
ʿAbod. Zar.	*ʿAbodah Zarah*
Adv. Marc.	Tertullian, *Against Marcion*
1 Apol.	Justin Martyr, *First Apology*
b.	Babylonian Talmud
Barn.	*Barnabas*
Ber.	*Berakot*
Carn. Chr.	Tertullian, *De Carne Christi* (*On the Flesh of Christ*)
Cher.	Philo, *On the Cherubim*
1 Clem.	*1 Clement*
Contempl. Life	Philo, *On the Contemplative Life*
De Orat.	Cicero, *De Oratore*
Dial.	Justin Martyr, *Dialogue with Trypho*
Did.	*Didache*
Embassy	Philo, *On the Embassy to Gaius*
Ep.	*Epistles*
Flacc.	Philo, *Against Flaccus*
Gos. Phil.	*Gospel of Philip*
Gos. Thom.	*Gospel of Thomas*
Haer.	Hippolytus, *Refutation of All Heresies*
Hist.	*History* (separate works by Herodotus, Polybius, Tacitus, and Thucydides)
Hist. eccl.	Eusebius, *Ecclesiastical History*
Hom.	*Homilies* (Pseudo-Clementines)
Hom.1 on Matt	John Chrysostom, *First Homily on Matthew*
Ign. Eph.	Ignatius, *Letter to the Ephesians*
Ign. Magn.	Ignatius, *Letter to the Magnesians*

Ign. *Phld.*	Ignatius, *Letter to the Philadelphians*
Ign. *Pol.*	Ignatius, *Letter to Polycarp*
Ign. *Smyrn.*	Ignatius, *Letter to the Smyrnaeans*
Ign. *Trall.*	Ignatius, *Letter to the Trallians*
Inv.	Cicero, *De Inventione*
Jub.	Jubilees
Ketub.	Ketubbot
Laws	Cicero, *On the Laws*
Life	Josephus, *The Life*
Lives	Diogenes Laertius, *Lives of the Eminent Philosophers*
Lives	Plutarch, *Lives of the Noble Grecians and Romans*
m.	Mishnah tractates
m. sanh.	Mishnah *Sanhedrin*
Mart. Pol.	*Martyrdom of Polycarp*
Meg.	*Megillah*
Menaḥ	*Menaḥot*
Mid.	*Middot*
Midr. Rab.	*Midrash Rabbah*
Mor.	Plutarch, *Moralia*
Nat. Hist.	Pliny, *Natural History*
Num. Rab.	Numbers Rabbah
Pan.	Epiphanius, *Panarion*
Pesaḥ.	*Pesaḥim*
Pol. *Phil.*	Polycarp, *Letter to the Philippians*
Praescr.	Tertullian, *De Praescriptione haereticorum*
Ps-Clem.	Pseudo-Clementines
1QS	Dead Sea Scrolls, *Rule of the Community*
Recog.	*Recognitions* (Pseudo-Clementines)
Roš. Haš.	*Roš Haššanah*
Sanh.	*Sanhedrin*
SBLEJL	Society of Biblical Literature Early Judaism and Its Literature
Sib. Or.	*Sibylline Oracles*
Spec. Laws	Philo, *On the Special Laws*
Strom.	Clement, *Stromateis*
Syb. Or.	*Sybilline Oracles*

Symp.	Plato, *Symposium*
t.	*Tosefta (Talmudic tractates)*
T12Pat	*Testaments of the Twelve Patriarchs*
Taʿan.	*Taʿanit*
TAdam	*Testament of Adam*
Testim. Truth	*Testimony of Truth*
V.Pyth.	Iamblichus, *Life of Pythagoras*
War	Josephus, *Jewish War*
y.	Jerusalem (or Palestinian) Talmud
Yad.	*Yadayim*
Yebam.	*Yebamot*
Zebaḥ.	*Zebaḥim*

MODERN WORKS

AB	Anchor Bible
ABD	*Anchor Bible Dictionary*
ABRL	Anchor Bible Reference Library
AnBib	Analecta biblica
ANF	*The Ante-Nicene Fathers*, edited by Alexander Roberts and James Donaldson. 10 vols. 1881–1887. Peabody, MA: Hendrickson, 1994
ANRW	*Aufstieg und Niedergang der römischen Welt*
ANTC	Abingdon New Testament Commentaries
ATR	*Australasian Theological Review*
AUSS	*Andrews University Seminary Studies*
BBR	*Bulletin for Biblical Research*
BC	*The Beginnings of Christianity*, Part I: *The Acts of the Apostles*, 5 vols.
BDAG	Frederick W. Danker, *A Greek-English Lexicon of the New Testament and Other Early Christian Literature.* 3rd ed. Chicago: University of Chicago Press, 2000

BEEC	Brepols Essays in European Culture. Turnhout, Belgium		Coggins and J. L. Houlden. London: SCM, 1990
BETL	Bibliotheca Ephemeridum theologicarum Lovaniensium	DJG	*Dictionary of Jesus and the Gospels*, edited by Joel B. Green and Scot McKnight. Downers Grove, IL: InterVarsity, 2002
BHT	Beiträge zur historischen Theologie		
BJRL	*Bulletin of the John Rylands University Library of Manchester*	DLNT	*Dictionary of the Later New Testament and Its Development*, edited by R. P. Martin and P. H. Davids. Downers Grove, IL: InterVarsity, 1997
BNTC	Black's New Testament Commentaries		
BTB	*Biblical Theology Bulletin*		
BZAW	Beihefte zur Zeitschrift für die alttestamentliche Wissenschaft	DPL	*Dictionary of Paul and His Letters*, edited by G. F. Hawthorne and R. P. Martin. Downers Grove, IL: InterVarsity, 1993
BZNW	Beihefte zur Zeitschrift für die neutestamentliche Wissenschaft		
		EDB	*Eerdmans Dictionary of the Bible*, edited by David Noel Freedman. Grand Rapids: Eerdmans, 2000
CAH	*The Cambridge Ancient History* (12 vols.), 1921–1939		
CBET	Contributions to Biblical Exegesis and Theology	EdF	Erträge der Forschung
CBR	*Currents in Biblical Research*	EvQ	*Evangelical Quarterly*
CCWJCW	Cambridge Commentaries on Writings of the Jewish and Christian World, 200 BC to AD 200	ExBC	*The Expositor's Bible Commentary*, edited by F. Gaebelein et al. 12 vols. Grand Rapids: Zondervan, 1979
CEB	Common English Bible	FBBS	Facet Books: Biblical Series
CEV	Contemporary English Version (Bible)	FF	Foundations and Facets
CH	*Church History*	GBS	Guides to Biblical Scholarship
CHB	*The Cambridge History of the Bible*	HBD	*Harper's Bible Dictionary*, edited by Paul J. Achtemeier. San Francisco: Harper & Row, 1985
CRINT	Compendia Rerum Iudiacarum ad Novum Testamentum		
CulDB	John J. Pilch, *The Cultural Dictionary of the Bible*, Collegeville, MN: Liturgical, 1999	HibJ	*Hibbert Journal*
		HNTC	Harper's New Testament Commentaries
CurTM	*Currents in Theology and Mission*	HTR	*Harvard Theological Review*
		HTS	*Hervormde Teologiese Studies*
DBI	*Dictionary of Biblical Interpretation*, edited by R. J.	HUCA	*Hebrew Union College Annual*

HUT	Hermeneutische Untersuchungen zur Theologie	JTS	*Journal of Theological Studies*
IB	*The Interpreter's Bible*, edited by G. A. Buttrick et al. 12 vols. Nashville: Abingdon, 1951–57	LCC	Library of Christian Classics
		LCL	Loeb Classical Library
		LCM	Loeb Classical Monographs
IBC	Interpretation: A Bible Commentary for Teaching and Preaching	LEC	Library of Early Christianity
		LSJ	H. Liddell, G., R. Scott, and H. S. Jones, compilers. *A Greek-English Lexicon*. 9th edition with revised supplement. Oxford: Clarendon, 1996
IBS	*Irish Biblical Studies*		
ICC	International Critical Commentary		
IDB	*The Interpreter's Dictionary of the Bible*, edited by G. A. Buttrick. 4 vols. New York: Abingdon, 1962		
		LXX	*Septuaginta: id est vetus testamentum graece juxta LXX interpretes*. 1935. Rev. ed. by R. Hanhart. 2 vols. in one. Stuttgart: Deutsche Bibelgesellschaft, 2006.
IDBSup	*The Interpreter's Dictionary of the Bible: Supplementary Volume*, edited by Keith Crim. Nashville: Abingdon, 1976		
		NA[27]	*Novum Testamentum Graece*. 27th edition, by Eberhard and Erwin Nestle, Barbara and Kurt Aland, et al. Stuttgart: Bibelgesellschaft, 1993
IRT	Issues in Religion and Theology		
ITSORS	Italian Texts and Studies on Religion and Society		
		NASB	New American Standard Bible
JAAR	*Journal of the American Academy of Religion*		
		NCB	New Century Bible
JBR	*Journal of Bible and Religion*	*NCBC*	*New Century Bible Commentary*
JJS	*Journal of Jewish Studies*		
JR	*Journal of Religion*	NCCS	New Covenant Commentary Series
JRS	*Journal of Roman Studies*		
JSHJ	*Journal for the Study of the Historical Jesus*	*Neot*	*Neotestamentica*
		NET Bible	*A New English Translation*
JSJSup	Supplements to the Journal for the Study of Judaism	NHS	Nag Hammadi Studies
		NICNT	New International Commentary on the New Testament
JSNT	*Journal for the Study of the New Testament*		
JSNTSup	Journal for the Study of the New Testament: Supplement Series	*NIDB*	*The New Interpreter's Dictionary of the Bible*, edited by Katharine Doob Sakenfeld. 5 vols. Nashville: Abingdon, 2001–2009
JSP	*Journal for the Study of the Pseudepigrapha*		
JSPSup	Journal for the Study of the Pseudepigrapha: Supplement Series	*NIDNTT*	*The New International Dictionary of New Testament Theology*, edited by Colin Brown. 4 vols.

	Grand Rapids: Zondervan, 1975–85	*SBLHS*	*The SBL Handbook of Style: For Ancient Near Eastern, Biblical, and Early Christian Studies*, edited by Patrick H. Alexander et al. Peabody, MA: Hendrickson, 1999
NIGTC	New International Greek Testament Commentary		
NIV	New International Version		
NJBC	*The New Jerome Biblical Commentary*, edited by Raymond E. Brown et al. Englewood, Cliffs, NJ: Prentice Hall, 1990	SBLMS	Society of Biblical Literature Monograph Series
		SBLSBS	Society of Biblical Literature Sources for Biblical Study
NovTSup	Supplements to Novum Testamentum	SBLSP	Society of Biblical Literature Seminar Papers
NRSV	New Revised Standard Version	SD	Studies and Documents
NTA	*New Testament Apocrypha*, edited by Wilhelm Schneemelcher. Translated and edited by R. McL. Wilson. Rev. ed. Louisville: Westminster John Knox, 1991	*Semeia*	*Semeia: An Experimental Journal for Biblical Criticism*
		SJT	*Scottish Journal of Theology*
		SNTSMS	Society for New Testament Studies Monograph Series
		SNTSU	Studien zum Neuen Testament und seiner Umwelt
NTL	New Testament Library	SP	Sacra Pagina
NTOA	Novum Testamentum et Orbis Antiquus	STDJ	Studies on the Texts of the Desert of Judah
NTS	*New Testament Studies*	*TDNT*	*Theological Dictionary of the New Testament*, edited by G. Kittel and G. Friedrich. Translated by G. W. Bromiley. 10 vols. Grand Rapids: Eerdmans, 1961–1976
NTTS	New Testament Tools and Studies		
OCD	*The Oxford Classical Dictionary*, edited by Simon Hornblower and Anthony Spawforth, 3rd ed. New York: Oxford University Press, 1996		
		TLNT	*Theological Lexicon of the New Testament*, edited by Ceslas Spicq. Translated and edited by J. D. Ernest. 3 vols. Peabody, MA: Hendrickson, 1994
OTP	*The Old Testament Pseudepigrapha*, edited by James H. Charlesworth. 2 vols. Garden City, NY: Doubleday, 1983–1985		
		TSAJ	Texte und Studien zum antiken Judentum
PRSt	*Perspectives in Religious Studies*	UBS⁴	*The Greek New Testament*, edited by Kurt Aland, et al. 4th rev. ed. Stuttgart: Bibelgesellschaft, 1998
PSB	*Princeton Seminary Bulletin*		
RB	*Revue Biblique*		
RelSRev	*Religious Studies Review*		
SBEC	Studies in the Bible and Early Christianity	WBC	Word Biblical Commentary

WDNTECLR	*The Westminster Dictionary of New Testament and Early Christian Literature and Rhetoric*, edited by David E. Aune. Louisville: Westminster John Knox, 2003	ZNW	*Zeitschrift fur die neutesta-mentliche Wissenschaft*
WUNT	Wissenschaftliche Untersuchungen zum Neuen Testament	ZPE	*The Zondervan Pictorial Encyclopedia of the Bible,* edited by M. C. Tenney. 5 vols. Grand Rapids: Zondervan, 1975

Preface to the Second Edition

This book is the second edition of the 1989 publication of the same title authored by Charles B. Puskas. Now C. Michael Robbins is coauthor of the new edition. More than 30 percent of the material has been revised, especially scholarly discussion after the first edition. Since the first edition, a host of diverse cultural, historical, social-scientific, socio-rhetorical, narrative, textual, and contextual studies have surfaced, and we have noted them when they are relevant to our study. Some scholars, uncomfortable with the redaction-critical quest for the intent of the author and his *Sitz im Leben*, even challenging a two-level hermeneutic of tradition versus redaction, prefer the narrative language of "implied author," "textuality," and "social location." We are sensitive to these trends, even though varieties of different opinions still abound in *all* areas of research. In the revision of this manuscript, certain lacunae have been filled, especially by the insightful Dr. Robbins, who revised chapters 1–11 and some sections of chapter 13 (the sections on Q, Mark, Matthew, and John). The reader will also appreciate his poignant and provocative chapter openings.

Attentive to the reviewers of the first edition, who have noted with appreciation the following chapters that were included, i.e., the chapters on "text criticism, form, redaction, and literary criticism . . .[,] introductory views of each of the gospels, New Testament literature . . .[,] information on the Christian origins . . . [and] Judaism in the Greco-Roman world, [on] New Testament Greek, the New Testament canon, and English versions" (W. R. Stegner, M. A. Seifrid), we have retained them in our original tripartite arrangement of parts: "The World of the New Testament," "Interpreting the New Testament," and "Jesus and Early Christianity." In agreement with another reviewer, we continue to supply the reader with "pertinent primary and secondary material" (*Evangelical Quarterly*). Our new edition carries on "a genuine effort to be non-sectarian" (Robert F. O'Toole, SJ). Although our work is more an *Einleitung* (German: a "critical introduction") than an *Einführung* (German: a "survey"), we still recommend its use not only "by college or seminary students, but also . . . anyone who simply wishes to be better informed about the New Testament, its origins, its literary forms, its reading publics, and its history of transmission, including modern texts and translations" (Frederick W. Danker's endorsement).

Many thanks to K. C. Hanson, Cascade Books editor-in-chief, who encouraged this second edition; Professor James Voelz, academic dean of Concordia Seminary–St. Louis, for similar emboldenings; Nancy Collins, who helped with permissions (never a given, even with a new edition); Jim Chiampas, who expertly recommended to us some high digital photos; Jeremy Funk and Heather Carraher at Cascade Books; Craig and Anne Noll, skillful indexers; and finally our wives, Susan Puskas and Annette Robbins, to whom this work is affectionately dedicated.

Introduction

THE INFLUENCE OF THE NEW TESTAMENT

Probably no group of religious writings has influenced the Western world more than the New Testament. Its appealing message of the life and work of Jesus Christ has profoundly influenced and even transformed millions of lives. It has inspired the authors of such literary classics as *The City of God*, *Paradise Lost*, and *Pilgrim's Progress*. New Testament stories are read, rehearsed, and recited during the Christmas and Easter holidays. The Protestant work ethic derived from the New Testament. In the academic areas of ethics and philosophy, this provocative collection confronts the contemporary person with the ageless questions of ultimate concern: Who am I? Why am I here? Is there a god? Do we have a soul? Is there life after death? The New Testament challenges each generation to formulate anew responses to these enduring questions. Finally, in the disciplines of historical and cultural studies, the New Testament serves as one significant source for understanding Second Temple Judaism, the early Roman Empire, and the origins of Christianity.

THE DIFFICULTIES IN READING THE NEW TESTAMENT

Even though it has been an influential document for much of human culture, the New Testament is a difficult book to read. Not only does this ancient collection assume social structures and customs different from our own, but many of its teachings reflect diverse perspectives on similar topics. Note, for example, the shocking saying in Luke 14:26 about hating one's family in order to become a disciple, and the authoritarian teaching about submission in the household in 1 Peter 3:1–6. Both passages presuppose social structures unlike our own, and both reflect distinct perspectives on faith and family issues.

DISTINCT FEATURES OF THIS BOOK

The focus of this volume is on the development of early Christianity in its historical context. A presentation of the Greco-Roman world and Jewish environment of early Christianity is essential to bridging the historical and cultural gap that separates us from the New Testament. An outline tracing early Christianity from Jesus to emerging orthodoxy is important for understanding the different New Testament teachings in their respective historical contexts.

Since the New Testament is our basic source for this historical inquiry, chapters on the New Testament language, text, methods of interpretation, and literary genres are included, as are chapters on the formation of the NT canon and on English translations. All these sections seek to answer fundamental questions, such as, In what type of language was the New Testament written? How reliable is our New Testament text? How do we interpret the New Testament? Why are there only twenty-seven books in the New Testament? What type of translation should I read?

Our focus is that of a general introduction (to the NT collection as a whole), so separate discussions for every book (as in special introductions) are minimal, but our own inclinations about questions of authorship and dating are stated in the historical presentation of Jesus and early Christianity (part 3). Some treatment of these issues is found in the footnotes, with alternate views noted. Illustrations and charts will greatly assist the reader in comprehending the material. Primary and secondary sources are also provided for further study. Select abbreviations at the beginning of the volume, and a bibliography with indexes at the end, should also prove helpful. Studying the New Testament can be a fascinating enterprise, but it takes time, tools, some expertise, and a determination to encounter this collection of writings on its own terms.

PART 1

The World of the New Testament

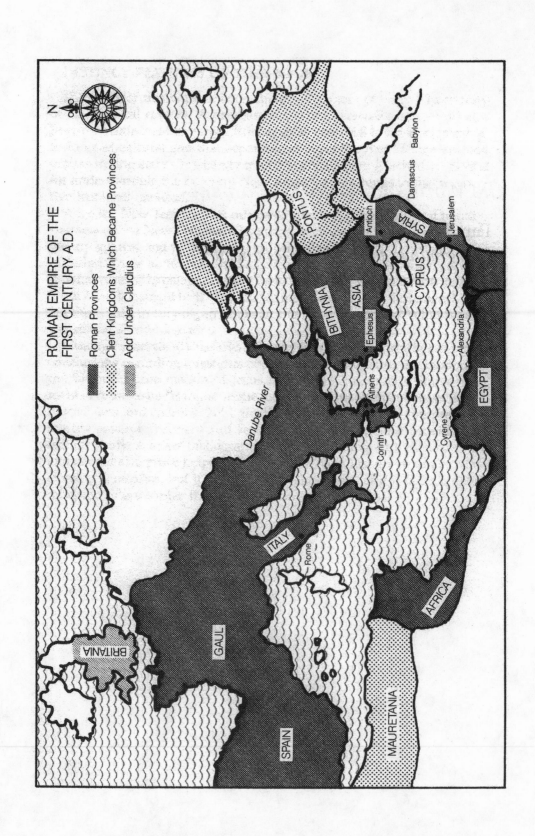

ROMAN EMPIRE OF THE
FIRST CENTURY A.D.

Roman Provinces

Client Kingdoms Which Became Provinces

Add Under Claudius

N

BRITANIA

SPAIN

GAUL

Danube River

ITALY

Rome

MAURETANIA

AFRICA

Corinth

Athens

Cyrene

Alexandria

EGYPT

PONTUS

BITHYNIA

ASIA

Ephesus

CYPRUS

Antioch

SYRIA

Damascus

Babylon

Jerusalem

1

The Greco-Roman Context of the New Testament

Understanding the historical context is crucial for the serious study of any important document, person, or event. Using a modern example, no earnest interpreter of the U.S. Constitution can ignore the importance of eighteenth-century mercantilism and the prevalent teaching of social contract and popular sovereignty. Historical context is crucial for understanding. We will return to this same analogy in chapter 5.

For an ancient example of the above point, note the apology of Plutarch (ca. 110) regarding his own limited presentation of the historical figure, Cicero. Plutarch pleaded with an aphorism of Ion of Chios: "Worthless on land is the dolphin's strength."[1] His plea is clear, and a point well made: A historian's weakness—even one as close as Plutarch—is his or her

ignorance. So it is also with readers of the New Testament (NT).

If we are to interpret perceptively these early Christian writings, the significant provincial policies of first-century Rome and the influential thought of both Judaism and Hellenism cannot be ignored. No documents are immune to the influences of their historical context; indeed they are the reflections of it. And any good appreciation of the texts will be the result of an absorption of the same.[2]

A PERVASIVE HELLENISM

The NT was not written in Aramaic, the native language of Jesus and his disciples, or in Latin, the language of Rome, but in a

---

1. *Demosthenes* III.2 (Plutarch *Lives* 7.6–7; Robbins's translation). Mestrius Plutarchus (AD 50–120), the Platonist philosopher and biographer, was from Chaeronea in northwest Boeotia, Greece. He visited Athens often and traveled to Egypt and Italy, lecturing in Rome.

2. Some excellent introductory texts to the task are Schaps, *Handbook*; Bell, *Guide*; Eder and Renger, *Chronologies*; Hedrick, *Ancient History*; Ferguson, *Backgrounds*; Heiken, *Seven Hills*; Robinson, *Sources*; Mousourakis, *Legal History*; Casson, *Everyday Life*; Lefkowitz, *Women's Life*; Malkin, "Networks."

common Greek dialect of the first century. Why was it written in Greek? This linguistic phenomenon is chiefly due to the efforts of one extraordinary man: Alexander of Macedon (356–323 BC).

Hellenization under Alexander the Great

Alexander's background is impressive and his achievements are astonishing.[3] As the son of an ambitious Macedonian ruler (Philip II), Alexander studied ethics, geography, and Homer's *Iliad* under the famous Greek philosopher Aristotle; he also received intensive military training from experienced warriors. When he succeeded his father in 336 BC, young Alexander sought to consolidate his father's power and launch a fantastic campaign eastward. Within ten short years, Alexander and his great army of thirty thousand infantry and forty-five hundred cavalry would conquer Asia Minor (modern Turkey), Syria, Palestine, Egypt, Babylonia (modern Iraq), Persia (Iran), and northwestern India.[4]

Alexander the Great.
From a first-century Roman mosaic depicting the battle of Issus where Alexander defeated the Persian king, Darius III. (National Archaeological Museum, Naples, Italy)

3. Primary sources for Alexander and his accomplishments are the works of Diodorus of Sicily (first century BC), Quintus of Curtius (first century AD), Plutarch of Chaeronea (early second century AD) and Arrian of Nicodemia (second century AD). Pertinent selections from the above are found in Austin, *Hellenistic World*, 8–46. For helpful surveys, see Tarn, *Alexander the Great*; for useful resources see Roisman, *Brill's Companion*; Heckel, *Who's Who*; Heckel and Yardley, *Alexander the Great: Historical Sources*; Carney, *Olympias*; Romm, *Landmark Arrian*.

4. The above military statistics from Diodorus, *Library of History* 17.7.3–4, are probably not an exaggeration. The geographical extent of Alexander's conquest is most evident (ironically) in the accounts narrating the division of his kingdom, e.g., fragment of Greek history attributed to Arrian 156F (in Austin, *Hellenistic World*, 41–43). See also Gergel and Wood, *Alexander the Great*.

As Alexander marched eastward, he brought his Greek culture with him. Although "Hellenization," or the spread of Greek culture away from its homeland, began centuries earlier with Greek traders and colonists, the process was greatly accelerated by Alexander's military campaigns, which began in 335 BC.

Intending initially (perhaps) just to free the Greek cities in western Asia Minor (Ionia), and then to further weaken the strength of Persia by breaking its control of more inland cities, Alexander eventually saw that much more was within his grasp. In 333 the Battle of Issus (close to Tarsus), where Alexander met (for the first time) with the great army of Darius and defeated it may have been a turning point; Alexander was offered, but rejected, terms of peace. He moved swiftly south down the Mediterranean coast, taking Sidon, Tyre, and then Lower Egypt, founding the famous city of Alexandria in 331. Controlling the entire Mediterranean coast, he moved the same year toward the heartland of Persia, taking in coming years all of Mesopotamia (Babylonia), western and central Iran, and eventually northern and western Iran. Traveling thus from the Mediterranean to the Persian Gulf to the Caspian Sea to the Kush mountain range and then down the Indus River to the Arabian Sea by 325, Alexander proved himself the greatest Greek military strategist ever, perhaps the greatest of all the ancient world.

As a student of Greek learning, he envisioned a union of the East and West through Greek culture and took definite steps to fulfill it. He dreamed of enriching Eastern culture with that of Greece, bringing the Greek language (see chapter 3 below), and building Greek cities along the trail, sixteen of which were called Alexandria. These cities would become centers of Greek culture. But Alexander was more willing than his soldiers (especially those loyalists from Macedonia) to acculturate himself in the East. For example, he married Persian women (including the daughters of both Darius III and Artaxerxes III) and encouraged his soldiers to do the same (Arrian, *Anab.* 7.4.4). Second, he and his successors built a network of Greek cities throughout the empire. These became centers of Greek culture. Many other Hellenistic aspirations and achievements of Alexander are highlighted, with some exaggeration, in Plutarch's *On the Fortunes or Virtues of Alexander the Great* 1.328C–329D. The ten years

of military invasion that so began would change the look of cultures east of Greece forever. Merely the use of Hellenistic Greek as a common language (see chapter 3 below) would last almost a millennium (322 BC—AD 529).

The type of Greek language disseminated by Alexander and his men was not the classical Attic of Aristotle (although it was dominant), but *koinē* or "common" Greek. This type was a vernacular Greek, a more vigorous and simplified form of Attic (the variety spoken in Athens) with elements of Ionic (the variety spoken in Ephesus). It may have evolved in the following manner. Alexander probably emphasized the Attic dialect in which he was schooled. It was later modified by his troops, whose native dialects were diverse, and it underwent further changes when adopted by the Eastern "barbarians" (non-Greeks). This simplified and adaptable Greek dialect soon supplanted Aramaic, the language of the Persian Empire. It became the international tongue of the Mediterranean world, just as Latin did in medieval Europe, and as English has done in our contemporary world.

Hellenization after Alexander the Great

Although the cultural impact of his conquests would endure long after his death, the political unity of the empire would not survive after Alexander. In 323 BC, burdened with administration and probably suffering from a fever, he died at the age of thirty-two with no legal heir (except one, as yet unborn, son). His generals struggled for control of his empire and soon dismantled it into small, petty kingdoms. Ptolemy took Egypt and southern Syria;

Antigonus claimed most of northern Syria and western Babylonia; Lysimachus held Thrace and western Asia Minor; and Cassander ruled Macedonia and Greece. The territory of Antigonus was taken by Seleucus I after the battle of Ipsus (301 BC), and the kingdom of Lysimachus was also absorbed into the realm of Seleucus. For centuries the dynasties established by Seleucus and Ptolemy fought against each other for more territory, For example, Palestine, caught in the crossfire, served as a buffer zone between the two kingdoms; it was first under Ptolemaic control and then under Seleucid rule after 198 BC.[5]

The Hellenization process begun by Alexander, however, continued under the Seleucid and Ptolemaic empires. Cities like Alexandria of Egypt, Antioch of Syria, and Seleucia on the Tigris River (near modern Baghdad) were model Hellenistic cities. Most of them had great walls that enclosed private homes, a central marketplace (Gk. *agora*) with temples and government buildings, a gymnasium, a theater, and a bathhouse. Alexandria of Egypt was a trade center with a great library and museum. Seleucia on the Tigris was a wealthy banking city, and Antioch of Syria later became the capital of the Seleucid Empire.[6] Although the luxuries of these Hellenistic cities were enjoyed by the king and his Greek associates, privileges were extended to influential non-Greeks who assimilated Greek language and customs. Upper-class non-Greeks formed their own associations, and the people were allowed to observe either Greek laws or their own statutes unless they conflicted with those of the king.[7] This arrangement also applied to Palestine, where numerous Hellenistic cities existed in Phoenicia (e.g., Ptolemais-Acco, Jamnia, Ascalon, Gaza) and the regions near Galilee (e.g., Sepphoris, Pella, Gadara, Scythapolis).[8] Because Greek became the language of commerce, every region concerned with business and education was affected. The conquests of Alexander set in motion cultural trends that could not be reversed despite the splintering of his empire among his generals and the continued rivalry among their own descendants. After centuries of political conflict, each small kingdom fell in turn to Rome in the first century BC. By that time, however, a distinctive culture had emerged: a curious blend of Greek and Eastern.

A STABLE ROMAN EMPIRE

The United States and China are two modern examples of world powers whose interests and concerns greatly affect the rest

---

5. Primary sources for this complicated period after Alexander are found in Austin, *Hellenistic World*; Shipley, *Greek World*. For helpful survey see Tarn and Griffith, *Hellenistic Civilisation*, 5–46; and Austin, *The Hellenistic World*.

6. An early (20 BC) description of the above three cities is found in Strabo, *Geography* 16.1.5 (Seleucis); 16.2.4–10 (Antioch); 17.1.6–10 (Alexandria); 16.2.5 (all three). For further discussion, see Koester, *Introduction* 1:67–73; Tarn and Griffith, *Hellenistic Civilisation*, 150–52, 183–86.

7. Hadas, *Hellenistic Culture*, 30–44; Koester, *Introduction* 1:56–58.

8. On the pervasive influence of Hellenism on the Jews of Palestine in late antiquity, see Hengel, *Judaism and Hellenism*, 1:58–88; but some groups, e.g., Khirbet Qumran (the third century BC to the first century AD) were more fluent in Hebrew and Aramaic than Greek; see Millar, "Background of the Maccabean Revolution"; Vermes, *Jesus in His Jewish Context*; and Vermes, *Jesus and the World of Judaism*, 26, 74; see also discussion in Grabbe, "Jews and Hellenization"; Collins, *Jewish Cult*; Bar-Kochba, *Image of the Jews in Greek Literature*.

of the world. The history of civilization is replete with such examples of world powers, and the time of the NT is no exception. The early Christian documents were written at a time when Rome controlled the Mediterranean world. With Rome's ascendance as a world empire it also became the heir to a Hellenized world.[9] By the sixth century BC, Rome had evolved[10] from a monarchy into a republic ruled by two consuls in cooperation with a senate and two assemblies. Because of their fear of invaders and additional reasons (e.g., economic interests, political mission), the Romans sought to neutralize their frontiers. By the third century they had gained control of Italy (275 BC) and had finally defeated Carthage (207 BC),[11] and secured domination of the western Mediterranean world. In the second and first centuries BC, when Rome expanded its borders eastward, it began absorbing the Hellenistic world founded by Alexander. Macedonia and Achaia (148 BC), Asia Minor (133 BC), Syria (64 BC), and Egypt (30 BC) all became Roman provinces. The Christian era thus begins with Rome as the political machine governing the Hellenized world of the Mediterranean. By the first century BC the eastern Mediterranean kingdoms linked together by Greek culture were absorbed into the one political entity of Rome.

Augustus Caesar[12]

After a half century of bitter power struggles involving Julius Caesar, Pompey, Mark Antony, and Octavian, Rome became an imperial government under Octavian, Caesar's grandnephew.[13] In 27 BC, when Octavian emerged as undisputed victor of the power struggle, the senate responded by granting him numerous titles and offices: he was Princeps or "first citizen," proconsul, tribune, and assumed the title Augustus, or "revered one." Although he pledged to restore the republic, in practice Augustus was head of state, governed the important provinces, and had veto power over the senate. Augustus also assigned to his imperial household the daily business of managing the government, which also lessened the influence of the Senate. Because the Roman republic was inefficient in handling its vast dominion, the transition to a strong central authority was a considerable improvement.[14]

In a testament prepared by himself, called the *Res Gestae*, or "achievements," Augustus could boast of (1) securing peace by extending and neutralizing the frontiers,[15] (2) encouraging religion by building temples and shrines, (3) strengthening morality by enforcing laws governing personal behavior, and (4) beautifying the city of Rome with

---

9. Primary sources for the history of Rome are Dio Cassius, *Roman History* (second century AD), the works of Livy (first century AD), C. Tacitus, *Histories* and *Annals* (first century AD), and Suetonius, *Lives of the Caesars* (early second century AD). For summaries of Roman history, see Kamm, *Romans*; Goodman, *Roman World*; Zoch, *Ancient Rome*; Grant, *World of Rome*; *Founders*; Hadas, *Imperial Rome*, 35–44, 57–68; Scullard, *From the Gracchi to Nero*; Champion, *Roman Imperialism*.

10. Cornell, *The Beginnings of Rome*.

11. Goldsworthy, *Fall of Carthage*.

12. Shotter, *Augustus*; Ehrenberg and Jones, *Documents*; Sherk, *Roman Empire*.

13. Kamm, *Julius Caesar*; Billows, *Julius Caesar*; Burns, *Great Women*.

14. Hadas, *Imperial Rome*, 44, 57–59.

15. Talbert, et al., *Barrington Atlas*; Stoneman and Wallace, *Classical Wall Maps*.

magnificent buildings.[16] Most of these achievements would serve as standard policy goals in the imperial administrations that would follow.

Augustus's reorganization of the provinces is noteworthy. The senate retained control of the pacified provinces (e.g., Macedonia, Achaia, Crete, Cyprus) without a standing army. Both Sergius Paulus, proconsul (Gk. *anthypatos*) of Cyprus (Acts 13:4, 7), and Gallio, proconsul of Achaia (Acts 18:12–17), were governors of senatorial provinces appointed for one-year terms. Those provinces, requiring legions of troops because they were newly acquired or frontier territories (e.g., Syria, Pamphylia, Galatia), fell under the direct control of the emperor, who appointed a legate as governor. In some districts (e.g., Egypt, Judea) the emperor ruled through a prefect or (after AD 41) a procurator. The Gospel of Luke identifies both the legate of Syria (Quirinius, 2:2) and the prefect of Judea (Pontius Pilate, 3:1), although both offices are given the general title of "imperial governor" (Gk. *hēgemōn*). All provinces were ruled by Romans, but certain responsibilities were delegated to local magistrates, especially in the senatorial provinces. The governors of the provinces had both financial and legal responsibilities. They supervised the collection of taxes and administered justice. Any lawsuit in the provinces could be transferred to the

Statue of Caesar Augustus located on the island of Capri in the Bay of Naples, Italy.
(iStock Photo)

imperial court. An appeal to Caesar was significant, for example, in cases of extortion against officials or for alleged crimes against the Roman people and their emperor (e.g., treason, conspiracy). Roman law was equitable for loyal, taxpaying provincials but harsh for those convicted of extortion or treason.[17]

Augustus also created new offices for the construction and repair of public buildings, roads, and aqueducts. The great network of roads built by Augustus and his successors was an impressive accom-

16. The *Res Gestae Divi Augusti* inscription (AD 13) was discovered in the temple of Rome and Augustus at Ancyra in Galatia (*Monumentum Ancyranum*). See Brunt and Moore, *Res Gestae Divi Augusti*. Other writings extolling the accomplishments of Augustus are Suetonius, *Augustus*; and Horace, *Secular Ode*, 51–52, selections of which are found in Barrett, *New Testament Background*, 1–8. See also Hadas, *Imperial Rome*, 58–59.

17. For more information on the Roman provincial system, see Stevenson, *Roman Provincial Administration*; Mousourakis, *Legal History*; Jones, *Studies in Roman Government and Law*; Sherwin-White, *Roman Foreign Policy in the East*; Sherwin-White, *Roman Society*.

plishment. Roads extended throughout the empire, making even the remote frontiers accessible. Durable and well constructed, some of these roads are still in use today. Military posts, postal stations, and inns were set up at regular intervals, and maps were provided indicating distances and major points of interest. This engineering feat greatly enhanced travel, trade, and communication in a manner unparalleled in ancient history. It also was a significant factor in the mission and expansion of Christianity.

The Julio-Claudian Emperors

Most of the emperors after Augustus (27 BC–AD 14) either continued or expanded his provincial policies.[18] The four who followed him are known as the Julio-Claudian emperors because they were descendants of the Julians and Claudians, two families of ancient Roman nobility.

Tiberius (14–37)

Tiberius was the stepson of Augustus. He assumed the office with an experienced military and administrative background. Luke mentions his reign (3:1). The Galilean tetrarch Herod Antipas was his client king. He appointed Pontius Pilate as governor from 26 to 36. Although he tried to emulate the accomplishments of

Augustus, domestic problems, fear of conspiracy (e.g., by his lieutenant Sejanus), and general indecision made his reign an unfavorable time for the senate and provincial governors like Pontius Pilate.

Gaius Caligula (37–41)

Caligula was the great-nephew of Tiberius, and his rule was at first popular (e.g., he pardoned political prisoners and reduced taxes), but his demand to be addressed as a god (the embodiment of Jupiter) offended the Romans and outraged the Jews (Philo, *Embassy*). He also drained the treasury with his reckless expenditures and was killed by his own guards, who then put forward Claudius as a puppet.

Claudius (41–54)

Caligula's uncle, Claudius, was an author of books in both Latin and Greek and proved to be at fifty years old a sensible and competent ruler., despite his problems with a physical paralysis. He expanded the offices of the imperial household into an efficient government bureaucracy and also extended Roman citizenship to many prominent provincials. He led the first successful invasion of Britain, for which the senate conferred on him the title Britannicus. He is mentioned as expelling the Jews from Rome for rioting (because of Christian preaching?) according to Acts 18:2 and Suetonius, *Claudius* 25. He was unfortunately poisoned by his second wife (and his own niece), Agrippina, who had previously forced him to adopt her son, T. Claudius Nero, as legal heir to the throne.

18. For primary sources on the Roman emperors see Suetonius, *Twelve Caesars;* Tacitus, *Annals* and *Histories;* Dio Cassius, *Roman History*. Selections with discussion are found in Charlesworth, *Documents*; Braund, *Augustas to Nero*; Smallwood, *Documents*; Wilkinson, *Caligula*; Shotter, *Nero*; Levick, *Tiberius the Politician*; Levick, *Claudius*; Seager, *Tiberius*; Balsdon, "Principates"; Williams, "Expulsion"; Millar, *Emperor in the Roman World*.

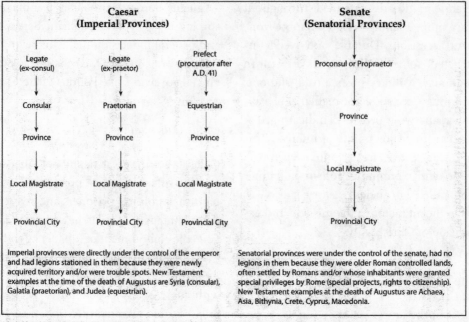

Caesar (Imperial Provinces)			Senate (Senatorial Provinces)
Legate (ex-consul)	Legate (ex-praetor)	Prefect (procurator after A.D. 41)	Proconsul or Propraetor
↓	↓	↓	↓
Consular	Praetorian	Equestrian	
↓	↓	↓	Province
Province	Province	Province	
↓	↓	↓	↓
			Local Magistrate
Local Magistrate	Local Magistrate	Local Magistrate	
↓	↓	↓	↓
Provincial City	Provincial City	Provincial City	Provincial City

Imperial provinces were directly under the control of the emperor and had legions stationed in them because they were newly acquired territory and/or were trouble spots. New Testament examples at the time of the death of Augustus are Syria (consular), Galatia (praetorian), and Judea (equestrian).

Senatorial provinces were under the control of the senate, had no legions in them because they were older Roman controlled lands, often settled by Romans and/or whose inhabitants were granted special privileges by Rome (special projects, rights to citizenship). New Testament examples at the death of Augustus are Achaea, Asia, Bithynia, Crete, Cyprus, Macedonia.

Adapted from Merland Ray Miller, "Timetables and Charts for the New Testament," ThM thesis (Portland, Ore.: Western Conservative Baptist Seminary, 1980), by permission.

Roman Political System

Nero (54–68)

Stepson of Claudius, Nero had a successful early reign beginning under capable advisors (Seneca, G. Burrus), but it began to deteriorate when he took full control. He had members of his own family murdered, emptied the treasury with his extravagant spending, and resorted to violence in replenishing it. He was accused of setting fire to Rome (64) but fixed the blame on the Christians (Tacitus, *Ann.* 15.44; Suetonius, *Nero* 16.2). According to tradition, Peter and Paul were executed then. After failing to lead a military campaign in the east, Nero, forced by his praetorian guards to flee the city of Rome, committed suicide.

After the Julio-Claudian emperors, a year of civil war saw the reign of three short-lived emperors from the military ranks: Galbo, Otho, and Vitellius.

The Flavian Dynasty[19]

The Flavian dynasty, unlike the Julio-Claudians, descended from an "equestrian" family, the middle class of military commanders and merchants.

T. Flavius Vespasian (AD 69–79)

Vespasian was an experienced general who was completing the campaign to end the Judean revolt of 66–70 (Josephus, *War* 3–4) when his supporters proclaimed him emperor. Leaving the siege against Jerusalem to his son, Titus, he seized Egypt, thereby controlling Rome's grain supply, and then proceeded to the city with his

19. Garnsey and Saller, *Early Principate*; Mc-Crum, *Select Documents*; Southern, *Domitian*; Morgan, *69 AD*; Botha, "Historical Domitian"; Jones, *Emperor Domitian*; Jones, *Emperor Titus*; Coleman, "Emperor Domitian."

army to receive from the senate their official confirmation of his imperial authority. His wise rule brought a new era of peace. He weakened the political control of the army by returning power to the emperor and senate. The bankrupt treasury was replenished, and appointments in the imperial household attracted equestrians and senators. He strengthened the frontiers through a system of new roads and forts, and the granting of Roman citizenship was made more available to provincials.

Titus (79–81)

Titus had replaced his father, Vespasian, as general, overseeing the destruction of Jerusalem in 70 (Josephus, *War* 5–6; 7.1–5; Tacitus, *Hist.* 5.1) before becoming emperor. His short reign, mainly concerned with relief work to victims of catastrophe (i.e., the volcanic destruction of Pompeii and Herculaneum, fire at Rome, plagues), was a popular one (Suetonius, *Titus* 8.3; 11). Pliny the Elder dedicated his *Natural History* to Titus (see his Prefatio).

Domitian (81–96)

Brother of Titus, Domitian was ambitious and autocratic. His extensive building projects and efforts to fortify the provinces depleted the treasury. He eventually controlled the senate and had many opponents murdered. He sought to revive the emperor religion and promote his own deification (Suetonius, *Domitian* 13). This last policy probably caused the persecution of certain Jews and Christians. The anti-Roman motifs in Revelation may reflect the circumstances of his reign (Rev 13; 17; cf. *1 Clem.* 1.1; Eusebius, *Hist. eccl.*

3.18.4; 4.26.29; Dio Cass. 67.14). Domitian was killed by members of his imperial household.

The Emperors of the "Golden Age"

The "five good emperors" that followed Domitian saw the "golden age" of the empire. Each emperor made provisions for his own successor, and special attention was given to the welfare of provincial cities during this time of peace and prosperity. All except Nerva were provincials.

Nerva (AD 96–98)

Nerva was a respectable old Roman lawyer who sought to rebuild the state treasury, distribute land to the poor, and encourage construction. He took definite steps in the choosing and training of a successor.

Trajan (98–117)

From an equestrian Roman family of Spain, Trajan was Nerva's appointed successor. Trajan was an ambitious ruler who waged war against the Parthians (115–117) and suppressed a Jewish revolt to expand the eastern frontiers. Under his reign the empire reached its peak geographically. To prevent abuse and extravagance, he appointed curators to supervise the local affairs of provincial cities. During this time of prosperity, Trajan also encouraged public and private philanthropy. His famous correspondence with Pliny the Younger, governor of Bithynia, provides insights regarding Rome's dealings with Christians (*Ep.* 10.96.5–6).

Hadrian (117–138)

Also from Spain, Hadrian was Trajan's adopted son and successor. Although he did not continue Trajan's policies of conquest, he sought to neutralize the frontiers through negotiation (with the Parthians) and fortification (e.g., Hadrian's wall in Britain). Hadrian was a cosmopolitan emperor who traveled extensively throughout the empire, promoting Greek culture and numerous building projects. He granted citizenship to a growing number of new towns and cities that applied for it and standardized Roman legal procedure throughout the empire. In reaction to Hadrian's attempts to rebuild Jerusalem into a Roman city with a temple dedicated to Jupiter, the Jews revolted under Simon Bar Kochba (132–135). The insurrection was suppressed after much effort, and it resulted in the expulsion of all Jews from Palestine.

Antoninus Pius (138–161)

From a Roman family of southern Gaul, Antoninus Pius was Hadrian's appointed successor. He quietly furthered the centralization of the government (e.g., he had an imperial cabinet of advisors) but maintained good relations with the senate. Despite border clashes in the northern and eastern frontiers, he enjoyed a reign of peace and prosperity as expressed in the oration *To Rome* by Aelius Aristides (tutor of Marcus Aurelius). Aristides, a provincial from Asia Minor, pictured the empire as a commonwealth of peaceful and prosperous city-states under Rome's beneficent leadership and protection.

Marcus Aurelius (161–180)

Marcus Aurelius was the adopted son of Antonius and came from a consular family of Spain. At an early age he gained the favor of Hadrian, who supervised his fine education. When he assumed the imperial throne, Aurelius was an accomplished soldier, administrator, and philosopher. He composed his *Meditations*, breathing high Stoic principles, between military campaigns. Despite wars on the Rhine, Danube, and Euphrates Rivers, there was a remarkable sense of unity in the empire. Grants of Roman citizenship were freely given, and qualified provincial citizens also served in the senate.

Despite the sporadic periods of tyranny in the reigns of Caligula, Nero, and Domitian, the emperors of Rome continued and even refined the fair provincial policies of Augustus. They maintained political order and economic stability in an otherwise turbulent Mediterranean world. By the Golden Age emperors were taking an active role in the safety and welfare of provincial cities. Early Christianity would benefit from such imperial policies. Full-scale persecution of Christians for refusing to pay homage to the emperor would not begin until the reigns of Decius and Valerian (250–260). These efforts ended with the reign of Constantine (324–337), who declared Christianity a legal religion of Rome.

AN AGE OF ANXIETY AND ASPIRATION[20]

Rapid change in any society can both inspire new hopes and arouse new fears.

20. The title, "Age of Anxiety and Aspiration,"

From the years following World War II to the present, our Western society has experienced great scientific and technological advances that have given it a sense of both achievement and anxiety. Our rocket systems are so advanced that we can make shuttle trips to the moon or send guided missiles to destroy any locality in the world. Genetic engineering capable of creating new life forms in a laboratory may help solve some current problems or produce many unforeseen ones. Our great advances in computer technology can enhance the productivity of some people or limit the employment opportunities of others. This paradox of aspiration and anxiety through rapid change was also characteristic of the NT world. With the cultural revolution caused by Hellenism and improved travel, goods and ideas were either exchanged or exploited; old traditions were either transformed or forgotten; and people left their native lands either as hopeful travelers or as despairing slaves. Rapid change in any age generates both aspirations and anxieties.

The Anxieties of the Age

Before looking at the new aspirations, we will survey some of the anxieties and the circumstances that produced them.

is derived in part from: Dodds, *Greeks and the Irrational* (1951) 44, 78, 97; Dodds, *Pagan and Christian in Age of Anxiety* (1965) 3–4, 133; also used in Kee and Young, *Understanding the New Testament* (1957), 7–8. Although the second title by Dodds mainly concerns the 2nd–4th centuries AD, much of it has relevance for our period of discussion (i.e., late antiquity). The English word, "anxiety," is derived from the Latin, *anxietas*, which denoted "worry, trouble" and "fear" in Latin literature; "aspiration" is likewise so derived from *aspiratio*, "exhalation," conveying the figurative meaning of "hope" or "aspiration."

Improved travel, improved trade, and pervasive Hellenism certainly produced favorable changes in the Greco-Roman world. But such changes also brought with them numerous problems or sources of anxiety. Improved travel not only enhanced communication and trade but also increased the spread of diseases, causing illness, death,[21] or the fear of disease.[22] Improved trade not only stimulated the accumulation of wealth for some but caused the exploitation and displacement of people from their homelands to serve as slaves for a new, prosperous merchant class.[23] Such a situation would produce in these oppressed peoples feelings of despair and vulnerability and would

21. Hope, *Death in Ancient Rome*; Toynbee, *Death and Burial*.

22. The movement of goods and people was easy and cheap in the empire; see for examples the travels of the Apostle Paul, Aquila, and Priscilla in Acts, and the accounts of traveling merchants, cited in Charlesworth, *Roman Empire*, 86–87. The spread of disease was also unprecedented; for example during the reigns of both Titus and Marcus Aurelius terrible plagues swept across the empire. Note also the diverse list of diseases in Edelstein and Edelstein; Jacob and Jacob, *Healing Past*; Nutton, *Ancient Medicine*.

23. The correspondence of Zeno, steward of a large estate in Fayum, Egypt, addressed to Apollonius, the finance minister under Ptolemy II (282–246 BC), and the king's extensive "Revenue Laws" indicate the vast amounts of trade in which moneymaking Egypt was engaged (Austin, *Hellenistic World*, 395–411). On prosperous Roman trading, see Charlesworth, *Roman Empire*, 81–91. The importance of slaves in labor and commerce cannot be underestimated. In the first century BC, one-third of Rome's population were slaves. Most were acquired through military conquest, e.g., the Jewish historian, Josephus, stated that Rome took 97,000 prisoners from Palestine during the Jewish revolt of AD 66–70, *War* 6.420. See Wiedemann, *Greek and Roman Slavery*; Kirschenbaum, *Sons, Slaves, and Freedmen*; Bradley, *Slavery and Society*; Hopkins, *Conquerors and Slaves*; Bartchy, "Slavery."

The temple of Athena Parthenos (maiden) built on the highest part of the Acropolis of Athens, 438 BC. The outer colonnades have been rebuilt in modern times. (iStock Photo)

result in the loss of ethnic identity. Pervasive Hellenism in the East resulted in the emergence of Eastern thought in Greek dress. Such a transformation brought new life to both Eastern religions and Greek philosophy, but it also carried with it a pessimism of the old traditions and an obsession with fate that would lead to moods of hopelessness and helplessness.[24]

Belief in fatalism dominated Hellenistic thought. Since the classical period, the Greeks believed that each person received his "appointed portion" in life (Gk. *moira* in Homer). But in Hellenism, human life was predetermined by higher powers (e.g., Stoicism, apocalypticism) which were often identified as fate (Gk. *heimarmenē* or *anankē*; Lat. *fatum*). Fate, sometimes personified, would determine the outcome of nations, individuals, and events, with little or no human control.[25] The preoccupation with fate was greatly influenced by astrology. The belief that the stars were deities which determined the destiny of humans probably began in Mesopotamia (700 BC) and spread

24. See the concern for deliverance from fate in Apuleius, *The Golden Ass* 11.6.15; Corpus Hermetica 12.9 (in Bultmann, *Primitive Christianity*, 154). For the view of the revival of Eastern religions in Greek language and thought-forms, see Jonas, *Gnostic Religion*, 3–27.

25. Examples of fatalism in Stoicism are Zeno, *Fragments* 175–76, and Chrysippus, *Fragment* 625 (both in Barrett, *New Testament Background*, 61–64); Seneca, *On Providence* 5.7–9 and *To Marcia* 18.5–6; see also: Pliny, *Nat. Hist.* 2.22 and the histories of Suetonius and Tacitus. The following are examples of the apocalyptic view that the events preceding the end are predetermined: Dan 9:24; *1 Enoch* 92:2; *4 Ezra* 4:36–37; 6:1–6; *2 Bar* 25; see also Jewish Wisdom: Eccl 3:2–8; Sir 23:20; 39:25, 30.

throughout the Mediterranean world after Alexander.[26] Astrology affected every aspect of society: religion, war, politics, trade, and personal matters. The old Greek gods were identified with the planets: Zeus = Jupiter, Aphrodite = Venus, Ares = Mars, Kronos = Saturn, Hermes = Mercury. Symbols of the Zodiac figure prominently in a sculpture of Zeus from Italy and in a relief of Cybele the Asian mother-goddess (from the Transjordan area) both dated in the early second century AD. Horoscopes were so prevalent in the early Roman Empire that Augustus sought to standardize them by publishing his own.

The Aspirations of the Age

Appearing as either symptoms of or responses to the above anxieties and obsessions were the aspirations of this age. They were numerous and diverse but primarily religious and philosophical. Many of these spiritual pilgrimages or quests for meaning are a resurgence of Eastern thought transformed by Hellenism. They represent a new synthesis of oriental

religion in Greek dress. For example, the ancient Egyptian cult of Isis (representing the earth) and Osiris (personifying the Nile) are Hellenized into Isis, the "Mother of all things," and Sarapis, who is portrayed in the likeness of Zeus.[27]

Most of these Hellenistic religions and philosophies offered people security, identity, and a sense of community in the midst of growing fears. They also provided ways of dealing with the problem of fate.

Astrology, Magic, and Divination

Specific attempts at circumventing one's fate were the practices of astrology, magic,[28] and divination. Although astrology led to the preoccupation with fate, it also sought to deal with the problem. If the order of the stars determines one's destiny, then a knowledge of one's fate could be gained by a study of the stars. This explains the wide use of personal horoscopes in such diverse places as the imperial household[29] and Jewish Qumran. It also accounts for the depiction of Hellenistic deities in the zodiac, implying their control of the stellar movements. Closely associated with astrology was

26. See examples of Hellenistic astrology: Betz, *Greek Magical Papyri*; Cicero, "Dream of Scipio" (*On the Republic* 6.13ff.); Plutarch "The Face of the Moon" (*Moralia* 920ff.) Papyri Tebtunis 276 (late second century AD) and Chrysippus, *Fragment* 625 (both in Barrett, *New Testament Background*, 35–36, 61–62); Philo, *Migr. of Abraham* 179 (early first century AD); 4Q186 and 4QMess (Qumran Scrolls). Note statues and reliefs of Greek gods and zodiac in Godwin, *Mystery Religions*, plates 2 (Jupiter in zodiac), 8 (zodiac and intermediate deities), 142 (Orphic deity and zodiac); see also plates 75 (Asian goddess Cybele and zodiac) 50 (Jewish zodiac, sixth century AD). For excellent discussions, see Segal, "Heavenly Ascent"; Beck, *Brief History of Ancient Astrology*; Cramer, *Astrology in Roman Law*.

27. See plates of oriental deities in Hellenistic dress with universalistic titles, in Godwin, *Mystery Religions*, plates ii (Mithra), ix (Isis), 63–71 (Mithra), 85–89 (Isis and Sarapis).

28. For ancient texts, see Luck, *Arcana Mundi*. For discussion, see Aune, "Magic"; Petropoulos, *Greek Magic*; Kee, *Medicine, Miracle, and Magic*, 95–125.

29. Most of the Julio-Claudian and Flavian emperors were believers in astrology. Suetonius (*Augustus* 94.5) reports that from the hour of Augustus's birth, prophecies were made of his notable destiny; in his life of Tiberius, Suetonius repeatedly references astrologers; Claudius's wife Agrippina and her son Nero were both astrologer supporters.

Public ceremony of Isis cult, with priest officiating; wall painting from Pompeii, first century AD. (National Archaeological Museum, Naples)

the practice of magic. It was an attempt to gain mastery over both the good and evil powers that determine one's fate. The Great Magical Papyri from Egypt (third century AD) contain various prescriptions and rituals to deal with the good and bad spirits (demons) that affect one's destiny.[30] Prophetic oracles were also consulted at places like the shrine of Apollo at Delphi, Greece, and divination was practiced to discern the future.[31]

30. Both Jewish and pagan magical texts are found in these Egyptian papyri, now preserved in the National Library of Paris. The texts are reproduced, translated, and discussed in Deissmann, *Light from the Ancient East*, 254–64.

31. Originally prophetic women, called sibyls, resided at places like the temple of Delphi and gave ecstatic predictions. Later, prophecies ascribed to these sibyls were published in books, called the *Sibylline Oracles*. See translations and critical

The Mystery Religions

The mystery religions sought to deal with the problem of fate and the fears of the age with the hope of a continuation of life after death and personal communion with a deity.[32] Although they were given the

discussion of the vast corpus of the Sibylline Oracles (second century BC—seventh century AD) by J. J. Collins, in Charlesworth, *OTP*, 1:317–472. Underscoring their popularity in the Roman world, the emperors also consulted oracles and participated in divination (e.g., Suetonius, *Julius Caesar* 81; *Vespasian* 5; Tacitus, *Histories* 5.13).

32. Primary sources for the mystery religions are from a variety of Greek and Latin authors and inscriptions. Selections are found in Meyer, *Ancient Mysteries*; Ferguson, *Greek and Roman Religion*; and Grant, *Ancient Roman Religion*. Informative illustrations of ancient artifacts and excavated sites are also found in Ferguson, *Religions of the Roman Empire*; Godwin, *Mystery Religions*; and Guirard,

name "mystery religions" because of secret initiations, many also included public processionals and celebrations. Most of these mysteries included both the recital and the reenactment of a myth celebrating the death and resurrection of a deity. Some of these myths corresponded to the annual vegetation cycle when life is renewed each spring and dies each fall. The mysteries also promised their initiates immortality or at least some knowledge of the end of life, personal communion with a deity, and membership in a close-knit organization of fellow adherents. Cicero (*Laws* 2.14.36) records the opinion that in them "we have gained the power not only to live happily, but also to die with a better hope." Although all of the mystery cults were influenced by Hellenism and circulated throughout the Mediterranean world, we have conveniently grouped them according to their places of origin.

GREECE

The cult of Demeter[33] (goddess of soil and farming) and Kore (her daughter) originated at Eleusis (near Athens) in the fifteenth century BC. The myth concerns the kidnapping of Kore to Hades, Demeter's search for her, and Kore's release as Persephone. These events were memorialized in great festivals. The departure of Kore/Persephone was celebrated in October and her return in February. In September a great procession from Athens to Eleusis was held in honor of Demeter. Rites of purification and initiation were

also performed. The cult of Dionysus[34] began in Thrace (modern Bulgaria) but came to Boeotia, Greece, at an early date. Originally Dionysus was the god of wine (Roman name: Bacchus) and later the god of vegetation, life, and pleasure. In the myth, Dionysius was born from a union between Zeus and a human mother (Semele) and was raised by the nymphs of Nysa. As an adult he discovered the art of making wine and shared this gift with mortals during his many travels. Cultic festivals were held in December (new wine offering) and late February (last vintage of wine). Animal sacrifices were also offered. In early March a great festival took place with dramatic representations. In addition, orgiastic revelries occurred (e.g., on the slopes of Mount Cithaeron). The Orphic cult identified Dionysus with the Cretan god Zagreus, son of Zeus and Demeter (or Kore), who was slain and dismembered by jealous Titans. His heart was rescued by Athena, and from it Zeus created Dionysus, the Orphic god of life and death. Later Orphics eliminated the orgiastic features of the early Dionysian cult and produced sacred writings of hymns and cosmological myths.

EGYPT

The Isis-Sarapis cult[35] (300 BC) utilized ancient myths about the deities Isis, Osiris, and Horus, as early as 3000 BC. In Plutarch's version, Osiris (the personification of the Nile) was slain and dismembered by the evil god Typhon (associated with desert and sea water). Isis, a goddess representing earth and the forces that

---

New Larousse Encyclopedia of Mythology.

33. Meyer, *Ancient* Mysteries, 15–45; Mylonas, *Eleusis*; Clinton, "Eleusinian Mysteries."

34. Meyer, *Ancient Mysteries*, 61–110.

35. Ibid., 155–96.

cause the Nile flood, recovered the scattered pieces of Osiris and revived him. As his waters began to flow once more over the land, the union of these two divine principles gave birth to Horus, the personification of Egypt. In the Hellenistic period Osiris took the name Sarapis and was often portrayed as Zeus-Jupiter. Isis also appeared as Juno or Venus and was regarded as a divine queen, the mother of all, savior, and ruler of fate. Temples of Isis and Sarapis were found throughout the Mediterranean world. For example, Hellenized sanctuaries of Isis (called Iseia) have been found in Pompeii, in Rome, and on the Aegean island of Delos. Temples of Sarapis (called Sarapeia) have been excavated at Alexandria, Ostia near Rome, Pergamum, Ephesus, and Miletus. Many of them had assembly halls to contain a large number of people. These temples indicate a structured organization under the leadership of priests. Membership was obtained through a rite of initiation, and participation in sacred meals also occurred. Elaborate public processions were also part of the Isis-Sarapis cult. As a Hellenistic mystery religion, it flourished from 300 BC to AD 400.

PERSIA

The origin of Mithraism[36] goes back to the Mitra of the Indo-Aryans with some modifications. The god Mithras appears to be lower than the Persian Supreme Deity of Light (Ahura Mazda) but higher than the visible sun. He was also a mediator between light and the power of darkness (Ahriman). In the cult's legend,

Mithras is born from a rock on December 25 as witnessed by shepherds with gifts. While hunting, Mithras encounters a bull, overcomes it, and carries it into a cave where he kills the bull with a short sword. From its blood and semen grows new life, but a snake tries to drink the blood, and a scorpion poisons the semen. The sun, the moon, the planets, and the winds witness the sacrifice; Mithras meets the sun (i.e., Helios/Sol), both eat the meat and drink the bull's blood and make a covenant; Sol kneels before Mithras, receives the accolade, and they shake hands. The initiation into the mystery comprised seven steps of endurance, which probably corresponded to the seven planets. The initiate was called "reborn," and through an oath he became a soldier of Mithras. Military discipline and subordination were part of the cult's hierarchical structure. The Mithraeia at Ostia and Rome are cave-like structures with carvings of Mithras slaying the bull. The caves had benches for worshippers. Mithraism was a cult restricted to males but had fraternal relations with the Cybele cult. Mithraism flourished in the Roman Empire from the first to the fourth century AD.

ASIA MINOR

Although the Cybele cult[37] had early connections with Syria, it expanded to Asia Minor by the second millennium BC, where it flourished for centuries. The goddess Cybele was viewed as the Great Mother of life and a mighty and fierce fertility goddess. Attis was a Phrygian shepherd or the son of a mountain deity, beloved by the Great Mother. Although

---

36. Ibid., 197–222; Ulansey, *Origins*; Beck, *Religion of the Mithras Cult*.

37. Meyer, *Ancient Mysteries*, 111–54.

the Hellenistic legends of the couple are diverse, they concern Cybele's vengeance at the infidelity of Attis and his tragic death by castration. Some legends included a death and restoration to life of Attis by Cybele. Her cult was accompanied by orgiastic rites leading to a climax during which devotees would castrate themselves in ecstatic frenzy. Although the cult came to Rome in the early third century BC, its worship was secret because it was too barbaric for the Romans. In Greece the castration rite disappeared. A well-known rite of the cult was the taurobolium, in which initiates were washed in the blood of a slaughtered bull.[38] The cult attracted many female devotees.

Because they were close-knit associations attempting to overcome fate and offer a new hope, the mystery religions spread widely throughout the Roman world. Hellenization and syncretism (mixing of religions) contributed to their massive popularity, but their appeal must also be understood as a way for the benefits of Greek philosophy to reach the poor, less-educated masses. Although a direct dependency of early Christianity on the mystery cults is difficult to establish, both Christianity and the mystery religions shared parallel patterns of development because they existed in the same cultural environment. In many cities of the empire, the Romans (e.g., Tacitus, Suetonius, Pliny the Younger) probably viewed early Christians as devotees of a new mystery cult.

38. A vivid account of the taurobolium is found in a Christian work from the second century, Prudentius *Peristephanon* 10.1011–50. For discussion of relevant source material and the inclusion of informative archaeological photographs and illustrations, see Vermaseren, *Cybele and Attis.*

Gnosticism

Another spiritual phenomenon that competed with the mystery cults was Gnosticism, a widespread religious and philosophical movement of the first three centuries AD.[39] This diverse movement (or movements), like the mystery cults, was the product of Hellenistic syncretism, the mingling of Greek and Eastern traditions and ideas (i.e., of Greek, Jewish, Iranian, and Christian influences). Although there was no uniform Gnostic system, certain myths and motifs were dominant. A first major concept was "knowledge" (Gk. *gnōsis*). It was a secret revealed knowledge to initiates, which had both liberating and redeeming effects. The content of this gnosis consisted of basic insights into the divine nature of humanity and the cosmos. The possession of it freed the individual from ignorance and bondage in the world.

A second characteristic was a central myth that certain humans possessed a divine spark, which proceeded from the divine realm and had fallen into our world. Second, the earth is the tragic result of a downward movement from the divine realm. Third, the recovery of this divine spark in the world by its own

39. Primary sources for Gnosticism are found in Robinson, ed., *Nag Hammadi Library;* Layton, *Gnostic Scriptures;* Foerster, *Gnosis;* Grant, *Gnosticism: A Source Book;* Schneemelcher, *NTA;* selections of Mandean, Manichean, and other Gnostic texts are found in Rudolph, *Gnosis;* Barnstone, *Other Bible.* For a brief survey, see Hedrick and Hodgson, ed., *Nag Hammadi, Gnosticism, and Early Christianity,* 1–11. For a comprehensive survey and critical discussion of sources, see Rudolph, *Gnosis;* Pearson, *Ancient Gnosticism;* Perkins, *Gnosticism;* Yamauchi, *Pre-Christian Gnosticism;* Logan, *Gnostic Truth;* Williams, *Rethinking Gnosticism;* Roukema, *Gnosis;* King, *What Is Gnosticism?;* Lupieri, *Mandaeans.*

divine counterpart is necessary for liberation and redemption.

Another concept presupposed in Gnostic systems is radical dualism (two opposite realms) interwoven with a monistic conception (a supreme, unknown God). The spiritual realm of the unknowable God which incorporates a "fullness" (*plērōma*) of subordinate angels and heavenly beings is in direct opposition to our own physical world, which is characterized by chaos, darkness, ignorance, and death. The structure of this scheme consists of the following elements: At the center is the earth, surrounded by air and eight heavenly spheres. The eight spheres consist of the seven planets and the fixed stars that close them off. The spheres were believed to be inhabited by demons, spirits, or "rulers" (Gk. *archōn*). Above them lies the realm of the unknown God and the *plērōma* ("fullness") with its graduated worlds (*aeons*). These Gnostic cosmologies (or schemes of the world) varied particularly in the number of heavenly beings and spheres and the different names ascribed to them. For example, the so-called Valentinian system consisted of pairs of aeons ("dyads") called Nous-Truth, Logos-Life, and Man-Church. The so-called Basilidian system gave prominence to the archons, called Ogdoad and Hebdomad. Yet the basic scheme mentioned above is presupposed in both systems.

Also connected with these cosmologies was a myth of the creation of the world (a cosmogony) offered as an explanation for the present dilemma of humanity remote from God. Most Gnostic cosmogonies are influenced by the Genesis creation stories and consist of a fall of a heavenly being (e.g., Sophia), who through a series of complicated or tragic circumstances brings about the creation of the world (often called the Abortion). Like a diamond in mud, a divine spark hides within human inhabitants of this dark and ignorant world. Salvation for humans and the cosmos is accomplished when people receive gnosis about their divine origins through a Gnostic Redeemer, and when the divine soul takes its heavenly journey through the hostile spheres to be reunited in the divine realm. This final phase of restoration also constitutes the Gnostic teaching of last things.

Our understanding of Gnostic cults and communities is derived from Gnostic writings, patristic reports (often exaggerated), and later manifestations found among the Manicheans (sixth through tenth centuries) and Mandeans (fourth through twentieth centuries). Gnostic practices are as diverse as the sources, ranging from ascetic and monastic to libertine and licentious activities. Our primary sources confirm the ascetic and monastic features whereas evidence for libertine activities is deduced from secondary reports of the church fathers. The Manicheans were an ascetic, communal organization with a common meal and a so-called mass for the dead. The practices of the Mandeans were similar but are distinguished primarily by their baptismal ceremonies in flowing ("living") water.

The origins of Gnosticism are difficult to ascertain since our earliest sources are from the second and third centuries AD. Evidence from church fathers like Justin Martyr and Irenaeus make it clear that Christian Gnostics were in conflict with early catholic Christians at that time. Some have concluded from the patristic data that Gnosticism began as a Christian heresy. However, the discovery of the Nag

Hammadi texts in southern Egypt in 1945 has challenged this view. The Nag Hammadi collection seems to indicate the existence of fully developed non-Christian and non-Jewish Gnostic systems that may have preceded Christianity. This is a significant point since some scholars believe that the concept of a Gnostic Redeemer may have influenced the way some early Christians portrayed Jesus (e.g., Philippians 2; John 1), although there is no consensus on this view. Later Mandean, Manichean, and Hermetic texts (second to sixth centuries AD) show the prevalence of Gnosticism in the East and possibly contain early traditions contemporary with the NT.

Gods and Divinized Heroes

The Greco-Roman world, as we have seen, had many gods and goddesses. Some were mythical deities who dwelt in the heavens or on some mythical mountain, and others were associated with the cycles of the seasons. Some of these immortal gods, like the Gnostic Redeemer figure, descended from heaven to earth or were sent to fulfill some important mission for the benefit of humanity.

Some human figures of both history and legend were so endowed with divinity that they performed miraculous deeds.[40] Some were believed to be the offspring of gods and humans. What is most characteristic of them is their wisdom and spe-

cial powers. Usually they were considered great benefactors of humanity. In this category were divinized rulers, military leaders, politicians, philosophers, physicians, and healers. The idea of emperor worship, for example, was an adaptation of Eastern beliefs about the divinity of the king or pharaoh. But Western conquerors fostered such ideas on their marches eastward; for example, in the eastern provinces the Roman emperor was often believed to be divine. At home, Greeks and Romans tolerated such views for political unity but were disillusioned with them. It was customary, however, to pay homage to emperors as gods after they died.

Especially widespread was the notion of a hero or philosopher revered for his ability to perform miracles or to impart great wisdom. These great abilities were believed to be a manifestation of deity, and some of these heroes, such as the legendary Hercules, were granted immortality after death. Another example was the itinerant Pythagorean philosopher Apollonius of Tyana (Asia Minor), who had a miraculous birth, gathered followers, taught, healed, and appeared to his followers after his death. He lived in the first Christian century, and shortly after AD 217, a *Life of Apollonius*, which resembles a Synoptic Gospel, was written by Philostratus.

Hellenistic Philosophies

Like the mystery religions and Gnosticism, Hellenistic philosophies also promised deliverance from the fears and uncertainties of life.[41] Unlike most reli-

---

40. A selection of primary sources and comments on gods and divinized heroes is found in Cartlidge and Dungan, *Documents*; F. C. Grant, *Ancient Roman Religion*, 169–243; Hadas and Smith, *Heroes and Gods*; Campbell, *Hero with a Thousand Faces*, 49–254, 315–64. See also the surveys in Holladay, *Theios Aner*; Talbert, *What Is a Gospel?*; Tiede, *Charismatic Figure*.

41. For the pragmatic focus in Greco-Roman philosophies, see Bevan, "Hellenistic Popular

gious cults, these philosophical schools offered a comprehensive picture of the origin and structure of the universe. Such teachings were not formulated in the interests of pure science but were intended to explain a person's place and destiny in the universe, and how that person might best conduct his or her life. By the Hellenistic period, the golden age of Greek philosophy was past. In a pragmatic age disillusioned with the past ideals of human reason, the Hellenistic philosophies were popular quasi-religious movements of wandering preacher-philosophers and healers. The influential ideas of Plato (d. 347 BC) were continued in what is labeled Middle Platonism (68 BC—AD 205).[42] These Platonists followed the three characteristic aspects of Plato's dualism: (1) A distinction was made between two levels of reality: the imperfect, temporal, changing, material world of particulars over against the perfect, eternal, unchanging, spiritual world of Forms. (2) True knowledge of the Forms could be attained only by reason, not by sense experience. (3) The immortal soul was imprisoned in the mortal body (this idea is also Pythagorean). Plato's theological speculations were also developed by his disciples and the later Platonists. Plato's conception of the Good as the highest of Forms was identified as a supreme Deity (Middle

Platonism). His Demiurge (Divine Craftsman in *Timaeus*) was equated with Aristotle's Unmoved Mover (by Albinus of Smyrna), and Plato's mention of intermediaries (*daimones*) between heaven and earth was delineated into good and evil demons (by Xenocrates of Chalcedon).

Platonism influenced Alexandrian Jews like Philo, the Gnostic movement, and early Christianity. A few examples will be given: Philo stated that an invisible plan of Ideas had been conceived by God before he created the world (*Creation* 4). Philo also used biblical stories, such as Abraham's migration to Canaan, to illustrate the soul's migration from physical bondage. Gnosticism regarded the soul ("inner spirit") as needing liberation from the body, made extensive use of intermediate beings, and went beyond Platonic dualism in viewing the earthly world and divine realm as irreconcilable opposites. The NT book of Hebrews may have been influenced by Platonic (or Philonic) dualism in its constant analogies between shadow and reality, earthly and heavenly, and transitory and enduring. Early catholic Christians like Justin Martyr, and Alexandrian Christians like Clement and Origen were especially indebted to Middle Platonism.

The founder of Epicureanism was Epicurus of Samos (342–270 BC). His basic teachings were rarely altered by his followers.[43] Although maligned by contemporaries for his professed hedonism, he advocated a rational pursuit of pleasures that would free one from pain and

---

Philosophy." For primary sources and comments, see Barrett, *New Testament Background*, 54–79; Clark, *Selections from Hellenistic Philosophy*; Ferguson, *Greek and Roman Religion* 90–117; Grant, *Ancient Roman Religion*, 59–156.

42. A selection of sources for Plato and Middle Platonism are Plato, *The Republic, Symposium, Timaeus, Parmenides*; Diogenes Laertius *Lives* bk. 3; Albinus of Smyrna (AD 150); Plutarch, *Platonic Essays* (AD 120). Helpful secondary sources are Dillon, *Middle Platonists*; Merlan, *From Platonism to Neoplatonism*; Shorey, *Platonism*.

43. Sources for Epicureanism are Leucippus and Democritus in Diogenes Laertius, *Lives* 9.30–49; life and teachings of Epicurus in Demosthenes Laertius, *Lives* 10; Lucretius, *On the Nature of the Universe* (50 BC). For secondary information, see Hicks, *Stoic and Epicurean*.

despair. In order to lead such a pleasant life, Epicurus believed that one must be released from groundless fears that cause mental anguish. For this reason, Epicurus based his ethics on a materialist view of the universe. Whereas Aristotle valued the perceptions of our senses, Epicurus regarded them as the only true source of knowledge (not unlike modern empiricism). Epicurus also adopted the atomistic view of reality from Democritus (405 BC). This atomistic theory gave a natural explanation of the origins of the universe without reference to the gods: everything originated from the determined movements of atoms (*atomoi*) in a vacuum (*kenos*). This view, Epicurus believed, could deliver one from the fear of the gods, from the dread of death, and from the terrors of superstition. It would liberate the individual from the fear of the gods since the gods did not create the world, are made of a different element, and are unconcerned with human affairs. His view would release one from the dread of death, because when the atoms and void that constitute a person come apart, there is nothing more to experience. (Both the body and soul, or vital spirit, are mortal.) Epicurus's view would finally set free the person from the terror of destiny, because everything that occurs is the result of either atoms colliding in a vacuum (chance) or our own human choices (modifying Democritus with the inclusion of human volition).

Stoicism was probably the most popular Hellenistic philosophy.[44] Its name was derived from the *Stoa Poikile* or "painted porch," a public hall in Athens where its founder, Zeno (336–263 BC), taught. Because of its diverse development, Stoicism has been divided into three periods: Early Stoa (300–185 BC), Middle Stoa (185–46 BC), and Later Stoa (46 BC—AD 180).

In the early period, Zeno and his students sought to develop a complete philosophical system of physics, ethics, and logic. In physics, he followed the teachings of Heraclitus (500 BC), who saw the world ordered by divine reason or Logos, which he identified with the primal element of fire, from which everything came and to which all would return. Zeno and his student Cleanthes identified the Logos with Zeus, the supreme (but impersonal) governor of the universe. Zeno's disciple Chrysippus believed that the world would perpetually undergo a process of destruction by fire and restoration to life (i.e., a universal and recurring conflagration). In ethics, Zeno and his followers viewed conformity with the natural laws of divine reason as imperative. One conforms to divine reason by pursuing the good (virtue) and avoiding evil (vice). Since all adversities are determined occurrences, they should be endured with self-control and composure. Destiny is overcome by not being emotionally swayed by the circumstances of life. In logic Zeno was influenced by his teachers: Diodorus for his dialectics and Antisthenes (fourth century BC) for his linguistic analyses. Logical discussion mainly concerned the nature and manner of perceiving and understanding reality.

44. The lives and teachings of Heraclitus, of Zeno, and of his students is found in Diogenes Laertius, *Lives* 7; 9.1–17. The works of Epictetus and Seneca are found in the LCL. Collections of Stoic writings are found in Arnim, *Stoicorum Veterum Fragmenta*; Clark, *Selections from Hellenistic Philosophy*, 50–105; Barrett, *New Testament Background*, 61–71. For discussion, see Sellars, *Stoicism*; Hicks, *Stoic and Epicurean*; Rist, *Stoic Philosophy*.

The Middle Stoa was characterized by further revisions and accommodations to contemporary philosophical and religious views. Panaetius (185–109 BC) rejected the doctrine of universal conflagration and advocated the (Peripatetic) belief in the eternal quality of the world. Posidonius (135–46 BC) believed that a "seminal reason" of the divine Logos dwelt within all humans, and that obedience to this "seed of the Logos" would bring one in harmony with the universe.

The later period was almost exclusively devoted to ethical teachings. Seneca (AD 60), Nero's advisor, wrote essays on practical moral topics. The ethical *Discourses* and *Manual* ascribed to the Roman slave Epictetus (130) utilize the so-called diatribe form of argumentation: i.e., objections by fictional opponents, rhetorical questions, hyperbole, and anecdote. This form of debate was also used by the Apostle Paul and by the author of the book of James. The *Meditations* of Marcus Aurelius (AD 121–180) includes Epictetus and Plato as its sources.

Much of Stoicism was derived from Cynicism. Zeno, the founder of Stoicism, was a student of Crates, a disciple of Diogenes (400–325 BC), whose detached and independent lifestyle gave him the label "dog" (Gk. *kyōn*), from which the sect derived its name. Diogenes based his teaching on the Socratic ideals of Antisthenes (445–360 BC), who advocated the independent pursuit of virtue. Crates developed in a moderate direction the teachings of Diogenes, who stressed self-sufficiency and individualism with little interest in theoretical or speculative knowledge.[45]

During this period, literary disciples like Bion and Teles developed the diatribe form of argumentation and the listing of vices and virtues. Both of these literary forms are found in the NT. By the first century AD, much of Cynicism had been absorbed into Stoicism, although the former persisted in its characteristic scorn of conventional morality and religion.

In the Hellenistic world, the teachings and practices of philosophical leaders were often preserved and continued in schools of disciples. By the sixth century BC, the followers of Pythagoras gathered around him in Italy, forming a close brotherhood. Many other schools were also established in Athens: for example, Plato's Academy and Zeno's public hall or *Stoa*. This school tradition was also prevalent among the Jewish Essenes and Pharisees, with roots in the prophetic guilds of the ancient Near East (e.g., 1 Sam 10:5–11; 19:20–24; Isa 8:16; Jer 36:4). It also seems apparent that early Christianity developed schools or communities along similar lines (e.g., the Johannine community and Origen).[46]

Hellenistic Judaism

In competition with the religious and philosophical aspirations of the Greco-Roman world was Hellenistic Judaism, especially the Diaspora Jews, who lived

---

45. For primary data on Antisthenes, Diogenes and his followers, see Diogenes Laertius, *Lives* bk. 6. See also the following Cynic writings, mostly

from the third and second cent. BC: Malherbe, ed., *Cynic Epistles*; Malherbe, "Cynics"; Kee, *New Testament Context*, 230–31.

46. For the best example of philosophical schools and the succession of tradition, see Diogenes Laertius, *Lives of Eminent Philosophers*. See also surveys and discussion in Culpepper, *Johannine School*; Talbert, *Literary Patterns* 89–110, 125–34; and especially Alexander, "Acts and Ancient Intellectual Biography."

outside of Palestine.[47] Despite its distinctive adherence to the law of Moses, Judaism was a Hellenistic religion. By the third century BC, most Jews of the Diaspora and Palestine had learned to speak Greek. Shortly afterward, a Greek translation of the Hebrew Bible, the Septuagint, was begun in Alexandria.[48] It was later used by early Christians. Jewish philosophers like Philo of Alexandria (AD 20–50) interpreted the Jewish Scriptures figuratively or allegorically to underscore biblical agreement with Hellenistic philosophy.[49] It was Philo who sought to present the religion of the Jews as a type of mystery cult (*Cher.* 48–50), although he was not favorably disposed to the pagan mysteries (*Spec. Laws* 1.319–21). Jews such as Josephus wrote histories of their people to show that their cultural heritage was as good as that of the Greeks (e.g., *Ag. Ap.* 2.164–71). Archaeological excavations have shown that synagogues, serving as gathering places for worship and instruction, were located throughout the Mediterranean world.

Jews maintained a belief in only one God (monotheism), who created the world and controls its future. For those who live according to the will of God as expressed in the Jewish law (Torah) there is everlasting life; for the disobedient there is everlasting judgment (e.g., Dan 12:2–3; *1 Enoch*; 1QS 4.6–14; *m. ʾAbot*). These beliefs were appealing responses to the fears and problems connected with fate in Hellenism. As a result, Judaism attracted converts and admirers (e.g., Acts 2:5–13; 13:43, 50; 17:4, 17). Some Jews were probably engaged in missionary activity (Matt 23:15; *Num. Rabbah* 8.3; *b. Yebam.* 47a, b). Converts became sons children of Abraham, the father of all nations, and adopted partners in a covenant relationship with the God of Israel. Judaism's greatest influence was upon early Christianity, which began as an apocalyptic (end-time-oriented) Jewish sect.[50]

SUMMARY

A common language in a world of many dialects, improved travel and political stability under a world power, combined with fears and aspirations in an age of rapid transition: these are major characteristics of the NT Greco-Roman world. It was an age when Koinē Greek was spoken from East to West, and when Greek culture penetrated every major city of the Mediterranean world. It was a Roman age when political peace and economic stability were long-awaited realities in a war-torn and politically fragmented world. Roman resourcefulness and efficiency improved travel and trade in an unprecedented manner. Despite the irrational actions of a few despots, most Roman emperors and provincial rulers were fair to and tolerant of those willing to live peaceably under their rule. This period was a

47. See the mention of Diaspora in Josephus, *Ant.* 14.110–18; Philo, *Flacc.* 73–77; Jews discussed in Tacitus, *Hist.* 5.4–5. See also Bartlett, *Jews in the Hellenistic World*; Schürer, *History* 3:1–176; Levinskaya, *Book of Acts*; Bar-Kochva, *Jews in Greek Literature*. For further discussion, see chapter 2 below.

48. *Letter of Aristeas* 1–12, 28–51, 301–11 (second century BC); Philo, *On the Life of Moses* 2.26–42 (first century AD).

49. Examples of Philo's allegorical exegesis can be found in his *On the Migration of Abraham*, 89–93; *On the Posterity and Exile of Cain*, 1–11.

50. Collins, *Apocalyptic Imagination*. See also section on "Jewish Apocalypticism" in ch. 2 below.

time of rapid change through improved communication and increased mobility.

The sudden and pervasive changes mentioned above also generated new fears and aspirations. New fears were caused by the spread of disease, the shift of wealth, the dislocation of peoples, and the breakdown of old traditions. These fears expressed themselves in a variety of ways: as anxieties about the future, through loss of social or ethnic identity, and especially in an obsession with fate or destiny. In this age of anxiety, a variety of human aspirations arose, which were either symptoms of or responses to the fears and uncertainties. These aspirations appear to have been either religious or philosophical. The popular religious responses to this anxiety attempted to provide security and community through personal experiences with the gods. The popular philosophical responses sought to provide security and tranquility through a comprehensive picture of the universe and a specific ethical orientation to life.

It was into such an environment of cultural exchange, increased mobility, political stability, and of new hopes and fears that Christianity was born and developed. Nevertheless, just as Freudian psychologists remind us that the behavioral development of a child cannot be determined solely by his or her environment but must include the genetic relationship to the parents, so also we must include the parent religion that gave birth to Christianity: Judaism. Although we have briefly surveyed the phenomenon of Hellenistic Judaism, it is now necessary to examine more closely the development of Judaism and its beliefs, especially in the context of its homeland, Palestine.

2

The Jewish World of the New Testament

Heredity or environment? Which of these factors most determines the behavioral development of a child? This question has been debated vigorously among psychologists and behavioral scientists. No doubt most would conclude today that both hereditary and environmental factors are important and that both should be considered. This is also the case with the development of early Christianity, if we may employ an analogy between human growth and the historical development of a religious movement. What later became rabbinic Judaism and Christianity were both developments out of Judean state religion. Jesus and his disciples were Jews, and for some time Christianity was a sect within Judaism. We cannot fully appreciate the beliefs and practices of first-century Judaism without a grasp of the history that shaped them.

THE TRAGIC HISTORY OF JUDAISM

From the sixth century BC to the second century AD, the history of Judah can be viewed as one of foreign dominance with a brief interlude of independence. This tragic history of Israel can be outlined in five series of events: the Babylonian exile, the problematic resettlement under Persia, Greco-Syrian oppression, a disappointing interlude of independence, and conflicts with Rome.[1]

1. The provocative title of this section is based primarily on the history of Israel as one of domination by foreign oppressors (e.g., Assyrians, Babylonians, Egyptians, Syrian Greeks, Romans). A secondary consideration is Israel's interpretation of its own history as one of disobedience to the God of Israel (see, e.g., Deut 32; 1 Kgs 22; Neh 9; Isa 6:9–10; 8:17; 64:5–7; Jer 5:20–31; Ezek 2–3; Damascus Document of Qumran [CD]). See also the early Christian interpretations of Israel (Acts 7; 28:24–28; Rom 9–11). The titles "Tragic History" and "Persistent Faith" have also been applied to Judaism in Spivey and Smith, *Anatomy*, 7, 13.

The Babylonian Exile

The Babylonian exile (587 BC) marked the end of a great period of Judah's independence under such notable kings as David, Solomon, Hezekiah, and Josiah. Although the northern kingdom had seceded from unified Israel in 922 BC and had fallen to the Assyrians in 722 BC, the southern kingdom of Judah (west of the Dead Sea and including Jerusalem) had a relatively stable government and economy before the fateful years leading to its conquest by the Neo-Babylonians under Nebuchadnezzar II.[2]

The Babylonian exile meant for the people of Judah the loss of a king, land, and temple. From 598 to 587 BC there was a rapid succession of three Judean kings who were deported or killed by the Neo-Babylonians.[3] By 587 BC, a large number of citizens had been deported as slaves to Babylon. The city of Jerusalem lay in ruins and the magnificent temple built by Solomon had been destroyed. The holy place of worship, the temple, where the God of Israel chose to dwell with the people, was no more. This terrible series of events, as indicated by the sources, produced negative responses of fear, loneliness, anger, and despair, and the loss of both cultural and religious identity among the people of Judah.[4]

But these fifty years of exile were also a time of reorganization and growth for Judaism.[5] It was a time when many old traditions were written down and collected as sacred literature. The rite of circumcision and the institution of Sabbath-day observance had a special binding force, as did the possession of Jerusalem (and all that it meant) through the experience of dispossession. The Jewish belief in only one God (monotheism) reached its classical definition. The emergence of the synagogue, the meeting place for prayer and study of the law of Moses, also occurred. Finally, in the course of fifty years, many of the Jews who were dispersed throughout the Near East as slaves soon earned their freedom and entered trade and commerce. The dispersal of the Jews is the beginning of what is called the Diaspora, or the Jews scattered throughout the world.[6] During the Greco-Roman period, the Diaspora is almost synonymous with Hellenistic Judaism.[7]

2. The rise and fall of the Israelite monarchy is narrated in the Hebrew Bible: 1 and 2 Samuel, 1 and 2 Kings, 1 and 2 Chronicles, and also by Josephus, *Ant.* 7–9. See the following modern studies: Bright, *A History of Israel*, 183–339; Hayes and Miller, *Israelite and Judean History*; Herrmann, *A History of Israel*; Kaufmann, *The Religion of Israel*; Grabbe, *A History of the Jews*.

3. For biblical accounts of the fall of Judah, see 2 Kgs 24–25; 2 Chr 36; Jer 52; and Lamentations. See also Josephus, *Ant.* 10.74–185. For modern studies, see Ackroyd, *Exile and Restoration*; Bright, *History of Israel* 343–59; Herrmann, *History of Israel*, 289–97; Klein, *Israel in Exile*.

4. See, e.g., Lamentations; Pss 44; 74; 79; 102; 137.

5. See the exilic and postexilic writings of the so-called Deuteronomistic Historian (Deuteronomy to 2 Kings), the Priestly Writer (Leviticus and related cultic legislation of the Pentateuch), "Second and Third" Isaiah (40–66), and Ezekiel. See also the following: Ackroyd, *Exile and Restoration*; Bright, *History of Israel*; Klein, *Israel in Exile*; Blenkinsopp, *Judaism*; and Blenkinsopp, "The Age of Exile," 416–39; Zadok, *The Earliest Diaspora*.

6. It is because of the dispersion that we later read of Jewish residents in Mesopotamia, Arabia, Egypt, Asia Minor, Thrace, and Rome (e.g., Acts 2:9–11; 11:20; 13:14; 14:1; 17:1; 18:8; 18:19; 28:14–15; 1 Pet 1:1; Josephus, *Ant.* 13.259; 15.14; Philo, *Flacc.* 45–46). See Zadok, *Earliest Diaspora*; Levinskaya, *Book of Acts*; Bartlett, *Jews in the Hellenistic and Roman Cities*.

7. Josephus, *Ant.* 10.186–87; 14.110–18; *War*

The Resettlement under Persia

Even though the conquest of Babylon by the Persians and the Edict of Cyrus (538 BC) permitted the Jews to return home, there were many problems involved in the resettlement.[8] First, not many exiled Jews wished to return to their homeland. Most of them were descendants of the exiles, comfortably settled in Babylon and elsewhere. Second, there was much work to be done if Palestine was to be reestablished as a Jewish nation. Jerusalem lay in ruins, and there was no holy temple to unify the Jews in worship. Third, the exiles who arrived in Palestine were not welcomed by the current inhabitants. There was conflict with the scattered Jewish communities not deported in 587 BC, who were practicing a form of Judaism less structured than that of the exiles. There also was opposition from the Samaritans, a Jewish-like people who claimed to be the descendants of the northern kingdom, although this area had been resettled by Assyrian colonists after the fall of the north in 722 BC. Finally, there was also armed conflict with Arab tribes of surrounding nations (e.g., Edomites).

Despite many problems, groups of exiles returned to Palestine from 536 to 444 BC. A modest temple of worship was constructed around 515 BC, and the walls of Jerusalem were rebuilt under Nehemiah (437 BC). About this time, Ezra, "a scribe skilled in the law of Moses" (Ezra 7:43; Philo, *Flacc.* 73–75. See also Safrai and Stern, *The Jewish People*, 1:117–215; Sanders, "Dispersion," 854–56; Zadok, *Earliest Diaspora*; Bartlett, *Jews in the Hellenistic and Roman Cities*.

7:6), arrived, bringing the sacred Torah, which contained laws for the life and faith of the people. By this time, not all Jews were conversant in Hebrew but instead spoke Aramaic, a related Semitic language. It became the international language of commerce in the western Persian Empire. Aramaic remained the chief native dialect of Palestine during the time of Jesus, although most also spoke Hellenistic Greek.

The Greco-Syrian Oppression

The Hellenization of the Near East began with the conquests of Alexander the Great (332–323 BC) and continued under his two generals: Ptolemy and Seleucus.[9] Both divided up Alexander's eastern empire after his death and established dynasties: the Ptolemies of Egypt and the Seleucids of Syria.

For one century the Seleucids sought control of Palestine from the Ptolemies, because it served as an excellent buffer zone between the two kingdoms. When the Seleucids under Antiochus III finally controlled Palestine in 198 BC, the Jews welcomed their new overlords, and Antiochus granted them special privileges.[10] Under the rule of his son, Antiochus IV Epiphanes, this peaceful coexistence would end.

Because of heavy taxation under the Seleucids and the political infighting of the priestly families of Jerusalem, Palestine was in a turbulent state under Antiochus IV. The situation reached a crisis

8. See Ackroyd, *Exile and Restoration*, 138–231; Blenkinsopp, "The Age of Exile," 416–39; Collins and Harlow, *Eerdmans Dictionary of Early Judaism*.

9. For further discussion of Alexander and his successors, see ch. 1 above.

10. See Josephus, *Ant.* 12.129–53. On the term "Palestine," see Hanson and Oakman, *Palestine*, xviii, 15.

Incised on a fourth-century column capital of a synagogue in Capernaum, this seven-branched menorah lampstand (cf. Exod 25:31–40) commemorates the Maccabean victory over the Syrian Greeks and the purification of the Jerusalem temple (164 BC) celebrated at Hanukkah, the festival of lights. (Photo by Charles B. Puskas)

in 168 BC, when Antiochus plundered the temple treasury of Jerusalem between campaigns against Egypt. Conservative Jewish factions revolted in response. By this time the Egyptian campaign of Antiochus ended in defeat because of Roman intervention. The humiliated Seleucid king then returned to Jerusalem intent on subduing the rebellion.[11] He captured Jerusalem, killed or expelled its Jewish inhabitants, and repopulated the city with Syrian Greeks. As a result, the Jewish temple was devoted to the worship of Zeus, the Jewish religion was outlawed in Judea, and pious Jews were persecuted.[12]

The Interval of Jewish Independence

In response to these tragic events, the Maccabean revolt of 167 BC occurred. Many Jews who defied the laws of Antiochus IV fled to the hills of Judea and joined the guerrilla forces of Judas called Maccabeus ("the Hammer").[13] This resistance was actively supported by the Hasidim ("pious ones"), who advocated traditional Jewish values, and discouraged Hellenistic

---

11. See 1 Macc 1; 2 Macc 4–5; Josephus, *Ant.* 12.242–64. See also Bickerman, *God of the Maccabees*; Koester, *Introduction* 1:210–15; Jagersma, *History of Israel* (1986), 44–67.

12. Because of his anti-Jewish legislation, the figure of Antiochus IV has been portrayed as the archetypal villain in Jewish apocalyptic and

historical writings: e.g., Dan 11:20–39; 1 Macc 1; 4 Macc 4:15—5:38; Josephus, *Ant.* 12.242–86; *TAdam* 4:6–7.

13. Judas appears to have been the founder of the resistance movement in 2 Macc 5:27; 8:1, whereas in 1 Macc 2–3, it seems to be Mattathias of Modein, the father of Judas. The discrepancy may be explained by the fact that 1 Maccabees was composed by a Hasmonean court historian. The Hasmonean dynasty was founded by Simon, who was also a son of Mattathias. See Portier-Young, *Apocalypse Against Empire*, 25, 169, 212–14.

reform. Judas waged effective guerrilla warfare against the Syrian Greeks. In 164 BC he and his forces captured Jerusalem and reestablished Jewish worship in the temple.[14] Judaism has commemorated this event in the Feast of Dedication or Lights, also called Hanukkah.[15]

The Maccabean revolt restored freedom of worship to Judea, but independence would not take place until the ruling house of Simon was established, also called the Hasmonean dynasty.[16] Shortly afterward, Simon was heralded by the Jewish people as both ruler and high priest (140 BC).[17] During the reign of his son John Hyrcanus (134–104 BC), Syrian interference in the Jewish state finally ended.[18]

The dynasty established by Simon had the appearance of Hellenistic royalty.[19] As rulers of the people, Simon and his descendants had full military and political power. Only they were permitted to be clothed in purple and wear a gold buckle. As high priests, they were in charge of the sanctuary and its priests. Although the establishment of the dynasty was a welcome alternative to foreign rule, certain priests regarded the Hasmonean office of high priest as illegitimate; they questioned whether the Hasmoneans descended from the priestly family of Zadok.[20] It was probably at this time that the Essenes, a faction of the Hasidim whose leader was a Zadokite priest (the "Teacher of Righteousness"), left Jerusalem to establish their own community near the Dead Sea: Qumran.[21] Another faction of the Hasidim, the Pharisees, would also be persecuted under a later Hasmonean, Alexander Jannaeus (104–78 BC).[22]

Under the reigns of John Hyrcanus and his son, Alexander Jannaeus, most of Palestine became a Jewish state through conquest. Although they were practicing Hellenists, the Hasmoneans compelled the inhabitants of the Greek cities to convert to Judaism or to emigrate. Under coercion, Idumean males were circumcised,

14. Jerusalem's temple was *officially* returned to traditional Jewish worship by Antiochus (probably Antiochus V, 2 Macc 11:22–26). The remaining correspondences in 2 Macc 11:16–38 presuppose a lengthy period of negotiation, probably 164–162 BC.

15. See 1 Macc 4:36–59; 2 Macc 10:5–8; Josephus, *Ant.* 12.323–26.

16. Simon was the brother of Judas and son of Mattathias of Modein. Josephus calls Simon's family the "Asmoneans," probably the name of one of Simon's ancestors, *Ant.* 16.187; 20.190, 238.

17. 1 Macc 14:41–49.

18. Josephus, *Ant.* 13.254–300.

19. 1 Macc 14:41–49; Josephus, *Ant.* 13.213–17.

20. In the Chronicler's history, Zadok was a descendant of Aaron (1 Chr 6:50–53) who was appointed high priest by King David (16:39–40; 29:22). Ezekiel underscores the case that only descendants of Zadok could serve as high priests (Ezek 40:46; 48:11). On the Hasmonean ruler Jonathan (152–142 BC) as the wicked high priest at Qumran, see Stegemann, *The Library of Qumran*, 104–6, 148–52, 185; and VanderKam, *The Dead Sea Scrolls*, 129–32.

21. Some of the writings of this Qumran community, called the Dead Sea Scrolls, underscore both the preeminence of the Zadokite priesthood (CD 3.184.4; 1QS 5.1–3) and the corruption of the Jerusalem (Hasmonean) priests (1QpHab 9.4–5; 12.7–9); references from Dupont-Sommer, *The Essene Writings*; and García Martínez, *Dead Sea Scrolls*. On the possibility that the Hasmoneans were Zadokites see VanderKam, *From Joshua to Caiaphas*, 270 n. 90.

22. Josephus, *Ant.* 13.372–76. Pharisees were probably among the thousands of Jewish rioters punished by Alexander Jannaeus since they were outspoken critics of Hyrcanus, his father. See *Ant.* 13.288–92.

A Chronology of Jewish and Christian History

Major Empires	General History	Jewish Events	Select Authors or Writings
Neo-Babylonian (597–538 BC)	587 BC Destruction of Jerusalem by Neo-Babylonians	Babylonian exile Jerusalem temple destroyed	Lamentations Job (?) Isaiah 40–55
Persian (538–336 BC)	538 Cyrus's edict of toleration 509 Founding of Roman Republic 507 Democracy at Athens 431–404 Peloponnesian Wars	Return of exiles to Palestine 445 Nehemiah governs 428 Ezra's reforms	Isaiah 56–66 Haggai/Zechariah Malachi Ezra/Nehemiah Herodotus, Thucydides, Plato
Hellenistic (336–148 BC)	336–323 Conquests of Alexander the Great 175–164 Rule of Selucid Antiochus IV Epiphanes	320–290 Onias I, high priest 171–161 Menelaus, high priest 167 Maccabean Revolt against Seleucids 167–163 Independent Jewish state	Cynics Aristotle Stoics, Epicureans Chronicles, Daniel(?) Apocalyptic writings, Greek Septuagint (LXX) 1 Maccabees
Roman (148 BC—AD 455)	150–146 Destruction of Carthage and Corinth by Rome 44 Julius Caesar killed	Hasmoneans 135–104 John Hyrcanus 103–76 Alexander Jannaeus; Pharisees and Sadducees emerge 63 Rome acquires Syria and Palestine	*Psalms of Solomon* Cicero (106–43) Virgil (70–19) Lucretius (60) Philo (30–42); Paul (50–62)
30 BC—AD 14 Augustus 14 Tiberius 37 Gaius Caligula 41 Claudius 54 Nero 66–70 1st Jewish Revolt 69 Vespasian, 79 Titus 81 Domitian 98 Trajan 117 Hadrian 132–135 Second Jewish Revolt		37–4 BC Herod the Great 6–4 BC Jesus is born 4 BC—AD 39 Herod Antipas 30–33 Ministry of Jesus 62 Paul in Rome 70 Fall of Jerusalem 70–5th century Yavneh (Jamnia) R. Akiba 130 Simon bar Kosiba	Synoptic Gospels (65–85) John's Gospel (90) Josephus (75–93) *1 Clement* (95) *Didache* (100) *Gospel of Thomas* (100) Ignatius of Antioch (115) *Letter of Barnabas* (132)

Section of Roman aqueduct on the outskirts of Caesarea, first century AD.
(Photo by Charles B. Puskas)

and Samaritans submitted to the religious jurisdiction of Jerusalem.[23] Much of this expansionism was more the result of political ambition than religious zeal, as indicated by the Jewish revolt against the policies of Alexander Jannaeus (94 BC).[24]

After the reigns of Jannaeus and his widow, Alexandra (76–67 BC), the Hasmonean dynasty came to a close with the intrigues and fighting of their two sons. In 65 BC, such a struggle for power ensued between Aristobulus II and Hyrcanus II that the latter asked Rome to intervene, thereby ending Jewish independence.[25]

The Roman Occupation

The Roman general Pompey ended the dispute between the two Hasmoneans in 64 BC, bringing Judea and Galilee under Roman control, and in the reorganization under Augustus (27 BC) Palestine became part of the imperial province of Syria.[26] Around AD 6, Samaria and Judea were governed directly by the emperor through his prefect (later procurator). Pontius Pilate served as prefect of these regions from AD 26 to 36. His chief responsibilities were to maintain order and collect taxes. Although the Jews were granted certain privileges by the emperor, these were not always honored by the provincial governors (e.g., Pilate or G. Florus).[27]

The Roman provincial system also used the services of local magistrates. In

23. For the conquests of Hyrcanus, see Josephus, *Ant.* 13.230–300.

24. *Ant.* 13.131–86.

25. *Ant.* 14.1–79.

26. For more discussion of the Augustan provincial policies, see the previous chapter.

27. All the prefects and procurators of Palestine are mentioned in Josephus, *Ant.* 18.1–108; 19.360–65; 20.1–53, 148–223; *War* 2.117–83, 204–49, 271–404. Pilate is also mentioned in Philo, *Embassy* 38. See also Stevenson, *Roman Provincial Administration. Palestinia* was the Roman designation for both regions of Judea and Galilee and the Jewish inhabitants were called Judeans (*'Ioudaioi*) or Israelites (John 1:47; Acts 2:22), Hanson and Oakman, *Palestine*, xviii, 11.

First-Century Emperors, Roman Prefects over Judea, and Rulers in Israel

Emperors	Prefects	Kings, Tetrarchs, Ethnarch
AUGUSTUS, 27 B.C.–A.D. 14	Coponius, A.D. 6–9	HEROD the Great, King over all Israel, 37–4 B.C. (Matt. 2:1–19; Luke 1:5)
TIBERIUS, A.D. 14–37	M. Ambivius, 9–12 Annius Rufus, 12–15	ARCHELAUS, Ethnarch of Judea, Samaria, and Idumea, 4 B.C.–A.D. 6 (Matt. 2:22)
	Valerius Gratus, 15–26 PONTIUS PILATE, 26–36 (Luke 3:1; 23:1)	HEROD PHILIP, Tetrarch of Iturea, Trachonitus, Gaulanitis, Auranitis, and Batanea, 4 B.C.–A.D. 34 (Luke 3:1)
		HEROD ANTIPAS, Tetrarch of Galilee and Perea, 4 B.C.–A.D. 39 (Mark 6:14–29; Luke 3:1; 13:31–35; 23:7–12)
Caligula, 37–41	Marcellus, 36–37	
CLAUDIUS, 41–54	Marullus, 37–41	HEROD AGRIPPA I, 37–44; by A.D. 41, King over all Israel (Acts 12:1–24)
Nero, 54–68 (Emperor at deaths of Paul and Peter) Galba, 68 Otho, 69 Vitellius, 69 Vespasian, 69–79 Titus, 79–81 Domitian, 81–96 Nerva, 96–98 Trajan, 98–117	Cuspius Fadus, 44–46 Tiberius Alexander, 46–48 Ventidius Cumanus, 48–52 M. Antonius FELIX, 52–60 (Acts 23:26–24:27) Porcius FESTUS, 59–62 (Acts 25) Albinus, 62–64 Gessius Florus, 64–66 Vettulenus Cerialis, 70–72 Lucilius Bassus, 72–75 M. Salvienus, 73–81 Pompeius Longinus, 86	HEROD AGRIPPA II, 50–100, Tetrarch of Chalcis and northern territory (Acts 25:13–26:32)

Names in caps are mentioned by name in the New Testament.

H. Wayne House. Copyright © 2009 by the Zondervan Corporation.

the case of Palestine, the Idumeans, Antipater and his son Herod ("the Great"), obtained this derived authority. These shrewd politicians were able to shift allegiances to a succession of Romans (e.g., Pompey, Julius Caesar, Antony, Octavian), and as a result Herod became ("the Great" and) a powerful vassal king of Rome (37–4 BC).

Herod was also a magnificent builder[28] and a ruthless tyrant.[29] Though he may have won the favor of Augustus as a passionate Hellenizer, and surrounded himself with Greek scholars to undertake many building projects,[30] the last years of his reign were characterized by suspicion and cruelty. He had many opponents and relatives executed, including his wife (a Hasmonean princess). Because of his acts of cruelty and the fact that he was an Idumean convert to Judaism, Herod was never greatly liked by the Jews. Before Herod died, Jesus of Nazareth was born.[31]

After Herod's death, his kingdom was divided among his three sons. Philip became tetrarch of the largely non-Jewish areas northeast of the Sea of Galilee (4 BC—AD 34). Herod Antipas was named

28. Roller, *The Building Program*. For a well-done series of entries on the Herodian temple done from an archaeological and cultural perspective, see Rousseau and Arav, *Jesus and His World*, 279–313.

29. Sandmel, *Herod: Profile of Tyrant*. However, one need only read Tacitus, Suetonius, or other historians reciting the rise and fall of rulers in the ancient world to see that Herod was uncivilly typical in his savage protection of civil authority.

30. An impressive fortified palace, the magnificent Jerusalem temple, the fortress of Masada (thirty-five miles south of Jerusalem), and numerous Greek cities with theaters, baths, and amphitheaters are examples of his complacent ambition.

31. For extensive material on Herod the Great, see Josephus, *Ant.* bks 14–17 and *War* 1.195–673. See also Grant, *Herod the Great*; Perowne, *Life and Times*; Kokkinos, *Herodian Dynasty*; Richardson, *Herod*.

tetrarch of Galilee and Perea across the Jordan River (4 BC—AD 39). Herod Antipas had John the Baptist executed (Mark 6:14–29), and it was before him that Jesus appeared (Luke 23:6–12). Antipas was eventually exiled by the emperor Caligula (AD 39). Archelaus was given Samaria and Judea. Because his rule was challenged by both his subjects and Antipas, and because general unrest was brewing in Galilee, Archelaus was dismissed by Rome and banished to Gaul in AD 6. Except for the short reign of Herod Agrippa I over all Palestine (41–44), the entire region was under Roman procurators after AD 44.[32]

According to ancient Jewish sources, life for the Jews under the prefects and procurators was difficult. Pontius Pilate ignored Jewish customs, confiscated temple monies, and killed many Jews and Samaritans.[33] Pilate was eventually sent to Rome to account for his actions and was exiled (AD 36). After the interim reign of King Agrippa I ended (AD 44), the situation under the procurators became worse. At this time arose Jewish revolutionaries who sought to rekindle the spirit of the Maccabean revolt. Self-styled prophets

and messiahs also appeared, as well as a radical group of assassins, the Sicarii.[34] The procurators Felix (AD 52–60) and Festus (AD 60–62), spent a great deal of time putting down Jewish revolts (both are mentioned in Acts 23–24).

Gessius Florus (AD 64–66), one of the last and worst procurators, fanned the flames of revolt in Palestine.[35] In AD 66, his embezzlement of funds from the temple treasury outraged the people. Florus responded to their outcries by having his troops plunder the city. When mediation attempts failed, a fierce struggle occurred in the area between the Roman fortress of Antonia and the temple court. Shortly afterward, sacrifices offered to Rome and the emperor ceased, and the fortress of Masada, thirty-five miles south, was captured. These events marked the beginning of the Jewish resistance party called the Zealots.[36]

---

32. For information on the later Herods, see Josephus, *Ant.* bks. 17–19; *War* bks. 1–2. See also Hoehner, *Herod Antipas*; Jones, *Herods of Judea*; Perowne, *Later Herods*. See also Safrai, *Economy of Roman Palestine*.

33. *Ant.* 18.55–59, 85–89; *War* 2.175–77; Philo, *To Gaius* 38.

34. For example, see Judas the Galilean who inspired the Zealot sect (*Ant.* 17.271–72; 18.1–10; *War* 2.117–18), Theudas the false prophet (Ant. 20.97–99), the Egyptian prophet (*Ant.* 20.167–72) and other false prophets (*War* 6.285–87). For data on the Sicarii and Zealots, see *War* 7.252–74; 7.407–19. See also Rhoads, *Israel in Revolution 6–74 C.E.*; on social banditry, see Hanson and Oakman, *Palestine*, 81–85.

35. Josephus, *War* 2.77–341. On Roman provincial administration of Palestine, see Hanson and Oakman, *Palestine*, 62–63.

36. *War* 2.405–56. Although many resistance groups existed before AD 66, a case can be made for the emergence of a specific Zealot party only after AD 66. See Josephus, *War* 2.441–48, 564; 4.158–61; 7.268–70; Rhoads, *Israel in Revolution*, 52–58, 97–110; Borg, "Currency of the Term 'Zealot'"; Hengel, *Zealots*; Goodman, *Ruling Class*.

The Arch of Titus on the Via Sacra of Rome was erected (ca. AD 94) to commemorate Titus's capture of Jerusalem in AD 70. On it, Jewish captives are shown marching in procession and carrying spoils from the temple.
(Photo by C. B. Puskas)

After some successful attacks by the rebels, Nero dispatched his able general, Vespasian, to quell the revolt that was spreading throughout Palestine. With the aid of his son, Titus, who commanded the forces of Egypt, Vespasian made a successful assault upon Galilee with a massive army.[37] Jerusalem at this time was caught in a bitter civil war between moderate and radical Jewish rebels. The experienced Vespasian subdued the surrounding areas and waited for the Jews to exhaust themselves in Jerusalem. But before Vespasian could end the revolt in Jerusalem, his actions were delayed by the death of Nero. In 69, Vespasian left his command post

to his son Titus and went to Rome to become its ninth emperor.[38]

In the spring of 70, Titus began his siege of Jerusalem.[39] Although the Jewish factions finally united in combat, the military entrenchment around the city made it impossible for the rebels to receive supplies. Hunger and thirst took their toll and the city was gradually taken. The great temple was lost to fire amid the battle.[40] Many men, women, and children died because the Jews refused to surrender. When the battle was over, the city and temple were in ruins, and Titus returned to Rome with hundreds of prisoners to exhibit for the victory parade through the city, commemorated (shortly afterward) by the arch of Titus, still standing in the Roman Forum today.[41]

Despite a decisive victory, the Romans needed to subdue several fortresses, particularly the fortress of Masada.[42] Built by Herod the Great on a mesa along the Dead Sea, the fortress was almost impregnable. The rebels occupying Masada were under the command of Eleazar son of Yair. Flavius Silva, the Roman commander, was forced to build a tremendous land bridge in order to transport a large battering ram to penetrate the wall. When Eleazar realized that the cause was lost, he addressed his garrison, and requested

38. *War* 4.486–502, 545–55, 588–663; Suetonius, *Vespasian* 4–6.

39. *War* 5.1–20, 39–46.

40. Ibid., 6.1–8, 15–53. On the impact of the destruction, loss, and calamity for the Jews, see Neusner, "Judaism in a Time of Crisis."

41. The Arch of Titus was completed after his death (AD 94). The following references recount his triumph over the Jews. *War* 7.116–162; Suetonius, *Titus* 4–5.

42. *War* 7.252–406; Yadin, *Masada: Herod's Fortress.*

37. *War* 3.1—4.120

Judaea Capta. (Photo by Art Resource)

that they kill their families and themselves rather than surrender. When the Romans finally breached the wall in AD 73, there was no battle left to be fought. According to Josephus, there were seven survivors: two women and five children.

The destruction of Jerusalem and the second temple was a terrible blow to Judaism. What survived was a reorganized religion under the Pharisees,[43] who gathered at the coastal town of Jamnia (Hebrew: Yavneh).[44] This religion without a temple and priests became known

as rabbinic Judaism.[45] Influential Jewish communities continued to develop outside of Palestine (e.g., in Egypt, in Babylon). Palestinian Judaism lingered until the Judean uprising led by Simon bar Kosiba or Kochba ("Son of the Star") between 132 and 135.[46] The revolt reacted to Emperor Hadrian's attempt to rebuild Jerusalem into a Greco-Roman city with a temple for Jupiter. Hadrian ended the revolt and carried out his plans, forbidding Jews to enter the city. From that time on, until the establishment of a Jewish state in

43. According to Cohen ("The Significance of Yavneh") Jabneh (Yavneh) should be seen as the development of a Jewish coalition of the sects. The rabbis who engineered the reorganization "saw themselves as members of the same philosophical school who could debate in friendly fashion the tenets of the school" (51).

44. The Hebrew name, Jabneh or Yavneh is mentioned in 2 Chr 26:6; the Greek name Jamnia in 1 Macc 4:15; 5:58; 2 Macc 12:8–9; Josephus, *War* 2.335. The Jewish Mishnah (ca. AD 220) mentions the transfer of the court ("Beth-Din") or college ("Yeshiva") of seventy-two elders from Jerusalem to Jabneh in the following tractates: *Roš Haš.* 4:1–2; *Zebaḥ.* 1:3; *Ketub.* 4:6. Yavneh (Jamnia) was the center of Judaism from AD 70 to the early second century. See Lewis, "What Do We Mean by Jabneh?" 125–32; Neusner, "The Formation," 3–42.

45. Third-century rabbinic sources containing earlier traditions are the Mishnah, legal interpretations of the Torah; the early *Midrashim*, commentaries on the Hebrew Bible; the Tosefta, additions to the Mishnah. See also Neusner, *Early Rabbinic Judaism*; and Neusner, *Method and Meaning in Ancient Judaism*. For a collection of texts with introductions see Schiffman, *Texts and Traditions*; and for a full discussion, see Schiffman, *From Texts to Tradition*; also Strack and Stemberger, *Introduction to the Talmud and Midrash*; Neusner, *Rabbinic Judaism*; Evans, "Judaism, Post–AD 70."

46. Spartianus, *Hadrian* 4; Dio Cassius, *Roman History* 69.12–15; Eusebius, *Hist. eccl.* 4.6.1–4; 8.4. See recently discovered letter from Simon Bar Kochba in Yadin, *Bar-Kochba*.

1948, Judaism was primarily a religion of the Diaspora.[47]

THE PERSISTENT FAITH OF JUDAISM

Although Judaism's history was characterized by foreign dominance, its traditions and beliefs persisted for centuries. Unlike their foreign conquerors, whose religions were diverse, the Jews retained their belief in only one God, offered sacrifices at only one temple, observed feasts that retold their history as a people, sought to follow laws of God written in sacred books, worshipped God and studied the laws in meeting houses called synagogues, and maintained confidence in their destiny as the people of God. Even though foreign thought forms (e.g., Babylonian, Persian, Greek, and Roman) influenced Jewish beliefs and practices, their appropriation into a complete system of monotheism, law, and religious history made Judaism a distinct religious phenomenon. We will now look more closely at these Jewish beliefs and practices.

The One God

Allegiance to only one God, or practical monotheism, came to its fullest expression in Judaism during the Babylonian exile, when the sovereignty of other gods was rejected.[48] However, stress on the oneness of God and on the need for exclusive obedience to him occurred before the exile, when Israel's classic expression of faith was framed: "Hear, O Israel, the Lord our God, the Lord is one" (Deut 6:4; cf. 4:35, 39). After the exile, God's name, Yahweh, became too sacred to be pronounced and was substituted with Adonai ("Lord").[49] The Jews also viewed their God in distinction from the world as its creator, yet as active in the world as provider and savior. During the Greco-Roman period, Jews were often accused of atheism by Gentiles (non-Jews), because Jews refused to recognize the sovereignty of any other deity except their own.[50]

Connected with the Jewish belief in only one God was the idea of a covenant that bound the people with their God. Many of the covenant formulations found in the Jewish Scriptures were based on secular treaties of the ancient Near East that had been instituted by kings for their vassal subjects.[51] These covenants or binding agreements with God usually included (1) a list of gracious acts that God had performed in Israel's behalf, such as delivering it from bondage in Egypt (Exod 19:4–6), and (2) stipulations that Israel was expected to carry out in response to God's acts of favor (20:1; 23:19). The circumcision of every male child was also required as a sign of the covenant (Gen

---

47. See the popular history that underscores this point: Eban, *My People*. See also Ben-Sasson, *History of the Jewish People*.

48. Second Isa 43:10–11; 44:8; 45:5–6, 21–22; 46:8–9. See also Anderson, "God"; Smith, *Early History of God*, 145ff.; Riley, *River of God*, 22–49.

49. Mishnah *m. Sanh.* 7:5; *Yoma* 6:2; *Sotah* 7:6; and Matt 5:34–35; 23:21–22.

50. For Roman suspicions of Judaism, see Seneca, *Ep. Mor.* 95.57; Tacitus, *Hist.* 5.2–13. For Jewish opposition to emperor worship, see Josephus, *Ant.* 18.257–68; Philo, *Embassy* (concerning the deification of emperors Caligula and Augustus).

51. For modern discussion with primary sources, see McCarthy, *Treaty and Covenant* and *OT Covenant*; Mendenhall, "Covenant Forms in Israelite Tradition"; Porter and de Roo, *Concept of the Covenant*.

Jerusalem viewed from the east, near the Mount of Olives. The Dome of the Rock (center) was built in AD 691 on the Herodian temple area. The current walls, rebuilt in the sixteenth century, follow roughly the contours of Herod's construction.
(Photo by Charles B. Puskas)

17:10–14). This covenant with God gave the people both a special status as God's elect and a sacred responsibility to carry out God's statutes and laws.

The Sacrificial System

Although attempts were made in Israel and Egypt to construct rival temples,[52] the temple of Jerusalem[53] remained the exclusive place of sacrificial worship for almost all Israelites. King Solomon built the first temple a thousand years before the Christian era, and it was destroyed by the Neo-Babylonians in 587 BC A modest temple was built by the returning exiles in 515 BC and rebuilt on a much grander scale in the

Herodian period. This temple was begun under Herod the Great (20 BC) but was not completed until AD 60—ten years before its destruction.[54]

The guardians of the temple and its worship were the priests. When temple worship was restored in 515 BC, they regained much of the influence they had lost during the exile—especially the high priest, who had both civil and religious authority. Under the Seleucid Greeks, the high priesthood became a political position sought after by competing priestly families (e.g., Jedaiah, Bilgah). During the brief interlude of independence, the Hasmoneans (of questionable Zadokite descent) assumed the prerogatives of both high priest and king. As a result, the

52. Stinespring, "Temple, Jerusalem"; Ben-Dov, "Temple of Herod"; Haran, "Priests and Priesthood."

53. When the Jerusalem temple was captured by Antiochus IV, the high priest, Onias IV, built a similar but inferior temple in Heliopolis, Egypt; see Josephus, *Ant.* 13.62–68.

54. The earliest descriptions of the Herodian temple and priesthood are Josephus, *Ant.* 15.380–425; high priests 20.224–51; *War* 5.184–247; *m. Mid.* ("Measurements" of the temple) 1–5; see for discussion Rousseau and Arav, *Jesus and His World*, 279–313.

pro-Zadokite Essenes withdrew from Jerusalem, and the pro-Hasmonean Sadducees (mostly of the house of Boethus) rose to power. In the Herodian period, high priests were appointed from priestly families of the Diaspora (e.g., Phiabi of Babylon, Boethus of Egypt). They presided over both the temple worship and the Great Sanhedrin, the high court of Judaism.[55] The power of the priesthood ended with the destruction of Jerusalem in AD 70.

administered by the priests, and sacrifices were offered on an altar at least twice daily.

Even the architectural design of the Herodian temple reflected the various degrees of holiness.[57] Only the outermost part of the temple was accessible to Gentiles. Moving toward the central buildings (for Jews) came the Court of Women; the Court of Israel (for men); the Court of Priests, where daily sacrifices took place;

Scale model of the Herodian Temple of Jerusalem reconstructed by Y. Aharoni and displayed at the Holyland Hotel of Jerusalem. (Photo by Charles B. Puskas)

The major religious functions of the priests were to maintain purity through the sacrificial system at the temple.[56] In ancient Israel a whole system of sacrifices had arisen to set sinful people right with the one, holy God. This system was

the Holy Place, where the priests regularly burned incense; and the Holy of Holies, which the high priest entered only once a year on the Day of Atonement.

Even though the temple was a holy center where the priest interceded for the people, it was also the center of commercial activity. It housed the national treasury collected from an annual temple tax that every Jew was expected to pay. The

55. For an excellent survey, see Mantel, "Sanhedrin."

56. Lev 1–10; 16; 21–23; 27; Ezek 44–46. See also Schiffman, "Priests."

57. Josephus, *Ant.* 15.380–425; *War* 5.184–247; *m. Mid.* 1–5.

priests were also responsible for the collection and allocation of these funds.

The Feasts

Closely related to the temple worship were the religious festivals and holy days of the Jews.[58] The Jewish civil year began around September/October whereas the religious year began in about March/April. Regula-tions for the feasts are prescribed in the books of the law (Exodus, Leviticus), with the exception of Hanukkah and Purim, which were instituted later. Pilgrims from outside Jerusalem and Palestine thronged to the holy city for the three main festivals: Passover/Unleavened Bread, Pentecost, and Booths. The biblical significance of the feasts was retained in the Herodian period.

Feast	Purpose	Date
Passover/ Unleavened Bread	Commemorates the exodus from Egypt and marks the beginning of the wheat harvest (Exod 12–13; Num 9; Deut 16; 2 Chr 30; 35).	Nisan 15 (March/April) 7 days
Pentecost or Weeks	Commemorates the giving of the Law on Mt. Sinai (Lev 23:15–16) and marks the end of wheat harvest (Exod 23:14–17; 34:18–24; Deut 16:10)	Sivan 6 (May/June) 50 days after Passover
Trumpets or Rosh Hashanah	Inaugurates both the civil year and the end of the grape and olive harvest (Lev 23:23–25; Num 29).	Tishri 10 (Sept/Oct)
Day of Atonement *Yom Kippur*	Day of national repentance, fast and atonement (not called a feast) (Lev 16; 23:26–32).	Tishri 10 (Sept/Oct)
Booths or *Succoth*	Commemorates the living in tents leaving Egypt for Canaan—a joyous festival when people would live in temporary huts made of branches (Exod 23:14–17; Lev 23:34–36).	Tishri 15–22 (Sept/Oct)
Lights or Dedication, Hannukah	Commemorates the rededication of the temple by Judas Maccabeus, with brilliant lights in temple area and Jewish homes (1 Macc 4:42–58).	Kislev 25 (Nov/Dec) 8 days
Purim or Lots	Commemorates the deliverance of Israel during Persian period, with public reading of book of Esther in synagogue (2 Macc 15:36).	Adar 14–15 (Feb/March)

58. Early sources outside the Bible are Josephus, *Ant.* 3.237–57; 11.109–13; 12.323–26; *War* 2.42–44; 6.423–27; *m. Moʿed* ("Set Feasts"), second major division. For a listing of some Mishnaic texts with comments, see Barrett, *New Testament Background*, 153–62.

The Law

After the exile, Judaism began to stress obedience to God's will in its collection of sacred writings.[59] By this time the Deuteronomistic History (the books of Deuteronomy through 2 Kings) had been added through Deuteronomy) and Prophets (Joshua through 2 Kings, Isaiah through Ezekiel, and twelve Minor Prophets) was closed by the second century BC (according to the prologue in the book of Sirach), but a third undefined group of other books (Writings) remained open. This

The ark of the covenant (Exod 25:10–22) incised on column capital of the synagogue of Capernaum. It was associated with the presence of God and supposed to have contained the tablets of the Ten Commandments. It disappeared at some time during the monarchy, although it is said that Jeremiah hid it from Nebucahadnezzar (2 Macc 2:4–8; 2 *Bar.* 6), see Neusner and Scott, *Dictionary of Judaism*, 59. (Photo by Charles B. Puskas)

to Genesis, Exodus, Leviticus, and Numbers to serve as Israel's primary history. Several prophetic books were also added: Isaiah 1–39, Jeremiah, Ezekiel, and some so-called Minor Prophets (i.e., Amos, Hosea, Micah). Supplements to Isaiah (40–66) and additional Minor Prophets were added in the exile and shortly afterward. This collection of the Law (Genesis third general category included such writings as the Psalms, the Proverbs, Esther, and Daniel.[60]

Obedience to the Torah ("instruction"), particularly to the legal material of the law collection (Exodus–Deuteronomy), was of primary importance in Judaism. To know the law was to know the will of God. To study and do the law was

59. Mantel, "Development of Oral Law," 41–64, 325–37; "Torah Scholarship," 314–80; and "Life and Law," 464–87; Strack, *Introduction to the Talmud and Midrash*.

60. Freedman, "The Canon of Old Testament"; and J. A. Sanders, "Torah"; Sundberg, "The 'Old Testament'"; Leiman, *Canonization of Hebrew Scripture*.

the greatest blessing. By the Hasmonean period, different attitudes had evolved regarding the Torah. The Pharisees were concerned with interpreting and applying the law in a manner applicable to contemporary problems. They held that God had given Moses two laws: a written one (Law, Prophets, and other Writings) and an oral one to interpret the written.[61] The Sadducees rejected the concept of oral law and did not regard the prophetic or other books (Writings) as binding in authority. The Essenes, like the Pharisees, devoted themselves to the study of the Law, Prophets, and Writings but focused on ascetic practices and prophetic predictions in their communities outside of Jerusalem.[62]

After AD 70, rabbinic Judaism assumed the position of the Pharisees. The practice of the Pharisees and their descendants—to expand the written word by oral tradition in order to apply it to new conditions—is documented in the Mishnah and Talmud. Rabbinic Judaism progressed by restatement and revision as a result of much discussion and debate. By the first century already differing schools of interpretation had formed within the Pharisees (e.g., Hillel and Shammai). Debate and discussion were necessary to make a hedge for the Torah, i.e., to keep it from being transgressed. To preserve the Sabbath commandment (Exod 20:11) one should not work. But what is work? Oral tradition, transcribed into the Mishnah

by AD 220, would set out to define precisely what activities constitute work. So important was the Torah to the Jews that all aspects of life and thought were to be inspired and guided by it.[63]

The Synagogue

The synagogue ("gathering place")[64] played an important part in the growth and persistence of Judaism. In the Roman period, synagogues were in most regions of the empire.[65] Although the Talmud mentions their origins during the exile,[66] the earliest archaeological evidence dates from the Christian era.[67] The synagogue was a meeting place for prayer, and an educational center for the study of the law. No sacrifices were offered there. The synagogue services probably consisted of a recitation of the Shema (Deut 6:4), Scripture readings, expositions, blessings, and

---

61. On Pharisees and oral law, see Josephus, *Ant.* 13.297. For an example of oral traditions codified in writing, see *m. ʾAbot*, selections of maxims in praise of the law handed down in the names of 60 teachers of the law who lived between 300 BC and AD 200.

62. Josephus, *Ant.* 18.18–22; *War* 2.119–61; the Dead Sea Scrolls of the Qumran community (an Essene sect).

63. Some English translations of major rabbinic works are Danby, *The Mishnah*; Neusner, *Mishnah*; Blackman, *Mishnayoth*; Epstein, *Babylonian Talmud*; Neusner, *Babylonian Talmud*; Guggenheimer, *The Jerusalem Talmud*; Freedman and Simon, *Midrash Rabbah*. The Mishnah and Talmud, contain *halakah* (exposition of law) and *haggadah* (stories and maxims). The Midrash is primarily *haggadah*.

64. Safrai, "Synagogue"; "Synagogue," in Schürer, *History* 2:423–63; Feldman, "Diaspora Synagogues"; Levine, *Ancient Synagogue*.

65. Allusions to these synagogues can be found in the Gospels, Acts, Josephus, Philo, and rabbinic sources.

66. *p. Meg.* 3.73d; *b. Meg.* 29d, alluding to Ezek 11:16, a "sanctuary" (*mikdash*) for the Diaspora.

67. See archaeological illustrations with comments about synagogues in Palestine, Babylon, Egypt, Asia, Greece, and Italy: Sonne, "Synagogue"; and Meyers, "Synagogue, Architecture"; Rousseau and Arav, *Jesus and His World*, 268–72.

Rabbinic Writings

Writings	Divisions	Dates	Contributors	Contents	Comments
Mishnah	Seeds Festivals Women Damages Holy Things Purifications	50 B.C.–A.D. 200	Tannaim	Curriculum for the study of Jewish law	The Mishnah was the basic document of Rabbinic Judaism and considered *Oral Torah*. The Mishnah was divided into six sections: *Seeds*, concerning ritual laws dealing with cultivation of the soil; *Festivals*, concerning rules and regulations on the Sabbath and holy days; *Women*, on marriage, divorce, and other family issues; *Damages*, mainly regarding compensation on damages; *Holy Things*, rules and laws on sacrifices, and other issues pertaining to the ancient temple and its ritual; *Purifications*, pertaining to the subject of cleanness and purity.
Tosefta		A.D. 100–300	Tannaim	Teachings not found in the Mishnah	Earliest commentary on the Mishnah
Palestinian Talmud	Mishnah Gemara	A.D. 300	Amoraim	Commentary on the Mishnah	Over ninety percent of the Palestinian Talmud focuses on the Mishnah.
Babylonian Talmud	Mishnah	A.D. 200	Tannaim	Legal portions commenting on Torah	The Babylonian Talmud contains more material that is unrelated to Mishnah than does the Palestinian Talmud. Also, the Babylonian Talmud includes many more scriptural units than the Palestinian Talmud.
	Gemara	A.D. 200–500	Amoraim	Commentary on the Mishnah	
Midrash	Halakah	100 B.C.–early Middle Ages	Tannaim and Amoraim	Legal sections commenting only on Torah	Halakah is the legal part of the Midrash, usually derived from OT.
	Haggadah			Narratives and sermons on any part of Old Testament	Haggadah embraces nonlegal interests infrequently encountered in the Mishnah.

H. Wayne House. Copyright © 2009 by the Zondervan Corporation.

prayers.[68] The popular Jewish sect of the Pharisees, whose members excelled in the study of the law, were closely associated with the synagogue.

The Final Destiny

Judaism was concerned not only with remembering the past and living faithfully in the present but also with understanding its future destiny.[69] In reaction to the tragic events of Jewish history (e.g., the Babylonian exile, Syrian oppression, and the disappointing Hasmonean rule), two alternative lines of thought developed about the future. First, Judaism could repeat the lofty, nationalistic hopes of the ancient prophets (e.g., Isa 11; Mic 4), and leave to God the time and circumstances under which these glorious promises would be fulfilled. Second, it could assess the national tragedies as the work of a demonic power opposed to God and shift

68. For the two versions of the "Eighteen Benedictions" (*Shemoneh 'Esreh*) used in early synagogue worship, see Schürer and Vermes, *History* 2:455–63; and other prayers with some Christian interpolations: Darnell and Fiensy, "Hellenistic Synagogal Prayers (Second to Third Century AD)," in *OTP* 2:671–97.

69. For primary sources, see *OTP*, vol. 1; Vermes, *Complete Dead Sea Scrolls*; García Martínez, *Dead Sea Scrolls*; Ryle and James, *Psalmoi Solomontos*; Charlesworth, *Dead Sea Scrolls*. For important studies, see Hanson, "Jewish Apocalyptic against Its Near Eastern Environment"; Hanson, *Dawn of Apocalyptic*; Koch, *Rediscovery of Apocalyptic*; Collins, *Apocalyptic Imagination*; Collins, *Origins of Apocalytpicism*; Collins and Fishbane, *Death, Ecstasy*; Collins, *Cosmology*; Hogeterp, *Expectations of the End*; Flusser, *Qumran and Apocalypticism*; DiTommaso, "Apocalypses and Apocalyticism in Antiquity"; McGinn et al., *Continuum History of Apocalypticism*; McGinn, et al., *Encyclopedia of Apocalypticism*; García Martínez, *Qumran and Apocalyptic*; García Martínez, *Wisdom and Apocalypticism*; Sandy, *Plowshares*; Parry and Tov, *Dead Sea Scrolls Reader* (6 vols).

Remains of a Capernaum synagogue with Corinthian caps and Doric-style columns, third or fourth century AD. It may have been built on the earlier site of the synagogue mentioned in Mark 1:21–23; Luke 4:31–33. (Photo by Charles B. Puskas)

the sphere of God's final triumph from a future time in plain history to the cosmic realms of heaven and earth at the end of time.

Nationalistic Hopes

By the first century BC, most Jews assumed the first alternative of repeating the nationalistic hopes of the earlier prophets. Documentation for this outlook is found in the *Psalms of Solomon*.[70] The unknown author was a Jew who longed for the establishment of a Davidic ruler as God's vice-regent over Israel (17:4–5, 32) and saw the Hasmonean Sadducees as the opponents of the devout (8:12, 22; 17:5–8, 22, 45). His teaching of divine providence (5:3–4) and final retribution (2:34–35;

70. The following text has been used: Wright, *Psalms of Solomon*; OTP 2:639–70.

15:12–13) reflects a Pharisaic or Essene viewpoint. But the book is probably Pharisaic instead of Essene, because it lacks those end-time features characteristic of Essene prophecies.[71]

Like the Essenes, Pharisees, and Zealots, most Jews hoped for a coming messiah ("anointed one") who would be of the dynasty of King David.[72] In contrast

71. The *Psalms of Solomon* contain no predictions about the "trials of the faithful" before the Messiah's coming nor any cryptic clues as to when the event will occur. God will establish the rule of the Davidic Messiah at a time determined by him (17:21). For more information, see Kee, *New Testament in Context*, 85–87; Ryle and James, *Psalmoi Solomontos*.

72. Jer 23:4–5; 33:14–22; Zech 6:12–13; 9:9–10; *Pss Sol* 17; Philo, *Rewards* 16.95–97 (conquering Messiah); Josephus, *War* 6.288–315 (6.312, on messianic oracles); Qumran scrolls on Davidic Messiah, 1QSa 2.11–27; 4QPatrBless 1–8; 4QFlor 1.11–13; and see Charlesworth, ed., *Qumran-Messianism*; Flusser, *Qumran and Apocalypticism*;

to the early Christian understanding, this Jewish hope concerned a political ruler who would defeat the foreign oppressors and establish Israel as a great political kingdom. Unlike for the revolutionary Zealots (who attracted many Pharisees and Essenes in AD 66), this would not come about through violent resistance to Rome but through the hand of God. In distinction from the views of Essenes and other esoteric groups of end-time orientation, this nationalistic hope would take place in the real politics of plain history, sometime in the future. Like the Sadducees, who did not entertain such hopes, the Pharisees were involved in Jewish politics.[73] However, the Pharisees did not espouse these future hopes out of patriotic interests alone. Pharisees (as well as Essenes, Zealots, and Christians) adhered to the teachings of a resurrection of the dead and a final judgment of both good and evil (Dan 12:2), although the Sadducees rejected these teachings (Mark 12:18; Acts 23:8).

Apocalyptic Eschatology

The Essenes, certain early Christians, and other related messianic or prophetic groups assumed the second alternative of apocalyptic eschatology or "mysterious unveilings about the end of the age."[74] They taught that God had revealed to them the secret schedule of his plan, by which the evil powers would be overcome and God's eternal rule established. They did not expect the restoration of all Israel or the world, but rather the vindication of a small faithful remnant, usually identical with the sect that propagated the teaching. The type of literature produced by these groups was highly symbolic and esoteric in style. It was filled with veiled references to historical events structured in a certain time-frame that led to a final conflict followed by a new age of salvation. All was predetermined by God, and only those within the group could decipher the revelations (apocalypses) and discern the movement of the divine purpose. Ultimate deliverance would come from God through a messianic figure: a Davidic king, a prophet like Moses, an ideal priest, a leader of eschatological (end-time) war, or a heavenly Son of Man.

Unlike the Pharisaic hope of national deliverance, the Essene vision viewed these disclosures of the end time as no longer translated in terms of plain history, real politics, and human instrumentality.

Hogeterp, *Expectations of the End*; Knohl, *Messiah before Jesus*; early Christian accounts of Jewish messianism: Mark 8:11–12; 12:35–37; 15:43; Luke 23:2–3; John 1:41, 49; 6:15; *m. Ber.* 1:5 and *Sotah* 9:15 (approaching age of the messiah); *Midr. Rab.* on Psalms 60.9–10, where Rabbi Akiba hails Simon Bar Kosiba as messiah in AD 132–135. For a challenge to a central focus upon Davidic descent for the messianic kingship, see Pomykala, *Davidic Dynasty Tradition*.

73. For example, the Pharisees opposed the policies of John Hyrcanus (*Ant.* 13.288–98), and a Pharisee named Zadok helped Judas the Galilean organize a resistance group against the Romans (*Ant.* 18.1–10).

74. For a convenient collection of the literature, see *OTP*, vol. 10. For studies, see Schmithals, *Apocalyptic Movement*; Special Issue on Apocalyptic Literature, *CBQ* 39:3 (1977); Hanson, "Apocalypse, Genre," 27–28; Hanson, "Apocalypticism," 28–34; Portier-Young, *Apocalypse Against Empire*. See footnotes 69 and 72 above for more bibliography. For a brief but articulate statement of the unique features of apocalyptic eschatology over against prophetic eschatology, see Reddish, *Apocalyptic Literature*, 20: "Hope was shifted from this world and this age to another world and another age. God would not employ ordinary means but supernatural forces to bring about the divine plan."

They were portrayed as cosmic battles between heaven and earth, between angels and demons, with ultimate salvation coming from God alone. Examples of apocalyptic literature are Daniel, *1 Enoch*, *2 Baruch*, *Testament of Moses*, *4 Ezra*, Mark 13, Revelation, and many of the Dead Sea Scrolls from Qumran. Most of the books listed above are written in the name of famous individuals like Daniel, Moses, and Enoch. Although the real authors are unknown, this procedure (called pseudonymity) was a feature of apocalyptic books, designed to lend the writing a certain authority.[75]

The origins of apocalyptic eschatology are complex, diverse, somewhat uncertain, and therefore debated.[76] One could speak of it as having a genealogy, for it manifests the influence of Hebrew prophecy and wisdom literature, Persian (Zoroastrian) dualism (angels vs. demons), Babylonian astrology (predetermined events), and even the Greek periodization and Hesiod's chain of being. It is also a product of both hope and despair. It resulted from the unswerving hope in the power of God and the ultimate plan he has established for his people. But it was also a product of despair in the course of Judaism's tragic history of foreign domination, which smashed hopes of establishing a successful independent Jewish nation.

THE COMPETING PARTIES WITHIN JUDAISM

The type of Judaism that persisted through a tragic history was one of competing parties. Despite basic agreement on such points as monotheism, Torah, Sabbath, and the feasts, there were diverse views about how to interpret and implement them. Since we have already discussed Hellenistic Judaism of the Diaspora, we will limit our discussion to the four major parties of Palestinian Judaism: the Sadducees, Pharisees, Essenes, and Zealots.[77]

The Sadducees

The Sadducees,[78] whose name was probably derived from Zadok, a high priest of

---

75. Frey, et al., *Pseudepigraphie und Verfassserfiktion,* esp. by Hogan, "Pseudepigraphy and the Periodization of History in Jewish Apocalypses" (61–84); Tigchelaar, "Forms of Pseudepigraphy in the Dead Sea Scrolls" (85–104); and Aune, "Reconceptualizing the Phenomenon of Ancient Pseudepigraphy" (789–824); Charlesworth, "A History of Pseudepigrapha Research"; Dunn, "Pseudepigraphy"; Brockington, "Problem of Pseudonymity"; Metzger, "Literary Forgeries."

76. Collins, *Origins of Apocalypticism;* DiTommaso, "Apocalypses and Apocalypticism in Antiquity," esp. Part II; see also Collins, *Apocalyptic Imagination.*

77. See the following studies: M. Simon, *Jewish Sects at Time of Jesus*; Schürer, *History*, 2:381–414, 562–90, 598–606; Avi-Yonah and Baras, *Society and Religion in the Second Temple Period*, 99–152, 263–302; Nickelsburg and Stone, *Faith and Piety in Early Judaism*, 24–40; Baumgarten, *Flourishing of Jewish Sects*; Flusser, *Qumran and Apocalypticism*, esp. ch. 16 "Pharisees, Sadducees, and Essenes in Pesher Nahum" (214–57). See also Schiffman, *Qumran and Jerusalem*, 337–38.

78. For primary sources, see Josephus, *Ant.* 13.171–73 (their denial of fate); 13.293–98 (adhere only to written law, not oral traditions of the fathers; 13.297); 18.16–17 (deny immortality of the soul); *War* 2.162–66 (only concerned with human free will and deny final rewards and punishments; 2.164–65); Mark 12:18; Acts 23:8 (they deny there is a resurrection from the dead); *m. Ber.* 9:5 (classified with "heretics" perhaps for denying a world to come); *Parah* 3:3, 7 (scrupulous in temple sacrifices); *Yad.* 4:6–8 (disagreements with Pharisees on legal issues); *Menah.* 10:3; *b. Pesah* 57a (identified with the house of Boethus, from Alexandria,

Solomon's time (1 Kgs 2:35, 950 BC), first made their appearance during the reign of the Hasmonean John Hyrcanus I (130 BC). They were the party of priestly, urban aristocrats favorably disposed to Hellenistic culture but conservative in politics and religion. In the area of politics, they were generally supportive of the ruling establishment. For example, they supported the policies of the Hasmoneans and later sought to secure the favor of the Herods and Romans. As priests, they officiated the sacrificial offerings at the temple, and it was from their ranks that the high priest was appointed. It was also their members who dominated the Jewish high court of the Sanhedrin. In both politics and religion they came into conflict with the popular Pharisee party, whose members were generally more antagonistic to Roman rule, and who tended to associate themselves with the synagogue and its particular emphases. In their understanding of Torah, the Sadducees and Pharisees were the most dissimilar. Moreover, the Pharisees adhered to a written Torah consisting of the Law and the Prophets, as well as an oral Torah of tradition, but the Sadducees regarded only the five books of Moses as binding. Whereas the Pharisees sought to apply the Torah to all aspects of life through the assistance of oral tradition, the Sadducees sought to limit the scope of the Torah by a more literal interpretation not employing oral tradition as an authoritative guide. Whereas the Pharisees held to belief in angels and a resurrection of the dead as derived from the authority of the written prophets and oral tradition, the Sadducees rejected these beliefs because

they were later formulations not derived from the authoritative books of Moses. After the destruction of the temple in AD 70, the priestly group of the Sadducees lost its power and eventually disappeared.

The Pharisees

The Pharisees[79] were probably the most influential and significant Jewish group of the Greco-Roman times. Their name is probably derived from the Hebrew *perushim*, meaning "the separated ones." Nevertheless it may have been a pejorative nickname—"Persian" (Aramaic *Parsh'ah*)—because they shared certain Persian beliefs (e.g., in resurrection, in angels and demons). Their intense devotion to the law makes them the spiritual descendants of the Hasidim ("pious ones"), who joined the Maccabean revolt to oppose religious persecution under the Syrian Greeks (1 Macc 2:42). Like the Sadducees, the Pharisees first appear under the Hasmonean reign of John Hyrcanus I. Unlike the Sadducees, most Pharisees were not priests but lay scholars responsible for the development and preservation

79. For primary sources, see Josephus, *Ant.* 13.288–98; 13.408–15; 17.32–45 (their politics, popularity, and adherence to the traditions of the fathers); 13.171–73 (fate is balanced with human freedom); 18.11 (their lifestyle of moderation, belief in immortality of the soul, final rewards and punishments); *War* 1.110–12 (their piety, precise interpretation of the law, and political influence); *Life* 189–94 (their accurate knowledge of Jewish law); Matt 23 (a Christian critique of their religious zeal and legalism). Much of the teaching of the Mishnah and Talmud that can be traced back to the so-called Tannaitic period (200 BC—AD 200) is from Pharisaic schools. See Neusner, *Rabbinic Traditions about the Pharisees before 70*; and Davies, *Introduction to Pharisaism*; Finkelstein, *Pharisees*; Weiss, "Pharisaios"; Kampen, *Hasideans*; Mason, *Flavius Josephus on the Pharisees*.

23 BC, *Ant.* 15.320); Goldin, *Fathers according to Rabbi Nathan*, 5 (supposed split of Boethusian and Sadducean parties over doctrine of final reward).

of the oral legal tradition. Therefore they were connected with the synagogue, known for pious living (prayer, fasting, almsgiving, tithing) and precise interpretations of the law, especially in the areas of food purity, crops, Sabbaths, festivals, and family affairs. In contrast to the Sadducees, the Pharisees accepted the larger notion of Scripture (Law and Prophets) as well as new doctrines about angels, demons, and the resurrection of the dead. The Pharisees also divided into various schools of interpretation: for example, the schools of Hillel and Shammai in the first century AD. It was the Pharisees who survived the war with Rome and reorganized Judaism along Pharisaic lines at the coastal town of Yavneh (Jamnia).

The Essenes

The Essenes[80] were an ascetic group who maintained a strict adherence to the law. Those who resided at Qumran near the Dead Sea were a strict monastic community with a profound eschatological perspective of themselves and the world.[81] Their name may have been derived from the Aramaic *Hasayyah* or "pious ones," reflecting their close associations with the Hasidim of the Maccabean revolt. They first appear when the Hasmonean Jonathan assumed the high priesthood (161–143 BC). Both Philo and Josephus mentioned that thousands of Essenes lived in towns and villages of Judea. The discovery of the Dead Sea Scrolls at Khirbet Qumran in 1947 revealed a monastic, end-time-oriented wilderness community that may have been a major Essene center. The location confirmed the reports of the Roman scholar Pliny the Elder (AD 70). The founder of the Qumran community was a Zadokite priest called the Teacher of Righteousness, who opposed the (non-Zadokite) Hasmonean priesthood and left Jerusalem with a sizable group of followers. Probably in fulfillment of the prophetic utterance "in the wilderness prepare the way of the Lord" (Isa 40:3), the group founded a center in the wilderness of Judea near the Dead Sea. There a community of scribes (experts in the law of Moses) under the direction of the Zadokite priest awaited the end of the age, interpreting future prophecies as if they spoke to its situation in an exclusive manner. Members worked, copied religious texts, composed religious books, worshipped according to the community's calendar and customs, baptized,

80. Primary sources: Josephus, *Ant.* 13.171–73 (fate governs everything); 15.373–79 (foreknowledge of the future and knowledge of divine revelations ascribed to Menahem the Essene); 17.345–48 (the interpretation of dreams ascribed to Simon the Essene); 18.18–22 (their belief in immortality and resurrection, strict ascetic and communal lifestyle, do not worship in the Jerusalem temple); *War* 2.119–36 (ascetic practices, abstain from marriage, communal living in towns of Judea, their study of ancient writings); Philo, *Good Person* 12.75–91 (they do not offer sacrifices, live in villages, ethical concerns, synagogues, sharing of goods and monies); Pliny, *Natural History* 5.15.73 (their community near the Dead Sea, celibacy, recruitment of members). The Dead Sea Scrolls and community discovered at Khirbet Qumran (1947) are from an Essene group. For English texts, see Dupont-Sommer, *Essene Writings*; Vermes, *Dead Sea Scrolls*; and Gaster, *Dead Sea Scriptures*. See also Cross, *Ancient Library of Qumran*; and Vermes, *Complete Dead Sea Scrolls*.

81. Some would question the association of Qumran with the Essenes, see Cansdale, *Qumran and the Essenes*; Schiffman, *Reclaiming the Dead Sea Scrolls*, 78–81. See helpful summaries of discussion in Schiffman, *Qumran and Jerusalem*, ch. 1; and Collins, *Beyond the Qumran Community*, ch. 4.

Cave 4 at Qumran where many of the Dead Sea Scrolls were discovered.
(Photo by R. Hodgson)

shared in a common meal, and sought to live undefiled, ascetic lives.[82] The Dead Sea Scrolls produced by this community are also important for understanding apocalyptic and messianic groups like early Christianity.[83]

The Zealots

The Zealots[84] were a Jewish resistance group that sought to revive the spirit of the Maccabeans in their revolt against Rome (AD 67–70). Their name is probably derived from Phineas, who was "zealous for God" (Num 25:13), or from statements like a "zealot for the laws" (2 Macc 4:2). Like the Pharisees, they envisioned Israel's national deliverance under a messiah. Unlike (most of) the Pharisees,

82. Although some Essenes in outlying towns ("camps") married and reared children (CD 7.6–8; 12.1, 2, 19; Josephus, *War* 2.160–61) and the bones of a few women and children were found on the periphery of the Qumran graveyard (where only adult male skeletons have been uncovered), the Qumran sect (Essene) was primarily a male celibate community. See 1QS 1.6; 11.21; Josephus, *War* 2.120–21; Philo; Pliny; Vermes, *Complete Dead Sea Scrolls*, 34, 44, 47–48, 83; Cross, *Ancient Library of Qumran*, 97–99.

83. For an important study offering another interpretation of the sect behind the scrolls, see Schiffman, *Reclaiming the Dead Sea Scrolls*; and Schiffmann and VanderKam, eds., *Encyclopedia of the Dead Sea Scrolls*.

84. Most of our information is from Josephus, see *War* 2.647–51 (their conflicts with the high priest; 2.651); 4.158–61 (they profess to be zealous for a good cause; 4.160–61); 4.300–304 (Zealot raids on Jerusalem); 4.556–76 (fighting against other Jewish factions); 5.1–10 (their seizure of the temple); 5.98–105 (more fighting in the temple); 5.248–57 (uniting with other factions to fight the Romans); 7.252–74 (their violent activities summarized). See also Rhoads, *Israel in Revolution*, 94–181; Stern, "Zealots," 135–52; Hengel, *Was Jesus a Revolutionist?*; Hengel, *Zealots*.

the Zealots sought to bring this about through armed resistance.

Even though the Zealot movement probably began in Jerusalem shortly after the revolt against procurator Florus (AD 66), it was influenced by many rebels and resistance movements that preceded it. An important ancestor of two Zealot lead-

identified with the Zealots at Masada (AD 72). They may have had some connection with the brigands and assassins that arose at the time of the procurator Felix (52–60). This earlier group was also called the Sicarii by Josephus because they mingled in the crowds and assassinated their opponents with concealed knives.

The western wall of the Jerusalem temple mount, with huge marginally dressed stones from the Herodian period, commonly called the Wailing Wall. (Photo by Charles B. Puskas)

ers, Menahem and Eleazar ben Yair, was Judas the Galilean.[85] In AD 6, for example, Judas rebelled against the Roman legate of Syria because of a provincial census. The Sicarii (Lat. "daggers, assassins")[86] were

The Zealot movement of 66–70 was one of several rival factions whose rebel leaders each sought control of Jerusalem. John of Gischala, who led a rebellion in Galilee, fled to Jerusalem in 67 to form another revolutionary faction. His group probably joined with the Zealots near the

85. *Ant.* 18.4–10, (author of the fourth sect of the Jews); 20.97–104 (concerning the rebel Theudas and the sons of the Judas the Galilean; 20.98, 102); *War* 2.117–18 (the revolt against Roman taxation; 2.118); Acts 5:36–37 (Theudas and Judas); Acts 21:38 (the Egyptian and Assassins). See also Farmer, *Maccabees, Zealots, and Josephus.*

86. *War* 2.254–65 (the rise of the Sicarii, rebels, and false prophets under the Roman procurator

Felix); 2.425–29 (Sicarii known for attacking opponents with concealed daggers; 2.425); 4.398–409 (their occupation of Masada and the banditry throughout Judea); 4.514–20 (their raids against the temple); 7.252–406 (their stand against the Romans at Masada); 7.407–25 (some fled to Egypt); 7.437–42 (some fled to Cyrene).

end of the war. Simon bar Giora was an Idumean guerrilla leader who fought the Zealots for control of the temple. He later joined forces with John of Gischala and the Zealots to feebly oppose the mighty Roman army under Titus. Many of the Zealots and Sicarii under Eleazar ben Yair fled to the Herodian fortress of Masada, where they all committed suicide rather than surrender to the Romans in 72. In reaction to the Hellenizing policies of Emperor Hadrian, the spirit of the Zealot resistance revived in the revolt under Simon Bar Kosiba (132–135). This rebel leader was also called Simon Bar Kochba by the famous Rabbi Akiba. *Bar Kochba* means "Son of the Star," a messianic title from Num 24:17. The messianic and apocalyptic overtones of this revolt were also characteristic of many rebel movements in first-century Palestine.[87]

Rebels and brigands, such as the Zealots and Sicarii, were part of life in the restless province of Palestine. Mention is made of rebels in the New Testament (Mark 15:7; Acts 5:36–37; 21:38). Even one of Jesus's disciples was thought to have been a Zealot ("Simon the Zealot," Luke 6:15; Acts 1:13).

87. See *Midr. Rab.* on Pss 60:9–10, where Rabbi Akiba hails Simon Bar Kosiba as Messiah, and also in Eusebius, *Hist. eccl.* 4.6.1–4; 8.4. See note 46 of this chapter.

SUMMARY

A tragic history of foreign dominance could not stifle the persistent faith of Judaism in the first Christian era. Through such tragedies as the Babylonian exile, the struggles in resettlement of Palestine, Syrian oppression, a disappointing interval of independence, and revolts against Rome, Judaism revived, readjusted, and reorganized as a monotheistic faith devoted to the law, the Sabbath, circumcision, and the feasts. This unifying faith of Judaism also persisted in a diversity of expressions, as we have seen in the parties of the Sadducees, Pharisees, Essenes, and Zealots. Emerging from this diversity after AD 90 was a consolidation of beliefs and practices brought about by the surviving Pharisaic party, a trajectory that leads to the complex legal systems of rabbinic Judaism. This trend from diversity to conformity, as we will note, also took place in early Christianity about the same time.

This was the situation into which Christianity emerged: in a Greco-Roman environment of pervasive Hellenism, under a stable Roman government, in an age of anxiety and aspiration, conceived and mothered by Judaism, its parent religion. Both the environmental and hereditary factors must be considered in our attempt to understand the growth and development of early Christianity and its written legacy, the New Testament.

3

The Language of the New Testament

In what language was the NT originally written? Almost all of the NT authors were Jews, but not a single book was written in Hebrew or Aramaic (a related Semitic language).[1] All of the NT books were written when Rome ruled the Mediterranean world, but none were written in Latin. Therefore we must turn to the one language prevalent during that period: ancient Greek. We have over five thousand manuscript copies of the NT written in Greek from the mid-second to the twelfth centuries. The earliest versions of the NT were in Syriac, Coptic, and Latin (as early as the second and third centuries); all presuppose a Greek original.

Unfortunately, the question of the NT language is not sufficiently answered with the statement that it was written in ancient Greek. This general statement prompts us to ask a more specific question: In what *dialect* of ancient Greek was the NT written? Or, stating it another way, was the NT written in the Old Ionic of Homer, the Attic of Plato, or the literary Koine of Philo? We will attempt to answer this complex question, first by reviewing

1. The Aramaic of first-century Palestine was a Semitic language closely related to Hebrew with a long historical development (from the twelfth century BC to the seventh century AD). It was the native language of Palestinian Judaism and was used by Jesus and primitive Jewish Christianity. See the classic discussion by Fitzmyer in his presidential address to Catholic Biblical Association, "Languages of Palestine." Although some scholars have argued that some NT texts were originally *composed* in Aramaic (e.g., Torrey, *The Four Gospels*), a consensus of scholars today rejects this thesis. Torrey also asserted that the Apocalypse of John was composed first in Aramaic: his commentary on it was published in 1956, fifteen years after his ideas about it first appeared in *Documents of the Primitive Church* (1941), and yet even after fifteen years, he could refer to no scholar who had been convinced by his arguments; still he speaks of his conclusions as fully established. An Aramaic influence on NT Greek is probable, however; see e.g., Fitzmyer, *A Wandering Aramean*; Evans, "Introduction: An Aramaic Approach"; Stuckenbruck, "An Approach to the New Testament through Aramaic Sources"; Casey, *An Aramaic Approach to Q*.

briefly the history of development of the Greek language up to the present, and then by briefly examining the characteristics of NT Greek.

THE HISTORY OF THE GREEK LANGUAGE[2]

Greek has been a spoken language for more than three thousand years. Like all spoken languages, it has experienced constant changes, generally from more complex to simpler linguistic forms.[3] However, Greek can also be observed to have moved from periods of dialect differentiation to periods of dialect homogenization.[4] The periods of Greek can be divided approximately into the following four categories:[5]

Classical period	from Homer to Aristotle (1000–322 BC)
Hellenistic period	from Alexander the Great to the Roman emperor Justinian I (322 BC—AD 529)
Byzantine period	from Justinian I to the fall of Constantinople (529–1453)
Modern period	from 1453 to the present.

The Classical Period (1000–322 BC)

The classical period was characterized by a variety of different dialects, resulting from differences in culture and geographical location. Some of the dialects of this early period were as follows:

Old Ionic. This dialect of Achaea was in use from the tenth to the eighth centuries BC. The epic writings of Homer and Hesiod employ this dialect of Greek.[6]
Ionic. Used throughout the classical period, it was the Greek of Herodotus the historian and Hippocrates the physician. Ionic was the dialect of the southwest Asia Minor coast.
Attic. This sophisticated Greek of Athens was dominant in the classical period and greatly influenced the Hellenistic dialect. Attic was the linguistic medium of the orator Demosthenes, the philosophers Plato and Aristotle, the historians Thucydides and Xenophon, and the tragedians Aeschylus, Sophocles, and Euripides. Attic was a smooth and harmonious dialect (like Ionic) in comparison with later NT Greek. It was also characterized by complex linguistic forms.

2. See Palmer *The Greek Language*; Horrocks *Greek*; Adrados, *A History of the Greek Language*; Christidis, *A History of Ancient Greek*. For some beginning texts in classical Greek studies, see Dickey, *Ancient Greek Scholarship*; Schaps, *Handbook for Classical Research*; Frede and Inwood, *Language and Learning*.

3. For further information, see Colwell, "Greek Language."

4. Thus Caragounis *The Development of Greek*, 21–60, lists five evolving phases of Greek:
1) Greek becomes differentiated from Proto-Aryan (before the Greeks come to the Hellenic peninsula)
2) The coming of the Greek to the Hellenic peninsula and the breakup into dialects (Ionic, Aiolic, Doric, Thessalic, Epirotic, etc.)
3) Hellenistic Period: Greek dialects reunited (Koine)
4) Byzantine and Late Byzantine: Greek again breaks up into dialects
5) Neohellenic: Greek reunites again (currently).

5. The four categories are from Metzger, "The Language of the New Testament," 44–46. These four periods suggested by Metzger correspond roughly to the last four periods of Caragounis in the previous note.

The grammar of Attic Greek was sophisticated and precise. It made ample use of the subjunctive and optative moods in verbs, the dual number in nouns and adjectives, and a bewildering maze of particles.[7] One example of preciseness in Attic Greek is that it could state in three words what would take ten in the English language: "I have been called up for service throughout the wars" (Thucydides). Such precision with an economy of expression was achieved by prefixes, suffixes, and infixes added to the three words. This compound formation of words is called synthesis.[8] In the next period with wider use among people of different cultures there would be a trend away from synthesis to analysis, e.g., some inserted a series of helping words rather then building on the same stem.

Attic Greek had an enduring influence for two reasons. First, it was the dialect of Athens, the city that had dominance over the other Greek communities after the Persian war. (It also took part in the colonization of the Aegean Sea region.) Second, the last great representative of the classical Attic dialect was Aristotle, the teacher of Alexander the Great. Although Aristotle's death marks the end of the classical period, the influence of Attic Greek continued.

The Hellenistic Period
(322 BC—AD 529)

Alexander's conquest of the eastern Mediterranean world began the Hellenistic period. Two developments took place after the establishment of Alexander's empire: (1) The Greek language and culture penetrated the Orient (for example, Palestine, Egypt, and Persia); and (2) a homogenization of the numerous regional dialects produced a new form of Greek called Hellenistic or Koine (common) Greek.

This new Koine Greek was the result of internal and external factors. The following might have been some of them: First, within Alexander's army were men from all parts of Greece. Their close associations during the campaigns played a significant role in the emergence of a new type of Greek (which had already begun through increasing contact between city-states). Those elements of speech most widely current and readily adapted from various dialects tended to survive, whereas the less functional were dropped. Since Attic was the predominant language also spoken by Alexander, a tendency arose to conform to Attic standards. Second, wherever the army of Alexander went, this language was disseminated and took root in oriental soil with all the adaptations and modifications that generally accompany such assimilation. It must be noted, however, that the use of native dialects continued alongside the newly acquired Greek. For example, in Palestine most of the people spoke their native Aramaic as well as the Koine Greek.

In a relatively short period of time Koine Greek became the common means of communication in the Hellenistic age. After Alexander's death the Greek

---

6. In *Homeric Whispers*, Price locates Troy on Croatia's Dalmatian Coast and develops the thesis that the epics were originally in a Slavic dialect—a thesis he first put forward in 1985 in *Homer's Blind Audience*.

7. White, "Greek Language," *ZPE* 2:827.

8. Colwell "Greek Language," *IDB* 2:480.

language spread extensively throughout the Mediterranean world so that by the first century AD, Koine Greek was spoken from Spain to northwestern India and was the chief language of "ca. 80% of the citizens of the eastern end of the empire."[9]

Varieties of Koine included literary Koine, Attic, and vernacular Koine. Literary Koine comes closest to being a natural development of Attic. It became the most suitable vehicle for formal literature. This was the Koine of Polybius the historian, Strabo the geographer, Epictetus the philosopher, and the Jewish writers Josephus and Philo.

The Atticist dialect was developed by a few literary men to imitate the Attic of the classical age. It was an artificial, literary language in reaction to Koine Greek and only lasted a short period. Some of the participants in this short-lived Attic revival were Dionysus and Dio Chrysostom.

Vernacular or nonliterary Koine was the most influential of the period. It was the language of the street, home, marketplace, and farm. In comparison with Attic Greek, it was crude, often ungrammatical. Egyptian papyri, pottery fragments, and inscriptions dating from the third century BC to the fourth century AD (discovered in the late nineteenth and early twentieth centuries) give us a wealth of information about this vernacular.[10]

Before the discoveries of the Egyptian papyri and their evaluation by such men as Grenfell, Hunt, Deissmann, and Moulton, scholars were divided in their understanding of the NT language into at least two camps of interpretation: One camp regarded NT Greek as a distinct Hebraic or biblical Greek because of its use of the Greek OT and its lack of extrabiblical parallels (at that time).[11] Critics accused this camp of advocating a "Holy Ghost Greek" for the NT. The second camp evaluated the language according to the high standards of classical Attic. They generally regarded the NT Greek as decidedly inferior to its classical ancestor and concluded that it was a vulgar imitation by writers who used Greek as foreigners.

Early Christianity (Ancient History Documentary Research Center, Macquarie University, New South Wales 1981; vol. 2, 1982; vol. 3, 1983; vol. 4, 1987; vol. 5, 1989; vol. 6, 1992; vol. 7, 1994; vol. 8, 1998). *New Documents* is not a lexicon or a grammar. It gives the papyrus text examined and its translation in its entirety. It divides the texts both generically and topically and includes essays regarding grammatical, lexical, and social interest. An ancillary objective of the project was to work toward the more focused goal of compiling a "new Moulton-Milligan" (see Hemer, "Towards a New Moulton and Milligan," 97–123). See now the two articles ("Lexicon of the New Testament with Documentary Parallels") installments 1 and 2 written by Horsley and Lee in vols. 10 (1997, 55–84) and 11 (1998, 57–84) of *Filologia Neotestamentaria* giving format and sample articles for their preparation of the new Moulton-Milligan.

11. The premier advocate of this position in the mid to late twentieth century is Nigel Turner, who wrote the third (*Syntax*, 1963) and fourth (*Style*, 1976) volumes in Moulton's celebrated *Grammar of New Testament Greek*. For a critical evaluation of Turner's work, see Horsley, "The Fiction of Jewish Greek," 5–40. For a history of the Hebraist-Purist debate going back to the seventeenth century, see Voelz, "The Language of the New Testament," in *ANRW* II, 25/2, 893–977.

---

9. Caragounis, *The Development of Greek*, 45.

10. For information on the discoveries of the Egyptian papyri and inscriptions, see Deissmann, *Light from the Ancient East*, 1–61. See also Hunt and Edgar, *Select Papyri*; Grenfell and Hunt, *New Classical Fragments*; Moulton and Milligan, *Vocabulary of the Greek Testament*, vii–xx. Many papyri continued to be found, and finally in 1981 a group of papyrologists at Macquarie University began publishing *New Documents Illustrating*

With the discovery of the Egyptian papyri our understanding of the NT language changed radically. No longer was the language of the NT viewed as a special biblical Greek or a vulgar imitation of Attic but as the colloquial language of the people of that day.

The Byzantine Period (AD 529–1453)

The Byzantine period continues the process of simplification typical of the Hellenistic period. The Byzantine period begins with the influential reign of Emperor Justinianus from Constantinople (who instigated the compilation of the Justinian Code of 529). He "declared Greek the official language of the Byzantium empire."[12] This period saw a low ebb in learning, and much of the distinctiveness of the Greek was lost through changes in syntax and through borrowings from other languages. The Turkish takeover in 1453 ended the Byzantine period. But during its twilight years, as a result of much political turmoil, a new period of dialectical differentiation began.

The Modern Period (AD 1453–Present)

This period, which Caragounis calls the Neohellenic period, continues a new phase of dialectical differentiation among Greek speakers, and though the number of dialects emerging from this period of "political and social isolation" of the Greeks is "impossible to calculate," he refers to estimates of "over seventy dialects."[13] Differentiation continued until the late eighteenth and early nineteenth centuries when Hellas was reconstituted as a free state (1828). This most recent political change for the Greeks led to many unsuccessful efforts at some linguistic unification through the use of a common dialect. The contentious period over "the language question" lasted until 1976 when Neohellenic Koine was finally adopted as the official language of Hellas.[14]

THE GREEK LANGUAGE OF THE NEW TESTAMENT[15]

Although they fit very comfortably into the common vernacular of the day, the literary qualities of the NT authors vary. Certain books, such as Hebrews and Luke-Acts, approach the literary Koine, but most fall within a broader vernacular spectrum of speech. The Gospels of Mark and John and the book of Revelation are typical of the popular colloquial Koine. They evidence a limited vocabulary and even a disregard for the ordinary rules of Greek syntax (e.g., Revelation). Mark, John, and Revelation also retain many Semitic and Aramaic idioms. The letters of Paul fit somewhere between literary and colloquial Koine. Although he is steeped in both the Greek OT and colloquial language, Paul speaks with the Koine of an educated man (e.g., Epictetus).

---

12. Caragounis, *Development of Greek*, 45.

13. Ibid., 49.

14. See the engaging discussion in Caragounis, *The Development of Greek*, 49–60.

15. Moulton, "Introduction," in Howard, *Accidence and Word Formation*, 1–34; Porter, *The Language of the New Testament*; Louw, "New Testament Greek," 159–72; Porter, "Greek Grammar and Syntax," 76–103. Beginning grammars are legion, but see Hewett, Robbins, Johnson, *New Testament Greek: Beginning and Intermediate Grammar*; see also the excellent introductory text to the subject of verbal aspect: Campbell, *Basics of Verbal Aspect*.

Semitisms

Because most NT books were written by Jews, reflect a Palestinian setting, or use Palestinian sources, NT books show evidence of Semitic influence. The Semitisms of the NT originate from a number of sources: (1) borrowings from the language of the Greek OT (see below), (2) the occurrence of Aramaic terms and constructions, and (3) possible Hebrew constructions. Most Semitisms are borrowings from the language of the Greek OT, which is translation Greek in the Koine tradition. A number of Aramaic terms are retained in the Gospels, especially Mark (e.g., *Gethsemane*; *abba*; *eloi, eloi, lama sabachtani*; *Golgatha*; and *rabbi*), and some alleged-Aramaic constructions occur.[16] Although many Jews of Jesus's day knew Hebrew, its influence on the NT is difficult to discern. Much of the Hebraic style in NT Greek was derived from the LXX rather than from the Hebrew Bible. Nevertheless, some have argued that such expressions as "with joy you will rejoice" (you will rejoice greatly, John 3:27) or "before the face of his way" (Acts 13:24) are Hebrew constructions.[17] However, it is difficult to refute the claim that these Hebrew constructions were conveyed through Greek translations of the OT.

Latinisms

Latinisms are sparsely represented in the NT. They are chiefly military and commercial terminology: e.g., *centurion, legion, speculator, denarius*, and *colony*. The occurrence of Latinisms in the NT is probably due to the presence of the Roman military throughout the Mediterranean world. These isolated terms probably filtered into the popular colloquial Koine.[18]

Christian Vocabulary[19]

The possibility of a specific Christian element in the NT language must be approached with some reservation. Upon the discovery of the Egyptian papyri, many special "biblical terms"[20] (Thayer) were actually found to be part of the everyday language of the people (Deissmann, Bauer). Thayer originally argued for over seven hundred "biblical terms" in the NT. Deissmann brought this special list down to fifty, and Bauer reduced this list even more.[21] Of course the Christian communities used popular vocabulary and gave it a different nuance in the context of their worship and proclamation.

18. There are also a number of NT phrases that seem awkward in Greek but resemble familiar Latin idioms, e.g., Mark 15:15, 19; 14:65; Luke 12:58; Acts 17:9; 19:38. See Moule, *An Idiom Book*, 192.

19. Notable recent sources for the study of Christian vocabulary include the following: Lee, *A History of New Testament Lexicography*; Danker's complete 2000 revision of Bauer's *A Greek-English Lexicon* (BDAG); and Silva's *Biblical Words and Their Meaning*.

20. See, for example, the long list of "Biblical or New Testament" Greek words in Thayer, *Thayer's Greek-English Lexicon*. 1889. (appendix 3), 693–710.

21. See how the list of "Christian terminology" is considerably shortened in BDAG, xix–xxviii.

16. A fine discussion can be found in Mussies, "The Use of Hebrew and Aramaic," 416–32.

17. Also paratactic constructions connecting a series of independent clauses by conjunctions (such as *and*) are considered to be (Semitic) Hebraic constructions.

But reservation should be maintained about the possibility of the *creation* of new Christian terms and phrases.

THE SEPTUAGINT, AQUILA, SYMMACHUS, THEODOTION[22]

Septuagint (*Septuaginta*; the full title was *Interpretatio septuaginta virorum*: "the interpretation of the seventy elders") means "seventy" in Latin. It is the abbreviated name given to a Greek translation of the Hebrew Bible made between the third century BC and the first century AD in Alexandria, Egypt, under the initial direction of Philadelphus, king of the Hellenistic kingdom in Egypt. It is usually abbreviated with Roman numerals as LXX (70). According to fanciful tradition, seventy or seventy-two Jewish elders from Jerusalem were brought to Alexandria (six from each of the twelve tribes of Israel) to do the work of translating the sacred texts into Greek for the great library at Alexandria. According to the *Letter of Aristeas*, the elders were brought to Philadelphus, who gave a banquet in their honor, during which he tested them as to their expertise and proficiency. Each of the seventy-two elders brought with him a copy of the Jewish Law written on animal skins in letters of gold. Shortly afterward the elders began the work of translation. According to Aristeas, they worked for seventy-two days, comparing their work with one another at intervals. In this manner the work was completed.

Early Christian historians repeat the story, though with some minor variations. According to some early Christian tradition, the seventy-two elders worked separately in total isolation. They all emerged seventy-two days later, and when their individual translations were compared, they all miraculously agreed, word for word. In this way divine inspiration (of sorts) was attributed to the translation. If nothing else, this elaboration of the story reflects the high esteem in which the early church held this translation. It is the translation most often used in the quotations of the OT in the NT texts.

In the postapostolic period (in the second and early third centuries) several other translations appeared (Aquila, Symmachus, and Theodotion). Aquila's translation was very literal, completed in AD 130, and was preferred by Jews as well as by the Jewish Christian sect called the Ebionites. Jewish scholars grew to object to the LXX especially as Christians used it for proof-texting doctrines such as the virgin birth of Jesus (through an appeal to Isa 7:14 in Matt 1:23: "Behold the virgin shall be with child and shall bear a son, and they shall call his name Immanuel"). In this case the Hebrew word translated into English as "virgin" means simply "young girl," but the LXX translated the Hebrew word with the Greek word for "virgin."

Origen, the great Alexandrian scholar of the late second and early third centuries, created a parallel text of the Old Testament with six columns; hence it was called the *Hexapla*. The six columns featured (1) the Hebrew text, (2) a transliteration of the Hebrew using Greek letters

---

22. Recent books on the LXX include Marcos, *The Septuagint in Context*; McLay, *The Use of the Septuagint in New Testament Research*; Hengel, *The Septuagint as Christian Scripture*; Dines, *The Septuagint*; Jobes and Silva, *Invitation to the Septuagint*; Wasserstein and Wasserstein, *The Legend of the Septuagint*.

(3) the Aquila translation, (4) the Symmachus translation, (5) the Septuagint, (6) the Theodotion translation. Eusebius in his *Hist. eccl.* (6.16) describes the work in some detail. Origen recognized the value of the other Greek versions of the Hebrew and wanted future Christian scholars to use them to check and correct the Septuagint. He also compiled a Tetrapla (four columns), eliminating the first two columns. Origen was perhaps the first Christian scholar not of Jewish birth who learned Hebrew so that he might interpret the Jewish Scriptures.

Thus the Septuagint emerged as one of the monumental Greek texts of the Hellenistic period. The complexity of its (alleged) origins and characteristics reflect something of the typical complexity of Hellenistic Greek as a whole: the LXX was undertaken in Egypt by Judeans and included translations of an ancient Semitic text as well as freely composed Greek. As a translation it varies in quality and readability. Sometimes its Greek barely betrays that a Semitic original lies covered beneath it; sometimes its Greek is so literal that the Semitic text is easily imagined behind it. Scholars value it for a plethora of reasons. It is of value to text critics, although sometimes the Hebrew text lying behind it is like nothing that we actually possess. It is of value to theologians, as it represents not only an interpretation of the Hebrew Bible itself (because every translation is an interpretation), but also because it was used by the early church in the expression and development of early Christian theology. It is of interest to philologists, as it is a broadly mixed specimen of Hellenistic Greek, though with many complex dimensions. It is of interest to lexicographers, as it often affected the meaning of lexemes used by the early church, and as it often reflects an understanding of an obscure Hebrew word or phrase. It is of interest to sociologists, as it represents a product of cultural contact. It is of interest to linguists who work currently in the area of Bible translation, because it is an example of what they aspire to do, however imperfectly it was done.

Codex Sinaiticus, a fourth-century uncial manuscript.
This folio includes John 21:1–35; approximate size 14" by 13".
(© British Library Board)

4

The Text of the New Testament

THE MANUSCRIPTS OF THE NEW TESTAMENT TEXT

Certain questions are essential for interpretation. One question to be addressed before asking what a text originally meant is, did the text originally state that? For example, if we want to understand what the author of 1 John originally meant by the phrase "the Spirit, the water, and the blood" (5:7–8), we had better be certain that the author of 1 John composed it.[1] How reliable are the Greek manuscripts on which our modern translations are based?

All extant (existing and known) Greek manuscripts of the NT are in codex (book) form, and those before the ninth century were written in uncial capital letters.[2] The codex (plural: codices), or leaf-form book, came into extensive use at least by the second century. Codices were folded sheets (quires) bound by waxed tablets and fastened together by a thong hinge. It was much easier to use than the older scroll, which was a roll of sheets fastened together up to thirty-five feet in length and wound around a stick. Some of the early writings of the NT may have been composed on a scroll, but we do not possess any of the originals.

---

1. The KJV in 1 John 5:7 has a long theological interpretation of these three (Spirit, water, blood) as symbols of the Trinity; this is derived from late manuscripts. The RSV, NEB, JB, NAB, NIV, NJB, REB, NRSV, and almost all other modern translations omit this statement. See Metzger, *Textual Commentary*, 647; Aland and Aland, *Text of the New Testament*, 311–12; Greenlee, *Text of the New Testament*, 78–80.

2. Material in this section has been derived from Aland and Aland, *Text of the New Testament*; Black, *Rethinking New Testament Textual Criticism*; Comfort, *Encountering the Manuscripts*; Elliott and Moir, *Manuscripts and the Text of the New Testament*; Fee, "Textual Criticism of the New Testament"; Finegan, *Encountering New Testament Manuscripts*; Greenlee, *Introduction to New Testament Textual Criticism*; Greenlee, *Text of the New Testament*; and Greenlee, "Text and Manuscripts of the New Testament"; Metzger and Ehrman, *Text of the New Testament*; Vaganay and Amphoux, *Introduction to New Testament Textual Criticism*.

Greek manuscripts before the ninth century were written in the literary uncial (or "majuscule") style. Uncials (Lat. "inch-high") were capital letters written with little or no punctuation and spacing between words. It was the style used for literary writing. At the same time a cursive (running) handwriting existed that was used for personal or nonliterary purposes (e.g., personal letters of the nonbiblical Egyptian papyri). Some of Paul's letters, for example, may have been written originally in a cursive handwriting, but we do not possess the originals.

There are over 5700 extant Greek

Papyri

The 116 or more extant papyri manuscripts of the Greek NT date from the early second to the eighth centuries. Most were discovered in the sands of Egypt in the late nineteenth century. These manuscripts are sheets of papyri made from the spongy center of the stalk of the papyrus plant grown mostly in marshy areas (Job 8:11) like that the Nile Delta region. The processed sheets usually ranged in size from 6 x 9 to 12 x 15 inches. All extant papyri texts are in the codex form. Although most are fragmentary, together they in-

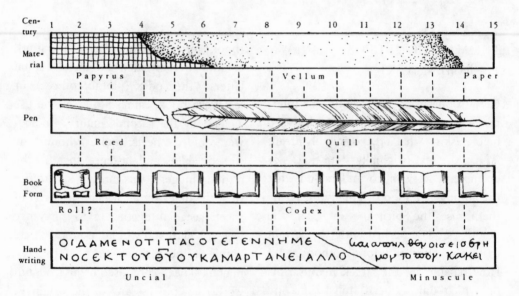

Paleographic Chart of the New Testament. J. Harold Greenlee, 1995.

manuscripts of the NT. This is a quantity greater than any other ancient body of literature. These Greek manuscripts fall under five major categories: papyri (116), parchments (270), uncials and minuscules (2877), ancient versions, and patristic citations. We will briefly examine all five.

clude a considerable part of the NT. Most of the papyri represent an early Alexandrian (Egyptian) text type. In spite of their early date, the reliability of the papyri is reduced by the fact that many of them were copied by nonprofessional scribes.[3]

3. Greenlee, *Text of the New Testament*, 7–9 and 702; Metzger and Ehrman, *Text of the New Testament*, 4–7; Epp, "Issues in New Testament

Chester Beatty Papyrus II (P[46], third century) showing the text of Romans 15:29–33; approximate size 6" by 9". (Chester Beatty Museum)

Two of the most important collections of NT papyrus manuscripts were acquired in 1930 and 1931 by Chester Beatty of London, and by M. M. Bodmer of Geneva in 1955 and 1956. The oldest known fragment of the Greek NT is P[52] of the John Rylands Library in Manchester. It contains a few lines of John 18 and is dated around AD 125.[4]

The Beatty collection is found mostly in Dublin, although some fragments are located at the University of Michigan and in Vienna. All of the papyri of the Beatty Collection date in the early third century. They include almost one-seventh of the Gospels and Acts (P[45]), a large portion of Paul's letters plus Hebrews (P[46]), and about one-third of the book of Revelation (P[47]).[5]

The Bodmer Collection is located in Geneva, Switzerland. The dates of the papyri range from the second century (P[66], P[75]) and third century (P[72]) to the seventh century (P[74]). They include a large portion of John's Gospel (P[66], P[75]); most of Luke (P[75]); Jude; 1 and 2 Peter (P[72]); Acts; James; and 1, 2, and 3 John (P[74]). The manuscript P[72] also includes a number of apocryphal writings (e.g., the *Nativity of Mary*, the apocryphal correspondence of Paul to the Corinthians).[6]

Parchment Uncials

The parchment uncials (majuscules) presently number about 310, varying in size from a few verses to the complete NT, and with dates ranging from the fourth to the tenth centuries. These manuscripts are durable sheets made from animal skins that were soaked, scraped, dried, and rubbed down to a smooth writing surface. Parchments are also called vellum, but sometimes the word *vellum* refers to a more refined parchment. This form of writing material replaced papyri by the

Textual Criticism," 27–29. For further discussion on the preparation and use of papyri, see Pliny, *Nat. Hist.* 13.68–83; Herodotus, *Hist.* 2.92; Barrett, *New Testament Background*, 23–25; Finegan, *Encountering New Testament Manuscripts*, 19–22; Ackroyd and Evans, *From the Beginnings to Jerome*, 30–32, 48–66; Lewis, *Papyrus*, 34–69.

4. For an introduction and complete text of P[52], see Comfort and Barrett, *Complete Text*, 355–58. For a survey and discussion of the major NT Greek papyri, see Metzger and Ehrman, *Text of the New Testament*, 53–61; Aland and Aland, *Text of*

the New Testament, 83–102 (includes several photos); UBS[4], 6–7.

5. On P[45]–P[47], see Comfort and Barrett, *Complete Text*, 145–341.

6. On the Bodmer collection, see ibid., 366–458, 468–598 (excluding apocryphal writings).

fourth century. All parchment uncials (majuscules) were kept in codex form. By the parchment and uncial period, Christianity had become a legitimate religion of the Roman Empire, and consequently most uncial manuscripts were copied by professional scribes.

The Codices Sinaiticus (‭א‬) Vaticanus (B), Alexandrinus (A), and Bezae (D) are four of the more significant or representative parchment uncials. Codex Sinaiticus, from the fourth century, contains all of the New Testament and most of the Old. It is located in the British Library of London. It is one of the most important manuscripts of the NT, and its discovery by Constantine von Tischendorf around 1840 is a fascinating story. Codex Sinaiticus belongs in general to the Alexandrian (Egyptian) text type with which most of the early papyri are identified.

Codex Vaticanus (B), written in the mid-fourth century, is located in the Vatican Library. It ranks with Sinaiticus as one of the two most important Greek manuscripts of the NT. It lacks part of the OT, and in the NT part of Hebrews and all of Titus, Timothy, Philemon, and Revelation are missing. Some speculate that Vaticanus may have been one (or a candidate for one) of the fifty copies of the Bible that Emperor Constantine ordered (331), but this is difficult to prove. Like Sinaiticus Vaticanus is considered a good representative of the Alexandrian (B) text type.[7]

Codex Alexandrinus (A), a fifth-century manuscript, lacks almost all of Matthew, most of 2 Corinthians, and part of John. It is displayed in the British Museum in London. It contains a mixed text type: the Gospels are of the later Byzantine type, and the rest of the NT (copied by a different scribe?) resembles the Alexandrian type.

Codex Bezae (D) is a sixth-century manuscript of the Gospels and Acts, now located in the Cambridge University Library. The text of Codex D (05), also known as Cantabrigiensis, has Greek and Latin facing each other on opposite pages (what is called diglot, for "two languages"). It is the chief representative of the Western text, known for its extensive paraphrases and additions, especially in Acts. Codex D (06), Codex Claromontanus, contains the Pauline letters and is located in Paris. Other minor Greek manuscripts are designated by letters of the Greek alphabet (Δ, Π) and numerals preceded by zero (048, 0242).

Minuscules

The third major manuscript category is that of the minuscules. These manuscripts outnumber the uncials ten to one and range in date from the ninth to the fourteenth centuries. The minuscule ("small letter") handwriting style was a ninth-century refinement of the early nonliterary cursive style which completely displaced the use of uncials in formal literature. Like the early cursive ("running") style the minuscule letters were connected (including words!), which made writing

---

7. For discussion of all major uncials (majuscules), see Metzger and Ehrman, *Text of the New Testament*, 62–86; Aland and Aland, *Text of the New Testament*, 103–28 (with photos); UBS[4], 9–16. On the development of the NT text in the Constantinian era and how conditions were right for church scriptoria to be established at such centers of learning as Alexandria and Antioch,

see Aland and Aland, *Text of the New Testament*, 64–67, 70–71.

(if not interpreting) much easier than the uncial style.[8]

The minuscule manuscripts are designated by numerals (33, 2127) and vary from one or two pages to the complete NT. Only two examples will be given: Manuscripts 1 and 13. Manuscript 1 is a twelfth-century manuscript containing the entire NT except Revelation. It is located in Basel, Switzerland. It was one of the manuscripts used by Erasmus in the preparation of the first published edition of the Greek NT. Manuscript 1 is closely related to a group of minuscules (118, 131, and 209) labeled "family 1" by Kirsopp Lake (1902).

Manuscript 13 is a thirteenth-century codex of the Gospels located in Paris. It is closely related to a group of minuscules (e.g., mss 69, 124, 346, 828) known as "family 13" (by William H. Ferrar, 1868) which is textually related to "family 1." In the family 13 group, the woman taken in adultery follows Luke 21:36 instead of John 7:52.

The lectionaries are also classed with the minuscules. They are selections from the Gospels and "apostolic writings" used for reading in worship services (both parish and monastic). There are over 2,300 of these lectionary minuscule manuscripts dating from the fifth to the eighth centuries. They are identified by the following symbols: *l* 60, *l* 680.[9]

Ancient Versions

In addition to the Greek manuscripts there were also early versions of the NT in other languages. Many were prepared by missionaries to spread the faith among peoples whose native language was Latin, Syriac, or Coptic.[10] The important Latin versions of the West date from the late second to the fourth centuries (Jerome's Vulgate, ca. 384). The Syriac translations of the East date from the mid-second century (Tatian's Diatessaron) to the seventh century (the Peshitta revisions). The Coptic versions of Egypt date from the early third century (Sahidic) to the fourth century (Bohairic). Through textual criticism, a version can sometimes indicate what type of Greek manuscript was used as well as its approximate date and geographical origin. The versions therefore make a significant contribution to the study of the Greek NT manuscripts. Designations for versions are, e.g., it^A, it^S (Latin), syr^S, syr^P (Syriac), cop^{SA} (Coptic).

Patristic Citations

A final source for recovering the original Greek text is the NT quotations or citations, commentaries, and intertextual allusions of the early church fathers. Most of their works are in Greek and Latin with a lesser amount in Syriac and other languages.[11]

---

8. On important minuscule manuscrpts, see Aland and Aland, *Text of the New Testament*, 128–58; Metzger and Ehrman, *Text of the New Testament*, 86–92.

9. On the major lectionaries, see Aland and Aland, *Text of the New Testament*, 160–70 (lists with some illustrations).

10. See Metzger and Ehrman, *Text of the New Testament*, 94–126; Aland and Aland, *Text of the New Testament*, 185–221.

11. Aland and Aland, *Text of the New Testament*, 171–84; NA^{27}, 72–76; Metzger and Ehrman, *Text of the New Testament*, 126–34; On the problems and procedures, see Fee, "Use of Greek Fathers," 191–207.

Although the NT quotations are extensive, a number of problems arise in attempting to recover the Greek text utilized by them. First, the Christian writers often cited the NT from memory, and it is therefore difficult to determine the actual wording of their Greek text. Second, a patristic writer may have used several different copies of the NT. Finally, most available texts of the patristic writings are also late and sometimes corrupt copies. Yet when the difficult task of reconstructing the NT text of the patristic writers is done, it is of great value, since it provides a datable and geographically identifiable witness to the NT available to an early Christian writer. Designations for church fathers are generally the first few letters of their names: e.g., Ir (Irenaeus), Tert (Tertullian), Hier (Jerome).

THE TRANSMISSION OF THE NT TEXT

The history of the transmission of the NT text will be surveyed from two major periods:[12] first, the period of the handwritten text (before 1516); second, the period of the printed text (1516 to present).

The Handwritten Text

The period of the handwritten text (before 1516) was characterized by three developments: a divergence of manuscripts, a convergence of texts, and the dominance of the Byzantine texts.

The Divergence of Manuscripts

The period of the divergence of manuscripts begins with the writing of the first NT books (ca. 55) and declines with the request for fifty copies of the Bible by Emperor Constantine (ca. 331). During this period of divergence, many errors in the copying of the NT took place. At this time NT books were generally copied by Christians who were not professionally trained scribes. These early copyists introduced thousands of changes in the text. The majority of their errors were unintentional and are easily discernible as slips of the eye, ear, or mind. Hundreds of changes, however, were intentional. Early scribes often "smoothed out" the Greek of the NT author by changing word order or tenses of verbs and by adding conjunctions. They also tended to clarify ambiguous passages by adding nouns or pronouns, by substituting common synonyms for uncommon words, and even by rewriting difficult phrases. There were tendencies to harmonize one passage with another, as with the Synoptic Gospels, and even to make certain liturgical or doctrinal changes.[13]

This period also saw the rise of local texts. Copies of NT books were carried to various localities by Christians, each manuscript containing its own characteristic textual variants. Over a period of time, the manuscripts circulating in a given locality would tend to resemble one another more nearly than manuscripts of any other locality. Different local texts (first

12. Material for this section has been adapted from: Greenlee, *Introduction to New Testament Textual Criticism*, 51–91; Vaganay and Amphoux, *Introduction to New Testament Textual Criticism*, 89–171; Metzger and Ehrman, *Text of the New Testament*, 137–94; Aland and Aland, *Text of the New Testament*, 3–47.

13. For outline of unintentional and intentional changes, see Greenlee, *Introduction to NT Textual Criticism*, 55–61; Black, *NT Textual Criticism*, 59–61. For discussion of deliberate and intentional scribal changes, see Epp, "Issues," 27–29, 52–61; Royse, "Scribal Tendencies," 239–52; Ehrman, *Orthodox Corruption of Scripture*.

argued by B. H. Streeter, 1924) may have been present in Egypt plus the eastern and western regions. From the surrounding areas dominated by the centers of local texts (e.g., Alexandria, Antioch, Rome, Constantinople) early translations of the Greek manuscripts also emerged. Translations of certain NT books into Latin (in North Africa) and Syrian (East) began in the mid-second century. By the third century, Coptic translations of the NT began in Egypt. This development contributed to the divergence of NT manuscripts.[14]

Some Convergence of Diverse Texts

The most important contribution to some convergence of NT Greek manuscripts was the commission by Constantine to produce fifty new copies of the Bible for churches of Constantinople (AD 331). Although other earlier causes were at work, like the toleration of Christianity and its sacred writings (AD 313), Constantine's imperial edict marked a period of standardization.[15] This imperial commission gave opportunity for official comparison of various manuscripts and indicated the need for uniting divergent local texts into a single text tradition. Professional scribes

could now be employed for copying the manuscripts, which helped reduce variations in the text. Therefore at Constantinople, the center of the Greek-speaking church, some convergence of Greek NT manuscripts took place that influenced most of the church. Despite the appearance of, e.g., western variants, the process of converging and displacing older text types continued from the fourth to the ninth centuries.[16]

The Dominance of Byzantine Texts

Factors such as the weakening of Christian influence in Egypt and the rise of the Byzantine Empire (where the Greek language was preserved) eliminated the competition of other local text types and contributed to the dominance of the Constantinople text tradition, or "Byzantine text," from the ninth to the fifteenth centuries. More than nine-tenths of the existing manuscripts of the NT are from the eighth century and later. Very few of these manuscripts differ from the Byzantine text. Although copying manuscripts by hand increased variations, the text after the ninth century was basically Byzantine. The printed Greek NT was also essentially a Byzantine type until the late nineteenth century.[17]

14. Greenlee, *Introduction to New Testament Textual Criticism*, 52–53; for discussion see, Aland and Aland, *Text of the New Testament*, 53–64; Vaganay and Amphoux, *Introduction to New Testament Textual Criticism*, 89–111; Metzger and Ehrman, *Text of the New Testament*, 276–80, but few critics follow Streeter's method in all its particulars, e.g., his so-called Caesarean text-type is difficult to establish, 216–18. On early manuscript diversity, see Parker, *The Living Texts*.

15. Eusebius *Life of Constantine* 4.36; Metzger and Ehrman, *Text of the New Testament*, 15–16; Aland and Aland, *Text of the New Testament*, 64–71. The city of Byzantium was renamed Constantinople, around AD 330.

16. Greenlee, *Introduction to New Testament Textual Criticism*, 54–55; Vaganay and Amphoux, because of different recensions, see it as a period of "limited control" (*Introduction to New Testament Textual Criticism*, 111–23).

17. Metzger and Ehrman, *Text of the New Testament*, 279–80; Greenlee, *Introduction to New Testament Textual Criticism*, 54–55; Vaganay and Amphoux, *Introduction to New Testament Textual Criticism*, 123–28.

The Printed Text

The next historical phase of the transmission of the NT text was the period of the printed text (1516 to the present). This period was characterized by at least four developments: (1) the establishment of the "received text," (2) the accumulation of textual evidence, (3) the struggle for the critical text, and (4) the period of the critical text.[18]

The "Received Text"

Johannes Gutenberg's invention of the printing press (ca. 1450) marked a new period in the history of the NT text. Although the first Greek NT to be printed was the Polyglot Bible edited by Cardinal Ximenes (1514), the first text put on the market was edited by the Dutch humanist Erasmus in 1516.

Unfortunately these first editions, which served as the basis for all subsequent editions until the nineteenth century, were derived from late medieval manuscripts of inferior quality. In fact, Erasmus's only manuscript of Revelation was so badly mutilated that he supplied the missing portions with the Latin Vulgate translated into Greek (the last six verses). These readings have never been found in any Greek manuscripts.

Three subsequent editions are of special importance in the history of the text.[19]

18. Outline from Greenlee, *Introduction to New Testament Textual Criticism*, 62–75; see also Metzger and Ehrman, *Text of the New Testament*, 137–94; Vaganay and Amphoux, *Introduction to New Testament Textual Criticism*, 129–59.

19. Fee, "Textual Criticism of the New Testament," 141–42; Aland and Aland, *Text of the New Testament*, 3–11; Metzger and Ehrman, *Text of the New Testament*, 150–52.

First, the third edition of Robert Stephanus, which was dependent on the text of Erasmus, served as the basis for the King James Version (1611). The fourth edition of Stephanus (1551) was also the first to be numbered into chapters and verses as they are today. Second, Theodore Beza (in whose library was Codex Bezae), Calvin's successor in Geneva, published nine editions from 1565 to 1604 that gave the text of Erasmus a stamp of approval. Two of his editions were also used in the King James Version. Third, a Greek text very similar to those of Erasmus, Stephanus, and Beza was edited by the Elzevir brothers in 1633. It became the standard Greek text of Europe. The term "received text" (*textus receptus*: TR) is from the preface of their 1633 edition: "You therefore have the text which is now received by all, in which we give nothing changed or corrupted." This boast held good for over two hundred years.

New Textual Evidence

The period from 1633 to 1831 was characterized by the accumulation of new evidence from Greek manuscripts, versions, and from patristic writers. During this period, the dominance of the TR was not broken, but evidence was collected that eventually led to a better Greek text.

At least three scholars made significant contributions in this period: Bengel, Wettstein, and Griesbach. In 1734, J. A. Bengel published a Greek text, reprinting the TR but not based on any single edition. Here he first suggested the classification of manuscripts into text types (African, Asiatic) and devised a system for evaluating textual variants (e.g., superior, inferior). J. J. Wettstein's edition of the Greek text (1751–52) presupposed certain principles of textual criticism and used a system for designating manuscripts by symbols. J. J. Griesbach, in his editions from 1774 to 1807, modified Bengel's classification of text groups to three (Western, Alexandrian, Byzantine), defined the basic principles of textual criticism, and showed great skill in evaluating textual variants (e.g., his fifteen canons of textual criticism). Although the above works followed the "received text," valuable new evidence was relegated to the critical notes.

Struggle for the Critical Text

The period from 1831 to 1881 saw the overthrow of the TR and the struggle for a new critical edition. The first important break with the TR came with the Greek text published by Karl Lachmann (1831). His was the first attempt to reconstruct a text from scientific principles instead of reproducing the medieval text.[20] The impressive work of Constantin von Tischendorf brought to light many unknown manuscripts (e.g., Codex Sinaiticus). He also published critical editions of the Greek text. The last edition (1872) gave a critical apparatus noting all the known variants of the uncials, minuscules, versions, and patristic readings.

The Critical Text

In 1881 two Cambridge scholars, B. F. Westcott and F. J. A. Hort, combined their efforts to produce a monumental critical edition of the Greek NT. The *New Testament in Original Greek*, 2 vols. (1881–82) It was based on the earlier research of Griesbach, Lachmann, and Tischendorf, and it established a foundation for further study. The Westcott-Hort text was the basis for the English Revised (1881) and American Standard (1901) Versions of the NT.

In the introduction to the critical edition, F. J. A. Hort laid to rest the TR with three basic arguments against the Byzantine text type.[21] First, manuscripts of the Syrian (Byzantine) text type contain readings that combine elements found in the earlier text types. Second, the readings peculiar to the Syrian text type are never found in Christian writings before the fourth century. Third, when readings peculiar to this text type are compared with rival readings, the Syrian claim to originality disappears.

After careful examination of the early text types and their variants, Westcott and Hort concluded that the Egyptian text (Sinaiticus, Vaticanus, which they called "Neutral") preserved the original text with minimal change. Their critical Greek text was therefore based on this "neutral" text type, except in cases where internal evidence was clearly against it.

Subsequent research after Westcott and Hort (1881) has seen further refinements in the reconstruction of the critical text. In 1913, H. von Soden published a massive work that included a critical text, an extensive apparatus (critical notes), and lengthy descriptions of manuscripts. Although his textual theories became

---

20. Aland and Aland, *Text of the New Testament*, 11; Metzger and Ehrman, *Text of the New Testament*, 170–71.

21. Summary of three points in Metzger and Ehrman, *Text of the New Testament*, 180–81; see also Aland and Aland, *Text of the New Testament*, 14–20; Greenlee, *Introduction to New Testament Textual Criticism*, 72–75.

controversial, von Soden's text is a treasure of information.[22]

Defenders of the Textus Receptus or Byzantine text, listed with publication date of their major works, have reacted to the work and legacy of Westcott and Hort. J. W. Burgon (1871), T. R. Birks (1878), E. F. Hill (1956), and similar "majority text" advocates W. N. Pickering (1977), A. L. Farstad and Z. C. Hodges (1982), and M. A. Robinson (2002) fail to overcome Hort's arguments, mentioned earlier, face late-dating issues, and have not made a credible case based on the accepted principles of textual criticism.[23]

Theories concerning the History of the Text

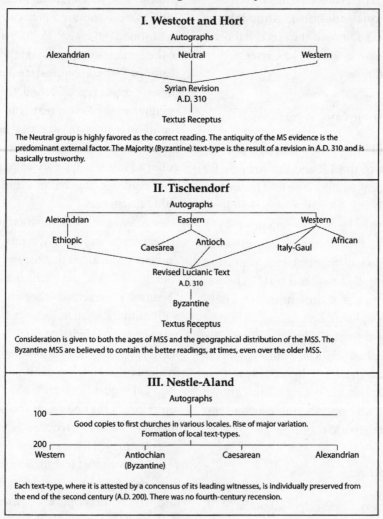

I. Westcott and Hort

Autographs

Alexandrian   Neutral   Western

Syrian Revision
A.D. 310

Textus Receptus

The Neutral group is highly favored as the correct reading. The antiquity of the MS evidence is the predominant external factor. The Majority (Byzantine) text-type is the result of a revision in A.D. 310 and is basically trustworthy.

II. Tischendorf

Autographs

Alexandrian   Eastern   Western

Ethiopic   Caesarea   Antioch   Italy-Gaul   African

Revised Lucianic Text
A.D. 310

Byzantine

Textus Receptus

Consideration is given to both the ages of MSS and the geographical distribution of the MSS. The Byzantine MSS are believed to contain the better readings, at times, even over the older MSS.

III. Nestle-Aland

Autographs

100

Good copies to first churches in various locales. Rise of major variation. Formation of local text-types.

200

Western   Antiochian (Byzantine)   Caesarean   Alexandrian

Each text-type, where it is attested by a concensus of its leading witnesses, is individually preserved from the end of the second century (A.D. 200). There was no fourth-century recension.

H. Wayne House. Copyright © 2009 by the Zondervan Corporation.

22. Greenlee, *Introduction to New Testament Textual Criticism*, 77–81; Aland and Aland, *Text of the New Testament*, 22–23; Metzger and Ehrman, *Text of the New Testament*, 185–90.

23. Greenlee, *Introduction to New Testament Textual Criticism*, 76–77; Metzger and Ehrman, *Text of the New Testament*, 181–82, 218–22; Robinson "Case for Byzantine Priority," 125–39,

Since 1898, pocket editions of the Greek NT began under the editorship of Eberhard Nestle (1851–1913) with subsequent editions (e.g., 13th ed., 1927) by his son, Erwin Nestle (1883–1972). Recently, a completely revised twenty-seventh edition (NA[27]) appeared in 1993 under the supervision of Barbara and Kurt Aland (Kurt worked on Nestle twenty-first edition, 1952). In this edition, as specified in the twenty-sixth edition, consideration is given to the geographical location of the text (e.g., Alexandria) as well as the reading that best explains the others (called the local-genealogical method).[24] This latter genealogical consideration is a modification of the Westcott-Hort local text theory. The critical apparatus remains extensive, devoting particular attention to the transmission of the text in the early period. In 1966 the United Bible Societies (New York, London, and Stuttgart) published a new handbook edition edited by K. Aland, Black, Metzger, Wikgren, and

later Martini. This text has been prepared especially for Bible translators and therefore only variants that make a difference in translation are included with more explanation. The fourth revised edition of this text (UBS[4] 1993) shares the same basic text with the Nestle-Aland, 27th edition, although it retains its more focused critical apparatus. Also, instead of the earlier Punctuation Apparatus, a Discourse Segmentation Apparatus (e.g., paragraph breaks) has been included (UBS[4], Intro. 39–45). A commentary on each textual variant of the United Bible Societies' Greek text was written by Bruce Metzger (1973), with a second edition published as a companion volume to UBS[4] (*The Textual Commentary on the Greek New Testament*, 1994).

Despite the advances beyond Westcott and Hort, the texts of Nestle-Aland (twenty-seventh edition) and the United Bible Societies (fourth edition) differ much more with the TR than with that of Westcott and Hort. The contribution of these Cambridge scholars appears to be enduring.

TEXTUAL CRITICISM OF THE NT

What principles are employed in deciding between variant readings of a text? What criteria are used for detecting the earliest possible reading? These questions are the concern of the science of textual criticism. We will now give a basic survey of the principles employed in this method of inquiry.[25]

---

with responses from Holmes (87–88) and Silva, (142–50). For more discussion and critique, see Wallace, "Majority Text Theory."

24. On the Alands' local-genealogical method and the classification of mss, see Comfort, *Encountering the Manuscripts*, 298–300; Metzger and Ehrman, *Text of the New Testament*, 237–38, and Metzger's judgment of variants according to text types, see Comfort, 300–302, and Metzger and Ehrman, 300–315. The Alands' method is also called the (reasoned) eclectic method because it presupposes a reconstruction of the earliest and best text variant by variant according to critical judgment without favoring any particular text type as preserving the original. See Fee, "Textual Criticism of the New Testament," 150; Aland and Aland, *Text of the New Testament*, 20, 22, 31–36, 43–47. See also Silva, "Modern Critical Editions," 285–91; on reading the NA[27] and UBS[4], see Greenlee, *Introduction to New Testament Textual Criticism*, 92–95; Comfort, *Encountering the Manuscripts*, 101–2; Elliott and Moir, *Manuscripts and the Text of the New Testament*, 20–25.

25. For a more complete discussion, see Aland and Aland, *Text of the New Testament*, 280–312; Fee, "Textual Criticism of the New Testament" 148–53; Finegan, *Encountering New Testament Manuscripts*, 54–75; Greenlee, *Introduction to*

One criterion above others affects the scholar's choice at every point of variation: the variation that best explains the origin of all the others is most likely to be the original. In order to "best explain the origin of the others," scholars must consider two factors: external evidence (the manuscripts themselves) and internal evidence (the authors or the scribes).

Concerning external evidence, one must first weigh the manuscript evidence supporting each variant. The age, quality, and geographical distribution of the witnesses and their text supporting each variant are important considerations for isolating the best readings and their documents. Internal evidence is of two types: (1) transcriptional probability, which deals with what kind of error or change the scribe probably made; and (2) intrinsic probability or what the author was most likely to have written. The detection of scribal errors (1) is based on inductive reasoning. For example, it is usually true that the more difficult reading is probably the original one, because scribes had a tendency to make the text easier to read. Also, the shorter reading is often the original one, because scribes tended to add to the text (although the scribes sometimes made omissions!). Finally, a textual variant differing from quoted or parallel material is almost always original, since the scribes tended to harmonize.[26] Detecting what the author most likely would have written (2) is the most subjective aspect of textual criticism. It has to deal with the style, vocabulary, and ideas of the author as they are found elsewhere and in the immediate context. (This aspect of internal evidence is given special weight by G. D. Kilpatrick.)

Not all the criteria mentioned above are equally applicable in every case; sometimes they even oppose one another. In such stalemates the text critic is usually forced back to the external evidence (the manuscripts themselves) as final arbiter. It is significant that for most scholars over 90 percent of all the variations of the NT text are resolved, since the variant that best explains the origin of the others is also supported by the earliest and best witnesses.[27]

New Testament Text Criticism, 111–31; Metzger and Ehrman, *Text of the New Testament*, 205–71, 300–315; Comfort, *Encountering the Manuscripts*, 321–29; Elliott and Moir, *Manuscripts and the Text of the New Testament*, 27–76.

26. Fee, "Textual Criticism," 149; Metzger and Ehrman, *Text of the New Testament*, 262–63.

27. Fee, "Textual Criticism," 150; Greenlee, *Introduction to New Testament Text Criticism*, 112; Aland and Aland, *Text of the New Testament*, 280. On the future direction of NT textual criticism, see Epp, "Issues in New Testament Textual Criticism."

PART 2

Interpreting the New Testament

5

The Historical Methods of Criticism*

Why does a "popular" collection of writings require such careful interpretation to be understood properly? Readers might raise this or a similar question after noting the technical title of this chapter. But this predicament of interpreting popular writings is not restricted to the NT. It also applies to the United States Constitution. To use a simple analogy: both the NT collection and the U.S. Constitution were written for the benefit of "common people," and both require careful interpretation to be understood properly.

The reasons for the predicament in interpretation are analogous for the two documents. First, both are a diverse collection of documents. The NT contains twenty-seven books. The Constitution contains seven articles and twenty-seven amendments. Second, both are products of a lengthy historical process. The NT includes almost a century of tradition and composition (AD 30–120). The Constitution and its amendments represent almost two centuries of tradition (1789 to the present). Third, both contain technical language belonging to specific communities: the religious communities that produced the NT and the legislative bodies that produced the Constitution.

The above reasons also substantiate two key points: (1) both the NT and the U.S. Constitution are difficult documents to read; and (2) a proper understanding of them necessitates the assistance of specialists. Despite the above difficulties and necessities, there are some positive aspects of the analogy: both sets of writings were compiled for the benefit of nonspecialists who are encouraged to be familiar with their contents. Therefore, these

* The word *criticism* means "judgment" or "discernment" (Gk. *kritikos*; *diakrisis* in 1 Cor 12:10). Just as an art critic enters a museum to appreciate with some discernment the paintings, so a "biblical critic" seeks a critical appreciation with discernment of the function or meaning of the text. Although the word *criticism* may sound malicious, it really is not. In the employ of a good exegete, these methods are heuristic (Gk. *heuriskein*, "to find").

documents of the common people, which require such careful interpretation, were also intended to be understood by common people.

TWO PRESUPPOSITIONS

The NT methods that concern us presuppose two kinds of historical distance: (a) that which exists between the modern reader and the ancient texts; and (b) that which exists between the time of writing and the events narrated.

Modern Reader and Ancient Texts

The first type of distance concerns the great span of about 2000 years that exists between the NT and us. On the one hand, there is our situation: we live in a modern industrial age of computer technology with air travel and space exploration. On the other hand, there is the NT period: it was an agrarian culture of wheel and plow with travel by sail or domesticated animal.[1] Clearly, these are two different worlds, separated historically by almost two millennia. The methods that we are about to discuss presuppose this historical distance. It is a basic premise of all objective historical study. It is also a necessary prerequisite for interpreting ancient texts. Once the historical gap is recognized, steps can be taken to establish a common ground of understanding between the modern reader and ancient documents. For example, in order to become acquainted with a foreign culture, one must also be able to understand the

differences between one's own culture and that foreign culture. This understanding of historical and cultural differences is presupposed in the historical methods of literary criticism. With this historical premise in view, we approach the NT in a manner different from that of reading the daily newspaper.

The Writings and the Events

Another type of distance which these literary methods presuppose is that between the time of writing (AD 65–95) and the time of the events narrated (e.g., the lives of Jesus and the apostles, AD 30–67). This is especially the case between the time when the four Gospels were written (AD 65–95) and the date of the ministry of Jesus (AD 30–33).

Why would historical distance imply a change in viewpoint from the time of Jesus to the time of the Evangelists? Did not the ancient person have a greater propensity to preserve and transmit old traditions than we do today? Were not some of the words and deeds of Jesus committed to writing during his lifetime? The historical gap of thirty-five to sixty-five years includes many social, cultural, and political changes. For example, the destruction of both the city of Jerusalem and its temple by the Romans in AD 70 is only one event that produced diverse changes in Palestinian Judaism, Diaspora Judaism, and early Christianity. Here is a reply to the second question: people of the ancient world did devote themselves to preserving and transmitting old traditions, but subtle and sometimes substantial changes took place in the process. Some changes took place to assist in memorization (e.g., mnemonics). The transmitters of the traditions

---

1. See Bailey, *Poet and Peasant*; Hanson and Oakman, *Palestine*; Malina and Rohrbaugh, *Social Science Commentary on the Synoptic Gospels*; Pilch, *CulDB*.

would also adapt the materials for their respective audiences or revise them when combined with other traditions. As a result, different versions of the same tradition appeared.

Several reasons can be given in response to the third question: were there not early written documents about Jesus that would minimize any different perspectives between Jesus and the

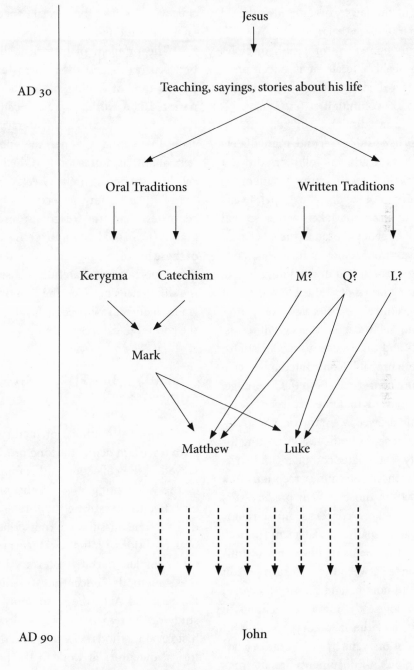

Development of the Gospels, C. B. Puskas and David Crump

Evangelists? First, we have no evidence that material about Jesus was committed to writing during his lifetime. It is clear from the Gospels that Jesus did not lecture in a classroom with students taking class notes. He taught where the common people of the Jews worked and gathered (e.g., marketplace, synagogue).

Although many of Jesus's disciples were probably literate, it is uncertain if any were skilled in writing documents for use in their communities (cf. Acts 4:13). Most of Jesus's disciples worked in manual trades like fishing. Second, immediately after Jesus's death, his followers did not devote themselves to writing his memoirs but rather to preaching the gospel. Evangelization was undertaken with a special sense of urgency, because they believed that Jesus would soon return as a conquering messiah and divine judge. Third, the writing down of oral traditions about Jesus became a great necessity only after the death of most of the eyewitnesses. Second- and third-generation Christians, who were probably confronted by diverse teachings, concerned about their heritage, and convinced that the return of Jesus would be delayed, were the ones who devoted themselves to the task of writing for posterity. These later compilers and writers had conceptions and perceptions that differed from those of their predecessors due to the new concerns and circumstances accompanying a later time period. Ancient documents that evidence a similar distance between the historical person and its author include Plato's *Dialogues*, which eulogize the life and teachings of Socrates; and the laudatory accounts of Apollonius of Tyana by Philostratus, a later disciple. Both documents are attempts by students to maximize the positive and

minimize the negative perceptions others may have had of their teachers. Socrates and Apollonius probably would have told their own stories differently. The above are some reasons why the writings of the gospel tradition were relatively late and why they would reflect the special concerns of later generations.

The problem of historical distance between (a) us and the ancient text and (b) the time of writing and of the events narrated is a working presupposition of the historical methods of literary criticism. In a similar manner, the science of textual criticism presupposed the historical distance between our Greek copies of the NT (e.g., from the second to fourth centuries) and the originals, or autographs (from the first century). Awareness of these historical gaps should underscore the importance of carefully considering the differences between the two time periods, before drawing conclusions about the common features.

COMMON OBJECTIVES AND CONCLUSIONS

The historical methods of literary criticism trace and define the long process involved in the collection and composition of the NT writings. It is their common objective to investigate the three periods of: oral transmission, the transcription of oral traditions, and their incorporation into complete narrative books. Although these methods concentrate on the four Gospels and Acts, they also apply to the study of the remaining NT books. These historical methods seek to reveal the historical dynamics at work in the production of ancient texts.

The historical methods of criticism enable us to view the NT books as intricate works with ingenious literary patterns and highly developed interpretations.[2] Before these insights the Gospels were often understood as simple recollections of events merely set together and told in a very straightforward manner. The story of Jesus, for example, was viewed as a verbatim report of the busy itinerary of Jesus narrated in a precise chronological order. The specific problems with this view will be discussed under form and redaction criticism. Learning to (re)appreciate the literary achievement of the Gospel writers is one of the important insights gained in the past two centuries of modern NT research.

Modern research draws certain historical conclusions about the NT books.[3]

First, they are not merely a collection of factual reports but reflect various sociological and religious concerns, different contexts, and different literary purposes. Second, the religious topics discussed in the text are not necessarily precise images of reality but reflect the faith and life of early communities and their authors. Third, the primary function of the Gospels is to bear witnesses to Jesus Christ and to what God has done in the person and work of Christ (Luke 1:1–4; Acts 1:1–5; John 20:30–31). Ignoring this point merely reduces the Gospels to a database for the reconstruction of diverse religious communities. Fourth, all historical reconstructions of modern research are subject to refinement and revision. Because every age has its biases, limited knowledge, and perspectives, one should avoid all cultural chauvinism. Uncritical loyalty to either our own contemporary era or the ancient culture of the NT hinders the interpretive process.

THREE METHODS OF CRITICISM: SOURCE, FORM, AND REDACTION CRITICISM

These methods were applied in an historically consecutive and logically necessary order. As historical critics of the late eighteenth and nineteenth centuries applied their craft to the early Christian texts (particularly to the Gospels), they asked

---

2. Old and new perceptions of the NT are from Dan Via, in his foreword to McKnight, *What Is Form Criticism?* v; see also Kelber, "Redaction Criticism," 14; Tuckett, *Reading the New Testament*.

3. Three points on modern biblical research are derived from Hayes and Holladay, *Biblical Exegesis* 116–17. Historical distance between Jesus (AD 30) and the written Gospels (post–AD 70) along with the very nature of Gospels (not mere factual reports) make necessary what is called a "two-level hermeneutic." Here the surface language of the Gospel is interpreted (decoded?) redaction-critically so that many of words and deeds of Jesus on the surface (tradition) are viewed as "symbolic" references written by the author (or redactor) for the historical situation of his Markan or Johannine community. See Martyn, *History and Theology*; and Weeden, *Mark*. Both Köstenberger, *Theology of John's Gospel*, 55–56; and Bauckham, *The Gospels for All Christians*, 19ff. take issue with this approach as deriving too much community situation from the Jesus storyline; but they fail to supply a better alternative that adequately takes into consideration the complexities of historical distance (30 and post-70) plus tradition (Jesus) with redaction (in Matthew, John). See a response to Bauckham: Sim, "The Gospels for All Christians?" 3–27; and the helpful survey of discussion in Collins,

Mark, 96–102. Meeks notes that our knowledge of the social dimensions of the Gospels has expanded greatly by means of sociohistorical analysis: "A Hermeneutics of Social Embodiment," 176–86. Perhaps also an understanding of the Gospels as *primarily* witnesses to Jesus Christ is a helpful corrective to the above concerns (see Barton, "Can We Identify the Gospel Audiences?" 194; see also ch. 6 below for discussion of the nature of the Gospels).

the simple question, what really happened? From the four Gospels they were sometimes offered different answers. Thus were they led to deal with the mysterious similarities and differences of the four canonical Gospels. Paramount to further progress was the determination of which of the *Synoptic* Gospels was prior to the others, as they were interested in finding the *oldest* source. Continuing this historical quest led them to the application of *source criticism* to these texts. This comparative analysis of texts sought to determine when sources were used, and which documents were sources (if we had access to them). Who wrote first . . . Matthew, Mark, or Luke? The answer given by many was Mark (this is called Markan Priority).

The next step back would then have to be done with preliterary traditions (oral tradition). The method known as form criticism was then applied to the Gospel texts. This method was an analysis of the "form" or "type" of individual pericopae.[4] Focus turned to the form of the individual stories, and interest shifted to the early life of the church and the use that it made of the stories in preaching the gospel and teaching. An axiom of form crticism is that form and function are related. At this point the interest of the analysts was not the Gospel compositions themselves, but the separate pericopae of which the Gospels were composed. The analysts were at a difficult place, for the ability of these collected forms to disclose

pristine historical data was extremely limited, and historical skepticism cast a shadow over the enterprise. The quest of the historical Jesus seemed to be at an impasse.

But new energy was infused into the enterprise by the next turn of events after World War II. With the rise of redaction criticism, the question changed from, "what really happened?" to what are the final editors or authors saying? This question was not a primary concern of form critics, who were more interested in the individual life of floating traditions. The redaction critics put the pieces back into the larger form that they had in the finished compositions and sought the editorial or authorial meaning there. They were initially intent upon seeing the authors as editors (German: *Redakteurs*) who used traditions and sources in particular ways.

Before they were used to interpret Scripture, these critical tools were employed in the study of classical Greek and early Western literature. Although they are technical approaches to the ancient texts, they can be understood and employed by the nonspecialists.

Before approaching a text with the historical methods it is important to be familiar with the literary, historical, and cultural context of the passage to be studied. First, consult and use modern English translations based on the most reliable Greek manuscripts (e.g., NRSV, NEB, NIV, CEB, NET Bible). A working knowledge of the Greek New Testament is, of course, most helpful! Second, read the passage carefully. Be alert to the literary relationship of your passage to its immediate context (e.g., paragraph, chapter, section), reading forward and backward, within the book in which it occurs.

---

4. *Pericope* (Greek) means "cut around" and refers to a section of text around which it is possible to cut and to view as an isolated piece of tradition. The theory was that these pericopae were used in early Christian preaching, and that they survived because of their usefulness and relevance to the early church. Their incorporation into the Gospels helped to secure for them a fixed form.

Familiarity with the general outline of the book is helpful. Some understanding of ancient rhetoric (Aristotle, Cicero) will benefit you here. Third, get acquainted with the names, places, concepts, and cultural practices in the passage. This can be done by consulting a current Bible encyclopedia, such as the *ABD, IDB, IDBSup, NIDB, HBD, CulDB, DJG, EDB, DPL, DLNT,* or *ZPE.* Fourth, outline the passage to discover and highlight the major points (i.e., grammatical analysis). Again, ancient rhetoric will also prove helpful here. Fifth, compare also writings by the same author (e.g., Luke and Acts) or contemporary writings (e.g., Paul's letters, the Pastorals). Sixth, check your research by consulting a Bible commentary on the NT passage: commentary series include, for example: HNTC, AB, Hermeneia, NCBC, NICNT, SP, Pillar, NJBC, and WBC.[5] This process of understanding the text need not be followed in the exact order listed above, nor does it have to be a long, time-consuming project since you will learn more as you utilize the historical methods of literary criticism. For more information consult the sections of **Reference Works** and **Commentaries** in our **Bibliography** at the end of this book.

Source Criticism

The method of source criticism seeks to determine the following in a written document: (1) the presence and meaning of sources, and (2) the author's use of these sources.[6]

The Importance of Detecting Sources

Knowing sources is especially important if one encounters startling information or conflicting accounts. Consider the following scenario: You are driving home from school and suddenly hear on the radio that the United States has invaded Iran. Certainly you would want to know the source of information for such startling news—especially if you are of a draftable age! When you arrive home to view the evening news on television, you hear that United States has not invaded Iran. A democratic revolution had successfully taken place within that nation! Certainly you would be interested in knowing the sources behind these two conflicting reports. You would want to either learn more about the event or to confirm the credibility of the sources used (e.g., foreign correspondents, Pentagon officials). Startling information and conflicting reports are at least two reasons why it is important to have access to primary sources.

5. See our abbreviation list and bibliography for further information on the above works. For specific books on tools for NT study, see Danker, *Multipurpose Tools*; Fitzmyer, *An Introductory Bibliography*; Scholer, *A Basic Bibliographic Guide.* On the practice of NT interpretation (Gk. *exegesis*), see Fee, *New Testament Exegesis*; Green, *Hearing the New Testament*; Porter, *Handbook to the Exegesis of the New Testament*; Kaiser and Kümmel, *Exegetical Method*; Hayes and Holladay, *Biblical Exegesis*; Green and McKnight, *Dictionary of Jesus and the Gospels*; McKnight, *Synoptic Gospels: An Annotated Bibliography*; Gorman, *Elements of Biblical Exegesis*; McKnight and Osborne, *Face of New Testament Studies.*

6. For introductions to source criticism, see Harrington, *Interpreting the New Testament*, 56–57; Wenham, "Source Criticism," in Marshall, *New Testament Interpretation*, 139–52; Tate, *Interpreting the Bible*, 347–48.

The above scenario is similar to the situation often faced in NT studies. For example, in the narrative of Matt 8:28–34, there are *two* demoniacs from *Gadarenes*; but in Mark 5:1–20 there is only *one* demoniac from *Gerasa* mentioned. Do the two accounts presuppose two different sources, or two variations of the same source? The issues raised by these two passages are part of the concern of source criticism.

The Basic Assumptions

Source criticism assumes that the NT authors used written as well as oral traditions in the production of their works.[7] In the Gospels, the gap of thirty-five to sixty-five years from the time of the events to the time of their written narration lends good support to this assumption. Because of this presupposition, source criticism excludes from its approach two extreme positions: First, is the view that the events narrated in the NT are complete literary

7. For background on the history of source-critical research, note the following scholars with dates of major works reflecting this concern: OT source criticism (mainly the Pentateuch) had a long history originating in the late seventeenth century, with R. Simon and later developed by, e.g., A. Kuenen (1860), K. H. Graf (1860), and J. Wellhausen (1870). Scholars of early European history also employed the method: e.g., B. G. Niebuhr (1811), L. von Ranke (1824). NT source criticism focused on the Synoptic Gospels, beginning with, e.g., J. J. Griesbach (1776), J. G. Eichhorn (1795), K. Lachmann (1835); and developed further by, e.g., H. J. Holtzmann (1863), Schweitzer (1906, 1968), B. H. Streeter (1924), W. R. Farmer (1964) D. Dungan (1999), M. Goodacre (2002). For more discussion of the above, see Kümmel, *The New Testament: A History*, 74–88, 144–61, 325–41; Neill and Wright, *Interpretation*; Baird, *History of New Testament Research*, vol. 1 (1992), vol. 2 (2002); McKim, *Dictionary of Major Biblical Interpreters*.

fabrications of the author. Many of them correspond too closely to what we know from archaeology and other ancient literature to support this view. Second, is the view that the NT writers were merely "stenographers for God" who wrote at his dictation. Such an extreme confessional position would require a much greater degree of uniformity in content, style, and purpose than exists in the NT. Source criticism presupposes that the NT was the product of a human process of collecting oral and written traditions and of committing them to writing. This assumption does not conflict with any view that is historically informed.

The NT writers made use of written traditions. This is evident, first of all, by the explicit use of passages from the Jewish Scriptures, especially the Septuagint (LXX). There are approximately 1600 citations in the NT of over 1200 different passages from the Jewish Scriptures, as well as several thousand allusions. The author of Luke-Acts explicitly mentions written accounts of Jesus, which he probably utilized in his own work (Luke 1:1–4). Unfortunately, he does not tell us when he is relying on these written Jesus traditions.

How to Detect Sources

How does one detect the presence of sources in the NT writings? Sometimes explicit reference is made to a source before it is cited. This is especially the case with citations of the Jewish Scriptures. They are often preceded by such formulas as "it is written" (Rom 1:17) or "as Isaiah predicted" (Rom 9:29). There are over two hundred instances of OT citations introduced by these formulas.[8] In another example of the explicit use of a written document, the Apostle Paul writes in his first letter to the Corinthian church, "now concerning the matters about which you wrote" (1 Cor 7:1). A final example is to introduce a source with a stereotyped phrase designating it as traditional material: "for I delivered to you . . . what I also received" (1 Cor 15:3). It is unclear in this last instance whether the author is using an oral or a written source.

When the use of sources is not mentioned, the task of deciphering them becomes more difficult. Source criticism suggests possible internal criteria for detecting them, although it is worth remembering that this process is as much an art as it is a science. The criteria include (a) the displacement or discontinuity of thought and literary style and (b) the use of unusual vocabulary uncharacteristic of the rest of the book. Other criteria will be introduced in our comparisons of Matthew, Mark, and Luke.

An example can be given: 2 Cor 6:1—7:4. If one carefully reads this entire passage, the contents of 6:14—7:1 seem to interrupt the thought pattern. The topic of 6:1–13 (an appeal for openness) abruptly changes at v. 14 and does not resume until 7:2. The vocabulary and style of 6:14—7:1 are also different from the rest of 2 Corinthians specifically, and from Paul's other letters generally. This has led some commentators to observe similarities between this seemingly displaced passage and certain teachings found in the Dead Sea Scrolls of Qumran; a few even go so far as to speculate that this passage came from an Essene document revised by Christians. As we have seen, displacement of thought and the presence of unusual vocabulary are two internal criteria for detecting possible sources, especially when the writer of a work does not identify them. The observable comparisons between Matthew, Mark, and Luke, however, offer more opportunities for identifying sources than Paul's letters do. Other significant examples will be given to better understand the methodology of source criticism.

A Case Study in Mark

Let us apply these principles of source criticism to a passage in the Gospel of Mark (the second Gospel) 1:1–3: "The beginning of the gospel of Jesus Christ, the Son of God. As it is written in Isaiah the prophet, 'Behold, I send my messenger before your face, who shall prepare your way; the voice of one crying in the wilderness. Prepare the way of the Lord, make his paths straight.'"

The source used by Mark in this passage is clearly introduced by the stereotypical formula "as it is written in Isaiah the prophet." Most modern translations indent the quotation. However, a difficulty arises in attempting to identify precisely what source or sources are used. The passage cited in Mark is from Isa 40:3, probably in a Greek translation of the Hebrew Bible:[9] "The voice of one crying in

8. Shires, *Finding the Old Testament in the New*, 15; Beale and Carson, *Commentary on New Testament Use of the Old Testament*; Archer and Chirichigno, *Old Testament Quotations in New Testament*; Porter, *Hearing the Old Testament in the New Testament*. See especially indexes of quotations, allusions, and parallels in *Novum Testamentum Graece*. 27th ed. corrected (1998), 770–806; UBS[4], 897–911.

9. Our translation of the LXX is based on Rahlfs, *Septuaginta*, 2:619.

the wilderness. Prepare the way of the Lord, make *our God's* path straight."

With only one modification (italicized), Mark makes use of the passage of Isa 40:3 in a Greek translation similar to the one from which we have translated it: i.e., the Septuagint, but the Isaiah 40 passage accounts for only the second part of the quotation. Nowhere in Isaiah 40 or in the entire book of Isaiah (1–66) is there found the first part of Mark's quote attributed to Isaiah! It is, however, found in Mal 3:1, and follows closely a Hebrew text similar to the one from which our OT is translated.[10] "Behold, I send my messenger before *my face* to prepare the way."

Some of the wording in Mark's quote may have been influenced by a Greek translation of Exod 23:20 since part of it agrees verbatim with Mark: "behold, I send my messenger before your face."[11] But the quote in Mark 1:2, ascribed to Isaiah, is clearly referring to the passage from Mal 3:1. As odd as this may appear to us, Mark provides an example of a common Jewish practice of biblical citation and interpretation called *conflation*. By "splicing" together pieces of two or probably three similarly worded OT passages, Mark identifies "the beginning of the gospel" with not one but three crucial moments in Israel's history of salvation: the exodus from Egypt (Exod 23:20), the return from Babylonian exile (Isa 40:3), and the yet-to-be-fulfilled expectation of a deliverer (Mal 3:1).[12]

The Synoptic Problem

Now compare Mark with the Gospels of Matthew and Luke.[13] All three are called the Synoptic Gospels because they share a "common" (Gk., *syn-*) "vision" (Gk., *-optic*) of the life of Jesus. Note that all three accounts deal with John the Baptist, and both Matthew and Luke cite the passage from Isaiah 40 found "The voice of one crying out in the wilderness." But what happened to that problematic Malachi passage found in Mark 1:2? It is omitted in the accounts of both Matthew and Luke. These two Gospels use the Malachi passage in another context, perhaps influenced by another source (Matt 11:10; Luke 7:27 = Q). Could it be that both Matthew and Luke eliminated Mark's Jewish practice of conflation (of Isaiah and Malachi) because it was problematic for their Gentile audiences? We can only surmise here.

We should also note how Matthew and Luke employ the Isaiah 40 quotation differently from Mark, by observing what precedes and follows in all three Gospel accounts. First, neither Matthew nor Luke employs Mark's superscription: "The beginning of the gospel." The basic reason for this omission is that Matthew and Luke begin their Gospels ("good news announcements") not with the account of John (cf. Mark) but with the birth and infancy narratives. Second, Luke begins his account of John with a chronological notation (Luke 3:1–2), endeavoring to

---

10. Our translation of the Hebrew Bible is based on Elliger, et al., *Biblia Hebraica Stuttgartensia*, 1084.

11. Translation based on Rahlfs, *Septuaginta*.

12. For a more detailed discussion, see Guelich, *Mark 1—8:26*, 10–12; France, *The Gospel of Mark*,

63–64; and esp. Beale and Carson, *Commentary on the New Testament Use of the Old Testament*, 113–20.

13. The following work has been used in our comparison: Throckmorton, *Gospel Parallels*; see also Swanson, *Horizontal Line Synopsis of the Gospels*.

Matthew 3:1–3	Mark 1:1–3	Luke 3:1–6
	[1] The beginning of the gospel of Jesus Christ, the Son of God.	
[1] In those days		[1] In the fifteenth year of reign of Tiberius Caesar, Pontius Pilate being governor of Judea, and Herod being tetrarch of Galilee, and his brother Philip tetrarch of the region of Ituraea and Trachonitis and Lysanias tetrarch of Abilene, [2] in the high-priesthood of Annas and Caiaphas, the word of God came to John the son of Zechariah in the wilderness; [3] and he went into all the region about the Jordan, preaching a baptism of repentance for the forgiveness of sins. [4] As it is written in the book of the words of Isaiah the prophet,
came John the Baptist, preaching in the wilderness of Judea		
[2] "Repent, for the kingdom of heaven is at hand:" [3] For this is he who was spoken of by the prophet Isaiah when he said,	[2] As it is written in Isaiah the prophet, "Behold, I send my messenger before thy face, who shall prepare thy way;	
"The voice of one crying in the wilderness: Prepare the way of the Lord, make his paths straight."	[3] "The voice of one crying in the wilderness: Prepare the way of the Lord, make his paths straight—"	"The voice of one crying in the wilderness Prepare the way of the Lord, make his paths straight. [5] Every valley shall be filled, and every mountain and hill shall be brought low, and the crooked shall be made straight, and the rough ways shall be made smooth; [6] and all flesh shall see the salvation of God."

link his narrative with secular history, a distinctive concern of Luke. Third, both Matthew and Luke feel it necessary to first acquaint their readers with the message of John's preaching before offering the Isaiah quotation, whereas Mark includes this after it (Mark 1:4). Fourth, although Luke retains Mark's phrasing of John's message ("preaching a baptism of repentance for the forgiveness of sins"), Matthew changes this to "Repent, for the kingdom of heaven is at hand," which is a special emphasis in his Gospel (e.g., Matt 3:11; 4:17). Fifth, only Luke expands upon the Isaiah quotation, citing 40:3–5 (LXX with two words, and a phrase omitted from 40:4–5). This

especially highlights the statement, "all flesh shall see God's salvation," which is another distinctive emphasis of the author of Luke-Acts (e.g., Luke 2:30; Acts 28:28). The five points raised above show how differently the Isaiah 40 passage in Mark is employed by Matthew and Luke.

It also appears from our comparison that Matthew and Luke are dependent on Mark. Several observations support this assertion, and problems are raised by resisting it. First, we saw that both Matthew and Luke, possibly influenced by a common source, omit the problematic Malachi passage that Mark had ascribed

Synoptic Parallels

	Matthew	Mark	Luke	John
Preaching of John the Baptist	3:1–2	1:1–8	3:1–20	1:19–28
Baptism of Jesus	3:13–17	1:9–11	3:21–22	
Temptation	4:1–11	1:12–13	4:1–13	
Beginning of Galilee ministry	4:12–17	1:14–15	4:14–15	
Rejection at Nazareth	13:53–58	6:1–6	4:16–30	
Healing of Peter's mother-in-law and others	8:14–17	1:29–34	4:38–41	
Cleansing of a leper	8:1–4	1:40–45	5:12–16	
Healing of the paralytic	9:1–8	2:1–12	5:17–26	
Calling of Levi	9:9–13	2:13–17	5:27–32	
Fasting	9:14–17	2:18–22	5:33–39	
Grain plucking on the Sabbath	12:1–8	2:23–28	6:1–5	
Healing of withered hand	12:9–14	3:1–6	6:6–11	
Choosing of the Twelve	10:1–4	3:13–19	6:12–16	
Parable of the sower	13:1–23	4:1–20	8:4–15	
Jesus' true family	12:46–50	3:31–35	8:19–21	
Calming of a storm	8:23–27	4:35–41	8:22–25	
Healing of demon-possessed man	8:28–34	5:1–20	8:26–39	
Jairus's daughter and woman with hemorrhage	9:18–26	5:21–43	8:40–56	
The Twelve sent out	10:5–15	6:7–13	9:1–6	
John the Baptist beheaded	14:1–12	6:14–29	9:7–9	
Five thousand fed	14:13–21	6:30–44	9:10–17	6:1–14
Peter's confession	16:13–19	8:27–29	9:18–20	
Jesus' foretelling of death and resurrection	16:20–28	8:30–9:1	9:21–27	
Transfiguration	17:1–8	9:2–8	9:28–36	
Casting out of unclean spirits	17:14–18	9:14–27	9:37–43	
Second Prediction of death and resurrection	17:22–23	9:30–32	9:43–45	
"Who is greatest?"	18:1–5	9:33–37	9:46–48	
Jesus and Beelzebub	12:22–30	3:20–27	11:14–23	
Demand for a sign	12:38–42	8:11–12	11:29–32	
Parable of the mustard seed	13:31–32	4:30–32	13:18–19	
Blessing of little children	19:13–15	10:13–16	18:15–17	
Rich young ruler	19:16–30	10:17–31	18:18–30	
Third Prediction of death and resurrection	20:17–19	10:32–34	18:31–34	
Healing of blind Bartimaeus (and another)	20:29–34	10:46–52	18:35–42	

The Final Week

	Matthew	Mark	Luke	John
Triumphal entry into Jerusalem	21:1–11	11:1–11	19:28–40	12:12–19
"By what authority …?"	21:23–27	11:27–33	20:1–8	
Vineyard and tenants	21:33–46	12:1–12	20:9–19	
"Render to Caesar"	22:15–22	12:13–17	20:20–26	
The resurrection	22:23–33	12:18–27	20:27–40	
David's son	22:41–46	12:35–37	20:41–44	
Sermon on the last days	24:1–36	13:1–32	21:5–33	
Passover plot	26:1–5, 14–16	14:1–2, 10–11	22:1–6	
Preparing of Passover	26:17–20	14:12–17	22:7–14	
Foretelling of betrayal	26:21–25	14:18–21	22:21–23	13:21–30
The Lord's Supper	26:26–30	14:22–26	22:14–20	
Prediction of Peter's denial	26:31–35	14:27–31	22:31–34	13:36–38
Gethsemane	26:36–46	14:32–42	22:39–46	
Arrest of Jesus	26:47–56	14:43–50	22:47–53	18:3–12
Sanhedrin (Peter's denial)	26:57–75	14:53–72	22:54–71	18:13–27
Jesus before Pilate	27:1–2, 11–14	15:1–5	23:1–5	18:28–38
Sentencing of Jesus	27:15–26	15:6–15	23:17–25	18:39–19:16
Crucifixion, Death, Burial	27:32–61	15:21–47	23:26–56	19:27–42
Resurrection	28:1–8	16:1–8	24:1–12	20:1–10

H. Wayne House. Copyright © 2009 by the Zondervan Corporation.

to Isaiah (Mark 1:2). Second, Matthew and Luke either arranged in different order or revised material they seemed to have gotten from Mark (e.g., the content of John's preaching). Third, there is an example of one Gospel's apparently expanding upon the quotation originally cited in Mark: Luke's expansion of the Isaiah 40 quotation in Mark. The theory of Markan priority (the idea that Mark's Gospel was written first and then used as the primary source for both Matthew and Luke) appears to provide the best explanation of the evidence as we have shown by the three observations listed above.

Resisting the conclusion of Markan priority raises additional problems.[14] First, why would anyone want to abbreviate or conflate Matthew and Luke to produce a Gospel like Mark's? Second, why would Mark have omitted so much material from Matthew and Luke? For example, why would Mark have ignored the infancy stories and postresurrection appearances? Third, what kind of author and religious teacher would Mark have been if he really had copies of Matthew and Luke but omitted so much from them? The above problems support the view that Mark was the first Gospel and that Matthew and Luke used Mark independently. This hypothesis, for a majority of scholars, best explains the phenomena of similarities and differences between Matthew, Mark, and Luke (called the Synoptic Problem).

There is also a second problem encountered in the Synoptic Gospels. This concerns the close similarities between Matthew and Luke that are not found in

14. The three points concerning Markan priority are from Harrington, *Interpreting the New Testament,* 61–62. For further arguments, see Fitzmyer, "Priority of Mark and the 'Q' Source in Luke," 1:131–70; Kümmel, *Introduction,* 35–63; Streeter, *Four Gospels;* Styler, "Priority of Mark," 223–32; Neville, *Arguments from Order in Synoptic Source Criticism;* Kloppenborg, *Excavating Q,* 11–54, 271–328; Black and Beck, *Rethinking the Synoptic Problem;* Evans, *Mark 8:27–16:20,* xliii–lviii; Kloppenborg, *Q: The Earliest Gospel,* 1–40. Note, however, the following works that favor Matthean priority (i.e., the Griesbach hypothesis) and argue for Markan dependency on Matthew and Luke: Dungan, "Mark—The Abridgement of Matthew and Luke," 51–97; Farmer, *Synoptic Problem;* Farmer, "Modern Developments of Griesbach's Hypothesis," 275–95; Longstaff, *Evidence of Conflation in Mark?;* Wenham, *Redating Matthew, Mark and Luke.*

Mark. Let us look again at our Synoptic comparison. After following Mark's account of John the Baptist and his ministry, both Matthew and Luke add an account that it is not found in Mark:

Matt 3:7–10	Luke 3:7–9
[7] But when he saw many of the Pharisees and Sadducees coming for baptism, he said to them, "You brood of vipers! Who warned you to flee from the wrath to come? [8] Bear fruit that befits repentance, [9] and do not presume to say to yourselves, 'We have Abraham as our father'; for I tell you, God is able from these stones to raise up children to Abraham. [10] Even now the axe is laid to the root of the trees; every tree therefore that does not bear good fruit is cut down and thrown into the fire."	[7] He said therefore to the multitudes that came out to be baptized by him, "You brood of vipers! Who warned you to flee from the wrath to come? [8] Bear fruit that befits repentance, and do not presume to say to yourselves, 'We have Abraham as our father'; for I tell you, God is able from these stones to raise up children to Abraham. [9] Even now the axe is laid to the root of the trees; every tree therefore that does not bear good fruit is cut down and thrown into the fire."

Despite the differences in the opening sentence between Matt 3:7 and Luke 3:7, the rest of the two passages are verbatim in the Greek, with the exception of one word and one case ending (cf. Gk. *doxēte* and *arxēsthe, axion* and *axious,* Luke also adds *kai*). These two passages show such close verbal similarities that it is probable that a common written source is used here. This parallel is only one of many (e.g., Matt 6:24/Luke 16:13; Matt 23:37–39/Luke 13:34–35). Often this common non-Markan material is arranged in different places by Matthew and Luke, indicating that both utilized this source independently. This common written source, not found in Mark, is often called "Q" from the German *Quelle*, meaning "source." It is also called the Synoptic Sayings Source, because it contains mostly sayings of Jesus, rather than stories about him.[15]

The Contents of Q as determined by the International Q Project[16]

Q 3:2b, 3, 7–9, 16b–17, 21–22

Q 4:1–4, 9–12, 5–8, 13, 16

Q 6:20–21, 22–23, 27–28, 35c–d, 29–30, 31, 32, 34, 36, 37–38, 39, 40, 41–42, 43–45, 46, 47–49

Q 7:1, 3, 6b–9, ?10?, 18–23, 24–28, 29–30, 31–35

Q 9:57–60

Q 10:2, 3, 4, 5–9, 10–12, 13–15, 16, 21, 22, 23–24

Q 11:2b–4, 9–13, 14–15, 17–20, 21–22, 23, 24–26, ?27–28?, 16, 29–30, 31–32, 33, 34–35, ?39a?, 42, 39b, 41, 43–44, 46b, 52, 47–48, 49–51

Q 12:2–3, 4–5, 6–7, 8–9, 10, 11–12, 33–34, 22b–31, 39–40, 42–46, 49, 51, 53, 54–56, 58–59,

Q 13:18–19, 20–21, 24–27, 29, 28, 30, 34–35

Q 14:·11, 16–18, ?19–20?, 21, 23, 26, 27

Q 17:33

Q 14:34–35

Q 16:13, 16, 17, 18

Q 17:1–2

Q 15:4–5a, 7, 8–10

Q 17:3–4, 6, 20–21, 23–24, 37, 26–27, ?28–29?, 30, 34–35,

Q 19:12–13, 15–24, 26

Q 22:28, 30

The theory that Matthew and Luke used both Mark and Q as sources is called the Two-Document Hypothesis. In addition to these two written documents, two oral (or written) sources have been postulated to explain the presence of distinctive Matthean and Lukan material. "M" refers to that material only found in Matthew, such as the Coming of the Magi, the Slaughter of Children by Herod, and the Flight and Return of Jesus and His Family from Egypt. "L" refers to that material only found in Luke, such as the Birth of John the Baptist, Mary's Magnificat, the Visit of the Shepherds, and the Presentation of the Infant Jesus in the Temple. This expanded version of the theory (postulating that M and L included additional written sources) is sometimes called the Four-Document Hypothesis.[17] However,

---

15. See Kloppenborg *Excavating Q*, for summary discussions (to 1999) of: the varieties of nomenclature of Q (*logia, Logienquelle*, Sayings Gospel Q, etc.), 402–8; the order of Q, 88–91; the extent of Q, 91–101, the language of Q, 72–80, 341–42; the people of Q, 166–213; the date of Q, 80–87. For a well-done history of Q scholarship, see Fleddermann, *Q: A Reconstruction and Commentary*, 3–39.

16. http://www.ntgateway.com/synoptic-problem-and-q/q-web-materials/; versification follows Luke's text (Q 14:11 = Luke 14:11). Chapter-verses separated by commas indicate separate sayings.

The order is Luke's with a few exceptions. Kloppenborg, *Q, the Earliest Gospel*, 123–44; Kloppenborg, *Excavating Q*, 100; Robinson, et al., *The Critical Edition of Q*; Robinson, et al., *The Sayings Gospel Q in Greek and English*. For a workbook on Q that contains Matthean and Lukan texts (Greek and English), extensive canonical and noncanonical parallels, a (Greek) concordance of Q, plus introductory discussions of proposed inclusions see Kloppenborg, *Q Parallels*.

17. Streeter, *Four Gospels*, 223–70.

unlike with Mark and Q, it is difficult to determine if M and L are (a) oral or written sources, or (b) the literary creations of the authors.

The documentary hypothesis we have outlined above has been followed by a majority of biblical scholars since the beginning of the twentieth century. Regarding Q it should be noted also that some scholars continue to dispute either the necessity of a Q document (some argue that the same results would be pro-

One problem raised by the Two-Document Hypothesis concerns the minor agreements of Matthew and Luke against Mark.[19] If they used Mark independently, they really should not agree in their modifications of it. Four responses to this problem can be given: First, on certain topics, Q and Mark may have overlapped, and here Matthew and Luke may have relied on Q instead of Mark. Second, Matthew and Luke may have had access to a slightly different edition of Mark from

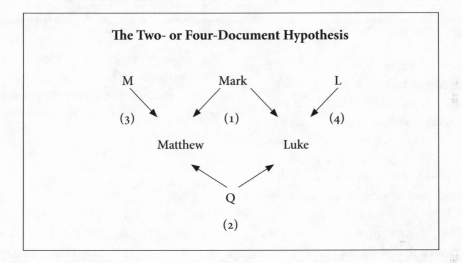

The Two- or Four-Document Hypothesis

duced by either Matthew or Luke copying from the other), or the *limitations* of a minimal Q especially with respect to the passion narrative.[18]

18. For example, Goodacre defends the order of Mark—Matthew—Luke in *Synoptic Problem* and in *Case against Q*. Others defend the order of Mark—Luke—Matthew, see Huggins, "Matthean Posteriority," 204–25; Hengel, *Four Gospels and the One Gospel*, 169–207. A few argue for common oral traditions and not literary dependence to explain the origins of the Synoptic Gospels, see Reicke, *Roots of the Synoptic Gospels*; Linnemann, *Is There a Synoptic Problem?* Thomas, *Three Views*, 226–309. There is a growing group of scholars convinced that while there was a Q, nevertheless circumscribing the *limits* of the document to *minimal Q* with the double tradition is an error in method. See, for example, Hultgren, *Narrative*

what we have. Third, those who copied the early Greek manuscripts may have har-

Elements, who argues for the presence of a passion narrative in Q based upon *minor agreements* between the passion narratives of Matthew and Luke. Another study by C. Michael Robbins, *Testing of Jesus in Q*, argues for a reflection on Jesus's death and enthronement (a virtual passion narrative) in Q on the basis of the pervasive eschatological tradition-history of the elements of the Temptation Narrative. Either approach drastically alters the theological profile of minimal Q, heralded by many as an early sayings source with no interest in Jesus's death.

19. Neirynck, *Minor Agreements of Matthew and Luke*; Simpson, "Major Agreements of Matthew and Luke against Mark," 273–84. For survey of the problem and responses, see Harrington, *Interpreting the New Testament*, 63.

monized the Matthean and Lukan texts. Fourth, just as two competent teachers independently reading a student's paper will naturally introduce many of the same corrections, so Matthew and Luke may have independently yet harmoniously corrected Mark's rough Greek style. The Two Document explanation of the Synoptic Problem is only a hypothesis, although it is a plausible explanation of the facts and explains more of the data than any alternate theories.

Source Criticism: Conclusions

Source criticism attempts to do three things: (1) to detect the presence of a source; (2) to determine the contents of the source; and (3) to understand how the source was used. Source criticism seeks to deal seriously with the NT as a historical document. Its importance is obvious to anyone who is confronted with startling or conflicting information. When the reader of the NT encounters a problem passage or two conflicting accounts of one event, the quest for sources can often help clarify or explain the problem. Although most of our examples of source criticism have been taken from the Synoptic Gospels, this method is used throughout the NT. The relationship of 2 Peter and Jude, for example, has raised several source-critical questions not unlike those of the Synoptic Problem. The usefulness of source criticism is augmented by the historical methods of form and redaction criticism.

Form Criticism

Form criticism concentrates on the traditional units that originated in an oral or preliterary setting. It attempts to get behind the written sources to the oral period before the literary forms were put into writing. Before discussing form criticism, the nature and significance of literary forms will be examined.

Literary forms are various modes of communication available to the writer for his readers.[20] There are numerous assortments of literary forms in every culture, ancient and modern. Note the diverse examples of literary forms in our culture: a personal letter, an obituary notice in the newspaper, a school drama script, and the love poem on a greeting card. All of the above examples are modes of communication used by writers for various audiences. As we see, literary forms are an important and pervasive phenomenon in human culture.

Basic Features of Literary Forms

There are at least five basic cultural characteristics of literary forms that can be reflected in form criticism. First, all literary forms have fixed patterns. In our culture, for example, even a personal letter will usually contain (a) an indication of place and date, (b) the name of the recipient (e.g., Dear Aunt Sue), (c) an apology for not writing sooner, and (d) a statement of the writer's health and expression of

20. The NT literary forms relevant to the Synoptic Gospels will be classified under the following categories: (1) Sayings (i.e., direct discourse, e.g., proverbs, parables) and (2) Stories (i.e., indirect discourse, e.g., miracle accounts, legends). Despite differences, see Dibelius, *From Tradition to Gospel*, xv (e.g., paradigm); Bultmann, *The History of the Synoptic Tradition*, vii–viii, 11 (apophthegm); Taylor, *The Formation of the Gospel Tradition* (pronouncement story); Stanton, *Jesus of Nazareth*; for a summary see Tate, *Interpreting the Bible*, 137–38.

hope that the recipient is in good health. In another example, newspaper obituary notices generally contain the following pattern: (a) the name of the deceased, (b) a brief description of the life and career, (c) a mention of surviving relatives, (d) a mention of age, (e) the date of death, and (f) mention of proposed funeral arrangements.[21] Every culture has fixed patterns for its literary forms of communication.[22]

Second, literary forms change throughout history. For example, a personal letter written in Egypt around the second century BC has features different from those of our own time and culture:[23]

> *Greeting:* Isias to her brother Hephaestion, greeting.
>
> *Thanksgiving:* If you are well and other things are going right, it would accord with the prayer which I make continually to the gods. I myself and the child and all the household are in good health and think of you always.
>
> *Body:* When I received your letter from Horus, in which you announce that you are in detention in the Sarapeum at Memphis . . .when all the others who had been secluded there have come, I am ill-pleased . . . please return to the city, if nothing more pressing holds you back . . .

> *Closing:* Goodbye. Year 2, Epeiph 30. (Addressed) To Hephaestion.

Although the basic pattern of a greeting, body, and closing are similar to our modern letter form, its basic arrangement and formal contents are different. The above features are typical of most personal letters written in the ancient Hellenistic world.[24]

Historians of literature, by studying the external and formal features (as well as language and style) can arrive at a relatively accurate date and location for the above literary forms, even when such information is not given. Sensitivity to the changes of a literary form in the history of a culture is an important concern in form criticism.

A third characteristic of literary forms is that each form has a unique linguistic intent associated with it. For example, personal letters are intended to renew acquaintances, obituary notices serve as memorial notices for the deceased and family, dramatic plays entertain, and love poems endear one individual to another.

Although there may be exceptions to the above generalizations, every literary form has a specific intent. This linguistic intent or purpose is also fully understood by the specific audience addressed. The intent of a literary form is usually so familiar to the audience or readers that it signals certain expectations in them. We are so familiar with our literary forms that we have some idea of their contents even before reading them! For example, we

---

21. Lohfink, *The Bible, Now I Get It!* 19.

22. Klauck, *Ancient Letters and the New Testament,* 2–7. Today, much of the personal letter form is still retained in personal email and social networking communications (b-d) with "Dear Sue" replaced by, e.g., "Hi Sue!"

23. What follows is a letter from a wife to her husband from 168 BC, found at Memphis; it is adapted from Letter no. 144 in Bagnall and Derow, *Greek Historical Documents,* 235.

24. On ancient letter forms, see White, *Form and Function*; and White, *Light from Ancient Letters*; Meltzer, *Letters from Ancient Egypt*; Stirewalt, *Paul, the Letter Writer*; Klauck, *Ancient Letters and the New Testament.*

approach a love poem differently from an obituary notice, a dramatic play with different expectations from those behind a special documentary report. Each literary form has a specific intent that is fully understood by the audience addressed, and that triggers certain expectations in them.

A fourth characteristic of literary forms is that they are connected with certain social and institutional settings. The setting of a personal letter, for example, would be a private relationship between two friends (in most cases). The setting presupposed in an obituary notice is that of grief shared by friends and relatives of the deceased. The setting of a dramatic play, in our culture, would be on a stage in a public theater. The setting generally presupposed in a love poem is a private relationship between two people in love. Literary forms are either the products of certain settings or only comprehensible in certain contexts.

A fifth and final characteristic of literary forms is that the setting for certain literary forms changes over a period of years. An illustration of this will be taken from the broad category (or genre) of drama. The modern setting of a dramatic play is generally on the stage of a public theater, a secular or popular setting. Originally, drama did not have such a setting. Both tragedy and comedy originated in the religious festivals of Greek cities of the classical and Hellenistic periods. Despite their diverse themes and plots, dramatic plays were performed in honor of the Greek god Dionysus, and they generally followed a private religious ceremony of the cult in a nearby temple of the god! Consider the origins of this literary category the next time you watch your favorite television drama. The settings of literary forms change in the history of a culture. This is an important observation in the study of those traditional units of folk literature that presuppose an oral setting (e.g., poems, songs, riddles). When these oral forms are put into writing, the literary context often differs from its original oral setting.[25]

New Testament Case Studies

Our discussion on the nature and significance of literary forms is a relevant preface to the form-critical study of the NT. This method was first applied to old European folk literature before its use in biblical writings.[26]

The popular and social character of both types of literature almost required such a method. Because of the nature of literary forms (as we have seen), form criticism seeks to comprehend the

25. See Lohfink, *The Bible, Now I Get It!* 45–51, for a similar example taken from a love poem. See also Lewis, *The Allegory of Love*.

26. Two early influences on form criticism of the Bible were von Ranke, *Geschichte der romanischen und germanischen Völker* (1824) and Norden, *Agnostos Theos* (1913). The following studies pioneered the approach in biblical studies: Gunkel, *Genesis*; and Gunkel, *Ausgewählte Psalmen* (1917); Dibelius, *Die Formgeschichte des Evangeliums* (1919); Bultmann, *Die Geschichte der synoptischen Tradition* (1921); and in English, R. H. Lightfoot, *History and Interpretation in the Gospels* (1935); both V. Taylor, *The Formation of the Gospel Tradition* (1st ed., 1933), and Riesenfeld, *The Gospel Tradition and Its Beginnings* (1st ed., 1957) assume more "remembered" past than "invented" past (contra Bultmann). See also Harrington, *Interpreting the New Testament*, 70–84; McKnight, *What Is Form Criticism?* Travis, "Form Criticism," 153–64 (contra Bultmann); Buss, *Biblical Form Criticism*; Sweeney and Ben Zvi, *The Changing Face of Form Criticism*; Carey, "Traditio-Historical Criticism," in Green, *Hearing the New Testament*, 102–21.

following: (1) the character of each literary form and the fixed patterns in which it is framed, (2) the linguistic intent that the readers were accustomed to expect, and (3) the social and institutional setting that produced the literary form. These three concerns of form criticism will be applied to two traditional forms found in Mark's Gospel: the miracle story of the healing of the leper (1:40–45) and the parable of the mustard seed (4:30–32). Each is a prevalent form in the Synoptic Gospels, each reflects an oral setting and has been the focus of much form-critical research.

Like all literary forms, the account of the healing of the leper in Mark 1:40–45 follows a fixed pattern, characteristic of most miracle stories of that period:

> *Diagnosis*: a leper in need of cleansing, v. 40
>
> *Therapy*: the healing touch of Jesus, v. 41
>
> *Proof of Restoration*: the leper left—cleansed! v. 42

Reading the entire account, one will note that the story centers upon this basic three-point pattern. All details are reduced to essential descriptions. Nothing is known of the leper's name or of the specific time or place, nor is anything else mentioned of him after his restoration to health. Why? Assuming that healings took place in the ministry of Jesus, we can assume that the incident was probably reduced after years of oral circulation to a simple, fixed pattern so that the story could be remembered easily and transmitted to others. This was an acceptable way of telling miracle stories in the ancient Mediterranean world (and elsewhere). For example, many similar stories

with the same fixed forms were circulated about the healer-philosophers Pythagoras and Apollonius.[27]

The essential points to which this miracle story is reduced make plain the linguistic intent of this form. The healing-of-the-leper story seeks to glorify Jesus as the instrument of God's power. It might also have sought to encourage its hearers by impressing them with Jesus's special ability to relieve a human affliction.

The sociological setting that produced the present framework of the miracle story is more difficult to ascertain. There are three (or more) stages in the history of the transmission of this gospel tradition (e.g., Jesus-church-gospel), and we will concentrate on the stages preceding the Gospel of Mark.[28] According to most form critics, many of the miracle stories of Jesus were widely circulated among urban Gentile communities attracted to Jesus as a divine miracle worker superior to other healer-philosophers. However, the concluding proof of restoration in the story

27. Iamblichus, *Life of Pythagoras* 36, 60–61, 134–36; Philostratus, *The Life of Apollonius* 2.4; 3.38; 4.20, 45; see also the healing accounts at the temple of Asclepius in the Epidaurus inscriptions (fourth century BC). All the above healing accounts are found in Cartlidge and Dungan, *Documents*, 151–55, 220, 225–26, 229–31. For studies on NT miracles, see Fuller, *Interpreting the Miracles*; Kee, *Miracle in the Early Christian World*; Keller and Keller, *Miracles in Dispute*; Theissen, *The Miracles*; Wenham and Blomberg, *Gospel Perspectives*; Hooker, *The Signs of a Prophet*; Twelftree, *Jesus the Miracle Worker*; Eve, *The Jewish Context of Jesus' Miracles*.

28. If we were to trace the history of the tradition from its inception to its final shape in the Gospel, it would be more appropriate to posit four or more stages, for example: (1) the ministry of Jesus; (2) the earliest followers after Jesus; (3) early Christianity adjusting to its environment; and (4) the writing of the Gospels. See our chart in this section on the growth of the Gospels.

indicates that it probably originated in a Jewish-Christian community of Palestine: "Go present yourself to the priest and offer for your cure what Moses prescribed" (Mark 1:44). Although the literary framework of the story is characteristic of many miracle stories in the ancient Mediterranean world, the vocabulary and religious contents reflect the beliefs and perceptions of Jewish Christians of Palestine. This proposed setting also lends some credibility to the view that the story points back to an incident that took place in the ministry of Jesus.[29]

The saying in Mark 4:30–32 is called a parable. Beginning in the nineteenth century, NT scholars attempted to distinguish the "simplicity" of Jesus's parables from the "complexity" of traditional allegory. According to this view, allegory encodes an elaborate set of symbolic comparisons into the numerous details of a story, whereas a parable focuses attention on *only one* central message illustrated by a familiar life-situation.[30] However, recent studies regard this view as reductionistic. The insistence on one point per parable appears to be a modernistic reaction to a less-disciplined, ahistorical reading

popularized by medieval allegory where even minor details carried great spiritual significance. Many contemporary scholars now urge a more flexible understanding of parable as an evocative metaphor, sufficiently imprecise that it will draw the hearers' or readers' minds and imaginations to actively wrestle with its elusive message.[31] Still others argue for striking a balance between the allegorical and the parabolic by allowing Jesus's parables to make at least as many points as there are, e.g., main characters in the story.[32]

Despite the above debate, Mark's parable of the mustard seed is simple enough to contain the following fixed pattern: (a) a starting point, usually with the opening phrase ("The kingdom of God is like"), (b) the illustration from life (e.g., a mustard seed), and (c) a central point (e.g., miraculous growth). The one central point aspect of this fixed pattern becomes problematic in the longer parables of Jesus that have more than one main character or theme (e.g., Luke 10:25–37; 16:19–31).

Many form critics believe that Jesus taught about the kingdom of God using concise and simple parables like that of the mustard seed (Mark 4:30–32). If this parable stems from the ministry of Jesus (as most scholars believe), it was probably

29. On the gospel tradition originating with Jesus himself: Riesenfeld, *Gospel Tradition;* Hooker, *Signs of a Prophet;* Twelftree, *Jesus the Miracle Worker.* For a cultural understanding of Mark 1:35–45 (e.g., skin disease, healing, holy men), see Malina and Rohrbaugh, *Social Science Commentary,* 151, 368; Pilch, *Healing in the New Testament.*

30. See the important work of A. Jülicher, *Die Gleichnisreden Jesu.* For studies on parables, see Dodd, *Parables of the Kingdom;* Jeremias, *Die Gleichnisse Jesu;* Tolbert, *Perspectives on the Parables;* D. B. Gowler, *What Are They Saying about the Parables?* Longenecker, *Challenge of Jesus' Parables;* Hedrick, *Many Things in Parables;* Schottroff, *Envisioning the Reign of God through Parables;* Snodgrass, *Stories with Intent.*

31. Funk, *Language, Hermeneutic, and Word of God;* McFague, *Speaking in Parables;* Perrin, *Jesus and the Language of the Kingdom;* Donahue, *Gospel in Parable;* Hedrick, *Parables as Poetic Fictions.*

32. See Funk, *Parables and Presence;* Borsch, *Many Things in Parables;* Blomberg, *Interpreting the Parables.* For example, the parables of the Hidden Treasure and the Pearl of Great Price (Matt 13:44–46) each make one point since there is only one "character" in the story. Parables such as the Pharisee and the Tax Collector (Luke 18:9–14) make two points, and the parable of the Prodigal Son (Luke 15:11–32) makes three points, one for each character (father, prodigal, and elder son).

intended as a defense of Jesus's ministry against Jewish critics. Many Jews of Jesus's day did not see the end-time glories of God's kingdom that they anticipated in Jesus's ministry. Telling a parable like the mustard seed would be an appropriate response of Jesus to that situation.

The following interpretation is a possible rendering of the original intent of Jesus's parable of the mustard seed: Although it is small and insignificant when it is planted, the mustard seed miraculously grows into a large bushy shrub providing shelter for the birds. So it is also with the kingdom of God in Jesus's ministry. Even though it appears small and insignificant, when God's reign is truly recognized in the ministry of Jesus, it will become something great, providing shelter for people. This emphasis on the small beginnings of God's kingdom with the promise that it would develop into something great would be an appropriate response of Jesus to the charges of his critics.

Form Criticism: Conclusions

Although much form-critical research has been done in the Synoptic Gospels, attention has also been directed to other areas, for examples: early Christian hymns (e.g., Phil 2:6–11; Col 1:15–20; 1 Tim 3:16; 1 Pet 3:18–22) and household rules (e.g., Eph 5:21—6.9; Col 3:18—4:1; Titus 2:1–10). Most of the hymns emphasize the divine mission of Christ and presuppose original oral settings in the life and worship of early communities. The household rules are drawn from the traditional ethics of the Hellenistic world. Other traditional forms analyzed in the NT epistles are creeds, confessions, baptismal formulas,

catechetical teachings, diatribes (or philosophical dialogues), and parenesis (i.e., moral exhortations).[33]

The special concerns of form criticism are significant for the study of early Christianity. First, it seeks to get behind the sources discovered by source criticism to learn something about the earliest communities and Jesus. Second, it takes seriously the fixed literary forms of the NT and seeks to understand their practical function within the communities that produced them. Third, it takes seriously the preliterary period of oral transmission as a time of growth and adaptation for the literary forms within the communities who used them. Finally, form criticism regards many of these literary forms with their long preliterary history as "windows" from which the existence of early Christian communities can be viewed and studied.

Redaction Criticism

Redaction is the process of putting information into a suitable literary form: the act of revising or editing. Using an example from our day, redaction is the work of a newspaper reporter who selectively organizes information from an interview and brings it together into a final written report. It is also the task of anyone today

33. For surveys of the various early Christian forms, see Doty, *Letters in Primitive Christianity*, 55–63; Lampe, "Evidence in the New Testament for Early Creeds," 359–63; Roetzel, *Letters of Paul*, 41–49. For specific form-critical studies, see Balch, *Let Wives Be Submissive*; Martin, *Carmen Christi*; Neufeld, *Earliest Christian Confessions*; Sanders, *New Testament Christological Hymns*; Stowers, *Diatribe*; Bailey and Vander Broek, *Literary Forms*; Aune, *WDNTECLR*. See also n. 24.

who revises a written proposal from a committee meeting by correcting it or adding important information that was overlooked. Redaction is concerned with the selection, omission, addition, correction, or abridgement of information to produce a final written document.

Basic Concerns

In the NT, redaction criticism is concerned with the activity of the final writer of a book: (1) how the writer employed (revised, edited) sources, (2) his or her particular emphases and distinctive viewpoint, and (3) the author's own life-setting

Mark 1:1–4	Luke 3:1–6
[1] The beginning of the gospel of Jesus Christ, the Son of God.	[1] In the fifteenth year of the reign of Tiberius Caesar, Pontius Pilate being governor of Judea, and Herod being tetrarch of Galilee, and his brother Philip tetrarch of the region of Ituraea and Trachonitis and Lysanias tetrarch of Abilene, [2] in the high-priesthood of Annas and Caiaphas, the word of God came to John the son of Zechariah in the wilderness; [3] and he went into all the region about the Jordan, preaching a baptism of repentance for the forgiveness of sins. [4] As it is written in the book of the words of Isaiah the prophet,

[2] As it is written in Isaiah the prophet,
 	
"Behold, I send my messenger before thy face, who shall prepare thy way;
[3] the voice of one crying in the wilderness:
 	
Prepare the way of the Lord, make his paths straight – "
	The voice of one crying in the wilderness.
	    Prepare the way of the
	Lord, make his paths straight.
	     [5] Every valley shall be filled,
	    and every mountain and hill
	      shall be brought low,
	    and the crooked shall be
	      made straight,
	   and the rough ways shall
	    be made smooth;
	[6] and all flesh shall see
	   the salvation of God."

[4] John the baptizer appeared in the wilderness, preaching a baptism of repentance for the forgiveness of sins.	

and the needs of the specific audience being addressed.[34]

Redaction criticism both draws upon the literary and historical concerns of source and form criticism and also goes beyond them by focusing on a different aspect of the text. It presupposes source criticism by investigating the author's use of sources but goes beyond this method by concentrating on the work of the *final author*. It serves as a complement to form criticism because it concerns the final stage of the history of tradition. However, it distinguishes itself from form criticism on at least three points: (a) redaction criticism focuses on the final text, not the pre-literary history of tradition; (b) it works toward a synthesis of the smaller literary units that form criticism seeks to analyze; and (c) it only deals with the final author's life-setting, and not with the various oral and written settings of the traditions.

A Case Study from Luke

Let us again look at our comparison of the Synoptic Gospels, concentrating on Luke 3:1–6 and its use of Mark. We see from the comparison chart that our analysis will presuppose from form criticism that Mark is a source for Luke. Even though redaction criticism can be undertaken

34. For redaction-critical studies, see Conzelmann, *The Theology of St. Luke*, transl. of *Die Mitte Der Zeit*, 1954; Bornkamm, et al., *Tradition and Interpretation in Matthew* (Ger. ed., 1948); Harrington, *Interpreting the New Testament*, 96–107 (survey); Marxsen, *Mark the Evangelist* (Ger. ed., 1956); Perrin, *What Is Redaction Criticism?*; Rohde, *Rediscovering the Teaching*; Stein, "What Is Redaktions-geschichte?" 45–56; Stein, *Gospels and Tradition*. For socio-rhetorical analysis of narrative that challenges certain theories of life-setting and community crises, see Robbins, "The Social Location," 305–32.

with documents whose sources are not clearly delineated (e.g., Mark's gospel and the Acts of the Apostles), the evidence of defined sources makes the analysis less complicated. Mark is a complete work in itself, but in the history of the synoptic tradition it, along with Q, functions as a precursor to the completed stages of the Synoptic tradition in which the Gospels of Matthew and Luke are classified.

As we concentrate on Luke's use of Mark, we would like to point out five redactional techniques employed by Luke: addition, omission, expansion, rearrangement, and inclusion. Some overlap may occur.

Let us look at *addition*. It is clear from the chapter headings that Luke does not begin his gospel at the same place that Mark does. Luke adds to his source two chapters of material not found elsewhere: a prologue with birth and infancy narratives (Luke 1:1—2:52) and a historical preface (Luke 3:1–2a). Luke's prologue (1:1–4) introduces not only his gospel but also his second volume, Acts of the Apostles (cf. Acts 1:1). The birth narratives also include accounts of John the Baptist (Luke 1:5–25, 57–80), who is also the subject of our comparison chart (Luke 3:1–6; Mark 1:1–4). This background of John is not found in Mark. Luke's additions (1:1—3:2a) provide much that is lacking in his Markan source and give Luke's Gospel ancient biographical or historical characteristics. The historical notations, found in 2:1–3 and 3:1–2, may signify Luke's special concern to place the stories of John and Jesus in the context of Roman secular history, since these notations are found elsewhere (e.g., Acts 11:28; 18:2, 12).

The second technique concerns a Lukan *omission*. Looking at our comparison chart, we note that Luke omits the Malachi passage found in his source (Mark 1:2/Mal 3:1). Luke's omission was probably influenced by Q since the Malachi passage appears elsewhere in a tradition common to both Luke and Matthew (Luke 7:27 and Matt 11:10 = Q).

Lukan *expansion* of his source is the third redactional technique. In Luke 3:5–6, the author expands his source by quoting more extensively the Isaiah 40 passage found in his Markan source. Luke continues to follow a Greek text similar to Mark. In his expanded citation of Isa 40:3–5, Luke omits a word ("all") and a phrase ("the glory of the Lord") and appears to underscore the statement, "all flesh shall see the salvation of God." This statement in the Greek resembles both Luke 2:30 (God's salvation anticipated) and Acts 28:28 (God's salvation extended to all people). This theme of worldwide salvation (for Jews and Gentiles) is an important concern for the author of Luke-Acts (e.g., Luke 2:32; 24:27; Acts 13:47; 26:23). On the basis of historical clues and such Lukan emphases as worldwide salvation, tension with Judaism, and appeals for Roman tolerance, one can draw some tentative conclusions about the situation of Luke and his readers. They appear to be part of a growing Gentile-Christian community that is experiencing a loss of identity or purpose as a result of Jewish and pagan antagonism (ca. AD 80–90).

The fourth device used by Luke in this passage is the *rearrangement* of his source. Luke makes it clear to his readers "about whom this prophet speaks" by relocating his source about John's preaching (Mark 1:4) before the Isaiah passage is cited (Luke 3:3). Luke also prefaces this Markan preaching summary with an introduction that appears to identify John as a prophet: "the word of God came to John" (3:2). John is identified as a prophet elsewhere (e.g., Luke 7:26–27; 20:4–6). By rearranging his source Luke provides a "topical sentence" to introduce and preview the discussion on John that follows.

Luke uses a fifth redaction technique in this passage: *inclusion*. Luke not only begins his discussion of John with a description of John's preaching (3:3) but concludes with it as well (v. 18). Substantial blocks of material on John's preaching are also included from Q, Luke's second source (Luke 3:7–9/Matt 3:7–10), and from Luke's own special material (Luke 3:10–14). All this extra material probably serves as Luke's interpretation of the Markan source. According to Luke, John is the prophet who preaches "repentance for the forgiveness of sins" in anticipation of God's worldwide salvation. John is both subordinate to Jesus the Messiah (3:15–16) and united with Jesus in his preaching and prophetic role (cf. 3:2b–20 with 4:16–30).

It has been evident from our study that much of the information on Luke's redactional activity was collected by approaching the text from two perspectives. First, by looking in the text for redactional changes, and then by looking *through* the text into the entire literary work to verify whether the themes of the text are typical emphases and concerns of the author. From this last perspective we sought to reconstruct the author's life-setting.

Redaction Criticism: Conclusions

As we have mentioned, redaction criticism can be applied to other books of the

NT. It is can be applied to books with no clearly delineated sources, such as Mark's gospel and the Acts of the Apostles. Here (without the close comparison of a specific written source) concentration must be placed on the unique vocabulary, style, structure, and key themes of each author. Redaction-critical study of the NT letters and homilies has also been done, especially where the use of traditional material can be detected (e.g., in hymns, confessions, creeds, and household rules).[35]

The method of redaction criticism concentrates on the time of the final authors, their setting and audience, their special concerns and intentions. It is not concerned with the preliterary, oral traditions but with the literary text in its *final form*. This focus of redaction criticism has also prepared the way, some argue, for more recent methods of literary criticism that are concerned with language, diction, structure, genre, style, imagery, and poetic analysis.

MORE RECENT METHODS OF STUDY

Since the 1960s, other approaches to the NT have been employed, especially from the fields of the humanities and social sciences. Whereas historical criticism originated in France and Germany, most of these current approaches are North American in origin. First, *sociological criticism* and *social-scientific criticism* utilize sociological and cultural anthropological methodology to understand the social context, social relationships (e.g., kinship, patronage), cultural values (e.g., honor, purity), and the symbolic universe (e.g., in-groups, zones of interaction).[36] Second, *social-rhetorical criticism* approaches a text in the ways that an anthropologist might "read" a village and its culture, examining its literary-rhetorical aspects, intertextuality, social and cultural dynamics, plus ideology.[37] Third, *narrative criticism* seeks to understand how the NT stories function. What are the roles of character, story setting, and plot? Who is the author as implied or derived from the narrative? Who is the ideal or implied reader? It focuses on the world of the text (e.g., plot, characters) with little concern for the "real history" outside the text, e.g., the historical situation.[38] Fourth, *postmodern criticism* examines contextualization, deconstruction, semiotics,

35. Redaction-critical research of the NT epistles is evident, for example, in the following commentaries of the Hermeneia series (Philadelphia: Fortress, 1971–): Conzelmann, *1 Corinthians*; Betz, *Galatians*; Lohse, *Colossians and Philemon*; Dibelius and Conzelmann, *Pastoral Epistles*; Dibelius and Greeven, *James*. A related approach, composition criticism, focuses on the final composition of the work, its distinct vocabulary, style, and theology, particularly where the specific use of sources is not clearly discernable, Haenchen, *Acts*, 90–110; O'Toole, *Unity of Luke's Theology*, 11–14. On its trajectory toward narrative criticism, see Donahue, "Redaction Criticism."

36. The pioneering studies of Weber (1919), Troeltsch (1911), Douglas, *Purity and Danger* (1966), and the NT research of E. A. Judge (1960–1992) in Scholer, *Social Distinctives*; Theissen, *Sociology of Early Palestinian Christianity*; Malina, *New Testament World*; Esler, *The First Christians*; Elliott, *What Is Social-Scientific Criticism?*

37. See Robbins, *Jesus the Teacher*; and Robbins, *Exploring the Texture of Texts*: these volumes are conversant with New Rhetoric; for surveys à la G. A. Kennedy, see Witherington, *New Testament Rhetoric*; and Tate, *Interpreting the Bible*, 342–46; helpful discussion of both are in Black, "Rhetorical Criticism," in Green, *Hearing the New Testament*, 2nd ed., 166–88.

38. Chatman, *Story and Discourse*; Genette, *Narrative Discourse*; Alter, *Art of Biblical Narrative*; Powell, *What Is Narrative Criticism?*; Fowler, *Let the Reader Understand*; Kurz, *Reading Luke-Acts*.

and political ideologies.[39] Fifth, *feminist criticism* focuses on the feminine characters portrayed or not portrayed in the narrative: Why are they depicted in this manner? Why are they omitted? Is there a certain bias here against women that limits their abilities or functions in society? What elements of a narrative can be resources for women's liberation? Can a more inclusive approach be found to guide our understanding of a narrative's overall patriarchy?[40] Sixth, *cross-cultural*

criticism tries to understand the social locations of the text (e.g., Hellenistic Jewish), the social locations of today's readers (e.g., North America), and how location influences the reading of the text today (by raising cultural biases or chauvinism, for example).[41]

All of the above critical methods approach the biblical texts with insightful questions. We see value in all approaches and judge their effectiveness by what they contribute to exegesis. At times they help to broaden, challenge, and even correct our perceptions and perspectives as we continue to employ the historical methods of literary criticism in a postmodern era.

---

39. Derrida, *Derrida Reader*; Foucault, *Language, Counter-Memory, and Practice* on, e.g., semiotics, poststructuralism, see Barthes, *Pleasure of the Text*; Sontag, *Barthes Reader*; in NT, see Moore, *Literary Criticism and the Gospels*; and Moore, *Poststructuralism and the New Testament*; Moore's work is often entertaining and deliberately obscure, using examples from the NT to illustrate how a postmodern reading deconstructs conventional biblical exegesis, see also Adam, *What Is Postmodern Biblical Criticism?*; and Adam, *Postmodern Interpretations of the Bible*.

40. Stanton, *Woman's Bible*; Russell, ed., *Feminist Interpretation of the Bible*; Tolbert, ed., *Bible and Feminist Hermeneutics*; Levine, ed., *Feminist Companion to Matthew*; and Levine and

Blickenstaff, eds., *Feminist Companion to the Acts*, citing two in the series; see also F. S. Spencer, "Feminist Criticism," in Green, *Hearing the New Testament*, 289–325.

41. Felder, ed., *Stony the Road*; Blount, *Cultural Interpretation*; Segovia and Tolbert, eds., *Reading from This Place*; De La Torre, *Reading the Bible from the Margins*; Yeo, *What Has Jerusalem to Do with Beijing?*

6

The Genres of the Gospels and Acts

A FEW WORDS ABOUT
LITERARY GENRE

> He once entertained the envoys
> from the Persian king who
> came during Philip's absence
> . . . He won upon them by his
> friendliness, and by asking no
> childish or trivial questions
> . . . [T]he envoys were there-
> fore astonished and regarded
> the much-talked-of ability of
> Philip as nothing compared to
> his son's eager disposition to do
> great things.[1]

This excerpt from Plutarch's *Life of Alexander* is a species of story similar to
the story of twelve-year-old Jesus in the
Temple (Luke 2:41–51). The heroes of
both stories were boys, precocious in that
they both spoke with relevance beyond
their years to the surprise of seasoned
specialists, in military strategy for Alexander and in theology for Jesus. The story

in Alexander comes between a narrative
of his birth and the exploits of his matu-
rity; likewise for Jesus. Such texts reveal
an example of text that illumines in a flash
why genre recognition is important. One
might call this a *child-prodigy story*. Its
form, content, and function seem clear.
It prepares the reader for an amazing life.
But as obvious as some examples are of
identifiable genre, it is naive to suppose
that the discussion in this chapter is a self-
evident one.

The question of the genre of the four
Gospels and Acts is, on the contrary, a difficult one. Some scholars have dismissed
all known generic categories for these
writings (the Gospels) and regarded them
instead as the distinct products (*sui generis*, Latin for "of their own kind") of early
Christian communities.[2] Others dismiss

---

1. Plutarch, *Life of Alexander* 5.1 (in Perrin,
Plutarch's Lives 7:235).

2. Guelich, "Gospel Genre." See also discussion
in Collins, *Mark*, 19–22; and Burridge, *What Are
the Gospels?* 7–15, who explain how form critics,
like Dibelius and Bultmann, concluded that the
Gospels were distinguished as nonliterary products of primitive Christian communities, and that

discussion of genre for other hermeneutical reasons.[3] In order to advance discussion we will first examine Luke and Acts, next Matthew and Mark, then treat the Gospel of John in a separate section.

Genre is commonly understood as the broad category of artistic, musical, or literary composition characterized by a particular style, form, purpose, or content. In modern literature, for example, there are the genres of fiction, nonfiction, drama, and poetry. These categories are often self-evident to the modern reader because he or she is accustomed to their style, form, content, and purpose. The classification of ancient writings (e.g., epic, tragedy, history) is more difficult because the modern reader is not as familiar with them. Nevertheless, the discipline of genre criticism is important for interpreting and understanding.[4] It greatly assists

our understanding of an ancient classic when we know what to expect from it and can discover what the work sought to accomplish.

One of the reasons why there is so much disagreement about the nature of the Gospels is because there is general confusion about the type of literature that one is reading. For example, certain laypeople read the prophecies of Mark 13 like weather predictions in today's newspaper. They also tend to read the ministry of Jesus in the Gospels like the daily itinerary of the pope. The general reader certainly does not treat modern literature in the same naive manner as the Gospels. For instance, most people correctly read *Titan: The Life of John D. Rockefeller, Sr.*, by Ron Chernow as biography, and Cormac McCarthy's *The Road* as fiction. Despite current fascination with historical novels, such as *The Rebels of Ireland* by Edward Rutherfurd, modern readers are cautious not to read too much fact into fiction. Why, therefore, is there so much confusion about interpreting the Gospels?

Reading the Gospels as ancient literature raises another problem. The Gospels are not only classic writings but are also part of a canon of religious literature. This fact tends to encumber the Gospels with various kinds of traditional interpretations. This point might explain some of the confusion about interpreting the Gospels. But whatever our attitude toward these sacred books, our common

---

many redaction critics, like Perrin and Vielhauer, favored this view despite the creative role that they assigned to the Gospel writers. For different reasons, both the Italian literary critic, Croce, *Aesthetics* and the avant-garde Paris journal *Tel Quel* (1962–1966) advocated critical theories that transcended all generic boundaries.

3. Since genre implies a sort of social contract of known, shared meaning between writer and reader and hence implies necessarily a perception of authorial intent, how we treat the identification/interpretation of genre may be problematic to some postmodern/deconstructionist readers. Jacques Derrida thinks that the impure nature of genres renders classification of them an uncertain and a less than useful enterprise ("The Law of Genre"). It is beyond the scope of this text to explore this subject, and clearly the authors are taking a position that genre is recognizable and valuable. For more discussion, see Eddy and Boyd, *Jesus Legend*, 16–21, 318–20; Thiselton, *Thiselton on Hermeneutics*.

4. See the ancient categories of epic poetry, tragic drama, dithyramb (1.1–3.6), and history (9.2; 23.2–3), in Aristotle's *Poetics*. "The critical theory of genres is stuck precisely where Aristotle left it" (Frye, *Anatomy*, 13, also 246–50). "Understanding

is genre-bound" (Hirsch, *Validity in Interpretation*, 78, also 80–81, 86, 98). See Todorov, *Structural Approach to Literary Genre*; Gerhart, "Generic Studies," 309–25, and "Generic Competence" in *Genre, Narrativity, and Theology*, 29–44; Strelka, *Theories of Literary Genre*; "genre establishes a relationship between author and reader . . . a generic contract" (Dubrow, *Genre*, 31).

goal is accurate interpretation (i.e., exegesis). The achievement of this objective requires some adherence to the basic methodologies discussed in chapter 5. Genre criticism also assists in this goal by complementing, correcting, or clarifying internal analysis through external classification.

In our discussion of genre, we will be looking at the Gospels of Mark and Matthew as well as Luke-Acts. From our study of source and redaction criticism, we have seen that Mark was probably the earliest Gospel, and that Luke-Acts was a two-volume work written by one author. Furthermore, Matthew, Mark, and Luke are called the Synoptic Gospels because they share a similar vision of the life of Christ.

Under what categories do we classify Matthew, Mark, and Luke-Acts? To illustrate the practical importance of this question, let us imagine ourselves in different roles at a different place and time. We are a group of librarians at the great library of Alexandria in the early third century AD. We have just received copies of Mark, Matthew, and Luke-Acts for the library. The head librarian orders us to categorize and shelve them with appropriate identifying tags.[5] We must go through

these documents and classify them according to the existing generic categories[6] and not according to some religious predisposition (i.e., canon). Under what genres do we classify these books? Three prevalent categories of the Hellenistic world might be suggested: history, biography, and tragic drama.[7]

---

5. Ptolemy II (285–247 BC) wants Demetrius of Phaelerum, his librarian, to collect all the books in the world for the library of Alexandria, Demetrius reports an inventory of twenty thousand volumes of scrolls, including, e.g., "works by poets and prose-writers, rhetoricians and sophists, doctors and soothsayers, historians and all others too" (Canfora, *Vanished Library*, 20). Demetrius also wants to include a copy of the Jewish law in a Greek translation, *Letter of Aristeas* (170 BC?) 1–11, 29–31; Charlesworth, *OTP* 2:7–16ff.; Canfora, *Vanished Library* 20–25, 45–50, 101, 147–60. In 250 BC, Ptolemy III had given Callimachus of Cyrene the great task of cataloging the ever-increasing mountain of books: they were classified as written by (1) dramatists, (2) epic and lyric poets,

(3) legislators, (4) philosophers, (5) historians, (6) orators, (7) rhetoricians, and (8) miscellaneous (Pollard and Reid, *Rise and Fall of Alexandria*, 146; Casson, *Libraries in the Ancient World*, 31–47). According to Casson, the library was in operation from the 4th cent. BC to AD 270 (under emperor Aurelian), see 31–47.

6. The Christian category of "gospel" is not helpful in this context. The word "gospel" (*euangelion*), for Hellenistic non-Christians, probably had the meaning of a joyful announcement connected with the eventful appearance or activity of a great ruler, BDAG, 402–3; LSJ, 704–5. The titles Gospel of Matthew, Gospel of Mark, Gospel of Luke, and Gospel of John were applied to the first four books of our NT by Christians of the mid-second and third centuries (e.g., Justin, *1 Apol.* 66.3) as convenient identifying labels; they do not represent a precise category of genre nor are they infallible indicators of authorship. Each of the Gospels and Acts should also be examined separately, since the source dependence of the Synoptic Gospels does not automatically mean genre dependence, see Shuler, *A Genre for the Gospels*, 30–31; Collins, *Mark*, 19–22. On the unity of Luke-Acts, see Puskas, *The Conclusion of Luke-Acts*, 2n3, 86n59.

7. Let us clarify our study with some preliminary remarks: (1) Other so-called genres could also be considered (e.g., historical romance, monograph), but most of them are modes of the three host ones that we have selected. To illustrate the dominance in antiquity of the genres of history, biography (or *bios*, "life"), and tragic drama or poetry, see, e.g., the mosaic (ca. AD 100) found at Hadrumetum in Africa (now in the Bardo museum) where Virgil is flanked by the muses of both history (Clio) and tragedy (Melpomene) as he composes the *Aeneid*. (See also "history" distinguished from "tragedy" in Polybius, *Hist.* 2.56.10–12.) Virgil describes his own work as an account of the deeds and hardships of Aeneas as he travels from Troy to found Rome (*Aeneid* 1.1–7; i.e., an epic *bios* of Aeneas, perhaps inspired by the muse Calliope).

THE HISTORICAL GENRE: A COMPARISON WITH LUKE-ACTS

Why would any of the Gospels or Acts be compared to ancient history? They are not secular or comprehensive in scope like the Greek and Roman histories. Even when compared to the more religious Israelite-Jewish histories, they are still not as broad and inclusive. In contrast to most ancient histories, the Gospels and Acts do not focus on politics and war or generals and kings. In comparison with the great Greek

histories of Herodotus, Thucydides, and Polybius, their style and composition is less cultivated. Finally, when Eusebius of Caesarea wrote his *Ecclesiastical History* in the early fourth century AD, he considered it to be the first of its kind (1.1).

Despite the above contrasts, Luke-Acts lends itself to some comparison with ancient history. At least seven points of analogy exist: (1) prefaces stating the author's method and purpose, (2) chronological notations, (3) attention to factual details, (4) political bias, (5) assumptions about fate or providence, (6) speeches that express the author's understanding of the events, and (7) selective arrangement of events in a line of progression related to the present.[8] Before discussing the points of comparison we will first identify some ancient histories, then mention the similarities and differences of Greco-Roman and Israelite-Jewish histories.

Jewish and Greco-Roman Histories

Examples of Israelite histories are the Deuteronomistic History (i.e., the final edition of Deuteronomy through 2 Kings, or 1 Kings to 4 Kings in the Greek

---

Furthermore, see distinctions made between history and laudatory biography (or encomium) in Lucian, *How to Write History*; Plutarch (*Alex.* 1.2), who states, "it is not Histories (*historias*) that I am writing but Lives (*bious*)"; and also Nepos, *Pel.* 1.1 (first century BC). (2) Our purpose here is not to develop specific criteria of "genre" and apply them consistently to each Gospel as in Talbert, *What Is a Gospel?* 2–5; and Burridge, *What Are the Gospels?* 105–23. These approaches seem overconfident with the clarity of the criteria, plus they assume too much uniformity of style, structure, and intent in all four Gospels. In this chapter we seek to introduce readers to a sampling of diverse (but prevalent) genre categories that a reading of the Gospels might have elicited from the ancient reader. Consistent with our purpose, we consulted the authors of antiquity (e.g., Aristotle, Lucian) and certain literary critics (e.g., Hirsch, Frye) for definitions of the genres and tentative criteria to understand their forms and functions. (3) Our study presupposes that the first four books of our NT are not necessarily of the same literary genre merely because they contain common traditions and were labeled "gospels" by later Christians. It also recognizes the difficulty of categorizing the Gospels according to one genre because each book seems to incorporate several (sometimes large) literary types or modes. See Perkins, *Introduction to the Synoptic Gospels*, 1–16, 23–26, where she surveys comparisons of the Gospels with ancient *bios*, apostolic memoirs (Justin Martyr), Mark as apocalyptic historical monograph, ancient novels, Homeric epic tales and other ancient epics, as well as ancient historiography. Blomberg adds midrash, aretalogy (*theios anēr*), and theological biography (favoring the last) *Historical Reliability*, 298–303. Keener has a similar list, *Historical Jesus*, ch. 5.

8. The above points are derived from comparisons of Luke-Acts with several ancient histories (e.g., Thucydides, Josephus, Herodotus, Polybius) and the following sources: Lucian, *How to Write History* §§7, 23–27, 40, 51–53, 58–60; Polybius, *Histories*, 10.21.8; "Historiography," in *OCD*, 714–17. Attridge, *Interpretation of Biblical History*; Cadbury, "Greek and Jewish Traditions of Writing History," in *BC* 2:7–29; Dibelius, *Studies in the Acts*, 125, 133–38; Gomme, *Commentary on Thucydides*, 1:1–2, 25–30; Grant, *Ancient Historians*; Momigliano, *Essays in Ancient and Modern Historiography*; Van Seters, *In Search of History*; Sterling, *Historiography and Self-Definition*, ch. 7; most Greek and Latin histories cited in this section are from the Loeb Classical Library series.

LXX) and the Chronicler's history (1 and 2 Chronicles or 1 and 2 Supplements in LXX, plus Ezra and Nehemiah). Examples of Hellenistic Jewish histories are 1 and 2 Maccabees, Artapanus, *Concerning the Jews*, Demetrius, and Josephus's *Antiquities* and *Jewish War*. Examples of Greek and Hellenistic histories are Herodotus, *Histories*, Thucydides's *History of the Peloponnesian War*, Diodorus of Siculus's *Bibliothēkē*, Dionysius of Halicarnassus's *Roman Antiquities* and Polybius's *Histories*. Examples of Roman histories are the works of Livy (*Ab urbe condita*), Sallust (historical monographs), and Tacitus (*Annals* and *Histories*).

Although the Israelite-Jewish histories are not as secular and anthropocentric as certain Greco-Roman histories (e.g., Thucydides, Xenophon), they have similarities. Both types deal with the similar topics of politics and wars of nations, as well as with the words and activities of rulers and generals. It was probably for this reason that Eusebius in the fourth century labeled his history of Christianity *Ecclesiastical History*, although he is selective in his mention of political events and the activities of rulers. Both Jewish and Greco-Roman histories attempt to be comprehensive in their recording of events and people in a linear progression of time (i.e., the origin and development of a people).[9] It also must be pointed out

that the pervasive influence of Hellenism made Jewish and Greco-Roman histories increasingly similar (e.g., works of Josephus and Tacitus).

Fate, providence, moralism, and value judgments can be found in both Israelite-Jewish and Greco-Roman histories with differences only in emphasis and interpretation. For example, the works of Herodotus (*Hist.* 1.53–56); Polybius (*Hist.* 1.4.1–2); Diodorus Siculus (*Bibliothēkē* 1.1.3); and Tacitus (*Hist.* 1.86) include instances where fate seems to rule in the affairs of people; in Israelite-Jewish histories, however, fate is explicitly ascribed to the providence of God and occurs more frequently in their accounts.[10] Value judgments and moralism appear more often in Israelite-Jewish histories (1 Kgs 11:4–6), perhaps because they are more religious in nature than most Greco-Roman histories (but see the judgment of Herodotus regarding a story in his *History.* 1.60.3).

The basic differences between Israelite-Jewish and Greco-Roman histories

---

9. It has been held that the basic difference between Israelite-Jewish and Greco-Roman histories consisted in their respective concepts of time. See Boman, *Hebrew Thought Compared with Greek*. But recent research has raised doubts about these distinctions. See Momigliano, *Essays in Ancient and Modern Historiography*, 184–89; Gabba, "True History," 50–62. For further critiques of the old view, see Barr, *Biblical Words for Time*; Hengel, *Judaism and Hellenism*; Brown, *Ancient Israel and Ancient Greece*, 1–48; Malina, "Christ and Time,"

1–31. Malina contrasts the modern Western future linear orientation with the Mediterranean present temporal orientation, where the past is viewed from its impact on the present (24–28). The past-orientation of Roman elites was often a result of ancestrism and the belief that history teaches us about the present life (Cicero, *De Orat.* 2.9), but long-range plans for the future were not part of the Roman agenda (Malina, "Christ and Time," 6 n. 16); see also Van Seters on ancient history writing in Israel (*In Search of History*, 4–5); and Greco-Roman "Time-reckoning," *OCD*, 1527–28.

10. For discussion of fate, prophetic oracles, and providence with primary sources, see "Divination," 487–88; "Dreams," 496–97; "Fate," 589–90; and "Oracles," 1071–72 in *OCD*; Aune, *Prophecy in Early Christianity*, chs. 2–5, 7, and 10; Talbert, "Prophecy and Fulfillment," 91–103; Talbert, *Reading Luke* 263–76; Sterling, *Historiography and Self-Definition*, 295–96, 358–59; Kurz, "Hellenistic Jewish Narratives," 147–70; V. Robbins, *Invention*, 253–60.

would be in the areas of religious or philosophical bias, reliability of evidence, and motives for writing history. Concerning bias, Israelite-Jewish histories give prominence to the role of the prophet who interprets the religious significance of the events. In certain Greco-Roman histories we find, e.g., oracles of Delphi (often cryptic) impacting the events.[11] When it came to attending to the reliability of evidence, Greco-Roman histories generally placed a higher priority on it as a criterion for writing history (e.g., Thucydides, Xenophon). Most Israelite-Jewish histories incorporated religious traditions without questioning their reliability (e.g., strange miracles: see 2 Kgs 2:24; 6:6). Some differences also included the motives for writing history. For Greeks it was to cherish the examples of the ancestors and to rescue what was in danger of being unknown (Herodotus, *Hist.* 1.1). For Israelite history, it was more a religious duty to remember the past (Exod 32:13; Deut 7:18). These motives for writing Israelite/Jewish history, however, are not profoundly different from those of the pagan Greeks and Romans.

It is with the above similarities and differences between Greco-Roman and Israelite-Jewish historiography in view that we compare Luke-Acts with ancient

history. Let us now look at the seven points of comparison.

Points of Comparison with Luke-Acts

Similar Prefaces

The first point of correspondence between Luke-Acts and ancient history is found in the prefaces: Luke 1:1–4 and Acts 1:1–2 (not to exclude parallels with the academic prose prefaces of e.g., Galen, Hermogenes, and Vettius Valens). Because papyri scrolls were limited in length, ca. thirty feet with about one hundred columns of words, an ancient author had to divide his work into separate volumes. He would prefix to the first a preface for the whole and add secondary prefaces to the beginning of each later one.[12] This is apparently the case with the Lukan prefaces. Both are addressed to Theophilus, probably a Roman patron to whom the work is dedicated (or e.g., the book's publisher, or even a fictional person: *theo-philus*, i.e., "lover of God").

Parallels to this practice occur in the work of the historians Josephus ("Epaphroditus" in *Ag. Ap.*, 1.1; 2.1; *Ant.*, 1.8) and Polybius (*Hist.*, 1.1 and 3.1). Like the preface in ancient histories (e.g., Polybius), Luke alludes to the narrative work of his predecessors (*diēgēsis*, Luke 1:1). The

11. See Herodotus, *Hist.* 1.46, oracles in numerous localities, 1.53, 91 (to King Croesus); discussion in Plutarch, *Pyth. orac.*; the Sybil at Cumae in Virgil, *Aeneid* 6.9–101; *OCD*, 1071–72. For additional similarities and differences, see Momigliano, *Essays in Ancient and Modern Historiography*, 194–95; Schmidt, "The Historiography of Acts," 417–27; Nielsen, *Tragedy in History*, despite his late date for the final redaction of Dtr Hist, helpful comparisons are made; see excellent overview in Aune, *New Testament and Its Literary Environment*, ch. 3.

12. For Lucian's views on writing prefaces, see his *Hist.*, §§16, 52–53. For comparisons with historiographical prefaces, see Cadbury, "Preface of Luke," in *BC* 2:491; Sterling, *Historiography as Self-Definition*, 339–46; for parallels to scientific and technical treatises of e.g., Galen, Hermogenes, see Alexander, *Preface to Luke's Gospel*; see helpful discussion in Moessner, *Jesus and the Heritage of Israel*, 9–23 (several essayists); Aune, *WDNTECLR*, 280–81 (Luke and Acts on two scrolls), 367–72 (prefaces); Puskas, *The Conclusion of Luke-Acts*, 96–99.

Lukan preface also reflects the historical concern to utilize eyewitness material (*autoptēs*, Luke 1:2; Polybius, Tacitus). "Events accomplished among us" (*pragma*: Luke 1:1) echoes the focus of ancient historiography on the facts of the near past (e.g., Herodotus, Thucydides, Polybius). Luke's concerns to "follow all things closely" and to "write an orderly account" (*akribōs, kathēchēs*: Luke 1:3) are in keeping with the practices of ancient historians to work carefully through reports and memoranda and arrange them in an orderly manner.[13] We know that Luke probably made use of at least two documents in his composition: Mark and Q. Like that of ancient histories, Luke's general purpose is to "preserve from decay the remembrance of what others have done" (Herodotus, *Hist.* 1.1).

Similar Chronological Notations

A second point of comparison is chronological notation. These synchronisms are found in Luke-Acts at numerous points. They link the birth of Jesus with the reign of Emperor Augustus and the census of Quirinius, legate of Syria (Luke 2:1). They also connect the ministry of John the Baptist with the rules of Emperor Tiberius, Pontius Pilate, prefect of Judea, and the Herodian ethnarchs (3:1). Further references are made to the famine under Emperor Claudius (Acts 11:28); the death of Herod Agrippa I (12:20–23); the expelling of Jews from Rome under Claudius (18:2); Paul's appearances before Gallio,

13. Lucian, *How to Write History*, §§43–44, 47–48; Dionysius of Halicarnassus, *On Thucydides*, ch. 6; Alexander, *Preface to Luke's Gospel*, 102–46.

proconsul of Achaia (18:12–17); the procurators Felix and Festus (chapters 24–25); and the ethnarch Agrippa II (25:13–14). Such chronological notes are characteristic of ancient histories (Thucydides 2.2; 4.135; Polybius, *Hist.* 1.3; 2.37; Josephus, *Ant.* 18.106; 20.1). They are also Luke's attempt to link his account of Jesus and early Christianity with the secular Roman world.

Similar Attention to Detail

Related to synchronisms is the third point: attention to factual details. This concern for specific names, dates, places, titles, and technical terms is especially evident in the histories of Herodotus, Thucydides, Polybius, and Josephus. However, Luke's concern for factual details is no guarantee of their accuracy. Discrepancies do occur, as in all ancient writing; inaccuracies occur, for example, with the linking of Jesus's birth (4 BC) and the census of Quirinius (AD 6) in Luke 2:1, with the conflicts between Josephus and Acts on the dating of Theudas the rebel (Acts 5:36; *Ant.* 20.97–98), and disagreements between Acts and Paul's letters on the apostle's visits to Jerusalem (cf. Acts 9, 11, and 15 with Galatians 1–2).

Despite the above discrepancies in its narrative, Luke-Acts includes many accurate details. The author's knowledge of the Aegean Sea region is extensive (Acts 15:36—19:20; cf., Thucydides), and numerous localities are correctly identified. Luke's account of Paul's basic itinerary finds many points of agreement with Paul's letters. The narrative of Paul's sea voyage to Rome is one of the most instructive accounts of ancient seamanship (Acts

27:12—28:15). The book of Acts alone contains more than one hundred personal names: Jewish, Christian, and pagan. The identities of many of the personages are corroborated by Paul's letters and ancient history (e.g., Paul's co-workers as well as Gallio, Claudius, Felix, and Festus).

Details of time and place, as well as concern for technical terms, also figure prominently. Note for example, the time and place notations on Paul's itinerary: three Sabbaths in the synagogue of Thessalonica (17:2), eighteen months in Corinth (18:11), three months in the synagogue of Ephesus (19:8), and three months in Achaia (20:3). Luke also has an impressive grasp of the technical terms of Roman administration. He correctly distinguishes between imperial provinces governed by legates and senatorial provinces ruled by proconsuls (e.g., Acts 13:7; 16:20, 22; 18:12). He is familiar with other titles of local provincial magistrates: "politarchs" (17:6), "city clerk" (19:31). Furthermore, he is informed about appropriate military titles (10:1; 21:31; 27:1).

Similar Bias

The fourth point of comparison is that of political bias. Since ancient history deals with politics and war, and all historians are partial to certain viewpoints, political bias often surfaces in their work. Herodotus and Thucydides were pro-Athenian, Polybius, Tacitus, and Josephus were pro-Roman. It is also the case with Luke-Acts. Despite some instances of cruelty and corruption (Luke 13:1; Acts 24:25–27), imperial Rome is portrayed in a favorable light. In Luke's Gospel both the Roman prefect Pilate and a Roman centurion, on

separate occasions declare Jesus innocent (23:4, 14, 22, 47). In Acts, prominent Roman officials are converted to Christianity (Acts 10–11; 13:7–12; 28:7–10), Paul himself claims to be a Roman citizen and enjoys all the privileges connected with that honor (16:37–39; 22:24–29), and in Rome Paul is permitted to live under house arrest and receive visitors (28:16, 30–31). Luke's motive for this pro-Roman bias is probably similar to that of the Jewish historian Josephus: to achieve a favorable standing with Rome for himself and his people. Luke sought to win Rome's favor toward Christianity, whereas Josephus had the same objective on behalf of Judaism.[14]

Similar Views on Providence

The fifth basis of comparison concerns assumptions about fate or providence. Even though Luke's notion of divine necessity in human affairs (e.g., Luke 17:25; 22:22; 24:26; Acts 4:28; 10:42; 13:48; 17:31) has similar functions to the Greco-Roman concept of fate in history, the best context for understanding this theme is Israelite-Jewish history. In Luke-Acts divine necessity is closely related to fulfillment of the Jewish Scriptures (Luke 24:26–27, 44–47; Acts 4:24–29; 10:42–43; 13:46–48). Although similar phenomena are found in pagan histories,[15] proof from prophecy

14. On Luke-Acts and Josephus as apologetic historiography seeking to establish their self-identity in the larger world, see Sterling, *Historiography as Self-Definition*, 16–19, 255, 297–98, 308–10, 385–93. See also Holladay, *Fragments from Hellenistic Jewish Authors*.

15. For example, Herodotus narrates the Delphic oracle's cryptic prophecy (one of many) to King Croesus of Miletus going to war and "destroying an empire," *Hist.*1.53–56, 91, the cosmic

in Luke-Acts is biblical. Much of Luke's thought on divine election is also informed by biblical texts (Luke 9:35; 23:35; cf. Isa 42:1; Luke 2:31–32; Acts 1:8; 13:47; cf. Isa 49:6).

In Israelite-Jewish history, the themes of divine necessity and election occur in the context of God's activity on behalf of his people—called "salvation history." Two examples of this divine activity are God's delivering Israel from Egypt and bringing Israel into the land of Canaan. In Luke-Acts, salvation history is identified with the appearance of Jesus as savior of the world (Luke 1:30–33; 2:10–14, 27–32; Acts 3:13–15; 4:10–12) and with the extension of salvation to the nations (Luke 24:46–48; Acts 1:8; 9:15; 13:47).[16]

Similar Use of Speeches

The sixth point of comparison is the use of speeches that express the author's

interpretation of the events. It was common practice in ancient times to adorn historical works with speeches of the actors that expressed the historian's perspective on the events narrated. Thucydides in his introduction to *The Peloponnesian Wars* (1.22.1) states his method of employing speeches. Although its was difficult for him to follow precise wordings, Thucydides would try to keep to the general sense of the word to make the speakers say, in his opinion, what was called for by each situation. Instances can be cited, however, when Thucydides falls short of his methodological objective. Let us look at some examples. The famous funeral oration of Pericles makes little reference to the minor occasion in which it is placed (2.34–46), detailed forensic speeches make little reference to the event that prompted the debate (3.36–50), and the favorite themes of Thucydides are repeated on the mouths of different speakers addressing different audiences (1.120–24, 140–44). Even though some of the above examples may capture the memory of the occasions, speeches as ancient history reflect the author's purpose and contain teaching to instruct the reader.[17]

consequences of a return to despotism in the speech of Socles to the Spartans, 5.92, and predictions in the visions/dreams of King Xerxes and Artabanos, his advisor, regarding their plans to fight the Greeks, 7.14–19. The prophecy of Vespasian becoming emperor of Rome is recounted in Suetonius, *Vespasian* 5; and Tacitus, *Hist.* 5.13; Josephus claims to have made this prophecy concerning Vespasian (*War* 3.399–408); See other predictions of a coming ruler in Virgil, *Ecologues* 4 and the *Sibylline Oracles* 11–12. For other Hellenistic prophecies (pagan and Jewish), see Aune, *Prophecy in Early Christianity*; Talbert, *Reading Luke*, 265–69.

16. The following works treat the themes of divine necessity, election, and proof-from-prophecy under Luke's salvation-history scheme: Conzelmann, *Theology of St. Luke*, 149–69; Dahl, "Story of Abraham," 139–58; O'Toole, *Unity of Lukan Theology*, 17–32; Squires, *Plan of God*, 34–36, 137–39, 187–88; Sterling, *Historiography as Self-Definition*, 358–59; Kurz, "Hellenistic Jewish Narratives," 148–55; Puskas, *Conclusion of Luke-Acts*, 5, 23, 75, 94, 100, 121–28. On biblical election from a Jewish perspective, see Kaminsky, *Yet I Loved Jacob*.

17. Cadbury, "Speeches in Acts," in *BC* 5:405 (402–27). See also on Lukan speeches Dibelius, *Studies in the Acts*, 138–91; Schweizer, "Concerning Speeches in Acts," 208–16; Bailey, et al., *Literary Forms in the New Testament*, 166–72; Soards, *Speeches in Acts*, 134–61; Aune, *WDNTECLR*, 447–49. Two examples from the Roman period revealing the authors' creative use of speeches will also be given. The speech of Caesar to his soldiers in Dio Cassius, *Roman History* 38.36–46 is very different from the brief address reported by Caesar himself in *Gallic Wars* 1.40. Josephus, reporting on the same event in different books, puts two different speeches in the mouth of Herod in *War* 1.373–79 and *Ant.* 15.53. On the proper use of speeches, see Thucydides, *Hist.* 1.22.1; and Polybius, *Hist.* 12.25a.5–25b.1.

Approximately one-fifth of the book of Acts, like the history of Thucydides, is speech material. In Acts, speeches proclaim the passion, resurrection, and exaltation of Jesus (e.g., Acts 2:14–39; 3:11–26; 4:18–22; 13:16–41) and defend Paul and the Christian mission to the Gentiles (22:3–21; 26:1–23; 28:16–28). As in ancient history, the speeches of Acts enhance the significance of the events, advance the action of the narrative, and allow the author to address his audience through his characters. Although some speeches may capture the essence of the original event, they primarily reflect the author's interpretation and perspective. Many speeches do not even apply to the specific settings in which they are found but go beyond the historical situation to address the readers of the book.[18]

Similar Arrangement in a Line of Progression

Both Greco-Roman and Israelite-Jewish histories basically follow a line of progression through time, and both were acquainted with a cycle of seasons and festivals (which complement this progression through time). For example, the Greek Herodotus begins his *History* with the rise of the Persian Empire from its beginnings to the sixth century BC (1.1—5.27). He then progresses to the Greek and the Persian wars of the sixth and fifth centuries BC (5.28—9.1). The Jewish historian Josephus, in his *Antiquities*, follows the progression of biblical history in his first eleven books: from creation, to the exodus (twelfth century BC), to the exile and restoration (sixth and fifth centuries BC). In the remaining nine books, Josephus continues from the death of Alexander the Great (fourth century BC) to the Maccabean and Hasmonean periods (second and first centuries BC), ending with the outset of the Jewish revolt (AD 66). *The Jewish War* by Josephus begins with a survey of events from Antiochus IV Epiphanes (168 BC) to the death of Herod the Great (4 BC). He continues from the death of Herod up to the time when Vespasian was sent to subdue the Jewish revolt (AD 66) and then focuses on the Jewish revolt in the remaining five books (AD 66–73).

Luke-Acts covers not the centuries outlined by Herodotus and Josephus but less than sixty years from the birth of Jesus to the imprisonment of Paul at Rome (4 BC—AD 62). The reason for this brevity is that Luke, like certain ancient historians (e.g., Thucydides, and Xenophon in *Hellenica*), is selective. He reports only what is "important, essential, personal or useful."[19] Luke-Acts, similarly to ancient histories, moves in a geographical and

---

18. The author of Luke-Acts appears to make creative use of his speeches as in ancient history. First, the speeches and narratives are dominated by the style and thought of Luke. Second, the author's favorite scriptural quotes occur in the mouths of different speakers on different occasions, for example: Ps 16 in both Acts 2:27 (Peter) and 13:35 (Paul); Deut 18 in both 3:22 (Peter) and 7:37 (Stephen); Exod 20 in both 4:24 (the disciples) and 14:15 (Paul). Third, a similar logic of interpreting biblical quotes is presupposed in all of the above speeches: (a) Scripture says this; (b) this must apply to the speaker's time or another era; (c) it does not apply to the speaker's time; (d) therefore since it was fulfilled in Jesus, it may be applied to him. All the Christian speakers of Acts interpret Scripture in a similar manner. Cadbury, "Speeches," *BC* 5:408; Soards, *Speeches in Acts*, 182–208.

19. Lucian, *How to Write History* §53; see also in Dionysius, *On Thucydides*, balanced treatment of content, 6, and avoiding excessive elaboration, 42.

chronological progression (in Luke-Acts) from Jesus to the Jerusalem church and Paul at Rome. The book of Acts begins with the emergence of Christianity in Jerusalem (1:15—8:3 [AD 33?]). It continues with the spread of Christianity into Samaria and the coastal regions of Palestine (8:4—11:18 [AD 34–36?]). Acts then focuses on the development of Christianity in Antioch, Asia Minor (11:19—15:35 [AD 37–48]), and the Aegean Sea region (15:36—19:20 [AD 48–55]). It concludes with the progression of Christianity from Jerusalem to Rome in the story of Paul's journeys, imprisonment, and appeal to Caesar (19:21—28:31 [AD 57–62]).[20]

THE BIOGRAPHICAL GENRE: A COMPARISON WITH MATTHEW

The second ancient genre to be examined is biography.[21] Why would any of

the Gospels or Acts be read as biography? Though Matthew refers to his composition as a "book" (*biblos*) and did not read Mark's opening use of "gospel" (*euangelion*) as a title or generic description (though Mark's opening lent itself to *engendering* the gospel genre), it is as biography that we will discuss it. The discourse among scholars since the Enlightenment over whether it is appropriate to call (any of) the Gospels biography has progressed like a game of verbal volleyball. Much ink has been spilt, but the evidence in favor of the Gospels' being some sort of recognizable biography is overwhelming. Still, we will discern other familiar or identifiable genres that have been added, forming a *mixtum compositum* or "mixed genre,"

---

20. Cadbury, "Greek and Jewish Traditions of Writing History," in *BC* 2:22–29; for other comparisons, see ibid., 2:7–21; Peterson, *Acts*, 32–39; Puskas, *Conclusion of Luke-Acts*, 3–4, 83–84, 125–27. See also our ch. 12 on the use of Acts in a chronology of Paul's life.

21. Most of the primary sources of ancient biography cited in this section are from the Loeb Classical Library. See also Athanassakis, *Life of Pachomius*; Aune, "Problem of the Genre of the Gospels," in France, *Gospel Perspectives*, vol. 2 (1981); Aune, "Greco-Roman Biography," in *Greco-Roman Literature and the New Testament*, 107–26; Aune, *New Testament in Its Literary Environment* (esp. 17–76); Klaus Baltzer, *Die Biographie der Propheten* (a study that works not from Greco-Roman biography but from biographies of the prophets, providing the stimulus for some of Dormeyer's work, and treated positively by Koester [below]); Barr and Wentling, "Conventions of Classical Biography," in Talbert, *Luke-Acts: New Perspectives*, 63–88; Berger, "Hellenistische Gattungen" (this essay contains a chronological list of Greek and Latin biographies); Burridge, *What Are the Gospels?* with an analysis of the problem and proposed solution

makes a strong case for the Gospels as ancient *bioi* (biographies) allowing this genre to be mixed even with other lesser "modes"; Burridge, *Four Gospels, One Jesus?* 5–8, for a quick summary of his conclusions); Cartlidge and Dungan, *Documents*; Cox, *Biography in Late Antiquity* (1983); Dormeyer and Frankenmölle "Evangelium als literarischer und als theologischer Begriff"; Dormeyer, *Evangelium als Gattung*; Eddy and Boyd, *Jesus Legend*, 309–61; Guelich, "Gospel Genre"; Gundry, "Recent Investigations into the Literary Genre 'Gospel,'" in Longenecker and Tenney, *New Dimensions in New Testament Study*, 97–114 (both Eddy and Boyd plus Guelich and Gundry argue that the Gospels are unique [*sui generis*] and kerygmatic expansions in origin); Hadas and Smith, *Heroes and Gods* (1965); Koester, *Ancient Christian Gospels* (The Gospels as Hellenistic biographies is especially challenged in ch. 1; the book proposes that there are seven different genres [or better, "forms"] dealing with the transmission of Jesus tradition: sayings-collections, miracle-story chains, parable collections, apocalyptic prophecies, birth legends, kerygma gospel, and dialogues); Koester, *From Jesus to the Gospels* (esp. ch. 4: "From the Kerygma-Gospel to Written Gospels"); Shuler, *A Genre for the Gospels*; Talbert, *Literary Patterns*; Talbert, "Prophecies of Future Greatness"; Talbert, *What Is a Gospel?*; Votaw, *Gospels and Contemporary Biographies*; Wardman, *Plutarch's Lives*.

and we will end our discussion in this section with an example of such.

Some Objections

Certainly questions can be raised against the genre biography. The gospel stories have "nothing to say about Jesus's human personality, his appearance and character, his origin, education, and development."[22] The Gospels and Acts are also not as cultivated in techniques of composition as great literature of this type.[23] Conversely, they are rich in traditions of divine activity and reflect a communal setting of worship, but this is not typical of ancient biographies.[24]

Though these are valid observations, their relevance must be assessed within the context of comparable literature. First, regarding silence about Jesus's human personality, appearance, character,[25] origin, education, and development, it will be shown that books following the three aspects of a *bios* pattern need not include all the above characteristics in order to be classified a biography. Second, concerning the literary quality of the Gospels, although they were not written in the Attic Greek of Polybius and Xenophon, they appear to be more loosely joined collections of folk traditions produced by sectarian communities. Redaction and literary criticisms have established that the final forms of the Gospels and Acts are the designed literary products of creative authors. The Gospels and Acts are not polished Attic Greek but reflect definite techniques of composition and style. Third, it can be shown that numerous ancient biographies (a) contain myths of immortals and divine men (e.g., Alexander the Great, Augustus, Pythagoras, Apollonius of Tyana) and (b) are linked to communities founded by, or connected with, the hero of the narratives (e.g., emperor cults of Alexander and Augustus, religious communities of Pythagoras, shrines and temples of Apollonius).[26]

Despite the above difficulties, the Gospels (especially Matthew) and most ancient biographies share a common *bios* or life pattern. The pattern manifests itself in at least three areas: (1) similar *topoi* or topics relevant to the praise of an individual; (2) analogous literary techniques of creative arrangement, amplification, and comparison; and (3) a common intent to praise and honor a great individual.[27] Be-

22. Bultmann, *History of the Synoptic Tradition*, 372.

23. Though the episodic and paratactic style often profiled as an example of this gracelessness is a signal feature of specific types of Greco-Roman biographical literature (cf. Aune, *Literary Environment*, 31–35).

24. Bultmann, *History of the Synoptic Tradition*, 371–74. F. J. Moloney even contends that John's Gospel (e.g. John 1:18) is a *bios Theou* or, better, a *bios patros* rather than a *bios Christou*, arguing that John's theology not be swallowed up in his Christology (*Gospel of John*, 47). Is this criticism directed at the christological focus of gospel *bios* study?

25. Character was indeed important to include as a feature of biography, but it was manifested in a person's words and actions (Xenephon, *Memorabalia* 1.1.20; where Socrates's words [*logoi*] and deeds [*prattein; praxis*] testify to his reverence *sebas*; cf. Luke 24:19; Acts 1:1), hence Bultmann's inclusion of this as a disclaimer is a misunderstanding of ancient literature on this point.

26. Talbert, *What Is a Gospel?* 25–113. The observation of Moloney that John is more a *bios* of God than of Christ is worthy of further investigation in the Synoptic Gospels as well (see footnote 24).

27. These three characteristics apply to a certain type of ancient biography, encomium, which was well known in late antiquity. The three points

fore discussing these patterns, with their Matthean analogues, we will profile the type of biography of interest and give examples of similarity.

Characteristics of Laudatory Biography

The type of ancient biography with which we are concerned is called encomium or laudatory biography. This was a distinct type of literature in the ancient Mediterranean world whose primary concern was to show individual greatness and merit.[28] The three characteristics of encomium (i.e., *topoi*, literary techniques, and common intent) are derived from Greek and Roman experts on rhetoric: Aristotle (fourth century BC), Cicero (first century BC), Quintilian (first century AD), Theon of Egypt (second century AD), and Hermogenes of Tarsus (second century AD). Because of the far-reaching influence of many of the above rhetoricians, the techniques of writing encomia would have been known in most areas of the first-century Mediterranean world.[29]

Similar Topoi

The first identifiable characteristic of ancient biography is *topoi* (i.e., "topics, common-places, or elements"). This feature of encomium consists of topics of birth, ancestry, character, deeds, virtues, and type of death. The use of such *topoi* was determined by the design of the author. Detailed explanations of them are given by Quintilian and Theon of Smyrna. Matthew's Gospel contains the following *topoi* in the accounts of Jesus's birth and infancy: (a) his illustrious lineage through his earthly father (1:17), (b) his upright earthly father (1:19), (c) the time and place of his birth (2:1), (d) his escape from death as an infant (2:13–15), and (e) his hometown (2:23). These *topoi* are accented by dreams, stellar illumination, and the adoration of the child. Many of these elements appear in ancient biographies (e.g., Isocrates, *Evagoras*; Philo, *Life of Moses*, Tacitus, *Agricola*).[30]

In Matthew 3–4, Jesus's baptism and temptation can be viewed as substitutes for stories about the virtues of his childhood and youth. In Matthew 3 Jesus is empowered by God's Spirit, and his identity is revealed as God's Son. After his messianic identity is disclosed, it is tried and proven in the next scene (4:3, 6). Matthew 4 presents Jesus as a strong messianic figure who can withstand temptation and provide spiritual leadership. In several laudatory biographies, heroes were

---

are derived from both the remarks of Greek and Latin rhetoricians and from a comparison of ancient biographies, as outlined in Shuler, *A Genre for the Gospels?* 85–87, 92–106. These characteristics would not include biographies that seek to discredit a teacher (e.g., Lucian, *Alexander the False Prophet*) or those that combine genres (e.g., *Life of Aesop*, a romantic type of biography).

28. On formal encomia and the characteristics of the laudatory-biography genre cf. Isocrates, *Helen*; Busiris, *Evagorus*; Tacitus, *Agricola*; Lucian, *Demonax*; Philostratus, *Life of Apollonius*; Shuler, *A Genre for the Gospels?* 57. For further discussion on the criteria for determining genre, see Barr and Wentling, "Classical Biography," *Luke-Acts*, 63–88.

29. See e.g., Marrou, *History of Education in Antiquity*, 198–99.

30. The above analysis of Matthew as ancient encomium is derived from Shuler, *A Genre for the Gospels?* 98–106. See also Burridge, *What Are the Gospels?* 67–123 for surveys of ancient and modern discussion with his recommended sequence of analysis (i.e., opening features, subject, external features [size, length, structure] and internal features [function, occasion, purpose]).

praised because their vocational choices were not altered by other tempting possibilities. For example, Agricola resisted fame, Moses his royal inheritance in Egypt, and Demonax wealth.

Other *topoi* of significance are connected with Jesus's death and resurrection. By focusing on these aspects that underscore Jesus's innocence, uprightness, and messianic identity, Matthew transforms a scandalous form of death into a victorious glorification. For example, the predictions of Jesus's impending death (16:21; 17:22–23; 20:17–19; 26:2) underscore its divinely planned significance. By emphasizing the following two points, Matthew also affirms Jesus's innocence: (1) his death was the result of a treacherous scheme by his opponents (26:3–5; 27:1), and (2) the betrayer, Judas, realized he was wrong and feebly tried to rectify it (27:3–10).

Just as they appear in the narrative of Jesus's birth, so supernatural events surround his death, affirming his innocence and messianic identity. Through his wife's dream (27:19) Pilate is warned to have nothing to do with the upright Jesus. Pilate, Jesus's judge, then becomes convinced of his innocence (27:24–26). The divine necessity of Jesus's death is indicated by darkness over the land at his death (27:45) and by the tearing of the temple curtain (27:51). There is also mention of an earthquake with a resurrection and appearances of the dead (27:51–53). A second earthquake also occurs on the first day of the week before the women visit Jesus's tomb (28:1). Even his humiliating death is presented in such a way as to elicit faith and praise from the reader. In response to the events connected with Jesus's death the centurion and his men exclaim in unison: "Certainly this was the Son of God" (27:54).

Finally, Matthew gives special evidence of the resurrection. In Matt 27:62–66, Pilate sets up guards to prevent the theft of Jesus's body and to squelch all rumors of a resurrection. Shortly afterward (28:4) it is the soldiers themselves who witness the magnificent angel rolling the stone away from the tomb, and their response is one of fear. Still later (28:11–15) the soldiers are bribed and told to falsify their testimony by stating that the disciples stole the body. Consequently, Matthew's readers can have confidence in the resurrection of Jesus through this carefully worked out defense.

Analogous Techniques

The second characteristic of ancient biography is found in the literary techniques of creative arrangement, amplification, and comparison. By creative arrangement we mean the subordination of geography and chronology to the author's design. For example, in *Agricola* by Tacitus, the author's apologetic is veiled in a conquest of Britain without a real concern for geographical accuracy.

In Matthew's Gospel there is no attempt to trace a chronology of Jesus's life. Matthew uses the *bios* form as an outline on which to organize the traditions that commend Jesus. Traditions that eulogize the hero are historicized—like the Sermon on the Mount and the speeches of both Calgarus and Agricola in *Agricola* 29–36. Matthew further validates his presentation with numerous Scripture quotations, each prefaced by a fixed formula (e.g., 1:22; 2:15, 17, 23). In a similar manner, Plutarch incorporates quotations from ancient poets to support the praiseworthiness of its subjects (e.g., Philopoemen 11.2–3; and Aristides 3.4 in *Lives*).

Matthew also tends to arrange materials thematically. For example, the Sermon on the Mount (chapters 5–7) concerns righteousness; miracle stories are combined in one unit (chapters 8–9); the mission charge (chapter 10) focuses on discipleship; the section on parables (chapter 13) concerns the kingdom and its growth; rules of church discipline are collected in chapter 18; teachings against the Pharisees are in chapter 23; and discourses on the return of the Lord and the final judgment are collected in chapters 24 and 25. Traditions are also organized in both Philo (*Life of Moses*) and Xenophon (*Agesilaus*) to convey special themes of the authors.

Amplification is the technique used by laudatory biographers to accent the positive attributes and minimize the negative qualities of their heroes. It is a basic feature of encomium. Polybius described it as a "somewhat exaggerated account of . . . achievements" (*Histories* 10.21.8). Cicero described it as eulogizing actions in a way that enhances merit to the point of exaggeration (*Letters* 5.12.3). Encomium seeks to magnify the merits of a great person and not to dissect or criticize that individual (cf. also Josephus, *Life*; Plutarch, *Lives*; Cornelius Nepos, *Lives of Great Men* [Pelopidas 16.1.1]).

Matthew often uses the literary technique of amplification. The progressive disclosure of Jesus's identity as the Son of God (chapters 1–4) and the extraordinary *topoi* surrounding his death (chapters 27–28) are two examples of amplification. Both sections are heightened by the use of dreams, supernatural phenomena, and the testimony of eyewitnesses. Amplification is also evidenced in the particular segments of Jesus's life chosen by Matthew for presentation. Following most ancient biographies, Matthew concentrates on certain segments of the adult years. Matthew includes Jesus's birth and the beginning of his ministry, but only as preliminary accounts. The ministry itself focuses on a small segment of Jesus's life in comparison with the accounts of his final week. From these concentrated traditions one can discern the identity and character of Jesus, his message proclaimed, his actions performed, the nature of the opposition as a rationale for his death, and the purposes of God throughout the entire process.

The literary technique of comparison was prevalent in laudatory biography. In Isocrates's *Encomium to Helen* 16, the technique is used to elevate Helen to a rank above the great Hercules. Much of Helen's praiseworthiness is also derived from the character of her suitors, like the noble Theseus (38). In Isocrates's *Evagoras*, Cyrus and Conon are compared to Evagoras, but neither excels him in greatness (33). In Philo's *Life of Moses* 2.19–20, the law of Moses is regarded as superior to that of other nations. It was Ptolemy Philadelphus, whose qualities are unequaled, who recognized the value of Moses's law and commissioned its translation into Greek (2.29–37).[31]

Comparison is evident in Matthew's Gospel. Impressive personages like John the Baptist, Jesus's opponents, and Roman

---

31. In the *Letter of Aristeas* Ptolemy Philadelphus (285–247 BC) is purported to be the backer of the Jewish translation of the Hebrew Bible into Greek (LXX) in Alexandria, Egypt.

officials are shown by comparison to neither excel nor equal Jesus in greatness or authority. In Matthew 3, John appears as an impressive figure: preaching, baptizing, and attracting disciples. His preaching is identical with that of Jesus (3:2; 4:17). The groups that John denounces become the opponents of Jesus (Pharisees and Sadducees, 3:7). These parallels, for Matthew, do not argue that John and Jesus are equals, or that Jesus was a disciple of John. In Matt 3:14, John's hesitation to baptize Jesus, and his own willingness to be baptized by Jesus, point to the superiority of Jesus over John. John's identification with Elijah (3:3; 11:14) also indicates Jesus's supremacy: John is the one preparing the way for another greater than he. Following the baptism, both the heavenly voice and the descent of the dove confirm this conclusion. The implication of this comparison is that, since John can be considered great, how much greater is Jesus![32]

Matthew's depiction of Jesus and his opponents also reveals comparison. Although direct conflict begins at Matthew 12, readers are alerted earlier to impending conflict. After the Sermon on the Mount it is stated that Jesus taught with authority, not as the scribes (7:28–29). In response to an indicting question (9:11) Jesus gives only a general answer (9:12–13), and to charges by the Pharisees (9:34) he gives a reply later in the narrative (12:24–32). When Jesus commissions his disciples, he warns them that they will encounter the same opposition that he is about to face (10:16–25). These clues alert readers to expect greater conflicts in the narrative between Jesus and his opponents. In Matthew 12–22 the conflict stories are more direct and intense. The Pharisees criticize Jesus for allowing his disciples to pluck grain on the Sabbath and even condemn him for healing on that sacred day (Matt 12:1–15a). Jesus's clever response to the accusations of his opponents (vv. 3–13) indicates his superiority over them. Therefore, since they are incapable of defeating him in debate, they must destroy him (v. 14). The conflict stories again become concentrated at Matt 21:23, and climax in 22:45–46. Now Jesus appears as the aggressor. After a series of confrontations, the Pharisees refuse to answer a question that Jesus initiates, and Matthew states that "no one dared . . . to ask him any more questions" (22:46). Readers therefore conclude that Jesus is superior to his opponents. Even though Jesus answers all his opponents' charges and questions, they are at a loss to answer his challenge, and so their only course of action is to seek his death.

In ancient biography, similar comparisons of the hero with his inferior opponents occur: the jealousy encountered by Moses prior to his first flight from Egypt (Philo, *Life of Moses* 1.46) and the envy successfully avoided by the humble actions of Agricola, which account for his longevity (Tacitus, *Agricola* 44), are two examples.

Similar Intent to Praise

The third element common to the encomium is the intent to praise and honor a great individual. Cornelius Nepos, in his life of Pelopidas, was concerned about building a case for greatness (16.1.1).

---

32. This type of comparison was frequently used in rabbinic interpretation. In the hermeneutical rules of Hillel (first century AD) it was called *qal wahomer*, or "inference from minor and major."

Xenophon in *Agesilaus* endeavored to write an "appreciation of Agesilaus" that would be "worthy of his virtue and glory" (1.1). Philo in his *Life of Moses* sought to present "the story of this greatest and most perfect of men" (6.1–2, 4). This chief aim of the laudatory biographers determined the content and arrangement of the materials with which they worked.

In a manner characteristic of encomium, Matthew sought to focus on the following: (1) Jesus's prominent identity, (2) the significance of his words and deeds, and (3) the kind of response his readers assume toward him (e.g., imitation, emulation). This threefold purpose has parallels in Philo's *Life of Moses*, Lucian's *Demonax*, and Philostratus's *Life of Apollonius*. Matthew's distinctive focus might be on the type of response he wished to inspire in his readers: e.g., faith, praise, and obedience.

In the narrative Matthew progressively unfolds the identity of Jesus as the "Son of God." The importance of this identification is evident from the key positions the title occupies in the text (e.g., 4:3, 6; 14:33; 16:16; 26:63; 27:40, 54). The authentication of this identity by numerous scriptural prophecies confirms for the reader the messianic identity of Jesus. The question asked of Peter, "who do you say I am?" (16:15), with its appropriate answer, "you are the Christ" (v. 16), is also asked of the reader.

The second laudatory focus of Matthew is the recognition of Jesus's messianic activity. The summary of Jesus's messianic activity in Matt 4:23–25 serves as a programmatic statement that introduces both the Sermon on the Mount (chapters 5–7) and the section on miracles (chapters 8–9). The proper response to this messianic activity is both heeding and doing what Jesus proclaims (7:24).

To inspire emulation of the messiah's activity, chapters 1–9 constitute a paradigm of discipleship. There is no direct conflict during this period in Jesus's ministry. For Matthew this time of Jesus seems to be identical with the time of the reader, who is being taught and trained before being sent out (in chapter 10).[33] After announcing Jesus's messianic identity, Matthew presents his teaching on the Sermon on the Mount (cf. Lucian, *Demonax*). Matthew concludes chapters 1–9 with important instruction for his readers on true discipleship (8:18–22; 9:10–13, 35–38). Only after such instruction is the disciple ready for commissioning (chapter 10). In a similar manner to Matthew 1–9, chapters 12–28 can be understood as providing a model for facing trials, since the teaching to the disciples in Matthew 10 includes warnings of future opposition (vv. 16–25).[34]

33. On Matthew and his audience, see Crosby, *House of Disciples*; Riches, "Synoptic Evangelists"; Keener, *Matthew*, 45–51.

34. In the *Lives of Eminent Philosophers*, the life of Plato (3.1–45) is recounted, followed by a listing of his disciples (3.46–47) and a summary of his doctrine (3.47–109). The same pattern is followed for other founders of philosophical schools (e.g., Pythagoras, Epicurus). In the Christian *Life of Pachomius*, the early part of the biography deals with the career of Pachomius, the founder of this particular monastic community. In section 117, he appoints Orsisius to succeed him. In sections 118–29 the life and teaching of Orsisius is recounted as emulating the life and teachings of Pachomius. Then Orsisius appoints Theodore as successor (130). For more discussion on these points, see the following works by Talbert: *What Is a Gospel?* 956; Talbert, *Literary Patterns*, 125–34; Talbert, *Luke-Acts*, 1–3.

The Hellenistic Genre *Synkrisis*

Compatible to the host genre of biography, and companionable with the *common intent to praise* is the skillfully integrated literary genre called *synkrisis* (Lat. *comparatio*). The basis of seeing a *synkrisis* operative in the Christian Gospels, especially in Luke but also probably in Q,[35] is the elaborate "comparison" made between Jesus and John.[36] *Synkrisis* is a strange name for a genre, but it is descriptive, made up of two words that imply the opposite of each other, making it something of a paradox: *syn* (meaning "together") and *krisis* (meaning "separating"). In this bringing together, a distinction or separation is made. The *bringing together* is John and Jesus, the *separating* or *distinguishing* is the purpose and achievement of the structure. Two characters are developed together in order to feature one or the other. In the pairing of the two in Luke (especially in the birth narrative), the goal is the exaltation of Jesus, a goal also of laudatory biography. To see the genre *synkrisis* operative in Luke where the host genre is some form of history or biography, and to see both history or biography and *synkresis* working toward the same goals is a good exemplar of the *mixtum compositum* mentioned earlier, which is a feature of all of the texts of the New Testament.

When two principal characters are conjoined in narrative as John and Jesus are, artful possibilities exist for dynamic interface. Some hero stories from antiquity, using *synkrisis* (visible in the pairing of Jesus and John), effect with the pairing of the characters what has been the "second-self" of the hero.[37] The narrative techniques, e.g., describing the nature of the hero, the direction and nature of his growth, and his weaknesses and strengths, all contribute to the ways that the hero confronts himself. In its most simple form, the hero is the subject of the story, and the "second self" is a foil for chronicling his development, preparing him for his destiny. The relationship that exists and is developed between the two is the narrative dynamic and can be as complex and strategic as the sophistication of the author and his tradition will allow.

35. See Robbins, *Testing*, esp. 92–95; 135–40. On *synkrisis*, see also "comparison," in Aune, *WDNTECLR*, 110 (includes a comparison of Christ and Melchizedek in Hebrews).

36. Aelius Theon of Alexandria (first century BC), in writing about *synkrisis* in his *Exercises* (*progymnasmata*) says "Whenever we compare persons we shall first put side by side their good birth and education . . . after this we shall compare their actions"; Hermogenes of Tarsus (AD 161–180), another contributor to ancient rhetoric of comparison, says, "Synkrisis is comparison of similar or dissimilar things . . . We compare the cities from which the men came, and family with family and nurture with nurture and pursuits and deeds and external factors and manner of death and what follows death" (translations in Kennedy, *Progymnasmata*, 53, 83–84). The term *synkrisis* occurs in Aristotle's *On Rhetoric*, in Dionysius's *Thax and Philodemus*, and is part of the discussions of comparisons along with the terms *eikōn*, *homoiōs* and *parabolē*, (see discussion by McCall, *Ancient Rhetorical Theories*). In NT, see *synkrisis* also in Hebrews regarding, e.g., Jesus and Melchizedek, Jesus and Moses (Witherington, *Letters and Homilies*, 48–49).

37. While not a pervasive motif, its presence in the *Epic of Gilgamesh* and the *Iliad* has been much discussed. Some of the literature on this theme: Van Nortwick, *Somewhere I Have Never Travelled*; Nagy, *Best of the Achaeans,* esp. ch. 2; N. Van Brock, "Substitution Rituelle," *RHA* 65 (1959) 117–146; Keppler, *Literature of the Second Self*, (1972); Campbell, *Hero with a Thousand Faces*, (1949); Devereux, "Achilles' 'Suicide' in the Iliad" *Helios* 6 (1978) 3–15; Rogers, *Double in Literature*, (1970); Griffin, *Homer on Life and Death* (1980).

Definitions are diverse but seem to be related. For Van Nortwick, the second self is essentially a hero's *companion* in the narrative. Enkidu is Gilgamesh's second self in the *Epic of Gilgamesh*; Patroclus is Achilles's second self in the *Iliad*. In both cases the second self is a comrade, friend, and mate. For Van Brock it is an alter ego, *un autre soi-même*. She traces the Greek word *therapōn* to the Hittite *tarpassa-/tarpan (alli)*—"ritual substitute," which converges upon the almost-universal presence of the motif of death, a historical connection with which Nagy concurs.[38] Tragedy, such as death, is usually a fundamental dimension of the experience of the hero and his significant other. Enkidu's death forces Gilgamesh to face his own mortality. Achilles refuses to face his own destiny as a hero of the Achaeans and to do battle with Hector, *until* Patroclus dies brutally at Hector's hands. This pairing and dynamic is visible in the interface between John and Jesus.

It is exhibitive, not eccentric, to base much of the interaction between John and Jesus upon this motif, especially in Luke, where there is sustained dialogue involving them both. John provides focus for our perception of Jesus, from the leap in the womb at their prenatal encounter (Luke 1:41)[39] to John's baptism of Jesus and John's declamation about this "coming one" who is "stronger"[40] (Luke 3) to his confused queries about what he is doing (Luke 7). But Jesus, in step, seems to be just as occupied with John: from his speech to the crowds about John's unparalleled greatness (Luke 7) to his repeated encounters with John's legacy of fame and fear from both the crowds (Luke 9:19) and political authorities (9:7) to his use of John as a foil of protection when under attack from the leaders in Jerusalem (20:1–8).

John is so important to Jesus that Jesus even hinges "ages" on him, as we have done with Jesus (Luke 16:16). So it would seem that *quantity* of material is not nearly as important as the structural relationship of the material. In the increasing complexity of the gospel stories of Matthew, Mark, and Luke, the potential of this relationship is enlarged.[41] From the leap

---

38. Nagy, *Best of the Achaeans*, 292. In the *Iliad* (16.241–45) Achilles prays to Zeus for Patroclus, who has donned Achilles's armor and is about to engage in battle with Hector: "Far-seeing Zeus! Let the glory of victory go forth with him. Make him breathe courage from inside, so that Hector too will find out whether our *therapōn* knows how to fight in battle alone, or whether his hands rage invincible only those times when I myself enter the struggle of Ares." Patroclus falls in battle, is unequal to Achilles, being "the recessive equivalent of the dominant hero" (Nagy, *Best of the Achaeans*, 292). But as *therapōn* to Achilles, Patroclus was far more than merely an attendant or companion (uses of the word otherwise attested in the *Iliad*) but apparently could not fight alone. He was Achilles's equal only as a shadow is the equal of the substance. But he compelled Achilles into the battle.

39. The *synkrisis* between the two begins in grand style with Luke comparing their births (see discussion in Nolland, *Luke 1—9:20*, 19–22).

40. This designation of Jesus as "stronger" (*ischyroteros*) in 3:16 is a recurring quality, perhaps even a title, which appears in contexts relating to both friend and foe (see 11:22, where it appears in the Parable of the Strong Man).

41. De Jonge, "Sonship, Wisdom, Infancy"; Kirchschläger, "Beobachtungen zur Struktur der lukanischen Vorgeschichten Lk 1–2"; Minear, "Luke's Use of the Birth Stories"; Stöger, "Spiritualität der lukanischen Kindheitsgeschichte"; Tatum, "Epoch of Israel"; Talbert, "Immortals in Mediterranean Antiquity"; Talbert, "Prophecies of Future Greatness"; Diefenbach, *Komposition des Lukasevangeliums*.

Minear reviews scholarly efforts at interpreting

in the womb to the role of John's death in changing the geographical route,[42] per-

sonal focus,[43] and pedagogical axis[44] of Jesus, John is a forerunner, helping to prepare Jesus for his destiny. Finding such a *synkrisis* in Luke does not surprise anyone. But finding it in Q might indeed!

The Biographical Genre: Conclusions

Much of what we have concluded about Matthew and laudatory biography is, as we have seen, applicable to the other Gospels and to Acts. One can hardly deny to Mark, Luke, and John the basic *bios* pattern that we find in Matthew. Mark's gospel, for example, is a major source for both Matthew's and Luke's outline of Jesus's ministry. Also, both Luke and Matthew contain redactional additions of a biographical nature (e.g., birth, infancy, ancestry), and employ many of the same *topoi* and literary techniques that seek to glorify Jesus.

---

the infancy narrative, criticizing the tendency to either study the Lucan corpus in isolation from these narratives (Conzelmann) or *vice versa*. He then reviews scholarship which has argued for the inclusion of "the childhood history" (*der Kindheitsgeschichten*) in the exegesis of the Lucan corpus. In any pairing of Jesus and John, the first two chapters of Luke are a programmatic introduction, without which an entire dynamic would be lost. The value of Talbert's essays for the proposal of a *synkrisis* here is the degree to which he helps verify Luke's familiarity with the complex generic characteristics of Hellenistic hero stories. While he may get a little ambitious at times, he has understood exactly the functions of these stories and has been willing to credit a NT author with the competence to understand as well.

Diefenbach provides a full-blown defense and exhibition (*Darstellung*) of Luke's competence in ancient rhetoric, and an interpretation of the text as a hero story focusing more on achievement than historical information. The role of the Baptist in this story is important. Describing Luke's "quasi-biography" of the Baptist as providing a sense of direction and paradigm to the developing narrative- life-path (*Jesuserzählkreises*) of Jesus, and quoting Cadbury who says "in birth, in ministry and in martyrdom he is the complete forerunner of Jesus" (Cadbury, *Making of Luke-Acts*, 44), Diefenbach provides this insightful macrostructure:

The commission from God to the Baptist (Luke 3:2)	The commission from God to Jesus (Luke 3:21—4:13)
Public works of the Baptist (Luke 3:7–18).	Public works of Jesus (Luke 4:14—19:48).
The imprisonment of the Baptist (Luke 3:19–20).	The passion of Jesus (Luke 20:1—23:56)
	The resurrection, appearances and ascension of Jesus Christ (Luke 24:1–53).

What is being suggested here is that this macrostructure, combined with the motif of Jesus's growth, development, and discourses about John, leaves John in the role of the hero's mentor, second self, and perhaps his guide. Diefenbach has apparently not made that claim.

42. It was after John's death (Matt 14:3–12;

Mark 6:17–29) that Jesus withdrew from Galilee, and, one may assume, from the crowds to Tyre and Sidon, and Caesarea Philippi (cf. Matt 15:21; 16:13; Mark 7:24; 8:27). This change in locale would have taken him (at least) out of Herod Antipas's jurisdiction, to the sanctuary of his (half) brother Philip's Tetrarchy. Several interesting things happen here.

43. It was during this retreat that Jesus asked his disciples about *himself*, and in response to their answers began speaking of his own death (Mark 8:31 par; 9:31 par; 10:33–34 par).

44. It is on this retreat also that Jesus articulates that to follow him requires the loss of one's life, the carrying of a cross (Mark 8:34—9:1 par), and servanthood to the point of death (Mark 9:33–37 par; 10:35–45 par).

THE DRAMATIC GENRE: A COMPARISON WITH MARK

Let us explore one final ancient genre: tragic drama.[45] Why would any of the Gospels be regarded as drama? Certainly the Gospels were designed for sectarian reading, not stage presentation. And they were written in colloquial prose, not in poetic verse as most dramas were; and even though large sections of the Gospels consist of dialogue, it is more conversational and less poetic than most dramatic dialogue. And finally, compared to tragic drama of the time, the Gospels were too long and lacked songs.

Reasons for a Comparison with Mark

Despite the above differences between the NT Gospels and tragic drama, a number of significant reasons can be given for comparing the Gospels, especially Mark, with tragic drama. First, both were religious in origin and dealt with religious questions. Second, drama was so prevalent and influential in the Roman era that the Gospel writers must have been acquainted with it. Third, by that time period, drama had become diverse enough in form and function to include a work like Mark's Gospel,

written by a religious teacher for a sectarian audience. Fourth, the Gospel of Mark tends to follow many of the basic components of Greek tragedy outlined in the influential Aristotle's *Poetics*.

A Well-Known Genre

By the Roman period, drama was prevalent throughout the Mediterranean world. Theaters, where comedies and tragedies were performed by a chorus and actors before a live audience, have been discovered in Italy, Greece, France, Asia Minor, Egypt, Syria, Palestine, and Phoenicia. Unlike its modern descendant, ancient drama was connected with religion. Drama was also studied in the classroom.[46] Wherever Hellenism took root, educational institutions transmitted the Greek literary heritage. Therefore the Gospel writers were probably familiar with ancient drama as well as other classical literature.

A Diverse Genre

The form and function of ancient drama also became diverse during the Roman period. Literary or "closet plays" were written for small select groups instead of the public theater. Most of these closet dramas were not written by dramatic poets but by philosophers and historiographers, who generally used them as a medium for propagating their teachings. Some of these closet plays reflected contemporary historical events. Some examples are the nine dramas attributed to the Stoic philosopher Seneca; the play by the Jewish

45. For English translations and critical discussions of Greek and Roman drama, see Oates and O'Neill, *Complete Greek Drama*; and Duckworth, *Complete Roman Drama*. For the Greek and Latin texts, see LCL. For comparisons of Mark and Greek tragedy, see Bilezikian, *Liberated Gospel*; Burch, "Tragic Action in the Second Gospel"; Stock, *Call to Discipleship*; Stone, "Gospel of Mark and *Oedipus the King*"; France, *Gospel of Mark*, 10–20; see discussion of "tragic history" in Aune, *New Testament in Its Literary Environment*, 83–84. Finally, see the majestic Balthasar, *Theo-Drama: Theological Dramatic Theory*, 4 vols. (1988–1994).

46. Marrou, *History of Education in Antiquity*, 161–65, 277–78, 403–4.

The Theater of Ephesus, western Asia Minor, which had a seating capacity of 25,000, was first constructed in the first century BC and modified by the Romans in the first two centuries AD. Reference is made to it in Acts 19:29. (Photo by Charles B. Puskas)

historiographer Nicolaus of Damascus based on the story of Daniel and Susanna; and the Latin drama *Octavia*, reflecting the turbulent reign of Emperor Nero. Therefore Mark's Gospel cannot be excluded from the category of drama simply because it was not written by a dramatic poet for public stage presentation.

A Misunderstood Genre

The Gospels, especially Mark, share more basic components with Greek tragedy than with comedy. Although some of his actions and his associations with the "riff-raff" might recall ancient comedy,[47] Jesus's purpose and fate in Mark qualify him as a tragic hero. This gospel also follows many of the components of tragedy outlined in Aristotle's *Poetics*. Whatever the relationship of the Gospels to Greek tragedy, it is an oversimplification to associate ancient tragedy only with disaster and misfortune. The religious soul of tragedy has been described as the affirmation of moral order, the assertion of transcendence, the mimesis of sacrifice, and faith in the overruling of justice. The tragic element does not necessitate the destruction of the whole world. In fact, "the stormy heavens may break to shed the light of salvation."[48]

Points of Comparison with Mark

Now we will see to what extent Mark follows the characteristics of Greek tragedy as outlined in Aristotle's *Poetics*. Although the views of this influential philosopher

47. Via, *Kerygma and Comedy*, 100.

48. Bilezikian, *Liberated Gospel*, 26–27. See also discussion in Hengel, "Literary, Theological, and Historical Problems," in Stuhlmacher, *Gospel and the Gospels*, 213–17.

of the fourth century BC are not infallible, they are a helpful guide to the basic features of Greek tragedy as understood in antiquity. Aristotle's *Poetics* reveals a keen perception of Greek tragedy, and it is possible that his widely acclaimed views on the subject influenced the subsequent writing of tragedy.

Aristotle held that tragedy was basically an imitation of human beings in action rather than the disposition of the characters (*Poetics* 6.2).[49] Therefore, for him, the most important component of tragedy is its plot, which supplies the action in the play (6.12–18).

According to Aristotle, the plot in a tragedy includes a complication and denouement (18.1). The complication, or "tying of the knot," includes the incidents from the beginning of the story to the point just before the change in the hero's situation. The denouement, or "untying of the knot," consists of everything from the beginning of the change to the end (18.1–3).

In Aristotle's plot-structure scheme, the transition between complication and denouement is called the crisis or turning point. It brings about the change in the course of action. A prologue or opening scene summarizes what has taken place before the beginning of the play. An epilogue also closes the play and is generally brief. Complication-denouement plot structure, prologue, and epilogue are evident in most Greek and Roman plays.

Like most Greek plays, Mark's Gospel begins with a prologue (1:1–13). This convention of providing an introduction and background for the contemporary audience is found in most tragedies (e.g., *Hippolytus, Ajax*). The entrance of the protagonist, Jesus, is announced by John the Baptist, who soon leaves the scene (1:2–9). The statements of the messianic identity of Jesus (1:1,11), the prophetic expectation (1:2–3), and the conflict with evil (1:13), set the tone and inform the audience of the subject matter.

In the complication (1:14—8:26) Jesus is unable to proclaim his messiahship because his contemporaries are unable to recognize the nature of his vocation. Instead, he discloses it only to those who have "eyes to see and ears to hear." Jesus proclaims God's reign and performs various miracles. But those around him fail to perceive the significance of his words and deeds. Their conceptions of a political messiah or great miracle worker have blinded their understanding.

The dramatic tension created by the complication of the unrecognized messiah is partially relaxed when the disciples begin to recognize the messianic identity of Jesus (8:27–30). This pericope of Peter's confession at Caesarea Philippi serves as the crisis, or turning point, of the narrative.

As a result of Peter's confession, the plot moves to its resolution or denouement (8:31—15:47). The ministry of Jesus now has a central focus: the accomplishment of his messianic task. The denouement unfolds along two lines: (1) Jesus prepares the disciples for his death, and (2) the opponents succeed in putting him to death. Jesus instructs his disciples about the necessity of his suffering and death, but they fail to understand, and desert him when he is arrested. After

---

49. Chapters and verses of Aristotle's *Poetics* follow the LCL volume. See also Lucas, *Tragedy: Serious Drama in Relation to Aristotle's Poetics.*

Jesus has effectively challenged the Jewish leaders, they succeed in their scheme to kill him. Even though the death of Jesus was a tragic act, it was also the accomplished goal of his messianic mission. It was a goal to which he, as a tragic hero, nobly submitted.

Mark 16:1–8 serves as an effective closure or epilogue. As in the prologue, the contemporary audience of Mark is addressed in the scene. The audience is informed of the successful outcome of the protagonist by a young man (messenger): "He has risen, he is not here . . . but go tell his disciples . . . that he is going before you to Galilee, there you will see him." (16:6–7). This finale is a dramatic counterpoint to the denouement (the necessity of the Messiah's death). The young man's message is directed to the audience as well as the women at the tomb. The audience also shares with the women the response of fear and awe at this final scene. The brief and sudden closure (16:8) appears to evoke a dramatic suddenness that leaves the audience pondering over the meaning of the story. A stage suddenly left vacant by the main character (the tragic hero) is an acceptable and effective device for ending tragedies.[50]

Following his essential component of plot, Aristotle's second component of tragedy is character or ethos (*Poetics* 6.9). Although his understanding is not limited to it, much of Aristotle's discussion presupposes one dominant figure or hero, which is typical in most tragedies. According to Aristotle, the tragic hero should be (a) characterized by moral purpose, (b) true to type (appropriate), (c) realistic, and (d) consistent in character throughout the play (15.1–6). Aristotle also mentioned that the main character or hero should be of high station and good fortune (13.6). He continues with his noteworthy statement: "This is the sort of man who is not pre-eminently virtuous and just," and yet it is through no evil or villainy of his own that he falls into misfortune but rather through some "flaw in him" (13.5). Aristotle's mention of a hero "not pre-eminently virtuous and just" coincides with his discussion of appropriate and realistic characterization. Aristotle's reference to the hero's falling into misfortune by some "flaw in him" does not connote moral deficiency but some error of judgment (Gk. *hamartia*). It may even consist of a moral bent or quality that is turned into a liability for the hero in unusual circumstances.[51]

In Mark's Gospel, Jesus appears as the tragic hero. His words and deeds are typical of a messianic prophet of first-century Palestine. Exclusive titles like Son of God are used to enhance the nobility of his character. The humanness of his feelings and perceptions gives us a realistic portrayal. The moral purpose of Jesus is consistently depicted in his unshakable determination to fulfill his work. Jesus's drive to complete his mission, his

50. This dramatic effect is achieved in the endings of Aeschylus's *Choerphoroe* (i.e., Libation Bearers), *Eumenides* (Benevolent Beings) and Seneca's *Troades* (Trojan Women). See also Bilezikian, *Liberated Gospel*, 135–36; Stock, *Call to Discipleship*, 50–53.

51. For example, in *Hippolytus* by Euripides, it was the determination of young Hippolytus to resist temptation and remain chaste for the goddess Artemis that caused his downfall. Also in *Oedipus the King* by Sophocles, it is the tragic hero's obsession to know the truth that revealed his own crime. See Bilezikian, *Liberated Gospel*, 110; Mandel, *Definition of Tragedy*, 114, Jesus had a certain hubris, passion or obsession, typical of prophets and tragic heroes.

refusal to escape his fate, and his passive acceptance of violence, however, can also be viewed as heroic moral qualities turned into liability and misfortune by an exceptional set of circumstances (i.e., *hamartia*).

Aristotle's third component of tragedy is the "element of thought," or the message of the play. It should be intelligible and evoke the appropriate response from the listener (19.2–8). The literary techniques of arrangement in Mark's Gospel also imply a concern for the proper transmission of ideas and the responses they should elicit from the reader.

Diction, or the choice of words, expressions, and style, figures prominently in Aristotle's discussion (19.7—22.19). He recommends that diction be clear and not commonplace, in a style worthy of tragedy but not so ornamental as to be unintelligible (22.1). This advice was important since ancient tragedy was intended for public, oral presentation.

The choice of vocabulary and style in Mark's Gospel accords with Aristotle's recommendation that clarity in expression should have priority over nobility in form: "Mark's style and syntax produce an effect of actuation similar to the animated reality of dramatic performances."[52] The following dramatic traits can be cited in Mark's Gospel: descriptive use of the Greek historical present, the impression of immediacy with auxiliary verbs of action, the use of direct discourse and

imperatives to intensify dramatic situations, vividly described scenes, and realism. The Koine Greek of Mark also has close affinities with the spoken dialect of everyday life. Aristotle himself pointed out the similarities between the typical "iambic meter" of Greek tragedy and conversational dialogue (*Poetics* 4.18–19). Furthermore, it was noted earlier that dramatic poetry contains colloquial expressions and descriptive verbs not unlike those in Mark's gospel.

Aristotle's fifth and sixth components of tragedy—spectacle and song—are not directly relevant to Mark's Gospel. Both melody (singing and dance) and spectacle (stage presentation) lost much of their prominence in the Roman period. The literary plays by Seneca, which do not emphasize these components, are an example of this minimization of music and dance. The Gospel of Mark also contains many literary techniques of tragedy mentioned by Aristotle. Concerning the plot (*Poetics* 11), Aristotle recommended achieving the ideal tragic effect (which was, for him, the arousing of pity and fear) by the following three ways: discovery (Mark 8:27–30), reversal of situation (8:31–33), and suffering or pathos (14:43—15:32). Concerning other literary devices, there are at least seven parallels: irony or paradox (1:11–13; 16:6); foreshadowings or forewarnings of disaster (3:6; 8:31); forensic debates between protagonists and antagonists (11:27–33; 12:13–27); *hyporcheme* (song and dance) or outbursts of joy (11:7–10); final oracles of judgment on antagonists (chapter 13); messengers (1:4–9; 16:5–7), and *deus ex machina* (Lat. "god from the machine"), a divine or human character brought out to

52. Bilezikian, *Liberated Gospel*, 113. Based on his discussion of the levels of "genre" and their mixing with other lesser "modes," in *What Are the Gospels?* 38–67, Burridge would allow Mark as a *bios* of Jesus to also contain or display a tragic "mode," 239–40. France sees Mark as a "Drama in Three Acts," *Gospel of Mark*, 10–15.

resolve quickly some desperate situation in the play (16:5–7).

The Dramatic Genre: Conclusion

The foregoing analysis indicates that Mark corresponds with many of Aristotle's characteristics of Greek tragedy. Furthermore, the prevalence of the genre in the Roman world and its diversity (which included literary or closet plays) contribute to the similarities of Mark's Gospel with the ancient category of tragic drama. Certainly Mark could be compared with other ancient genres. Our purpose in this section has been to show that the content of Mark's Gospel is diverse enough to include characteristics from the genre of tragic drama.

THE GOSPEL OF JOHN AND GENRE

John and the Synoptics: A Comparison

Differences

When we read the Gospel of John, we seem to enter a different narrative world from that of the Synoptic Gospels. In contrast to the Synoptics, John introduces us to a distinctly different Jesus: the pre-existent *Logos* (Word), who is God's only Son, the Lamb of God, messiah, and king of Israel (John 1). In the Fourth Gospel, we do not find the straightforward Synoptic parables of Jesus but rather a few complex allegories. The concise synoptic aphorisms have become extended discourses in the form of dramatic dialogues or monologues (John 4; 9; 10). The miracle stories are limited to seven "signs" that glorify Jesus and teach the meaning of

belief. John's emphasis on the Judean ministry of Jesus is evident by the five trips Jesus makes to Jerusalem (2:13; 5:1; 7:10; 10:22, 23; 12:12) in contrast to one visit in Mark (Mark 11) and two in Luke (Luke 2:22; 19:45). In Mark 1:14, Jesus's ministry begins as John the Baptist is imprisoned whereas in John 3:24 the two preachers work side by side.

According to the Synoptic Gospels, the temple was cleansed at the close of Jesus's ministry (Matt 21:12–13; Mark 11:15–19; Luke 19:45–46). In John's account the temple cleansing occurs at the beginning (2:13–22). The dialogue on the eating of Jesus's flesh and the drinking of his blood (John 6) replaces the Last-Supper words in the synoptic tradition (e.g., Mark 14:17–25). John also includes a long farewell discourse of Jesus (chapters 13–17) related to the Synoptic prayer at Gethsemane (e.g., Mark 14:32–42). The Synoptic Gospels agree that the crucifixion of Jesus took place on the Passover (Nisan 15), but John has it before the Passover to coincide with the sacrifice of lambs (John 1:29, 36; 19:30–37). Finally, the length of Jesus's ministry in John is at least three years, whereas in the synoptic tradition it appears to be only one.

It becomes evident from a comparison of John with the Synoptic Gospels that the structural arrangement and thematic emphases of the former are distinctive. John 1:19—12:50 seems to be built on the theme of signs (2:11; 4:54; 12:37); chapters 13–17 are thematic discourses and a prayer, and chapters 18:1—20:31 are a passion narrative. In distinction from the synoptic tradition, we also find in John a high Christology (e.g., the pre-existent Word), a moral dualism (light vs.

darkness, life vs. death), an emphasis on faith, the presence of the Paraclete (chapters 14–16), and realized eschatology (e.g., 3:17–19; 11:25–26).

The Gospel of John also contains stories and discourses not found in the Synoptic Gospels: the wedding at Cana (2:1–11), the narratives concerning Nicodemus (3:1–21) and the Samaritan woman (4:7–42), the healing at the pool of Bethzatha (5:1–9), the healing of the man born blind (9:1–12), the raising of Lazarus (11:1–44), and Jesus's farewell discourse and prayer (chapters 13–17).

Similarities

Despite numerous differences, John and the Synoptics have noteworthy similarities. Narratives that John has in common with the Synoptic Gospels are the call of the disciples (1:35–51), the healing of the official's son (4:46–53), the feeding of the multitude followed by a sea crossing miracle (6:1–21), Peter's confession (6:66–70), the entry into Jerusalem (12:12–15), the cleansing of the temple (2:13–22), the anointing at Bethany (12:1–8), the Last Supper with a prophecy of betrayal (13:1–11), and the basic story of the passion. Events in John that follow Mark's sequence are

(1) The work of the Baptist
(2) Jesus's departure to Galilee
(3) The feeding of a multitude
(4) Jesus's walking on the water
(5) Peter's confession
(6) The departure to Jerusalem
(7) The entry into Jerusalem and the anointing
    (order rearranged in John)

(8) The Supper with predictions of betrayal and denial
(9) The arrest and the passion narrative

The feeding and sea miracles followed by a discourse on bread in John also has parallels with a double cycle tradition in Mark:

Event	Mark	Mark	John
Feeding	6:30–44 (five thousand)	8:1–10 (four thousand)	6:1–14 (five thousand)
Sea crossing	6:45–56	8:10	6:16–21
Controversy	7:1–13	8:11–13	6:15
Teaching on bread	7:14–23	8:14–21	6:22–51

Even though there are verbal differences in the above three accounts, the similar order and themes seem to indicate a common cycle of tradition.

There are also similarities between the Markan and Johannine Passion Narratives:

Event	Mark	John
Anointing for burial	14:3–9	12:2–8, with similar vocabulary
Prediction of betrayal	14:18–21	13:21–30
Prediction of denial[53]	14:27–31	13:36–38
Trial before the high priest	14:54 [55–65]	18:15–18 [19–24]
Trial in context of Peter's denial	14:66–72	18:25–27
Pilate and "the king of the Jews"	15:2–15	18:33–39
Aspects of the crucifixion	15:20–37	19:16–30

53. The bracketing of John's account of the trial by the narrative of Peter's denial, precisely as it appears in Mark, argues favorably for John's dependency on Mark or on a pre-Markan tradition.

Verbal Parallels

Phrase	Mark	John
"Rise, take your pallet, and go home" (different paralytics addressed)	2:11	5:8
Bread worth two hundred denari	6:37	6:7
"a pound of costly ointment or pure nard"	14:3	12:3

The use of identical words and phrases lends further support to the view that John was familiar with either Mark's Gospel or traditions used by Mark. Some think that John knew of Luke's Gospel. See the review essay of Klaus Scholtissek who says that concensus is swinging toward John's familiarity of the Synoptic Gospels (p.445).

Another literary source relationship seems apparent when John and Luke are compared in the story of the anointing (Luke 7:36–50; John 12:3–8). In John 12, the two unusual actions of Mary are explainable if John knew Luke's simpler version. In John she first anoints the feet of Jesus then dries them with her hair (!), whereas in Luke the woman wipes Jesus's feet with her hair before anointing them. John's version seems more complicated and unusual. Luke's account is simpler and less problematic. Luke is also the earliest gospel to include the two ritualistic acts. In Mark 14:3–9, for example, the woman anoints only Jesus's head with no mention of wiping his feet with her hair. Therefore, it seems plausible that the author of John derived both acts of footwashing and anointing from Luke and added his own curious changes which we read in Jn 12:3–8. Even if John was familiar with the Synoptic Gospels, he did not follow them closely.[54]

The Dramatic Genre: A Comparison with John's Gospel

In our comparison of the Gospel of Mark with Greek tragedy, we stressed the similarities between ancient drama and gospel. Like the Gospel of Mark, John's Gospel may also be viewed as a tragedy.[55] An application of Aristotle's theory of tragedy to the Fourth Gospel is likewise appropriate.

An Application of Aristotle's Theory

JOHN'S PROLOGUE

John's prologue (1:1–18), like the prologues of most Greek tragedies, provides an introduction and background for the contemporary audience. John's stylistic use of third-person singular and plural is reminiscent of the prolegomenon recited by the chorus in Aeschylus's *Supplicants*. The content of the prologue also recalls the opening speech in Euripides's *Hippolytus*, where the goddess Aphrodite describes her power and reign before sketching

54. See discussion on John and the Synoptics in Kysar, *Fourth Evangelist and His Gospel*, 54–66; Kysar, "The Gospel of John in Current Research"; Keener, *Gospel of John* 1:40–42; Scholtissek, "Johannine Gospel," 444–72.

55. See the following works on the dramatic character of John: Brant, *Dialogue and Drama*; Connick, "Dramatic Character of the Fourth Gospel"; Lee, "The Drama of the Fourth Gospel"; Domeris, "The Johannine Drama"; Flanagan, "The Gospel of John as Drama"; Smalley, *Evangelist* 192ff.; Witherington, *John's Wisdom*, 4–5. See theo-drama, christo-drama, sēmeio-drama and cruci-drama employed in Köstenberger, *Theology of John's Gospel*, 48, 124, 168–69.

some of the events up to the drama. In John's prologue, the divine identity and preexistence of the *Logos* (Word) set the tone and inform the audience. Then John the Baptist announces the entrance of Jesus the central character.

JOHN'S PLOT COMPLICATION

The Gospel of John conveniently breaks down into the plot structure of: complication (John 1:19—12:19), crisis (12:20–26), and denouement (12:27—20:31). In the complication (1:19—12:19), the audience is immediately drawn into the drama of the divine mission of Jesus the Son of God. The different characters (e.g., Nathanael, Nicodemus, the Samaritan woman, the Jews) typify the responses of belief or unbelief to Jesus's identity and mission. The "hours" (2:4; 8:20; "time" 7:6, 8, 30) unfold the story's plot by raising the questions: When will the hour of Jesus arrive? Why could he not attend a certain feast or be arrested—before his time had come? The statements that flank the complication section (1:14 and 11:40) raise the question, How will God's glory be revealed? The "signs" that Jesus performs manifest God's glory (2:11) but reach a climax in "the hour" when "the Son of Man should be glorified" (12:23).

Suspense in the drama is caused by the unbelief and hate of both the Jews and the world (5:16–18, 42–47; 8:37–59; 10:19–20, 31–33). The schemes and attempts to kill Jesus appear to both jeopardize (8:59; 10:31–33, 39; 11:8) and expedite (11:47–53) the accomplishment of Jesus's mission. Although his disciples are given clues about the "hour" of Jesus's glorification (11:40; 12:7) before

12:20–26, the audience has been informed throughout the drama (1:29; 3:14–15; 8:28; 10:11, 17; 11:50; 12:16). The disciples and other characters in the story are like those in Sophocles's *Oedipus the King* who follow their roles unaware of the full story known to the audience.

JOHN'S PLOT CRISIS

The crisis occurs with the coming of the Greeks (John 12:20–26). Their entry is hinted at in John 7:35. The many references to the "hour/time" (of glorification: 2:4; 5:25,28; 7:6, 30; 8:20) make the statements in John 12:23 a climactic discovery: "the hour has come for the Son of Man to be glorified!" In accordance with Aristotle's recommendations of achieving ideal tragic effect in the plot (*Poetics* 10–11), the crisis of John (as in Mark 8:27–33) consists of the discovery of the hero's tragic role (John 12:23), the anticipated reversal of the hero's situation (life to death, 12:24, 25), and his subsequent pathos or suffering (12:27; 13:21; chapter 19).

JOHN'S PLOT DENOUEMENT

As a result of Jesus's disclosure, the plot moves to its resolution or denouement (12:27—20:31). The denouement has two lines of development: (1) preparing the disciples for Jesus's glorification and departure (chapters 14–17) and (2) the success of the opposition in putting Jesus to death (chapters 18–19). The Fourth Evangelist, like Sophocles, uses the well-known farewell-discourse form to accomplish the denouement of his plot. Despite its numerous ancient parallels (e.g., Gen 47–49;

Deut 31–33; *T12Pat*; Plato, *Phaedo*), the farewell discourse of Jesus (e.g., John 14:18–21) seems to recall the farewell address in Sophocles's *Oedipus at Colonus*: To his grieving daughters he says, "My children, this is day that ends your father's life. All that I was on earth is gone: no longer will you bear the heavy burden of caring for me. It was hard, I know, my children, but one word alone repays you for the labor of your lives—love, my children. You had love from me as from no other man alive, and now your must live without me all your days to come" (lines 126–34, translated by Robert Fagles).

Both John 14:18–21 and the passage from *Oedipus at Colonus* speak of the departure of the father/master, the nearness of the end, and the importance of the ethic of love. Even though the parallels are typical of the genre and the differences are evident (e.g., Oedipus leaves little hope of his return), the concentration of similar themes in two similar passages is noteworthy. Both John and Sophocles appear to use a similar farewell-discourse form to accomplish the denouements of their respective plots.

The chief antagonist who brings about Jesus's arrest is Judas, whom Satan has possessed (John 6:70–71; 13:2, 26–27). It is through Judas (and his Jewish collaborators) that the "ruler of this world," the "evil one," is revealed (14:30; 16:11; 17:12, 15). The trial scenes provide the forensic debates with the accusers and judges serving as foils for the hero (18:12—19:16). The forensic setting of John is similar to that of Aeschylus's *Prometheus Bound*. In that play, the attention is on Prometheus and the question of his guilt for breaking a rule of Zeus, i.e., giving humans the knowledge of making fire.

The "hour" of glorification (17:1, 4) is accomplished with Christ's being lifted up on the cross (19:25–27). The somber setting of the burial scene (19:38—20:11) is enlivened by the surprise appearance of the Lord (20:16ff.: cause for song and dance, *hyporchēma*). He now affirms the faith of his disciples and bestows on them the Holy Spirit (20:21–22).

JOHN'S EPILOGUE

The epilogue, or closing narration (20:30–31),[56] functions like the brief concluding chorus in a Greek tragedy, which often summarizes its contents (e.g., see Sophocles's *Antigone* or Euripides's *Medea* or *Hippolytus*).

Common Motifs

John's gospel also shares at least six motifs with Greek tragedies, some of which we have already mentioned. First, the content of the prologue (1:1–18) resembles of the opening speech in Euripides's *Hippolytus*, where the goddess Aphrodite describes her power and reign before sketching some of the events leading up to the drama. Second, the sign performed by Jesus at Cana (2:1–11) recalls the actions of the god Dionysius, who also transforms water into wine (Euripides, *Bacchae*, lines 704–7). Third, the motif of the vicarious suffering of Jesus (1:29; 10:11, 17–18; 11:50; 12:16, 23–24; 15:13; 19:36–37) is reminiscent of the self-sacrifice of Alcestis, who dies in place of her husband, Admetus (Euripides, *Alcestis*).

---

56. We regard John 21 to be a later addition to the tragic drama of which John 1:1–18 was already an intrinsic (although added) part.

Fourth, the farewell discourse of Jesus (e.g., 14:18–21) recalls the farewell address in Sophocles's *Oedipus at Colonus*. In this play, a messenger relays to the daughters of Oedipus the king's farewell words explaining the necessity of his absence from them, the great love he has for them, and the need for them to carry on without him (lines 1585–1658).[57] Even the theme of universal love (e.g., John 15) is found in Sophocles's *Antigone* (lines 522–23). The motif of union with God (John 14; 17) also has parallels in Sophocles's *Oedipus the King*, line 314, and *Oedipus at Colonus*, line 247.

Fifth, the trial scenes in John (18:12—19:16) are reminiscent of the forensic debates in Aeschylus's *Prometheus Bound*. The play focuses on the question of the guilt and punishment of Prometheus for his breaking a rule of Zeus by giving humans the knowledge of making fire. Sixth, the motif of the risen Christ, who avoids being touched (John 20:17), recalls the play *Alcestis*, by Euripides. Alcestis is brought back from the dead but cannot speak to her husband until she is consecrated after three days (lines 1140–50).

The above six motifs are only a selection of similarities between John's Gospel and Greek tragedy.[58] Some may be coincidental, and others could reflect John's acquaintance with Greek tragedy, since this form of drama was prevalent in the Roman world. It would also be understandable for the Fourth Gospel to share some motifs with other Greek plays, if John is a type of Greek tragedy.

CONCLUDING SUMMARY

In conclusion, we have looked at several generic possibilities in our attempt to understand the Gospels in their ancient context. The Gospels as ancient biographies and Acts as Hellenistic historiography, for example, carry generic weight for many today and perhaps did for those in antiquity. Nevertheless, Walter J. Ong's cautionary note about literary genre has relevance for both ancient and modern literature: "Just as a poem or other work of art as word resists complete framing as an 'object' thought of as clearly and distinctly outlined in space, so it resists complete framing in terms of types and genres. For these represent an attempt to define, to delimit, to mark off . . . which can never be entirely satisfactory."[59] Father Ong's warning should not discourage the pursuit of genre studies of the New Testament books, but rather should mitigate our attempts to limit or define through overconfidence in the clarity of our criteria about the style, structure, or intent of these ancient writings of renown that still challenge each generation of readers with the question, "what does this mean" (Acts 2:12b)?

---

57. Oates and O'Neill, *Complete Greek Drama* 1:664–65.

58. For other similar motifs of John and Greek tragedies see Barrett, *John*, 380, 444, 474, 520; Brant, *Dialogue and Drama* studies both classical and theater criticism notes that dialogue in tragedies is always between two or three actors and a collective voice—the same style of dialogue used in John's Gospel, which functions in many ways as a performance text.

59. Ong, "A Dialectic of Aural and Objective Correlatives," originally published in 1958, and later reprinted in *20th Century Literary Criticism*, 505.

7

The Ancient Letter Genre

In the previous chapter we looked at NT books composed in a basic narrative framework: the four Gospels and Acts. Although they include large amounts of direct discourse, such as sayings, speeches, and dialogues, the Gospels and Acts mostly contain narrative materials (e.g., miracle stories and historical legends). Also, the direct discourse in these books is joined by narrative comments and summary statements that permeate each work. The epistolary literature is primarily direct discourse. Its small amount of narrative material is mostly autobiographical. Much of its hymns, sayings, and teaching material is part of a dialogue between author and reader. Both the audience and the author are generally specified in this genre. The pronouns that dominate it are characteristic of direct discourse: "I," "we," and "you" (sing. and pl.). Subsumed within the broader category of ancient letter are homilies and expositions. These categories are mostly practical exhortation and doctrinal expositions of

Scripture typical of Jewish homilies (e.g., 4 Maccabees; Tob 4; Wis 1–5) and early Christian sermons (e.g., Acts 13:15–43; Hebrews; 2 *Clement*).[1] Also classified under "letter" are the so-called epistles of John. This is merely a convenience, since all do not exhibit the formal characteristics of letters (e.g., 1 John has no elements of letter form).[2]

THE LETTER GENRE: ITS IMPORTANCE

In the NT twenty-one of the twenty-seven books are labeled letters, and both Acts and Revelation contain them (Acts 15:23–29; Rev 1:4—3:22). Despite its prevalence

1. See Stegner, "Ancient Jewish Synagogue Homily," in Aune, *Greco-Roman Literature*, 51–70; Malherbe, *Moral Exhortation*; Schroeder, "Exhortation"; Schroeder, "Paranesis"; Koester, *Hebrews*; Witherington, *Letters and Homilies*, 20–21, 40–50.

2. See R. E. Brown, *Epistles*, 86–100; Kruse, *Letters of John*; Köstenberger, *Theology of John's Gospel and Letters*, 125–26.

in the NT, all twenty-one books are not complete letters, and the types we find are diverse. The letter to the Hebrews is actually a homily (or sermon), and both 2 Timothy and 2 Peter are farewell discourses with epistolary features. First Peter, Ephesians, and Jude appear to be homilies in letter form; 1 Timothy, Titus, and James are basically exhortations on worship and ethics. First John seems to be a midrash of John's Gospel, and 2 and 3 John are typical letters. Even the undisputed letters of Paul show diversity: Philemon is a combination of personal/pastoral and recommendation/official correspondence, and Romans is a long letter essay. The forms of argumentation or rhetoric used by Paul in his letters are also varied.

Basic Characteristics of Ancient Letters

The basic characteristics of the letter genre have changed little in history. Letters are a form of written communication between two parties when person-to-person contact is impossible or inappropriate. Letters presuppose a sender and addressee; everyone else is a third-party outsider. The sender's side of the dialogue dominates the letter. The addressee's conversation can be inferred but is not fully articulated until the addressee responds in written form as a sender. Letters are also occasional, written in response to some situation or set of circumstances. Something prompts the sender to write, even if it is merely the fact of physical distance. Letters are often spontaneous, written in reaction to an incident. The above observations apply to all letters, whether they are informal, personal, and private, or formal, official, and public.

Six Basic Types

From the hundreds of letters of antiquity, at least six basic letter types have been discovered.[3]

1. Person-to-person letters: love letters, letters of friendship, private business letters, recommendation or introduction letters between family or friends (e.g., *Letters to Friends* from Cicero, 3 John and Philemon [recommendation], papyri letters from Egypt).

2. Business letters: dealing with trade taxes, wills, land (e.g., Egyptian papyri).

3. Official letters: from political or military leaders to constituents, subservients, or superiors (e.g., letters from Augustus, letters of Pliny to Trajan, all of Paul's authentic letters according to Stirewalt).

4. Public letters: literary, public pleas and philosophical treatises (e.g., letters from Isocrates, Plato; "epistle," according to Deissmann).

5. Fictitious letters: these may purport to come from heaven, or be an epistolary novel or pseudonymous (letters of Hippocrates, *Letter of Aristeas*, 2 *Clement*, Revelation 2–3 [according to Deissmann]).

6. Discursive or essay-exposition of teaching letters, monographs (e.g., 2 Macc 1; *Mart. Pol.*; Romans [according to Deissmann])

---

3. On functional "letter" and literary "epistle," see Deissmann, *Light from the Ancient East*; Brown, *Introduction*, 410–12; on letter types, see Doty, *Letters*; Roetzel, *Letters*; Klauck, *Ancient Letters*; Evans, *Ancient Texts*, 287–328; on Paul's official letter style, see Stirewalt, *Paul*, chs. 2–3.

There is some overlapping of the above categories. We find personal letters of Roman officials written to friends and family. Fictitious letters include those of a novelistic type (Themistocles, Chion of Heraclea), letters purporting to come from heaven (Revelation 2–3, according to Deissmann), and pseudonymous documents or homilies written in the name of or attributed to some famous individual (*Letter of Jeremiah*, *Letter of Aristeas*, *2 Peter*, *2 Clement*). The contents of these subcategories vary greatly. In the New Testament, Philemon is a combination of personal/pastoral and recommendation/official correspondence. Although it has a specified sender and addressees, Romans is a lengthy letter essay or essay-letter. Ephesians, regarded by many as Deutero-Pauline, reads more as a theological treatise and literary "epistle" than a genuine letter.

Fixed Patterns

Letters of antiquity followed a basic pattern as they do today. In modern personal letters we see the following fixed forms:

(1) Indication of place and date: Boston, MA; May 18, 2010

(2) Name of recipient: Dear Ahmed

(3) Apology for not writing sooner

(4) Statement of writer's good health and the hope that the recipient is in good health

(5) Body

(6) Salutation: "yours truly" with name of sender.

In ancient letters we detect the following pattern:

(1) Opening (sender, [co-sender], addressee[s], greeting)

(2) Thanksgiving, wish for health

(3) Body (formal opening, background, followed by the business that occasioned the letter)

(4) Closing (greetings, [notation of autograph], wishes for other people, final greeting, wish or prayer, sometimes a date)

Here is an example of an ancient person-to-person letter (of a son to his father) using the above fixed form:

> **Opening:** Apion to Epimachus, his father and lord, heartiest greetings. *Thanksgiving;* First of all I pray that you are in health and continually prosper and fare well with my sister and her daughter and my brother.
> **Body:** I thank the lord Sarapis that when I was in danger at sea he saved me. Straightway upon entering Misenum I received traveling money from Caesar, three gold pieces. And I am well. I beg you therefore, honored father, write me a few lines, first regarding your health, secondly regarding that of my brother and sister, thirdly that I may welcome respectfully your hand [writing] . . .
> **Closing:** Greetings to Capito, to my brother and sister, to Sernilla and to my friends. I send you by Euctemon a little portrait of myself. My military name is Antonius Maximus. I pray for your good health. Athenonike Company.[4]

Paul's letters also have elements of official correspondence (e.g., a ruler to

---

4. Derived from Deissmann, *Light from the Ancient East*, 179–83; Klauck, *Ancient Letters*, 9–14 (with commentary).

his constituents) that include co-senders (e.g., Timothy, Silvanus, Sosthenes), a lengthy letter body offering background for and explanation of the pertinent business to be discussed, and a closing subscription that may include an autograph notation (1 Cor 16:21; Gal 6:1).[5] Paul also expands various portions and adds new features to the above person-to-person letter pattern. First, the thanksgiving section is usually expanded (e.g., Phil 1:3–11; 1 Thess 1:2—2:16). Second, pastoral or theological features are added: (a) an eschatological comment that concludes certain sections (1 Cor 1:8–9; 4:6–13; 1 Thess 3:11–13); (b) mention of travel plans (Phil 2:19–24; 1 Thess 2:17—3:13); (c) a section of parenesis or ethical exhortations (Rom 12:1—15:13; Eph 4:1—6:20; 1 Thess 4:1—5:22); and (d) a doxology or benediction is included (Rom 15:33; 16:20, 25–27; 1 Thess 5:28). With these features in view, the following outline will be presented on the basic pattern of early Christian letters.

(1) Opening (sender, co-sender, addressees, greeting)

(2) Thanksgiving (often with a prayer of intercession and an eschatological ending)

(3) Body (formal opening, background, explanation of business, often mentioning travel plans and an eschatological ending)

(4) Parenesis (ethical exhortation)

(5) Closing (greetings, autograph notation, doxology, benediction)

THE USE OF THE LETTER FORM BY EARLY CHRISTIANS

What type of letters were written by early Christians like the Apostle Paul? From two examples within his undisputed letters we find a diversity of types. Paul's letter to Philemon is a personal and pastoral letter of recommendation with some aspects of official correspondence (e.g., co-sender Timothy). It does not appear to be written as an epistle for a literary public but instead to Philemon, Apphia, Archippus, and his house-church. Similar kinds of letters are found among the Egyptian papyri and elsewhere. Paul's Letter to the Romans, although a genuine letter, is a letter-essay similar to the literary epistles of Epicurus, Cicero, and Plutarch.[6] This lengthy exposition of religious teaching and ethics was probably intended to be circulated in Rome and elsewhere.

Four Features of Official Correspondence

Early Christian letters share at least four features mentioned earlier, which give them an official quality: (1) the frequent

5. See Stirewalt, *Paul*, Appendix, for sample letters of official correspondence, e.g., Josephus, *Life* 216–18, 226–27; *Ant* 13.127–28; Demosthenes, *Or.* 18 (*De Corona*) 39; *Oxyrhynchus Papyrus* 2108 (AD 259). On the imperial letter of Claudius to the Alexandrians (with commentary), see Klauck, *Ancient Letters*, 83–101. See also our "Four Features of Official Correspondence" below.

6. The letters attributed to the third-century-BC Greek philosopher Epicurus are in Diogenes Laertius, *Lives of Eminent Philosophers* 10.35–38, 84–116, 122–35; Klauck, *Ancient Letters*, 149–55. On the letters of Roman orator and philosopher Cicero (first century BC), see Letters to Atticus and also to Quintus and Brutus, discussed in Klauck, 156–65; those of the first-century-AD Greek biographer Plutarch are in his *Moralia* 478A; 502B; 783A, see also Aune, *The New Testament in Its Literary Environment*, ch. 5 and his *WDNTECLR*, 162–68, 267–72; Evans, *Ancient Texts*, 298–300.

use of an amanuensis or executive secretary (Rom 16:22; 1 Cor 16:21; Gal 6:11; Col 4:18; 2 Thess 3:17); (2) the mention of co-senders or co-workers as messengers who deliver the letters (e.g., Rom 16:1–2; 1 Cor 16:10; 2 Cor 8:16–18; Phlm 10–12; Eph 6:21; Col 4:7); (3) the mention of the sender's apostolic authority, making the letter an official pronouncement (Rom 1:1, 11; 1 Cor 1:1; 2 Cor 1:1; Gal 1:1; Eph 1:1); and (4) mention of the sender's associates, often in the opening (1 Cor 1:1; 2 Cor 1:1; Phil 1:1; Col 1:1; Phlm 1). The use of secretaries (Lat. *amanuenses*) and messengers was typical with ancient letters. The presence of an amanuensis, the presence of the sender's co-worker, and the sender's apostolic authority combined to give most early Christian letters an official quality not unlike that of a ruler's correspondence to his constituents.

Eight Literary Forms

In the letters of Paul and other early Christians we find numerous literary forms, for instance:

1. *Autobiography.* These are statements about the sender's experiences and situation. In the case of Paul they refer to the travels and experiences of his apostolic ministry (2 Cor 1:8–10; 7:5; 12:1–10; Phil 1:12–14; 1 Thess 2:1–12). Some accounts also seek to defend his apostolic authority (Gal 1:11—2:14; 1 Cor 9).

2. *Apocalyptic material.* These unveilings of the end time refer to the Lord's coming, to apostolic afflictions and trials, and to other more typical features of the apocalyptic (e.g., angels, demons, the new Jerusalem, final judgment). Apocalyptic features symbolic language and may include visions, blessings, and special revelations. See, e.g., 1 Thess 4:13—5:11; 2 Thess 1:5–10; 2:1–17; 1 Cor 15:12–28; Jude; 2 Pet 2–3; Heb 1–2; Revelation; cf., Daniel, 2 Baruch, 4 Ezra.

3. *Catalogues and lists.* These include the Hellenistic lists of vices and virtues (e.g., Gal 5:19–23; Col 3:5–15; cf., Diogenes Laertius, *Lives* 7.92–95; Plutarch, *Mor.* 3–4), household rules (e.g., Col 3:18—4:1; Eph 5:21—6:9; Titus 2:1–10), and rules for the community (e.g., 1 Tim 2; 5; 1 Pet 2:13—3:7). Some lists are merely descriptive and lead to threats of condemnation or to a contrast with Christian behavior (Rom 1:18–32; 1 Cor 6:9–11). Other lists are parenetic and are utilized for teaching a moral code of behavior (Gal 5:16–24; Col 3:5–11).

4. *Catechesis.* Specific accounts of teaching on Christian holiness are found in 1 Thess 4:1–9 and 1 Pet 1:13–22. Other passages teach abstinence from evil and the pursuit of righteousness (Eph 4:22–25; Col 3:8—4:12).

5. *Confessional statements.* These brief honorific titles confessing faith in Jesus as God's agent are found in Rom 10:9; 1 Cor 11:23; and 1 Tim 3:16.

6. *Hymns.* These traditional elements are probably fragments of songs originally used in worship. There are hymns about Christ (Phil 2:2–11; Col 1:15–20; 1 Pet 2:21–24) and baptism (Romans 6; Eph 2:19–22; Titus 3:4–7), to use two examples. Hymn-like passages usually distinguish themselves

from their context by a conscious parallelism, unique vocabulary, and special grammatical features.

7. *Kerygma.* This pertains to specific preaching accounts about Christ. These accounts often refer to prophetic fulfillment accomplished by Christ, his crucifixion, resurrection, and exaltation, and point to the promise of this coming with a subsequent call to repentance (e.g., Rom 1:1–3; 1 Cor 15:1–7; Gal 1:3–4; see also Acts 2:14–29; 10:36–43).

8. *Prophetic denouncements.* Like the denouncements in the Hebrew prophetic writings, prophetic denouncements in NT letters can include: (a) an introduction, (b) a statement of offense, (c) a punishment threatened, and (d) a hortatory conclusion (e.g., Gal 1: 6–9; Rom 1:18–32; 1 Cor 5:1–13; 2 Thess 1:5–12; cf., Amos 8:4–8; Hos 4–5; Mic 6).

Four Stylistic Features

It is no surprise that the early Christian letters are replete with the stylistic habits and thought patterns of late antiquity. This diversity of literary and stylistic features includes (1) principles of literary balance, (2) figures of speech, (3) rhetorical devices, and (4) grammatical and stylistic peculiarities.

Literary Balance

Two types of literary balance found in Hebrew poetry and Hellenistic literature are evident in early Christian letters:

regular and inverted parallelism.[7] Regular parallelism follows the AB:A′B′ pattern, where the elements of the second group are repeated in the same order as in the first. In early Christian letters, as in Hebrew poetry, regular parallelism is usually confined to smaller units and involves contrasting as well as synonymous correspondence. The following pattern from 1 Cor 9:20 is an example of synonymous parallelism:

(A) To the Jews

  (B) I become as a Jew

    (C) in order to win the Jews

(A′) To those under the law

  (B′) I became as one under the law

    (C′) that might win those under the law.

Here the thoughts of the first stanza (A–B–C) are repeated with different words in the second stanza (A′–B′–C′). Examples of antithetical or contrasting parallelism are found in Rom 4:25; 5:10; 1 Cor 7:29–34; 10:6–10; 2 Cor 5:13.

Inverted parallelism, or chiasm, is another principle of balance detected in early Christian letters. This introverted A–B:B′–A′ pattern also occurs in Greco-Roman and other early Christian literature (e.g., Herodotus, *History*; Virgil, *Aeneid*; Luke-Acts). In Rom 2:6–11 we find the following chiastic pattern:

7. Gottwald, "Poetry, Hebrew"; Bauer, "Chiasm"; Lund, *Chiasmus in the New Testament*; Breck, *Shape of Biblical Language*; Talbert, *Reading Corinthians*, 16–17, 85–86.

(A) God judges all (v. 6)

    (B) the righteous receive eternal life (v. 7)

        (C) the wicked receive wrath (v. 8)

        (C′) the wicked experience distress (v. 9)

    (B′) the good experience glory (v. 10)

(A′) God is impartial (v. 11)

Figures of Speech

The language of the early Christian letters, and human language in general, abounds with symbolic words and images.[8] Therefore only a few examples of this nonliteral use of language will be given. We will look at the figures of comparison and contradiction, as well as at rhetorical questions and assertions.

Figures of comparison occur when familiar images are employed to clarify, highlight, or dramatize the speaker's ideas through analogy or illustration. Comparisons are drawn from family relations, the human body, sickness and death, nature, various trades, war, and athletic contests. Figures of comparison include the simile, where the comparison is expressed, and metaphor, where it is implied. Paul's use of simile can be seen in 1 Thess 2:7: "like a nurse (Gk. *trophos*) tenderly caring for her own children." Other examples are found in Rom 9:27–29; 1 Cor 3:1; 4:13; 2 Cor 6:8–10; Gal 4:14; Phil 2:15, 22. First Peter and James also contain many similes. Metaphors carry greater semantic power. In Gal 5:1, Paul states, "do not submit again to a yoke of slavery," and employs the imagery of slave constraints (cf. Sir 33:25–26) to describe the Galatians' futile lapse into Jewish legalism. Paul also uses slave imagery positively to depict his obligatory relationship to Christ: Paul, a "slave (Gk. *doulos*) of Christ" (Rom 1:1; Gal 1:10). Other metaphors used by Paul are "sowing and reaping," "fruit of the Spirit," "body of Christ," and "stumbling block." These familiar images of everyday life were effective vehicles for conveying Paul's teaching.

Figures of contradiction are irony and paradox. Irony, a statement that intends to convey its opposite meaning, occurs frequently in 2 Cor 10–13. In these chapters Paul's dialogue with the boastful charlatans of Corinth is full of irony and sarcasm in the Socratic tradition (Plato *Symp*. 175E; see also 1 Cor 4:8; 6:4; 2 Cor 5:3).

Paradox, or an apparent contradiction that may reveal some profound truth, occurs often. For Paul, the crucifixion is a foundational paradox (1 Cor 1:22–25). Paradoxical statements are also found in Rom 7:15, 19; 1 Cor 7:22; 2 Cor 4:8–11; 5:17; 6:9–10; 12:10; Phil 3:7.

Rhetorical questions require no direct answer but attract the attention of the hearer. This provocative use of interrogation was widely employed by Hellenistic philosophers like Seneca and Epictetus. Paul in Rom 6:15 asks: "What then? Should we sin because we are not under law but under grace? By no means!" The answer, generally given, is self-evident, but the rhetorical device itself is

8. For further study, see Bullinger, *Figures of Speech*; Caird, *Language and Imagery*; Soulen, *Handbook*; Turner, *Style*, vol. 4 in Moulton, *Grammar*; Williams, *Paul's Metaphors*; Tate, *Interpreting the Bible*; see, e.g., Stowers on Romans 7 in Meeks, *The Writings of St. Paul*, 525–38.

effective in evoking a response. Rhetorical questions occur frequently in Romans (2:3–4, 21–23; 3:1–9, 27–29; 4:1; 6:1; 9:19; 11:1) and James (2:4, 6–7, 20–21, 25; 4:1, 4, 14). Rhetorical assertions are numerous, so only a few examples will be given. Hyperbole, or exaggeration for the sake of emphasis, is found in Gal 1:8, "But even if we or an angel from heaven should proclaim to you a gospel contrary to what we preached to you, let that one be accursed!" See also Gal 4:15; 5:12. Hyperbole is used often in prophetic denouncements or judicial indictments (e.g., Matt 23; Jas 5:1–6). Assertions of understatement, called *meiosis*, are also found in Gal 5:23: "There is no law against such things," and in Rom 1:16: "For I am not ashamed of the gospel." Those understatements, the opposite of hyperbole, are used for emphasis or convey a certain effect. Another form of understatement is *litotes*, which affirms a fact by denying its opposite: "they make much of you, for no good purpose" (Gal 4:17). *Litotes* is also used in Acts (Acts 12:18; 19:11; 21:39). This cautious use of language was effective in courtroom rhetoric (e.g., in the case of Lysias against the thirty tyrants: Cicero, *Inv.* 2.26–27).

Rhetorical Devices

Rhetorical devices coincide with the previous category, since ancient techniques of effective speaking and persuasion employed much figurative language. First, we will examine those dialogical and rhetorical features that Paul shares with the Hellenistic diatribe, then briefly look at the types of Hellenistic oratory with which the letters of Paul coincide.

Some early Christian letters, e.g., Romans 2–11 and James 2, seem to employ the dialogical features of the diatribe.[9] This form of discourse and discussion probably originated in philosophical schools, where a teacher would try to expose the errors of his students and lead them into truth. It was previously thought that the diatribe was a form of Cynic propaganda for the masses, but this viewpoint only finds some support in a few sources (e.g., Bion, Dio of Prusa). Most of the primary documents for the diatribe were written by teachers of philosophical schools: e.g., Teles Bion (third century BC); Epictetus *Discourses* (first century AD); Musonius Rufus (first cent. AD); Plutarch (first cent. AD); Seneca *Moral Essays* (first century AD). Since the diatribe presupposes a student-teacher setting, it was probably not addressed to outsiders and does not contain polemics against opponents, as some scholars have previously held.

The diatribe envisions two audiences: one real and one imagined. The real audience comprises disciples of the author who are in need of further enlightenment. The imagined audience includes a fictitious dialogue partner or objector, who represents a false viewpoint. The dialogue opens with an address of indignation (apostrophe) to this imaginary interlocutor, who is usually a caricature of a proud or pretentious person and represents the false views of the real audience. A dialogical exchange follows in which the author resolves objections to his viewpoint or corrects false conclusions drawn from his line of reasoning. These objections and false conclusions are usually raised by the imaginary interlocutor. The purpose of

9. See Stowers, *The Diatribe*; Song, *Reading Romans as Diatribe*; Malherbe, "*Mē Genoito* in the Diatribe and Paul"; Jewett, *Romans*, 25–27; Aune, *WDNTECLR*, 127–29.

the dialogue is to lead the real audience into truth by exposing false thinking or behavior.

The above discussion of diatribe has significance for understanding the argumentation in Romans and James. Both contain many of its dialogical features. In Rom 1–11, for example, the dialogical style is central to the letter's message. Paul and the author of James probably used the diatribe to expose error and to lead their readers into a deeper commitment to the Christian life. It is probable that the diatribe was one of the major teaching techniques of early Christianity.

Since the NT letters are primarily written dialogues and discourses, and many are sermons in letter form, they have close affinities with Hellenistic oratory. According to the influential works on persuasion and public speaking by Aristotle, Cicero, and Quintilian, different types of speeches are characterized by a certain arrangement.[10] Political speeches and funeral orations concerned with merits and honor were called *epideictic* or demonstrative. Their function to display common virtues and values is similar to the purpose of Paul's letter to the Romans (cf. Colossians, Ephesians, 2 Timothy, 2 Peter, and Jude). Courtroom or judicial speeches concerned with justice (accusatory or defensive) coincide well with the *apologetic* functions of Galatians 1–4 and 2 Cor 10–13. Speeches that provide advice

for future decisions were labeled *symboleutic* or deliberative. First Corinthians 7–16, where Paul provides specific advice to his readers, seems to fit this category (cf. 2 Corinthians 8–9, Philemon, 1 Timothy, Titus, Hebrews, and James).

The arrangement of these types of speeches falls into the basic pattern of: (a) introduction or *exordium* (e.g., Rom 1:1–15; Gal 1:6–10; Heb 1:1—4:16); (b) *propositio*, or thesis to be demonstrated (Gal 1:11–12); (c) the facts of the case, or *narratio* (Gal 1:11—2:14; Heb 5:1—6:20); (d) argumentation, called *probatio* (Gal 3:1—4:31) or *confirmatio* (Rom 1:18—15:13; Heb 7:1—10:18; and (e) closing summation, or *peroratio* (Gal 6:11–18; Rom 15:14—16:23; Heb 10:19—13:21).

Stylistic Peculiarities

The following examples of stylistic peculiarities will be examined: (a) abrupt changes in syntax and thought, (b) unclear idioms, and (c) borrowings from the Septuagint (LXX). Abrupt changes in syntax and thought occur frequently in Paul's letters. The technical term for such a sudden break is *anacoluthon* (Greek), but some of the phenomenon could be interpreted as either a parenthesis (i.e., a clause inserted into a sentence without regard for its syntax) or an interpolation (i.e., a block of inserted material by the author or a later editor).

An example of anacoluthon is found in Rom 2:15–16, where Paul is talking about the conscience of the Gentiles serving as their moral umpire before he suddenly breaks in with "on that day when, according to my gospel, God judges the secrets of men by Christ Jesus." The change of both thought and sentence structure is

10. On Hellenistic rhetoric and the NT, see Betz, *Galatians*; Kennedy, *Interpretation through Rhetorical Criticism*; and Kennedy, *Progymnasmata*; Wuellner, "Where Is Rhetorical Criticism Taking Us?"; Porter and Stamps, *Rhetorical Criticism*; Witherington, *New Testament Rhetoric*; Aune, *WDNTECLR*, 414–25; for rhetorical outlines of Paul's letters (disputed plus undisputed) and Hebrews, see Puskas, *Letters of Paul*.

sudden and unexpected. It may be either intentional or unintentional—either a stylistic device to arouse the reader's attention or the result of an author's losing his previous train of thought as a new idea is suddenly pursued. Other examples of anacolutha are 2 Cor 1:22–23; Gal 2:4–6; and a large digression in 2 Cor 6:14—7:1.

Parenthetical phrases are often noted in English translations: e.g., Rom 1:13 ("but thus far have been prevented"); 2 Cor 11:21 ("I am speaking as a fool"); 2 Pet 2:8 (entire verse). An interpolation (or gloss) is a larger insertion of material disrupting the original flow of thought. It is either the work of the author or of a later editor. In 2 Corinthians it has been argued that 6:14—7:1 is an interpolation by a later editor, because (a) there is no direct connection of 6:14—7:1 to what precedes or follows, (b) 2 Cor 6:13 and 7:2 connect smoothly without the passage, and (c) the vocabulary and conceptions are never or rarely used by Paul elsewhere (leading to the hypothesis that the section is non-Pauline). Examples of other possible interpolations are Phil 3:2—4:3 (a later polemical fragment by Paul?) and 1 Thess 2:13–16 (a post-70 denouncement of the Jews?).

Idiomatic expressions are unclear to modern readers for at least two reasons. First, they are cultural statements foreign to us. Second, the sender often assumes that intended readers are already familiar with their meanings. Remember that we are outsiders reading these ancient letters from a third-party perspective. One random example is in Gal 3:20, translated literally: "now the mediator involves more than one party, but God is one." In v. 19 Paul speaks of the law as being ordained by angels through a mediator, but com-

mentators are unsure about what inference Paul is trying to establish in v. 20. For other examples of unclear idioms, the meanings of which are important for understanding the overall arguments, see Rom 3:7; 8:22; 1 Cor 2:16c; 15:29 (the last reference probably reflects an ancient practice).

Borrowings from the LXX are numerous in early Christian letters. Over seventy direct quotations from the Jewish Scriptures (from Greek and perhaps from Hebrew texts) are made in Paul's letters, as the discussion on source criticism in chapter 5 pointed out. Sometimes explicit mention is made of a source (e.g., Rom 1:17; 9:29), and frequently sources are not stated (e.g., Rom 10:13; 1 Cor 2:16; 5:13; 10:26). In some places Paul's entire discussion is permeated with a wide variety of lengthy scriptural quotations: e.g., Romans 9–11 (citing Isaiah, Jeremiah, Hosea, Joel, Deuteronomy, the Psalms, Leviticus, Exodus, Proverbs, and 1 Kings). Generally such passages are the most difficult to interpret, because the modern reader is unfamiliar with Paul's rabbinic methods of interpreting the Jewish Scriptures.[11] Many of Paul's awkward sentence constructions are also due to his use of septuagintal or Semitic phrasings (Rom 10:5–17). What has been mentioned here of Paul's letters also applies to the non-Pauline correspondence, since all make ample use of the LXX, although the selection of passages and their interpretations are usually different.

11. Weingreen, et al., "Interpretation, History of"; M. P. Miller, "Midrash"; Ellis, *Paul's Use of the Old Testament*; Stegner, "Rom 9:1–29—Midrash"; Longenecker, *Biblical Exegesis*, 6–35, 88–139; Hays, *Echoes of Scripture*, chs. 1–2, and his *Conversion of Imagination*, 25–49; Beale and Carson, *Commentary on the New Testament Use of the Old Testament*.

8

The Genres of the Apocalypse (Revelation)* of John**

As we tried to imply in the last two chapters, the disclosure of literary genre is intended to be a momentous event in the introduction of a text, tantamount perhaps to the discovery of an edible species

* *Apocalypse* is a close but not-exact transliteration of the Greek word *apokalypsis*, which suggests *the uncovering of something* (like your head when you remove a cap). The Vulgate (Latin translation) of this book of visions begins this way: *Apocalypsis Iesou Christi*, transliterating *apokalypsis* (rather than translating) from the Greek word; elsewhere the Vulgate gives *revelatio* as a Latin gloss for the word. In most English translations the word is, even here in the *Inscriptio* (the inscription or title of the book itself) translated with the gloss "revelation." Hence the book is known in much of the English-speaking world as Revelation or the book of Revelation or the Revelation of John, Saint John, St. John the Divine, etc.; and sometimes incorrectly as Revelations! Here in this chapter we will call it Revelation, the book of Revlation, or the Apocalypse. It is referred to in academic literature in most all these ways, and so will it be here. Let the reader understand.

** For commentaries on Revelation see Beasley-Murray (1974); Caird (1966); Charles, 2 vols. (1920); Ford (1975); Mounce (1977); Harrington (1993); Talbert (1994); Beale (2000); and Aune, 3 vols. (1997–1998); Malina and Pilch (2000).

of plant by a starving explorer. Despite the promise of such an occasion, however, in actual practice it can sometimes be frustrating, offering less of a hermeneutical advantage than is sometimes anticipated. But take courage! It is a bit like the great dialogue of Plato, *Theaetetus*, where knowledge and understanding are discussed and debated. One begins by thinking s/he knows what knowledge is, but by the end not only is one certain that one does not know the meaning, but one feels as though one actually *knows less* than when one began! Plato, however, is kind enough to leave us with words of comfort from Socrates, which I think are pertinent here. Despite the frustration of having thoughts disturbed or even jumbled, at least we will next time have the good sense "not to fancy you know what you do not know," and in the future any thoughts that we do have will be "better as a consequence of today's scrutiny."[1] But, back to the frustration.

1. Excerpts of *Theaetetus* (Gk. "asked of the

Reasons for it are numerous. Worthy of mention first is the definition of genre itself. Rolf Knierem said in 1973 (in a discussion of Hermann Gunkel's work), "One of the facts is that we are no longer so clear as to what exactly a genre is. More pointedly: It is doubtful whether this has ever been clear."[2] *Genre* is the French word for the Latin *genus*,[3] used in English as a technical term in scientific classification and sometimes translated with the gloss "species." So, to be rather simplistic, *literary genre* is a species of literature having characteristics in common with other literary works with which it can then be understood as "kin." But the difficulty is just what *kind* of characteristics, and *how long to make the list* of characteristics that one species of literature must have to be "kin" to another.[4]

Second, one should understand that while almost any text comprises *numerous* genres and *literary forms* in combination,[5]

in the case of the Apocalypse the mixture has turned it, generically, into the most challenging text in the New Testament corpus. Since the 1970s[6] there has been an almost global effort by a group of scholars of apocalyptic literature to analyze apocalyptic texts and to forge from their discourse a description of the difficult genre of apocalyptic.[7] Slowly but surely they have emerged from their discussions with a description that is somewhat satisfying to them all, though it has not been easy or even a quick decision.

The three elements in bold type below are fundamental features of their definition of *genre*, the rest a generic description of an apocalypse that is fuzzy enough around the edges to permit the existence of an acceptable variety:

> In *form* an apocalypse is a
> first-person prose recital of
> revelatory visions or dreams,
> framed by a description of the
> circumstances of the revelatory
> experience, and structured to

gods"), quoted from F. M. Cornford's translation in Hamilton, *Collected Dialogues*, 919.

2. Knierem, "Old Testament Form Criticism Reconsidered," in *Interpretation* 27 (1973) 435–68.

3. The following group of Indo-European words may help one to see relationships: Latin (*gen, genus*); French (*genre*); English (*genus, gender, kin*); Greek (*genos*). The German word used in this discourse (*Gattung*) is less helpful here.

4. For example W. G. Doty says, "Generic definitions ought not to be restricted to any one particular feature (such as form, content, etc.), but they ought to be widely enough constructed to allow one to conceive of a genre as a congeries of (a limited number of) factors. The cluster of traits charted may include authorial intention, audience expectancy, formal units used, structure, use of sources, characterizations, sequential action, primary motifs, institutional setting, rhetorical patterns, and the like" (Doty, "Concept of Genre," 439–40; quoted in Aune, *Apocalypticism, Prophecy, and Magic*, 39).

5. Aune (*The New Testament in Its Literary Environment*, 13) says that each of the four major

literary types found in the NT text (gospels, acts, letters, apocalypse) "is a 'complex' or 'inclusive' literary genre used to frame a variety of shorter literary forms."

6. Osborne calls the years 1979–1989 a "creative decade" for analysis of the genre apocalyptic ("Recent Trends," 475).

7. Important studies of apocalyptic, apocalypticism, and the Apocalypse of John have appeared throughout the twentieth century, witnessing to a stream of scholarly interest that has frequently changed direction and focus but has continued nevertheless. The subject of genre is a rather recent change of direction evident, for example by a simple look at the bibliographies of articles written by some of the contributors. The article by A. Y. Collins ("Introduction: Early Christian Apocalypses") introducing *Semeia* 36 (1986), an issue devoted to the subject of genre, has twenty-two items in the Works Cited, none of which is earlier than 1976 save a text on early Christian martyrs by Musurillo (1972).

emphasize the central revelatory message. The *content* of apocalypses involves, in the broadest terms, the communication of a transcendent, often eschatological, perspective on the human experience. Apocalypses exhibit a threefold *function*: (1) to legitimate the message . . . through an appeal to transcendent authorization, and (2) to create a literary surrogate of revelatory experience for hearers or readers, (3) so that the recipients of the message will be motivated to modify their views and behaviors to conform to transcendent perspectives.[8]

When applied to the Revelation of John the description gets (even) more complicated, for there are other major literary forms in that book, which some scholars think are primary (see below), and some exceptions in that text to what many consider typical of apocalypses generally (such as pseudepigraphy). These are the sorts of things that have made the genre-based discourse about the Apocalypse interesting, if not exasperating.

Indeed, the intricacy of their debate[9] has not inspired perseverance among some monitoring it from the margins; and the generality of their conclusions has not inspired endorsement from others who see "diminishing returns" from all the discourse.[10] So some interpreters engage

only minimally in the genre debate, making it less than a specific starting point.[11] Reasons for their disengagement vary, but judging from the creativity of their insights into this bizarre book, some accounting of their work and their methods deserves a place here (see below under the heading Literary Techniques), for it is

---

8. Aune, *The New Testament in Its Literary Environment*, 230–31.

9. See, for example, the essay in *Semeia* 36 by David Hellholm: "The Problem of Apocalyptic Genre and the Apocalypse of John" (13–64).

10. These are Beale's words (*Revelation*, 41) as he reviews their advancement. He voices the opinion, shared also by others (Michaels, *Revelation*; Mazzaferri, *The Genre of Revelation*;

Court, *Revelation*), that little change resulted "in terms of new interpretative insights into the book of Revelation."

11. For example, Hemer, *The Letters to the Seven Churches*. Aune wrote the foreword to the 2001 reprint of Hemer's *The Letters to the Seven Churches* and discusses there why Hemer "virtually ignored scholarship on the genre of Revelation." Hemer felt that its identification with the genre apocalypse had been overstated, "reflecting a widespread English discomfort with apocalyptic reflected in the work of C. H. Dodd and G. B. Caird" (xviii). Beale spends six pages of a 1200-page (superb) commentary on the topic of genre. He says there, "it is best to understand apocalyptic as an intensification of prophecy. Too much distinction has typically been drawn between the apocalyptic and prophetic genres. Indeed, some Old Testament books combine the two to one degree or another" (37). John Barton is an OT scholar who writes about just this mixture. In *Oracles of God*, Barton has a chapter on "Modes of Reading the Prophets." He is interested in how the prophets and other Scripture were read once there was a pervasive understanding that a primary "prophetic age" had come to an end. His contention is that *genre* had little to do with it, and that genre sensitivities moderated neither reading nor writing. He even says, "No one in our period if asked to define a 'prophetic book' would have said anything about genre . . . only about divine origin, and the sort of book they would produce would be merely an imitation of the sort that they liked to read. And most of those were composite, redacted, inconsistent works" (147). This explains (for Barton) many of the puzzling features in works from the Second Temple period! These postexilic writers did not trouble themselves about genre at all. Criticism of genre-intensive studies also comes from another direction in recent history: from the deconstructionists. Mixed genres mark a forfeiture of their value as a classification device for interpretation (see discussion in Osborne, "Recent Trends," 474).

a literary analysis that does not begin with an indefatigable analysis of genre. Aune, on the other hand, as one of the several premier interpreters of Greco-Roman oracular literature, Christian prophecy, apocalyptic, and Hellenistic literary genres in general, seems to be of the opinion that it *is* a necessary hard labor, and he is simply not going to give up (on the difficulty of it) "without a struggle."[12]

SOCIAL SETTING

Social setting is a subtopic of "literary genre," sometimes discussed in relation to "function" since it involves the reader, reader expectation, authorial intent—insofar as one believes these can be discovered. The subject can be problematic in light of postmodern literary theory and the issues of authorial intent and reader response. It is wide-ranging, tenuous,

and charged with hermeneutical twists and turns (nothing is easy!). In a simpler vein, (for example) is the (social-setting) issue of whether the churches to whom the Seer was writing were living during the reign of Domitian, and whether or not there was during this reign an aggressive persecution of Christians.[13] As one might expect, the date of the book is debated (though the two popular options are both in the first century AD: one during the reign of Nero, the other during the reign of Domitian), and the setting-in-life is debated (though most all agree that the readers or hearers were experiencing some measure of persecution, and that from the Roman Empire).

DIVERSE GENRES

Apocalypse

The book of Revelation is apocalyptic in point of view.[14] While it has characteris-

---

12. Aune, "Apocalypse of John and the Problem of Genre," 67. He says there about the phenomenon of "mixed genres": "if the notion of a *mixtum compositum* is too quickly applied to a problematic text, the possibility of achieving a generic understanding of the structure of the entire text is given up *without a struggle*" (italics added). A century ago, when the Apocalypse was called composite, it was meant that the Apocalypse was not a literary unity but a collection of disparate sources. At the beginning of the twenty-first century it is not a mixture of sources that challenges the reader, but a mixture of genres. Aune ("Apocalypse of John and the Problem of Genre," 80) discusses the issue more broadly under a section subtitled "The Whole and the Part," noting that there are many examples of texts containing apocalyptic sections, and so he discusses a "host genre" which can contain a variety of other literary forms (following Dubrow, *Genre*). Collins (*Daniel*, 3) traces the composite (generic) nature of apocalyptic texts to Gerhard von Rad (*Old Testament Theology*, 2:330), who says that "'apocalyptic' is not a literary genre at all but a *mixtum compositum*" (Collins, *Daniel*, 54).

13. A Domitian date (as opposed to the other favorite: Neronian date) is less debated than the related issue of persecution. Thompson says, "Few students of the Apocalypse today accept Eusebius of Caesarea's comments about a widespread persecution under Domitian (*Hist. eccl.* 3.17–20, 39; 4.18; 5.8, 18; 6.25; 7.25)." (Thompson, "Sociological Analysis," 153; see also Thompson, *The Book of Revelation*, 95–115). Some students do, however. While Thompson argues that later Roman writers accuse Domitian of such offenses wrongly out of bias, Beale says it is equally possible that Roman authors contemporary with Domitian showed bias in the other direction (*Revelation*, 6). See Strand, "Review of Thompson" for a similar argument; and Riley, *One Jesus*, 196–97, for a reading of the Roman sources.

14. See Collins, *The Combat Myth*; Hanson, *Dawn of Apocalyptic*; Koch, *Rediscovery of Apocalyptic*; Pilch, *What Are They Saying about the Book of Revelation?*; Russell, *Message and Method*; Russell, "Apocalyptic Literature"; Schmithals, *The Apocalyptic Movement*. See also ch. 2, above: "The

tics of prophecy, its conceptual outlook is apocalyptic. For example, most of the Hebrew prophetic literature awaited a future political ruler over Israel. Revelation, however, does not court nationalistic hopes. Like other apocalyptic writings, it paints the future political scene as hopeless and the human world dominated by angels and demons. According to this perspective, a radical transformation of the world with cosmic catastrophes and a final punishment of the wicked are needed to vindicate the faithful. Examples of apocalyptic literature are Daniel 7–12, *1 Enoch* 1–36 (the *Book of the Watchers*) and *1 Enoch* 72–82 (*Book of the Heavenly Luminaries*), 2 Esdras, *2 Baruch*, *3 Baruch*, *Testament/Assumption of Moses*, with apocalyptic elements in some of the Qumran texts such as the War Scroll (1QM), the Psalms of Thanksgiving (1QH), and the commentary of Habakkuk (1QpHab).[15]

Apocalyptic literature can be generally characterized by the following literary and thematic features: First, discourse cycles or visions occur between a seer and a heavenly being, revealing the secrets of human destiny (e.g., Dan 10; 2 Esd 11–12; Rev 4–5; 17). Second, the visions often contain mythical images rich in symbolism: a four-headed leopard with four wings (Dan 7:6), an eagle with twelve wings and three heads (2 Esd 11:1), and a beast with ten horns and seven heads (Rev 13:1). Third, the theme of cosmic catastrophe's preceding the end is mentioned:

war, fire, earthquake, famine (2 *Bar* 25–27; 2 Esd 5:1–13; War Scroll, 1QM 1; Rev 6:1—9:21). Fourth, the events of history are regarded as predetermined in fixed periods of time (Dan 9:24; 2 Esd 4:36–37; 2 *Bar* 25; Rev 6:11; 4:1; 10:7). Fifth, there is to be an end of the present evil order and the beginning of a new age inaugurated by a royal mediator or son of man (Dan 7:1–14; 2 Esd 13; *1 Enoch* 69:27–29; Rev 19:11–21). Sixth, there is to be a final judgment of the wicked (*TMos/As Mos* 10; War Scroll, 1QM 18–19; Daniel 12; Revelation 20) and a vindication of the righteous to a state of bliss (*1 Enoch* 48–50; 1QM 19, Messianic Rule fragment from Qumran; Revelation 21–22).

Prophecy

To discuss the Apocalypse as prophecy, either as Christian prophecy or as classical Old Testament prophecy,[16] or as over against the genre of apocalypse[17] or in some combination with the genre apocalypse,[18] invokes diverse discourses

Jewish World of the New Testament."

15. For primary sources, see Charlesworth, *OTP*, vol. 1; Vermes, *The Complete Dead Sea Scrolls*; Dupont-Sommer, *The Essene Writings*. For discussion of the genre apocalypse among the Dead Sea Scrolls, see Collins, *The Apocalyptic Imagination*, 115–41.

16. For example David Hill's "Christian Prophets," "Prophecy and Prophets," and "Creative Role." Hill argues that John's self-understanding and authority is not that of an early Christian prophet but rather that of a *classical* prophet, and that this can be evidenced by his use of the Scriptures (an incredibly complex subject by itself, see more below under "Solecism"). He was engaged in these arguments by Schüssler Fiorenza, "Apokalypsis and Propheteia." Also, see Aune's discussion of the recent (since the 1970s) surge of interest in Christian prophecy in *Prophecy in Early Christianity*, 114, 174–288; and Mazzaferri, *The Genre of the Book of Revelation*; see also note 19, below.

17. Mazzaferri (*Genre of the Book of Revelation*) argues that the Revelation of John belongs strictly to the genre of prophetic writings of the OT and is not an apocalypse at all.

18. This is a common position taking various forms. Beale (*Revelation*, 37–39) whose discus-

from a plethora of wide-ranging biblical scholars. It is quite easy in their nuanced argumentation to get lost in the forest of details and speculations. It is certainly best to start out at a more fundamental level and see why the Apocalypse is talked about as a piece of prophecy at all.

The *prophetic character* of Revelation can be detected first of all from the book's description of itself. Revelation describes its own contents as "prophetic" at the beginning and ending of the book (1:3; 22:7, 10, 18–19). There is also the prophetic, oracular character of the letters to the seven churches and the use of the verb "to prophesy" in 10:11. Less direct, but no less noticeable, are the many allusions,[19] some simply verbal and others more fundamentally structural to the prophetic literature in the Hebrew Bible. A few examples will have to suffice, since books, even tomes, have been written in explication.

Second, the opening title and motto of Revelation are reminiscent of, for example, the prophetic book of Amos (Rev 1:1–3, 7–8; cf. Amos 1:1–2). The messages of both Amos and Revelation are ascribed to obscure individuals (e.g., not to Moses, Adam, or Enoch), and both are described as visions or divine disclosures. Third, Revelation has three visions that commission the prophet or seer to do an appointed task. The first, in Rev 1:9–20, is similar to the inaugural vision of Isaiah 6. The second, in Revelation 4–5, is like the commissioning vision in Ezek 1:5–20. The third, in Rev 10:8–11, has parallels to Ezek 3:1–3 ("eating the scroll") and functions as the center of the book's concentric outline. Fourth, the denouncements upon the churches for misbehavior (Rev 2:1—3:22, excluding the constructive directives) are similar to the prophetic judgment speeches in Amos (1:3—2:6; 4:1–2). Fifth, the following literary forms in Revelation also have parallels in the prophetic books: vision reports (e.g., Rev 4:1–11; 6:1–18; 7:1–8; 14:1–5; cf. Amos 7:1–9; 8:1–3), woe oracles (e.g., Rev 8:13; 12:12; cf. Amos 5:18–20; 6:1–7; Isa 5:8–23; 28:1—38:8; Mic 2:1–4), and a funeral dirge (e.g., Rev 18; cf. Amos 5:1–3; Ezek 26–27). The above are only some of the prophetic features found in Revelation.[20]

Epistle, Epistolary

The primary reason for asserting an epistolary classification is that the Apocalypse is enclosed within a recognizable letter framework. "John to the seven churches . . . from . . ." (1:4–5) as an opening (prescript) and "The grace of the Lord Jesus be with you all. Amen." (22:[10–]21) as a

---

sion of this is brief and good, refers to Schüssler Fiorenza (*The Book of Revelation: Justice and Judgment*) and an older study by Ladd ("Why Not Prophetic-Apocalyptic?") from 1957.

19. The Apocalypse never quotes directly from the OT, but allusions abound. Some count as many as a thousand (van der Waal, *Openbaring*); Nestle-Aland (27th ed.) text index cites 635; UBS[4] text index, 394; Swete (*The Apocalypse of St. John*) cites 278; Charles (*A Critical and Exegetical Commentary*) cites 226; Bratcher (*Old Testament Quotations*) lists only eleven OT citations. I am grateful to Beale for some of these statistics (Beale, "Revelation"). The range of opinion is due to different criteria for inclusion of course, but it is fair to say that the book is full of allusions to the OT.

20. Some scholars don't trace random similarities, but rather major structural units to prophetic books of the OT. For example, Beale (*The Use of Daniel*); and also for the book of Daniel, Vanhoye ("L'Utilisation"); and for Ezekiel: Ruiz (*Ezekiel in the Apocalypse*); and for Genesis: Skiadaresis, "Genesis and Apocalypse."

closing (postscript) are difficult to misapprehend.[21] The salutation identifies the recipients as the churches of Asia and the sender as John (1:4a) with a blessing: "grace and peace" (1:4b–5a) and a doxology: "to him be glory" (1:5b–6). The book's ending has a concluding greeting like an early Christian letter: "the grace of the Lord Jesus Christ be with you all. Amen" (22:21). In fact, Rev 22:18–21 has parallels to 1 Cor 16:22–24. Both have a conditional formula ("if anyone") (1 Cor 16:22; Rev 22:19) followed by an anathema or curse on the disobedient and the prayer "come Lord Jesus" or *maranatha* (1 Cor 16:22; Rev 22:20). Both conclude with the wish of grace (1 Cor 16:23; Rev 22:21). The epistolary beginning and ending of Revelation appear to bracket 1:4—22:21 as a complete unit.

In addition, the letters to the seven churches in the opening scenes of the book (1:4—3:22) provide an epistolary summary of the happenings upon earth. The seven letters are similar to 2 and 3 John which contain: an opening address, praise or warning, threats and rewards, promise of a future visit, and a final greetings. Upon close examination, the seven letters in Revelation have five sections:

(1) an address and commission to write (2:1, 8, 12, 18; 3:1, 7, 14);

(2) a messenger formula ("these things says the One who . . .") similar to the pronouncement of the Hebrew prophets: "thus says the Lord," and followed by a description of the heavenly Christ in the inaugural vision (same verses as above);

(3) an exhortation introduced by "I know," which includes some or all of the following:

(a) a description of the situation with "I know that . . ." (2:2–3, 13, 19; 3:1, 8, 15)

(b) a censure with the formula, "but I hold it against you . . ." (2:4, 14, 20) and without this formula (3:2, 16–17)

(c) a call to repentance (2:5, 16, 21; 3:3, 19c)

(d) a revelatory saying introduced by "see" or "behold" (Gk. *idou*—2:10, 22; 3:8, 9, 20)

(e) announcement of the Lord's coming (2:5, 16, 25; 3:3, 11)

(f) an exhortation to hold fast (2:10c, 25; 3:2–3, 11)

(4) a call to hear the message directed to all: "let him who has ears to hear" (2:7, 11, 17, 29; 3:6, 13, 22), and

(5) an end-time promise: "to the victor I will give . . . ," or "he who overcomes will be . . ." (2:7, 10c, 17b, 26; 3:5, 12, 21).

The seven letters are addressed to seven specific churches that were once located in the ancient province of Asia, which is now the western part of modern Turkey. Although they are an integral part of the book's structure, these letters mirror the problems of early Christians at a particular place and time.

Narrative

While the genres apocalypse, epistle and prophecy have been featured ingredients in the generic discussion by specialists

---

21. "In this respect the Apocalypse is unique: *no other apocalypse is framed by epistolary conventions.*" (Aune, *The New Testament in Its Literary Environment*, 240; italics original).

for a long time, rather more recently the proposal has been made that the book of Revelation is also narrative.[22] Insofar as this proposal discusses the Apocalypse as being a story about Jesus, it is very interesting.

LITERARY TECHNIQUES AND DEVICES

> The Apocalypse of John is a work of immense learning, astonishingly meticulous literary artistry, remarkable creative imagination, radical political critique, and profound theology. Yet among the major works of early Christianity included in the New Testament, it remains the Cinderella. It has received only a fraction of the amount of scholarly attention which has been lavished on the Gospel and the major Pauline letters.[23]

This quotation from a well-known interpreter of the Apocalypse and apocalyptic literature surely causes one to pause. Although Bauckham does not avoid questions of genre (see his discussions of it dispersed throughout *The Climax*, such as in chapter 8: "The Apocalypse as a Christian War Scroll"),[24] he certainly does not

spend a great amount of time on it, and the contents of his kind of literary analysis need a place for presentation and review here, although we may not be quite sure what to call it. Some of the observations border upon being structural in nature, others stylistic; others point out literary forms, and others, such as Gematria, are not really symbols, not really numbers, and not really numerology. The many observations that might be unearthed during close reading prove interesting, especially to those with vivid and quick imagination.

We will begin with *intercalation* and *interludes*. An analysis of the structure of Revelation will show that the author did not arrange it in a linear-temporal manner, but in a topical-thematical way. This observation finds some support in the author's techniques of arrangement and composition.

Intercalation[25]

First, the author employs the method of inclusion or intercalation throughout the book. This technique of bracketing material (A-B-A') was discussed in our analysis of Mark's gospel. The author frames small segments, large sections and the entire book by this device.[26] In the prophetic introduction, we have the superscription (1:1–3, A) and a motto (1:7–8, A'), which brackets the epistolary prescript

---

22. Barr, *Tales of the End*; Barr, "The Apocalypse of John," 259–71; Michaels, *Interpreting the Book of Revelation*; Hedrick, "Narrative Asides"; and see Osborne "Recent Trends," 479, for brief discussion.

23. The opening words to Richard Bauckham's book *Climax of Prophecy*.

24. He does not want to say that it belongs to the genre of which 1QM (the War Scroll in the Dead Sea Scrolls) is a specimen. And he later says, "The Apocalypse *is* an apocalypse in form, but it also has a formal peculiarity in that it combines

the genres of apocalypse and *letter* (see especially 1:4–5)" (213, italics original).

25. For discussion see Aune, "Intercalation," in *WDNTECLR* 230–32.

26. Schüssler Fiorenza organizes the entire structure of the book with the author's intercalations ("Composition," 360ff.).

(1:4–6, B). In Revelation 8, the announcement (v. 2, A) and description (vv. 6ff., A') of the seven angels with seven trumpets brackets a heavenly liturgy (3–5, B). The reader is therefore required to view these elements as part of an indivisible whole. In larger sections the technique of intercalation is also employed. Between the Babylon visions in 17:1—19:10 (A) and the Jerusalem visions in 21:9—22:5 (A') is inserted the parousia judgment series in 19:11—21:8 (B). Finally, as mentioned earlier, the entire book (B) is bracketed by an epistolary prescript (1:4–6, A) and conclusion (22:21, A').

Interludes

Closely connected to the technique of intercalation are interludes. These interrupt the progression of the narrative with *visions* and *hymns* of end-time salvation (7:1–17; 11:14–19; 12:10; 14:15; 15:24; 19:1–8; 20:4–6). Combined with intercalations, the interludes become part of a double intercalation. For example: Rev 10:1—11:14 is clearly marked as an interlude inserted into the cycle of seven trumpets (8:6—9:21, A; 10:1—11:14, B; 11:15–19, A'). At the same time, however, Rev 10:1—11:14 serves as an introduction to the following section (Revelation 12–14), since it refers to the same period of persecution by the beast (11:7ff.; 13; 17).

The vision of the small scroll is also held together by the pattern A (10:1—11:14), B (11:15–19), A' (12–14); and is tied to the trumpet septet of the seven-sealed scroll by the same pattern. By the method of intercalation it is tied at the other end to the bowl septet. The introduction to the bowl septet (15:1–8) is patterned analogously to that of the trumpet septet: the appearance of the seven angels 15:1 (A), the heavenly liturgy 15:5–8 (B), and the execution of the plagues 16:1ff. (A'). In this sequence 15:2–4 is an interlude that at the same time represents an intercalation (Revelation 14, A; 15:1, B; 15:2–4, A'). The vision of the small prophetic scroll thus reaches a climax in 15:2–4—a climax that at the same time ties the vision to the bowl septet of the seven-sealed scroll. These examples show that the author does not divide the text into separate sections but interlocks material from one section to the next. Thus the author joins sections together by interweaving and interlacing them through this method of intercalation.

Chiasm

Another method of composition somewhat similar in feel to both intercalation and interlude, inasmuch as modes of parallelism are achieved, is chiasm (A-B-C-D-C'-B'-A'). Chiasm is an extremely common literary configuration not only in Jewish, but also Greek literature.[27] It is so common and such an apparently comfortable way to express thoughts that it can be found in both aphorisms and long narratives. It provides the basis for the structuring of entire texts. Such a chiastic structure was proposed earlier for the opening section of Q, and even as the structure for short pieces within texts, as

27. For example, in *The Second Discourse on Kingship* 19 by Dio Chrysostom: *mythōn te rhētēr emenai prēktēra te ergōn* / "as to speech—speaker; doer—as to deeds" (quoting Homer, *Iliad* 9.443, translated by C. Michael Robbins); text of Dio Chrysostom from Loeb Classical Library series, vol. 1.

in the three temptations of the Q temptation narrative. Even as Paul wrote or dictated an epistle such as the first to the Corinthians, his speech took form in chiasm.[28] In Greek tragedy, as we have seen, the play unfolds by means of a complication (A), climax (B), and denouement (A). Revelation shares many other similarities with Greek tragedy.[29] Roman architecture was often characterized by this pattern. Even the seven-branched lampstand, i.e., the menorah used in Jewish liturgy, follows the A-B-C-D-C'-B'-A' pattern.[30]

In the Apocalypse both the introduction (1:1–8, A) and closing of the work (22:10–21, A') contain a letter form, prophetic statements, and a blessing. The inaugural vision and letter septet (1:9—3:22, B) correspond to the visions of final salvation (19:11—22:9, B') in the following manner: several points of comparison exist between (a) the introductory vision of Christ in Rev 19:11–16 and the inaugural vision (1:9–20) with its recur-

rence in 2–3; and (b) the promises to the victorious in Revelation 2–3 find its fulfillment in 19:11—22:9. The vision of seven bowls (15:1; 15:5—19:10, C) clearly continues the vision of the seven seals and seven trumpets (4:1—9:21; 11:15–19, C), both of which bracket the central section (10:1; 15:4, D) of the small prophetic scroll.

Numerical Arrangements[31]

The Apocalypse is like a labyrinth or maze of numbers and numerical structures. The book has two scroll visions (Rev 5; 10) and four septets or cycles of seven (seven letters 2:1—3:22; seven seals 4:1—8:1; seven trumpets 8:2—9:21; 11:15–19; seven bowls 15:1; 15:5—16:21). The three plague septets are related to one another as prelude, crescendo, and climax, whereas the letter septet points forward to the visions of end-time salvation. "The most significant numbers in Revelation are seven, four, three, and twelve (and in some cases multiples of these)."[32] Thus does Bauckham draw one into the complex and finely configurative world of numerology in this text: "The number four is the number of the world (31) . . . Three seems to be a number without a consistent symbolic significance (32) . . . Twelve is the number of the people of God" (36).[33]

The subject of numbers or numerology, and the larger subject of symbolism

28. It is possible that some of the textual variants between P46 and Codex Sinaiticus in 1 Corinthians can be resolved based upon the presence of chiasm, as Gunther Zuntz argued half a century ago (*The Text of the Epistles*, 91).

29. The following studies compare Revelation with Greek tragedy: Bowman, *The First Christian Drama*; Bowman, "Revelation: Its Dramatic Structure"; Spinks, "Critical Examination"; Bowman "Revelation, Book of"; Brewer, "Influence of Greek Drama on the Apocalypse of John"; Palmer, *Drama of the Apocalypse*; Blevins, "Genre of Revelation." Blevins points out that six of the seven cities of Asia Minor addressed in Revelation had Greek theaters. Ephesus had the largest with a seven-windowed stage. Greek plays also had prologues and epilogues, a number of choruses, interludes, and hymns similar to those in Revelation.

30. For illustrations of this concentric symmetry in other works, see: "Greek Art," in *Encyc. Brit.* (1971) 10:837–40; Richmond, "The Temples of Apollo and Divus Augustus on Roman Coins."

31. Bauckham, *Climax of Prophecy*, 29–37; Collins, "Numerical Symbolism"; Beale, *Revelation* 58–64.

32. Bauckham, *Climax of Prophecy*, 30.

33. So spans an eight-page discussion of numerical symbolism (29–36) that covers these numbers, combinations of these numbers and even discussion of the Seer's parody of these numbers in reference to the devil and impotent evil.

in the Apocalypse, is a somewhat recent interest. Moffatt, who wrote a fine introduction to the book in his *Introduction to the Literature of the New Testament*, criticizes near-contemporary interpreters of the book for their preoccupation with *sources* but then spends not a small amount of time on them as well, calling "source-criticism of some kind is necessary in order to account for the literary and psychological data."[34] The data that need accounting for seem to be primarily things that Moffat did not understand: "incongruities and vacillations in the symbolism, isolated allusions, unrelated predictions left side by side and episodical passages and atmospheres of historical outlook, differing not simply from their context but from one another . . . variations of Christological climate, the juxtaposition of disparate materials, and the awkward transitions at one point after another."[35] In the twentieth century, *things not understood* in this unusual book have steadily decreased, and this is encouraging. One would like to think that it is due to hard work and creative imagination.

Moffatt devotes little time to the subject of numerical symbolism, mentioning gematria (see below) and isopsephia only in a note on page 487. Today one cannot find an introduction to the New Testament or a commentary (even a brief one) that does not give considerable attention to symbolism, especially to numbers.[36]

Symbols, Symbolism

A common stock of symbols and images are employed throughout the book. For example, the image of the throne has to be seen in connection with other expressions and symbols of kingship in order to grasp its full impact. Symbolic colors (like purple as royalty or luxury, black as death, and white as joy or victory) as well as symbolic numerals (above) are used similarly throughout the book, with exceptions that are almost always important. Finally, the notion of end-time war is intensified and enhanced by a variety of terms and symbols of war.

Gematria

Gematria is the assignment to each letter of the alphabet (of any desired language) a numerical quantity so that names or words can be referred to as numbers. The most well-known example of this is 666 in the Apocalypse, and since the early 1800s it has been suspected that this referred to (Caesar) Nero. Transliterating this name from Greek into Hebrew letters and using the numbers of the Hebrew alphabet for the calculation gives the number 666; transliterating from Latin into Hebrew will give you the number 616 (a textual variant of 666).

The world of *gematria* is mysterious[37] and to enter into it is to immediately find several other dimensions of meaning to words and especially to numbers as the numbers pick up additional related

---

34. Moffatt, *Introduction*, 488.

35. Ibid.

36. See for example Reinhold, *Number Seven*.

37. Even the derivation of the word is a bit of a mystery. Some trace it to a Hebrew word, others to a Greek word. Some feel it was a Hebrew word built up from a combination of words from other languages. It was a common practice in antiquity.

mathematical characteristics traceable to Pythagoreanism and geometric forms.[38]

Allusion

Allusion is an elusive term, but what is meant is that the author uses subtle means to inform and contextualize prophecy using texts and traditions. In footnote 19 above, mention was made of the "seer's" allusion to the sacred texts of the Jews. Other words are sometimes used to describe this: *echo, intertextuality, mimesis.* The point is no longer considered to be just a footnote in studies of the Apocalypse. The range of possible allusions mentioned in this previous note discloses a datum itself, namely, that this is a highly subjective discourse. How much intertextual knowledge would a skilled first-century reader of a text like Revelation have processed? How much did the author intend to convey by such allusions? Does it even matter what the author intended? Good questions, these. In biblical studies, the notice of such things as allusion and the like has been growing in importance.[39] Some of the energy to do so can be traced to the discovery of the Dead Sea Scrolls.

The echo in Plato's Myth of the Cave (*Republic* 5.516c–d) of Odysseus's conversation with Achilles in Hades compares as and certainly illustrates a prolific allusion pregnant with pretext. One can hardly read the Myth in the same way once the allusion is recognized. The discussion

between Odysseus and Achilles is well known. Achilles, though the Achaean hero who won fame and immortality as a warrior on the battlefield, is here claiming that he would much rather be a servant on earth than a hero in Hades. With allusions to this talk between these two warriors, Plato implies that *all* those alive on earth chained in the cave are at best like the hero in Hades.

Demetrius ("On Style" §§287–88) refers to another sort of subtlety—this time in Plato's *Phaedo* 59c, where two men (Phaedo and Echecrates) are discussing the last hours of Phaedo's teacher, Socrates. Echecrates is ascertaining who stayed beside Socrates (faithfully) to the end. After hearing the list of those present with Socrates at his death, Echecrates asks "Weren't Aristippus and Cleombrotus there?" Both the question and the response, says Demetrius, are examples of "allusive verbal innuendo" (§287); the question presumes to disparage the two men with "They were in Aegina," a rather short distance away. As a result, the phrase "they were in Aegina" carries with it distasteful insinuations of unfaithfulness and questionable loyalty.[40]

Solecism[41]

A solecism is the sort of thing that a reader of a Greek text would stop and reread, or that the editor of a text would correct:

38. See Bauckham, *Climax of Prophecy,* ch. 11: "Nero and the Beast" (384–452) for a generous sampling of the process, the theory, and the unusual trails down which such speculation leads.

39. For example in studies of the Hebrew Bible: Fishbane, *Biblical Interpretation*; and in New Testament studies: Hays, *Echoes.*

40. Hugh Tredennick preserves the sharp edge of the comment with his translation "No, they were in Aegina, apparently." Hamilton, et al., *Collected Dialogues of Plato,* 42.

41. *Solecism* is a pejorative, nontechnical reference to a grammatical blunder given by the Greeks to residents of Soloi in Cilicia who misspoke the Greek language. It has for a long time been applied to the similar errors in the Apocalypse.

"Mary was so hungry that he ate two sand-wiches" contains such an error, for *Mary* is a feminine name and should have "she," not "he," as the pronoun. Since Greek is a highly inflected language with critical demands for concord or agreement within sentences, it is a candidate for numerous kinds of solecisms. These are so frequent in the Greek text of the Apocalypse that modern scholars, who rarely use the word "unique" anymore, nevertheless use it with regard to the language of this book of visions.[42]

But is it a mistake to call them mistakes? Some scholars look at them now as something different. Beale argues that they are, at least sometimes, markers to Old Testament allusions.[43] It is at least curious that the Seer inconsistently makes these so-called mistakes, and that some of them have a high degree of order and pattern to them. Take, for example, his use of the comparative particle *homoios*, used by the Seer twenty-one times as an adjective introducing a comparison or metaphor, often alongside the comparative particle *hōs*[44] (1:14–15, where *hōs* is used five times, *homoios* one time; 9:7 where both are used twice; and many others).

Herein is a good test case for consistency. The grammatical case following *hōs* is *always* the case that precedes it;[45] the grammatical case following *homoios* is *always* the dative case, with two (identical) exceptions. Twice the title "Son of Man" is introduced with *homoios*; once in 1:13 and once in 14:14. In both these cases *homoios* takes, rather, the accusative case: "Like a son of man" or "like the Son of Man": both passages are allusions to Dan 7:13, but they do not conform grammatically to Daniel. There is some other reason for this surprising solecism. And if this example exists, how many others do?

Cross-References and Repetition with Slight Variation

Cross-references are evident, for example, when the characterizations of Christ in the inaugural vision (1:9–20) recur in Rev 2–3; 14:14ff. and 19:11–16. This device enables the reader to readily identify the character in the narrative. Such repetitions occur quite frequently in this book, at times with slight variations, and at times with numerical significance.[46]

---

42. "stand alone in the history of literature" (Torrey, *Apocalypse of John*, 16); "absolutely unique in the three thousand years during which Greek has existed since the time of Homer" (Charles, *Lectures*, 72); "*the linguistic character of the Apocalypse is absolutely unique*" (Charles, *A Critical and Exegetical Commentary*, cxliii [italics original]); "the most sustained body of violation of the rules of Greek grammar that exists anywhere" (Beardslee, *Literary Criticism*, 59); "The Seer's Greek is uniquely bizarre" (Farrer, *Revelation*, 50); "stands alone among Greek literary writings in its disregard of the ordinary rules of syntax" (Swete, *Revelation*, cxxv); "not only barbaric but scarcely literate" (Bloom, *Revelation*, 5—though Bloom's harsh comments are less about the book's Greek than its content). Goodspeed disagrees with these sentiments, saying it is much ado about nothing and that the book reads powerfully as it is; a comment I remember vividly reading, but have not been able to locate the source (C. Michael Robbins).

43. See his "The Use of the OT in the Apocalypse" (*Revelation*, 76ff.).

44. Used seventy times in the book.

45. The single exception to this (4:7) has a complex text history.

46. Bauckham does some exploring into these repeated references (22–29), and even quotes Mealy (*After the Thousand Years*, 5), who talks of "the extensive network of cross-references and allusions which affect the interpretation of virtually every passage in Revelation."

Contrasts

Contrasts occur between the Beast and the Lamb, between the great harlot and the woman, in chapter 12, as well as between the harlot and the bride of the Lamb, the New Jerusalem. Contrasts effectively distinguish the identity and role of each character, and the nature and function of each object or image. Consider, for example, what Bauckham calls the "satanic trinity":[47] the Dragon (12:13–17), Beast number 1 (13:1–10), and Beast number 2 (13:11–18). Or even more interesting is the tripartite formulaic title given to the beast in 17:8: "the beast that you saw *was and is not and is about to come*"—a parody of the divine name.

THE MYTHICAL WORLDVIEW

Because Revelation is apocalyptic in outlook and style, it employs much mythical and symbolic language. Like other ancient writings, Revelation assumes the mythic worldview of a three-storied universe (heaven, earth, Hades) inhabited by angels and demons. Like other apocalyptic writings, it visualizes a radical transformation of the world through cosmic catastrophe. Revelation also makes use of well-known mythologies of antiquity. The story of the queen of heaven with the eternal child in chapter 12 is one example. The elements of myth are (1) the woman, (2) the child, (3) his birth and ascension, and (4) the dragon. This myth is international—found in Egypt (involving Isis, Horus, and Seth), Babylon (involving Demkina, Marduk, and Tiamat), Greece (involving Letho, Apollo, and Python), and Palestine (involving Israel, Messiah, and Satan or Leviathan). Other examples of popular mythologies are the heavenly council portrayed as the assembly of the gods (chapter 5), the holy wars of the archangel against the serpent (12:7–12), and the god of heaven, who defeats the monster of chaos and death to bring forth a new creation (19:11—22:5). In the ancient Combat Myth, the chaos monster was ocean dwelling, and so it is not surprising that in the new creation "there is no longer any sea" (21:1).

Our discussion of myth in the book of Revelation is not to be understood in a negative or denigrating light but in a positive and functional sense.[48] The word *myth* as we are using the term here names stories about the "world beyond" (religious reality) told in language of "this world" (human reality). Myths are expressed in symbolic language because the realities they convey are too profound or complex to be rationally explained. Myths are important in human culture because they (a) order human experience with a foundational vision of reality, (b) inform humanity about its identity and destiny, (c) express a saving power in human life, and (d) provide patterns for human actions.[49]

47. Bauckham, *Climax of Prophecy*, 32.

48. Some conservatives feel that to mention myth in relation to the Bible is to denigrate the Bible's authority.

49. For the difficulty of defining *myth* see Robbins, *Testing*, 21–25. Some want to discard the word as useless since it is adopted as a technical term by psychoanalysts (Freud), cultural anthropologists (Durkheim), psychological theorists (Jung), historians of religion (Eliade), linguistic symbolists (Ricoeur), and others but means something different to all of them. Levenson (*Sinai and Zion*, 102) says that *myth* is "amorphous and vulnerable to misuse," but yet these are reasons he prefers it. Its primary adequacy is the inadequacy of history. This is a clarifying comment. For him it

seems that, within reason, myth is what you make it. If the biblical scholar is going to use the term, the scholar must define it in a way that is appropriate to the material s/he is interpreting, and must employ it consistently. Levinson's working definition of *myth* is a "cast of mind that views certain symbols in terms of an act of unlimited scope and import that occurred, in Brevard Child's words, 'in a timeless age of the past.'" (103) Thus he talks of mythical time (borrowing the language of Eliade), which transcends the historicity of the moment.

Events within time can thus be spoken of as occurring *in illo tempore* ("in that time") as either protological or eschatological. The continuing relevance of protological events can be imputed to any moment. Thus a function of myth is transcending time, and reveals quite well its power for theological meaning. "Mythic symbols are thought to be by their very nature invulnerable to obsolescence. On the contrary, they are more 'real' than the flux and change of history." Levenson, *Sinai and Zion*, 103.

PART 3

Jesus and Early Christianity

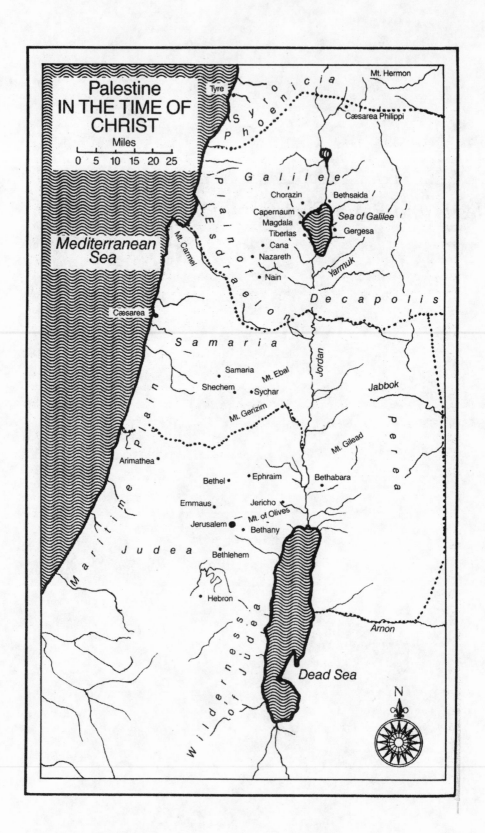

Palestine
IN THE TIME OF
CHRIST

Miles

0 5 10 15 20 25

Mt. Hermon

Tyre

Cæsarea Philippi

Syro

Phoenicia

Mediterranean
Sea

Mt. Carmel

Plain

Esdraelon

Galilee

Chorazin   Bethsaida
Capernaum   Sea of Galilee
Magdala
Tiberias   Gergesa
Cana
Nazareth

Nain   Yarmuk

Decapolis

Cæsarea

Samaria

Jordan

Jabbok

Samaria
Shechem   Mt. Ebal
•Sychar

Mt. Gerizim

Mt. Gilead

Perea

Arimathea

Bethel •   • Ephraim   Bethabara

Emmaus •   Jericho
Jerusalem ●   Mt. of Olives
          • Bethany

Judea   Bethlehem

Hebron

Wilderness of Judea

Arnon

Dead Sea

N

9

Reconstructing a Chronology of Jesus's Life

How challenging is this venture? First, if our interest is in the last few years of a life lived two thousand years ago, of which we have multiple records (with challenging parallels), any one of which can be read in one to four hours; second, if they may be based upon numerous different ancient calendars in the target multicultural world each with different cultural points of interest and different annual calendar systems, both lunar and solar; and third, if our goal is to develop a chronology of that life with this diverse information, then many may conclude that it is a difficult (even pointless) venture.[1]

Furthermore, the details of the life of interest are anything but helpful here. The preserved sayings of this person are of necessity fragmentary,[2] vintage, and representative[3] rather than exhaustive. The focus of the records left is topical and typical with an emphasis hard to miss on the hero's death. Indeed, some basic chronological work can be done prima facie. For example, it is certain that before Jesus died, he was born; and that before he worked with John, he was baptized by him; and it is fairly certain that before he was known as a worker of miracles, he

1. This is so simply because the gaps left in such a reconstruction will be larger than the life observed. So for the modern historian interested in specificity there is little hope of satisfaction; for the apologist of faith interested in legitimation there is not much hope of laudation; and for the dogmatist interested in credulity there is little hope of corroboration. The complexity of ideas in these opening statements are deliberate—to illustrate the difficult subject matter pursued in this chapter!

2. The "words of Jesus" in Mark total just over 5,000; in Matthew almost 14,000; in Luke almost 13,000; and in John almost 9,000. (The count was done in an English translation: the NASB.)

3. The sermons or discourses, for example, are strategically presented. For example, the Sermon on the Plain in Luke (6:20–49) is found at the end of a long narrative section that pictures Jesus as an amazingly influential teacher, but that lacks any sample of what he teaches! By the time the reader gets to the sermon, a significant anticipation has been generated and one is quite ready to hear what this man is teaching!

was known as an ordinary worker; that before he was arrested and tried, he was in some way incendiary; and that before he was betrayed he had merited friendship, and that before he was scourged he had earned enemies.

Some of our chronological work has to do with synchronizing the hero's life (such as his birth and death) with other known historical events. This data may be useful for historical contextualization and reimagining, even creating, cultural context. But even with these events, there is still a contest of data and interpretation today among historians. In developing a chronological scheme, one can establish no certain fixed dates, only probable or plausible ones based on available evidence. And since educated speculations differ among specialists in chronological studies, our views will reflect our own effort to reach astute conclusions within the realm of other possibilities. This can be illustrated below with respect to the date of Jesus's birth.

Early Christians were not as concerned about exact dating as we are. The synchronism "in the fifteenth year of the reign of Tiberius" (Luke 3:1) was sufficient to mark the beginning of John the Baptist's ministry. Julius of Africanus (AD 160–240) placed the birth of Jesus in a year he reckoned as the 5,500th from creation. In AD 525 Pope John I asked Dionysius Exiguus, a Scythian monk, to prepare a standard calendar for the Western church using the Roman dating scheme of AUC, *anno urbis conditae* (Latin for "from the foundation of Rome"). Dionysius calculated that the Christian era was January 1, AUC 754, and Christ's birth was thought to have been on December 25

immediately preceding it.[4] Therefore, AUC 754 equaled AD 1 in the calendar of Dionysius. The years before this date are denoted BC (before Christ") and after by AD (Latin: *anno Domini* = "in the year of our Lord"). However, later research has shown that the latest year for Herod's death was 750 AUC,[5] and Christ's birth, according to Matthew, occurred before Herod's death (Matt 2:1–8). Therefore the birth of Christ must have been prior to 750 AUC or 4 BC. Josephus also places the death of Herod before a Jewish Passover.[6] This would place the Nativity sometime before March/April of 4 BC.[7]

---

4. The traditional day of Christ's birth as December 25 was stated in Hippolytus, *Commentary on Daniel* 4.23.3 (AD 220) and by Chrysostom (ca. AD 386). In the Eastern church, January 6 became the date for both Jesus's birth and the visit of the Magi on his second birthday. See MacCulloch, *Christianity*, 82; Declercq, *Anno Domini*; Mosshammer, *Easter Computus*.

5. Josephus (*Ant.* 17.164–67) says that before Herod died, there was an eclipse of the moon, which occurred in AUC 750, in the second week of March. (Following much of classical scholarship, we have retained BC instead of opting for BCE ["before the Common Era"]; we have retained AD in place of CE ["Common Era"], not out of sectarian preference, but from the pragmatic convenience of convention.)

6. Josephus, *Ant.* 17.206–33; *War* 2.1–13.

7. See Marshall, *Gospel of Luke*, 99–104; Stein, *Jesus the Messiah*, 52–56; Meier, *Marginal Jew*, 1:375–76; Theissen and Merz, *Historical Jesus* 153–55; Finegan, *Handbook of Biblical Chronology*, 279–328, for good discussions on the birth of Jesus and the census of Quirinius (Luke 2:1–2). We consider the historical difficulty of Luke 2:1–2 to be too problematic for any attempt to reconstruct a chronology of Jesus's life. Scholars are reasonably close to each other in their estimation of the date of Jesus's birth: e.g., Stein: "sometime during the years 7–5 BC" (53); Meier: "a few but only a few years before 4 BC" (377); Theissen, and Merz, *Historical Jesus*: "in the year 6 BCE at the latest," and "the last years of the reign of Herod the Great are a possibility" (155).

THE MINISTRY OF JESUS: AD 29–33

An important chronological notation for the commencement of Jesus's ministry is found in Luke's Gospel:

> In the fifteenth year of the reign of Tiberius Caesar, when Pontius Pilate was governor of Judea, and Herod was ruler of Galilee, and his brother Philip was ruler of the region of Iturea and Trachonitus, and Lysanias ruler of Abilene, during the high priesthood of Annas and Caiaphas, the word of God came to John the son of Zechariah in the wilderness. He went into all the region about Jordan preaching a baptism of repentance for the forgiveness of sins. (Matt 3:1–3)

The "fifteenth year of the reign of Tiberius" marks the beginning of John's ministry. At the time John was baptizing the people, he also baptized Jesus, which marked the commencement of Jesus's ministry. Therefore the ministry of Jesus began sometime (perhaps shortly) after that of John. The "fifteenth year of Tiberius's reign" was probably reckoned from the death of Caesar Augustus (AD 14).[8] Therefore the date would be AD 28 or 29 for the beginning of John's ministry.[9] This date coheres adequately with the text's other chronological notations, and the dates we have established for them. Pilate served as prefect of Judea from AD 26 to

36 or 37,[10] Herod Antipas was tetrarch of Galilee until AD 39; Philip died in AD 34; and Caiaphas was high priest from AD 18 to 37.[11] Therefore, Jesus probably began his ministry around AD 29.

According to Luke 3:23, at the commencement of his ministry Jesus was "about thirty years of age." However, this need not mean that Jesus was exactly thirty but "around (*hōsei*) thirty," which could mean any age from about 30 to about 33.[12] John 8:57 also states that in the midst of his ministry, Jesus was "not yet fifty years old," which is probably a generalized statement on Jesus's age in contrast to his claim that he existed before Abraham.[13] Therefore, for Jesus to begin his ministry at the age of 33 (4 BC—AD 29) would not conflict with the mention of his age in Luke 3:23.

Even though arguments on the duration of Jesus's ministry range from one to four years,[14] those for a two- or three-year ministry seem more plausible. The two-year position argues that John's Gospel mentions three Passovers (2:13; 6:4; 11:55), implying at least a two-year

---

8. The view that the "fifteenth year of Tiberius's reign" included a co-regency with Augustus is not supported by the evidence that reckons Tiberius's reign from the death of Augustus (AD 14), see Josephus, *Ant.* 18.224–37; *War* 2.181–83.

9. For discussion, see Meier, *Marginal Jew*, 1:383–86; Finegan *Handbook of Biblical Chronology*, 329–48 (esp. 329–36).

10. Josephus, *Ant.* 18.88–89. Pilate served ten years and was dismissed shortly before Tiberius's death (AD 37). The coinage issued in Judea under Pilate also supports this date.

11. Josephus, *Ant.* 18.29–35; 18.90–95.

12. Hoehner, *Chronological Aspects*, 37; Stein, *Jesus the Messiah*, 58, suggests that this age could have been (1) to parallel David's age at the inception of his reign (2 Sam 5:3–4) or (2) to parallel other Jewish leadership figures (Joseph [Gen 41:46], Ezekiel [Ezek 1:1], or leaders at Qumran [4Q267, fr. 9 v, 11 in Vermes, *Complete Dead Sea Scrolls in English*, 143]).

13. Hoehner, *Chronological Aspects*, 23.

14. See Hoehner's discussion on the various positions (*Chronological Aspects*, 45–60).

ministry.[15] This position also transposes John 5 and 6 to make better geographical sense:

Passage in John	Place or Event in Ministry
John 4	Cana of Galilee
John 6	Sea of Galilee (v. 4: "Passover" approaching)
John 5	Jerusalem ("festival" mentioned in v. 1 is Passover)
John 7	Recently had left Judea for Galilee

Advocates for the three-year ministry of Jesus make the following case.[16] First, if John's version is correct, certainly more than two years are involved with the mention of three Passovers in John (e.g., at least one year has already passed between John 2:13 and 6:4!). Second, a plausible case can be made for the death of Jesus at AD 33 instead of AD 30. The last point will be argued in the next section. The following outline supports the three-year ministry of Jesus.[17]

I. Ministry before the First Passover
The beginning of Jesus's ministry was AD 29, after John baptized him, he was tested in the wilderness, called his first disciples, and ministered in Capernaum.

II. Ministry from the Passover of 30 to the Passover of 31

After the AD 30 Passover, Jesus may have ministered in Judea (John 3). When John was imprisoned (Mark 1:14), he returned to Galilee.

III. Ministry from Passover of 31 to Passover of 32
The story about plucking grain on the Sabbath may reflect this period (Mark 2; Luke 6; Matt 12). The Sermon on the Mount and extensive healing activity in Galilee also took place here. John the Baptist is beheaded at this time.

IV. Ministry from Passover of 32 to Passover of 33
This is probably Jesus's period of retirement from public ministry (Matt 15:21–28; Mark 7:24–30). The confession at Caesarea Philippi also takes place here (Mark 8:27–30). Jesus's last journey to Jerusalem was to celebrate the Passover of AD 33.

If one were to interpret the Parable of the Barren Fig Tree (Luke 13:6–9) as a commentary on the ministry of Jesus, then the additional year requested by the vineyard keeper (Jesus) to the three years already attempted would give Jesus's ministry an additional year. This three-plus year ministry would fit within the chronological confines of John's Gospel if one understood the "festival of the Jews" (5:1) as another Passover. We are still far below the duration suggested for Jesus's ministry in *Adv. Haer.* 2.22.6, where Irenaus suggests that Jesus was in his forties when the Jews in John 8:57 said, "you are not yet fifty years old . . ."

15. Two-year advocates are Epiphanius, *Panarion* 51.30; Schnackenburg, *The Gospel according to St. John* 1:345; Caird, "Chronology, New Testament," in *IDB* 1:601–2.

16. Three-year advocates are Eusebius, *Hist. eccl.* 1.103–4; Hoehner, *Chronological Aspects*, 55–63; Guthrie, *New Testament Introduction*, 294–95.

17. Hoehner, *Chronological Aspects*, 60–62.

CRUCIFIXION, AD 33

Before we try to determine the year of Jesus's crucifixion, it is important to clarify on what day he died. First, we will discuss the day of the week and month, then examine the year of his death.

Although both Thursday and Wednesday crucifixions have been argued,[18] the traditional Friday crucifixion of Jesus is perhaps most tenable. The three chronological considerations for this position are

(1) The four Gospels argue that Jesus's body was laid in the tomb on the evening of the day of the preparation (Friday), the day before the Sabbath (Matt 27:62; 28:1; Mark 15:42; Luke 23:54–56; John 19:31, 42);

(2) Luke tells us that the women returned home and rested on the Sabbath (Saturday, Luke 23:56).

(3) The four Gospels agree that early on the first day of the week (Sunday) the women went to the tomb (Matt 28:1; Mark 16:1–2; Luke 24:1; John 20:1).

The argument from Matthew 12:40 that Jesus would be in the heart of the earth for three days and three nights is parabolic and should not be pressed as a detailed description. There are OT examples where "three days" and "three days and nights" are approximations signifying less than the full seventy-two-hour period (e.g., Gen 42:17–18; 1 Sam 30:12–13; 2 Chr 10:5, 12; Esth 4:16; 5:1;). Therefore, concerning Jesus's death and resurrection there is little difficulty in viewing "three days and three nights" as fractions of days:

18. Hoehner, *Chronological Aspects*, 65–71.

i.e., part of Friday, all of Saturday, and part of Sunday.

Now that we have discussed the day of Jesus's crucifixion, we will examine the day(s) of the month that Jesus ate the last Passover and was crucified. According to the four Gospels and Paul, Jesus ate the Last Supper the day before his crucifixion (Matt 26:20; Mark 14:17; Luke 22:14; John 13:2; 1 Cor 11:23). On what day did Jesus eat the Last Supper? The Synoptics see Jesus celebrating the Last Supper as a Passover meal on Thursday, Nisan 14, with the trial and crucifixion on Friday, Nisan 15 (Matt 26:17; Mark 14:12; Luke 22:7–8), whereas in John the Last Supper was not a Passover meal (John 13:1–4). It was celebrated on Thursday, Nisan 13, with the trial and crucifixion on Friday, Nisan 14 (John 18:28; 19:14).

According to John, the time of Jesus's death was when the Paschal lambs were slain (John 1:29; Nisan 14), just before the evening Passover meal (i.e., Nisan 15). This explanation assumes that John reckoned "days" from sunset to sunset (e.g., Exod 12:18; Lev 23:32). John's version finds support in a diversity of independent sources: Paul, the Babylonian Talmud, and the extracannonical *Gospel of Peter*.[19] Therefore we favor John's version.

19. John's account agrees with (a) the Babylonian Talmud, *b. Sanh.* 43a: "on the eve of the Passover, Yeshu was hanged"; (b) Paul, 1 Cor 5:7: "Christ, our paschal lamb has been 'sacrificed'" (presupposing that Christ died just as the paschal lambs were slain for the Passover); and (c) the *Gospel of Peter* 6: Jesus was delivered to the people "on the day before the unleavened Bread, their feast." These traditions agree with John, although he specifies that Jesus's time of death (Nisan 14) was only a few hours before the "day the Passover" (Nisan 15), which began at sunset. Jesus probably hung on the cross for most of the day (Nisan 14) before he actually expired a few hours before sunset (before Nisan 15).

The Reckoning of Passover

Galilean Method Synoptic Reckoning used by Jesus, His disciples, and Pharisees	Judean Method John's Reckoning used by Sadducees
Thursday	
Midnight	
Sunrise	
Nisan 14 3–5 p.m. Slaying of Passover lamb	
Sunset	
Last Supper Jesus arrested	Nisan 14
Friday	
Midnight	
Sunrise	
Nisan 15 6 a.m. Jesus before Pilate 9 a.m. Crucifixion 12–3 p.m. Darkness 3 p.m. Death of Jesus Burial of Jesus	3–5 p.m. Slaying of Passover lamb
Sunset	
	Nisan 15
Saturday	
Midnight	

This presentation is a matter of debate. Annie Jaubert, for example, has offered a Tuesday Passover for Jesus and his disciples and a Friday crucifixion on the official Passover, in agreement with the Book of Jubilees, in which the Passover was always celebrated on Tuesday.

Adapted from Harold W. Hoehner, 1978, and H. Wayne House, 2009, Zondervan Corporation.

Several different explanations have been given to account for the discrepancies in the Synoptics and John concerning the time of the Last Supper (i.e., whether it occurred during or before the Passover. The Synoptics may have been observing the solar calendar like the Qumran sect; the solar calendar would date the Passover earlier than the official day according to the Jewish lunar calendar.[20] Second,

20. 1QH 12.4–7; *CD* 6.18–19; cf. *1 Enoch* 72; 74; *2 Enoch* 1:1–2; 14–16; 48; Jaubert, *Date of the Last Supper*; Vermes, *Complete Dead Sea Scrolls* 176–77; Cross, *Library of Qumran* 46 n. 71; 103 n. 123; 235 n. 87.

perhaps the Synoptics followed the Pharisaic dating of the Passover, whereas John observed the Sadducean scheme (following closely Lev 23:15).[21] Third, the Synoptics adhere to the Galilean method of reckoning a day from sunrise to sunrise (e.g., Deut 16:4; Matt 28:1), but John observes the Judean method of calculating the day from sunset to sunset (e.g., Exod 12:18; Neh 13:19; Mark 4:27; 5:5).[22] According to the Galilean method, the slaying of the Passover lamb would happen between 3 and 5 p.m. on Thursday (Nisan 14), whereas the Judean method would place the ritual between 3 and 5 pm on Friday (Nisan 14). The last explanation appears to satisfy the data of both the Synoptics and the Gospel of John. The custom is also substantiated by the Mishnah, which prohibits Galileans from working on the day of the Passover. But Judeans worked until midday (*Pesah.* 4:5).

Although the death of Christ was one of the most significant events of history, disagreements still persist about its date. In this century alone dates have been postulated from the broad range of AD 21–36. However, from previous discussion and other significant data, AD 30 or 33 are probable dates for Jesus's crucifixion. First, Pontius Pilate, under whom Jesus was crucified, served as prefect in Judea from AD 26 to 36.[23] Second, both John and Jesus began their ministries around AD 29 according to our interpretation of Luke

3:1–3.[24] Third, according to astronomical calculations, the Passover (Nisan 14) took place on Friday in both AD 30 and 33.[25]

A Chronology of Jesus's Life

Jesus is born (7–4 BC).
Herod the Great dies (March or April of 4 BC).
Prefects begin to rule over Judea and Samaria (AD 6).
Caiaphas becomes high priest (AD 18).
Pilate arrives in Judea (AD 26).
John and Jesus's ministries begin (AD 29).
Jesus observes his first Passover after his baptism (AD 30).
John the Baptist is imprisoned (AD 30 or 31).
Jesus celebrates his second Passover (AD 31).
John the Baptist dies (AD 31 or 32).
Jesus observes his third Passover (AD 32).
Jesus starts his final week (March–April AD 33).
Jesus enters Jerusalem (March AD 33).
Jesus eats the Last Supper; is betrayed, arrested, and tried (Thursday, April 2, AD 33).
Jesus is tried and crucified (Friday, April 3, AD 33).
Jesus is laid in the tomb (Saturday, April 4, AD 33).
The risen Jesus appears to his followers (April 5, AD 33).

We favor AD 33 as the most plausible date for the following reasons. First, it allows for at least a three-year ministry from 29 to 33. Second, it places both the deaths of John and Jesus closer to the

---

21. Strack and Billerbeck *Kommentar zum Neuen Testament aus Talmud und Midrasch*, 2:812–53.

22. A sunrise-to-sunrise reckoning for the Passover is presupposed in Josephus, *Ant.* 3.248–51, and a sunset-to-sunset reckoning is presupposed in the *m. Pesah.* 10:9; *Zebah.* 5:8; see Hoehner, *Chronological Aspects*, 85–90.

23. See n. 10 above.

24. We reckon the "fifteenth year of Tiberius's reign" after the death of Augustus (AD 14).

25. See the following work for the contribution of astronomy for dating the death of Christ: Jeremias, *The Eucharistic Words of Jesus*, 36–41. For a helpful discussion of both the difficulties of dating events in antiquity and the problems posed by the luni-solar calendar of the Jews, especially for dating the crucifixion of Jesus, see Sanders, *Historical Figure*, 282–90; Keener, *Historical Jesus*, 372–74, 597–98.

defeat of Herod Antipas by Aretas in 36. Aretas waged war with Antipas to avenge the death of John and especially the divorce of his daughter by Antipas in order that Antipas could marry Herodias.[26] Third, the accommodating attitude of Pilate toward the Jews at the trial of Jesus is best understood after AD 31. In the fall of that year, Lucius Sejanus, a friend of Pilate, was executed under Tiberius for seizing control of the government from 26 to 31.[27] As a result, the anti-Jewish policies (practiced by Pilate)[28] were lifted, and all friends of Sejanus (e.g., Pilate) were in danger of banishment. The situation after AD 31 would make Pilate very accommodating toward the Jews (e.g., John 19:12). Fourth, the crucifixion date of AD 33 coheres adequately with the statement in John 2:20. It seems to refer to the temple edifice (not the temple precincts completed AD 63) that was completed ca. 18/17 BC or "one year and six months"

after Herod began his great temple reconstruction (ca. 20/19 BC: Josephus, *Ant.* 15.380–87, 421–23) and probably asserts that the temple edifice has been standing for "forty-six years," i.e., AD 29/30. This calculation assumes that the statement in John 2:20 was made at the outset of Jesus's ministry. Fifth, the reference to Jesus's being "about thirty years of age" (Luke 3:23) at the start of his ministry can be adequately explained as an approximate age (i.e., 30–35). As a result of our discussion we favor Friday Nisan 14 (April 3) AD 33 as the date of Jesus's crucifixion.[29]

A chronology of Jesus is at best tentative. It is an historical attempt, working mostly from literary sources of limited self-evident historical value to construct a historical chronology of the life of Jesus. Differences of informed opinion abound, as we have shown above. We have endeavored here, nevertheless, to make a credible case for a workable chronology based on the data and interpretive resources now available to us.

26. Josephus, *Ant.* 18.109–19. John disapproved of Antipas's divorce from the daughter of Aretas to marry Herodias and was beheaded as a result (Mark 6:14–29).

27. Tacitus, *Annals* 6.48; Suetonius, *Tiberius* 36; Josephus, *Ant.* 18.179–94.

28. For the cruel anti-Jewish policies of Pilate, see Josephus, *Ant.* 18.55–59; *War* 2.169–77; Philo, *Embassy* 301–2.

29. The following scholars support AD 33 for the death of Christ: Reicke, *New Testament Era*, 183–84; Hoehner, *Chronological Aspects*, 103–14; Maier, "Sejanus, Pilate, Crucifixion," *CH* 37 (1968) 3–13. For survey of discussion, see Declercq, *Anno Domini*; Mosshammer, *Easter Computus*.

10

The Historical Jesus

We began in the previous chapter with the task of recovering a chronology of the life of Jesus with its challenges of minimal external points of reference, multiple calendrical systems within which to insert data, multicultural varieties of fixing days or holy days or years within an annual calendar, and the like. Knowing as much as possible about Jesus and his world certainly makes the venture worthwhile, but the writers of the early "biographies" of Jesus seemed little concerned about certain time issues and quite unsuspecting of the obsessions that we as their eighteenth- through twenty-first-century readers would entertain.

Furthermore, known details of Jesus's life are both blessing and bane. His preserved sayings are of necessity *fragmentary*[1] rather than exhaustive; and

vintage—even *representative*[2]—rather

comparatively large collection of Jesus's words can be read in the time (one and a half hours) devoted to many university lectures on any given day.

For us a useful range of representative teaching styles recur. The Synoptics contain forms of teaching typical of a Jewish sage: aphorisms, proverbs, parables, and riddles. All these forms of speech fall within the range of the *mashal,* a word for the typical teaching form of wise men in ancient Israel, and also a word translated in LXX by many different Greek words (*parabolē, logos, paroimia,* and *ainigma* are four that occur in just the first six verses of Proverbs [titled *mishlē*; but also *problēma, mythos* and *diēgēsis*). In the Gospels, the Greek words that communicate this meaning are very restricted (*parabolē* mostly, but also possibly *logos* [Mark 4:14] in the Synoptics and *paroimia* in John [10:6; 16:25, 29]). It wouldn't take long in early Christianity for Jesus himself to become the parable, enigma, and problem (*parabolē, ainigma, problēma*). See also Snodgrass, *Stories with Intent,* 1–60, 567–77.

2. In chapter 9, we noted that the sermons and discourses are placed strategically. For instance, the Sermon on the Plain in Luke (6:20–49) is found at the end of a long narrative section (4:14—6:19) that tells of Jesus as an amazingly influential (and inflammatory) teacher, but that lacks any sampling of what he really teaches! By the time the reader gets to the sermon, a significant anticipation has

---

1. As we mentioned earlier, the words attributed to Jesus in Mark total just over 5,000; in Matthew almost 14,000; in Luke almost 13,000; and in John almost 9,000. (The count was done in an English version: the NASB.) This count is itself an interesting diversity, considering that Mark talks often about Jesus's being a teacher. Even Matthew's

than random. The focus of the records left is topical and typical with an emphasis hard to miss on the hero's death. But indeed some basic chronological work can be done prima facie. For example, it is certain that before Jesus died, he was born; that before he worked with John, he was baptized by him; that before he was known as a worker of miracles, he was known as an ordinary worker; that before he was arrested and tried, he was in some way incendiary; that before he was betrayed, he had merited loyal friendship and even messianic hope; that before he was scourged and crucified, he had earned enemies (both political and religious); and finally, if we may, that after he was entombed (bringing an end to some hopeful scenarios), he was resurrected—giving birth to others. Debate over whether to include an account of the *risen* Jesus in discussion of the *historical* Jesus continues with energy.[3] It is an important discussion, because without the risen Jesus, would we really have the Gospels to argue about, and would we have early Christianity or the Epistles as well as any other NT and early Christian literature?

With such examples before us of our own focus and interest (with many of our questions) differing from theirs, and with our picture of Jesus determined by the portrait left by the Gospels, it should make our caution and humility both easier and more urgent. At some point ahead any student of the Gospels will have to address the question of an *author's* interests, the quest for which may be more successful as well as more meaningful, in surprising ways.

THE CULTURAL PROBLEM

What was Jesus of Nazareth really like, especially in his views and teaching? Was he a sentimental teacher of love? A pacifist contemplative? An activist provocateur? A plotting and scheming political messiah? A para-Zealot revolutionary? An

---

been generated by the hoarding of the masses and the silence of the sage, and now one is quite ready to hear what this man is teaching! This artful work of the Gospel writers can (and should) be viewed positively, but frequently it is not since it reveals an authorial agenda to which the reader (and Jesus) is subject.

3. Sanders, *The Historical Figure*, discusses the resurrection as an epilogue (276–81), though he also has a chapter (10) on miracles; Stein, *Jesus the Messiah*, makes it the final chapter of his book roughly of equal length with all the others; Theissen and Merz, *The Historical Jesus*, devote a chapter to it titling it, however, "The Risen Jesus: Easter and Its Interpretations" (474–511), making it a bridge to the final chapter on the beginnings of Christology in the early church; Chilton and Evans, *Authenticating the Activities*, have contributions by scholars on the arrest, the foot washing, and the burial but none on the resurrection (see, however, the contribution by Bruce Malina on miracles in general, specifically on the walking upon water [351–71]; and the opening essay by Evans with the same title as the book [3–29, esp.

12–15]; Wright, *The Resurrection*, is a massive discussion; and Keener, *Historical Jesus*, makes "The Resurrection" (330–48) his final chapter, with also a separate appendix ("What Really Happened at the Tomb?" [379–88]). There are also numerous popularly written books on Jesus such as, by Philip Yancey, *The Jesus I Never Knew*. Yancey discusses the resurrection in the eleventh of fourteen chapters. (The last three chapters are instructive for both Jesus scholars and lay Christians.) Both L. T. Johnson, *Will the Real Jesus*, 133–40; and Keener, *Historical Jesus*, 330–48, discuss the debate and defend different perspectives. For a critical discussion of skeptical modern historiography, see "Miracles and Method," 39–90 in Eddy and Boyd, *Jesus Legend*; for a plea to better understand the dilemma, see Allison, "Miracles Here, There, and Everywhere," in Allison, *Historical Christ*, 66–78; and Chilton and Evans, *Authenticating the Activities*, 11–16.

existentialist rabbi? A cynic-like philosopher-sage? A Gnostic heavenly revealer? A mix of "all or some of the above"?[4] Can we know what he was like? If yes, then how? and what sort of limits would there be to our knowledge? If no, then why not?

The quest for the historical Jesus is not an easy one, because every person has his or her own conception of Jesus based on a particular cultural and religious context. The history of religious art, for example, provides many different faces of Jesus: a beardless Roman shepherd, a Cynic Greek philosopher, a Byzantine divinity, a grueling and tortured human of medieval Germany, Rembrandt's Renaissance-Man, a pious and sentimental-looking white Anglo-Saxon, and an angry black man from an American ghetto. In nineteenth-century Western theology, Jesus was described as a liberal teacher of brotherly love, before Albert Schweitzer argued impressively that he was an urgent preacher of apocalyptic doom.[5] Schweitzer's study

effectively ended the vigorous and prolific nineteenth-century quest with a fair amount of historical skepticism, for he showed that the historical-critical specialists, who had valiantly liberated themselves from the controlling strictures of dogmatic theology, ended up deviously controlled by something else: their own purview.

---

see Klausner, *Jesus of Nazareth*; Jeremias, *Problem of the Historical Jesus*; J. M. Robinson, *New Quest of the Historical Jesus*; Flusser, *Jesus*; Flusser and Notley, *Sage from Galilee*; Conzelmann, *Jesus*; Aulen, *Jesus*; Bornkamm, *Jesus of Nazareth*, 1–26; Bowman, *Which Jesus?*; Braun, *Jesus of Nazareth*; Käsemann, "'Jesus of History' Controversy," in Käsemann, *New Testament Questions of Today*, 23–65; Marshall, *I Believe in the Historical Jesus*; McArthur, *In Search of the Historical Jesus*; Perrin, *Rediscovering*, 15–53; Reumann, *Jesus*; Sanders, *Jesus and Judaism*; Vermes, *Jesus the Jew*; Vermes, *Jesus and the World of Judaism*; Crossan, *Historical Jesus*; Meier, *Roots of the Problem*; Meier, *Mentor*; Meier, *Companions*; Wright, *New Testament and the People of God*; Wright, *Jesus and the Victory of God*; Wright, *The Resurrection*; Allison, *Jesus of Nazareth*; Bock, *Studying the Historical Jesus*; Witherington, *Jesus Quest*; Witherington, *Jesus the Sage*; Keener, *Historical Jesus*; Levine et al., *Historical Jesus in Context*; Evans, *Fabricating Jesus*; Evans, *Life of Jesus Research*; Hengel, *Four Gospels*; Horsley, *Jesus and the Spiral of Violence*; Theissen and Merz, *Historical Jesus*; Crossan and Reed, *Archaeology*; Borg, *New Vision*; Chilton, *Rabbi Jesus*; Twelftree, *Miracle Worker*; L. T. Johnson, *Real Jesus*; Mack, *Myth*; Mack, *Lost Gospel*; Rousseau and Arav, *Jesus' World*; W. Craig, "Tomb"; W. Craig, "Historicity"; W. Craig, *Assessing*; Evans, *Fabricating Jesus*; Evans, *Life of Jesus Research*; Evans, "Non-Christian Sources"; Bockmuehl, *This Jesus*; Porter, *Criteria*; Powell, *Jesus as a Figure in History*. The study of the historical Jesus has as a discipline generated an entire subgenre of historical-critical-apologetic literature. As a consequence, sometimes those authors who produce technical, exegetical, and theological commentaries are sometimes neglected. It was for this very reason that Keener decided to write *Historical Jesus of the Gospels* so that his outsider and (hopefully) broader approach would be read by those who have become students of the subgenre just mentioned.

---

4. To begin with such a familiar list of extreme possibilities seems so clichéd. But scholars (still) do such things in their sleep. The layperson does them also, but usually with much less panache, and the resulting Jesus thumbnail usually looks like someone (e.g., the Good Shepherd) with whom they are comfortable (just as certain scholars are content with a "radical Jesus" that they have created). The point is made in the diversity. The intended pause is created by the possibility of it. See a discussion titled "Disparate Views about Jesus" in Keener, *Historical Jesus*, 1–69.

5. Schweitzer, *Quest of the Historical Jesus*. In 2000, SCM Press (and in 2001, Fortress Press) published the complete English edition based on the 1913 edition. Although W. Montgomery translated the earlier edition, a new translation was provided by Susan Cupitt and John Bowden (editor), with an appreciation of Schweitzer written by Marcus Borg. See also recent assessment by Porter in Charlesworth and Pokorný, *Jesus Research*, 16–35. After Schweitzer, further quests for the historical Jesus have ascended and descended. For example,

But not even the New Testament Gospels are immune from conceptualizing Jesus from a certain perspective. Indeed, they are even bold in their own interpretation of history.[6] Furthermore, the Gospel writers were quite good at embellishing historical data and "creating symbolic narratives."[7] John explicitly, but the others no less so, writes about Jesus from the vantage point of Easter. In John's Gospel it is an explicit motif, beginning in 2:17, 22; and continuing in 12:16 and 14:26 the disciples "remember" the events and words of Jesus with much more cognition (and courage) from the other side of the empty tomb. One must say then that a resurrection hermeneutic informs the writing of these texts, making them both confessions of faith and prompters of it.

So then, we do not have in them anything like pure historical recitation. Rather, the Gospel writers are more like tellers of history in the service of Christology,[8] and while the Christology at times is embedded in such things as titles, at other times it is embedded in theological reflection on the Jewish Scriptures, sacred tradition, and even interpreted events. This manner of communication can be quite subtle and itself culturally conditioned. Such things require the twenty-first-century reader to be cautious, alert, and informed.

THE SOURCE PROBLEM

Another challenge in our quest pertains to the nature of our sources: reliable data outside the NT are scarce. The NT sources are permeated by the literary techniques and theological perspectives of the authors.

Sources outside the NT

The sources outside the New Testament provide only bits of information about Jesus.[9] We will first look at Jewish and Roman and then Christian (including Nag Hammadi).

Jewish and Roman Sources

Only briefly is Jesus alluded to by Jewish and Roman writers. And while early Christian writers refer to Jesus and his teaching more frequently, few of them are independent of NT influence (attesting to some sort of canonical priority[10]). The

---

6. See Eddy and Boyd, *Jesus Legend*, for a recent, sophisticated discussion and defense of the (nevertheless) historical reliability of the synoptic tradition, as well as Bauckham, *Jesus and the Eyewitnesses*, for an original and insightful defense of the Gospels as eyewitness testimony. Another stimulating recent work, informed by wide learning, on Jesus as an apocalyptic prophet is Allison, *Jesus of Nazareth*. See also our chart "Development of the Gospels" in ch. 5, above.

7. Nolland, *Matthew*, 13.

8. Some of the most suggestive and productive Jesus scholarship on the person of Jesus and the early Jesus movement has then come from the solid, provocative perspective of this starting point, especially in coordination with the fast growing scholarship on first-century Judaism and the Greco-Roman world in which both religions grew and changed. For a sampling of such work, see Dunn, *Jesus Remembered*; Riley, *One Jesus*; Hurtado, *Lord Jesus Christ*; Hurtado, *One God, One Lord*; Charlesworth, *Jesus and the Dead Sea Scrolls*.

9. For further information, see Bruce, *Jesus and Christian Origins*; Crossan, *Sayings Parallels*; Jeremias, *Unknown Sayings of Jesus*; Schneemelcher, *NTA*, 1:77–133; Evans, "Jesus in Non-Christian Sources"; Van Voorst, *Jesus outside the New Testament*.

10. For example, two early birth or youth

Babylonian Talmud (AD 500) contains an early tradition about "Yeshu of Nazareth," who "practiced sorcery," "led Israel astray," and "was hanged" [crucified?] as a false teacher "on the eve of the Passover" (*Sanh.* 43a). Even though the tradition seems unreliable in other details, it corresponds with John's account of Jesus's execution before the Passover, and the derogatory description of Jesus's activities might reflect his great reputation as a miracle worker and teacher among the Jews. In a passage attributed to the Jewish historian Josephus (AD 94), the ministry, death, and resurrection of Jesus are reported (*Ant.* 18.63–64), but the report is probably a later Christian interpolation, because it reads like a creedal statement.[11]

The Roman historian Tacitus (AD 112–113) mentions that in the reign of

narratives about Jesus and the holy family, *Protoevangelium of James* and *Infancy Gospel of Thomas* (Schneemelcher, *NTA*, 1:421–39, 439–51), both show dependence upon the canonical Gospels. The former for curiously supplying information absent from the tradition, such as how John the Baptist survived Herod's slaughter of the innocents, and how Jesus came to have siblings. By filling in (very creatively) some hypothetical events from the boy Jesus's youth between the ages of five and twelve, these narratives fill the gap of silence left by Matthew on the one hand (after Jesus's returning from Egypt at around five years of age) and Luke on the other (the temple incident when Jesus is about twelve). Such creative insertions can be enlarged to such an extent that these texts can be effectively read intertextually.

11. Quite often such interpolations can be found in essentially non-Christian texts, especially in the collection of Pseudepigrapha. Early Christians were often quite transparent in their christological intrusions. Worth mention but not worth taking seriously is the sort of eccentric theory put forward by Thiering (*Jesus and the Riddle of the Dead Sea Scrolls*). She proposes that early Christian history is embedded in the Scrolls so that John the Baptist is the Teacher of Righteousness, and Jesus is the Wicked Priest! No more space than that will be given here.

Tiberius Caesar "Chrestus" was given the death penalty by Pontius Pilate, and that the prefect momentarily suppressed the Chrestus sect until it broke out again in Judea and Rome (*Ann.* 15.44). This information, however, may have been derived ultimately from Christian tradition since Tacitus probably based his account on police interrogations of Christians.

Christian Sources

In Christian sources other than the NT, we have a number of isolated sayings of Jesus, or *agrapha*. As examples, we will look at some sayings in Codex Beza, the *Gospel of Thomas*, the *Apocryphon of James*, Clement of Alexandria, and Tertullian.[12] In the Codex Beza (D), a sixth-century NT manuscript, an independent Jesus saying occurs after Luke 6:4, stating, "When on the same day he saw a man doing work on the Sabbath, he said to him: Man! if you know what you are doing then you are blessed. But if you do not know what you are doing then you are cursed and a transgressor of the law."

This saying, as will be shown, coheres well with what many scholars believe to be an authentic feature of Jesus's teaching: the challenge to make one's own decisions. The apocryphal *Gospel of Thomas* (AD 200), discovered along with other Gnostic writings at Nag Hammadi, Egypt, contains some isolated sayings that could have originated with Jesus. Translations of these sayings are from the Nag Hammadi Library in English.[13]

12. Schneemelcher, *NTA*, 1:91.
13. Robinson, *Nag Hammadi Library*.

Jesus said: "He who is near me is near the fire, and he who is far from me is far from the kingdom" (82; Origen).

Jesus said: "The kingdom of the Father is like a man who wishes to kill a powerful man. He drew the sword in his house, he stuck it into the wall in order to know whether his hand could carry through. Then he slew the powerful man" (98; cf. Luke 14:28–32).

The *Apocryphon of James* (AD 200?) is another Gnostic writing discovered at Nag Hammadi. The translations of these sayings are derived from an article by a Nag Hammadi scholar.[14]

"Do not cause the kingdom of heaven to become desolate by you (or among you)" (13.17–19).

"For the kingdom of heaven is like a spike of wheat, that sprouted in a field. And after it ripened, he (the farmer) sowed its fruit and again filled the field with wheat for another year" (12.24–26).

In the writings of the third-century catholic Christians Clement of Alexandria and Tertullian of Carthage we find the following independent Jesus sayings:

"No one can attain the kingdom of heaven who has not gone through temptation" (Tertullian, *On Baptism* 20.2 [Ernest Evans, ed.], translated by Charles Puskas). "Ask for great things, and God will add to you what is small" (Clement of Alexandria, *Stromateis*, 1.24.158).[15]

The above examples are considered isolated Jesus sayings because they show no clear dependency on the NT Gospels, yet their contents cohere substantially with the teaching of the historical Jesus as most scholars understand it.

14. Hedrick, "Kingdom Sayings and Parables."

15. *ANF*, 2:336.

New Testament Sources

The earliest literary witnesses to the historical Jesus are Paul's epistles. But his information is brief and, as letters are, circumstantial. From him we have cursory allusions to Jesus's ancestry, family, ministry, disciples, betrayal, death, and resurrection; many are found in kerygmatic and confessional traditions.[16]

Paul's letters contain some sayings attributed to Jesus, like those in 1 Thess 4:15; 1 Cor 7:10–11; 11:23, 25, but only the first two appear to be independent of the synoptic tradition.[17] The most authentic agraphon is found, not in Paul's letters but in Acts of the Apostles: "it is necessary to remember the words of the Lord Jesus, that he said, 'it is more blessed to give than to receive'" (20:35).

Even though the four Gospels provide the most information about Jesus, problems arise when (1) the Synoptic Gospels are compared with John and (2) the pervasive religious and literary features are detected in all four.

16. The Pauline traditions about Jesus's betrayal, death, and resurrection will be consulted in our discussion of these topics in a later chapter. For a more-extensive treatment of the Pauline traditions about Jesus, see Goguel, *Jesus and the Origins of Christianity*, 1:105–26; Dunn, "Jesus Tradition and Paul," in *Studying the Historical Jesus*, 151–78; Allison, "Pauline Epistles and the Synoptic Gospels."

17. See Patterson, "Paul and the Jesus Tradition," for an interesting discussion of the possibility of connections between Paul and communities that preserved the sayings traditions. One point suggested by Patterson is that there is an almost-playful familiarity with the Sayings Tradition evident in 1 Corinthians, suggesting both more awareness on Paul's part and also a little of what he might have done with the time "in Arabia" during his early years as a follower of Jesus.

The Gospel of John

The differences (which are more substantial than the similarities) between John and the Synoptic Gospels raise some difficulties for any harmonization, as well as historical reconstruction.[18] In John we do not find concise synoptic sayings or parables but long discourses in the form of dramatic monologues or dialogues.[19] The length of Jesus's ministry in John is three or four years, whereas in the synoptic tradition it is one or two. The Synoptic Gospels regard Galilee as the main area of ministry, whereas in John it is Judea. John has Jesus make (at least) three visits to Jerusalem during his ministry, whereas the synoptic tradition mentions only one. The Synoptic Gospels have Jesus crucified on the Passover, but John has the crucifixion before the Passover (cf. *b. Sanh.* 43a). Finally, John includes many unusual stories, themes, and symbols not found in the other Gospels. These sharp differences make attempts at harmonization a futile enterprise.

18. See Goguel, *Jesus and the Origins of Christianity*, 150–57; Brown, *John*, 1:xli–li; Keener, *John* 1:40–47; Smith, *John among the Gospels.*

19. The longest sayings groups in Matthew are The Sermon on the Mount (ca. 2435 words [NRSV the source of all the following stats]) and the sayings group of 23:1—25:46 (ca. 2900). The collected sayings groups of Matthew look quite different from the long discourses in John (most with minor interruptions, structural markers, etc.): 5:19–47 (ca. 641 words); 6:32–70 (ca. 597 words); 8:34–58 (ca. 648 words); 10:7–38 (ca. 611 words); 14:1–31 (ca. 711 words); 15:1–27 (ca. 615 words); 16:1–33 (ca. 704 words); 17:1–26 (ca. 656 words). The last four discourses in John are somewhat continuous, making them almost 2700 words, or comparable to the collections in Matthew. It is the way that the complexes are used that creates the significant difference (see Keener, *John*, 1:68–80).

The similarities between John and the Synoptic Gospels concern some general agreements in sequence and a few close parallels. For example, John and Mark follow a similar sequence at certain points: the work of the Baptist, Jesus's departure into Galilee, Jesus's feeding a multitude, Jesus's walking on water, Peter's confession, Jesus's departure to Jerusalem, Jesus's Jerusalem entry and anointing (rearranged in John), the supper with predictions of betrayal, the arrest and the passion. Some close parallels include the account of Jesus's anointing (John 12:3–8; Luke 7:36–50); the cycle of feeding, lake crossing, and dialogue (John 6:1–51; Mark 6:34—8:21); and the trial scene enveloped by the story of Peter's denial (John 18:15–27; Mark 14:53–72). These parallels contribute something to source-critical discussions, but historical-Jesus research isn't much advanced beyond the circumstance of parallel traditions. If we weight the synoptic tradition historically, then we find here in John some episodes that have (thereby) imputed to them a historical credibility.

Some contributions that John's gospel might provide for our historical quest are: (1) additional information about the relationship between Jesus and John the Baptist, (2) the plausibility that Jesus's ministry lasted longer than one year and involved more than one trip to Jerusalem, (3) the focus on the alleged political crimes of Jesus as the main grounds for his execution (19:12,15); (4) his death on the eve of the Passover; (5) an assortment of Jesus's sayings that have some stamp of authenticity (e.g., John 3:3, 5; 4:32–38, 48; 12:24–26; 13:16); (6) accurate information in chapter 4 about the Samaritans, their theology and worship on Gerazim, and the seemingly correct location of Jacob's well; (7) precise information in chapter 5 on the pool of Bethesda, accurate as to the name, location, and construction; (8) theological themes brought up in relation to Passover and the Feast of Booths (Tabernacles) reflect some accurate knowledge of festal ceremonies and the synagogue readings associated with the feasts; (9) some remarkable details about the city of Jerusalem (destroyed in AD 70) with respect to: the pool of Siloam (9:7), Solomon's portico as a winter shelter (10:22–23), and stone pavement to Pilate's Praetorium.[20] The above data, however, are difficult to distinguish from the pervasive literary and symbolic concerns in the Fourth Gospel. The statement of the author's purpose in writing John also has relevance for our discussion of the literary-religious character of the Synoptic Gospels:

> Now Jesus did many other signs in the presence of his disciples, which are not written in this book. But these are written so that you may believe that Jesus is the Messiah, the Son of God, and that through believing you may have life in his name. (John 20:30–31)

Selective use of data, especially to proclaim and magnify Jesus the Messiah, appears to be an overriding emphasis of

John. We will find that this point is also true of the Synoptics, though the difference may be one of focus, spiritual insight, and literary style. Clement of Alexandria called John the spiritual gospel, while the Synoptics recounted the "bodily facts."

The Synoptic Gospels

Leaving John for the Synoptics is less like going from nonhistory to history than like simply to gazing at a different kind of art. In many ways, pure history still seems a good distance away in the Synoptics; interpreted history unfolds right before our eyes.

What we know with fair certainty about these texts may be usefully summarized here. First, they are narrative constructs skillfully and selectively composed by people of faith wanting to produce faith. They use material that has been fondly preserved by eyewitnesses, oral proclamation, written sources, and keepers of tradition most probably from a variety of geographical locations. The actual live history of the events of Jesus's life has been considerably collapsed so that any chronology is tentative and hard to determine.[21] The date of composition of these texts in the first century is almost impossible to determine,[22] but it is reasonable to

---

20. Since the end of the nineteenth century, points 6 through 9 above have represented historical particulars providing some vindication for the Gospel of John as historically competent with regard to Palestine, especially pre-70 Jerusalem. For further examples of specific points of historical skepticism about the Gospels as sources along with counterpoints to each, see Theissen and Merz, *Historical Jesus*, 90–121. See our bibliography (commentaries section) for information on the commentaries on John by Barrett, Brown, Carson, Keener, and Moloney.

21. Sanders (*Historical Figure of Jesus*, 69) has even reasonably proposed that "perhaps none of the authors knew what took place when . . . or perhaps they did not care about chronological sequence and arranged the material according to some other plan. This would have resulted in chronological clues being scattered at random, and we could not draw good inference from them."

22. There is a fair consensus that Mark preceded Matthew and Luke, and that John is from the late first century, possibly during the reign of Domitian. Whether one or any or all of the Synoptics are from before the destruction of Jerusalem in 70 is debated. John Nolland in writing about

assume that all the texts had a historical context involving life experiences of communities that would help to explain some of their features. They are also all attempts to preserve the works and words of Jesus in a way that would be relevant to the communities' life of faith.

The presence of eyewitnesses, multiple testimonies, Aramaic substrata, and geographical familiarities add weight, but not certainty, to the historical credibility of the traditions. In fact, *certainty* in the study of ancient history, even of sacred history or tradition, is not something that can be achieved. To say this does not make one a skeptic. There are many degrees of historic possibility and probability. Some scholars of the Gospels are relentless in their application of tests to the Jesus traditions, believing that analysis, critical reading, and patient inquiry will always produce learning and an increase in knowledge. They are usually correct. Those scholars who undertake this investigative mission with malice or even with dishonest intent do not usually survive the encounter and the test of time with intellect intact. To satisfy the questioning mind, in the history of this study numerous tests have been proposed, used, wrongly trusted, imperfectly applied, and eventually discarded. But it seems that something useful is always learned even in the presence of abuse. This sequence in fact is a part of the story of New Testament scholarship. And it is the reason why the history of scholarship should be studied and understood.[23]

Next we will survey some of the criteria used to separate the more probable from the less probable elements of the Jesus tradition. Some of these elements have been events or acts of Jesus; some have been words of Jesus. Similar criteria are used in the analysis of historical events recorded in the texts. But since the goal of this chapter is simply the historical Jesus, our coverage will be limited to him. The discussion of these criteria as a heuristic method lends itself to criticism and debate, and we welcome this, will even feel compelled to encourage it. The next chapter is on the *message* of Jesus.

THE CRITERIA OF AUTHENTICITY[24]

While the "criteria of authenticity" have been used by form critics of the Gospels throughout the twentieth century (but mostly in the last half of it), the discussion of them has never been static. In the last forty years, the numbers of criteria have both risen and fallen; the opinion regarding their cogency has both waxed and waned; and the conviction regarding their relevance has both ebbed and flowed. This may seem paradoxical, given the logical nature of their conception

---

Matthew feels there is nothing in Matthew that requires a post-70 date, and so he dates it (along with Mark) before the war. Luke, however, he dates after the war for reasons delicately deduced from the text. All reasons must be delicately deduced.

23. See, for example, the classic histories of

interpretation by Kümmel, *New Testament*; Neill and Wright, *Interpretation of the New Testament, 1861–1986*; Schweitzer *Quest*; Bruce, "The History of New Testament Study," in Marshall, ed., *New Testament Interpretation*, 21–59.

24. Theissen and Merz, *Historical Jesus*, 90–124; Meier, *Marginal Jew*, 1:167–95; Stein, *Gospels and Tradition*, 153–87; Allison, *Historical Christ*; Allison, "Historian's Jesus," in Gaventa and Hays, eds., *Seeking the Identity of Jesus*, 79–95 (for a frontal assault on the criteria as a whole); Allison, *Historical Christ*, chs. 1–3 (also a critique of the criteria); Keener, *Historical Jesus*, 155–61; Porter, *Criteria* (2000).

and application, but if one remembers that they are criteria used to assess and evaluate data about the historical Jesus and theological Christ, then some of the mystery disappears. Everything about Jesus is potentially controversial.[25] The goal here then is to give both a primary and a secondary list of the criteria, briefly discussing the former. The primary list represents the criteria that many consider to be the most important, and includes more discussion. The secondary list is provided to illustrate the development of the discussion.

Primary Criteria

(1) **Embarrassment.** This criterion determines material—either actions or sayings—that would have been an embarrassment to the early church.[26] Such material can hardly be considered as a creation of the church for its proclamation, because it may have caused theological or moral difficulty for them. Examples are the baptism of Jesus by John (Matt 3:13ff.), the rumors that Jesus was a "glutton and a drunkard" (Matt 11:19; Luke 7:34) and had "gone out of his mind" (Mark 3:21), his crucifixion (Mark 15:25; cf. Deut 21:23), and finally the cry of desperation from the cross (Mark 15:34).

(2) **Dissimilarity or Discontinuity.** This criterion assumes that authentic Jesus material can be gleaned from what is dissimilar to or discontinuous with (perceived) post-70 theological tendencies and community-development issues reflected in the four Gospels. For example, Jesus's announcement of the coming reign of God (Mark 1:15), his radical ethics (Luke 14:26), apocalyptic teaching (Mark 13), and simplicity in prayer (Luke 11:2–4) appear dissimilar to what is perceived in the four Gospels as a later time of community development (Matt 16:18; 18:17), creedal formulation (Matt 28:19), separation from the synagogue (John 9:22; 16:2), and adaptation to life in the Roman Empire (ca. AD 65–90). In its quest for distinctiveness, this criterion is related to number 1, but it can also be too speculative and subjective for the following reasons. First, granting a historical distance from the time of Jesus to the time of the Gospels' composition, the distinctions between "early tradition" and "later redaction" cannot be easily discerned (contra, e.g., Fuller or Perrin). Second,

25. The most (in)famous example of controversial use of the criteria in recent years is by a group of scholars named by their organizer Robert Funk the Jesus Seminar. These scholars, largely from North America, met biennially from 1985 through 1991 to discuss, assess, and vote on the authenticity or inauthenticity of Jesus's sayings. They published their results in 1993 in a text titled *The Five Gospels* (the fifth being the Coptic *Gospel of Thomas* found among the Nag Hammadi Codices). They concluded that 82 percent of the sayings of Jesus in the Gospels are inauthentic, and also that 84 percent of his deeds (Funk, et al., *Five Gospels* 5; Funk, and the Jesus Seminar, *The Acts of Jesus*, 1). For a description of their methods and results see Funk, et al., *Five Gospels*, and Funk and the Jesus Seminar, *Acts of Jesus*. For responses to the Jesus Seminar, see Birger Pearson, "The Gospel according to the Jesus Seminar"; and Pearson, "Exposé of the Jesus Seminar"; Witherington, *Jesus Quest*; Hays, "Corrected Jesus"; Johnson, *Real Jesus*. Responses to the Seminar critics are Robinson, "The Real Jesus of the Sayings Gospel Q"; Miller, *Jesus Seminar*. Crossan's bestselling *Historical Jesus*, and Borg's popular *Meeting Jesus Again* are two titles that agree with many conclusions of the Jesus Seminar.

26. A criterion (from Greek *kritēs*) is a standard, rule, or test by which a judgment can be formed.

how much of the Gospels is really tendential and apologetic? Is the presentation of "Jesus the teacher of Israel" (Luke 4:15; 21:37–38) merely a creative response to Jewish accusations about "the founder" of the early church? Why would the historical Jesus not be one of the best representatives of his contemporary Jewish culture? Third, how defensible is it to conclude that most of the high estimations of Jesus (say as messianic prophet and the Wisdom of God) or that most of his prophetic criticisms of the temple (e.g., Mark 11:15ff.) merely reflect the creative responses of the early church to its own authority and self-identity problems but have little or no connection to the remembered past of his earliest followers? (On this question, see also footnote 8 above.) Finally, our information and understanding of first-century Palestine have developed significantly in the last 150 years, but especially in the last fifty (e.g., with the discovery of Qumran, prophetic messianism, Hellenistic Judaism, divine-wisdom theology, and the importance of memory and tradition). As a result of these findings, making clear distinctions between, e.g., Judaism and Hellenism, early and later Christologies, pre-70 and post-70 theology or praxis[27] are difficult to establish with any degree of credibility.

(3) Multiple Attestation. This criterion is a cross-sectional test used with the others, and it focuses on themes or concerns behind a particular saying or parable. If a concern or practice ascribed to Jesus can be traced to several independent sources (to Mark, Q, M, L, or John) and different literary forms (parable, wisdom saying, controversy story), it probably is an early Jesus tradition. Thus, Jesus's fellowship with tax collectors and outcasts, which has been established as authentic by the criterion of dissimilarity (both the Jews of Jesus's day [*m. Ṭehar* 7:6] and the early church [Matt 18:17] scorned them), is also verified by the criterion of multiple attestation. His association with tax collectors and sinners occurs in prophetic (Matt 11:19/Luke 7:34) and wisdom (Matt 5:46/Luke 6:33) sayings of Q, and in pronouncement (Mark 2:14) and controversy (2:15–16) stories of Mark. The authenticity of this practice of Jesus is attested in two independent sources (Q and Mark) and in four different literary forms.

(4) Coherence or Consistency. The criterion of coherence functions as a positive test that builds upon the other criteria. Early material can be accepted as authentic if it coheres or is consistent with material already established as authentic by the other criteria. For example, once the distinctive message of Jesus has been established by the other criteria, Jesus traditions consistent with this message can be regarded as authentic.

(5) Rejection and Execution. This criterion is different in nature but fundamental to the understanding of Jesus's life. It is not necessarily specific to sayings or events but rather is based upon the fact that Jesus's life was on a trajectory toward violent death at the hands of the Jewish

---

27. For example, Martyn, *History and Theology*, has argued for a post-70 separation of synagogue and church (John 9), appealing to the *birkat ha-minin* (the twelfth of eighteen *Amidah*) used in the late first-century synagogues, but Schiffman, "At the Crossroads," 115–56; and Kimelman, "*Birkat-Ha-Minim* and the Lack," have argued against such formal separation this early. See also in support, Katz, "Issues in the Separation of Judaism and Christianity."

leaders and Roman officials. Therefore, it seeks this large and primary context to be fulfilled in our understanding of the course of his life. This is why we said at the beginning of this chapter, "before he was arrested and tried, he was in some way incendiary." The claim of this criterion to authenticity is also related to criterion number 1: why would the church include this controversial material (e.g., Acts 5:30; Gal 3:13) in its teaching and preaching unless it was inseparable from the life and ministry of Jesus?

Secondary Criteria[28]

(6) **Traces of Aramaic.** Despite the prevalence of Hellenistic Greek, a Palestinian dialect of Aramaic was the household speech of Jesus's compatriots preserved in Greek transcription, especially Mark 5:41; 7:34; 15:34 (cf., Matt 27:46) but also Rom 8:15; 1 Cor 16:22; Gal 4:6. Even a Galilean Aramaic was recognized (Matt 26:73).

---

28. Items **6–11** are considered secondary. Further discussion of these criteria can be found in note 24 of this chapter. See also point **6**, "Traces of Aramaic"; and Meier, *Marginal Jew*, 1:178ff.; Stein, *Gospels and Tradition*, 163–64; Keener, *Historical Jesus*, 158–59; for point **7**, see Meier, *Marginal Jew* 1:180; Stein, *Gospels and Tradition*, 166–67; Keener, *Historical Jesus*, 157–58; for point **8**, see Meier, *Marginal Jew*, 1:180–81; Keener, *Historical Jesus*, 159–60; for point **9**, see Meier, *Marginal Jew*, 1:182; Stein, *Gospels and Tradition*, 168; for point **10**, see Meier, *Marginal Jew*, 1:183; Stein, *Gospels and Tradition*, 154–55, 186–87; for point **11**, see Stein, *Gospels and Tradition*, 162; Meier, *Marginal Jew*, 1:174–75.

The Son of Man title appears to make better sense in Aramaic (*bar 'enasha*) or Hebrew (e.g., Mark 2:28; 8:38; 9:9, 31) than in Greek or Latin (*Filius hominis*).

(7) **Palestinian Environment.** See below.

(8) **Vividness of Narrative.**

(9) **Tendencies of Synoptic Tradition.**

(10) **Historical Presumption.**

(11) **Multiple Forms.**

Because Jesus was a great person of history (not excluding his other attributes); and because the Gospels are literary, historical, and theological; and because the historical data about Jesus are limited, distant from its subject, and separated from us culturally, ideologically, and chronologically, some criteria of discernment are necessary. Because the NT writings are primarily rhetorical and theological, and because all of us who interpret them do so from certain perspectives and orientations, our findings and conclusions must remain tentative. Although our methodologies are continually subject to revision and (hopefully) improvement, perhaps the historical presentation of Jesus that is the *most* socio-rhetorically informed, the *most* culturally conversant with the remembered stories, and the *most* attentive to the theological and christological message of the Gospels probably can make the *best* claim for some historical credibility in our postmodern era.

11

The Message of Jesus

Judging from the Apostles' Creed, which jumps from the birth of Jesus to his death (Lat. *Natus ex Maria virgine; passus sub Pontio Pilato*), the details of neither Jesus's life nor his teaching carried much creedal significance. But if one important function of such a creed was for baptismal instruction and for profession at baptism when the convert renounced the devil and his works, and if part of Jesus's life was in fact a battle with evil (victory's being a fait accompli through his death and resurrection), then perhaps in the loosest terms one can see Jesus's life suggested between the semicolon and the word "suffered" (Lat. *passus*). It is difficult however, to accept such an attenuation of the Lord's life and words in the light of what was said and done by him.

For example, in Luke 6:46 Jesus says, "Why do you call me, 'Lord, Lord,' and do not do what I tell you?" This certainly sounds like a question one should avoid having to be asked! But indeed how would it be avoided if Jesus's words were not known? This saying is dramatized by Jesus in the parable of the Sheep and the Goats in Matt 25:31–46. In this passage, a group thinking they are his disciples are caught in the difficulty of having failed to do what he had required, and they learn that in a sobering sense the judgment will not pertain to what one *says* about Jesus, but instead to what one *does* because of him. Jesus cares about obedience, about "bearing fruit" to use a metaphor favored by him.

Other sayings of Jesus are equally alarming when seen in this context of the importance of his life and words. In the Sermon on the Mount, in the section that we call traditionally the antitheses (Matt 5:21–48), Jesus restates the mandates of Moses to an almost impossible degree. Instead of forbidding murder, Jesus forbids hate; instead of forbidding adultery, Jesus forbids lust. What the Torah required or forbade in action, Jesus requires or forbids in thought.

But the intensity of Jesus's preeminence goes beyond what he expresses as his will. It extends to the significance and enigma of who he is. The Jews had the great collection of Wisdom literature—that grand peripatetic tradition of how to live a skillful life according the "Way": the *ḥokmah* or "wisdom" of God by which the Almighty had founded the very order of creation. A grand tradition in Israel founded by the master sage himself, Solomon. But pay attention, for "something greater than Solomon is here" (Matt 12:42; Luke 11:31)! The Jews had the prophets, those anointed spokespersons for YHWH, who with their warnings guided Israel. Among these was Jonah, that prophet sent to proclaim YHWH's love even to Israel's enemies. But "something greater than Jonah is here" (Matt 12:41; Luke 11:32)! The Jews had the temple, the dwelling place of God on earth. But, behold, "something greater than the temple is here" (Matt 12:6)! The Jews had the Torah given through Moses, that man of whom, Philo says, no one born of woman is greater. The Gospel of John, however, says, "The Torah was *given* through Moses, but grace and truth were 'born' [Gk. *ginomai*] through Jesus Christ" (John 1:17, our translation). The confession of the Evangelist is that Jesus was an embodiment of revelation while the Torah through Moses was a record given.[1] Finally, the Jews had as their founding patriarch Abraham, but "before Abraham was, I am" (John 8:58). It is clear in this early Christian gospel tradition that Jesus in his person (i.e., acts) and in his words

was of such significance that to neglect either would be the worst kind of folly.

It should be said at the outset also that students of the Jesus traditions are coming to recognize the important corollary between Jesus's "deeds and words." What he teaches in aphorism and *chreia* and poetic style on ethics, reciprocity, *imitatio dei*, possessions, and the like can be demonstrated in other forms of teachings such as the parable collection. In Luke 6:20–49, a section of teaching known as the Sermon on the Plain, such a collection of topics and forms can be found in one place. This minicollection of Jesus's sayings from the Q tradition is vintage Jesus. It contains his teaching about sacrificial love, nonviolence, imitation of God ("Be merciful, just as your Father is merciful," v. 36), nonreciprocity (i.e., don't do things for others to incur a debt from them), possessions (you should gather and possess *material things* just so you have something to give to those in need). The list could be enlarged, but the point is made. A further point should be made, however: that almost all these admonitions can be dramatized from the parable collection.

Christians have developed some skill in muting Jesus. One maneuver has been called "the christological dodge."[2] Some construct chronological charts that put Jesus's ethical teaching in a completely different theological corridor, and hence reduce its importance for "the church." Some just use their incredible ingenuity to engineer elaborate systems of justification

---

1. It is possible that the Evangelist is implying that Jesus is the living Torah. The commentary on John by Craig Keener discusses this idea in this verse.

2. Robinson, "Real Jesus," 139ff. The point (well) made is that attention away from ourselves and our behavior is sometimes negotiated by changing the emphasis to *what we believe* about Jesus, our Christology, rather than *how we respond* to the radical ethical demands that Jesus makes upon our lives.

for almost any kind of behavior imaginable. The modest goal of these introductory paragraphs has been subversion. While there are numerous good reasons to study Jesus, one of the best is to aspire to follow him, and to do so on his terms (as the Gospels contend). It requires close attention to his teachings as we find them in the New Testament.

THE CULTURAL CONTEXT: MESSIANISM

At the time of Jesus, Palestine had many prophets and messiahs.[3] In Josephus's *Antiquities* and in the biblical Acts of the Apostles we read about end-time oriented prophets like Judas the Galilean (*Ant.* 18.1–10, 23–25; cf. Acts 5:37), Theudas (*Ant.* 20.97–98; Acts 5:36), the Egyptian prophet (*Ant.* 20.167–72: Acts 21:38), and John the Baptist (*Ant.* 18.117; Acts 13:24–25). All these except John advocated armed resistance against Rome. The followers of Judas the Galilean did not seek a coming messiah, since "they accepted God alone as their leader and master" (*Ant.* 18.169). John the Baptist advocated water baptism as an end-time seal for those who repented and practiced

3. The following works discuss prophets and messiahs of first-century Palestine: Hanson and Oakman, *Palestine*, 80–89; Horsley, "Ancient Jewish Banditry"; Horsley, "Early Christian Movements"; Horsley, *Jesus and the Spiral of Violence*; Bammel and Moule, eds., *Jesus and the Politics of His Day*, 1–68, 109–28; Schürer, *History of the Jewish People*, 2:488–513; J. J. Collins, "An Essene Messiah?"; J. J. Collins, *Scepter and the Star*; Riley, *River of God*, 205–12; Charlesworth, "Concept of the Messiah in the Pseudepigrapha"; Charlesworth, "From Messianology to Christology," in Charlesworth, *The Messiah*, 3–35; and also in this volume, Roberts, "Messianic Expectations," 39–51; Schiffman, "Messianic Figures," 116–29.

righteousness (*Ant.* 18.116–19). The Egyptian prophet emerged from the wilderness, performed miracles and signs, and gathered a large following of people at the Mount of Olives (*Ant.* 20.167–72). Although differences exist between Jesus and these other messianic figures, some general similarities between Jesus and these end-time prophets include an end-time orientation, use of prophetic imagery, the performing of miracles, little or no interest in a coming messiah (unlike the disciples of some), and large followings of people.

Whereas such similarities appear to situate Jesus in the end-time prophetic tradition, the following differences highlight his distinctive emphasis: (1) Unlike most end-time prophets, Jesus (like John) did not advocate any program of political resistance, despite his Roman execution for sedition. (2) Although Jesus was initially affiliated with the ministry of John, it is uncertain if Jesus continued John's practice of water baptism (see, e.g., John 3:22; 4:2). (3) Jesus did not emphasize the coming of God for judgment but the dawning of God's rule in his own ministry. It was John the Baptist who stressed the coming of God's final judgment and the need for repentance and conversion to escape this "baptism with fire" (Matthew 3; Mark 1:2–8; Luke 3). (4) As a result, the conduct of Jesus's disciples was not motivated by the threat of coming judgment but by the invitation to participate in God's rule (Mark 2:18–20). This last difference underlines the more affirmative and celebrative aspects of Jesus's message when compared with John's, which conforms to the old prophetic tradition (e.g., Elijah, Amos). The wisdom, piety, and great deeds attributed to Jesus are also reminiscent of other Jewish holy men of the Second Temple period. Like Elisha the prophet, Onias the righteous procured rain during a famine by his prayers (Josephus, *Ant.* 14.22). Healings and other miracles were also attributed to the prayers of Hanina ben Dosa, the Jewish sage (*b. Ber.* 33a, 34b; *b. Pesaḥ.* 112b; *b. Taʿan.* 24b; *b. Yoma* 53b).[4] But like some of the Gospel miracles, these embellished accounts tell us more about the convictions of later admirers than about the historical situations of these holy men.

THE RHETORICAL TECHNIQUES

Before developing the content of Jesus's message, it is necessary first to understand the imagery and rhetorical techniques central to his teaching. The most important imagery used by Jesus is that connected with God's rule. The phrase "kingdom of God" (Gk. *basileia tou theou*) would call up in the consciousness of any Jew of Jesus's day, the entire experience of Israel under God's sovereignty.[5] In Israel's

history, God was regarded as a great king who created the world, called the patriarchs, delivered Israel from Egypt, guided them through the wilderness, gave them the law, defeated their enemies, and brought them into the promised land. Before the Babylonian exile (587 BC) God's reign over Israel and the nations was envisioned as a future hope in history (ancient prophecy). After the exile and up to the first century AD, especially under the duress of foreign oppression and political dominance, the Jews believed that God's kingdom would be revealed at the end of the age in connection with cosmic catastrophes and spiritual warfare between angels and demons (apocalyptic eschatology). God will then judge the wicked (both foreign oppressors and all evildoers), vindicate the righteous (the faithful remnant), reestablish the divine covenant with Israel, and bring a new age of peace and blessing to all people. Such vivid and awesome imagery characterized Jesus's announcement that "God's reign is upon you" (Luke 11:20, translation by C. B. Puskas).

The rhetorical techniques of Jesus are evident to anyone who reads his parables and sayings. He often employed hyperbole or overstatement to impart both the dread of first encountering the awesome rule of God and the carefree joy of discovering and participating in it. To concretize his ideas and skillfully transport them to his listeners' situation, Jesus often used figures of analogy, especially parables. He also employed euphemism to instruct his listeners in matters of prayer and forgiveness (e.g., Mark 11:22–25). The teaching of Jesus would have produced in his

4. For further discussion of Jesus and "charismatic Judaism," see Vermes, *Jesus the Jew*, 58–82; Vermes, "Hanina ben Dosa"; Vermes, *Religion of Jesus*, 46–75; Green, "Palestinian Holy Men"; Buechler, *Types of Jewish-Palestinian Piety*; Flusser, *Jesus* 69–70, 93, 95; Flusser and Notley, *Sage from Galilee*. On the bold claims and resurrection faith of Jesus's followers, see Johnson, *Writings of the New Testament*, chs. 4–5; Keener, *Historical Jesus*, 339–48, 585–90.

5. Chilton, *The Kingdom of God*; Evans, "Kingdom of God, of Heaven," in *IDB* 3:17–26; Klappert, "King, Kingdom," in *NIDNTT* 2:372–90; Kleinknecht et al. "*Basileus, Basileia,* etc.," in *TDNT* 1:564–93; Perrin, *Kingdom of God in the Teaching of Jesus* (1963); Vermes, *Religion of Jesus*, ch. 5 (with biblical and intertestamental references); Willis, *Kingdom of God*; Meier, *Marginal Jew*, 2:237–506; Mack, "The Kingdom That Didn't Come"; Wright, *Jesus and the Victory of God*, part 2; Horsley, *Jesus and Empire*; Hanson and Oakman,

Palestine, 144–45; Chilton, "Regnum"; Chilton, "Kingdom of God in Recent Discussion."

listeners a wide range of human impressions and moods: intensity, seriousness, conviction, irony, mystery, joyfulness, reverence, and aspiration.

THE CONTENT OF JESUS'S MESSAGE

We will summarize the content of Jesus's message by examining the following five themes, which are all related to the proclamation of God's reign: (1) God's rule is present; (2) God alone accomplishes divine rule; (3) God's rule defies human standards; (4) God's rule challenges conventional wisdom; and (5) God's rule reveals God as a merciful father. In order to capture some of the original impressions conveyed by these themes, as well as to perceive the vividness and relevance of Jesus's teaching, some application to our own contemporary situation will be made. Material discussed below is as "authentic" as we can discern from the use of the (limited) criteria discussed in our previous chapter.

God's Rule Is Present

To anyone reading the sayings of Jesus in Mark 1:15, Matt 11:12; Luke 11:20; and 17:21, the sense of immediacy is striking: God's end-time rule is breaking in! The climax of God's saving activity is at hand! The sense of utter urgency that this message must have imparted to Jesus's listeners might be compared, in our own day, to the horrifying news of nuclear attack or the shocking report that we have terminal cancer. Throughout Israel's history, it must be remembered, the reign of God was viewed as a time of both judgment

and salvation. According to Jesus, there is an impending irruption now making itself felt. Speculations about the future coming of God's rule did not concern him. Jesus proclaimed the reign of God as a reality to be experienced in the lives of his listeners.[6] They were to recognize the reality of God's saving activity in the healings and exorcisms he performed (Luke 11:20), in the fate of John the Baptist (Matt 11:12), and in acts of mercy and love (Matt 5:39–41, 44–48).

God Alone Accomplishes Divine Rule

Unlike the contemporary end-time prophets who advocated armed resistance to effect God's reign, Jesus saw the new order instituted only by God. Although, like his contemporaries, he would have been critical of foreign rule. Jesus often communicated his views about the development of God's reign by speaking in parables.

Beginning in the nineteenth century, NT scholars attempted to distinguish the "simplicity" of Jesus's parables from the "complexity" of traditional allegory. According to this view, allegory encodes an elaborate set of symbolic comparisons into the numerous details of a story, whereas a parable focuses attention on *only one* central message illustrated by a familiar life situation.[7] However, recent studies regard

6. For further study on the present aspect of the kingdom of God, see Perrin, *Rediscovering*, 63–77; Perrin, *Jesus*, 15–34; Chilton, *God in Strength*; Dodd, *Parables of the Kingdom*, 21–84; Meier, *Marginal Jew*, 2:398–506; Stein, *Jesus the Messiah*, 123–40; Theissen and Merz, *Historical Jesus*, 246–80; Evans, "Inaugurating the Kingdom."

7. See the classic critical work of Jülicher, *Gleichnisreden Jesu*. For further studies and analyses, see Dodd, *Parables of the Kingdom*; Jeremias, *Parables of Jesus*; Tolbert, *Perspectives on the Parables*;

this view as reductionistic. The insistence on one point per parable appears to be a modernistic reaction to a less-disciplined, ahistorical reading popularized by medieval allegory where even minor details carried great spiritual significance. Many contemporary scholars now urge a more flexible understanding of parable as an evocative metaphor, sufficiently imprecise that it will draw the hearer's or reader's mind and imagination to actively wrestle with its elusive message.[8] Still others argue for striking a balance between the allegorical and the parabolic by allowing Jesus's parables to make at least as many points as there are, e.g., main characters in the story.[9]

Despite the above debate, a number of Jesus's parables (e.g., Mark 4:30–32) are simple enough to contain the following pattern: (a) a starting point, usually with the opening phrase, "the kingdom of God is like"; (b) the illustration from life (e.g., a mustard seed); and (c) a central point (e.g., miraculous growth). Finding "one central point" presents some challenges in some of the longer parables (e.g., parables with two or more characters).

Two parables illustrating the divine activity that accomplishes God's rule, the Seed Growing Spontaneously (Mark 4:26–29) and the Seed Being Sown (4:3–8), fit the pattern well. In the first parable, God's reign (a) is compared to seed growing spontaneously (b), to develop the main point of the miraculous growth of the kingdom (c). Just as the spontaneous growth of the seed into wheat ripe for harvest is not dependent on the farmer (b*), so is the dawning of God's rule not dependent on human activity (a*)—all are the direct result of God's miraculous activity (c). Since the ancient understanding of horticulture was prescientific, this parable of Jesus, highlighting the "mysterious" in nature, would have made an effective point to his listeners.

The other parable illustrating the dawn of the kingdom as an act of God alone is that of the seed being sown (Mark 4:3–8). Here the reign of God (a) is compared to seed scattered on a field (b) in order to illustrate again the miraculous growth of the kingdom (c). Just as some of the seed fails to grow even with an immense harvest (b*), so it is with God's rule: despite its apparent weaknesses, it will blossom into full glory (a*). In both parables, the human element is passive and dependent on a mysterious, divine force for the results. This miraculous growth, in the understanding of Jesus's listeners, could only be caused by God.

God's Rule Defies Human Standards

Jesus believed that God's emerging reign would bring a crisis to the human

Gowler, *What Are They Saying about the Parables?*; Longenecker, *Challenge of Jesus' Parables*; Hedrick, *Many Things in Parables*; Schottroff, *Envisioning the Reign of God through Parables*; Snodgrass, *Stories with Intent*. For more discussion of the parables, see our ch. 5 under "Form Criticism."

8. Funk, *Language, Hermeneutic, and the Word of God*; McFague, *Speaking in Parables*; Perrin, *Jesus*; Donahue, *Gospel in Parable*; Hedrick, *Parables as Poetic Fictions*.

9. See Funk, *Parables and Presence*; Borsch, *Many Things in Parables*; Blomberg, *Interpreting the Parables*. For example, the parables of the Hidden Treasure and the Pearl of Great Price (Matt 13:44–46) each could make one point since there is only one "character" in each story. Parables such as the Pharisee and the Tax Collector (Luke 18:9–14) make two points, and the parable of the Prodigal Son (Luke 15:11–32) makes three points, one for each character (father, prodigal, and elder son).

situation of his listeners. It would result in a radical self-questioning and a complete reversal of human values. In our own day, complete and sudden changes of priorities occur in crisis situations, like war and terminal illness. This new situation announced by Jesus threatened the security and stability provided by the Jewish worldview. Jesus's challenge of radical self-questioning can be illustrated by the parables of the Good Samaritan (Luke 10:30–36), the Unjust Steward (16:1–7), and the Pharisee and Tax Collector (18:9–14); and by those sayings that confront the hearer with a complete reversal of priorities (Luke 9:60; Matt 5:39–41; Mark 8:35; 10:23, 25, 31; Luke 14:11, 26).

In the parable of the Good Samaritan (Luke 10:30–36), Jesus demands that his listeners "conceive the inconceivable."[10] Only the parable appears to be from Jesus. Therefore, we have separated it from its present context, since the discussion with the lawyer (10:25–29, 37) is probably a conflation of Markan and Q material.[11] The focal point of the parable is on the goodness of the Samaritan: "which of these three . . . became a neighbor to the man who fell among the robbers?" The parable challenges Jesus's listeners to conceive the inconceivable because (a) both Jesus and his audience were Jewish, and (b) Samaritans were despised by the Jews on both racial and religious grounds. It was not the respectable Jewish priest or Levite that was a neighbor to the injured man, but the hated Samaritan! In order to comprehend better the original impact of Jesus's parable, let us retell the story for modern North American readers.

One night as a man was driving home from church in a suburban neighborhood, his car was stopped by a gang of youths. He was beaten, his car was stolen, and he was left on the side of the road unconscious. Now by chance a respected Protestant minister was driving by, but because his schedule was pressing, he drove on (planning to telephone the police later). So also a well-liked deacon at the minister's church passed by the man in his car. But then came a Shiite Muslim, an immigrant from Iran, suspicious of "Christians." As he drove to where the injured man was, he stopped his car, lifted the injured man into it, and drove him to the nearest hospital. Since the man's wallet and identification had been stolen, the Muslim signed all the admittance papers, contacted the police, and patiently waited at the hospital for the man to regain consciousness. Which of these three became a neighbor to the man who was beaten and robbed?

In the parable of the Unjust Steward (Luke 16:1–8), Jesus shows how even actions contrary to accepted human standards can be an acceptable response to the crisis of God's emerging reign. It is a surprising message in an honor-shame culture. The focal point of the parable is the reversal of moral values conveyed by the actions of the steward. In the story, an estate manager realizes that his absentee landlord is about dismiss him for negligence. Unable to see any future work opportunities, the manager pursues a bold course of action. Summoning the landlord's debtors (tenants or merchants with promissory notes), the manager

10. Funk, *Language, Hermeneutic, and Word of God,* 199–223; Crossan, "Parable and Example"; Crossan, *In Parables,* 57–66.

11. Hultgren, *Parables of Jesus,* 94–95. This conclusion does not rule out the probability that Jesus, on other occasions, debated with legal scribes and Pharisees.

drastically reduces the amount of each debt, and so is given the hope that they will reciprocate by welcoming him into their homes. As in the parable of the Good Samaritan, so in this parable Jesus "says what cannot be said," and advocates "doing what cannot be done."[12]

In the parable of the Unjust Steward, Jesus compels his listeners to applaud an act of mercy that is also dishonest. In our own situation it would be like a bank official reducing the home loans of his clients by 40 percent! In the context of Jesus's message, this rash decision becomes an acceptable response to the crisis of God's dawning rule: a reign that defies all human conceptions of honesty and justice. The parable of the Pharisee and the Tax Collector (Luke 18:9–14) discloses how God's rule reverses all religious values. The Pharisee is a respected member of the Jewish community whereas the tax collector is viewed by the Jews as a Roman sympathizer and a swindler. In our day, we might compare these two characters to a respectable Protestant minister and a "suspicious-looking" Shiite Muslim (in our post-9/11 era). The Pharisee's prayer began as an acceptable prayer of thanksgiving (v. 11; cf. Ps 17:1–5) but it appears to deteriorate into boasting and self-congratulations at the expense of the other person's defects.[13] The tax collector's

prayer is a typical petition of mercy, but because of his humility and sincerity he alone receives God's approval. Although it probably circulated independently of its present context, the following reversal saying of Jesus is an appropriate summary of the parable: "For all who exalt themselves will be humbled, but all who humble themselves will be exalted" (Luke 18:14).

In addition to parables, Jesus employed short wisdom sayings to challenge his listeners to radical self-questioning and a complete reversal of values. We will quote the sayings and only make a brief comment when necessary.

> Leave the dead to bury their own dead. (Luke 9:60)

> But if anyone strikes you on the right cheek, turn the other also; and if any one wants to sue you and take your coat, give your cloak as well; and if anyone forces you to go one mile, go also the second mile. (Matt 5:39–41)

In making these impossible demands to shun one's religious and social responsibilities for the dead or to become indecently exposed for the legal satisfaction of another and allow oneself to be forced indefinitely into the service of another (by a Roman soldier!), Jesus jolts

---

12. Funk, *Language, Hermeneutic, and Word of God*; Crossan, *In Parables*; see also similar interpretations by Via and Porter in Snodgrass, *Stories with Intent*, 406–7, 719. Some of the urgency of these sayings fits well, at times, with Schweitzer's view of an apocalyptic Jesus facing the immediacy of God's coming kingdom, Schweitzer, *Quest*, 322ff.

13. Danker, *Jesus and the New Age*, 184–86. Some scholars, however, see no deterioration in the Pharisee's prayer (Luke 18:11–12) but see both characters as caricatures: e.g., Downing, "Ambiguity of the Pharisee and Toll-Collector"; Hedrick,

Parables as Poetic Fictions, 227–35, causing us to ponder our relationships with God. Modern readers, however, must grasp how stunning was the news that a tax collector was declared righteous by Jesus (on unfair taxation, see Hanson and Oakman, *Palestine*, 106ff.). The paradox of a righteous tax collector coheres well with other related statements by Jesus, e.g.: "I have not come to call the righteous, but sinners to repentance" (Luke 5:32), or "many that are first will be last, and the last, first" (Mark 10:31); see Snodgrass, *Stories with Intent*, 467–68, 474.

his listeners into making real decisions about their lives and values. The crisis of God's in-breaking rule necessitates radical self-examination.

> For those who want to save their life will lose it; and those who lose their life for my sake and the sake of the gospel will save it. (Mark 8:35)

> How hard it will be for those who have wealth to enter the kingdom of God . . . It is easier for a camel to go through the eye of a needle than for someone who is rich to enter the kingdom of God. (Mark 10:23, 25)

> But many who are first will be last, and the last will be first. (Mark 10:31)

> For all who exalt themselves will be humbled, and those who humble themselves will be exalted. (Luke 14:11)

> Whoever comes to me and does not hate father and mother, wife and children, brothers and sisters, yes, and even his own life, cannot be my disciple. (Luke 14:26)

Like the parables examined in this section, these sayings advocate a complete reversal of human values and priorities as a result of the invasion of God's reign in human existence. The contrasts in these sayings are deliberately exaggerated by Jesus to challenge his listeners to reexamine their lives and values in the present. Whom does God accept? What am I to do about it?

Even though it is probable that early Palestinian followers of Jesus sought to practice many of these radical sayings (and created some of their own), we are not convinced that Jesus wanted everyone to be poor, homeless, wandering preachers like himself and his followers.[14] This type of lifestyle, however, was typical of many religious and philosophical movements in the Mediterranean world. Jesus's obvious appeal to the peasantry and artisans of his day, and his threat to the powerful elites and to religious boundaries, suggests that Jesus did not envision an ascetic and sectarian community like the Essenes. This observation leads us to believe that Jesus intended a response like radical self-questioning in his use of hyperbole and paradox. It certainly had political implications, as Richard Horsley and others have pointed out. The kingdom of God is *God's* empire, not that of Caesar or of any other foreign power. Furthermore, associations with "exile under a foreign empire" and the hope of deliverance from it (see the work of N. T. Wright) is implicit in the message and meaning of the kingdom of God's emerging in the words and deeds of Jesus.

God's Rule Challenges Conventional Wisdom

Closely related to the radical self-questioning of human values was Jesus's challenge to the old ways of comprehending human relations and the world itself. This challenge is best illustrated by the antitheses of the Sermon on the Mount (Matt 5:21–48) and the sayings on religious observance and purity (Mark 2:19, 21; 7:15). Because these sayings of Jesus, set against the law of Moses ("You heard that it was

14. Theissen, *Sociology*, 1–24; Theissen and Merz, *Historical Jesus*, 168–234; see also Hanson and Oakman, *Palestine*, on the "pyramids of power" involving patrons, brokers, and clients, with their effects on the peasantry, ch. 3.

said . . . but I tell you"), are so demanding, some were qualified in later traditions: e.g., "without a cause" (Matt 5:22 KJV); "except for the matter of unchastity" (Matt 5:32).[15] However, these challenges to the common sense values of Jewish law (e.g., eternal liability for anger, not just murder—contra Exod 20:13; adultery of the heart, not just the body—contra Exod 20:14) are more than radical demands to be modified and implemented. These antitheses of Jesus were intended to challenge one's secure and complacent view of the world. Like the wisdom sayings mentioned earlier, they were intended to produce a radical questioning of one's present existence because of the in-breaking of God's rule. Since God's future has arrived, humankind's present must be changed. Jesus's understanding of the present affected by God's future is also evident in his statements on religious observance and purity. The in-breaking of God's rule in Jesus's ministry marks a time of release from normal religious obligations (e.g., fasting) and a time of rejoicing in the experience of God's presence and activity (Mark 2:19). Jesus's ministry also marks a new point of departure, bursting the bonds of those traditions that oppress (2:21). Finally, one of Jesus's most radical challenges to the old way of understanding the world is found in Mark 7:15. The statements in this verse challenge Jesus's

listeners to reexamine a basic premise of the Jewish religion: the distinction between sacred and secular.[16] One must now question the presumption that any external circumstances in the world can separate a person from God. According to Jesus, only the individual person (i.e., his or her own attitude and behavior) is the defiling agent, not foods or other externals. The in-breaking of God's future in the present necessitates such a radical rethinking of the world. Thus religious power brokers of Judean religion could easily perceive this teaching as a threat.

God's Rule Reveals God as a Merciful Father

Jesus's constructive teaching on God as a merciful, understanding, and forgiving Father alleviates some of the urgent, confrontational, and deconstructive aspects of his teaching. Borrowing the modern illustrations used in our discussion in the section called "God's Rule Is Present," the sense of relief and gratitude conveyed by this teaching might be compared to learning that the approaching nuclear attack was a false report or that one's cancer is in complete remission! Even though some of this teaching may have provided positive incentives for those initially confronted with the challenge of God's rule, much of it seems to be addressed to those who have subsequently responded to it. For those early Palestinian Christ followers who sought to emulate the lifestyle of Jesus, this constructive teaching helped to

---

15. In Matt 5:22 the KJV contains the interpolation "without a cause" (Gk. *eikē*); widespread by second century, it was probably "added by a copyist to soften rigor of the precept," Metzger, *Textual Commentary*, 11. It has also been argued that the phrase "except for the matter of unchastity" (Gk. *porneia*) in Matt 5:32 may even be a redactional interpolation of Matthew, see, e.g., Reumann, *Jesus*, 339 n. 7; for survey of discussion, see Keener, *Commentary on the Gospel of Matthew*, 189–92.

16. Perrin, *Rediscovering*, 149–50. See esp. Bonhoeffer, *Discipleship*; and Bonhoeffer, *Life Together*, written in Hitler's Germany in the late 1930s.

solidify, inspire, and assure them in their zealous endeavor.

This section will explore Jesus's understanding of God by examining (1) the common way he addressed God as Father (Mark 14:36), (2) the simplicity of one of his prayers (Luke 11:11–13), (3) his teaching about God as Creator and Provider (Matt 6:25–34; Luke 11:11–13), (4) parables illustrating God's love for sinners (Matt 20:1–16; Luke 15:1–10, 11–32), and (5) the divine blessings invoked upon the humble pursuers of justice and mercy (Matt 5:3–8). Some sayings and parables illustrating radical reversal and self-examination also impart the image of God as a merciful Father (e.g., Luke 18:9–14) and the challenge to imitate the Father with human acts of mercy (e.g., Matt 5:39–41, 44–48; Luke 10:30–36). Therefore, some previous statements may be alluded to in this section.

In contrast to the elaborate epithets used of God in Jesus's day, such as, "O Lord, our God, who art the Creator of heaven and earth, our Shield and the Shield of our fathers," Jesus's forms of address to God invoked the familial name *father* (in Aramaic, *abba*: Mark 14:36). [17] The name *abba* was probably the original form of address used by Jesus in his prayer and sayings about the "heavenly Father" (Matthew 6; Luke 11).

The original simplicity of Jesus's prayer is well illustrated in Luke 11:2–4

when compared with a selection of one of the synagogue prayers dating back to the Second Temple period:

> Blessed art thou, O Lord, God of Abraham, God of Isaac and God of Jacob, the great mighty and revered God, the most high God who bestows loving kindness and possesses all things; who remembers the pious deeds of the Patriarchs and in love will bring a redeemer to their children's children for their names' sake. Forgive us, O our Father, for we have sinned; pardon us, O our King, for we have transgressed; for thou dost pardon and forgive. Look upon our affliction and plead our cause and redeem us speedily for thy name's sake; for thou art a mighty redeemer. Bless this year unto us, O Lord our God, together with every kind of produce thereof, for our welfare; give a blessing upon the face of the earth. O satisfy us with thy goodness, and bless our year like other good years. Blessed art thou, O Lord the redeemer of Israel, who art gracious and dost abundantly forgive, O King, Helper, Savior and Shield. [18]

The prayer, replete with biblical terminology, is not offensive, but the

---

17. On "Abba," see BDAG, 1, and *TDNT*, 1:5–6. The way to understand *abba* is debated still. While it seems certain that there was something distinctive and intimate in the way that Jesus addressed God in prayer, some English glosses propose, e.g., "daddy, papa" are criticized as too childish or disrespectful: see Stein, *Jesus the Messiah*, 131–34; Barr, "Abba Isn't Daddy"; Vermes, *Religion of Jesus*, 152–83; Keener, *Historical Jesus*, 272.

18. The lengthy prayer is adapted from Benedictions 1, 6, 7, 9 of the Shemoneh 'Esreh or "Eighteen Benedictions," some of which may date back to the time of Jesus (Barrett, *New Testament Background*, 162–63). See also the following collection of ancient and modern prayers in Simpson, *Jewish Prayer and Worship*. For balanced treatment of God's fatherhood in both the Gospels and Second Temple Judaism, see Vermes, *Religion of Jesus*, 152–80. See also helpful discussion on Jesus's statements and prayer in Jewish context: Keener, *Commentary on the Gospel of Matthew*, 210–26.

elaborate epithets and laudatory language seem to presuppose a formal distance between God and humanity that the petitioner is attempting to bridge through pleas of appeasement and pacification. Jesus of Nazareth might have criticized the language and assumptions behind such prayers (Matt 6:2, 5, 7). In contrast to the rather sanctimonious petition above, we have the simpler prayer of Jesus (Luke 11:2–4, CEV): "Father, help us to honor your name. Come and set up your kingdom. Give us each day the food we need. Forgive our sins, as we forgive everyone who has done wrong to us. And keep us from being tempted."

Both the concise language and conversational (nontheological) style of this prayer presuppose a God who is near and readily responds to the needs of people. This is the image of God that Jesus had, the one who Mark identified as the "carpenter" from Nazareth (Gk. *tektōn*, 6:3). It would appeal to the peasantry of Palestine. It would also become the spiritual focus of this "renewal movement" of Jesus's followers in Galilee and surrounding areas.

The teaching of Jesus about God as Creator and Provider (Matt 6:25–34; Luke 11:11–13) combines images of God from Jewish wisdom tradition (e.g., Job 12:7–10; 38:41) and his own emphasis on faith in God's future (e.g., Matt 6:33; Luke 11:9). According to the rationale of this teaching, since God has cared for creation from the past to the present, the Provider can also be trusted to continue this care in the future. God is a trustworthy caretaker of all creation (Matt 6:26, 28–29) and is more concerned about its welfare than a human father is for his own son

(Luke 11:11–13). This message not only alleviates some of the anxiety conveyed by Jesus's radical challenges but brings assurance to those who participate in God's rule. The early itinerant Jesus preachers also would have found great consolation in these sayings as they wandered throughout rural Palestine, challenging the power structures by proclaiming the imminent return of their Lord.

In his parables illustrating God's love for sinners (Luke 15:1–10, 11–32; cf. Matt 20:1–16), Jesus again confronts his listeners with a radical reversal of values. What kind of respectable father would run down the street joyfully to meet his misfit son and would slaughter the fatted calf for him? When would a responsible employer hire idlers on the street to do half a day's work yet pay them the same amount as the full-day workers?[19] It is precisely because of this motif of radical reversal that the theme of God's love for outcasts is so forcefully conveyed. The setting for these parables in the ministry of Jesus appears to be correctly identified in Luke's gospel. They are Jesus's responses to the Jewish leaders who criticized his ministry to tax collectors and sinners (Luke 15:1–2). In the parables of the Lost Sheep and the Lost Coin (Luke 15:3–10), Jesus reveals God's love for even the most obscure sinner and the great joy experienced by God and his people when even one sinner repents: "Just so, I tell you, there will be more joy in heaven over one sinner who repents than over ninety-nine righteous persons who need no repentance" (Luke 15:7).

---

19. See Second Temple attitudes toward prodigals and extravagant behavior in Snodgrass, *Stories with Intent*, 120ff., 364–65.

Both the parables of the Prodigal Son and of the Laborers in the Vineyard can be outlined in a similar manner. Both seem to highlight the theme of God's love for sinners. In Jesus's parable of the Prodigal Son (Luke 15:11, 32), the vindication of God's love for sinners theme (c) is developed in the following way: just as the prodigal son (b) was graciously welcomed back by his father despite the protests of the elder brother (b*), so also sinners and outcasts (a) are recipients of God's love despite the protests of the "righteous" Jews (a*). The starting concept (a) and its development (a*) are derived from Luke 15:1–2: i.e., Jesus's associating with tax collectors and sinners. Luke 15:1–2 also provides the appropriate historical context for Jesus's ministry.[20] In the parable of the laborers (Matt 20:1–16), the same theme of God's mercy for sinners (c) unfolds. Just as the owner who hires workers for his estate (b) picks idlers and gives them the same pay as the regulars, despite protests (b*), so also is God's love (a) extended freely to sinners and outcasts despite the protests of the "righteous" Jews (a*). The dawning of God's rule in Jesus's ministry results in acts of divine compassion toward Israel's outcasts. These are acts that defy all human standards and expectations.

Our final comments on Jesus's teaching about God concerns the Beatitudes (Matt 5:3–8 / Luke 6:20–22). In them Jesus invokes divine favor upon the poor, hungry, and oppressed. The blessings are pronounced as already present.

They provide comfort and assurance to those who respond to the challenge of God's reign:

> Blessed are you who are poor,
> for yours is the kingdom of God.
>
> Blessed are you who are hungry now,
> for you will be filled.
>
> Blessed are you who weep now,
> for you will laugh.
>
> Blessed are you when people hate you,
> and when they exclude you, revile
> you, and defame you . . .
>
> Rejoice in that day, and leap for joy,
> for surely your reward is great in
> heaven; for it is what their ancestors
> did to the prophets. (Luke 6:20–23)

From our discussion in this section, we observed that the God of Jesus was personal and accessible, good to the poor, glad when the lost are found, overflowing with a father's love for a returning child, and merciful to the despairing and needy. Those who participate in God's reign are not only beneficiaries of the Father's love but also benefactors who extend God's mercy to others in need. Relief and gratitude would be appropriate responses to such good news. So also would be the responses of Jesus's listeners to the experience of divine forgiveness and mercy as participants in God's rule.[21]

---

20. Called by Snodgrass, the "Compassionate Father and His Two Lost Sons," the parable certainly has other points of interpretation, Snodgrass, *Stories with Intent*, 126–41, although the themes of compassion toward lost sinners is a central concern here, 140.

21. For further discussion on the teaching of Jesus, see Bornkamm, *Jesus*, 64–143; Braun, *Jesus of Nazareth*, 36–136; Bultmann, *Jesus and the Word*, 27–220; Bultmann, *Theology of the New Testament*, 1:3–32; Conzelmann, *Jesus*, 51–81; Flusser, *Jesus*; Flusser and Notley, *Sage from Galilee*; Jeremias, *New Testament Theology*; Klausner, *Jesus of Nazareth*; Manson, *Sayings of Jesus*; Perrin, *Rediscovering*, 54–206; Perrin, *Jesus*, 40–56; Snodgrass, *Stories with Intent*; Keener, *Historical Jesus*, chs. 13–17; Theissen and Merz, *Historical Jesus*, part 3. See also the studies about Jesus and his teaching listed above in ch. 10 n. 5.

We conclude with the words of Albert Schweitzer, an accomplished interpreter of the Gospels and a Bach musician, who abandoned fame in Europe to become a medical missionary in West Central Africa: "He comes to us as one unknown, without a name, as of old, by the lakeside, he came to those . . . who did not know who he was. He says the same words, 'Follow me!' and sets us to those tasks which he must fulfill in our time. He commands. And to those who hearken to him, whether wise or unwise, he will reveal himself in the peace, the labours, the conflicts and the suffering that they may experience in his fellowship, and as an ineffable mystery they will learn who he is."[22]

22. Schweitzer, *Quest*, 487. Despite his controversial view that Jesus was a mistaken apocalypticist (see Matt 10:23), Schweitzer grounded "the truth of Christianity" in the "present experience of Christ as a living spiritual reality," writes Marcus Borg, in Schweitzer, *Quest*, ix. A recipient of the 1952 Nobel Prize and a proponent of "reverence for life," Schweitzer was admired by many, including Geza Vermes, who grouped him (for his medical work in Africa) with both Francis of Assisi and Mother Teresa of Calcutta as one of those who sought to practice "the piety of Jesus, such as his purity of intention and generosity of heart" (Vermes, *Religion of Jesus*, 214).

12

A Chronology of Paul's Life

The problems of Pauline chronology are similar to those in the study of Jesus. Evidence is sparse and scattered, and the sources are often dominated by literary and religious purposes. Factors that are distinctive for a chronology of Paul are that (a) we have the apostle's own words about certain events in his life; (b) references to Paul's life in Acts sometimes coincide with statements in Paul's letters; and (c) an ancient inscription confirms the Lukan account of Paul's appearance before Gallio (Acts 18:12–17).

The document of primary importance in determining a chronology of Paul is the Gallio Inscription found at Delphi, Greece (Achaia). Gallio's proconsulship of Achaia, mentioned in Acts 18:12–22, is independently attested by this document and can be dated within narrow limits. The inscription, with conjectural supplements [in square brackets] reads as follows:

> Tiberius [Claudius] Caesar Augustus Germanicus [Pontifex Maximus, in his tribunician] power [year 12, acclaimed Emperor for] the 26th time, father of the country, [consul for the 5th time, censor, sends greetings to the city of Delphi.] I have long been zealous for the city of Delphi [and favorable to it from the] beginning, and I have always observed the cult of the [Pythian] Apollo, [but with regard to] the present stories, and those quarrels of the citizens of which [a report has been made by Lucius] Junios Gallio my friend, and [pro]consul [of Achaea].[1]

Knowledge of stereotyped titles in official inscriptions confirms that the addresser is Claudius, who became emperor on January 25, AD 41. The acclamations were irregular, but from other inscriptions, we learn that he was acclaimed emperor for the twenty-second,

---

1. Barrett, *New Testament Background*, 48–49; and *BC* 5:461; for helpful discussion, see Riesner, *Paul's Early Period*, 202–11.

Statue of the Apostle Paul at the Constantinian Basilica of St. Paul, Outside-the-Walls, Rome; the fourth-century basilica was destroyed by fire and rebuilt in the nineteenth century. (Photo by Ralph Harris)

twenty-third, and twenty-fourth times in the eleventh year of his reign (AD 51), and that the twenty-seventh acclamation took place in the second half of the twelfth year of his reign (AD 52, before August).[2]

The twenty-sixth acclamation must therefore have taken place at the close of the eleventh year (AD 51) or probably the first half of the twelfth year: between January 25 and August 1, AD 52. Achaia was a senatorial province governed by a proconsul, who was customarily appointed by the senate for a one-year term. The one-year appointments were made in early summer (on July 1 under Emperor Tiberius). Even though alternative dates have been suggested within the AD 50–53 limit, a convincing case has been made for the Gallio proconsulship of Achaia from

July 1, 51, to July 1, 52.[3] Paul's appearance before Gallio (Acts 18:12–17) was probably soon after his accession to office (July 51). It would have been an opportune occasion for Paul's opponents to gain a fresh hearing and possibly to influence the decision of the new proconsul.

Before examining key events in Paul's life, we must state at the outset that priority will be given to the data found in Paul's letters. There are a number of reasons for proceeding in this manner.[4] First, Paul's letters are the earliest data available,

2. Lake "Chronology of Acts," in *BC* 5:462–63; Riesner, *Paul's Early Period*, 208.

3. Jewett, *A Chronology*, 38–40; Lüdemann, *Paul*, 163–64, 185–86.

4. Derived from Jewett, *A Chronology*, 22–24; *NIDB*, 1:634–36; see also Knox, *Chapters in a Life of Paul*, 13–29; Lüdemann, *Paul*, 1–43. For a survey of different approaches, see Riesner, *Paul's Early Period*, 3–28. On the composition of Acts in the late first century, see our ch. 13 under "Lukan Christianity."

predating the Acts of the Apostles by a few decades. Second, the details of the letters are not motivated by chronological considerations or by any assumption about the periodization of the church's history. Third, material from the letters is primary historical data and therefore has intrinsic priority over the more secondary information we find in the Acts of the Apostles (which is apologetical history from a later perspective).

These reasons do not imply that the data in Paul's letters are free from apologetic and theological influences, or that Acts does not include historical information. The data in the letters, however, are closer historically to the events; they are the apostle's own words about his own life, and thus they qualify as eyewitness material. Therefore a general outline of Paul's life will be first worked out from the data of the letters of Paul. Material from Acts is usable in our Pauline chronology only when it does not seem to conflict with the evidence found in the letters.[5]

CONVERSION AND CALL: AD 34

The primary data for Paul's conversion and call are found in Gal 1:15–16 and 1 Cor 15:8. Later evidence supporting this event is narrated in a more idealized and dramatic manner is Acts 9:1–9; 22:6–21; 26:12–18.[6] In Gal 1:15–16, this is identified as the initial event of Paul's missionary career. It includes a call from God (1:15) and a revealing of God's Son to Paul (1:16). This revelation is identified in 1 Cor 15:8 as a final appearance of the resurrected Christ to his followers. Even though the data from Acts do not include the appearance of Christ as the last of the post-Easter appearances, and though Acts includes details (e.g., the Lord's appearance to Ananias, Paul's blindness, charismata) not mentioned in Paul's letters, Acts and the Letters agree in the following areas. First, Paul was previously a persecutor of the church (Acts 9:1–5; 26:9–11; 1 Cor 15:9; Gal 1:13). Second, the vision of Christ is connected with Paul's missionary call to the Gentiles (Acts 26:16; Gal 1:16). Third, the whole event is connected with the Syrian city of Damascus (Acts 9; 22; 26; Gal 1:17).

The Pauline connection to the appearance of Christ as the last post-Easter appearance (not found in Acts) has extrabiblical support. From Gnostic and early Christian sources there is a tradition of the postresurrection appearances of Christ extending eighteen months. The Gnostic traditions found in Irenaeus's *Against Heresies* state that postresurrection appearances lasted eighteen months.[7] The second-century Christian work the *Ascension of Isaiah* mentions post-Easter appearances lasting 545 days (9:16).[8] The second-century Christian Gnostic *Apocryphon of James* refers to 550 days of resurrection appearances (2:20–21).[9] This eighteen-month (ca. 540-day) period may

---

5. On the alleged discrepancies between Acts and Paul's letters, see Vielhauer, "On the 'Paulinism' of Acts," in Keck and Martyn, eds., *Studies in Luke-Acts*, 33–50; and Lüdemann, *Paul*, 23–29, 41–43. For a chronology based on the framework of Acts, though, see Hemer, *Book of Acts*, 251–70.

6. For discussion of the similarities and discrepancies of Acts 9, 22, and 26, along with Paul's letters, see Lohfink, *Conversion of St. Paul*, 20–26; Hedrick, "Paul's Conversion/Call."

7. This tradition is found among the Gnostic Ophites (Irenaeus, *Against Heresies* 1.30.14) and the Gnostic disciples of Ptolemaeus (1.3.2).

8. Schneemelcher, *NTA*, 2:615.

9. Robinson, *Nag Hammadi Library*, 30

be a historical recollection derived from Pauline tradition.[10]

Basing the dating of Paul's conversion/call on the argument for Jesus's crucifixion at AD 33,[11] we arrive at October of AD 34, eighteen months after the Passover (April). As we proceed in dating the other key events in Paul's life, the AD 34 conversion/call will find further support.

FIRST JERUSALEM VISIT: AD 37

Paul states in Gal 1:17–18 that after his conversion/call, he went into Arabia, returned to Damascus, then "after three years" went to Jerusalem for the first time. Second Corinthians 11:32–33 describes this departure from Damascus as an escape from the ethnarch of King Aretas, who guarded the city to seize him. Acts 9:22–26 supports the Damascus-Jerusalem sequence of Galatians without referring to the Arabian trip, and also describes the Damascus escape without mentioning the ethnarch of King Aretas.

If Paul's conversion/call occurred in AD 34, and if he left Damascus for Jerusalem "after three years," the first Jerusalem visit would have taken place around 37. Is there any datum to substantiate the date for this trip? The historical allusion to the ethnarch's of King Aretas guarding Damascus to seize Paul (2 Cor 11:32) may provide this support. The crucial issue will concern the extent of Aretas's rule around AD 37.

Did the Nabatean king Aretas have jurisdiction over Damascus around 37? His rule over Nabatea and other regions was from 9 BC until his death in AD 39.[12] If Aretas had control over Damascus, it probably did not begin until after the death of Tiberius Caesar (March of AD 37). Tiberius discouraged native client kingdoms and favored Herod Antipas over Aretas in a border conflict between the two in AD 36. However, after the death of Tiberius in March of 37, a change in frontier policy seems to have occurred under Emperor Gaius Caligula. This change of policy would provide a favorable setting for Nabatean control of Damascus. Gaius reestablished a system of client kings in the east, refrained from any punitive measures against Aretas for the 36 border dispute, and even adopted a friendly attitude toward the Nabatean king.[13] It was probably during this favorable change of policy after March 37 that Damascus would have been transferred to Nabatean control (2 Cor 11:32). Paul's escape therefore occurred sometime within the two-year span up to the death of King Aretas in 39.

Our discussion provides some support for dating Paul's first Jerusalem visit at AD 37 (or 38). It also helps to substantiate the AD 34 conversion/call date three years earlier (Gal 1:15–18). Further confirmation for these dates will be provided when interlocked with other events in Paul's life.

---

10. Jewett, *Chronology* 29. See also Riesner, *Paul's Early Period*, 64–74.

11. Scholars defending an AD 33 crucifixion are Reicke, *New Testament Era*, 183–84; Hoehner, *Chronological Aspects*, 103–14; and Jewett, *Chronology*, 26–29, 119 n. 28.

12. Josephus, *Ant.* 16.293–99; 18.109–15; *War* 1.574–77; Jewett, *A Chronology*, 30–33, 121; but Riesner, *Paul's Early Period*, 75–89, is less confident here.

13. See Jewett, *Chronology*, 31–33, although Riesner finds evidence lacking here: *Paul's Early Period*, 82–83.

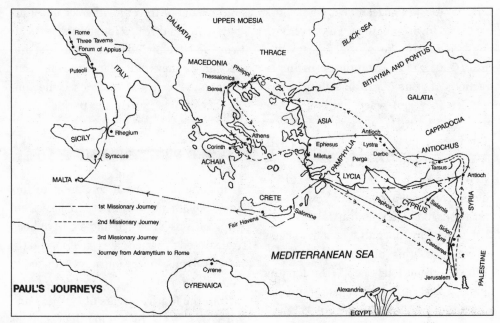

Paul's Mediterranean Journeys

MISSIONARY ACTIVITY: AD 37–51

The time frame for this period is based on the fourteen-year span between the two Jerusalem trips, mentioned in Gal 1:21; 2:1. After the first Jerusalem trip, Paul goes into the regions of Syria and Cilicia (1:21), and "after fourteen years" returns to Jerusalem (2:1).[14] In Acts the references to Syria and Cilicia in Gal 1:21 find specific support (the Acts allusions to Paul's trip to Tarsus of Cilicia [9:30] and to Paul and Barnabas's visit to Antioch of Syria [11:25–26; 13:1–2]). However, Gal 1:21 gives no indication that Paul is attempting to be exhaustive about his travels.[15]

Therefore, most of the missionary activities graphically portrayed in Acts 13–14 and from Acts 15:36 to 18:22 probably occurred at this time.

The date of Paul's second visit to Jerusalem coincides with Paul's appearance before Gallio in Corinth (AD 51). According to Acts 18, after Paul was acquitted by Gallio, he sailed for Syria (v. 18), stopping at Ephesus, Caesarea, and the church in Jerusalem (v. 22). As we have argued at the beginning of this chapter, the summer of AD 51 would have been an opportune time for Paul's opponents to present the apostle before the newly appointed proconsul. The most we can miscalculate on this point is one year (e.g., 50 or 52).

We have placed both missionary journeys of Paul (Acts 13–14; 15:36;

---

14. The Jerusalem trips mentioned in Acts 11:27–30; 15 and Gal 2:1–10 will be discussed under "Second Jerusalem Visit: AD 51."

15. Betz regards Gal 1:13—2:14 as the *narratio* of Paul's apologetic letter. According to Cicero, the *narratio* ought to be brief, clear, and plausible (*De Invent.* 1.20.28); Quintilian adds that some cases require a brief summary instead of a full statement of facts (*Inst.* 4.2.5). See Betz, "Literary

Compositions," *NTS* 21 (1975) 362–67; Lüdemann also concurs, *Paul*, 54–59. Kennedy sees *narratio* here but in the context of deliberative, not apologetic, rhetoric, *New Testament Interpretation*, 145–46.

18:22) into the fourteen-year framework for the following reasons. First, we have taken seriously the fourteen-year time span (Gal 1:21; 2:1) without resorting to fractions of years (e.g., calculating twelve or thirteen years) where part of a year may be reckoned as a whole year.[16] Second, our schema takes seriously Paul's busy itinerary in Acts 15:31—18:1. This "second missionary journey" of Paul includes over fifteen stops and covers over two thousand miles. Because Paul traveled on land by foot and by sea in ancient Roman boats, this journey would probably take three or four years.[17] This lengthy time of travel poses problems for anyone attempting to follow the order of Acts and reconcile it with the Gallio inscription.

The order of Acts places the first missionary journey (13–14) before the Jerusalem conference (15). The second journey follows the Jerusalem conference and ends with Paul leaving Corinth (15:36—18:22). The Jerusalem conference and Paul's departure from Corinth limit the time span of the second journey to two or three years.[18] But the distance of

and means of travel for the second journey requires three to four years.[19] This is why we have included both the first and second journeys of Paul into the fourteen-year time frame and transposed the conference of Acts 15 to a later period.

SECOND JERUSALEM VISIT: AD 51

It may be necessary at this point to further explain (a) why the two Jerusalem trips of Acts 11:27–30 and 15 have been transposed to a later date (AD 51), and (b) why both missionary journeys depicted in Acts 13:14 and 15:30–18:22 are included within the fourteen years of Gal 1:21 and 2:1 (AD 37–51). By linking the Galatians 2 conference (cf. Acts 15) with Paul's trip "up to" Jerusalem (Acts 18:22), we escape the necessity of positing seventeen empty years at the beginning of Paul's ministry and crowding virtually all that is known about his activity into the last few years.[20]

The Jerusalem offering (Rom 15:25–27; 1 Cor 16:1–8), designed to bridge the economic gap between the Palestinian and Hellenistic churches, provided Paul's motivation for the final trip to Jerusalem, although Luke omits reference to it except for one detail (Acts 25:17). In order to account for the general knowledge in the early church that Paul had indeed brought an offering to Jerusalem, Luke placed the trip back in the early life of

---

16. For example, counting fractions of years as whole years, one might declare that he or she attended college for four years because classes were taken in the years 2006, 2007, 2008, and 2009. However, this may actually be only three school years: (1) fall 2006–spring 2007, (2) fall 2007–spring 2008, and (3) fall 2008–spring 2009.

17. Jewett, *A Chronology*, 59–62; on Paul's rate of travel, see Riesner, *Paul's Early Period*, 307–17, and Rapske, "Acts, Travel," in Gill and Gempf, eds., *Book of Acts in Its Graeco-Roman Setting*, 6–14.

18. Most scholars date the Jerusalem conference of Acts 15 between 48 and 50, and Paul's departure from Corinth (based on the Gallio inscription) between 51 and 52 (see Riesner, *Paul's Early Period*, 208–11; Downs, "Chronology of the New Testament," in *NIDB*, 1:634–35). This time frame usually puts a limit of two to three years on Paul's second missionary journey (Acts

15:36—18:22).

19. Jewett, *Chronology*, 59–62.

20. Jewett, *Chronology*, 79. Although he dates the Jerusalem or apostolic conference earlier (AD 47, but possibly 50), Lüdemann, *Paul*, 64–75, finds indications that a Pauline mission (Gal 2:7–8) and even Paul's conflict at Antioch (2:11–14) occurred before the conference. Riesner favors 48/49: *Paul's Early Period*, 280–81.

Paul in connection with a famine (Acts 11:27–30). Paul is careful to mention only an "acquaintance" trip and a "conference" journey, and this may be sufficient to overrule Luke's chronology at this point.[21]

The following is a chart of the Jerusalem trips in both Paul's letters and Acts, reflecting our interpretation:

Jerusalem visit (Year)	Purpose of visit	Paul	Acts
First visit (AD 37)	Getting acquainted	Gal 1:18–20	Acts 9:26–27
Second visit (AD 51)	Attending apostolic conference	Gal 2:1–10	Acts 15
Final visit (AD 57)	Offering the collection; Paul is arrested	Rom 15:25–27	Acts 21:17–26 Acts 11:27–30

The dating of the Jerusalem conference will be determined by the relationships of the following texts: Acts 11:27–30; Acts 15:1–35; and Gal 2:1–10. Is Galatians 2 Paul's version of either the Jerusalem conference in Acts 15 or the famine relief visit of Acts 11:27–30? Note the chart of similarities and differences:

The similarities between Galatians 2 and Acts 15 are the most significant (numbers 1, 3, and 4). The differences (numbers 2, 5, and 6) between Galatians 2 and Acts 15 can be explained as two different versions of the same event (numbers 2 and 6) or as two different meetings on the same occasion (number 5). Paul's omission of the apostolic decrees (Acts 15:19–20; 21:25) may have been due either to Paul's own difficulties with such "legalistic" stipulations (Gal 2:6) or to the possibility (we think) that these decrees were introduced after the conference when Paul made his final trip to Jerusalem (Acts 21:25).

It seems unlikely that Gal 2:10 ("remember the poor") is an allusion to the famine relief visit (Acts 11:27–30). We regard the relief visit as a displaced reference to the collection that Paul brought on his final visit to Jerusalem (Acts 24:17; Rom

Topics	Galatians 2	Acts 11	Acts 15
1. Associates of Paul	Barnabas, Titus (Gal 2:1)	Barnabas (Acts 11:30)	Barnabas and others (Acts 15:2)
2. Appointment	Revealed by God (Gal 2:2)	Sent by the church (Acts 11:30)	Appointed by the church (Acts 15:2)
3. Occasion	Insistence by false brothers on Gentile circumcision (Gal 2:3–4)	Famine relief (Acts 11:28–29)	Insistence by men from Judea on Gentile circumcision (Acts 15:1)
4. Jerusalem officials	James, Cephas, John (Gal 2:9)	None	Peter, James, apostles, and elders (Acts 15:4)
5. Meeting type	Private	None	Public (Acts 15:4, 12–14)
6. Mention of poor?	"Remember the poor" (Gal 2:10).	Remember relief for famine victims (Acts 11:29)	None

21. Downs, "Chronology," in *NIDB*, 1:634–35.

15:25–27).[22] In his letters, Paul's concern for a famine relief is the collection for "the poor among the saints at Jerusalem" (Rom 15:26). The admonition to "remember the poor" in Gal 2:10 may even be an indication that the collection for the Jerusalem saints had already begun.[23]

We link the Galatians 2 and Acts 15 conference with Paul's trip "up to" Jerusalem after his second missionary journey (Acts 18:22; AD 51) for the following reasons. First, it best conforms to the fourteen-year gap between the two Jerusalem visits (Gal 1:18; 2:1). Second, it allows enough time for Paul to undertake his extensive missionary travels described in Acts 13–14; 15:35—18:22. Third, it takes seriously the priority of Paul's letters over Acts for a Pauline chronology. Because of these reasons, we date the Jerusalem conference at AD 51 (Gal 2 = Acts 15 = Acts 18:22) instead of between 48 and 50 as many scholars have.

FURTHER MISSIONARY ACTIVITY: AD 52–57

This period includes Paul's twenty-seven-month stay in Ephesus (Acts 19:8–10; 2 Cor 1:8; Phil 1; 4; Phlm) with brief visits to Corinth (2 Cor 2:1; 12:14; 13:1), Troas (2 Cor 2:12), Macedonia (Acts 20:1; 1 Cor 2:13), Illyricum (Rom 15:19), and

22. Knox, *Chapters in a Life*, 53–57; Jewett, *Chronology*, 79. Lüdemann *Paul*, 149–57, however, views Acts 11:27ff. as part of a tripling of Paul's second visit to Jerusalem (cf. Acts 15:1ff.; 18:22). Nevertheless, in all of the above cases, Acts 11:27–30 is viewed as a Lukan insertion that seems chronologically out of place in the narrative. See the appendix on chronologies of Paul in Patte, *Paul's Faith*, 352–61.

23. Nickle, *Collection*, 59–62; Lüdemann, *Paul*, 77–81; Joubert, "Collection," in *NIDB*, 1:698–99.

Achaia (Acts 20:2–3; Rom 15:25; 16:1), before Paul's final trip to Jerusalem (Acts 20:16; Rom 15:25). During these years, Paul's "collection for the saints" was begun (spring of 55; 1 Cor 16:1–8), continued among the churches of Macedonia and Achaia (2 Cor 8–9), and was completed for delivery to Jerusalem (AD 57: Rom 15:25–27). All of Paul's undisputed letters were also written at this time, with the exception of 1 Thessalonians (in AD 50 from Corinth).

FINAL JERUSALEM VISIT: AD 57

This last journey to Jerusalem is anticipated in Rom 15:25–27 and described in Acts 20:16; 21:1–18. According to Acts, the following events take place in Jerusalem.

(1) Conference with church and participation in a Jewish ritual at the temple (21:17–26)

(2) Paul is seized by a mob in the temple and taken into Roman custody (21:27–36)

(3) Paul addresses multitude and stands before Sanhedrin (21:39—23:10)

(4) A conspiracy is discovered, and Paul is transferred to Caesarea (23:11–31)

(5) Paul stays in Caesarea for two years (24:27) where he appears on trial before the procurators Felix and Festus (24–25) and also before the Herodian king, Agrippa II (26).

(6) Paul appeals to Caesar (25:10–12) and is sent to Rome (27:1—28:16).

Some verification for Paul's arrival in Jerusalem at AD 57 can be attained by dating the procuratorships of Felix and Festus

The Corinthian marketplace (*agora*) with the temple of Apollo in the background.
Paul worked with Aquilla and Priscilla for eighteen months when founding the church in Corinth
(Acts 18:1–11; 1 Cor 16:19). (Photo by Charles B. Puskas)

(Acts 24–25). If one favors the reports of Josephus over the report of Tacitus (as most scholars do), the arrival of Felix as procurator of Judea can be established around AD 52–53.[24] If one follows the progression of Roman procurators in the years prior to the Jewish war (AD 66–70), a date of AD 59 or 60 can be maintained for the arrival of Festus as the successor to Felix.[25]

24. Emperor Claudius appointed Felix as Cumanus's successor around the twelfth year of his reign (ca. 53), according to Josephus, *Ant.* 20.134–40; *War* 2.245–49. In Tacitus, *Ann.* 12.54 Felix and Cumanus were procurators at the same time over a divided Palestine; see Riesner, *Paul's Early Period*, 219–21.

25. Because there are dating problems connected with Josephus's own report on the circumstances immediately following the dismissal of Felix (*Ant.* 20.182–85), we prefer to work back from Josephus's reports on the procurators of Judea from the Jewish War (66–70) back to the years

Acts 24:27 states that when two years had elapsed (since Paul's transfer to Caesarea as a prisoner), the Roman procurator was succeeded by Porcius Festus. Based on our dating of these procuratorships, Paul's arrival in Caesarea would have been around AD 57. According to Acts, Paul's transfer from Jerusalem to Caesarea took place about two weeks after his arrival in Jerusalem around Pentecost, the summer of 57 (Acts 20:16; 21:17, 26–27; 22:30; 23:11–12, 31–33).

As a result of our discussion we can outline the chronology of this phase as follows:

(1) Paul arrives in Jerusalem (Acts 21:17) in summer of 57

of rule shared by Felix and his successor, Festus (ca. 52–62). Festus served for a brief period until his death in AD 61 or 62 (*Ant.* 20.197–203); Hemer, *Book of Acts*, 171; Jewett, *Chronology*, 43.

(2) Paul appears before Felix in Caesarea (24:10–22) in summer of 57

(3) Paul appears before Festus and Agrippa (25–26) after two years (24:27) in summer of 59

(4) Paul departs Caesarea for Rome (27:1–8) in late summer or early fall of 59

JOURNEY TO ROME: AD 59–60

After his appeal to Caesar had been granted (Acts 25:10–12; 26:32), Paul and other prisoners set sail for Italy under Roman custody (27:1). The sea voyage was probably undertaken before the dangerous season for sailing (before mid-September). Paul and the others boarded a sailing vessel to Myra of Lycia (southern Asia Minor), where they transferred to a larger grain ship en route to Italy (27:7–8). As the summer months came to an end, sailing became difficult on the eastern Mediterranean.[26]

Paul and company stayed at Fair Havens after the Day of the Atonement "fast" (Acts 27:9). According to the solar calendar, in AD 59, the Day of Atonement (Tishri 10) took place on October 5.[27]

Since the dangerous sailing season had begun, the pilot and ship owner attempted to winter at a seaport in Crete (27:9–12). The ship, however, was caught in a gale and driven westward (vv. 13–20). Following the chronological notations of Acts (27:20, 27, 33, 39), the boat shipwrecked at Malta in early November of 59

(27:39—28:1). After staying at Malta for three months and three days (28:7, 11), they sailed for Rome in early February of 60 and arrived there within two weeks (28:11–16).

According to Acts 28:30, Paul stayed in Rome for "two whole years." He awaited his appeal to Caesar with some degree of freedom. The apostle was also under house arrest and able to receive visitors (28:16–17, 23, 31).[28]

EXECUTION: AD 62

The evidence about the end of Paul's life is related to the question of the authorship of the Pastoral Letters. References to the "first defense" in 2 Tim 4:16 and the author's "rescue" in 2 Tim 4:17 have led some scholars to conclude that Paul was released after the two-year imprisonment in Acts 28:30. Since we contend that the Pastorals were probably not written by Paul, this evidence should be excluded.[29] The references to Paul's journey to Spain in the Muratorian Fragment and *1 Clement* 5 are probably derived from Rom 15:24, although the allusion in *1 Clem.*

---

28. If the variant reading of Acts 28:16 in the Western text (fifth century) is correct (that Paul and the prisoners were handed over to the *stratopedarch*), and it refers to the emperor's pretorian guard, then the last single office holder was Afranius Burrus, who died in AD 62. This variant would establish a latest possible date for Paul's arrival in Rome (Jewett, *A Chronology*, 44). For discussion of Acts 28:16, see Puskas, *Conclusion of Luke-Acts*, 19 nn. 43–44; Rapske, *Book of Acts*, 174–77.

29. On authorship and date of the Pastorals, see Kümmel, *Introduction*, 370–84; Donelson, *Pseudepigraphy*; R. F. Collins, *Letters That Paul Did Not Write*.

26. Smith, *Voyage and Shipwreck*, 74–81; Hemer, "Euraquilo and Melito"; Rapske, "Acts, Travel," in Gill and Gempf, eds., *Book of Acts in Its Graeco-Roman Setting*, 22–29.

27. Bruce, *Book of the Acts*, 506; Peterson, *Acts*, 684–85; but see Pervo, *Acts*, 656–57.

A Chronology of Paul's Life

AD 34: Conversion/Call (Gal 1:15–16; 1 Cor 15:8; Acts 9:1–9)
AD 37: First Jerusalem visit (Gal 1:18–19; Acts 9:26–28)
AD 37–51: Missionary activity (Gal 1:21; Acts 13–14; 16:1—18:22)
AD 51: Second Jerusalem visit (Gal 2:1–20; Acts 15) Apostolic Conference, Jerusalem
AD 52–57: Further missionary work (Acts 19–20; 1 Cor 16:1–8; e.g., collection for the saints, 2 Cor 8–9; Rom 15:25–27)
AD 57: Final visit to Jerusalem (Acts 21:17–18, 27–33) arrest and imprisonment
AD 60: Arrival in Rome (Acts 28:16, 30–31)
AD 62: Execution of Paul (*1 Clem.* 5; Euseb., *Hist. eccl.* 2.22)

5.7 does not require a mission to Spain interpretation.[30]

The decisive evidence for the death of Paul is in Acts 28:30–31 and 20:24, 38. The author of Acts appears to bring his work to a positive conclusion (28:30–31), but seems aware of Paul's death (20:24, 38). In all probability the execution of Paul took place immediately after his two-year stay in Rome, under Nero.[31]

The reign of Nero in AD 62 was marked by growing suspicion and the restoration of treason trials. Early in AD 62, the efficient administrator Afranius Burrus had died (Tacitus, *Ann.* 14.51), and the wise advisor Seneca was dismissed. In the summer of AD 62 Octavia, Nero's former wife, was executed. Because Nero's government had changed from one of judicial fairness to treachery and suspicion in early 62, it is unnecessary to link Paul's death with the later persecution of Christians in connection with the great fire of Rome (AD 64).[32]

For further study on Paul see Stendahl, *Paul among Jews and Gentiles*; Käsemann, *Perspectives on Paul*; Jervell, *The Unknown Paul*; Davies, *Paul and Rabbinic Judaism*; Sanders, *Paul and Palestinian Judaism*; Meeks, *The First Urban Christians*; and Meeks, *The Writings of St. Paul*; Dunn, *The New Perspective on Paul*; Dunn, *The Theology of Paul*; Hays, *Echoes of Scripture in Letters of Paul*; Hays, *The Faith of Jesus Christ*; Boyarin, *A Radical Jew*; Malina and Pilch, *Social-Science Commentary on the Letters of Paul*; Puskas, *The Letters of Paul*; Gorman, *Apostle of the Crucified Lord*; Wright, *The Climax of the Covenant*; and Wright, *Paul in Fresh Perspective*; Horsley, *Paul and Empire*; Wilson, *Pauline Parallels*; Ware, *Synopsis of the Pauline Letters*.

30. *1 Clem.* 5.7 states that Paul "reached the limits of the west" before his death." This phrase could refer to Illyricum, Rome, or Spain ("farthest limits"). The death of Peter is also mentioned as contemporary with that of Paul (5.2–5), which cannot be verified.

31. Although influenced by the Pastorals in asserting that Paul was released and retried, Eusebius (early fourth century) does state that Paul "suffered martyrdom under Nero" in Rome (Eusebius, *Hist. eccl.* 2.22).

32. On Nero, the fire in Rome, and the local persecution of Christians, see the Roman historian Tacitus, *Ann.* 15.44 (early second century) and Christian source Sulpicius Severus, *Chronicle* 2.29 (early fifth century); Barrett, *New Testament Background*, 15–17.

13

The Major Phases of Early Christianity

What can be learned about the origins and development of Christianity from the NT and other relevant documents? Along with its presentation of the life and work of Jesus Christ, the NT also includes useful data for reconstructing the beginnings of Christianity. Who were the earliest followers of Jesus? What did it mean to follow Jesus the Messiah in the first century? How can the NT and related writings help us to understand these questions? In this chapter, we will attempt to respond to these and other queries.

Historical reconstruction (to underscore previous discussion) is a difficult but necessary task. It is difficult because the results of this historical inquiry are tentative and (at best) plausible. Some criticize the task because they allege that the message of and about Jesus is neglected in the quest for the social and historical dimensions of the New Testament. It is a necessary task, however, precisely because it takes seriously the social and historical dimensions of these ancient writings

deemed sacred by millions for over two millennia.

THE CONTROVERSIAL SUBJECTS

Controversial subjects in our study are (1) determining the authentic sayings of Jesus, (2) distinguishing the teachings of Jesus from those of his earliest followers (e.g., the "Jesus movement"), (3) identifying the earliest forms of both Jewish and Gentile Christianity, and (4) postulating plausible social locations from the limited results of form criticism and sociological analysis.[1] The above subjects are controversial because (a) our data for early Christianity are minimal, (b) questions still arise about the appropriateness and critical results of our methods, and (c) the

1. On "sociological interpretation," see Holmberg, *Sociology and the New Testament*; Elliott, *What Is Social-Scientific Criticism?*; Osiek, *What Are They Saying about the Social Setting?*; Barton, "Social Scientific," in Green, *Hearing the New Testament*, 34–64.

pluralistic expressions of both Judaism and followers of Jesus (in NT times) raise doubts about the *identities* of the communities addressed plus the Jewish and Gentile ethnic *distinctions* within primitive Christianity. The problems connected with controversial subjects (1), (2), and much of (4) were discussed in previous chapters;[2] therefore we will limit our explanation here to point (3).

The controversy surrounding the early distinctions between Jewish and Gentile Christianity basically involves the detection of "pagan" religious motifs in the NT. It is noteworthy that Paul's earliest converts, e.g., had turned to God from idols (1 Thess 1:9); the Galatians had formerly worshipped "beings that by nature are not gods" (Gal 4:8); the Corinthians had worshipped "idols that could not speak" (1 Cor 12:2; cf. 6:9–11); the Philippians were not circumcised (Phil 3:2). As a result, one school of thought finds NT motifs that parallel Gentile/pagan religions (e.g., mystery religions) perhaps appealing to an interpretive frame of reference for this audience.[3] An opposing

school of thought is skeptical of either establishing parallels with "pagan" religions or of restricting these parallels to "Gentile" religions because Paul and most NT authors were Hellenistic Jews.[4] The controversy continues concerning the nature and extent of the parallels to pagan religions and whether certain motifs or characteristics can be labeled as non-Jewish or pagan.

At least three conclusions can be derived from the controversy of distinguishing between early Jewish and early Gentile Christianity. First, Judaism was a diverse phenomenon in the first century AD. Research has shown the prevalence of Hellenistic culture and religion in Palestine since the third century BC.[5] The

---

2. The problems of points (1) and (2) were discussed in ch 10 (above), "The Historical Jesus." Although point (4) was discussed in ch 5, under the sections on form and redaction criticisms, we will continue the discussion as it relates to the Gospels and the particular communities that they address, under, e.g., Markan Christianity, Matthean Christianity, and the like later in this chapter. N.B.: As ch. 5 stated, the primary function of the Gospels is to bear witnesses to Jesus Christ (Luke 1:1–4; John 20:30–31; Acts 1:1–5). Ignoring this self-evident observation might lead one to reduce the Gospels to a mere database for the reconstruction of diverse religious communities.

3. Studies advocating this "history-of-religions" position are Reitzenstein, *Hellenistic Mystery-Religions*; Bousset, *Kyrios Christos*; Heitmueller, "Hellenistic Christianity," in Meeks, *The Writings of St. Paul*, 308–23; Bultmann, *Theology*

of the New Testament; Nock, *Early Gentile Christianity*; Lüdemann, *Opposition to Paul*; Schmithals, *Theology*.

4. Studies that criticize the above "history-of-religions" approach (a) are skeptical of "pagan" parallels and evolutionary schemes of Christology presupposed, e.g., in Machen, *The Origin of Paul's Religion*; Kim, *Paul and the New Perspective*; Hengel, *Between Jesus and Paul*; Hurtado, *Lord Jesus Christ*; (b) detect methodological weaknesses in the approach: Tiede, *The Charismatic Figure*; Holladay, *Theios Aner in Hellenistic Judaism* (1977); see also Hengel and Hurtado; (c) are critical of any sharp distinction between Judaism and Hellenism: Hengel, *Judaism and Hellenism*; Hengel, *Between Jesus and Paul*; Marshall, "Palestinian and Hellenistic Christianity"; Brown and Meier, *Antioch and Rome*, 1–9 (also in *CBQ* 45 [1983] 74–79); (d) focus instead on social-rhetorical or social-scientific approaches to the data: e.g., Robbins, *Exploring the Texture*; MacDonald, *Pauline Churches*; Neyrey, *Social World*; Barton, "Social Scientific," in Green, *Hearing the New Testament*, 34–64.

5. Hengel, *Judaism and Hellenism*, 58–106, 255–66; however, the widespread use of Hebrew and Aramaic at, e.g., Khirbet Qumran (from the third century BC to the first century AD) raises questions about the prevalence of Hellenism in parts of Judea: see Millar, "The Background of the Maccabean Revolution"; Vermes, *Jesus in His*

study of the Nag Hammadi documents has also revealed an independent form of Jewish Gnosticism predating or at least contemporary with Christianity.[6] Second, it must be granted that the earliest Gentile Christians were converts of Jewish Christians, since Jesus's earliest followers were all Jews.[7] Third, all outlines of early Christianity are tentative and subject to revision, but reconstruction is preferable to deconstruction. Our presentation of the major phases of Christianity will take into account these conclusions.[8]

We have divided our presentation into three periods:

(1) Before the destruction of Jerusalem in AD 70

(2) From AD 70 to the end of the first century

(3) From the late first to the early second century AD

Jewish Context; and Vermes, *Jesus and the World of Judaism*, 26, 74; see also Grabbe, "Jews and Hellenization"; J. J. Collins, *Between Athens and Jerusalem*; Collins and Sterling, eds., *Hellenism in the Land of Israel*.

6. Rudolph, *Gnosis*, 51–52, 277–82; sources examined in Pearson, "Jewish Gnostic," in Hedrick and Hodgson, *Nag Hammadi, Gnosticism, and Early Christianity*, 15–35; survey in Perkins, *Gnosticism*, 20–28.

7. Brown and Meier, *Antioch and Rome*, 1–9; Sanders on Paul's Gentile converts in Sanders, *Paul: A Very Short Introduction*, 23.

8. Our presentation agrees to some extent with the revised history-of-religions approach in Schmithals, *Theology*, viii–xii; Becker, *Christian Beginnings*, chs. 2–4; Kee, *Beginnings*, 435ff.; Wedderburn, *History*; and (sociohistorical) Theissen, *Religion of the Earliest Churches*, 323–24. We have also taken into consideration the theological concerns of Schnelle, *Theology of the New Testament*, 45–49; Schnelle, *History and Theology*, 349–64. Discussion of Judaism and Hellenism in J. J. Collins, *Between Athens and Jerusalem*, ch. 7, is also noteworthy.

PHASE 1 (AD 30–70)

In this earliest period of Christianity we note two major groups that emerge: rural itinerant charismatics and urban community organizers.[9] Both types persist after AD 70, although the rural itinerant element surfaces only as a minority group afterwards (e.g., Agabus: Acts 11:28; 21:10; traveling prophets in the *Didache*).

The Rural Itinerant Charismatics

This group was comprised of charismatic prophets who traveled through the towns and villages of Palestine, and whose authority derived from a particular message and lifestyle. Like the Cynic itinerant preachers, they left both their families and their homes and renounced all wealth and property (Matt 10:37; Luke 14:26).[10] Like the Essenes, they were end-time oriented, criticized the Jerusalem authorities, and traveled in the rural areas of Palestine.[11] Their authority was not based on noble origin (Luke 14:21–22; 1 Cor 1:26) or past achievements, but was vindicated by

9. These sociological categories are derived from Theissen, *Sociology*; Theissen, *Social Setting of Pauline Christianity*; Theissen and Merz, *Historical Jesus*, esp. 163–239—sections where one will find masterful coverage of the geographical and social framework of Galilee, and of Jesus as a wandering charismatic and the social relationships that would have been typical for him in that place and in that lifestyle. See also Hanson and Oakman, *Palestine*, 13–14, 60–61.

10. See Downing, *Cynics and Christian Origins*; and Downing, "Cynics," in *NIDB*, 1:816–17; Malherbe, *Cynic Epistles*.

11. On similarities between Essenes, the Qumran sect, and the early followers of Jesus, see Wedderburn, *History*, 28–40; Colpe, "The Oldest"; Brooke, *Dead Sea Scrolls and the New Testament*, 7–26.

their teaching and style of life. Those who would be categorized in this group are Jesus of Nazareth and his immediate followers, the "Jesus movement."

Jesus of Nazareth

Although much more can be said of him from our discussion of the historical Jesus in chapters 9–11, one may at least conclude that the ministry of Jesus has similarities to that of a rural itinerant charismatic prophet.[12] This much can be deduced from both his sayings and the basic information we know about him.

First, Jesus grew up in the insignificant town of Nazareth and spent most of his time in the fishing villages of Galilee surrounding the Sea of Galilee (Mark 1:9, 16, 23). The town of Nazareth is rarely mentioned by ancient geographers and historiographers (LXX, Josephus, Philo, Pliny, Talmud) and has little importance in the time of Jesus (e.g., John 1:46; 7:41). In his Galilean ministry, Jesus frequented the fishing villages of Capernaum, Gennesaret, and Bethsaida-Julias. Although two larger cities of Galilee (Sepphoris and Tiberias) were close to where he grew up and preached (Sepphoris was six kilometers from Nazareth; Tiberias was sixteen kilometers from Capernaum), to sources contemporary with Jesus it is as if neither existed. Jesus also spent time in the rural areas of Galilee, Perea, and Judea. Although Jesus probably visited Jerusalem about three times during his ministry, his denouncement of both the temple ritual

(e.g., Mark 11:15–19; 14:58) and the Jerusalem authorities (Matt 23:23; Luke 10:31–32; 18:11) reflects the attitudes of a Jew living in agrarian Palestine.[13]

Second, Jesus was a traveling preacher. This point is evident, not only from his busy itinerary in rural Palestine, but also by what can be deduced from his teaching. Jesus spoke about leaving family and home (Mark 10:28–30; Luke 9:60; 14:26) as a response to God's emerging empire. He exhorted his disciples, in their preaching itinerary, to rely on the hospitality of friends in the villages and towns they visited (Matt 10:9–11). Many of the radical sayings of Jesus that advocate radical self-questioning and a reversal of values also seem to presuppose the lifestyle of a poor, homeless, wandering prophet (e.g., Matt 5:29–41; Mark 10:23; Luke 6:20–22).

Third, Jesus was a charismatic prophet. His authority was authenticated by his words and deeds. It was not legitimized by noble lineage (e.g., Matt 13:55) but by his message that God's empire had emerged in his words and deeds (Mark 1:15; Luke 11:20; 17:21). Even though he had distinctive emphases, Jesus shared similarities with other end-time prophets like John the Baptist (Mark 1; Luke 3). Jesus also refers to himself as a prophet (Mark 6:15; 13:33).[14]

---

12. See also Theissen and Merz, *Historical Jesus*, for discussion of Jesus as charismatic (ch. 8), prophet (ch. 9), healer (ch. 10), and poet of the parable (ch. 11); several of these titles or functions are also surveyed in Keener, *Historical Jesus*, ch. 3.

13. See "Galilee and Jerusalem" in France, *The Gospel of Mark*, 33–35; Freyne, *Galilee*; Horsley, *Christian Origins*, 1:30–39; Hanson and Oakman, *Palestine*.

14. See also Hurtado's survey of these various titles, roles, and functions ascribed to Jesus and his ministry in *Lord Jesus Christ*, 54–60; and Hurtado, "Christology," in *NIDB*, 1:612–22.

The Jesus Movement

Soon after the death of Jesus, a group of "Jesus preachers" arose who, like their master, traveled through villages and towns of Palestine preaching and healing. They were also convinced by his empty tomb and subsequent appearances that God had raised Jesus from the dead, and that he would soon return as end-time savior and judge. Despite their efforts to emulate the teaching and lifestyle of the Lord Jesus, their eschatology was much more futuristic, since they expected the imminent return of Christ (Matt 10:23; Mark 9:1; 13:30; Luke 17:23–24). In belief and practice, the Jesus movement may have been closer to John the Baptist, whose ascetic practices resembled those of the Essenes, and who also awaited the future, coming judgment of God (Matt 3; Mark 1; Luke 3).

It was also at this early stage that Jesus the proclaimer became the one proclaimed. Devotion to Christ was included in their worship of the one true God (as Hurtado points out). Along with the authentic words and deeds of Jesus, a kerygma about Jesus's suffering, death, and resurrection developed (Rom 1:2–3; 1 Cor 15:3–4; cf., Acts 2:22–24; 10:36–41). Both the kerygma and the teaching on the imminent *parousia* functioned as interpretive grids through which the Jesus material was filtered. As a result, authentic Jesus sayings are difficult to ascertain, but does not the Spirit of Jesus direct the words of his prophets (e.g., Acts 20:35)?

The contents of the Q document or synoptic-sayings source reflect the beliefs and practices of a rural, itinerant, charismatic, end-time community like the Jesus movement.[15] Such a group would have been responsible for the preservation of the authentic Jesus sayings and the composition of eschatological, prophetic, and wisdom sayings found in the Q collection.

These wandering charismatic missionaries who awaited the imminent return of Jesus were also countercultural, or skeptical of the Jewish establishment. They were ambivalent about the Jewish aristocracy of Jerusalem and favored theocracy ("rule by God alone"). Denouncements against the Pharisees in Q (those that are not from Jesus) are derived from this group (Luke 11:42/Matt 23:23; Luke 11:49–52/Matt 23:34–36).

Since this earliest group of Jesus preachers was probably Aramaic speaking (the dialect was Middle Aramaic of Jewish Palestine), they were probably responsible for the preservation and composition of several Aramaic confessions and slogans. From Jesus they preserved the *Abba* form of address for God. From Judaism they borrowed the Hebrew *amen* and *hallelujah* vocabulary of worship. To this group can also be ascribed the creation of the confession *Maranatha* ("Come, Lord"). Finally, the title "Son of man" (Aramaic: *bar ʾenasha*), replete with apocalyptic meaning from Daniel and Enoch, was probably employed by this group.[16]

The best representative of this rural, itinerant, charismatic movement would be the prophet Agabus (cf. *Did.* 12; 13). In Acts 11:28 he "foretold by the Spirit that there would be a great famine over the

15. See Kloppenborg, *Excavating Q* for the discussions that have taken place in the last ten to twenty years about Q, itinerant radicals (not to mention Cynics!), social factions in Galilee, and the ever-mysterious Q community.

16. See Guinan, "Aramaic," in *NIDB*, 1:229–31; and Fitzmyer, "Aramaic," 5–21.

world; and this took place in the days of Claudius." Foretelling was only one role of the Christian prophet, who primarily was a spokesman for Jesus (Acts 2:14–36). The daughters of Philip also prophesied (21:9). In Acts 21:10–11, Agabus the prophet predicts Paul's arrest by the Jews and his imprisonment under the Romans in Jerusalem. This passion prediction recalls those about Jesus in Luke 9:22 (that Jesus would be rejected by Jewish leaders) and 18:31–32 (that Jesus would be "delivered to the Gentiles").[17] Although Agabus is first mentioned as coming down from Jerusalem (Acts 11:27), he travels throughout Palestine and Syria to Antioch (Acts 11:27). He later journeys to Caesarea "from Judea" (Acts 21:10). Agabus seems to fit the category of an itinerant, rural, charismatic prophet.

The Urban Community Organizers

This category involves several different groups or factions in urban centers, such as in Jerusalem and Syrian Antioch. Each faction made converts, developed networks, and organized communities according to its own particular teachings and praxis. Most of the groups or factions were well integrated into the sociopolitical structure of clients, brokers, and patrons in the Roman world.[18]

---

17. In Acts, both Peter and Paul are also portrayed as itinerant prophets, but both function primarily as "urban community organizers." For more information on early Christian prophets, see Aune, *Prophecy*, 189–232; Aune, *Apocalypticism, Prophecy, and Magic*, 1–38 (apocalyptic), 300–319 (prophecy).

18. Meeks, *First Urban Christians*; Overman, "First Urban Christians?"; on factions, patrons, brokers, and clients, see Hanson and Oakman, *Palestine*, chs. 3–4. For Paul and others as community

According to Acts 6:1, the earliest Christians were first distinguished linguistically and culturally: (a) those who conversed in Hebrew and Aramaic, as well as in Greek (the "Hebrews") from Palestine, and (b) those who were only Greek speaking (the "Hellenists") from the Diaspora.[19] Since they are all Jewish Christian, each group or faction can be defined in relationship to the Jewish law. Also, within the Hebrew- and Aramaic-speaking group, three types can be distinguished by their interpretation and application of the Jewish law.[20]

---

builders and stabilizers, see, e.g., MacDonald, *Pauline Churches*; and our opening discussion in ch. 14 below: "Emerging Christian Orthodoxy: Part 1."

19. Hengel, *Between Jesus and Paul*, 1–29; and Hengel, *Acts*, 71–80. See an excellent survey of discussion in Paget, "Definition of Terms," in Skarsaune and Hvalvik, *Jewish Believers*, 22–52. Hill, *Hellenists and Hebrews*, would caution us about how much theological division can be derived from these two different linguistic and cultural groups mentioned in Acts 6 (contra F. C. Baur's view); Bauckham (underscoring division among Hellenistic Jews) reminds us that some Greek-speaking Jews of the Diaspora (Acts 6:9) may have been even more zealous in their devotion to Torah and temple than certain Palestinian Aramaic-speaking Jews: Bauckham, "James," in Skarsaune and Hvalvik, *Jewish Believers*, 63–65. Although specific identities of certain factions are disputed, a Jewish crisis about torah observance in the first century is undisputed in the NT and related sources: e.g., Josephus; Philo; 4 Ezra 8:20ff., see Theissen, *Religion of the Earliest Churches*, 214–17. Therefore, Schnelle, *Theology of the New Testament*, maintains that linguistic and cultural differences led to separate worship services (Acts 6:9; *y. Meg.* 73d) and involved theological differences explained by the different origins and cultural backgrounds of each group or faction; on synagogues of the Freedman and of the Alexandrians (Acts 6:9) see Chance, *Acts*, 106–7.

20. The above outline is derived from Brown and Meier, *Antioch and Rome*, 1–9; Brown, "Types of Jewish/Gentile Christianity." See also Esler, *Community and Gospel*, 139–45; Dunn, *Beginning from Jerusalem*, 625, 872, 932; Skarsaune and

Hebrew- and Aramaic-Speaking Groups

These factions conversed in Hebrew or Aramaic as well as in Greek. They were mostly Christians of Palestinian Jewish descent. Their ties to the Jewish torah and temple were (at least by proximity to Jerusalem) closer than those of the Greek-speaking (Hellenistic) Jewish Christians from the Diaspora. There are three types within this category distinguished by their relationship to Jewish law.

The first type believed that close observance of the Mosaic law, especially *kashrut* (dietary laws: Leviticus 11; Deuteronomy 14) and the practice of circumcision as the sign of God's covenant with Abraham (Gen 17:10–14). By participation in this covenant all nations would receive God's blessings promised to Abraham (Gen 12:3; 17:8 cf. Luke 1:59; 2:21; Acts 16:1–3). This movement of so-called Judaizers originated in Jerusalem (Acts 15:1, 24) and had some success in both Galatia (Gal 1–2) and Philippi (Phil 3). Their law-observant mission to the Gentiles came in conflict with Paul, who did not regard *kashrut* or circumcision as binding for his Gentile converts (Gal 2:3, 11–12). Even though this group did not appear to survive after AD 70, its practices of Torah observance (Justin, *Dial.* 46–48) and its opposition to Paul's teaching (plus a low Christology) continued among the Ebionite Christians of the second through fourth centuries (e.g., Irenaeus, *Adv. Haer.* 1.26.2; Eusebius, *Hist. eccl.* 3.27).

The second type of Hebrew-Christian faction had the following features.

Members did not insist on circumcision as necessary for the salvation of Gentiles but did require them to keep at least four Jewish purity laws (Acts 15:19–21; 21:25) similar to the seven (later) Noachic laws for Gentiles (Lev 17–18; *Jub.* 7:20–21; *b. Sanh.* 56–60; *t. ʿAbod. Zar.* 8.4–8). This type was a mediating position between that of the Judaizers and Paul, and exerted influence on both. It was headquartered in Jerusalem and its chief spokesmen and leaders were Peter and James (Acts 15; Gal 1:18–19; 2:9). It was probably from this group that the traditions about Jesus's Last Supper and the passion of Jesus with its scriptural fulfillments (Pss 22; 69) were preserved and developed.

This second faction also sought to convert Gentiles as well as Jews. Even though Paul states that Peter's mission was to the Jews (Gal 2:7), Acts 10:1; 11:18; and 15:7–11 tell the story of Peter's going to the Roman Gentile Cornelius. Also, both the presence of a "Cephas party" at Gentile Corinth (1 Cor 1:12) and the fact that 1 Peter is addressed to Gentile Christians in northern Asia Minor make little sense unless Peter missionized Gentiles. This Petrine movement, which originated in Jerusalem, became dominant in Antioch of Syria, Rome, and northern Asia Minor.[21]

Hvalvik, *Jewish Believers*, 105, 212, 644. On Hebrew and Aramaic language in first-century Palestine, see also footnote 5. On Aramaic influence on NT Greek, see our ch. 3, note 1.

21. These localities are deduced from 1 Peter (Petrine Christianity) and Acts 2:4–10, mostly nations of the Jewish Diaspora. Daniélou saw this faction of Torah-observant Jews, like the first apostles, as orthodox in Christology, who did not impose their Judaism on Gentile converts. In later church history the sect of the Nazarenes as described by Jerome and Epiphanius (*Pan.* 29) were closest in religious identity and function, see Daniélou, *Theology of Jewish Christianity*, 9. See also Luomanen, "Nazarenes," in Marjanen and Luomanen, *Companion*, 279–314.

The third type of Hebrew Christians included those who neither insisted on circumcision as necessary for the salvation of Gentiles nor required their observance of Jewish food laws. This type of Hebrew Christianity is associated with Syrian Antioch and the Apostle Paul.[22] In our chronology of Paul's life, we regard the apostolic decrees of Acts 15:19–20 to be an interpolation of what later was instituted at Paul's last visit to Jerusalem (Acts 21:25). Paul's conflict with Peter in Antioch (Gal 2:11–14) reflects the viewpoints of both type-2 and type-3 groups about the observance of Jewish food laws. Paul's concern for the collection of the Jerusalem saints (Rom 15:25, 31; 1 Cor 16:1–3) shows that he still maintained ties to the type-2 Hebrew Christians of Jerusalem. Also, Paul even concedes that circumcision has *cultural* value for the Jew if accompanied by faith (Rom 2:25—3:2; 4:2).[23] Although Paul himself rarely mentions the temple, except mostly to symbolize the holiness of the Christian body (1 Cor 3:16–17; 6:19; 9:13; 2 Cor 6:16), in Acts, Paul and the group associated with him maintain some connection with the Jerusalem temple (Acts 20:16; 21:26; 24:11).

This third faction was probably more missionary minded than group 2, since its base of operation was Antioch (Acts 11:19–26; 13:1–3; Gal 2) and its leading spokesman was Paul. As we note from Paul's letters and Acts, this group visited the cities of the Jewish Diaspora, where they sought to win both Jewish and Gentile converts, and to build a community of believers. Members were conversant in Greek, and some leaders probably had an understanding of Aramaic and Hebrew (e.g., Paul: Acts 26:14; 1 Cor 16:22; Phil 3:5; also Silas and Barnabas). They were fully integrated into the political structure of the Roman Empire. This third type of Hebrew Christianity organized Christian communities throughout the Mediterranean world. Paul is the best example of the goal-oriented community organizer breaking new ground with a community of believers composed of Gentile believers and a remnant of Jewish believers who are the Israel of God, yet who are separate from those who do not regard Jesus as the promised messiah. This group will grow and develop after AD 70.

Members of this type of Hebrew Christianity appeared to be more theologically venturesome. For Paul it is the gospel of Christ that calls forth a people of God connected to Israel by divine grace and yet separate from those Jews who do not respond (Rom 9–11). Therefore in their missionary work, titles like "Son of God" and "Lord" were preferred over titles such as "messiah" and "Son of Man,"

22. Paul appears to be a Hebrew Christian, since he calls himself a Hebrew (2 Cor 11:22; Phil 3:5) and is portrayed as a Hebrew Christian in Acts (22:2; 26:4–5). Daniélou describes this faction as including those who either had never been associated with or had broken from the Jewish world although they continued to think in Jewish terms. It also was the predominant group of *Jewish* Christianity up to the Bar Kochkba revolt of 132–35 (Daniélou, *The Theology of Jewish Christianity*, 9). On the significance of Antioch, see Schnelle, *Theology of the New Testament*, 196–98. For a bibliography on Paul, see discussion at the end of our ch. 12, "Chronology of Paul's Life."

23. In Galatians Paul sees no value in the circumcision of his Gentile converts. Based on his views in 1 Cor 7:14; 9:19–20; Gal 5:6, Paul may not have forbidden Timothy, born of a Jewish mother (and a Greek father who probably forbade it while he was alive) to be circumcised in Acts 16:3 for its *cultural* rather than soteriological significance, Johnson, *Acts*, 289; Skarsaune and Hvalvik, *Jewish Believers*, 135–39.

which were less understandable to their receptive Gentile audiences. In response to God's grace, it is obedience to Christ that fulfills the righteous requirements of Torah. Jesus Christ, the name above every name (Phil 2:9ff.) in Christian worship, was no longer a mere title for Jesus the Messiah from Nazareth. It signified his lordship and divinity.

In this third group of Hebrew Christians, greater stress was also laid on God's vindicating Jesus and his messianic claims by raising him from the dead (Acts 13:30–39; Rom 1:4–5; 8:34; 1 Cor 15:3ff.). The portrait of Jesus as a divine man in whom God worked great miracles (cf., Apollonius of Tyana, Pythagoras) was also emphasized in worship and witness by this missionary-focused group. Finally, the confession "Jesus is Lord" (Rom 10:9; Phil 2:11), important in Christ devotion, was also an appropriate corrective in a Greco-Roman context of emperor worship. Helpful in their evangelizing, the christological titles embraced by these early missionaries (e.g., Son of God, Lord) were also expressions of their devotion to Christ.[24]

Greek-Speaking Jewish Christians

This faction came from more Hellenistic families and did not converse in Hebrew or Aramaic (Acts 6:1). Like the two Hebrew-Christian groups associated with James and Paul, this group did not insist on circumcision as necessary for Gentile salvation. Like Paul, its participants did not require Gentiles to observe Jewish food laws (cf. Mark 7:12–23). In addition, many Greek-speaking Jewish Christians saw no abiding significance in the cult of the Jerusalem temple (Acts 6:13–14, an accusation; but see 7:47–51; 17:24–25; cf., symbolic view of the temple).[25] Later a more radicalized version of this faction of Christianity is encountered in John's gospel (John 2:19–21; 11:47–53; 19:14–15) and also in Hebrews (Heb 4:14—10:18), where the Levitical sacrifices and priesthood are obsolete (both the Gospel of John and Hebrews date from post-70—after the temple's destruction).

The Hellenistic faction began at Jerusalem and was associated with Stephen (Acts 6:1–5, 8–14). The group was scattered throughout Judea after Stephen's death (8:1). It spread to Samaria with Philip (8:4–6), to Phoenicia (8:26, 40), to Cyprus and Antioch (11:19–20), and eventually to Ephesus (18:19)—possibly the place of writing for John's gospel—, and then to Rome (28:14ff.), where the book of Hebrews may have originated).

Since this Jewish-Christian faction was the most Hellenistic of all the

---

24. See Hurtado, *Lord Jesus Christ*, 98–118.

25. Because the Lukan narrative tends to portray the temple in a positive light (Luke 1:5–23; 2:22–51; 24:53; Acts 2:42, 46; 3:1; 21:24–26) one might justifiably read Stephen's speech (7:48ff.) to say that the temple has *become* an instrument of idolatry (cf. 17:24–25), see Chance, *Acts*, 118–19. See also a similar critique in *Sib. Or.* 4:6–11, probably updated by a Hellenistic Jew confronting polytheism in the first century: Charlesworth, *OTP*, 1:381–84. See at Qumran the Teacher of Righteousness vs. the wicked high priest (possibly Hasmonean Jonathan), and the spiritual sacrifices of "Essenes" distinguished from those offered in the temple (Philo, *Good Person* 75; VanderKam, *Dead Sea Scrolls Today*, 129–32); Collins, *Beyond the Qumran Community*, 126, 132. After the temple's destruction, rabbinic Judaism, following the precedent of the Pharisees (and Essenes), reaffirmed the belief that the world is God's temple (Isa 66:1; Acts 7:49) and focused on the holiness of Israel's life, which formerly had centered on the Jerusalem temple (Pervo, *Acts*, 193; Neusner, *Rabbinic Literature: An Essential Guide*, 30–31).

Christian groups, members both experienced and communicated their faith in ways different from the ways of Hebrew Christians. They worshipped Jesus from a more discernibly Hellenistic viewpoint; so they saw him as a divine miracle-working hero or as the descending and ascending redeemer of humanity (i.e., in the spirit of late antiquity). Much of this thought is retained in the synoptic miracle stories (e.g., Mark 4:35—5:43) and early Christian hymns (e.g., Phil 2:6–11; Col 1:15, 20; 1 Pet 3:18–19, 22). In competition with or as a corrective to the popular cults of the day, this group may have been organized as a superior mystery religion, with baptism as an initiation rite and the Lord's Supper as a sacred meal; or as a philosophical school, with a succession of teachers and students. This development of Christianity as a Hellenistic religion probably occurred in cities like Antioch, Ephesus, Thessalonica, Corinth, and Rome. The worship of these Christians was grounded in Israel's faith but developed in its own distinctive, Hellenistic context.

Although Paul was a Hebrew Christian (2 Cor 11:22; Phil 3:5), much of his universal missionizing would have paralleled that of the Hellenistic Jewish Christians. Paul also rarely mentioned the temple (1 Cor 9:13) except as a symbol for the body of believers (1 Cor 3:16–17; 6:19; cf. Stephen). For Paul, the death of Christ is also the fulfillment of the temple sacrifices (*pascha*: 1 Cor 5:7; *hilastērion*: Rom 3:24–25; cf. Acts 6:13–14). In fact some overlap would be expected between the type-3 Hebrew Christians and the Greek-speaking Christians (type 4). After the destruction of the temple in AD 70 and the eventual break with Judaism that followed, these two groups probably

solidified into a movement since disagreements were minor.[26]

It was probably the Gentile converts of both the Greek-speaking Jews and Paul's Hebrew Christians that made the biggest contribution to emerging orthodoxy. However, the moderating spirit of consolidation and preservation within emerging orthodoxy may also have been influenced by the more tradition-embracing Hebrew Christianity of James and Peter.

PHASE 2 (AD 70–95)

In this second phase, early Christian factions are responding to: the crisis of the fall of Jerusalem in AD 70, the delay of the Lord's return (the *parousia*), the increasing conflicts with Judaism, the emergence of Gnostic threats, and sporadic persecution from the Roman government. This period was also characterized by: the writing down of Jesus sayings and stories into Gospels,[27] attempts to mediate between

26. Schiffman points out that post-70 Judaism did not close ranks against the Jewish Christians: "At the Crossroads," in Sanders and Baumgarten, *Jewish and Christian Self-Definition*, 2:115–56. Kimelman, in Sanders and Baumgarten, *Jewish and Christian Self-Definition*, 2:226–44, argues that the *birkat ha-minim* ("blessing for the heretics"), the 12th of the 18 Benedictions (*Amidah*, ca. 100), did not address Jewish Christians in particular. Louis Martyn had used the *birkat ha-minim* to argue for a post-70 break of the synagogue with the church (Martyn, *Gospel of John*; Martyn, *History and Theology*).

27. It should be understood, that with respect to such comments about the dating of the Gospels, some scholars (e.g., Nolland, *Luke 1—9:20*; Nolland, *Matthew*) date Matthew before the war, and hence Mark also. Nolland does date Luke after the war. See also Reicke, "Synoptic Prophecies," in *Studies in the New Testament*, 121–34. Clearly the only reason that scholarship can still not fasten a

various Christian factions, early efforts to combat false teachers, and the endeavor to reassert the influence of the apostles in the late first century. In this section we will examine the following groups: (1) Markan Christianity, (2) the community of Matthew (Matthean Christianity), (3) Lukan Christianity, (4) Deutero-Pauline Christianity, and (5) the community of John (Johannine Christianity).

Markan Christianity

This early movement of Christianity is deduced from what we know about the author of Mark's Gospel and the community he is addressing. In this Gospel, which reads like a Greek tragedy, the author is attempting to address the following issues: the fall of Jerusalem (or at least the growing threat of war from hostile Jewish factions); tribulation and persecution of Christians, related either to the war or to the savagery of Nero in Rome in the 60s; the necessity of Jesus's suffering and death; and the importance of discipleship. The gospel reflects the viewpoint of Gentile Christians, who saw little significance in the Jewish law and tradition.

If in Mark 13 the author is responding to the fall of Jerusalem and its subsequent tribulation, then the reference to the "desolating sacrilege" (v 14), derived from Daniel (11:31; 12:11), probably refers to the destruction of the Jerusalem temple by the Romans in AD 70.[28] Roman persecution of Palestinian Jews followed this catastrophe, and many Jewish Christians fled Judea.[29] At the very least, this chaos in Judea in the years leading up to the war are incorporated by Mark within the time frame between the resurrection of Jesus and his return from heaven. Additionally, Mark's gospel likely reflects the Neronian persecution and the emergence of Nero as an antichrist figure within the Christian communities (*Sib. Or.* 3:63; 4:119, 138; Rev 13:3, 12). During this period many will be led astray by false messiahs (Mark 13:5–7)—maybe by zealot leaders?—and others will undergo persecution for their faith (vv. 9–13). Despite these calamities, Mark assures his readers that the end is near, and that the Son of Man will soon return in power and glory (v. 26). For Mark and his readers, the war with Rome, the fall of Jerusalem, the madness of the emperor, and the accompanying persecu-

---

hard-and-fast date to these even with reference to such a cataclysmic event as the destruction of Jerusalem in 70 is twofold (at least): first, the documents give little away as to time of composition, and second, even though the war must have been on everyone's mind and in daily conversation, it does not appear as a discussion topic in texts with the exception of several apocalypses, and even in these it is often masked with figurative imagery and allusion. A further illustration of the softness with which we must discourse on these stages of historical development is the debate over Q. By some accounts of Q scholars, the Temptation Narrative is a very late addition to Q. Mack says it was added after AD 70, but Theissen argues that it comes from the 40s, during the reign of Gaius! If much preceded it (because it has a developed Christology and a late type genre), and if it yet comes from the 40s, then whence does Q derive? From the above debate, one can deduce that what some scholars insist came late may have come remarkably early; for discussion, see Robbins, *Testing of Jesus in Q*; Mack, *Q and Christian Origins*; Theissen and Merz, *Historical Jesus*, 23–24, 27ff.

28. Josephus, *War* 6.220–70. On the tragic impact of the temple's loss for Jews (and Christians) see Neusner, "Destruction of the Second Temple," *Judaica* 21 (1972) 313–27; Goodman, "Diaspora Reactions," in Dunn, *Jews and Christians*, 27–38.

29. Mark 13:14; flight to Pella: Eusebius, *Hist. eccl.* 3.5.3; Mark 13:2; and Roman capture of the temple: Josephus, *War* 6.413; 7.1. See Mark 13 and dating of the Gospel in Collins, *Mark*, 11–14.

tions are part of the tribulation that will precede the end.

Mark's emphasis on Jesus's suffering and death may reveal his attempt to address extreme tendencies in his community. Because the author incorporates material on Jesus's messiahship and miracles and material on Christian discipleship in the context of suffering and death, he may be correcting triumphalist interpretations of these teachings. Perhaps factions arose preoccupied with teachings about Jesus the divine worker of miracles (4:35—5:43) and the healing authority he bestows on his followers (3:14; 6:7, 13). Perhaps Mark's community, which was experiencing the hardships of persecutions (13:9, 14), saw no significance in the prospects of suffering and death (8:31–37; 10:33–45). Certainly the dramatic staging of Peter's inquisition in 14:66–72 alongside Jesus's inquisition by the high priest in 14:53–65 would communicate to readers and hearers the need to be courageous in the face of suffering and even death. Jesus was asked who he was, and during his trial, for the first time in the story, he admits to being the Son of God, though this will mean certain death. He speaks the truth in the face of danger. Peter, on the other hand, is asked thrice who he is, and to save his life he lies. Who is the hero here? Who is the model of courage and truth?

Mark's community seems to include Gentile converts of Hellenistic Jewish Christians who see little significance in Pharisaic traditions and temple rituals.[30]

30. For helpful survey of discussion on "audience and purpose" in Mark, see Collins, *Mark*, 96–102. Although, we have not focused on geographical *Sitz im Leben*, the problem of Mark's audience is an early one. Even though Clement of Rome, Gregory of Nazianzus, et al. state that Mark

Mark's portrait of Jesus's authority to abrogate Jewish law and tradition (2:15—3:6; 7:1–13) demonstrates the radical stance of Mark's community concerning Jewish legalism. Also, Mark's concern for Gentiles (5:1–20; 7:24–30; 15:39), his predominant setting of ethnically mixed Galilee (14:28; 16:7), and his attempt to explain Jewish customs for his readers presuppose a Gentile audience for whom the Jewish customs have little value.

Matthean Christianity

The author of Matthew's Gospel seems to have been a Greek-speaking Jewish Christian writing to a community in Syrian Antioch at the end of the first century. The author has made use of Mark's Gospel (ca. AD 70) and the statement about a king's sending troops and burning a city (Matt 22:7) may refer to Jerusalem's fall. Ignatius of Antioch appears to be the first to cite Matthew's Gospel. Although the author of Matthew is more sensitive to Jewish customs than is the author of Mark, Matthew 23 seems to reflect specific disagreements with the Pharisees and related factions. Are all the conflicts recorded here from the time of Jesus, or do they point to some later conflicts? Furthermore, how pervasive were they?

Writing from a period later than that of Mark, Matthew responds to both the delay of the Lord's return as well as Jerusalem's historic fall. For Matthew and his community, the ministry of Jesus is the new sacred time, which has fulfilled the hopes of Judaism. Therefore,

wrote in Rome for the people there, John Chrysostom believes that Mark left his writing for those in Egypt (*Hom.1 on Matt*); Collins, *Mark*, 98.

Jerusalem no longer has significance for the Christian as the sacred place.[31] The Lord's return is still expected, but in the meantime the church must discipline itself (16:18–19; 18:15–20) and make disciples of all nations (24:14; 28:19–20).

Matthew's Gospel seems to represent an attempt to mediate between the conservative Hebrew and radical Gentile elements in his community.[32] The inheritance of the extreme Judaizers is represented by sayings rejecting a Gentile mission (Matt 10:5–6; 15:24) and affirming the law's enduring validity (Matt 5:18/Luke 16:17; Q).

The James faction that remained in the church would have stressed strict observance of Mosaic law according to Jesus's teaching. This position would have

been represented by the Sermon-on-the-Mount sayings not contrary to Mosaic law (Matt 5:21–24, 27–29; 6:7), and the exhortation to remain subject to synagogue authorities (23:2–3).

Traditions favoring the Gentile mission (28:16–20) and opposing Pharisaic devotion to the law (6:1–6, 16–18; 15:12–14; 23) might be fostered by many of the Hellenistic Jewish Christians. Teaching on the radical moral demands that seem to revoke the letter of the Mosaic law may also have come from this group (5:33–39).

It was the task of Matthew to embrace, reinterpret, and synthesize the competing traditions of Antioch for a new situation. His portrait of Jesus the Messiah and Son of God, who fulfilled Jewish prophecy and properly interprets the law for the church, might have served as the standard by which to mediate these divergent traditions. The traditions of Christ's ministry as the new sacred time and the continuity of the church with Christ the Son of God seem to reflect the view of liberal Hebrew Christianity (e.g., Acts 11:19–26). Although Matthew's approach to the law is less abrasive than Paul's, both advocated a mission to the Gentiles without legal restrictions, and both saw the death and resurrection of Jesus as a pivotal end-time event.[33]

Matthew also works well as the church's Gospel. There is much concern within its pages for the community and its healthy life. It includes instruction for dealing with discord, with false teaching, with leadership failure and subversion. It would be and truly has been useful for the organized community of faith. Matthew

---

31. The debacle of the war created opportunities for the Christians, removing opposition from Jerusalem leadership and providing propaganda by explaining the temple's fall as divine judgment for rejecting Jesus (Matt 24:2; Luke 23:28ff.; 1 Thess 2:13ff.); see P. S. Alexander, "Parting of Ways."

32. See Brown and Meier, *Antioch and Rome*, 51–57. Because of historical distance (33 and post-70) plus the nature of the Gospels (not mere reporting), we are to employ a "two-level hermeneutic." Here the surface language of the gospel is interpreted redaction-critically, where some of the words and deeds of Jesus (tradition) are understood to reflect or symbolize some historical situations of the Markan (or here, the Matthean) community (redaction). See also Martyn, *History and Theology*. Köstenberger, *Theology of John's Gospel*, 55–56; and Bauckham, *The Gospels*, 19ff., take issue with this approach but fail to supply a better alternative that takes into account these factors. See response to Bauckham: Sim, "Gospels for All Christians?" 3–27; and even Nolland, *Matthew*, 18 n. 14. These problems do not mean that the quest for the audiences of the gospel and their social locations should be abandoned. Our knowledge of textual data and its social dimensions has greatly expanded in recent years. Caution and sensitivity to our endeavor as well as an understanding of the Gospels as primarily proclamations of Jesus Christ are important here.

33. Brown and Meier, *Antioch and Rome*, 62–63; Riches, "Synoptic Evangelists," in Becker, *Christian Beginnings*, 222–27.

is also often seen as the community tradition that embraced and preserved the remains of the Q community.[34]

Lukan Christianity

The author of Luke-Acts appears to have been a third-generation Christian (Luke 1:1–4; Acts 2:39) perhaps from the Aegean Sea region (Luke's geographical familiarity here is reflected in Acts 16–21). He and his readers appear to be a growing Gentile community (with a Jewish minority) in need of self-identity and direction as a result of Jewish and pagan antagonism. The author appears to be influenced by Pauline Christianity, although he also preserves traditions stemming from both moderate Hebrew Christians (James and Peter: Acts 15:1–35) and Gentile-missionizing Hellenists (Stephen in Acts 6:13–14 and 7:47–51; Philip in Acts 8:40; Antioch in Acts 11:19–20).

The author of Luke-Acts, like Matthew, responds to both the historic fall of Jerusalem and the delay of the *parousia*. Luke's description of Jerusalem's capture and destruction is more detailed and coincides with the accounts of Josephus.[35]

For Luke, Jerusalem is the city that rejected and persecuted the prophets (Luke 9:51; 13:33–34). It is the place of both Jesus's passion and Paul's passion (Luke 19:31–33; Acts 21:10–14). Therefore the destruction of Jerusalem was a consequence of the city's rejection of the prophets, Jesus, and Paul (Luke 19:41–44).

In Luke's Gospel, the close proximity of Jerusalem's destruction to the *parousia* (so in Mark) has been minimized. The reference to Jerusalem's destruction is more specific (21:20, 24a), but Luke omits the reference to the false prophets (placing it in a more realized-eschatological context: Luke 17:20–23) and adds here a reference to an interim period: "until the times of the Gentiles are fulfilled" (Luke 21:24b). Luke has thereby lengthened the time between the signs connected with Jerusalem's fall (21:7–24) and those of the *parousia* (21:25–28).[36] Luke gives other indications of the delay of the *parousia* throughout his corpus. Although certain passages reflect an imminent *parousia* (Luke 3:9, 17; 10:9–11; 18:7–8; 21:32), Luke identifies the "the time is at hand" slogan with false prophets (Luke 21:8) and modifies his source in stating that "these

---

34. Robinson, "The Q Trajectory," in Pearson, *The Future of Early Christianity*, 178–89. See also Nolland, *Matthew*, 20–21.

35. C. H. Dodd notes some Lukan images that may reflect OT accounts of Nebuchadnezzar's capture of Jerusalem in 587 BC, "Fall of Jerusalem and 'Abomination of Desolation,'" *JRS* (1947) 52. Nevertheless, the mention of Jerusalem's being encircled by armies (Luke 21:20) and the mention of building the palisades or ramps around the city (19:43) coincide with the accounts in Josephus, *War* 5.446–526. The references to Jerusalem leveled to the ground (Luke 19:44) and to people slain by swords and led away captive (21:24) coincide nicely with Josephus, *War* 6.220–357). See arguments in Puskas, *Conclusion of Luke-Acts*, 31–32.

36. Tiede, *Luke*, 355–60; Carroll, *Return of Jesus*, 37–40; and Carroll, *Response*, 109–12, 117ff.; Chance, *Jerusalem*, 120–21, 133ff. Allison raises questions about whether Luke addresses a specific community or situation, "Was There a Lukan Community?"; Moxnes adds that although we can anlyze the social relations, ethos, and symbolic universe of Luke's narrative world, we do not have a "window" that opens onto the social situation of Luke's historical community: "Social Context of Luke's Community"; see also Riches, "Synoptic Evangelists." Note, however, Esler's sociohistorical response to these criticisms in his "Community and Gospel"; and see Bovon's careful (albeit sparse) reflections on Luke and his audience, *Luke 1*, 5–11, which are developed further in his masterful commentary.

things [wars, insurrections] must take place *first*, but the end will not follow *immediately*" (Luke 21:9).[37] For Luke-Acts, there is an extended interim in which the church is to carry on its work and witness in the world (e.g., Acts 1:6–8).

In response to Jewish accusations of heresy and apostasy, the author of Luke-Acts presents Christianity as founded by a faithful Jew (Jesus), carried on by loyal Jews who worshiped in the temple (the Twelve), and extended to the Gentiles by a dedicated Pharisee, Saul of Tarsus (Paul). With this presentation Luke makes his case for Christians as the people of God and recipients of God's promises. In reaction to Roman suspicions about Christianity as a political threat (and facing the potential for more Roman cruelty and corruption: Luke 13:1–3; 21:12; Acts 24:26–27), Luke makes his case for Roman tolerance. All who live under Rome must not regard the Christian sect as a rebel group (Acts 5:36–37; 21:38) but as a harmless religion (18:14, 15) that proclaims a faith that has some appeal even with Romans (10:1—11:18; 13:7–12).

In order to explain to his readers how Christianity became a Gentile religion that has separated from its parent faith, Luke shows them how a worldwide mission was God's plan from the beginning. Universal salvation was inaugurated with the coming of Jesus, who fulfilled the Hebrew prophecies (Luke 2:32/Isa 49:6; Luke 3:6/Isa 40:5). These same Hebrew prophecies are also fulfilled in the Gentile mission of Paul (Acts 13:47/Isa 49:6; Acts 28:28/Isa 40:5). A mission to the Gentiles, however, is previewed in Jesus's opening

sermon (Luke 4:25–27), and at both the end of the Gospel and the beginning of Acts the resurrected Christ commands his disciples to preach salvation to the nations (Luke 24:47; Acts 1:8). Saul of Tarsus is called to carry the name of Jesus "before Gentiles and kings," and even Peter preaches the gospel to the Roman centurion Cornelius (Acts 10:1—11:18). Finally, in the missionary travels of Paul, the worldwide mission to the Gentiles becomes a major focus (Acts 13:46–47; 18:6; 19:9–10; 28:28). Luke provides this "insider information" for those in the church to instruct them, and for them to share with outsiders with whom these believers are in contact or seek to evangelize.

Even though Luke-Acts incorporates traditions from both Hebrew and Hellenistic Christianity,[38] the author and his community are most influenced by the theologies of both the James and Paul factions, i.e., moderate and more mission-focused Hebrew Christianities. It is clear that the life of Paul was known and revered by the author and his community, because of (a) the large amount of space given to him in Acts, (b) the flattering portrait of his activities, and (c) the information about Paul that the author assumes is already known by his readers.[39]

It is also clear that the author and the readers of Luke-Acts are influenced by the theology of the James group. In Acts 15, all are made to agree with James's view that circumcision is not necessary for the

---

37. Brackets [*polemos, akatastatos*, nouns, v. 9a] and *italics* [*prōton, eutheōs*, adverbs, v. 9b] are our interpolations in Luke 21:9.

38. Type 1, the Judaizers (Acts 15:1, 5; Gal 2:12; Phil 3:4–5); type 2, the James and Peter factions (15:12–21, 28–29; 21:17–26; Gal 2:6–9); type 3, the Paul group (15:1–5, 22, 36ff.; Gal 2:1–2); and type 4, the Hellenists (Stephen: 6:13–14; 7:48–51; Philip: 8:4–40; Antioch: 11:19ff.).

39. For example, his letters, his death; Pervo, *Dating Acts*, ch. 4.

salvation of the Gentiles but that Gentiles should be required to keep some Jewish purity laws (vv. 19–20, 28, 29; cf. Acts 21:25). The historical Paul might have taken issue with some of these extra conditions (Gal 2:6, 12). Also, the portrait of Paul in Acts favors the James group. First, Paul seems dependent on the Jerusalem apostles, especially James (9:27; 11:29–30; 15:2, 22; 21:17–26). Second, Paul complies with Jewish rituals regarded as unimportant in his letters: (a) he circumcised Timothy, whose father was a Gentile, (Acts 16:3; contra Gal 5:2, although Timothy's mother was Jewish); (b) he participated in a Nazirite vow on the advice of James (Acts 21:23–26, contra Phil 3:2–9; but see also 1 Cor 9:20).

With the above data several alternative conclusions can be made. First, Luke and his readers were probably too distant from the times of James and Paul to distinguish with precision their theologies or practices. For Luke in his day, the observance of Jewish law as necessary for salvation was no longer an important issue. The Jewish temple in Jerusalem was destroyed. Second, Luke may have wanted to reconcile the more-universalistic Pauline theology with the more-moderate Jacobian theology. In doing this, Luke might have wanted to reconcile Christian factions of his day with a presentation of a more harmonistic development of the church. Third, Luke might have been attempting to claim Paul for a more conservative version of Hebrew Christianity, defending the apostle against attacks from Jews and conservative Hebrew Christians (e.g., Acts 21:21; later, the Ebionites in Irenaeus, *Adv. Haer.* 1.26.2; Eusebius, *Hist. eccl.* 3.27.4).

If Luke-Acts, as we argue, was written in the late first century when early Christianity began to consolidate its traditions and establish more normative standards of behavior for congregations, the Gentile church of Luke might be moving in a more conservative direction similar to that of the James group or even to Judaism around the Yavneh period (AD 90–100).[40] This suggestion might explain the tendency in Luke-Acts to present Paul as a conservative Hebrew Christian in close agreement with James and Peter.

Deutero-Pauline Christianity

We note from Paul's letters and Acts that he had co-workers and helpers (1 Thess 1:1: Paul, Silvanus, Timothy; 1 Cor 1:1; 2 Cor 1:1: Gal 1:1–2; Phil 1:1; Phlm 1; Acts 15:22). Some co-workers may have functioned as coauthors. Some may have survived the apostle and sought to continue and develop his teaching (Col 1:1; 2 Thess 1:1; cf. Tertullian, *Adv. Marc.* 4.5; Iamblichus, *V.Pyth.* 31.198). This practice of teacher-student succession was also found in the philosophical schools of Hellenism and the rabbinic schools of Judaism (*b. Ber.* 62a). The best examples of a Pauline school are the Deutero-Pauline letters: 2 Thessalonians, Colossians, and Ephesians.[41] These books were written

---

40. For the development of a conservative community-protecting spirit in early Christian orthodoxy, see our discussion of emerging orthodoxy in chs. 14–15 below. On consolidation at Yavneh (where we see a parallel development in early Christianity), see Cohen, "Significance of Yavneh."

41. On the Hellenistic school tradition, see Alexander, "Ancient Literary Biography," in *Book of Acts*, 1:31–63. The Pastoral Letters are more distant to Paul's thought and are therefore classed among

in the name of Paul and are close to his thought yet sufficiently different from it for us to conclude that they were probably not written by the apostle.[42] These writings reflect how the Pauline school dealt with the delay of the *parousia*, how they confronted false teachings, how they handled relations with the Jews, how they thought about the nature of the church in the world, how they understood Christian ethics, and how they sought to maintain the general stability of the faith community.

In 2 Thessalonians the delay of the *parousia* is explicitly addressed, whereas in Colossians and Ephesians it is presupposed. In response to either apocalyptic enthusiasm or Gnostic realized eschatology ("the day of the Lord has come": 2:2), the author of 2 Thessalonians speaks of a series of events that must *precede* the end: (1) the apostasy, (2) the appearance of the rebel, and (3) the disappearance of the "restrainer." This "apocalyptic timetable" in 2 Thessalonians 2 both affirms the distance of the present time from the end and appears to legitimize the delay of the *parousia* up to the time of writing.[43] The *parousia* has not arrived, because the three prior conditions have not been met. Nevertheless, hope in the future return of the Lord is maintained (1:7–8).

In both Colossians and Ephesians we mostly find a realized eschatology as a response to the delay of the *parousia*. In both books, the present benefits of salvation take precedence over the future hope. The future *parousia* is viewed as either a final day of reward and punishment (Col 3:6, 24; Eph 5:6, 27; 6:13) or the completed phase of one's salvation (Col 1:22; 3:3–4). There is no trace of an imminent *parousia*.

In these writings, the emphasis is clearly on the future benefits of salvation that can be experienced in the present or have already been experienced in the recent past. God "has delivered us from the dominion of darkness" (Col 1:13); you "were buried with him in baptism, in which you were also raised with him" (Col 2:12; Eph 2:6); "you who were dead in trespasses . . . God made alive" (Col 2:13; Eph 2:5). Those "once estranged" are "now

the late 1st and early 2nd cent writings of emerging orthodoxy. See Dibelius and Conzelmann, *The Pastoral Epistles*; Donelson, *Pseudepigraphy*, 1–66; Collins, *1 and 2 Timothy and Titus*, 1–15.

42. Since the nineteenth century, disagreement among scholars about the authorship of 2 Thess, Col, Eph, and the Pastoral letters have made them the disputed letters of Paul. They reflect a considerable linguistic, stylistic, historical, and theological departure from Paul's undisputed writings (Rom, 1, 2 Cor, Gal, Phil, 1 Thess, Phlm). Attempts have been made to explain these problematic features as changes in Paul's thinking over the years, Paul's developing a new theology for a new situation, or Paul's acquiring a new secretary (amanuensis) (e.g., Guthrie, *New Testament Introduction*). The vocabulary, style, and theology, however, are too distinctive to be explained as simply a change in Paul's thinking or his addressing a new situation. If a secretary was employed, his influence was so dominant that it would be more appropriate to identify him as the author. Furthermore, just as each person has distinctive fingerprints and a voiceprint that cannot be imitated completely by anyone else, so each person has a "language print" (Sampley and Krodel, *The Deutero-Pauline Letters*; J. A. Bailey, "Who Wrote II Thess?"; on the issue of pseudonymous writings see Donelson, *Pseudepigraphy*; Rist, "Pseudepigraphy and Early Christians," in Aune, *Studies in the New Testament*, 3–24; Metzger, "Literary Forgeries"; Guthrie, *New Testament Introduction*, 671–84; Sumney, *Colossians*, 1–9; see the five types of authorship in Cicero's letters: Talbert, *Ephesians and Colossians*, 7–11).

43. The emphasis is different from Paul's in 1 Thessalonians, which affirmed the imminence of Christ's return (4:15, 17; 5:1–5). Richard, *First and Second Thessalonians*, 231–32; Jewett, *Thessalonian Correspondence*, 181–86.

reconciled" (Col 1:22; Eph 2:14–15). In these Deutero-Pauline letters the future dimension almost disappears, and hope becomes a symbol of assurance rather than anticipation for the end of the age.

The false teachings alluded to in the Deutero-Pauline writings appear to be Gnostic, although other possibilities have been given.[44] If 2 Thessalonians opposes Gnostic realized eschatology (2:2), this would also explain the admonitions against idleness and disorderly conduct (3:6–13). Since these "troublemakers" have now experienced the final resurrection, they are freed from the bondage of this world and all obligations connected to it. This would be the position of libertine Gnosticism (e.g., Irenaeus, *Adv. Haer.* 1.6.2–3). The statements in Colossians that those whom Christ has now reconciled "in his body of flesh by his death" (1:22), and that in Christ "the whole fullness of deity dwells bodily" (2:9) also appear anti-Docetic. The denouncement of the "worship of angels" (Col 2:18) may be directed against the *aeons* of Gnostic cosmologies. Even the admonition against those who scrutinize "eating and drinking or in regard to a feast or new moon or sabbaths" (Col 2:16) may be interpreted as rebuking Jewish Gnostic asceticism. The general harangues against false teachers in Ephesians (4:14–15; 5:6) could apply to any group opposed by the author and his community (e.g., *Apocalypse of Peter* 79.23–31).

Except for *Ioudaioi* (v. 14) in 1 Thess 2:13–16, the mention of the Jews, Israel, or the circumcised mainly concerns Hebrew Christians from the past or present. The Deutero-Pauline interpolation in 1 Thess 2:13–16 denounces "the Jews" (Judeans) for killing Jesus, and probably connects the destruction of Jerusalem with God's wrath.[45] In 2 Thess 1:4–5 there is reference to persecutions and afflictions, but it is unclear if the oppressors are Jews or Roman Gentiles.

In Colossians and Ephesians we find Christian reinterpretations of Jewish rites and symbols. Colossians 2:11 refers to a circumcision of Christ made without hands. Ephesians 2:11–16 mentions the reconciling of both Jews and Gentiles together in the church through Jesus Christ. In Eph 2:21, the church is also viewed as God's new temple.

The nature of the church is developed in Colossians and Ephesians with some allusions found in 2 Thessalonians. In 2 Thessalonians the Pauline concept of the church as a local assembly is found, but the situation of persecution and false teaching appears to be post-Pauline. In Colossians and Ephesians, there is added to the Pauline concept of "body of Christ" the motif of Christ as the "head" of the church/body (Col 1:18, 24; 3:15; Eph 1:22–23; 4:15–16; 5:23), who is also the "head" over principalities, powers (Col 2:10), and the entire cosmos (Col 1:18, 20; Eph 1:22). In Ephesians, the church is no longer a house assembly (Phlm 2; Col 4:15) but a universal entity embracing all Christians (Eph 1:22–23; 2:11–22; 3:6,

44. For a survey of opinion, see Gunther, *Opponents*, 3–9; Lüdemann, *Opposition to Paul*; Sumney, *Identifying Paul's Opponents*; Porter, *Paul and His Opponents*, 1–58.

45. Pearson, "1 Thess 2:13–16: Interpolation," 79–94; Schmidt, "1 Thessalonians 2:13–16," 269–79; Schlueter, *Filling Up the Measure*. On the impact of the temple's loss for Jews (and Christians) see Neusner, "Destruction of the Second Temple"; Goodman, "Diaspora Reactions." On the Jews as "Judeans," see Hanson and Oakman, *Palestine*, 11, 162.

20; 4:4, 12; 5:24–25, 29–32). The church's mission embraces both heaven and earth (Eph 1:22–23; cf. Col 1:18–20).

In Colossians and Ephesians, the church has assigned offices (Col 1:25; Eph 4:11), and its foundation is built upon the "apostles and prophets," with Christ as the cornerstone (Eph 2:20). In Ephesians, the church is not only the body of Christ but the household of God, the bride of Christ, and the holy temple. The focus is on the stability of the faith community.

Christian ethics in the Deutero-Pauline writings reflect the situation of a church adjusting to the world. Second Thessalonians adds to its Pauline admonitions the following: "hold to the traditions . . . taught by us" (2:15; cf. 3:6), the avoidance of evil teachers (3:1–3), and a golden rule of labor (3:6–12). Colossians and Ephesians incorporate many ethical exhortations into baptismal instructions for new converts (Col. 3:15–17; Eph 4:17—5:20) and household rules for Christian families (Col 3:18—4:5; Eph 5:21—6:9). The ethical admonitions in the baptismal instructions are conveyed by numerous metaphors (e.g., "put off"/ "put on," "old man"/"new man," "death"/"life") illustrating the process of sanctification. The household rules presuppose a hierarchy of authority typical in ancient Hellenistic society: Christ-husbands-wives-household servants-children.

Although the conservative tone of the Deutero-Pauline writings may parallel a similar stabilizing mood in contemporary Judaism and may echo the spirit of conservative Hebrew Christianity, their Hellenistic view of Jewish law and customs places them in the tradition of liberal Hellenistic Christianity. The conservative posture of avoiding false teachings, holding to apostolic traditions, and adjusting to the world as an institution is similar to that of post-Javneh Judaism (AD 90–100) and may recall the conservative mind-set of the James and Peter group. However, the influence of the teaching of Paul (a liberal Hebrew) is obvious, and a break with Judaism is evident (1 Thess 2:13–16). A Gentile majority emulating the teachings of Paul yet distant from the concerns of Hebrew Christianity is presupposed in the Deutero-Pauline writings.

These books of the Deutero-Pauline school contain the following teachings, which are characteristic of Hellenistic Christianity separate from Judaism: The legal traditions and feasts are abolished (Col 2:14–17, 20–23; Eph 2:15). All that matters is the circumcision of Christ (baptism?) made without hands (Col 2:11). The Christian church is now the holy temple (Eph 2:21). Although conservative in spirit and Pauline in tradition, the Deutero-Pauline writings share the views of Gentile-oriented Hellenistic Christianity separate from Judaism.

Johannine Christianity

In the Gospel and letters of John, as in the Synoptic Gospels, we seem to find a community addressing the issues of Jerusalem's fall, the delay of the *parousia*, and conflicts with Judaism. Unlike in the synoptic tradition, we encounter a high Christology and realized eschatology arising from a complex Hellenistic-Jewish environment (e.g., sectarian, Gnostic). The Johannine community is the product of diverse groups of Hebrew and Hellenistic Christians in conflict with the Jews and one another because of their beliefs about Jesus. Let us explain these points.

In John's Gospel there is a reference to the destruction of the Jerusalem temple by the Romans (11:48). In John 2 a denouncement of Jesus against the temple (v. 19) is spiritualized ("the temple of his body": v. 20) and adapted to the post–AD 70 situation when the temple did not exist. Also, Jesus is now the place of divine tabernacling (1:14). Finally, a time is coming when worship in a particular temple will be obsolete (4:21). The last three references reflect the same anti-temple beliefs as the Hellenistic Jews held who made converts in Samaria (Acts 6:13–14; 7:47–49; 8:45). This Hellenistic group seems to have influenced the Johannine community more than any other type.

John's gospel responds to the delay of the *parousia* by reinterpreting many of the future hopes as present realities. Even though the author retains some futuristic beliefs (5:28–29; 6:39–40, 44; 12:48b), many of them—resurrection, judgment, eternal life, *parousia*—are described as realities already present for the believer in the encounter with Jesus (3:17–19, 36; 5:24; 6:26–27, 40, 54; 11:25–26; 12:31).

Conflicts with Judaism are detected at various stages in the development of the Johannine community. There seem to be early conflicts with the Jews over the divine status of Jesus (5:16–18; 8:58–59; 10:33; 19:7), over the violation of the Sabbath and the law of Moses (5:16; 7:14, 22–24), and over the meaning of the Eucharist (6:52). It was probably the confession of Jesus as Messiah that caused the Jews to expel some of the Johannine Christians from the synagogues they attended (9:22; 12:42–43; 16:2–3). As a result of this expulsion, "the Jews" (Judeans)

were regarded by those expelled as outsiders hardened by God and under Satan's control (8:44; 9:41; 12:37–40; 15:25).[46]

Rejection by the local Judeans and probable difficulty with a Gentile mission (John 12:20–23 with 15:18–19) may have convinced the Johannine Christians that the world opposed Jesus (3:19; 7:7; 15:18–19; 16:20), that they should not belong to this world (15:19; 17:16), which is under the power of Satan (12:31, 35–36; 14:30).[47]

This situation of rejection that they faced might explain the world-negating attitude encountered in the Fourth Gospel (typical of Gnosticism and other sectarian movements).[48] The unfavorable references to the world (1:29; 3:16; 4:42; 6:33, 51; 10:36;

46. On a reexamination of church and synagogue (*birkat ha-minim*) with conflicts facing the Johannine community, see Köstenberger, *Theology of John's Gospel*, 55–59, 514–15; Katz, "Issues in the Separation." See also Boyarin, "*Ioudaioi* in John."

47. Although Wisse sees problems in deriving too much Johannine community from the Johannine story of Jesus, "Historical Method," 35–42, Hurtado still maintains several crises within and without the Johannine community related to the divine status of Jesus and devotion to him, *Lord Jesus Christ*, 423–26. Meeks indicates how much our knowledge of the social dimensions of the Gospels has expanded by means of sociohistorical analysis, "Hermeneutics of Embodiment," 176–86. Nevertheless, the message of John should not be lost in our quest for Johannine communities.

48. Regarding the world of John, Irenaeus claimed that John wrote his gospel to refute Cerinthus, an early Gnostic, *Haer.* 3.11.1; Perkins observes that both John and Gnosticism "may point to a common background," 120, in her *Gnosticism and the New Testament*, chs. 8–9. Hellenistic and sectarian Judaism (exemplified in the Dead Sea Scrolls community) are still rich with many similar themes (Hurtado, *One God, One Lord*, chs. 1–5; J. J. Collins, *Scepter and the Star*, 139–64). On the labels *faction*, *sect*, and *schism* and how scholars use them (often without clarification) to describe the diverse factions within both Judaism and Christianity, see Sanders, *Schismatics*.

12:47; 17:21) presuppose its evil state and magnify the love of God, who sent his Son to save it.

As a result, the feasts of "the Judeans" (5:1; 6:4 [Passover]; 7:2 [Tabernacles]; 10:22 [Lights]) find fulfillment in Jesus, who is the "Lamb of God" (1:29), who has "tabernacled (*skēnoō*) with us" as the "Light of the world" (8:12). Jesus is also the "king of Israel," and believers are "Israelites" (1:47, 49; 12:13; 19:19). Entry into God's community is not by natural birth but by the will of God (1:12–13; 3:3–7). Jesus is the new temple, which replaces the old that is no more (2:19–21; 4:21–24). This theological position appears to reflect the beliefs of certain Greek-speaking Jewish Christians and their Samaritan converts (Acts 6:13–14; 7:47–49; 8:4–5).

In addition to external conflicts with "the Jews," internal strife developed among members of the Johannine community. A high Christology and universalistic emphasis (John 3:16–17, 18–21; 4:24; 1 John 4:8–9) brought tension with conservative Hebrew Christians.[49] A defensive concentration on Christology against both "the Jews" and Jewish Christians eventually led to a split within the community.

Emphasis on the divinity of Jesus sharpened through polemics against the Jews and Jewish Christians probably left the question of Jesus's humanity unchallenged and undefined in relation to his divinity. Therefore one group within the Johannine community probably saw the human existence of Jesus as only a stage in the career of the divine Logos and not as a significant part of redemption. The only important doctrine for them was that eternal life had been brought down to people through a divine Son, who passed through the world.[50] Knowledge of this doctrine gave one a special communion with God that freed one from worldly duties and responsibilities. These early concepts of the group are on a trajectory toward Docetism (the notion that Christ only appeared to be human) and libertine Gnosticism (the belief in freedom from worldly responsibility). Christological broadness and inclusivity more than anything else is what characterizes the theological strength of this gospel. This community, unlike most early Christian groups, was able and willing to assimilate many views of Jesus. In the words of Greg Riley, "So he was the Logos, the Light of the World, the Only Begotten Son, the Prophet Like Moses, the Lamb of God, the Son of Man, the Son of God, Jacob's Ladder, the Good Shepherd, and more. There was little or no constraint. As long as Jesus occupied the spiritual center of

---

49. There also seems to have been conflicts with adherents from a sect founded by John the Baptizer. Note the number of negative statements disqualifying John as "the light" (1:9), the Messiah, Elijah, the prophet (1:19–24; 3:28), the bridegroom (3:29), or a miracle worker (10:41). See Riley, *Resurrection Reconsidered*, where a dispute between the Johannine community and a "Thomasine community" over resurrection of the body is proposed. It assumes that some early community material can be gleaned from the Gnostic writings of *Gospel of Thomas*, *Thomas the Contender*, in Robinson, *Nag Hammadi Library*, 124ff., 199ff.; and *Acts Thom.*, in *NTA* 2:322ff.). See critical reviews in Hurtado, *Lord Jesus Christ*, 452–85; Johnson, "John and Thomas in Context," 288–99.

50. Brown, *Community*, 103–44, and the contextual insights of Carter, *John*, 210–17. Note the caution in Carson, *Gospel according to John*, 35–37, and the controversies discussed in Köstenberger, *Theology of John's Gospel*, 53–59; and Barton, "Can We Identify the Gospel Audiences?" in Bauckham, *Gospels for All Christians*, 189–94; for survey and critical evaluation, see Brodie, *Quest for the Origin of John's Gospel*, 15–21.

his followers, he became identified with whatever could evoke that center. We should not be surprised then to find as we do a dozen or more Christologies in John. Among them we observe that some Christians saw Jesus on the model of Dionysus, the Son of God as Son of Zeus, who turns water into wine and whose very flesh and blood brings immortality."[51]

The author of the Johannine letters saw the beliefs and practices of this divine Logos group as a danger to the community. He reaffirms the importance of Jesus's humanity by exaggerating the error of the other group (1 John 4:2–3, 15; 2 John 7, 10–11) and by attacking their elitism and perfectionist ideas (1 John 1:6, 8; 2:4, 9–11).[52] This reaction caused a schism between the two groups (2:19) and forced the first group (secessionists) toward Gnosticism. Those recipients of the letters who adhered to the concerns of John the Elder and shared his anti-Gnostic stance eventually linked up with the Great Church.[53]

51. Riley, "'I Was Thought to Be What I Am Not,'" 22.

52. We favor the view that the same author wrote 1, 2, and 3 John, but may not have been the same author as the author of the Fourth Gospel. See Brown, *Epistles of John*, 14–35. See, however, the noteworthy argument that the Beloved Disciple is not John the son of Zebedee, but John the Elder (his disciple?), who authored the Johannine Letters and most of John's gospel, Bauckham, *Jesus and the Eyewitnesses*, ch. 16.

53. For more information, see our discussion of Docetism in ch. 14: "Emerging Christian Orthodoxy: Part 1."

14

Emerging Christian Orthodoxy: Part 1

"Christianity Adjusting to the World and Becoming an Institution," "The Period of Consolidation," "Early Catholicism," and "The Emerging Great Church"—these are some descriptive titles that have been given to this formative stage of early Christianity. This phase was characterized by a general loss of expectation for Christ's immediate return, a break with Judaism as the "parent religion," doctrinal solidarity, and a fixed organizational structure.[1]

Historian Adolf von Harnack (1851–1930) described this period of early Christianity as a time when (a) the inner dynamics of the apostolic period were exchanged for laws and rules, (b) the original spontaneity gave way to theological reflection, and (c) the apostolic priority on proclamation became subordinate to the defense of the faith. Harnack's

observations found independent support in the work of the social theorist Max Weber (1864–1920), who constructed a similar social model from his comparative study of world religions.[2] The first generation of founders could be regarded as the pioneers and pilgrims: those original visionaries who were usually counterculture sectarians led by "charismatic leaders." The second generation includes the settlers and builders, those community

---

1. See critical overview in Marshall, "'Early Catholicism' in the New Testament," 217–31; J. H. Elliott, "A Catholic Gospel"; and recent discussion in Harding, *What Are They Saying about the Pastoral Epistles?* 46–65; and Margaret Y. MacDonald, "Early Catholicism," in *DBI*, 182–83.

2. Harnack, *What Is Christianity?* 190–209; see also Harnack, *History of Dogma*, 2:169–77 for differences between emerging orthodoxy and its opponents. Harnack saw this phase as a result of growth in Greco-Roman world and reaction to opponents but did not label it early catholic. See *NJBC*, 66:94. The social model constructed by Weber consisted of an early charismatic phase of spontaneity and a later phase of routinization: Weber, *Economy and Society* and *From Max Weber*; White, *From Jesus to Christianity* outlines four generations: 1. Sectarian Beginnings (Jesus, Jesus Movement, Paul); 2. Birth Pangs and New Horizons (gospel trajectories); 3. From Sect to Church (e.g., John, Hebrews, 1 Clement, Ignatius); 4. Coming of Age in the Roman World (e.g., Pastorals, Gnostics, 2 Peter).

organizers who develop and expand the work of the founders. The third generation includes the landed aristocracy, who seek to preserve the traditions of their predecessors, who live in a phase of "routinization." The values and priorities of this last faction have changed the most in comparison with the original and the transitional groups.

It must be noted, however, that this social model accounts for the major trends and tendencies. The construct also accounts for such factors as the existence of reactionary factions in the later phases. These "restoration advocates" seek to call the movement back to the original days of spontaneity and charismatic leadership. These reactionaries would either be tolerated or opposed by the movement, depending on whether they are perceived as constructive prophets or destructive sectarians. When this and other qualifying factors are incorporated, the above categories remain adequate in explanations of a religious movement.

In our broad overview of "emerging orthodoxy" we will utilize the following early Christian writings: the Pastoral Letters; James; 1 and 2 Peter; Jude; 1, 2, and 3 John; Revelation, *1 Clement*, the *Didache*; the letters of Ignatius; and the works of Justin Martyr. Even though it will be argued that these writings share common characteristics as documents of "emerging orthodoxy," differences in doctrine and organization will also be noted, such as the divergent views of the episcopate in the Pastorals and Ignatius. It is our contention, however, that such differences are best explained when viewed on the same trajectory of thought, with earlier formulations moving toward later refinements. This discussion also assumes that

the above writings were composed in the same general period of AD 90–150.[3]

We have also labeled this period "emerging Christian orthodoxy" because the communities who identified with this movement appear to be on a trajectory of ideology moving toward the theology of a catholic Christianity in the fourth century characterized by the teachings of Eusebius and Athanasius. It is labeled "emerging orthodoxy" because distinctions between "right" and "wrong" beliefs are not completely discernible in the late first and early second centuries. This phase transitions from community stabilizing to community protecting institutionalization.[4]

In our discussion of emerging orthodoxy we will look at the following

3. Käsemann, "Paul and Early Catholicism," 236–51; Conzelmann, "Luke's Place in Early Christianity," in Keck and Martyn, eds., *Studies in Luke-Acts*, 302–9; but see concerns about "early Catholicism" and Protestant bias in *NJBC*, 94–95; for more nuanced sociohistorical approaches, see MacDonald, *Pauline Churches*, who is indebted to the sociological models of Weber as developed by Holmberg, *Paul and Power*; plus Berger and Luckmann, *Social Construction of Reality*; social historian Judge, skeptical of most social models, sees an urban Christianity compromised (i.e., adjusting to its world) by Roman occupation in Scholer, *Social Distinctives*, 1–56, 127–35. Burtchaell, *From Synagogue to Church*, sees a greater influence from the synagogue model and its institution of elders than from the house-church model, e.g., Balch and Osiek, *Families in the New Testament World*.

4. On p. 258, see our discussion of "orthodoxy" in the formation of the NT Canon. See also Kraft, "The Development of the Concept of 'Orthodoxy,'" in Hawthorne, *Current Issues*, 47–56; Hurtado identifies the ideology and praxis of this type of second-century Christianity as "proto-orthodox" in Hurtado, *Lord Jesus Christ*, 563–648. MacDonald employs the sociological models "community-building" (authentic Paul), "community-stabilizing (Colossians, Ephesians), and "community-protecting" (Pastorals) in her analysis of the institutionalization of early Christianity (MacDonald, *Pauline Churches*).

characteristics of this phase: conflicts with "false teachings," fixed organizational structure, preservation of the apostolic tradition, creedal statements and confessions of faith, developing patterns of worship, normative Christian ethics, and the collecting of a distinctive literature. Because of its importance for understanding emerging orthodoxy, we will concentrate on conflicts with "false teachings" in this chapter and on the other developments in the next one.

CONFLICTS WITH "FALSE TEACHINGS"

One major reason for the emphasis on doctrinal solidarity and structured organization in the late first and mid-second centuries was the presence of sectarian groups or factions in the church communities that the majority viewed as a threat. As early as the mid-first century, we detect the presence of Judaizing Christians in Galatia and Hellenistic Jewish Christians in Achaia (Gal 2:4; 2 Cor 11:26), both of which groups Paul viewed as threats to his ministry. The size and influence of these factions is uncertain. Other "false teachers and teachings" in the churches are alluded to in Mark, Matthew, John, Colossians, and Revelation.[5]

Introductory Concerns

Because most of these "opponents" in the early Christian writings are not specifically named, their exact identities are uncertain.[6] Some tentative conclusions, however, can be drawn from analyzing the invectives and harangues in the NT and other early Christian literature. This analytical procedure, however, must be cautiously followed, because a statement about "godless defilers of the flesh," for example, is probably polemical rhetoric with no historical reference intended.[7] Lucian of Samosata, the second-century-AD satirist, was well known for such rhetorical invectives: "Even before his attempt upon me, I detested him and held him in bitter enmity on account of the vileness of his character. So I undertook to prosecute him" (*Alexander Pseudomantis* 57). Lucian and the early Christian writers were merely following a common literary convention. Such exaggerated accusations might be compared to the rhetorical language of political slander in modern times.

Despite these cautionary concerns, the discovery of the Nag Hammadi Codices in southern Egypt in 1945 has provided us with primary texts of a diverse religious and philosophical movement (or phenomenon) of the third century, which was opposed by the Great Church. Many scholars who have studied these texts are also convinced that they contain

---

5. See Weeden, *Mark—Traditions in Conflict*; Francis and Meeks, *Conflict at Colossae*; Pokorný, *Colossians*; Georgi, *Opponents of Paul*; Gunther, *St. Paul's Opponents*; Desjardins, "Portrayal of the Dissidents"; Sumney, *Identifying Paul's Opponents*; Martin, *By Philosophy and Empty Deceit*. On factions, movements, and institutions, see Hanson and Oakman, *Palestine*.

6. The following works list a diversity of opinions on the matter: Gunther, *St. Paul's Opponents*, 1–9; Sumney, *Identifying Paul's Opponents*; Arnold, *Colossian Syncretism*; Porter, *Paul and His Opponents*, 1–58 (for an overview of perspectives).

7. Wisse, "Epistle of Jude," 133–43; Vallée, *Study in Anti-Gnostic Polemics*; Desjardins, "Portrayal of the Dissidents."

traditions much earlier than the third century, since fully developed non-Christian and Jewish-Gnostic systems have been detected. Perhaps the ideology of those opposed in these early "orthodox" writings is on a trajectory with what is found in the later Nag Hammadi writings, when an intertextual relationship can be established. As a result, one might label such factions as early Gnostic or gnosticizing Christians. The writings of Irenaeus and Epiphanius indicate that Gnosticism was regarded as an opponent by the late second and third centuries. Nevertheless, some caution must be used when we assert that the Gnostics were the opponents of emerging orthodoxy in the late first and early second centuries. The evidence of that period is sparse.

Other candidates for "opponents" of emerging orthodoxy (AD 90–150) are:

- **Ebionites.** Anti-Pauline and Torah-observant Jewish Christian factions that believed Jesus was born of Mary and Joseph (no virginal conception) but empowered by God at baptism. Sources for these factions are found in the second century (Irenaeus, *Adv. Haer.* 1.26.2; 5.1.3) and third century (Tertullian, *Carn. Chr.* 14; Pseudo-Clem. *Hom., Recog.* 1.27–71 ["Kerygmata of Peter"]; the *Gospel of the Hebrews* [both sources contain some Gnostic influences]; and the fourth-century Eusebius: *Hist. eccl.* 3.27.1–6).

- **Marcionites.** Led by a radical Paulinist of the mid-second century, Marcion of Pontus. He rejected the Hebrew Bible (as containing an inferior creator god) and believed that the true interpretation of Christ and the Father was preserved only in ten letters of Paul (minus the Pastoral Letters with the Laodiceans, which is probably Ephesians), plus the Gospel of Luke (ascribed to Paul's companion). Both the gospel and apostolic writings were edited and abridged by Marcion (Irenaeus, *Adv. Haer.* 1.27.2; 3.11.17). Despite opposition from Irenaeus and others (e.g., Eusebius, *Hist. eccl.* 5.13; Tertullian, *Adv. Marc.* 4.5; *Praescr.* 30), the radical, ascetic teacher from Pontus may have been the first to draw up a collection of Christian Scriptures with the two divisions: gospel and apostolic writings (although Luke and Acts might be precursors to these two divisions). See also Marcion, *Antitheses*; Justin Martyr, *1 Apol.* 1.26; 58; Hippolytus, *Haer.* 7.38.1–5 (see our discussion of Marcion in the formation of NT canon, pp. 262–63).

- **Montanists.** A prophetic movement from Asia Minor (ca. 170–230) that anticipated an imminent end of the world. Montanus, the founder, and his two prophetesses, Maximilla and Priscilla, claimed to utter new prophecies directly from God. Some of their utterances (similar to John 14–17) are found in the catholic writings of Tertullian (ca. 200) and Epiphanius (ca. 400). Although no Montanist books survive and the identity of the prophecies as "Scripture" is unclear, the new revelations of Montanism were refuted by the Great Church as an attempt to add to the four Gospels and apostolic writings (Epiphanius, *Pan.* 48.3.2; Hippolytus, *Haer.* 8.19; 10.25; Eusebius, *Hist. eccl.* 5.16–19; 5.18.5; 6.20.3).

- **Cerinthians.** A late first-century sect whose founder, Cerinthus, believed that Jesus was a man who had received the divine Christ when the supreme power descended upon him at baptism, but that it subsequently left him when he was crucified (Docetism; see Irenaeus, *Adv. Haer.* 1.26.1; 3.21.1; Eusebius, *Hist. eccl.* 3.28). The Ebionite view of Christ was associated with that of Cerinthus in Irenaeus, *Adv. Haer.* 1.26.2.

From the mid-second to the fourth centuries it became evident that these factions were opposed by orthodox and catholic Christianity, but it is also possible that some incipient forms of these "heresies" surfaced in the late first and early second centuries.

Gnosticism

In this section we will concentrate on the data that correspond closest to what we believe to be some early form of Gnosticism.[8] Reference will also be made to other opponents when the data suggest it.

The data that lend support to early catholic Christianity's opposition to Gnosticism in AD 90–150 are (1) references to "cleverly devised myths" and to "endless genealogies"—possible allusions to Gnostic cosmogonies; (2) opposition to ascetic practices characteristic of

8. See King, *What Is Gnosticism?*; Perkins, *Gnosticism and the New Testament*; Perkins, "Gnosticism," in *NIDB*, 2:581–84; Williams, *Rethinking Gnosticism*; Pearson, *Ancient Gnosticism.* NB: Citations of Gnostic books are from Robinson, *Nag Hammadi Library*, and used with permission. Additions to both NT and Gnostic texts by us or by a Nag Hammadi translator will be noted by parentheses ( ) or brackets [ ]. All words italicized for emphasis in the citations are ours. NT citations are from the NRSV unless noted otherwise.

Gnosticism; (3) denouncements of libertinism, which may have been the lifestyle of *some* Gnostics; (4) counterarguments to the belief that the final resurrection is already here; and (5) refutations of Docetic Christology, which was (or became) a Gnostic doctrine.

References to Cleverly Devised Myths

References to the "cleverly devised myths" and "endless genealogies," which may be allusions to Gnostic cosmogonies ("origins of the world"), are numerous: "cleverly devised myths" (2 Pet 1:16), "myths and endless genealogies" (1 Tim 1:4), "profane myths" (1 Tim 4:7), "strange doctrines or old myths that are useless" (Ign. *Magn.* 8.1).

Two other supportive references are "worship of angels" (Col 2:18) and "contradictions (*antitheseis*) of what is falsely called knowledge (*gnōseōs*)" (1 Tim 6:20).

The above references are taken from different contexts and some of them could be alluding to the practices of (non-Gnostic) Jewish factions. Nevertheless, as this section will indicate, there is sufficient evidence to support our original claim that these are anti-Gnostic texts.

From such apologists as Irenaeus (ca. 180) and Hippolytus (ca. 220), with some confirmation from the Nag Hammadi writings (third century), we learn about elaborate Gnostic conceptualizations of the cosmos. For example, the Valentinian-Gnostic system (according to Hippolytus) begins with the Unbegotten Father who creates a Dyad: *Nous* and Truth, which bring forth *Logos* and Life, and these produce Man and Church. Ten *aeons* derive from *Nous* and Truth, and twelve from *Logos* and Life. The last *aeon* of the twelve, *Sophia*, defects and brings forth the earth: an "abortion" without form and incomplete. She also produces the Demiurge from her union with the Fruit of the *Plērōma*. Thereafter the Father brings forth *Horos* so that the *aeons* may no longer be disturbed by the abortion.[9] This is only a brief summary of the elaborate Valentinian-Gnostic system.

If the authors of the early catholic writings were confronted with such elaborate Gnostic systems, it would be difficult to imagine that their response to be different from the statements we have listed above. The references in 1 Timothy are striking, because the opponents are accused of "contradictions and what is falsely called knowledge (Gk. *gnōseōs*: 6:20). This statement is a plausible allusion to an early form of Gnosticism. The reference in Colossians to the "worship of angels" (2:18) may also be an allusion to the *syzygies*, or pairs of semidivine beings (e.g., *Nous* and Truth), which are a major feature in the Gnostic systems.

Both the Valentinian and Basilidian systems would have easily been identified with "cleverly devised myths" and "endless genealogies" by early catholic writers.[10] The mention of "genealogies" in 1 Tim 1:4 could apply to the groups of aeons in the Gnostic systems. Even if "genealogy" in this context has the literal meaning of Jewish lists of family descent (Gen 5; 10–11), this does not rule out any possible Gnostic allusions. We must remember that both Gnostic systems mentioned above contain Jewish as well as Christian elements. Several writings from Nag Hammadi are also Jewish Gnostic (e.g., *Apocalypse of Adam, Eugnostos, The Thunder, The Three Steles of Seth, The Paraphrase of Shem*).

Asceticism

A second reason for regarding the Gnostics as a faction (or network of factions) opposed by emerging orthodoxy is that ascetic practices are denounced that are similar to those of the Gnostics. Two examples from Colossians and 1 Timothy will be given. The letter to the Colossians urges its readers to let no one pass judgment on them in matters of "food or drink or of observing festivals, new moons, or sabbaths" (2:16). The reference to "sabbaths" has led some scholars to conclude that a Judaizing heresy is being condemned; however, this assertion would not necessarily rule out a Gnostic influence since there were Jewish Gnostics. Also, this denouncement occurs in

---

9. On Valentinus (ca. 140–160), see Hippolytus, *Haer.* 29–36; Ptolemy, *Flor.*; Irenaeus, *Haer.* 1.1–11 (Valentinus and his pupil Ptolemaeus). On the teaching of Basilides (ca. 132), see Irenaeus, *Haer.* 1.24.3–7; Hippolytus, *Haer.* 7.20–27. For introductory discussion, see Rudolph, *Gnosis,* 53–274, 308–26; Perkins, "Irenaeus and the Gnostics," in Hedrick and Hodgson, eds., *Nag Hammadi, Gnosticism and Early Christianity,* 221–38; Pearson, "Basilides the Gnostic."

10. In some NT passages Gnostic stories and motifs appear to have been employed in a Christianized or demythologized form: e.g., the descent and ascent of the heavenly Redeemer in John 1; 6;

Phil 2:5–11; Col 1:15–20; Eph 2:14–16; 4:8–10, 13 has parallels with the Gnostic Redeemer myth; and the following texts contain various Gnostic motifs: 1 Cor 2:6–16 (aeon, *gnōsis, pneumatikos*), John 3:18; 9:39; 11:25–26 (note the realized eschatology). See Wilson, *Gnosis and the New Testament*; Yamauchi, *Pre-Christian Gnosticism*; Hedrick and Hodgson, eds., *Nag Hammadi, Gnosticism, and Early Christianity*; Perkins, *Gnosticism and the New Testament*; and Perkins, "Gnosticism," in *NIDB,* 2:581–84.

the same context as both the reference about the "worship of angels" (= aeons?: v. 18) and the anti-Docetic statement about Christ: "in him the whole fullness (Gk. *plērōma*) of deity dwells bodily" (v. 9). The meaning of Col 2:9 will be discussed later in this section.

The passage in 1 Timothy that also condemns ascetic practices occurs in a noteworthy context: "forbidding to marry and to abstain from foods which God created to be partaken with thanksgiving by those who believe and know (*epiginōskō*) the truth; because everything created by God is good and nothing is to be rejected if it is received with thanksgiving" (1 Tim 4:3–4, translation by C. B. Puskas).

The author's disapproval of practices that forbid marriage and that urge abstinence from certain foods is substantiated by the appeals to God's good creation and to believers, who know the truth and partake of God's creation with thanksgiving. Both points of the argument appear to be anti-Gnostic. First, in Gnostic thought the physical world is in complete opposition to the transcendent God; it is therefore inferior, deficient, and doomed to extinction. In both the Valentinian- and Basilidian-Gnostic systems, the creation of the cosmos is attributed to the work of the Demiurge, an inferior and ignoble divine being. Second, believers who gratefully partake of God's good creation are described as those who "know the truth." The assertion can be understood to be a specific reproof of Gnostics, who profess to "know" divine secrets. The word *epiginōskō* ("I know"), used in our passage, is a cognate verb form of the noun *gnōsis* ("knowledge") from which the Gnostics get their name (e.g., *Gos. Phil.* 84.8–13; *Apoc. Adam* 82.24–25).

Most Gnostics followed the ascetic practices condemned by the early Christian writers mentioned above. For example, regarding the Gnostics Saturninus and Basilides Irenaeus states: "They declare also, that marriage and generation are from Satan . . . Many of those, too, who belong to his school, abstain from animal food, and draw away multitudes by a reigned temperance of this kind" (*Adv. Haer.* 1.24.2).

"Springing from Saturninus and Marcion, those who are called Encratites (self-controlled) preached against marriage, thus setting aside the original creation of God, and indirectly blaming Him who made the male and female for the propagation of the human race. Some of those reckoned among them have also introduced abstinence from animal food, thus proving themselves ungrateful to God, who formed all things" (*Adv. Haer.* 1.28.1).

A similar statement equating marriage and sexual pleasures with the work of Satan can be found in the report of Epiphanius about the Gnostic leader Severus (*Pan.* 45.2.1–3). The following Nag Hammadi Codices advocate an ascetic lifestyle free from fleshly passions, jealousies, and other human vices: *Authoritative Teaching* (VI,3) 23–24; *The Teachings of Silvanus* (VII,4) 84, 94, 105, 108; *The Sentences of Sextus* (XII, 1) 172, 320, 345, 363; *The Book of Thomas the Contender* (II,7) 139, 140–41, 145 (see Robinson, *The Nag Hammadi Library*).

For most Gnostics rigorous abstinence was a desired goal. Since both the human body and the physical world were corrupt, it was necessary to gain some mastery over the evil desires of the body and to protect oneself from the allurements of a corrupt world. Although the emerging Great Church certainly valued the virtues of, e.g., self-control, purity, and sexual morality (Titus 2:2; 2 Pet 1:6), the views of the Gnostics were extreme and were based on false beliefs about God and the world, according to emerging orthodoxy.

Libertinism

A third reason for viewing Gnostics as the opponents of early orthodoxy is that the orthodox denounce libertinism, which may have been the alternative lifestyle of some Gnostics. The patristic evidence shows that unrestrained license was a second practical response to the Gnostic position that "matter" was corrupt (e.g., see Clement of Alexandria: *Strom.* 3.5; Epiphanius: *Pan.* 40.2.4). Since matter was evil and doomed to extinction, Gnostics could also treat their bodies and the physical world as something alien to themselves, toward which they had no obligations and could use or abuse as they please. Irenaeus described their position in the following manner:

> For just as it is impossible that the choic [earthly man] should participate in salvation—since, they say, it is incapable of receiving it—so again it is impossible that the spiritual [person]—and by that they mean themselves—should succumb to decay regardless of what kind of actions it performs. Just as gold, when placed in mud, does not lose its beauty but retains its own nature, since the mud is unable to harm the gold, so they say that they themselves cannot suffer any injury or lose their spiritual substance, whatever material actions they may engage in. For this reason the most perfect among them freely practice everything that is forbidden . . . For they eat food that was offered to idols with indifference, and they are the first to arrive at any festival party of the gentiles that takes place in honor of the idols, while some of them do not even avoid the murderous spectacle of fights with beasts and single combats which are hateful to God and man. And some, who are immoderately given over to the desires of the flesh, say that they are repaying to the flesh what belongs to the flesh, and to the spirit what belongs to the spirit. And some of them secretly seduce women who are taught this teaching by them . . . And some, openly parading their shameless conduct, seduced any women they fell in love with away from their husbands and treated them as their own wives. (*Adv. Haer.* 1.6.2–3)

Lengthy descriptions of unusual practices attributed to the libertine Gnostics have been compiled by orthodox writers. Epiphanius, bishop of Salamis (ca. 370), wrote about the *sperma* cult of the Borborites in his book *Panarion* (*Medicine Box* [for those afflicted by heresies]), chapters 25 and 26. A central ritual of this cult concerned the consumption of semen and menstrual fluids as a sacramental action. The exchanging of sexual partners during a drinking party is also mentioned (26.4.3–4). Clement of Alexandria (ca. 200) alludes to similar unrestrained practices at an agape feast in his *Stromateis* (or *Miscellanies* 3.2.4; 7.7.17). It must be noted that evidence is lacking from primary sources (for instance, from the Nag Hammadi Codices) to confirm the existence of such libertine practices. Most Gnostic factions were strictly ascetic, but two factors make the secondary patristic evidence compelling. First, the rationale for libertine Gnosticism, reported by Irenaeus, substantiates this practice as a viable Gnostic option. Second, the detailed descriptions of the *sperma* cult by Epiphanius, a zealous defender of orthodoxy and orthopraxy, cannot be easily dismissed as lustful inventions of the religious author.

We will now examine the denouncements of libertinism by emerging orthodoxy. Although we must be cautious about deriving historical reconstructions from statements resembling polemical rhetoric, a striking correlation surfaces when these harangues are compared with the patristic reports of libertine Gnosticism. We will first list the invectives (I translated the first quote below; the rest are from the RSV which captures well the vindictive tone), then comment on the most important texts:

> That each of you know how to control your own body in consecration and honor,) not in the passion of lust like the heathen who do not know God. (1 Thess 4:4–5)

> Ungodly who pervert the grace of our God into licentiousness . . . indulged in sexual immorality and pursued unnatural lust (*or* went after strange flesh) . . . these dreamers also defile the flesh, reject authority . . . But these people slander whatever they do not understand, and they are destroyed by those things that, like irrational animals, they know by instinct . . . These are blemishes on your love feasts, while they feast with

you without fear, feeding themselves . . . These are grumblers and malcontents; they indulge their own lusts; they are bombastic in their speech, flattering people to their own advantage . . . In the last time, there will be scoffers, indulging in their own ungodly lusts. It is these worldly people devoid of the Spirit, who are causing divisions (Jude 4, 7, 8, 10, 12, 16, 18–19).

> But false prophets also arose among the people, just as there will be false teachers among you, who will secretly bring in destructive opinions (*haireseis*) . . . Many will follow their licentious ways . . . Those who indulge their flesh in depraved lust of defiling passion, and despise authority . . . They count it pleasure to revel in the daytime. They are blots and blemishes reveling in their dissipation, while they feast with you. They have eyes full of adultery, insatiable for sin. They entice unsteady souls. They have hearts trained in greed . . . For they speak bombastic nonsense, and with licentious desires of the flesh they entice people who have just escaped from those who live in error. They promise them freedom, but they themselves are slaves of corruption. (2 Pet 2:1–2, 2:10, 2:13–14, 2:18–19)

> But I have a few things against you: you have some there [in Pergamum] who hold to the teaching of Balaam, who taught Balak to put a stumbling block before the children of Israel, that they would eat food sacrificed to idols and practice fornication [Num 25:1–2; 31:16]. So you also have some who hold

to the teaching of the Nicolaitans (See Rev 2:6, where the
sect is also mentioned at Ephesus.) . . . But I have this against
you [in Thyatira]: you tolerate
that woman Jezebel, who calls
herself a prophet and is teaching and beguiling my servants
to practice fornication and to
eat food sacrificed to idols. I
gave her time to repent, but she
refuses to repent of her fornication. Beware, I am throwing
her on a bed, and those who
commit adultery with her I am
throwing into great distress,
unless they repent of her do-
ings . . . But to the rest of you in
Thyatira, who do not hold this
teaching, who have not learned
[*ginōskō*] what some call the
deep things [*bathos*] of Satan,
to you I say, I do not lay on you
any other burden . . . The beliefs and practices of the cult at
Thyatira are similar to those of
the Nicolaitans. (Rev 2:14–15;
2:20–22, 2:24)

Although the invectives of Jude
and 2 Peter appear to derive from stock
phrases of false prophets in Jewish and
early Christian literature, the practices of
libertine Gnostics provide the best historical occasion for such polemical rhetoric.[11] One would expect these exaggerated
harangues if the early orthodox writers
of Jude and 2 Peter were confronted with
unrestrained Gnostic behavior.

The references to a specific faction
called the Nicolaitans in Revelation (2:6,
15) provide more certain grounds for

identifying a sect with practices similar
to the libertine Gnostics. Since the same
practice and teaching of immorality and
idolatry appear in the church at Thyatira,
the Nicolaitans, although not named, were
probably present in this church (2:20, 25).
Although his belief that Nicolaus of Acts
6:5 was its founder is questionable, Irenaeus states that the Nicolaitans forsook
true Christian teaching and lived in unrestrained indulgence (*Adv. Haer.* 1.26.3).
Clement of Alexandria (although he also
regarded Nicolaus as the founder) mentioned that the Nicolaitans, like goats,
abandoned themselves to pleasures in a
life of shameless self-indulgence (*Strom.*
2.20; 3.24). The earlier beliefs and practices of the Nicolaitans in Asia resemble
those of the later Borborites in Egypt (reported by Epiphanius).

Realized Eschatology

A fourth apparently anti-Gnostic motif
is opposition to the belief that the final
resurrection is already here; this belief
articulates a "realized eschatology." For
most Gnostics, the resurrection of the
dead became a personal eschatology and
was subject to spiritual interpretation.[12]
The resurrection from the dead not only
meant the release of the soul through revealed knowledge but also its ascent to
the *plērōma* (the "fullness" of the divine
realm). Therefore the one who receives
gnōsis has already spiritually attained the
resurrection from the dead. (That is, the
so-called dead ones are non-Gnostics.)
This symbolic and personal interpretation

11. Wisse, "Epistle of Jude"; Richard, *Reading 1
Peter, Jude, and 2 Peter*, 259–64, 268–71, 278–81,
286–89, 347–71; Kraftchick, *Jude, 2 Peter*. On the
libertine heresy, see Gero, "With Walter Bauer on
the Tigris," in Hedrick and Hodgson, eds., *Nag
Hammadi, Gnosticism, and Early Christianity*,
287–307.

12. Rudolph, *Gnosis*, 189–95. See *Gos. Thom.*
51, 113; *Ap. John* 19:15–34; *Exeg. Soul* 134.6–15.

of the resurrection has also been called realized eschatology.

The Gnostic *Exegesis on the Soul* from Nag Hammadi (II,6) explains this spiritual resurrection in the following manner:

> Now it is fitting that the soul regenerate herself and become again as she formerly was. The soul then moves of her own accord. And she received the divine nature from the Father for her rejuvenation, so that she might be restored to the place where originally she had been. This is the resurrection that is from the dead. This is the ransom from captivity. This is the upward journey of ascent to heaven. This is the way of ascent to the Father. (134, 7–16)

It is with this spiritual understanding of the final resurrection that some of the paradoxical statements in the *Gospel of Philip* (II,3), such as the following statement, can be understood: "Those who say they will die first and then rise are in error. If they do not first receive the resurrection while they live, when they die they will receive nothing" (73,1–5).

Although *The Treatise on the Resurrection* (I,4) discusses three types of resurrections, the spiritual one is the most important:

- "What, then, is the resurrection? It is always the disclosure of those who have [already] risen." (48, 4–7)
- "Therefore, do not think in part, O Rheginos, nor live in conformity with this flesh for the sake of unanimity, but flee from the divisions and the fetters, and already you have the resurrection." (49,10–17)

In the *Gospel of Thomas* (II,2) we have the following statements:

- "His disciples said to Him [Jesus], 'When will the repose of the dead come about, and when will the new world come?' He said to them, 'What you look forward to has already come but you do not recognize it.'" (saying 51)
- "His disciples said to Him, 'When will the Kingdom come?' [Jesus said,] 'It will not come by waiting for it . . . Rather, the Kingdom of the Father is spread out upon the earth, and men do not see it.'" (saying 113)

Although forms of realized eschatology appear in several NT books,[13] emerging orthodoxy saw this symbolic and personal interpretation as a threat to the doctrine of a final resurrection of the dead at the return of Christ. The realized eschatology of the NT probably did not find too much disagreement with emerging orthodoxy, because this motif often combined with that of future eschatology, resulting in a modified position, which contrasted with the radical realized eschatology of the Gnostics.[14] It is this extreme symbolic and personal interpretation of eschatology that the writers of emerging orthodoxy attack.

In the Deutero-Pauline writing of 2 Thessalonians (ca. 70–90), for example, the readers are warned not to become

13. For examples of realized eschatology, see John 3:17–19, 36; 5:21–26; 6:26–27, 40, 54; 9:39; 11:25–26; 12:31; 20:22–23, see also Carter, *John*, 203–9. This motif is like that already cited in Gnostic literature.

14. For examples of futuristic eschatology in John, see 5:28–29; 6:39–40, 44; 12:48b. The reader must also be reminded that John's Gospel was a favorite among Gnostics. The first commentary on the Fourth Gospel was written by the Valentinian teacher Heracleon (ca. 170–180; cited in Origen, *Comm. Jo.* 2.8, 15; 6.2, 13, 23; 10.9, 19).

excited about a letter purporting to come from the author stating that "the day of the Lord has come" (2:2). If this teaching of "realized eschatology" is Gnostic, it also explains the additional problem in the letter concerning idleness and disorderly conduct (3:6–13). Since these "troublemakers" have now experienced the final resurrection, they are freed from the bondage of this world and all obligations connected with it. This position would therefore reflect that of the libertine Gnostics.

The early orthodox writing of 2 Timothy (ca. 100–140) warns its readers of Hymenaeus and Philetus, "who have swerved from the truth by claiming that the resurrection has already taken place" (2:18). Hymenaeus is probably the same person denounced in 1 Tim 1:20. The later *Acts of Paul and Thecla* (ca. 190) attributes a similar viewpoint to both Demas and Hermogenes the coppersmith: "And we shall teach thee concerning the resurrection which he [Paul] says is to come, that it has already taken place in the children whom we have, and that we are risen again in that we have come to know the true God" (14).[15]

Although the author of 2 Peter (ca. 120) seems to be refuting general doubts about the *parousia* (3:3–4), such scoffing of the second coming could stem from a Gnostic interpretation of the final resurrection. Since the resurrection can already be experienced in the present, the Gnostic need not await a future event. These sneering men are also "indulging their own lusts" [= a reference to libertine

Gnostics?] (3:3). It is for such "godless" that a final day of judgment is reserved (3:7; see also: 2:17; Jude 7, 15; Ign. *Smyrn.* 6.1).

Polycarp, bishop of Smyrna (ca. 150), after alluding to 1 John 4:2–3, states that "whosoever perverts the sayings of the Lord to suit his own lusts and says there is neither resurrection nor judgment—such a one is the first-born of Satan" (Pol. *Phil.* 7.1).

Because the datum of realized eschatology in Gnosticism corresponds closely to the viewpoint opposed in emerging orthodoxy, it seems likely that the above texts of 2 Thessalonians, 2 Timothy, 2 Peter, and Polycarp's letter are all anti-Gnostic.

Docetism

A fifth reason why the writings of emerging orthodoxy appear to be anti-Gnostic is that we find refutations of a Docetic view of Christ. The term *Docetism* is derived from the Greek verb *dokeō*, which means "to appear," or "have the appearance of." Applied to the study of Christ (called Christology), it is the doctrine that Christ only had *the appearance of* a human (or "flesh") and consequently neither suffered nor was crucified. Docetism was a necessary part of Gnostic anticosmic dualism. Since the divine realm is perfect and cannot be tainted by the material world, which is inferior and evil, it was necessary that the divine Christ not appear in real human flesh and not be subject to the human experiences of suffering and death ("God cannot die"). In reaction to such a doctrine, emerging orthodoxy argued that Christ had come "in the flesh."

15. Schneemelcher, *NTA*, 2:241. The above passage appears to be a polemic against Paul in the *Acts of Paul*, who is portrayed as Gnostic there; Dibelius and Conzelmann, *Pastoral Epistles*, 112.

Docetic Christology plays a significant role in Christian Gnostic cosmogonies ("origins of the world"). As a Gnostic Redeemer, Christ adapts himself to earthly conditions, but only for a short time, and only in terms of external appearance since he is the representative of the higher, "unworldly" realm.[16] In these cosmogonies, the Redeemer adapts himself to the various spheres (or *aeons*) inhabited by the angelic beings (*archons*). Through a change in his outward appearance, he outwits the Demiurge (the ruler of the world). Then, after completing his task of redemption, he is able on his return to overcome them openly and triumphantly.[17]

The *Gospel of Philip* illustrates this "magic hood" motif found in many Gnostic cosmogonies:

> Jesus took them all by stealth, for he did not reveal himself in the manner [in which] he was, but it was in the manner in which [they would] be able to see him that he revealed himself. He revealed himself to [them all. He revealed himself] to the great as great. He [revealed himself] to the small as small. He [revealed himself to the] angels as an angel, and to men as a man. Because of this his word hid itself from everyone. Some indeed saw him, thinking they were seeing themselves, but when he appeared to his disciples in glory on the mount he was not small. He became great, but he made the disciples great that they might be able to see him in his greatness. (57, 29—58, 10)

All of the above adaptations and appearances of Jesus are merely resemblances of various forms that the Gnostic Redeemer assumes. To humanity, Jesus takes on only the appearance of a human being, because those "who wear the flesh" are "naked" and cannot "inherit the kingdom" (*Gos. Phil.* 56, 29–34).

The Gospel of Truth speaks of the "spiritualized flesh" of Christ visible only to the initiates: "For the material ones were strangers and did not see his likeness and had not known him. For he came by means of fleshly appearance while nothing blocked his course because it was incorruptibility (and) irresistibility" (31, 1–9).

The Docetic doctrine that states that Christ was not the one who suffered and died is illustrated in the *First Apocalypse of James*: "The Lord said, 'James, do not be concerned for me or for this people [who conspired against me]. I am he who was within me. Never have I suffered in any way, nor have I been distressed. And this people has done me no harm. But this (people) existed as a type of the archons, and it [my substitute] deserved to be (destroyed) through them'" (31,15–26).

The motif of a substitute for Christ on the cross is found in several Gnostic writings. Two examples will be given. In the *Second Treatise of the Great Seth*, Simon of Cyrene suffers and dies instead of Christ (55, 9—56, 19). According to the *Apocalypse of Peter*, it is the "fleshly likeness" of Jesus that is nailed to the cross (81, 3—82, 14).[18] In both cases, the substitute serves

---

16. Rudolph, *Gnosis*, 157.
17. Ibid.

18. *The Acts of John* 97–102 also has Christ as an onlooker while the Jesus substitute is crucified, in Schneemelcher, *NTA*, 2:184–86. Cerinthus of Asia (ca. 100), considered the first Docetist, also held this view, according to Irenaeus, "but at last Christ departed from Jesus, and that then Jesus

as a deliberate sham to outwit the *archons* and rulers of the world. This is why, as an onlooker, Christ is often portrayed as the laughing savior.

The early orthodox writings react against a Docetic interpretation of Christ. The numerous statements in the NT about "Christ coming in the flesh" seem to presuppose such a controversy about Christ's humanity. In the writings of Ignatius and Polycarp, the Docetic view is more clearly identified and denounced. We will list the texts and discuss only the most important passages.

- "Every spirit which confesses that Jesus Christ has come in the flesh (*sarx*) is of God and every spirit which confesses not Jesus, is not of God; this is the spirit of the antichrist." (1 John 4:2–3; also quoted in Pol. *Phil.* 7.1 against Docetism)

- "For many deceivers have gone out into the world, who will not acknowledge the coming of Jesus Christ in the flesh (Gk. *sarx*); such a one is the deceiver and the antichrist." (2 John 7)

- "In the beginning was the Word (*Logos*), and the Word was with God, and the Word was God . . . All things were made by him; and without was not anything made that was made." (John 1:1–3; see also 1 John 1:1–2)

- "And the Word became flesh (Gk. *sarx*) and dwelt among us." (John 1:14)

- [The resurrected Christ says to his disciples,] "See my hands and my

feet, that it is I myself; handle me, and see; for a spirit has not flesh and bones as you see that I have." (Luke 24:39; also quoted in Ign. *Smyrn.* 3.1–2 to counter Docetism)

- "For Christ also died for sins . . . being put to death in the flesh but made alive in the spirit." (1 Pet 3:18)

- "Since therefore Christ suffered in the flesh, arm yourselves with the same thought, for whoever has suffered in the flesh has ceased from sin, so as to live for the rest of the time in the flesh no longer by human passions but by the will of God." (1 Pet 4:1–2)

- "And you, who were once estranged and hostile in mind . . . he has now reconciled in his fleshly body through death." (Col 1:21–22)

- "For in him [Christ] the whole fullness of deity dwells bodily [Gk. *sōmatikōs*]." (Col 2:9)

- "He [Christ] who was revealed [*phaneroō*] in flesh." (1 Tim 3:16)

In all of the above examples, the words "flesh" (*sarx*) and "body" (*sōma*) denote Christ's actual physical humanity during his earthly existence. We have indicated elsewhere that other motifs in Colossians and 1 Timothy are anti-Gnostic. We also mentioned that the Gospel of John was acquainted with certain Gnostic concepts.

The letters of Ignatius are more explicit in their denouncements of Docetic Christology. Ignatius's *Letter to the Smyrnaeans* states: "He truly suffered even as he also truly raised himself, not as some unbelievers say that his Passion

suffered and rose again, while Christ remained impassible, inasmuch as he was a spiritual being" (*Adv. Haer.* 1.26.1).

was merely in semblance (*to dokein*), but it is they who are merely in semblance (*to dokein*)" (2.1; see also 4.2 and Ign. *Trall.* 10.1 for similar anti-Docetic statements).

In that same letter Ignatius also writes, "For what does anyone profit me if he praise me but blaspheme my Lord, and do not confess that he was clothed in flesh? But he who says this has denied him absolutely and is clothed with a corpse" (*Smyrn.* 5.2).

The Docetic position is here plainly articulated and denounced. The explicit anti-Docetic motifs in the letters of Ignatius are significant since they are contemporary with some of the later NT writings (e.g., the Pastoral Letters and 2 Peter).

In reaction to Docetism both the appearance of Jesus in the flesh (Gk. *sarx*) and his suffering and death are affirmed. Ignatius *To the Trallians* (9.1–2) states, "Jesus Christ was truly born, both ate and drank, was truly persecuted[,] . . . was truly crucified and died." Ignatius *To the Smyrnaeans* (1.2) adds that Christ was "truly nailed to a tree in the flesh" (cf. 1 Pet 3:18). It is also affirmed that Christ was in the flesh after his resurrection, and that he both ate and drank with the disciples (Luke 24:39) as a being of flesh [Gk. *sarkikos*] (Ign. *Smyrn.* 3.1–3). Like the NT writings, these affirmations are both reactions to and implicit denouncements of Docetism.

15

Emerging Christian Orthodoxy: Part 2

In reaction to the internal threats of Gnosticism and in response to external pressures from both Judaism and the Roman government, early Christianity began to consolidate and define itself as a distinct institution. The passage of time, which brought further delay to the hope of Christ's near return, also prompted some rethinking about the church's identity and mission in the world. What resulted from these developments is typical of most religious groups of the third and fourth generations.

In this chapter we shall look at the following characteristics of emerging orthodoxy: a fixed organizational structure, efforts to preserve the apostolic traditions, emphasis on confessions and creeds, the establishment of specific worship patterns, concern for normative Christian ethics, and the emergence of a distinct collection of sacred writings.

A FIXED ORGANIZATIONAL STRUCTURE

In the previous chapter we noticed the great threat that "false teachings" like Gnosticism must have posed for those churches of emerging orthodoxy. One effective measure against false teaching was to establish qualified leadership to preserve the faith. The appointing of bishops and elders, who were to continue the teaching of the apostles, became a normative procedure of this period. Criticisms of orthodoxy in the Nag Hammadi Codices reflect this organizational development:

- "And there shall be others of those who are outside our number who name themselves bishops and deacons, as if they have received their authority from God. They bend themselves under the judgment of leaders. Those people are dry canals." (*Apoc. Pet.* 79.23–31)

- "For many have sought after the truth and have not been able to find it; because there has taken hold of them the old leaven of the Pharisees and the scribes of the Law . . . For no one who is under the Law will be able to look up to the truth." (*Testim. Truth* 29.13–16, 23–25)

The first quotation is probably a Gnostic reaction to the early orthodox hierarchical organization. Perhaps these Gnostics believed that there was too much dry organization among these early orthodox churches and felt that the dynamic spirit of the apostolic period was active in their own group. Although the second quotation seems to criticize Judaism, it is probably a Gnostic criticism of orthodox Christianity (with its creedal statements, traditions, and ethical rules). This analogy to Judaism is significant since developments in early catholicism parallel those in post-Yavneh Judaism (post–AD 70).

A major tendency in the organizational structure of emerging orthodoxy was for leadership to derive its authority from the office rather than personal ability or charisma. In earliest Christian writings, leaders often gained their authority from special abilities and endowments of the Spirit (Rom 12:3–8; 1 Cor 12:8–10, 28–30); overseers and assistants also surfaced (Phil 1:1), but these roles were yet undefined.

By the late first century, the titles of bishop (*episkopos*: "overseer"), elder (*presbyter*), and deacon (*diakonos*: "assistant") denoted specific leadership and service functions in the churches (James, 1 Peter, 1 Clement, Didache). These officials often coexisted with the more ecstatic (and itinerant) teachers and prophets (*Didache,*

Shepherd of Hermas). By the early second century, certain organizational developments took place. Even though the Pastorals make no clear distinction between bishop and elder (as in *1 Clement*), the ethical qualifications and doctrinal duties of these office bearers are emphasized. They are to be worthy role models for the church, and are to preserve the apostolic teachings against misinterpretation. The letters of Ignatius, however, distinguish the office of bishop from the office of elder, and they underscore the preeminence of the bishop in a hierarchical scheme (a hierarchy already mentioned in *1 Clement*). Therefore, in the writings of Ignatius, the organizational tendency to ascribe authority to the office independent of personal ability and charisma becomes a major emphasis.

The following texts from the Pastoral Letters discuss the ethical qualifications and general responsibilities for the offices of bishop, elder, and deacon. Most contain general virtues required of public officials.[1]

Bishop	Elder	Deacon
1 Tim 3:1–7	1 Tim 4:14	1 Tim 3:8–10, 12–13
Titus 1:7–9	1 Tim 5:17–20	[Rom 16:1; Phil 1:1]
	[1 Pet 5:1–4; Acts 20:17, 28–30; Jas 5:14]	

1. See a list describing the good military general (e.g., "temperate, self-restrained, vigilant, frugal") in Onosander, *Strategikos* (first-century AD), cited in Dibelius and Conzelmann, *Pastoral Epistles*, 159–60. See also discussion in Levine, ed., *A Feminist Companion to the Deutero-Pauline Epistles*, 151. On factions, ideology, and institutions, see Hanson and Oakman, *Palestine*.

In 1 Tim 5:17–18 elders are described as engaging in the same activities ascribed to the bishop in 3:1–7 and Titus 1:7–9. These activities are governing, preaching, and teaching. Also in Titus 1:5–7, *elder* and *bishop* are used interchangeably. The Pastorals also assume a council of elders in the congregation (1 Tim 4:14). However, the nature of their leadership role is unclear. The acquiring of leadership positions seems to have been controlled by the already-established leadership. Prospective leaders were tested before being admitted to office (1 Tim 3:10). The Pastorals evidence a synthesis of charisma and office. In 1 Tim 4:14 and 2 Tim 1:6, we note that the office bearer is recognized as having a prophetic gift. Associating prophecy with church leadership may have been an attempt to weaken the position of charismatic leaders ("false prophets"), who are outside the official structure. The Pastorals specify only the qualifications for the office, but certain conclusions can be drawn about some responsibilities of bishops and elders. They had pastoral responsibility for the membership (1 Tim 5:1–2). They exercised disciplinary authority in the community (1 Tim 5:19–20), and they represented the church to the outside world (1 Tim 3:7).[2]

The office of deacon included deaconesses (not wives of deacons [1 Tim 3:8–13]). No separate title of deaconess was used, because there is no feminine form of *diakonos*. The basic role of the deacon was that of assistant. Deacons probably assisted in worship and in works of charity. Although 1 Peter uses the expression "elders" to denote the older generation (5:1; see also 1 Tim 5:1; Titus 2:2), by the time of the Pastorals, already a fixed circle of elders appears to exist (1 Pet 5:1–3). The exhortations on ministry (vv. 2–3) presuppose that elders are already engaged in ordered ministry.[3]

In the third letter of John, someone who appears to be an influential bishop (Diotrephes) is portrayed as an opponent of God (v. 9). He opposes the work of the presbyter (vv. 1, 9–10) and is possibly trying to gain control over the congregation.[4]

In *1 Clement* we see that bishops and deacons were appointed by apostles and were therefore part of a divine hierarchy (42.1–4; 44.2). Obedience to the church officials is therefore enjoined (1.3; 3.3; 21.6). However, no distinctions are made between bishops and presbyters (1.3; 21.6; 44.4–5; 47.6).

The *Didache* mentions bishops and deacons, but not presbyters (15.1, 3). The more ecstatic prophets and teachers also coexist with the ministry of bishops and deacons (11.1–2; 12.3ff.; 13.1–2). This mutual regard for (or toleration of) both the prophet and office bearer is also found in the *Shepherd of Hermas*.[5]

In the letters of Ignatius we note the fullest type of divine authority ascribed to the hierarchy of bishop, elders, and deacons (Ign. *Smyrn.* 8.1; *Phld.* 7.1; *Magn.* 6.1; *Trall.* 7.2). Even though the relationship of the bishop and elders is close (Ign. *Eph.* 4.1; 20.2; *Magn.* 2; 7.1; *Trall.* 2.2; 13.2), their offices are distinct, and the prominence of the bishop over the presbytery (council of elders) is evident (Ign. *Magn.* 2; 3.1; *Phld.* 7.2; 6.1; *Trall.* 12.2).

2. Verner, *Household of God*, 149–50, 159–60; for a survey of discussion, see Harding, *What Are They Saying about the Pastoral Epistles?* 46–65.

3. Schweizer, *Church Order*, 111.

4. Ibid., 128.

5. Ibid., 157–58; Niederwimmer, *Didache*, 200–201; Osiek, *Shepherd of Hermas*, 22–23.

In this hierarchy of divinely ordained offices, the presbytery is subordinate to the bishop (Ign. *Trall.* 12.2), and the deacon is subordinate to both the bishop and presbytery (Ign. *Magn.* 2; *Eph.* 2). It seems that over each local church (and region) there was a bishop and council of elders, assisted by deacons. The bishop probably functioned as prophet, chief liturgist, and administrator (Ign. *Phld.* 7; *Pol.* 2.2).[6] No worship service or church gathering was valid without the sanction of the bishop and the presbytery (Ign. *Smyrn.* 8–9; *Magn.* 4; 7; *Phld.* 12.2; *Trall.* 3.1; 7.2). The church must cling to the bishop as it clings to Christ and as Christ clings to the Father (Ign. *Eph.* 5.1; *Magn.* 4; 6.2; *Trall.* 7).

THE PRESERVATION OF THE APOSTOLIC TRADITIONS

From our previous discussions on opposition to false teachings and fixed organizational structures, it is understandable that emerging orthodoxy would have been concerned with "sound doctrine" (1 Tim 1:10, 6:3; 2 Tim 1:13; 4:3; Titus 1:9, 13; 2:1, 8) and with "guarding the deposit of the faith" (1 Tim 6:20; 2 Tim 1:14). What were these teachings, and why were they regarded as authentic? The question of content will be more fully addressed in the next section, on confessions and creeds. The related issues of a standard to measure authentic teachings and the procedures for safeguarding them will concern us here.

The content of the traditions we can easily deduce to be anti-Gnostic: the coming of Christ in the flesh; the necessity of his suffering, death, and (bodily) resurrection; hope in the second coming of Christ; and belief in one God. These teachings are expressed in creedal statements and confessions of faith (e.g., 1 Cor 15:3–7; 1 Tim 3:10; 1 Pet 3:18–19, 22).

It is the succession of tradition or the "apostolic transmission of the faith" that serves as both the standard and safeguard for authentic teachings in emerging orthodoxy. This succession-of-tradition motif prevails in Christian literature after the second century but is also evident in late first century writings.

It generally assumes the following pattern: Jesus Christ, who was sent from God, commissioned apostles to spread his teachings; they in turn appointed bishops and deacons to preserve this teaching for the church. Similar succession-of-tradition patterns are found in both the philosophical schools of Hellenism[7] and the rabbinic schools of Judaism.[8]

6. Richardson, *Early Christian Fathers*, 76; Schoedel, *Ignatius*, 238–44.

7. For example, the prologue of Laertius, *Lives* (1.12–14) attempts to give almost an exhaustive list of philosophical schools from the time of the Sages (e.g., Thales, Solon, Pherecydes) to the Ionian (Anaximander) and Italian (Pythagoras) schools to the diverse schools named according to cities (Elians), specific localities (Academics, Stoics), incidental circumstances (Peripatetics), their teachers (Socratics, Epicureans), and those with functional names (Moralists, Dialecticians); each school contains lists of teachers and their students in respective lines of succession. For a survey see, Algra, et al., *Cambridge History of Hellenistic Philosophy*; Alexander, "Acts and Ancient Intellectual Biography," in Winter and Clarke, *Book of Acts*, 31–63; Ferguson, *Backgrounds*, 319–95.

8. For example, the rabbinic tractate ʾAbot ("Fathers") in the Fourth Division of the Mishnah (AD 200) opens with the following succession of tradition: Moses-Joshua-Elders of Israel-Prophets-Men of the Great Synagogue (the Sopherim), (1:1). The Sopherim ("Wise Men"), represented by Ezra the scribe, were regarded as the founders of

In the first letter of Clement to Rome (AD 96) we note the typical pattern of the apostolic succession of tradition:

> The apostles received the gospel for us from the Lord Jesus Christ; Jesus, the Christ, was sent from God. Thus Christ is from God and the apostles from Christ. In both instances the orderly procedure depends on God's will. And so the apostles, after receiving their orders and being fully convinced by the resurrection of our Lord Jesus Christ and assured by God's word, went out in the confidence of the Holy Spirit to preach the good news that God's Kingdom was about to come. They preached in country and city, and appointed their first converts, after testing them by the spirit, to be the bishops and deacons of future believers. (42)

Ignatius (ca. 110) often utilized the succession motif, as in the following letter: "Defer to the bishop and to one another as Jesus Christ did to the Father in the days of his flesh, and as the apostles did to Christ, to the Father and to the Spirit" (Ign., *Magn.* 13). Other examples where the apostolic succession of faith is employed are in the teachings of Papias (ca. 100 in Eusebius's *Hist. eccl.* 3.39.3–4), in Justin Martyr (*1 Apol.* 66–67), and in Irenaeus (*Adv. Haer.* 1.10; 3.3.4). By the mid- and late second century the motif becomes elaborate and detailed (e.g., Irenaeus, Tertullian, *Praescr.* 21).

---

the rabbinic tradition (in the Tannaitic period). This Tannaitic phase, which overlapped with early Christianity, had its own teachers who founded their own schools: e.g., Hillel, Shammai, Gamaliel, Akiba. See Neusner, *Four Stages of Rabbinic Judaism*; Evans, *Ancient Texts*, 216–55; Ferguson, *Backgrounds*, 490–501.

In the Pastoral Letters, we note the following pattern:

(1) Paul has been entrusted with the "glorious gospel of the blessed God" (1 Tim 1:11; 2 Tim 1:12)
(2) Paul has publicly entrusted the gospel to Timothy (2 Tim 1:13–14; 1 Tim 6:20)
(3) Now Timothy is exhorted to pass it on to faithful men who will be able to teach others (2 Tim 2:2)

An apostolic succession from Paul to Timothy to elders and bishops is therefore evident. Paul is given special prominence in the Pastoral Letters (1 Tim 6:3; 2 Tim 1:13). First Timothy also has the appearance of being the apostle's last will and testament for the church.

In 2 Peter the letters of Paul are regarded as authoritative (3:15–16), and special prominence is given to Peter, the eyewitness of Christ's transfiguration (1:12–15). Second Peter also reads like a last will and testament of the Apostle Peter.

In Luke-Acts (ca. AD 90) we have several succession motifs. In Acts 20:17, 38, Paul, who was commissioned by Jesus Christ (Acts 9; 22; 26), appoints the Ephesian elders as his successors (Acts 20:28–32). In the preaching summaries of Luke-Acts a continuity of proclamation is also detected: Jesus (Luke 4:34; 8:1), disciples (Luke 9:1–2), the Twelve (Acts 4:33; 5:44), others in the early church (Acts 8:4–14), and Paul (Acts 18:11; 19:8; 28:23, 31). Luke 1:1–2, the preface to Luke-Acts, also presupposes three successive levels of tradition: (a) the events about Jesus, (b) eyewitnesses and servants of the word, and (c) Luke and his readers.

From these succession-of-tradition motifs we note two things: only that which is authentic can be passed on from

Jesus to the apostles to the church, and the recipients are to participate in the succession of the tradition to preserve and safeguard it. Therefore, the apostolic transmission of the faith serves as both a standard of measurement and the model for preserving it.

This procedure for defining the faith and guarding it is a reaction to the more visionary and individualistic groups like the Montanists and Gnostics. They superseded the chain of command (apostles and bishops) and claimed to receive their authority and teaching directly from Christ through visions and dreams.[9] Although itinerant charismatic prophetic types were tolerated in early catholic communities, precautions were taken to guard against extremists or "false teachers" (*Did.* 11–12).

FORMULATED CREEDS AND CONFESSIONS

The creeds and confessions of emerging orthodoxy derive from the earliest stratum of Christianity. Kerygmatic and creedal statements (Rom 1:14; 1 Cor 15:3–7) as well as hymns (e.g., Phil 2:6–11) are found in Paul. Most creeds and confessions originated as hymns in early worship settings (e.g., 1 Tim 3:16) or were summaries of early Christian sermons (Rom 1:1–4; 1 Cor 15:3–7). From these origins, the creeds developed into the standard formulation of the fourth-century Great Church (e.g., the Apostles' Creed, the Nicene Creed). We will first give examples of creeds and confessions found in the NT (quoting the NRSV); next we will reproduce a "rule of faith" by Tertullian, then an "Old Roman Creed" of the fourth century. Examples of hymns with strong creedal content are:

Phil 2:6–11:

who, though he was in the form of God,
 did not regard equality with God
 as something to be exploited,
but emptied himself,
 taking the form of a slave,
 being born in human likeness.
And being found in human form,
 he humbled himself
 and became obedient to the point of
   death—
 even death on a cross.
Therefore God also highly exalted him
 and gave him the name
 that is above every name,
so that at the name of Jesus
 every knee should bend,
 in heaven and on earth and under the
   earth,
and every tongue should confess
 that Jesus Christ is Lord,
 to the glory of God the Father.

Col 1:15–20:

He is the image of the invisible God,
 The firstborn of all creation;
for in him all things in heaven
 and on earth were created,
 things visible and invisible . . .
all things have been created through
 him and for him.
he himself is before all things,
and in him all things hold together.
he is head of the body, the church;
he is the beginning, the firstborn from
 the dead,
so that he might come to have first
 place in everything.
For in him all the fullness of God was
 pleased to dwell,
and through him God was pleased to
 reconcile to himself all things . . .

9. See, for example, the Nag Hammadi writings *Apoc. Pet.* 79:23–31; *Testim. Truth* 29.13–25.

1 Pet 3:18–19, 22:

He was put to death in the flesh,
  but made alive in the spirit,
  in which also he went and made a
        proclamation
  to the spirits in prison . . .
  who has gone into heaven and
  is at the right hand of God,
with angels, authorities, and powers
        made subject to him.

Eph 2:14–16:

For he is our peace;
in his flesh he has made both groups
    into one
and has broken down the dividing
    wall . . . between us . . .
that he might create in himself one
    new humanity
in place of the two, thus making peace,
and might reconcile both groups to God in
    one body through the cross . . .

Heb 1:3:

He is the reflection of God's glory and the
        exact imprint of God's very
        being,
    and he sustains all things by his
        powerful word.
    When he had made purification for sins,
    he sat down at the right hand of the
        Majesty on high . . .

1 Tim 3:16:

He was revealed in flesh,
    vindicated in spirit,
        seen by angels,
proclaimed among Gentiles,
    believed in throughout the world,
        taken up in glory.

Examples of kerygmatic statements derived from primitive Christian preaching are

1 Cor 15:3–5:

Christ died for our sins in accordance with the scriptures, and . . . he was buried, and . . . he was raised on the third day in accordance with the scriptures, and . . . he appeared to Cephas then to the twelve.

Rom 1:1–4:

. . . the gospel of God, which he promised beforehand through his prophets in the holy scriptures, the gospel concerning his Son, who was descended from David according to the flesh and was declared to be the Son of God with power according to the spirit of holiness by resurrection from the dead, Jesus Christ our Lord.

Rom 10:8b–9:

The word of faith that we proclaim [is] . . . If you confess with your lips that Jesus is Lord and believe in your heart that God raised him from the dead, you will be saved.

The kerygmatic speeches of Acts also contain some of the basic elements of Christ's death, resurrection, and exaltation, even though it is disputed whether these speeches reflect primitive or late first-century preaching (Acts 2:14–39; 3:13–26; 4:10–12; 5:30–32; 10:36–43; 13:17–41). The following NT statement is a formula similar to a pre–Nicene Creed: "For there is one God; there is also one mediator between God and humankind, Christ Jesus, himself human, who gave himself as a ransom for all—this was attested at the right time" (1 Tim 2:5–6).

As a transition from the creeds of emerging orthodoxy to those of the Great

Church, we give an example of the "rule of faith" by Tertullian of Carthage:

> We, however, as always, the more so now as better equipped through the Paraclete, that leader into all truth, believe (as these do) in one only God, yet subject to this dispensation (which is our word for "economy") that the one only God has also a Son, his Word who has proceeded from himself, by whom all things were made and without whom nothing has been made: that this [Son] was sent by the Father into the virgin and was born of her both man and God. Son of man and Son of God, and was named Jesus Christ: that he suffered, died, and was buried, according to the scriptures and having been raised up by the Father and taken back into heaven, sits at the right hand of the Father and will come to judge the quick and the dead: and that thereafter he, according to his promise, sent from the Father the Holy Spirit, the Paraclete, the sanctifier of the faith of those who believe in the Father and the Son and the Holy Spirit. That this rule has come down from the beginning of the Gospel, even before all former heretics, not to speak of Praxeas of yesterday, will be proved as well by the comparative lateness of all heretics as by the very novelty of Praxeas of yesterday. (Tertullian, *Praex.* 2.1–3 in *ANF*)

The Old Roman Creed, which later was developed into the traditional Apostles' Creed (eighth century), was probably that of Marcellus, bishop of Galatian Ancyra, delivered to Julius, bishop of Rome (ca. 340).[10]

1 I believe in God almighty

2 And in Christ Jesus, his only son, our Lord

3 Who was born of the Holy Spirit and the Virgin Mary

4 Who was crucified under Pontius Pilate and was buried

5 And the third day rose from the dead

6 Who ascended into heaven

7   and sitteth on the right hand of the Father

8 Whence he cometh to judge the living and the dead

9 And in the Holy Spirit

10 The holy church

11 The remission of sins

12 The resurrection of the flesh

13 The life everlasting.

The creeds and confessions of emerging orthodoxy can be viewed as moving on a trajectory toward the creeds of the Great Church. In both Tertullian's "rule of faith" and the Old Roman Creed, elements of earlier creedal statements from both 1 Corinthians 15 and 1 Peter 3 can be detected. These particular NT motifs were probably utilized in the creeds of the Great Church because they coincided best with the beliefs of fourth-century orthodoxy.

ESTABLISHED WORSHIP PATTERNS

By the late first century distinct liturgical patterns are noticeable. Meetings are on the Lord's Day, Sunday, the day of Christ's resurrection (Acts 20:7; 1 Cor 16:2; Rev

---

10. Bettenson, *Documents of the Christian*

Church, 23–24. On creeds and confessions in the first three centuries, see Clifford, *"One Teacher,"* 1–14, 80–89.

1:10; *Did.* 14.1). Gatherings of families in house churches still continued (Rom 16:5; 1 Cor 16:19; esp. Col 4:15; Phlm 2). The ceremony of the breaking of the bread (1 Cor 11:23–25; *Did.* 9) was maintained. The practice of water baptism also continued (Matt 28:19; Acts 8:36–37; *Did.* 7).

Three examples of worship patterns in emerging orthodoxy and the Great Church will be given. The first is from a non-Christian source: Pliny's letter to Trajan (AD 110). The second is from Justin Martyr, *1 Apol.* 65–67, and the last is from Hippolytus's *Apostolic Traditions* (ca. 220).

Pliny was the Roman governor of Bithynia (AD 110) when he wrote to Emperor Trajan concerning the Christian sect. Although the letter primarily concerns prosecution and punishment of Christians, it includes a glimpse of early catholic worship patterns. "They were in the habit of meeting on a certain fixed day before it was light, when they sang in alternate verses a hymn to Christ, as to a god, and bound themselves by a solemn oath, not to do any wicked deeds, but never to commit any fraud, theft, or adultery, never to falsify their word, nor deny a trust when they should be called upon to deliver it up; after which it was their custom to separate, and then reassemble to partake of food—but food of an ordinary and innocent kind" (Melmoth, *Letters of Pliny the Younger* 96).

From these verses, we learn that the Christians of Asia Minor met early on Sunday, sang antiphonal hymns to the divine Christ, and bound themselves to a baptismal vow or Eucharistic confession (cf. *Did.* 14). The mention of what appears to be a separate *agape* or fellowship meal later in the day presupposes an earlier

Eucharist celebration: "reassemble to partake of food—but food of an ordinary and innocent kind" (cf. 1 Cor 11:17–34; Justin Martyr, *1 Apol.* 65–67).

In the writings of Justin Martyr (150) we have a more extensive treatment of the worship service:

> And on the day called Sunday there is a meeting in one place of those who live in cities or the country and the memoirs of the apostles or the writings of the prophets are read as long as time permits. When the reader has finished, the president in a discourse urges and invites [us] to the imitation of these noble things. Then we all stand up together and offer prayers. And as said before, when we have finished the prayer, bread is brought and wine and water, and the president similarly sends up prayers and thanksgivings to the best of his ability, and the congregation assents, saying the Amen; the distribution and reception of the consecrated [elements] by each, takes place and they are sent to the absent by the deacons. Those who prosper and who so wish contribute each one as much as he chooses to. What is collected is deposited with the president, and he takes care of orphans and widows, and those who are in want on account of sickness or any other cause and those who are in bonds and the strangers who are sojourners among [us] . . . We all hold this common gathering on Sunday. (*1 Apol.* 67)

By the time of Justin, the *agape* or fellowship meal had been separated from the Eucharist (*1 Apol.* 66–67; *Did.* 9–10). Earlier they had been combined (1 Cor 11:17–34).

The last example is derived from a community document ascribed to Hippolytus, bishop of Rome (220). It is a condensed outline of an elaborate Roman baptismal service (*Apostolic Traditions*, 20).

1   Examination of catechumens by presbyter and deacon.[11]

2   Exorcism—by presbyter and deacon with the use of holy water.

3   Fasting and prayer—catechumens to fast on Friday and continue in prayer on Saturday.

4   All night vigil of reading Scripture.

5   Prayer over the waters by presbyter at sunrise on Sunday.

6   Candidates appear in the nude—first children, next men, then women.

7   Candidates are anointed by presbyter with the oil of thanksgiving and oil of exorcism.

8   Candidates descend into the water with presbyter.

9   They confess the common faith of the church: a version of the Old Roman Creed.

10   Triune baptism—they are baptized three times.

11   Candidates are then clothed in white garments.

12   The bishop lays hands on the candidates to receive the Holy Spirit.

13   They are sealed on the forehead to symbolize the seal of the Spirit.

14   They receive the kiss of peace from the bishop.

15   Then they pray together with the congregation.

16   Finally, they participate with the congregation in the celebration of the Eucharist.

Even though this Roman service is quite elaborate, specifications about water baptism are found as early as the *Didache* (7). It has also been argued that both Ephesians and 1 Peter are baptismal liturgies with epistolary features.[12]

NORMATIVE CHRISTIAN ETHICS

To prevent false teaching and ensure sound doctrine ("orthodoxy"), emerging orthodoxy focused on the importance of right living ("orthopraxy"). The ethical exhortations (*parenēsēs*) of Paul are emphasized. Paul's list of vices and virtues becomes a list of prohibitions and commandments.[13] Catalogues of ethical duties are now provided for every member and class in the congregation. These ethical norms exemplify the period of Christianity's adjusting to its environment.

In emerging orthodoxy, household rules emerged for husbands (Col 3:19; Eph 5:25–28; 1 Pet 3:7), wives (1 Cor

11. Catechumens here were converts to Christianity receiving training in doctrine and discipline before baptism. They were also called candidates for baptism. See discussion of this document from a Hippolytan community in Ferguson, *Baptism*, 327–33.

12. See Dahl, "The Concept of Baptism," in Hellholm et al., *Ephesians*, 413–39; Ysebaert, *Greek Baptismal Terminology*; Cross, *1 Peter*; and Selwyn, *First Epistle of St. Peter*; on 1 Pet, see Beasley-Murray, *Baptism in the New Testament*, 251–58; and Ferguson, *Baptism*, 161–62 (for Ephesians), 189–93 (for 1 Peter). On worship in the *Didache* and in the *1 Apol* of Justin Martyr, see Neyrey, *Give God Glory*, ch. 7.

13. These ethical lists were common in the philosophical preaching of the Hellenistic period (e.g., Dio Chrysostom, *Orations* 1.4, 6; 3.5; 4.83–96). See, Aune, *The New Testament in Its Literary Environment*, 194–96; Malherbe, *Moral Exhortation*, 138–41.

7:10–11; Eph 5:22–24; Col 3:18; 1 Pet 3:1–6), parents (Eph 6:4; Col 3:21;), children (Eph 6:1–3; Col 3:20), household servants (Col 3:22–25; Eph 6:5–8; 1 Pet 2:18–20; *Did.* 4.11), and masters of the household (Eph 6:9; Col 4:1). These rules are based on a hierarchical and patriarchal structure cemented by the principle of obedience. Therefore they represent an adaptation of early Christianity to the social ethics of the first century.[14]

There were also rules for the congregation. There were specified qualifications and duties for bishops (1 Tim 3:1–7; Titus 1:7–9; *Did.* 15.1–2), elders (= bishops: 1 Tim 5:17–20; 1 Pet 5:1–4; Acts 20:17, 28–32), and deacons (1 Tim 3:8–10, 11–13; *Did.* 15.1–2). Responsibilities were also delineated for the rich (1 Tim 6:5–10, 17–19), the young (1 Tim 5:1; 1 Pet 5:5–9), the old (1 Tim 5:1–2; Titus 2:2–3), and women in the congregation (1 Tim 2:9–15; 3:1; Titus 2:4–8). Care for widows was also enjoined (1 Tim 5:3–16; Jas 1:27). General admonitions were directed to all members (Col 4:1–8; 1 Pet 1:22–23; 2:11–12; *Did.* 4.9–10), and instructions on responsibilities to the state were specified (Rom 13:1–7; 1 Pet 3:13–17). Specific rules of church discipline were also provided (Matt 18:15–18).

Finally, church manuals like the *Didache* (ca. 100) were provided. The *Didache* contains ethical norms for the congregation (1–6), directions for church ordinances and liturgy (7–10, 14), guidelines for discerning false prophets (11–12), and procedures for electing church officers (15).

Lists of vices and virtues compiled for congregations since the time of Paul were also utilized (Gal 5:19–23; Eph 4:25—5:20; Col 3:5, 8, 12; *Did.* 1–6). These ethical lists are found in the parenetic sections of early Christian letters and resemble the Cynic and Stoic ethics of Hellenism (e.g., Epictetus, *Discourses* 1; 4; Seneca, *Ep.* 94–95).[15] Parallels to these ethical norms can also be found in rabbinic Judaism (e.g., numerous tractates of the Mishnah).

A DISTINCT COLLECTION OF WRITINGS

By the late first and early second centuries, a collection of Christian writings alongside the authoritative Jewish Scriptures begins to take shape. We will examine this development of a distinctive literature in three phases: (1) the original authorities, (2) the earliest collections, and (3) the emergence of NT collections.

The original authorities of Christianity were the Jewish Scriptures; they included the Law, Prophets, and "other books." The last category was undefined in Judaism until the late first century, and many early Christians utilized such writings as the Wisdom of Solomon, *Enoch*, and Judith in their worship, preaching, and teaching.

---

14. For Greco-Roman examples, see Philodemus, *Concerning Household Management* 29–30, 38; Arius Didymus, *Epitome* 148–49; Seneca, *Epistles* 89, 94–95; see also Soulen and Soulen, *Handbook*, 83; Balch, *Let Wives Be Submissive*; Balch, "Household Codes," in Aune, *Greco-Roman Literature*, 25–50; Osiek and Balch, *Families in New Testament World*; and Balch and Osiek, *Early Christian Families*. Lampe and Luz view this "civilized behavior" as "apologetics through action," in Becker, *Christian Beginnings*, 263.

15. Malherbe, *Moral Exhortation*, 68–85, 138–41; and Malherbe, *Cynic Epistles*; Klauck, *Ancient Letters*, 166–82.

Along with the Jewish Scriptures was the teaching of Jesus, Paul, and other recognized Christian leaders. The words of Jesus are cited as a new norm on matters of faith and practice by Paul (1 Cor 9:14; 1 Thess 4:15) and other NT writers (Acts 20:35; Revelation 2–3). Since Paul and certain recognized teachers were commissioned by Jesus and possessed God's Spirit, they also spoke with God's authority (1 Cor 7:25, 40; 1 Thess 2:13; 1 Tim 6:13–14; Rev 1:1–3; *1 Clem.* 63.2; Ign. *Phld.* 7.1–2).

From the late first century to the time of Marcion (140), the following developments took place: The sayings of Jesus were cited with equal authority as Scripture (2 Pet 3:2; *1 Clem.* 13.1–2; 46.2–8). Paul's writings were also circulated (Col 4:16). Clement of Rome made use of Romans, 1 Corinthians, and Hebrews. Ignatius of Antioch was familiar with Romans, 1 Corinthians, and Ephesians. The author of 2 Peter also mentions an unspecified collection of Paul's letters (3:15–16).

At this period it is unclear either if written gospels were employed or if independent oral sayings of Jesus used. However, the *Didache* seems to quote directly from Matthew's Gospel (*Did.* 8.2; Matt 6:9–13). Papias of Phrygia (120) is acquainted with Mark's Gospel and a Matthean sayings collection supposedly written in Aramaic (Eusebius, *Hist. eccl.* 3.39.15–16).

The first authoritative collection of Christian writings was compiled by Marcion of Pontus. Because he made a sharp distinction between the just, wrathful creator of the Jewish Scriptures (whom he rejected) and the Good Father of Jesus (whom he sought to follow), Marcion rejected the Jewish Scriptures and adhered only to his own edited versions of the Gospel of Luke and ten letters of Paul (Galatians, 1 and 2 Corinthians, Romans, 1 and 2 Thessalonians, Ephesians, Colossians, Philippians, and Philemon).

The period from Marcion to Origen of Alexandria was characterized by several new developments. In reaction to both the selective Scripture of Marcion and the additional Gnostic writings and Montanist prophecies, catholic Christians began to specify what writings were authoritative for them.

By the mid to late second century, we have Justin Martyr, Irenaeus, Tertullian of Carthage, and Clement of Alexandria supporting the authority of the four Gospels of Matthew, Mark, Luke, and John (although John was avoided in the Syrian churches).

Concerning the use of the letters of Paul and his students in catholic congregations we note the following developments: Polycarp, the bishop of Asia Minor, was familiar with seven or eight of Paul's letters and alludes to 1 and 2 Timothy. Irenaeus of Lyons made use of Paul's ten letters as well as 1 and 2 Timothy.

The letter to the Hebrews was cited early in *1 Clement* 36 and Polycarp *Phil.* 6.3, but its authority in the West was contested until the fourth century. Certain of the General Epistles circulated during this period. Polycarp was familiar with 1 Peter and 1 John, and Irenaeus cites 1 Peter and 1 and 2 John. The earliest use of Jude is found in 2 Peter.

Justin Martyr was one of the first to cite the book of Revelation as Scripture (*Dialogue with Trypho* 81). Irenaeus also supported Justin's position. In the East, Clement of Alexandria and Origin regarded Revelation as authoritative, but

Dionysius (a student of Origen) questioned its authorship and authenticity.

The NT collection of Origen (250) marks the beginning of canonical lists that culminated in the fourth century. It stated the books of undisputed authority to be those of the four Gospels, the thirteen letters of Paul and his students, 1 Peter, 1 John, Acts, and Revelation. Those books whose authority was disputed (or "spoken against") by various catholic congregations were 2 Peter, 2 and 3 John, Hebrews, James, and Jude. False writings were those Gnostic books like the *Gospel of Thomas*, the *Gospel of the Egyptians*, and the *Gospel of Basilides*. Origen also regarded as authoritative the *Gospel and Preaching of Peter*, the *Acts of Pilate*, the *Didache, Barnabas*, the *Shepherd of Hermas*, *1 Clement*, and the letters of Ignatius.

By the fourth century, we begin to see a trend toward the acceptance of the twenty-seven books of the present NT, although some are still disputed (James, Jude, 2 Peter, 2 and 3 John), and other extra books are recommended (Wisdom of Solomon, Sirach, the *Didache*, the *Shepherd of Hermas*). The Easter letter of Athanasius (367) becomes the first canonical list to recommend the twenty-seven books of our NT as authoritative. He permits the use of the extra books in the churches.

At least four factors forged the formation of the NT canon. First, the development of the canon may have been a response to Marcion's limited Scripture and to the extra writings of the Gnostics and perhaps of the Montanists. Second, the canon developed as a result of imperial pressure: Emperor Constantine (325) ordered fifty new copies of the Bible for use in catholic churches. Third, the public reception of the twenty-seven books by the congregations of the Great Church was an important deciding factor. Fourth, these books adequately reflected the beliefs and perceptions of orthodox Christianity in the fourth century.[16]

16. For further discussion on the formation of the NT canon, see Appendix A, below.

Appendix A
The Formation of the New Testament Canon

Why twenty-seven books—no more or less? There have been numerous attempts at answering this crucial question of the NT canon. Mid-twentieth-century archaeological discoveries, such as the Dead Sea Scrolls and the Nag Hammadi Library, as well as current scholarly research, have challenged many simplistic answers to the problem.[1] Before addressing the question about the twenty-seven books, it is necessary first to clarify three misconceptions concerning the subject and to define important terminology involved in the discussion. The question, why twenty-seven books? will then be answered by a

historical sketch of the formation of the canon.

SOME MISCONCEPTIONS

Original Unity

The first misconception is the assumption of an early church unified in doctrine and practice. Even though the emphasis on ecclesiastical solidarity in early catholic writings (e.g., the Pastoral letters, *1 Clement*, Ignatius) seems to convey the idea of an initial unity, it might be a response to a situation of diversity originating from the apostolic period. The NT supports this view of original diversity in the three examples that follow: First, it is evident that Paul, the apostle to the Gentiles, did not find much agreement with the Jewish Christians in Jerusalem (Gal 2:11–14; cf. Acts 21:17, 21). Second, it is clear from the letter of James and Paul's letter to the Romans that there was some difference of

---

1. Examples of past and recent challenges to more simplistic views of the past include Campenhausen, *Formation of the Christian Bible*; Dungan, "New Testament Canon in Recent Study"; Farmer and Farkasfalvy, *Formation*; Kalin, "Inspired Community"; Kalin, "Re-Examining New Testament Canon History"; Sundberg, "Bible Canon and the Christian Doctrine of Inspiration"; Sundberg, "Canon of the New Testament," in *IDBSup*, 136–40; McDonald and Sanders, eds., *Canon Debate*; McDonald, "Canon of the New Testament," in *NIB*, 1:536–47.

opinion concerning the important teaching of justification by faith (Rom 3:28; Jas 2:24). Third, in the NT we encounter a variety of diverse but noteworthy religious interpretations and observances from different social and ethnic groups, e.g., Hellenistic Jewish and Gentile; apocalyptic and early catholic; churches of Judea, Asia, Greece, and Rome. Early Christianity from its inception was characterized by a variety of beliefs and practices.[2]

New Testament Orthodoxy and Heresy

The second misconception can be explained in the following three statements: The first builds on the previous discussion of diversity in the NT. Because earliest Christianity was characterized by a variety of teachers and preachers advocating differing views, self-evident distinctions between "right" and "wrong" beliefs are not always that discernible to us today.[3] Second, *orthodoxy* defined as "correct opinion" and *heresy* as "false religious views" are terms characteristic of the period after the NT. The Greek term *orthodoxia* ("correct opinion/belief") is not found in the NT but is frequent in the fourth century.[4] The term *hairesis* generally had a neutral

sense in the first century.[5] The technical, negative usage of *heresy* as "false religious belief" rarely occurred until the second and third centuries.[6] Third, rigid orthodox and heretical labels obscure historical study by prejudging the positions of both concerned parties before they are examined. For example, we want to give the so-called Judaizers a chance to be heard, as well as the Apostle Paul, who opposed them (Gal 1–2). Therefore in our discussion of early Christianity, we speak of an emerging orthodoxy in belief and practice without prejudging this group as true and all dissenters and opponents as false. Our discussion in chapters 14–15 indicated that misunderstandings arose on both sides.

Canonical and *Apocryphal* in Early Christianity

The third misconception relates to the use of the labels *canonical* and *apocryphal* when discussing early Christian literature. As we have shown with *orthodoxy* and *heresy*, the above labels are also technical terms used after the NT period that tend to prejudice a critical study of the

2. For an early survey of original diversity, see Bauer, *Orthodoxy*, xxi–xxv, 229–40, and a critique of some aspects of Bauer's "geography of heresy," see Robinson, *The Bauer Thesis*. For some groundbreaking sociological and anthropological studies on plurality, see Meeks, *The First Urban Christians*; Stark, *The Rise of Christianity*; Theissen, *Religion of Earliest Churches*.

3. This point is carefully argued in Kraft, "The Concept of 'Orthodoxy,'" in Hawthorne, ed., *Current Issues*, 48–56.

4. For example, in the writings of Eusebius, *Hist eccl.* 3.31.6; and especially 6.2.13–14 (ca. 320).

5. The neutral sense of *hairesis* as a group with beliefs distinctive to it, e.g., a Jewish sect or party (Acts 5:17; 15:5; Josephus, *Ant.* 13.171; 18.11) or Christian group (Acts 24:5; 28:22, somewhat pejorative); the usage of *hairesis* with some negative connotation as a "faction" or as a source of "schism" in the church: 1 Cor 11:19; Gal 5:20; 2 Pet 2:2, and Titus 3:10; BDAG, 27–28; Reis, "Heresy," in *NIDB*, 2:798–99.

6. Ignatius, *Eph.* 6.2; *Trall.* 6.1 (ca. 118); Irenaeus, *Haer.* 3, preface and 1.1.3 (ca. 180). In 2 Pet 2:1, *hairesis* denotes "destructive opinions," but many scholars date this book in the early second century; see discussion in Kraftchick, *Jude, 2 Peter*; Kümmel, *Introduction*, 429–34; Guthrie, *New Testament Introduction*, 814–51 (first century).

literature. The word "canon" (Gk. *kanōn*, "straight rod, reed") was often used to signify a rule or norm (e.g., Gal 6:16). Later applied to the Bible itself, *canon* denotes an official list of authoritative writings (e.g., see the Easter letter of Athanasius, ca. 367).

Apocrypha (in Greek meaning "kept hidden") was a term often applied to secretive or objectionable literature. In the late second century it was used by Irenaeus in his denouncements of Gnostic writings he considered to be apostolic forgeries. Despite the attempts at censorship by Irenaeus and other Christian polemicists, the circulation of apocryphal writings, such as the *Gospel of Peter* and the *Acts of Paul*, continued for centuries.

Now that three misconceptions relating to the NT canon have been addressed, a historical sketch will be provided in response to the question: why are there twenty-seven books—no more or less? First, the authorities and collections of early Christianity will be examined. Second, the emergence of NT collections will be studied. Third, the canonical lists and their influences will be surveyed. Finally, lingering issues from the Reformation to the present will be addressed.

THE FORMATION OF THE NT CANON

The History of the NT Canon: AD 30–140

What were the written and oral authorities of the earliest Christians before the NT was written? What comprised some of the earliest collections of Christian teachings? These are some of the questions that will be treated in this section.[7]

The Authority of the Jewish Scriptures

Jesus and primitive Christianity were never without a Holy Scripture, since they relied heavily upon the authoritative writings of Judaism. Although all three parts of the later Hebrew Bible were quoted, it is uncertain whether there was a closed collection of Jewish Scriptures before the first century. Throughout the Mediterranean world of that time, the Jews used as Scripture the two closed collections of the Law and Prophets and also a third undefined group of "other books."[8] This undefined category was later called the Writings (*b. Sanh.* 90b), although this later rabbinic division omitted many widely circulated books, e.g., the Wisdom of Solomon and the *Psalms of Solomon*, 1 Enoch, and 1 and 2 Maccabees. There is no clear evidence of a closed collection of Jewish Scriptures until after the fall of Jerusalem in AD 70

---

7. The following designations of Christianity will be used in this study: (1) earliest or apostolic Christianity ca. 30–70, from the approximate dates of Jesus's ministry to the deaths of most of the apostles; (2) early orthodox or postapostolic Christianity, 70–150, after the apostles to the time of Marcion and Justin Martyr; (3) orthodox Christianity on its way to becoming the "Great Church" from the mid-second century until the reign of Constantine (324) and the Council of Nicaea (325); after 325 catholic Christianity becomes the Great Church. Some overlap will occur on the above categories.

8. These undefined "other books" are alluded to in the prologue of the book of Sirach and are exemplified in the broader collections of Scripture in the Dead Sea Scrolls (Qumran) and the Greek Septuagint (LXX). All the above writings were composed before the NT. See a helpful series of articles on the old/first canon in McDonald and Sanders, eds., *Canon Debate*.

(cf., Luke 16:29, 31; 24:27, 44 (ca. AD 80?); Josephus, *Ag. Ap.* 1.38–46; Philo, *Contempl. Life* 25; 4 Ezra 14:45–48). This final stage of consolidation possibly resulted from the late first-century rabbinic discussions at Yavneh. By this time early Christianity had begun to break away from Judaism and did not adhere completely to a fixed Jewish Bible, since books like the Wisdom of ben Sira, Wisdom of Solomon, *1 Enoch*, and Judith appeared to be used authoritatively in early Christian writings (e.g., Matt 11:25–30/Sir 51; Rom 1:18–32/Wis 13–14; Jude 14–15/*1 Enoch* 1:9; *1 Clem.* 27.5/Wis 12:12; 55:4–5/Jdt 8–13; *Barn.* 4.3/*1 Enoch*).

The Authority of Jesus

This broad view of Scripture in early Christianity is understandable since the sacred writings were subservient to the authoritative sayings of Jesus (e.g., Matt 5:21–45; John 5:39–47).[9] As early as the writings of Paul (50–62), words of Jesus are cited as a new norm on matters of faith and practice (e.g., 1 Cor 9:14; 11:23–25; 1 Thess 4:15). The citation of Jesus sayings is also evident in the early catholic literature (Acts 20:35; Rev 2–3).

The Authority of Paul and Others

Since Paul and other early Christian leaders were commissioned by Jesus and possessed God's Spirit, they also spoke with God's authority (e.g., 1 Thess 2:13; 1 Cor

7:25, 40; Rev 1:1–3; 1 Tim 6:13–14; *1 Clem.* 47.3; 63:2; Ign. *Phld.* 7.1–2. It was a charismatic living authority that developed in the activities of both proclamation and leadership.[10] Even though the author of Revelation claimed inspiration for himself (22:18–19) and Paul intended for certain of his letters to be circulated among the churches (1 Thess 5:27; Col 4:16), it is no indication that these writers were conscious of producing "canonical" Scriptures.[11]

The Earliest Collections

In the discussion above, we have seen that the authorities of earliest Christianity were the Jewish Scriptures, the sayings of Jesus, the teachings of Paul, and the words of certain early catholic writers. We will now look at some of the earliest collections of sayings and writings that preceded the NT lists of catholic Christianity (ca. 140–419). The authoritative use of Jesus sayings and certain letters of Paul was characteristic of post-apostolic Christianity before Marcion (140). The sayings of Jesus were cited with equal authority as

9. Kümmel, *Introduction*, 477–78; Ackroyd and Evans, *From the Beginnings to Jerome*, 286–88; McDonald, "The Canon of the New Testament," in *NIB*, 1:538–39; McDonald and Sanders, eds., *Canon Debate*, 332–40.

10. See especially Kalin, "Inspired Community"; McDonald and Sanders, eds., *The Canon Debate*, 435–39.

11. McDonald and Sanders, eds., *The Canon Debate*, 11–15, 25–35, 291–94. Trobisch, *Paul's Letter Collection*, based on his dissertation, argues from external manuscript evidence and internal analysis that Paul authorized certain of his letters for publication (Romans, the Corinthian correspondence, and Galatians); this assumption leads to an extended edition (by his disciples) after his death (of Ephesians, Philippians, Colossians, 1–2 Thessalonians), culminating in a later comprehensive edition (Hebrews, 1–2 Timothy, Titus, and Philemon). According to this argument, Paul's letter collection is analogous to the letter collections initiated by Cicero or Seneca.

Scripture (*1 Clem.* 13.2; 46.8; 2 Pet 3:2). Certain writings of Paul, including the vaguely Pauline letter to the Hebrews, were also circulated. Clement of Rome (AD 96) makes use of Romans, 1 Corinthians, and Hebrews. Ignatius of Antioch (ca. 110) was familiar with Romans, 1 Corinthians, and Ephesians. The author of 2 Peter (AD 110?) also mentioned an unspecified collection of Paul's letters (2 Pet 3:15–16). Data used to support an early collection of written gospels must be cautiously examined. It is not always clear whether a written gospel or an independent oral saying is cited by early catholic writers, like Clement of Rome and Ignatius. However, the *Didache* (ca. AD 90) appears to quote directly from Matthew's Gospel (*Did.* 8.2/Matt 6:9–13), and Papias of Phrygia (120) is acquainted with both the Gospel of Mark and a Matthaean sayings collection in Hebrew or Aramaic (Eusebius, *Hist. eccl.* 3.39.15–16). It appears that at least one or two written gospels were being circulated by the early second century. The appearance of Marcion from Pontus (ca. 130–160) marks a high point in the study of early Christian collections, since he appears to have been the first to undertake the task. Influenced by Paulinism (Romans, Galatians) and possibly Gnosticism,[12] Marcion made a sharp

distinction between a wrathful, inferior creator of the Jewish Scriptures (whom he rejected) and the Good Father of Christ (whom Marcion sought to follow). As a result, he rejected the Hebrew Bible and believed that the true interpretation of Christ and the Father was preserved only in ten letters of Paul, with the Pastoral letters excluded, and Laodiceans, which is probably Ephesians, plus an amended Gospel of Luke, ascribed to Paul's companion. Both the gospel and apostolic writings were edited and abridged by Marcion (Irenaeus, *Adv. Haer.* 1.27.2; 3.11.17). Despite opposition from Irenaeus and others (e.g., Eusebius, *Hist. eccl.* 5.13; Tertullian, *Adv. Marc.* 4.5; *Praescr.* 30), the radical, ascetic teacher from Pontus may have been the first to draw up a collection of Christian Scriptures with the two divisions gospel and apostolic writings (although Luke and Acts might be precursors of these two divisions).

The History of the NT Canon: 140–250

This period of identifying authoritative Christian writings in catholic Christianity was probably motivated by two negative influences: (1) the selective Scripture of Marcion, and (2) the circulation of new Gnostic books and Montanist prophecies.

---

12. It was clearly Paul's teaching on law vs. gospel that influenced Marcion's *Antitheses* (ca. 143). This work consists of a series of contrasts between the inferior teachings of the Creator/Moses/Law and the superior words and deeds of Christ. See "Marcion," in Meeks, *The Writings of St. Paul*, 284–90; Farmer and Farkasfalvy, *Formation*, 58–64, 134–41; McDonald and Sanders, eds., *Canon Debate*, 341–54; May, "Marcion"; Hall, "Marcion," in *DBI*, 423–24. If Gnosticism also influenced Marcion, it is difficult to understand what type. His distinction between the inferior creator and the

Good Father and his claim of a relationship with the Father for those who attain a new recognition of him through Christ have affinities with Gnosticism. But Marcion's teaching lacked the mythological and allegorical characteristics of Gnosticism (he was a literalist), a diverse movement based on both Jewish and Christian writings. S. G. Hall regards Marcion as an ascetic who was also a radical biblicist. On Gnosticism, see Pagels, "Gnosticism," in *IDBSup*, 366; Williams, *Rethinking Gnosticism*, 23–26, 269–70; Perkins, *Gnosticism and the New Testament*.

Although the use of Christian books by the emerging Great Church is apparent, the ambitious efforts of noncatholic Christians provide some explanation for the specific mention of Christian collections in the writings of Justin Martyr (150) and Irenaeus (180). Therefore the influences of Marcion, Montanism, and Christian Gnosticism will be discussed as background to our study of emerging NT collections.

Negative Influences

Marcion's rejection of the Jewish Scriptures and his exclusive allegiance to his editions of Luke's Gospel and Paul's ten letters have already been mentioned. Marcion's ambitious attempt was a deliberate restriction of a much broader use of Christian authorities already evident in the writings of Clement of Rome, Ignatius, and Papias. As a result, Marcion's teachings were denounced by Justin Martyr and Irenaeus, both of whom made use of a broader group of Christian books. The continuing revelations of Montanism were an opposite extreme from Marcionism, which early catholics also sought to avoid. Montanism was a prophetic movement from Asia Minor that anticipated an imminent end of the world (ca. 170–230). Montanus, the founder, and his two prophetesses, Maximilla and Priscilla, claimed to utter new prophecies directly from God. Some of their utterances (influenced by John 14–17) are found in the catholic writings of Tertullian (ca. 200) and Epiphanius (ca. 400). Although no Montanist books are extant, and though the identity of the prophecies as Scripture is unclear, the new revelations of Montanism were regarded by the Great Church as an attempt to add to the four Gospels and apostolic writings (Eusebius, *Hist. eccl.* 5.16–19; Epiphanius, *Pan.* 48).

Another extreme position or worldview that seemed to threaten the authoritative writings of catholic Christianity was that of Gnosticism.[13] Gnostics (a diverse movement) advocated spiritual liberation from the material cosmos and identity with the divine through revealed knowledge (*gnōsis*). This process of salvation was revealed in elaborate myths of heavenly beings emanating from a transcendent, unknowable deity; the myths generally involved a story of separation from the material cosmos (created by one or more demiurges) and restoration to the divine realm of the unseen God. Christian Gnostic systems utilized writings from the Synoptic Gospels, John's Gospel, and Paul (plus certain OT texts), but interpreted them allegorically for deeper religious truths. Some of the many Christian Gnostic writings produced in the second and third centuries were the *Gospel of Thomas* (90?), the *Gospel* and *Apocalypse of Peter*, the *Gospel of Philip*, and the *Gospel of Truth* (Nag Hammadi texts). The circulation of such Gnostic Christian writings posed a threat to the Great Church and its interpretation of the sacred writings. Therefore, Irenaeus (*Adv. Haer.* 2–3) and other catholic apologists (Tertullian, Epiphanius, Hippolytus) considered them to be a distortion of their Gospels, apostolic writings, and the Old Testament. Gnostic religious interpretation posed a

13. On Gnosticism, see ch. 14, also Pagels, "Gnosticism," in *IDBSup*, 366; Williams, *Rethinking Gnosticism*; Perkins, "Gnosticism," in McDonald and Sanders, *The Canon Debate*, 355–71; and Perkins, *Gnosticism and the New Testament*.

greater threat here than the fear of their supplanting sacred texts with Gnostic ones.

The Gospels

With the appearance of Marcion's influential collection and the wide circulation of Gnostic gospels, catholic Christianity began to specify which gospels and apostolic writings were considered authoritative. First, the use of specific gospels and apostolic writings will be noted. Then, the lists of Origen and the Muratorian fragment will be analyzed.

Although the four Gospels were probably used by mid-second century, no consensus was reached concerning their exclusive use in catholic Christianity. Justin Martyr of Palestine (ca. 150; *Dial.* 103.8; 106.2) cites the written Gospels of Matthew, Mark, Luke, and (possibly) John as Scripture (*Dial.* 105.1), calling them the "memoirs of the apostles" (*1 Apol.* 66.3). Irenaeus of Lyons, Gaul (180), employed fantastic numerology to argue for a closed collection of four Gospels (*Adv. Haer.* 3.11.8). This closed collection of Matthew, Mark, Luke, and John was supported in the West by Tertullian of Carthage (200 in *Adv. Marc.* 4.2.2) and in the East by Clement of Alexandria (170 in *Strom.* 3.93.1; Eusebius, *Hist. eccl.* 6.14-17, ca. 330) and Origen (230 in Eusebius 6.25.3-14). However, the exclusive use of four Gospels was contested by the Syrian churches for several centuries.

One reason for the dissension of Syria concerning only four Gospels was the work of Tatian from Syria (150). Tatian composed a harmony of four (possibly five) gospels, which was called the *Diatessaron*. Although this Gospel harmony has

been cited as an early witness to a fourfold gospel, the use of four separate gospels was not a general practice in Syria until the fifth century. Justin Martyr may even have relied on a harmony of the Synoptic Gospels (a precursor to Tatian's work). It should also be noted that reluctance to use certain individual gospels, especially John's Gospel, may have been in reaction to its Gnostic appeal. For instance, the Valentinian Gnostic Heracleon (170) produced the earliest commentary on the Gospel of John. The Montanists also favored John. Anti-Gnostic or anti-Montanist churches (most of which were catholic) would therefore have been reluctant to use such a writing. This may explain why the anti-Gnostic Syrian churches were reluctant to use separate gospels but favored the harmonistic arrangement by Tatian.[14]

Although a collection of Paul's letters existed before Marcion (Romans, 1-2 Corinthians, Galatians, Ephesians, Philippians, Colossians, 1-2 Thessalonians), the complete edition of this collection (fourteen letters) did not seem to appear before the third century. Polycarp, bishop of Smyrna (150), was familiar with seven or eight of Paul's letters (also found in Marcion's collection) and alludes to passages

14. The popularity of the *Diatessaron* continued in Syria until the fifth century. But the following circumstances contributed to the decline in its use: Tatian (a pupil of Justin Martyr) later joined a noncatholic, ascetic group (the Encratites) that was condemned by Irenaeus (*Adv. Haer.* 3.23.8) and Eusebius (*Hist. eccl.* 4.28-29). Hippolytus of Rome (220) accused Tatian of being a pagan Cynic (*Elenchus* 10.18). Bishop Theodoret of Cyrrhus (425) destroyed many copies of the Diatessaron because he suspected Tatian of heresy (Peterson, *Tatian's Diatessaron*; McDonald and Sanders, *Canon Debate*, 280, 302; Hengel, *Four Gospels*, 24-26, 223-24).

from 1 and 2 Timothy (not in Marcion's collection). First and Second Timothy, along with most of Paul's ten letters, were quoted in the writings of Irenaeus (180). After this period the Pastorals (1 and 2 Tim and Titus) are often quoted as the works of Paul.

Hebrews was cited early by both Clement of Rome (*1 Clem.* 36.1–6) and Polycarp (Pol. *Phil.* 6.3). It is also included in the Chester Beatty Papyrus (P^{46}, ca. 200) along with Romans, 1–2 Corinthians, Galatians, Ephesians, Philippians, Colossians, and 1 Thessalonians. Nevertheless, uncertainty about the authorship of Hebrews raised questions of its authenticity in the West until the fourth century. Tertullian, however, defended its authenticity by arguing that its author was Barnabas, a companion of the Apostle Paul.

This period also marks the circulation of the NT Catholic Letters. Polycarp appears to quote from 1 Peter and 1 John in his letter to the Philippians. Traces of 1 Peter have also been detected in Gnostic writers like Basilides (ca. 125). Irenaeus cites 1 Peter with the words: "Peter in his epistle," and also quotes 1 and 2 John, ascribing their authorship to the Apostle John. The earliest use of Jude is found in 2 Peter (ca. 120).[15] Clement of Alexandria and Origen were also familiar with most of the Catholic Letters.

Justin Martyr was one of the first to cite the book of Revelation as Scripture, ascribing its authorship to the Apostle John (*Dial.* 81). Irenaeus also supported Justin's position. When the Montanists

used this book to support their own ideas, it became controversial among catholic Christians in Asia Minor and Rome. In the East, Clement of Alexandria and Origen considered Revelation to be authoritative, although Dionysius (a disciple of Origen) questioned its authorship and authenticity.

The List of Origen

Origen of Alexandria (ca. 250) made use of a large group of early Christian writings. He composed commentaries, homilies, and theological treatises on every OT and NT book that was currently used in the Egyptian churches. From his numerous works, Eusebius (320) drew up a list of NT books that Origen had used.[16] In this composite list, Eusebius mentions the four Gospels, Paul's letters (in his writings, Origen alludes to twelve letters, excluding Philemon), Hebrews (whose authorship was unknown to him), 1 Peter (Origen doubted the Petrine authorship of 2 Pet), 1 John (he conceded that 2 and 3 John may not have been genuine), Acts, and Revelation.[17] Elsewhere, Origen rejects the following writings as heretical: the *Gospel of the Egyptians*, the *Gospel of*

---

15. For further discussion of the view that Jude was a source for 2 Peter, see Bauckham, *Jude, 2 Peter*, 141–43; Kraftchick, *Jude, 2 Peter*; Reese, *2 Peter and Jude*, 7–15, 115–23; Guthrie, *New Testament Introduction*, 919–22.

16. Most of Origen's works are found in *ANF* 4. Origen's list is found in Eusebius, *Hist eccl.* 6.25.3ff.; *Hist. eccl.* also includes an OT list that contains most of the extra books of the Greek or books not found in the Hebrew Bible (e.g., the books of Maccabees). For further discussion on Origen and the NT, see Kalin, "Canon of Origen"; Kümmel, *Introduction*, 495–96 (contrary to Kümmel, it appears that Eusebius, not Origen, divided the NT into three categories); see Sundberg, "Making of the New Testament Canon," 1223.

17. Doubts about James and Jude are also mentioned in Origen's commentaries on John (20.10.66) and Matthew (17.30).

Thomas, the *Gospel of Basilides*, and the *Gospel of Matthias*.

The list compiled by Eusebius, however, did not serve as a fixed canon for Origen.[18] Like his predecessor, Clement of Alexandria, Origen used a broader group of Christian writings in an authoritative manner: e.g., the *Gospel and Preaching of Peter*, the *Acts of Pilate*, the *Didache*, *Barnabas*, the *Shepherd of Hermas*, *1 Clement*, and the letters of Ignatius. Irenaeus also utilized *1 Clement*, the *Shepherd of Hermas*, and the writings of Ignatius. Tertullian likewise made use of the *Shepherd of Hermas*. Such widespread circulation of postapostolic and pseudonymous writings indicates the fluidity and open-endedness of authoritative Christian documents in the second and third centuries.

The Muratorian Fragment

The NT list in the fragment discovered by L. A. Muratori (1740) is significant.[19] Although the beginning and end of the so-called Muratorian Fragment are lost, the fragment appears to affirm a fourfold gospel. The fragment begins with Luke as the "third gospel book," presupposing Matthew and Mark, and it mentions "the

---

18. Sundberg, "Making of the New Testament Canon," 1223; McDonald and Sanders, eds., *Canon Debate*, 591.

19. The fragment discovered by Muratori in the eighteenth century is an early list of authoritative Christian writings found in a mutilated eighth-century Latin manuscript. For further information, see Kümmel, *Introduction*, 491–93; and Schneemelcher, "History of New Testament Canon," in Schneemelcher, *NTA*, 1:42–45. For important recent discussion, see Sundberg, "Muratorian Fragment," in *IDBSup*, 609–10, and Sundberg, "Canon Muratori: A Fourth-Century List"; Hahneman, *Muratorian Fragment*, and his essay in McDonald and Sanders, *Canon Debate*, 405–15.

fourth gospel . . . by John." The Acts of the Apostles is mentioned next. In conformity to the seven letters to churches in Asia Minor found in the book of Revelation, Paul is said to have written to seven congregations: Corinth, Ephesus, Philippi, Colossae, Galatia, Thessalonica, and Rome. The total number of Paul's letters here is probably nine, since the apostle wrote two letters each to the Corinthians and Thessalonians. Philemon and the Pastoral Letters are classed together as letters to individuals.

The Muratorian fragment also rejects two forged letters of Paul to the Laodiceans and Alexandrians, which are ascribed to the sect of Marcion. First John is mentioned with the Fourth Gospel. It is unclear precisely what are the two letters "with John's inscription" (e.g., 1 and 2 John, or 2 and 3 John?). The letter of Jude is also mentioned later in the manuscript; the Revelation of John is listed again with the Revelation of Peter, although the text states that some do not allow (both of) them to be read in the church. The Wisdom of Solomon is included without a word of caution or endorsement. The book recommended for private and not public reading is the *Shepherd of Hermas*. The Muratorian fragment gives the date and setting of the *Shepherd of Hermas* as "in our time . . . in the city of Rome, when his [Hermas's] brother Pius was seated as bishop of the church . . . of Rome." This allusion dates *Hermas* between about 140 and 150, and the composition of the Muratorian fragment within a generation of that date ("in our time"). Reference to the "catholic church" and the "city of Rome" has been interpreted as reflecting Roman origin.

However, the contents of the Muratorian fragment raise problems concerning its early Roman origin, and some have postulated a fourth-century date in the East.[20] First, if the Muratorian list comes from second-century Rome, it had little influence on the early collections of the West.[21] Western sources of the second century reveal no definite acquaintance with the fragment. Second, the contents of the Muratorian fragment are characteristic of fourth-century lists in the East. For example, the questionable status of Revelation, the disapproval of reading the *Shepherd of Hermas* in public, and the classification of the Wisdom of Solomon with early Christian writings are all features of fourth-century Eastern lists (cf. Eusebius). If the above criticisms are correct, then the Muratorian fragment preceded and possibly influenced several fourth-century lists, especially the collection of Eusebius (320). The Muratorian fragment, according to this viewpoint, moved West in a codex with other Christian documents (e.g., a book by Chrysostom, AD 350) in order to justify the inclusion or exclusion of certain writings in the West (e.g., Hebrews is omitted in the fragment).[22]

20. For the later Eastern dating and problems of early Roman origin, see Sundberg, "Muratorian Fragment," 609–10, and Sundberg, "Canon Muratori," 12–25, 34–41; Hahneman, *Muratorian Fragment*.

21. Sundberg, "Canon Muratori"; cf. Daniélou, *Origins of Latin Christianity*, 13–15.

22. Sundberg, "Canon Muratori," 38–41; Sundberg, "Muratorian Fragment," 609–10.

The History of the New Testament Canon: 320–419

The actual formation of a NT canon begins with the compilation of Eusebius (320). It reaches some degree of uniformity with the Easter letter of Athanasius (367) and the councils of North Africa (393–419), although uncertainty concerning the limits of the canon continued in the Syrian churches until the seventh century.

Eusebius

In his *Ecclesiastical History* (3.25), Eusebius of Caesarea provides a list of Christian Scripture. We will first examine his three categories of writings and then discuss the criteria he used in his categorization. Eusebius divides his canonical list into three categories: acknowledged, disputed, and "heretical." The accepted (Gk. *homolegoumena*) writings are similar to his compilation of Origen's list (6.25.3ff.), except that the body of Paul's letters is listed, and Hebrews is added to it; Eusebius also has reservations about Revelation ("if appropriate"). The "disputed writings" (Gk. *antilegomena*) are subdivided into disputed books "known to many" (James, Jude, 2 Peter, and 2 and 3 John) and "spurious" or forged apostolic writings: the *Acts of Paul*, the *Shepherd of Hermas*, the *Apocalypse of Peter*, *Barnabas*, the *Didache*, and Revelation "if appropriate." The third category, the "heretical" documents, are those books that are "completely senseless and impious": the *Gospels of Peter, Thomas, Matthias* (and others), the *Acts of Andrew*, the *Acts of John*, and other pseudonymous books that claimed apostolic authorship.

Three observations of the above criteria should be made. First, Eusebius regarded only the acknowledged writings as genuine and canonical. Second, although the disputed and spurious writings were rejected by some, they were read publicly in many churches. Therefore most of the disputed writings could be interpreted as quasi-canonical literature. Third, the heretical writings were "totally spurious and foreign to apostolic orthodoxy."[23] The criteria presupposed in the categorization of Eusebius appear to be three: (1) acceptance by all the churches, (2) apostolic and orthodox contents, and (3) apostolic authorship or origins. The heretical writings were probably rejected because they did not adequately meet the above criteria. Eusebius had little difficulty regarding Hebrews as an acknowledged writing since he ascribed its authorship to the Apostle Paul (unlike Origen or Tertullian). But Eusebius had reservations about the apostolic authorship of the Revelation of John. He was probably influenced by the skepticism of Dionysius of Alexandria concerning the book's authenticity. Acceptance by the churches was probably the most important criterion that helped gain canonical status for James, Jude, 2 Peter, and 2 and 3 John. Because the above books (including Hebrews) did not adequately meet all three criteria, their status remained disputed in the Western churches until the fourth century.[24]

23. *Hist. eccl.* 3.31.6. As noted in this discussion, Eusebius identifies his position with "apostolic orthodoxy and refers to his opponents as "heretics" (3.25.6). By the fourth century, the lines between true and false religious beliefs were more clearly defined; see also Kalin, "Eusebius," in McDonald and Sanders, *Canon Debate*, 386–404.

24. These books were disputed in the writings by Cyprian of Carthage (ca. 250) and Hilary of Poitiers, in France (ca. 350). There were probably other theological and sociopolitical factors that induced the skepticism in the West about the status of Hebrews and certain Catholic Letters.

Athanasius

The first list to have all twenty-seven books of our NT "canonized" (Gk. *kanonizomena*) was the Easter letter of Athanasius (367), bishop of Alexandria. There was, however, a list of additional books to be read by those being instructed in Christianity: the Wisdom of Solomon with four other Jewish books of the Septuagint (LXX) and the Christian writings of the *Didache* and the *Shepherd of Hermas*. Heretical writings that are falsely assigned an early date and "deceive the innocent" are labeled "the apocrypha" and rejected.

Syria

The twenty-seven-book canon of Athanasius greatly influenced the Western synods but had little effect on the Syrian churches. The church councils and synods of North Africa (at Hippo in 393 and in Carthage in 397 and 419) differed in arrangement but agreed in number with the canon of Athanasius. But the following developments took place in the Syrian churches, which challenged the Athanasian canon for centuries. In the fourth century, the *Diatessaron* of Tatian was favored over the four Gospels. The Catholic Letters and the book of Revelation were also omitted. In the fifth century the four Gospels were included, but four Catholic Letters and Revelation were omitted (in the Peshitta or "Syrian Vulgate"). During the sixth and seventh centuries, some degree of conformity to the twenty-seven-book canon was eventually attained.[25]

25. See, e.g.: the revision of the Peshitta. For further discussion, see Kümmel, *Introduction* 501–3; Ackroyd and Evans, *From the Beginnings to Jerome*, 364–68.

The History of the NT Canon: 1546–Present

During the Reformation period, Erasmus, Cardinal Cajetan, and Martin Luther, despite their theological differences, shared doubts about the apostolic origins of Hebrews, James, 2 Peter, Jude, and 2 and 3 John. Although Luther placed Hebrews, James, Jude, and Revelation at the end of his NT as the least esteemed books, his estimation of 2 Peter, and 2 and 3 John was more favorable than the estimations for these books by Erasmus and Cajetan.[26]

The Council of Trent

In response to lingering doubts about the status of certain NT books and other important factors,[27] the Roman Catholic Church issued a decree on the canon of Scripture at the Council of Trent (1546). Its basic contents and the later responses of Protestantism will be examined. The decision at Trent maintained that the books of the Latin Vulgate were "sacred and canonical in their entirety, with all their parts."[28] This decree affirmed the equal authority

of all twenty-seven books, in contrast to Luther, who categorized books as more esteemed and less esteemed. The council also reaffirmed a broader canon of the OT, which included books labeled by the Reformers as belonging to the Apocrypha (e.g., 1 and 2 Maccabees, Wisdom of Solomon, Sirach). Although the Lutheran and Anglican traditions encouraged the reading of these "additional books" for devotional but not doctrinal purposes, the Reformed churches have traditionally rejected them altogether (e.g., in the Westminster Confession, 1647).

The Post-Trent Situation

Despite occasional problems raised by the contents and authorship of such books as James and 2 Peter, all major bodies of Christendom reached general agreement on the canonical status of the twenty-seven books of the NT after Trent. Ecclesiastical agreement, however, did not settle academic debates on the limitations and binding force of the Christian canon.

Academic Debates concerning the Canon

Since the eighteenth century, questions concerning the dogmatic concept of a canon have been raised by scholars like J. S. Semler.[29] Why should historical investigation of early Christianity regard these twenty-seven books as special in comparison with other primary sources? Can the church regard as binding certain writings

---

26. Guthrie, "Canon of the New Testament," in *ZPE* 1:741.

27. The special status Luther ascribed to certain NT books (Romans, Galatians, Ephesians, John, 1 John, and 1 Peter) and the secondary status Luther and other Reformers assigned to the OT books of the Latin Vulgate outside the Hebrew Bible were two key factors.

28. The Latin Vulgate was a fourth-century translation of both the OT and NT by Jerome (ca. 345–419) made from earlier Latin, Greek, and Hebrew manuscripts available to him. The OT contains most of the books of the LXX that are not found in the Hebrew Bible. On the Vulgate, see Ackroyd and Evans, *From the Beginnings to Jerome*, 518–23. Quotation from the decree at Trent is from Brown, "Canonicity," in *NJBC* 67:91.

29. Kümmel, *Introduction*, 506; Rollman, "Semler," in McKim, ed., *Dictionary of Major Biblical Interpreters*, 910–13.

whose inclusion into the canon was based essentially on false assumptions (e.g., that Paul wrote Hebrews or that Peter wrote 2 Peter)?[30] With the discovery of dissimilar outlooks and differing theologies in the NT (e.g., James vs. Romans), the question is raised, Which early Christian viewpoint should be valued over the others? Is it possible to have an "actual" canon within a formal canon?[31] Harmonization of diverse NT theologies obscures the real issue or fails to address it. Often the principle of a canon within a canon is applied, for example, when certain parts of the NT are favored over others (1) because of their compatibility with church doctrine and practice (e.g., Paul's justification by faith and Lutheranism), or (2) because of their chronological closeness to the original apostolic witness (e.g., the letters of Paul and the study of Christian origins). The above questions concerning the limits and the normativeness of the NT canon are still being asked today.

THREE EXPLANATIONS OF THE CANON'S FORMATION

Why twenty-seven books—no more or less? The best explanations are found in the history of the Great Church, which collected them. First, in reaction to both a selective collection (Marcion) and additional supplements (Gnostics), the Great Church adhered to those writings that originated, they believed, from apostolic times and reflected their apostolic "rule of faith."[32] Second, Constantine, the first "Christian" emperor of the Roman Empire, ordered fifty new copies of the Bible for churches of Constantinople (ca. AD 331). This imperial edict played an important role the decision of which authoritative writings the Great Church would include in its Bible. Third, the public reception of certain books among the communities of the Great Church also influenced the limits of the NT canon. For example, the doubts of Eusebius concerning James, Hebrews, and Revelation were always qualified by statements about their popularity in the churches. In the case of the above books, this acceptance is what ultimately prompted their inclusion in the canon.

---

30. For discussion of the authorship of Hebrews and 2 Peter, see Guthrie, *New Testament Introduction*, 685–89, 820–28; Kümmel, *Introduction*, 401–3, 430–34; Bauckham, *Jude, 2 Peter*, 158–62; Dinkler, "Hebrews, Letter to," in *IDB*, 2:572–73; Becker, "Peter, 2nd Letter of," in *IDB*, 3:767–69; Koester, *Hebrews*.

31. The problem of the degrees of canonicity was raised acutely by Martin Luther (1520), because he gave preeminence to the letters of Paul, John's Gospel, 1 Peter, 1 John, and secondary rank to Hebrews, James, Jude, and Revelation. In the twentieth century Käsemann followed a similar position with his "center of the New Testament" (Paul's letters) and peripheral writings (Pastoral and Catholic Letters), *Essays on New Testament Themes*, 94–107.

32. The apostolic rules of faith (or truth) were summaries of the Christian faith, common in the mid-second century (e.g., Irenaeus, Tertullian), before the formal creeds of Nicaea. Although varied in content, they generally contained accounts of the life, death, and resurrection of Jesus Christ derived from oral and written traditions. They served as a basis for instructing converts, a guide for interpreting Scripture, and a defense against heretics: see Soulen and Soulen, *Handbook*, 165. Barton questions how much of a reaction Marcion really caused in his use of Scripture (McDonald and Sanders, eds., *Canon Debate*, 341–44, 354).

SUMMARY

The nature and limits of the twenty-seven books of the NT reflect fundamentally the beliefs and perceptions of the Great Church of the fourth century. This church of the Constantinian era supported its particular convictions about Jesus and the apostles, and rejected literature that did not satisfactorily express those beliefs. The modern commitment to a NT canon of twenty-seven books is basically a "vote of confidence" for the decision of the Great Church in the fourth century.[33]

The establishment of the NT canon, then, has favorable and precautionary aspects. The favorable aspect concerns the encapsulized portrait in the canon: a portrait of early Christianity in its diversity and multiplicity. The institution of a canon appears to legitimize a diversity of fresh and creative responses to Jesus Christ in the modern world. A pluralism of early Christian beliefs and practices (e.g., some apocalyptic, some early catholic) are canonized as models for modern readers to evaluate, assimilate, or set aside in their attempts to comprehend the NT teachings.[34]

The precautionary point concerns the negative historical consequences of elevating this "classical portrait" of Christian origins at the exclusion of other important primary sources of study (e.g., the Dead Sea Scrolls, the Apocrypha, Gnostic writings). As the possession of the Great Church, the NT achieved a place of reverence and respect in the church and world. Nevertheless, we must not overlook in our study the literature of that period that influenced the NT books, attempted to supplement them, or sought to provide alternative viewpoints of Jesus and early Christianity.[35]

33. The argument that the NT books attained canonical status not from church councils but because of their inherent spiritual and moral contents does not hold up well for books like Jude, 2 Peter, and 2 and 3 John, whose rather meager contents are overshadowed by such "quasi-canonical" books as the informative *1 Clement* or the dynamic letters of Ignatius.

34. This concept of canonized diversity is developed in Käsemann, "The New Testament Canon and the Unity of the Church," in Käsemann, *Essays on New Testament Themes*, 103–7; but see the cautionary note on the NT canonical limits of acceptable diversity: e.g., the Gospel of Matthew but not the *Gospel of the Ebionites*; the Gospel of John but not the *Gospel of Thomas*, the Acts of the Apostles but not the *Acts of Paul*; the Apocalypse of John but not the *Apocalypse of Peter*, in Dunn, "Canon, A Continuing Function," in McDonald and Sanders, eds., *Canon Debate*, 558–79; and Dunn, *Unity and Diversity in the New Testament*.

35. This precautionary note is not suggesting a reopening of the NT canon (supporting Dunn in McDonald and Sanders, eds., *the Canon Debate*, 578–79) but pleads to explore, with critical interest, all relevant ancient sources of the books of the NT canon within their own historical, political, social, religious, and cultural contexts. Such an approach may involve, e.g., the intertextual study of canonical and noncanonical, extrabiblical or nonbiblical texts of the Jewish and Greco-Roman world.

Appendix B:
English Translations of the New Testament

Why are there so many English translations of the Bible? Which ones are the
best? Is it important to know what is a
reliable English translation and why it is
reliable?

BEFORE THE KING JAMES VERSION

The translation of the NT from Greek into
the vernacular languages of Europe was
the aim of Renaissance humanism, and it
gained impetus in the Reformation. Luther's translation of the NT into German
was published in 1522. It was an example
followed in other lands.[1] In England, William Tyndale (1494–1536) undertook the
task of translation but faced difficulties
because of English hostilities to Luther,
led by Henry VIII (who remained Roman
Catholic until 1534). He carried out his

work in Reformed Europe and finally got
his English translation printed in Worms,
Germany, in 1526.[2] Although all of the
NT and most of the OT were completed,
Tyndale died in 1536, leaving unpub-
lished certain manuscripts of the OT. He
was proficient in both Greek and Hebrew,
and his translation influenced subsequent
English versions.

The Great Bible (1539)

This translation was a thorough revision of Matthew's Bible (1537; edited by
J. Rogers) undertaken by Miles Coverdale (1488–1569), both based on Tyndale's translation. Coverdale's revision
was completed in 1539 and was called the

---

1. See Bluhm, *Martin Luther, Creative Translator*; and Bluhm, "Martin Luther, Creative Bible
Translator"; Metzger, "Versions, Medieval and
Modern," in *IDB*, 4:773–74; Greenslade, *West from
the Reformation*, 94–103, 432–36.

2. See Mozley, *William Tyndale*. For further
information on English translations from 1450 to
1650 see Bruce, "Transmission and Translation of
the Bible," 48–53; Bruce, *English Bible*; Branton,
"Versions, English," in *IDB*, 4:760–68; Reumann,
Four Centuries of the English Bible; Greenslade,
West from the Reformation, 141–68; Metzger, *Bible
in Translation*, 58–60.

Great Bible. It was appointed for use in the churches and was the first "authorized version." From 1539 to 1569 it underwent numerous editions.

The Geneva Bible (1560)

The production of the Geneva Bible was begun by English Reformers exiled in Geneva, Switzerland, during the reign of the Catholic Queen Mary (1553–1558). The Bible was completed in 1560 and presented to Elizabeth I. Its publication was simultaneous with the establishment of Reformed religion in Scotland. It remained in use long after the KJV and was used by the Pilgrims when they came to America in 1620. To the Pilgrims the KJV was a "fond thing vainly invented." They considered the older version to be the better. The Geneva Bible was favored during the Elizabethan age and was even the Bible of William Shakespeare. The last edition appeared in 1644.

The Bishop's Bible (1568)

Because the radical Reformed and anti-Catholic sentiments of the Geneva Bible were offensive to many, a revision of Coverdale's Great Bible was made in 1568 by Matthew Parker, the Archbishop of Canterbury. Called the Bishop's Bible, it omitted many of the controversial notes found in the Geneva Bible. The whole Bible underwent nineteen editions from 1568 to 1606.

THE KING JAMES VERSION (1611)

When Elizabeth died in 1603, the crown of England passed to James I, who had ruled Scotland as James VI. To regulate the affairs of the church, he called a conference of clergymen and theologians at Hampton Court (1604). The most important project that resulted from the conference was that a new translation of the Bible should be made, and that it should be authorized for use in the churches of England.[3] The new translation was formally a revision of the 1602 edition of the Bishop's Bible. Many other helps and versions were used by the translators, who paid attention throughout to the original text. Forty-seven scholars divided into six panels: three for the OT, two for the NT, and one for the Apocrypha. The draft translation provided by the six panels was finally revised by a committee of twelve. Miles Smith helped to see the work through the press and also wrote the preface. Although it did not receive instant acceptance, this translation became a landmark in the religious history and English-speaking people. Its influence upon piety and culture in English has lasted a full four hundred years.

There are at least two reasons for the enduring use of the KJV. First, absence of controversial notes gave it broader ecclesiastical appeal. Second, it was a literary masterpiece. Its prose rhythms and avoidance of harsh combinations of sound made it useful for public reading. But much of this tribute must be paid to William Tyndale, since he had established the stylistic pattern of the KJV. Nine-tenths of the NT in the KJV is from Tyndale's translation.

---

3. Bruce, "Transmission and Translation of the Bible," 49–52; Lewis, *English Bible* 27–30; Branton, "Versions, English," in *IDB*, 4:766–68; Greenslade, *West from the Reformation*, 164–68.

REVISIONS OF THE KING JAMES VERSION

Although the so-called Authorized Version[4] established itself at the heart of English-speaking piety and culture, the following three facts remain. First, the translation was based on late and comparatively poor Greek manuscripts, and with the passage of time earlier and better Greek texts were discovered. Second, the translation was based on an inadequate understanding of Hellenistic Greek, something which has greatly improved with the discovery of the Koine Greek papyri from Egypt in the nineteenth century. Third, the English-language usage has also changed, so that while some of the phrases of the KJV proved unforgettable, others became unintelligible. The result was that in England in 1870 a revision of the KJV was undertaken.[5]

The English Revised Version (1881), ASV (1901), and NASBU (1995)

The English Revised Version of the Bible (ERV) was initiated by the Anglican convocation of Canterbury in 1870. There were two committees of revisers, one for the OT and one for the NT. Although stylistically inferior to the KJV, it was textually superior,[6] because its translation was based on the Alexandrian text advocated by B. F. Westcott and F. J. A. Hort in their *The New Testament in Original Greek*. The ERV was therefore more precise in its rendering of the Greek text. Hort and Westcott were on the NT committee, as was also F. H. A. Scrivener, who had some disagreements with the Westcott and Hort Greek text. The NT was completed in 1881 (the OT in 1885 and the Apocrypha in 1894).

American scholars involved in the ERV project were unhappy with the conservative conditions imposed on the revisers. The ERV appeared to use no expression that was not current in 1611. The American scholars worked on a new version (based on the best and earliest Greek manuscripts) without this archaizing policy. They agreed, however, to wait until 1901 to publish it. It was titled the American Standard Version (ASV).[7] The translators of the English and American revised versions, like their predecessors with the KJV, sought to keep as closely as possible the exact words and phrasings in the original language. This theory of translation is called formal equivalence.

The New American Standard Bible (NASB [with the NT completed in 1963 and the OT in 1972]) claims to be

---

4. We have no evidence when it was "authorized" and by whom, other than from the king's own privy council; see Bruce, "Transmission and Translation of the Bible," 52; see also Greenslade, *West from the Reformation to the Present Day*, 361–63.

5. Greenslade, *West from the Reformation*, 371–73. The New King James Bible (1980) is merely an updating of some of the KJV's archaic English expressions with some improvements on translation of the NT Koine Greek. However, the entire translation retains the late and poor Greek text behind the KJV (the "received text"). The NKJV imposes on the form and base of the KJV current English terminology and some recent insights from biblical research. See Kubo and Specht, *So Many Versions?* 273–307; Lewis, *English Bible*, 331–39; Moody, "NKJB," *RevExp* 77 (1978) 110–13.

6. There are over five thousand differences in the Greek text underlying that of the KJV and that of the RV (ASV), Lewis, *The English Bible*, 336. On Hort and Westcott with Scrivener on the ERV NT translation company, see Metzger, *The Text of the New Testament* (1992), 129–30, 137–38; and Metzger, *Bible in Translation*, 100–101.

7. Branton, "Versions, English," in *IDB*, 4:769–70; Lewis, *English Bible*, ch. 4.

a revision of the 1901 American edition, sponsored by the Lockman Foundation of California. The NT is a word-for-word (formal equivalence) translation of the Greek and maintains a conservative Protestant bias. In 1995, the NASB Update (NASBU) was published. It updated much of the archaic English (removing, e.g., "thee," and "thou"), made some changes in gender-inclusive language (a total of eighty-five such changes), and consulted newer scholarly editions of the Hebrew, Aramaic, and Greek texts (NA^{26}).[8]

The Revised Standard Version (RSV, 1946) and the NRSV (1989)

Plans for a new revision of the ASV (1901) were begun in 1937 in America. The result was the Revised Standard Version (RSV) of the Bible. The NT was completed in 1946 and the OT in 1952. The entire Bible was revised in 1962 and 1972. It was produced by American and Canadian scholars and copyrighted by the Division for Christian Education of the National Council of the Churches of Christ in the U.S.A. The Common Bible of the RSV was produced in 1972 with the Roman Catholic and Eastern Orthodox portions of the OT (the Protestant Apocrypha). As a revision of the KJV, the RSV comes closest to fulfilling the broad purpose once filled by the KJV. Alongside the KJV in the Tyndale tradition stand the ERV, the ASV, and the RSV. The RSV, which was also a committee translation, is stylistically superior to the ERV and the ASV, and is based on

the earliest and best Greek manuscripts of that time, reconstructed by modern textual criticism.[9]

In light of recent discoveries of additional Dead Sea Scroll fragments (for the OT) and further early Greek papyrus manuscripts (for the NT), a thorough revision of the RSV was proposed in 1974 by the National Council of Churches, to be carried out by the Standard Bible Committee, chaired by Bruce M. Metzger. The NRSV (1989) includes changes in punctuation and paragraph structure; elimination of archaisms from the Tyndale-KJV tradition; greater accuracy, clarity, and euphony; and the elimination of masculine-oriented language so far as it could be done without distorting the historical situation of the of the biblical cultures and societies.[10] The NRSV remains a more literal or formal equivalence translation but uses some idiomatic expressions to attain clarity, euphony, and gender inclusivity.

---

8. On the NASB, see Kubo and Specht, *So Many Versions?*, 222–30; Greenslade, *West from the Reformation*, 373–74. On the NASBU, see Sheeley and Nash, *Bible in English Translation*, 41; Metzger, *Bible in Translation*, 150–51.

9. Like the KJV and revised versions (ASV), the RSV attempts to keep as close as possible to the exact words and phrasings in the original language (formal equivalence), although the RSV has sought to be more intelligible to its modern-English readers. It therefore is a less literal translation. See Branton, "Versions, English," in *IDB*, 4:770–71; Metzger, "RSV Bible"; Greenslade, *West from the Reformation*, 377–79; Fee and Strauss, *How to Choose a Translation*, 147–48; De Regt, "Bible, Translation Theory," in *NIDB*, 1:452–53.

10. Metzger, *The Bible in Translation*, 155–56; Metzger et al., *Making the NRSV Bible*.

BREAKS WITH THE KING JAMES VERSION

The New English Bible (NEB, 1961) and the Revised English Bible (REB, 1989)

Two examples of translations that break with the KJV tradition are the New English Bible (NEB) and the Good News Bible (Today's English Version). The New English Bible (the NT completed in 1961, the OT in 1970) marked a genuine departure in the history of English translations. A team of British Protestant scholars under the general direction of C. H. Dodd, a NT scholar, set out to produce a "faithful rendering of the best available Greek text into the current speech of our time."[11] The NEB adopts the translation theory of dynamic equivalence: "we have conceived our task to be that of understanding the original as precisely as we could . . . and then saying again in our own native idiom what we believed the author was saying in his."[12] The NEB is not a free paraphrase but has sought to replace Greek constructions and idioms with those of contemporary English. Both C. S. Lewis and T. S. Eliot were consultants. Whereas the RSV follows the formal equivalence practice of reflecting the ambiguity of the original texts, the NEB is concerned to say what the biblical writers meant in the words of contemporary English.[13]

The Revised English Bible (REB) was completed in 1989 under the direction of W. D. McHardy, working with nineteen revisers and twelve literary revisers, including Roman Catholic, Salvation Army, and Moravian scholars. The English style is fluent and appropriate for liturgical use while maintaining intelligibility for worshippers over a wide range of ages and backgrounds. More inclusive gender reference was preferred without compromising scholarly integrity or English style.[14]

Good News for Modern Man (1966) and the *Contemporary English Version* (CEV, 1995)

The break with the KJV tradition in America came from the American Bible Society. In 1966 a NT translation titled *Good News for Modern Man* (Today's English Version) appeared. It was the work of Robert G. Bratcher, submitted for suggestions and approval to translation consultants of the American Bible Society and (later) the British Foreign Bible Society. The OT translation appeared in 1971 and the deuterocanonical books (the Apocrypha) in 1979 with four subsequent NT editions. The complete work is called the *Good News Bible* (GNB). The GNB (and the NEB, somewhat) follow the dynamic (or functional) equivalency theory of translation. This theory applied to the GNB is stated by Eugene Nida: "to try to stimulate in the new reader in the new language the same reaction to the text that the original author wished to stimulate in

11. Dodd, "Introduction to the New Testament," v. See also Greenslade, *West from the Reformation*, 379–82.

12. Dodd, "Introduction to the New Testament," vii. See also Ray, "Formal vs. Dynamic Equivalent," 46–56; De Regt, "Bible Translation Theory," in *NIDB*, 1:452–53; On NEB and REB as a mediating position between formal and functional equivalent translations, see Fee and Strauss, *How to Choose a Translation*, 25–28, 151–52.

13. Harrington, *Interpreting the New Testament*

26–27; Roberts, "Dynamic Equivalence," 7–20; Sheeley and Nash, *Bible in English Translation*, 73–75.

14. Metzger, *Bible in Translation*, 153–55; Coleman, *New Light and Truth*.

his first and immediate readers."[15] The GNB seeks to confront the modern reader with the meaning of the original texts in today's standard, everyday English.

The *Contemporary English Version* (1995) began as a modern-speech translation for early youth and sought to produce a version that could be understood more easily than even the *Good News Bible*. Theological terms such as *justification, sanctification,* and *righteousness* are replaced by other expressions or phrases appropriate to the context. "Story" is the preferred rendering for *parable* and "hooray" for *hosanna*. Where men and women are intended, gender-inclusive language is employed.[16]

The New English Translation (2005)

The *NET Bible* is an online Bible translation (also in print) sponsored by the Biblical Studies Foundation (http://www.Bible.org/) and produced by more than thirty biblical scholars, among them Darrell L. Bock and Daniel B. Wallace on the NT. The translation takes a mediating path between formal equivalence (RSV) and functional equivalence (REB). The *NET Bible*'s most distinctive feature is its inclusion of almost sixty-one thousand notes that provide interpretive options, alternate renderings, and other insights into the Hebrew and Greek texts. In addition

to translation notes, it has study notes, text-critical notes, and map notes.[17]

The Common English Bible (2010–2011)

Abingdon Press of Nashville is producing a fresh, new, ecumenical, international, and multicultural translation of the entire Bible, accessible to a broad range of people. One hundred fifteen biblical scholars from twenty-two faith traditions worked as translators for the CEB. The board of editors includes David L. Peterson (OT), Joel B. Green (NT), and David Silva (Apocrypha). The NT was published in 2010 and the complete Bible is available, 2011. For more information, see online: http://www.commonenglishbible.com/

PRIVATE TRANSLATIONS

The translations reviewed above have all been produced by committees or societies representing major churches, yet anyone at any time can publish a translation of the NT. Many private translations have appeared in the twentieth century; we shall look at five, by Moffatt, Goodspeed, Phillips, Taylor, and Peterson.

The Moffatt Translation (1913)

James Moffatt, a Scottish NT scholar, published a NT translation in 1913 and the OT in 1924 and titled it *The Bible: A New Translation*. Although the NT version was based on the questionable Greek text reconstructed by H. von Soden, it is a fresh and vigorous translation. Moffatt does not

---

15. On dynamic equivalence, see Nida and Taber, *Theory and Practice of Translation*, 175. On TEV, see Nida, *Good News for Everyone*; Sheeley and Nash, *Bible in English Translation*, 82–85.

16. Metzger, *The Bible in Translation*, 170–71; Fee and Strauss, *How to Choose a Translation*, 154–55; Newman, et al., *Creating and Crafting "The Contemporary English Version."*

17. See Fee and Strauss, *How to Choose a Translation*, 151.

hesitate to trust his scholarly judgment in such matters as rearranging the text of John's Gospel.[18]

The Goodspeed Translation (1927)

The American counterpart to Moffatt is *The Complete Bible: An American Translation* (1927, revised 1935) by Edgar J. Goodspeed, a scholar from the University of Chicago. His first edition of the NT was begun in 1923. Goodspeed based his NT translation on the more-acceptable Greek text of Westcott and Hort, with some modification. Using the then-current studies on the Koine Greek, Goodspeed sought to cast the original thought of the NT writers in the "simplest and clearest of present-day English."

The Phillips Translation (1958)

J. B. Phillips, a vicar of the Church of England, published between 1947 and 1957 a NT translation which was later published in one volume: *The New Testament in Modern English* (1958). Making use of the "best available Greek text" (Westcott and Hort), Phillips produced a very lively and readable translation for the ordinary reader. Although he attempted to achieve a dynamic (functional) equivalence translation, he frequently approaches paraphrase, translating the ideas from one language to another with less concern for the exact words of the original.

Nevertheless, his translation of Paul's letters (*Letters to Young Churches*, 1947) was a very popular and successful attempt to clarify the writings of the Apostle Paul. C. S. Lewis read Phillip's rendering of Colossians and commented, "it was like seeing a familiar picture after it's been cleaned."[19]

The Living Bible (1971)

The popular *Living Bible Paraphrased* (1971) was the work of Kenneth Taylor, founder of Tyndale House Publishers in Wheaton, Illinois. It differs from the above translations because it is a true paraphrase of the Bible (mostly of the ASV). In his attempt to explain what the NT writers meant, e.g., Taylor simplifies, expands, and updates the NT idioms and thought patterns in terms roughly equivalent to our modern English usage. It is a very readable and simple paraphrase but at numerous points gives the English reader something that the original language did not intend to convey. Although the *Living Bible* (LB) is helpful for young people and casual readers, it was never intended for serious academic study.[20]

The Message (1994)

This bestselling idiomatic translation by Eugene Peterson, pastor, and professor emeritus at Regent College in British Columbia, was published in 1994 by NavPress. *The Message* is a "contemporary rendering of the Bible from the original languages" in everyday language. In the

18. Moffatt, e.g., transposes John 3:22–30 between 2:12 and 2:13; next 7:15–24 is placed after 5:47; finally, 12:45–50 is placed in the middle of v 36. On Moffatt's translation, see Metzger, *Bible in Translation*, 112–13; on Von Soden's Greek NT, see Aland and Aland, *Text of the New Testament*, 22–23, 40.

19. Sheeley and Nash, *Bible in English Translation*, 68.

20. Comfort, *Essential Guide to Bible Versions*, 184–85.

NT, Peterson sought to "convert the tone, rhythm, events, and ideas of the Greek text into the way we actually think and speak in English" (preface). Recent editions since 2005 have included verses for easy reference.[21]

DENOMINATIONAL OR CONFESSIONAL TRANSLATIONS

The Jerusalem Bible (1966) and the New Jerusalem Bible (1985)

The denominational or confessional translations can be divided into two basic categories: Roman Catholic and Protestant evangelical. Until recently, Roman Catholic translations of the Bible were generally from the Latin Vulgate.[22] Then from 1948 to 1954 a translation of the whole Bible with an introduction and footnotes appeared in French under the editorship of Jerusalem Dominicans (*La Bible de Jérusalem*). A special English translation and revision of this French Bible was begun by British Catholic scholars under A. Jones, and was called the *Jerusalem Bible* (1966). The introduction and footnotes were translated into English and updated. J. R. R. Tolkien also served as a consultant (on Job). The biblical books were usually translated from the original languages in comparison with the French Bible. The Jerusalem Bible (JB) has a twofold objective: to translate the Bible into the language we use today and to provide notes that are neither sectarian nor superficial. Although the JB is more restrained than the NEB or GNB concerning the theory of dynamic (functional) equivalence, it is written in modern English and avoids the "biblical English" of the KJV tradition.[23]

In 1985 the New Jerusalem Bible was completed under the general editorship of Henry Wansbrough. It is an entire revision and updating of the Jerusalem Bible, based on new insights from the last twenty years of biblical scholarship.

The New American Bible (1970)

The New American Bible (NAB) is the American counterpart of the British JB. It was the project of members of the Catholic Biblical Association of America, with some assistance by Protestant scholars. The OT and deuterocanonical books were completed in 1969, with the NT finished in 1970. The NT is based on the Nestle-Aland Greek text, the twenty-sixth edition (NA[26], 1963). The footnotes of the NAB are even less Roman Catholic than the JB (although both attempt to be nonsectarian). Even though it is translated in modern, readable English, it seeks to retain many of the words and phrasings of the original language. The NAB therefore tends to follow a mediating path between the formal equivalence of the RSV and the dynamic equivalence of the NIV. In 1986, the *Revised New Testament* of the NAB was completed, seeking to be as faithful as possible to the meaning of the Greek original and to maintain its formal-equivalence

---

21. Ibid., 197–98; Sheeley and Nash, *Bible in English Translation*, 90–92.

22. On the Latin Vulgate, see Metzger, *The Text of New Testament* (1992), 75–79; on English translations from Vulgate (e.g., *Douay-Rheims*, 1582–1609, *Confraternity Rev. of NT*, 1941), see *NJBC* 68:208–11. In 1935 an English translation from the Greek NT was completed in the UK, called the Westminster Version (*NJBC*, 68:212).

23. Crim, "Versions, English," in *IDBSup*, 935; Harrington, *Interpreting the New Testament*, 27; *NIDB*, 1:452–53.

approach. Furthermore, where the meaning of the original is gender inclusive, the translators have sought to reproduce it as far as this is possible in normal English (Metzger, *The Bible in Translation*, 152–53; *NJBC*, 68:214).

The New International Version (1973) and Today's New International Version (TNIV, 2005)

A major translation produced by an international group of Protestant evangelicals is the New International Version of the Bible. The NT was completed in 1973 and the OT in 1978. All translators were committed to the "full authority and complete trustworthiness of the Scriptures." The translators were primarily concerned with the accuracy of the translation and its fidelity to the thought of the NT writers. Therefore the NIV ranks with the RSV and NAB in espousing the formal-equivalence theory of translation. A revision, *Today's New International Version* (TNIV) was completed in 2005.[24] Two biblical scholars were assigned to each biblical book, and their proposed revisions were submitted to the Committee on Bible Translation, where an 80-percent majority was needed to make a change. About 7 percent of the entire NIV was changed, with one third of the changes related to gender-inclusive language and with the rest related to greater exegetical accuracy

(e.g., 1 Cor 7:1). Gordon Fee, a member of the revision committee, regards the TNIV as a mediating version between formal equivalence and functional (or dynamic) equivalence.[25]

The New Living Translation (1996)

With the sponsorship of the Tyndale House Publishers, the *Living Bible* of Kenneth Taylor (a private translation; see above) underwent a thorough revision. More than ninety Protestant evangelical scholars from various theological traditions (e.g., including Reformed and Wesleyan) worked on it for seven years. In the NT, they used the most current critical editions of the Greek New Testament (NA^{27}/UBS^{4}). Grant Osborne and Norman Ericson are general reviewers of the NT translation team. The translation method has been described as dynamic or functional equivalence, to produce in English the closest natural equivalent of the message of the Hebrew and Greek texts—both in meaning and style, resulting in a carefully rendered thought-for-thought translation. A revision of the NLT was published in 2004.[26] "May God's grace be with you all" (Hebrews 13:25, NLT).

25. On the NIV, see Barker, *The NIV*; Kohlenberger, *Words about the Word*; Comfort, *The Essential Guide to Bible Versions*, 189–93. On the TNIV, see Fee and Strauss, *How to Choose a Translation*, 149–50.

26. On the NLT, see Comfort, *Essential Guide to Bible Versions*, 199–201; Fee and Strauss, *How to Choose a Translation*, 153–54, 157; Sheely and Nash, *Bible in English Translation*, 79–82.

24 An updated version, *The New International Version Bible* is available, 2011.

Bibliography

REFERENCE WORKS

Abbegg, Martin Jr., et al., editors and translators. *The Dead Sea Scrolls Bible: The Oldest Known Bible Translated for the First Time in English.* San Francisco: HarperSanFrancisco, 1999.

Achtemeier, Paul J., editor. *Harper's Bible Dictionary.* San Francisco: Harper & Row, 1985.

Ackroyd, Peter R. *Exile and Restoration: A Study of Hebrew Thought in the Sixth Century.* OTL. Philadelphia: Westminster, 1968.

Ackroyd, Peter R., and C. F. Evans. *From the Beginnings to Jerome.* Cambridge History of the Bible 1. Cambridge: Cambridge University Press, 1970.

Aharoni, and M. Avi-Yonah, *The Macmillan Bible Atlas.* New York: Macmillan, 1977.

Aland, Kurt. *Synopsis of the Four Gospels. A Greek-English Edition of the Synopsis Quattuor Evangeliorum.* 6th rev. ed. New York: United Bible Societies, 1983.

———, editor. *Synopsis Quattuor Evangeliorum.* 12th ed. Stuttgart: German Bible Society, 1982.

Aland, Kurt, et al., editors. *The Greek New Testament.* 4th rev. ed. Stuttgart: Bibelgesellschaft, 1998.

Alexander, Patrick, et al., editors. *The SBL Handbook of Style: for Ancient Near Eastern, Biblical and Early Christian Studies.* Peabody, MA: Hendrickson, 1999.

American Bible Society. *The Holy Bible: Contemporary English Version.* New York: American Bible Society, 1995.

Anderson, R. Dean Jr. *Glossary of Greek Rhetorical Terms Connected to Methods of Argumentation, Figures and Tropes from Anximenes to Quintillian.* CBET 24. Leuven: Peters, 2000.

Archer, Gleason L., and Gregory Chirichigno. *Old Testament Quotations in the New Testament: A Complete Survey.* 1983. Eugene, OR: Wipf & Stock, 2005.

Aristotle. *The Poetics.* In *"The Poetics," by Aristotle; "On the Sublime," by Longinus; "On Style," by Demetrius.* LCL. Cambridge: Harvard University Press, 1932.

Arnim, Hans Friedrich August von. *Stoicorum Veterum Fragmenta.* 4 vols. Lipsiae, Germany: Teubneri, 1921–1924.

Athanassakis, Apostolos, translator. *The Life of Pachomius,* with an introduction by Birger A. Pearson. Missoula: Scholars, 1975.

Aune, David E. *The New Testament in Its Literary Environment.* LEC 8. Philadelphia: Westminster, 1987.

———. *The Westminster Dictionary of New Testament and Early Christian Literature and Rhetoric.* Louisville: Westminster John Knox, 2003.

Bagnall, Roger S., and Peter Derow. *Greek Historical Documents: The Hellenistic Period.* SBLSBS 16. Chico, CA: Scholars, 1981.

Barnstone, Willis, editor. *The Other Bible*. San Francisco: Harper & Row, 1984.

Barrett, C. K. *The New Testament Background: Selected Documents*. New York: Harper & Row, 1961.

Bauer, Walter, et al., editors. *A Greek-English Lexicon of the New Testament and Other Early Christian Literature*. Rev. and ed. by W. F. Danker. 3rd ed. Chicago: University of Chicago Press, 2000.

Bettenson, Henry Scowcroft, editor. *Documents of the Christian Church*. 2nd ed. London: Oxford University Press, 1963.

Betz, Hans Dieter, editor. *The Greek Magical Papyri in Translation, Including the Demotic Spells*. 2nd ed. Chicago: University of Chicago Pres, 1996.

BibleWorks for Windows. Hermeneutika Software. Online: http://www.bibleworks.com/.

Blackman, Philip. *Mishnayoth: Pointed Hebrew Text, English Translation, Introductions, Notes, Supplement*. 7 vols. New York: Judaica, 1964.

Blass, Friedrich W., and Albert Debrunner. *A Greek Grammar of the New Testament and Other Early Christian Literature*. Translated and revised by Robert. W. Funk, with supplemental notes of A. Debrunner. Chicago: University of Chicago Press, 1961.

Bratcher, Robert G. *Old Testament Quotations in the New Testament*. Helps for Translators 3. London: United Bible Societies, 1967.

Braund, David C., compiler. *Augustus to Nero: A Source Book on Roman History, 31 BC–AD 68*. Totowa, NJ: Barnes and Noble, 1985.

Brown, Colin, general editor. *The New International Dictionary of New Testament Theology*. 3 vols. Grand Rapids: Zondervan, 1975–1978.

Brown, Raymond E., et al., editors. *The New Jerome Biblical Commentary*. Englewood, Cliffs, NJ: Prentice Hall, 1990.

Bruce, F. F. *Jesus and Christian Origins Outside the New Testament*. Grand Rapids: Eerdmans, 1974.

Brunt, P. A., and J. M. Moore, editors. *Res Gestae Divi Augusti: The Achievements of the Divine Augustus*. London: Oxford University Press, 1967.

Bullinger, E. W. *Figures of Speech Used in the Bible, Explained and Illustrated*. 1898. Grand Rapids: Baker, 1968.

Buttrick, George A., general editor. *The Interpreter's Dictionary of the Bible*. 5 vols. Nashville: Abingdon, 1962.

Caragounis, Chrys C. *The Development of Greek and the New Testament: Morphology, Syntax, Phonology, and Textual Transmission*. WUNT 167. Tübingen: Mohr/Siebeck, 2004.

Cartlidge, David R., and David L. Dungan, editors. *Documents for the Study of the Gospels*. Rev. and enl. ed. Minneapolis: Fortress, 1994.

Champion, Craig. *Roman Imperialism: Readings and Sources*. Interpreting Ancient History. Malden, MA: Blackwell, 2003.

Charlesworth, James H., editor. *The Old Testament Pseudepigrapha*. 2 vols. Garden City, NY: Doubleday, 1983–1985.

Charlesworth, James H., et al., editors. *The Dead Sea Scrolls: Hebrew, Aramaic, and Greek Texts with English Translations*. Princeton Theological Seminary Dead Sea Scrolls Project. Tübingen: Mohr/Siebeck, 1994.

Charlesworth, M. P. *Documents Illustrating the Reigns of Claudius and Nero*. Cambridge: Cambridge University Press, 1939.

Coggins, R. J., and J. L. Houlden, editors. *A Dictionary of Biblical Interpretation*. London: SCM, 1990.

———. *The SCM Dictionary of Biblical Interpretation*. 2nd ed. London: SCM, 2003.

Collins, John J., and Daniel C. Harlow, editors. *Eerdmans Dictionary of Early Judaism*. Grand Rapids: Eerdmans, 2010.

Common English Bible. New Testament. Nashville: Abingdon, 2010.

Conzelmann, Hans, and Andreas Lindemann. *Interpreting the New Testament: An Introduction to the Principles and Methods of N. T. Exegesis*. Translated by S. S. Schatzmann. Peabody, MA: Hendrickson, 1999.

Cook, S. A., et al., editors. *The Cambridge Ancient History*. 12 vols. Cambridge: Cambridge University Press, 1921–1939.

Crim, Keith, editor. *The Interpreter's Dictionary of the Bible Supplementary Volume*. Nashville: Abingdon, 1976.

Danby, Herbert. *The Mishnah: Translated from the Hebrew with Introduction and Brief Explanatory Notes*. Oxford: Clarendon, 1933.

Danker, Frederick W. *Multipurpose Tools for Bible Study*. Rev. and exp. ed. Minneapolis: Fortress, 2003.

Deissmann, Adolf. *Light from the Ancient East: The New Testament Illustrated by Recently Discovered Texts of the Graeco-Roman World*. Translated by Lionel R. M. Strachan. Reprinted, Grand Rapids: Baker, 1978.

Derrida, Jacques. *The Derrida Reader: Writing Performances*, edited by Julian Wolfreys. Stages 15. Lincoln: University of Nebraska, 1998.

———. "The Law of Genre." *Critical Inquiry* 7 (1980) 55–81.

Dickey, Eleanor. *Ancient Greek Scholarship: A Guide to Finding, Reading, and Understanding Scholia, Commentaries, Lexica, and Grammatical Treatises from Their Beginning to the Byzantine Period.* American Philological Association Classical Resources Series 7. Oxford: Oxford University Press, 2007.

Dines, Jennifer M. *The Septuagint*. Edited by Michael A. Knibb. Understanding the Bible and Its World. London: T. & T. Clark, 2004

DiTommaso, Lorenzo. *A Bibliography of Pseudepigrapha Research 1850–1999.* JSPSup 39. Sheffield: Sheffield Academic, 2001.

Doenges, Norman A. *The Letters of Themistokles.* Monographs in Classical Studies. New York: Arno, 1981.

Duckworth, George E., editor. *The Complete Roman Drama.* 2 vols. New York: Random House, 1982.

Dupont-Sommer, A. *The Essene Writings from Qumran.* Translated by Geza Vermes from the 1961 ed. Gloucester, MA: Smith, 1973.

Edelstein, Emma Jeannette, and Ludwig Edelstein, editors. *Asclepius: A Collection and Interpretation of the Testimonies.* Johns Hopkins University; Institute of the History of Medicine; Publications: 2nd ser., Text and Documents. Baltimore: Johns Hopkins University Press, 1945.

Eder, Walter, and Johannes Renger, editors. *Chronologies of the Ancient World: Names, Dates and Dynasties.* Brills Neue Pauli. Supplements 1. Leiden: Brill, 2006.

Ehrenberg, Victor, and A. H. M. Jones, editors. *Documents Illustrating the Reigns of Augustus and Tiberius.* 2nd (enlarged) ed. Oxford: Clarendon, 1976.

Electronic Resources for Classicists: The Second Generation. Online: http:/www.tlg.uci.edu/index/gateways.html/.

Elliott, J. K. *The Apocryphal New Testament.* Oxford: Clarendon, 1993.

Epstein, I., translator and editor. *The Babylonian Talmud.* 34 vols. London: Soncino, 1935–1952.

Evans, Craig A. *Ancient Texts for New Testament Studies: A Guide to Background Literature.* Peabody, MA: Hendrickson, 2005.

———. "Jesus in Non-Christian Sources." In *Studying the Historical Jesus: Evaluations of the State of Current Research,* edited by Bruce Chilton and Craig A. Evans, 443–78. NTTS 19. Leiden: Brill 1994.

———. *Life of Jesus Research: An Annotated Bibliography.* NTTS 24. Leiden: Brill, 1996.

Ferguson, John. *Greek and Roman Religion A Source Book.* Noyes Classical Studies. Park Ridge, NJ: Noyes, 1980.

Fitzmyer, Joseph A. *A Guide to the Dead Sea Scrolls and Related Literature.* Rev. and exp. ed. Studies in the Dead Sea Scrolls and Related Literature. Grand Rapids: Eerdmans, 2008.

———. *An Introductory Bibliography for the Study of Scripture.* 3rd ed. Subsidia Biblica 3. Rome: Pontifical Biblical Institute, 1990.

Foerster, Werner. *Gnosis: A Selection of Gnostic Texts.* 2 vols. Translated by R. McL. Wilson. Oxford: Clarendon, 1972.

Freedman, David Noel, et al., editors. *The Anchor Bible Dictionary.* 6 vols. Garden City, NY: Doubleday, 1992.

Freedman, David Noel, et al., editors. *Eerdmans Dictionary of the Bible.* Grand Rapids: Eerdmans, 2000.

Freedman, Harry, and Maurice Simon, editors. *Midrash Rabbah.* 10 vols. 2nd ed. London: Socino, 1951.

Funk, Robert W., Roy W. Hoover, and the Jesus Seminar. *The Five Gospels: The Search for the Authentic Words of Jesus.* New York: Macmillan, 1993.

Funk, Robert W., and the Jesus Seminar, editors. *The Acts of Jesus: The Search for the Authentic Deeds of Jesus.* San Francisco: HarperSanFrancisco, 1998.

García Martínez, Florentino. *The Dead Sea Scrolls Translated: The Qumran Texts in English.* Leiden: Brill, 1994.

García Martínez, Florentino, and Eibert J. C. Tigchelaar, editors. *The Dead Sea Scrolls Study Edition.* 2 vols. Leiden: Brill, 1997–1999.

Gergel, Tania, and Michael Wood, editors. *Alexander the Great: The Brief Life and Towering Exploits of History's Greatest Conqueror as Told by His Original Biographers.* London: Penguin, 2004.

Goldin, Judah, translator. *The Fathers according to Rabbi Nathan.* Yale Judaica Series 10. New Haven: Yale University Press, 1955.

Gomme, A. W. *A Historical Commentary on Thucydides.* Vol. 1, *Introduction and*

Commentary on Book 1. Oxford: Clarendon, 1956.

Gramcord for Windows/Bible Companion. Gramcord Institute/White Harvest. Online http://www.gramcord.org/windows.htm/.

Grant, Robert M. *Gnosticism: A Source Book of Heretical Writings from the Early Christian Period.* 1961. New York: AMS, 1978.

Green, Joel B., and Scot McKnight, editors. *Dictionary of Jesus and the Gospels.* Downers Grove, IL: InterVarsity, 2005.

Greenslade, S. L. *The West from the Reformation to the Present Day.* Cambridge History of the Bible 3. Cambridge: Cambridge University Press, 2008.

Grenfell, Bernard P., and Arthur S. Hunt, editors. *New Classical Fragments and Other Greek and Latin Papyri.* Oxford: Clarendon, 1897.

Guggenheimer, Heinrich W., editor. *The Jerusalem Talmud. First Order: Zeraim Tractate Berakhot.* Studia Judaica 18. Berlin: de Gruyter, 2000.

Guirard, Felix, editor. *New Larousse Encyclopedia of Mythology.* New ed. Translated by Richard Aldington and Delano Ames. London: Hamlyn, 1968.

Hamilton, Edith, et al., editors. *The Collected Dialogues of Plato: Including the Letters.* 1961. Reprinted, Bollingen Series 71. Princeton: Princeton University Press, 2005.

Hammond, N. G. L., and H. H. Scullard, editors. *The Oxford Classical Dictionary.* Oxford: Clarendon, 1970.

Hanson, K. C. "K. C. Hanson's Home Page." Online: http://www.kchanson.com/.

Harmless, William, compiler. "Bibliographies for the Study of the New Testament." Online: http://moses.creighton.edu/harmless/ bibliographies_for_theology/New _Testament_0.htm/.

Hawthorne, Gerald F., and Ralph P. Martin, editors. *Dictionary of Paul and His Letters.* Downers Grove, InterVarsity, 1993.

Hayes, John H., editor. *New Testament: History of Interpretation.* Nashivlle: Abingdon, 2004.

Heckel, Waldemar, and H. C. Yardley, editors. *Alexander the Great: Historical Sources in Translation.* Blackwell Sourcebooks in Ancient History. Oxford: Blackwell, 2003.

Heiken, Grant, Renato Funiciello, and Donatella de Rita. *Seven Hills of Rome: A Geological Tour of the Eternal City.* Princeton: Princeton University Press, 2007.

Hercher, Rudolphus, editor. *Epistolographi graeci: recensuit, recognovit, adnotatione critica et indicibus Instruxit.* 1873. Reprinted, Amsterdam: Hakkert, 1965.

Hewett, James Allen. *New Testament Greek: A Beginning and Intermediate Grammar,* revised by C. Michael Robbins and Steven R. Johnson. Rev. ed. with CD. Peabody, MA: Hendrickson, 2009.

Hock, Ronald F., and Edward N. O'Neil, editors. *The Chreia in Ancient Rhetoric.* Vol. 1, *The Progymnasmata.* Texts and Translations 27. Graeco-Roman Religion Series 9. Atlanta: Scholars, 1986.

———, editors. *The Chreia in Ancient Rhetoric: Classroom Exercises.* Writings from the Greco-Roman World 2. Atlanta: Society of Biblical Literature, 2002.

Holladay, Carl R., compiler and translator. *Fragments from Hellenistic Jewish Authors.* 4 vols. Texts and Translations 20, 30, 39, 40. Pseudepigrapha Series 10, 12, 13, 14. Chico, CA: Scholars, 1983.

Holmes, Michael W., editor. *The Apostolic Fathers: Greek Texts and English Translations.* 3rd ed. Grand Rapids: Baker Academic, 2007.

Hornblower, Simon, and Anthony Spawforth, editors. *The Oxford Classical Dictionary.* 3rd ed. New York: Oxford University Press, 1996.

Horsley, G. H. R, S. R. Llewelyn, et al., editors. *New Documents Illustrating Early Christianity.* A Review of the Greek Inscriptions and Papyri. Published in 1971–87 (in separate vols.). 9 vols. North Ryde, N. S. W., Australia: The Ancient History Documentary Research Centre of Macquarie University, 1981–2002. Grand Rapids: Eerdmans, 1991–2002.

Howard, Rebecca Moore. "Michel Foucault: A Bibliography for Composition and Rhetoric." The Writing Program of Syracuse University. Online: http://wrt-howard.syr.edu/Bibs/ Foucault.htm/.

Howard, Wilbert Francis. *Accidence and Word Formation.* A Grammar of New Testament Greek 2, by James Hope Moulton. Edinburgh: T. & T. Clark, 1929.

Hunt, Arthur S., and C. C. Edgar. *Select Papyri.* 2 vols. LCL. Cambridge: Harvard University Press, 1932.

Jeremias, Joachim. *Unknown Sayings of Jesus.* Translated by Reginald H. Fuller. 2nd English ed. London: SPCK, 1964.

Jewish Encyclopedia.com. Online: http://www .jewishencyclopedia.com/view .jsp?artid=543&letter=J.

Jobes, Karen H., and Moisés Silva. *Invitation to the Septuagint*. Grand Rapids: Baker Academic, 2000.

Kee, Howard Clark. *The New Testament in Context: Sources and Documents*. Englewood Cliffs, NJ: Prentice Hall, 1984.

Kennedy, George A., translator. *Progymnasmata: Greek Textbooks of Prose Composition and Rhetoric*. Writings from the Greco-Roman World 10. Atlanta: Society of Biblical Literature, 2003.

Kilburn, K, translator. *Lucian*. Vol. 6. LCL. Cambridge: Harvard University Press, 1999.

Kittel, Gerhard, and Gerhard Friedrich, editors. *Theological Dictionary of the New Testament*. Translated by Geoffrey W. Bromiley. 10 vols. Grand Rapids: Eerdmans, 1964–1976.

Kittel, Rudolf, et al., editors. *Biblia Hebraica Stuttgartensia*. Revised by Hans Peter Rüger, et al. 5th ed. Stuttgart: Deutsche Bibelstiftung, 1997.

Klauck, Hans-Josef. *Ancient Letters and the New Testament: A Guide to Context and Exegesis*. Translated and edited by Daniel P. Bailey. Waco, TX: Baylor University Press, 2006.

———. *The Religious Context of Early Christianity: A Guide to Graeco-Roman Religions*. Translated by Brian McNeil. Minneapolis: Fortress, 2003.

Kloppenborg, John S. *Q Parallels: Synopsis, Critical Notes and Concordance*. Foundations & Facets. New Testament. Sonoma, CA: Polebridge, 1988.

Lampe, G. W. H. *A Patristic Greek Lexicon*. Oxford: Clarendon, 1976.

Lanham, Richard A., *A Handlist of Rhetorical Terms*. 2nd ed. Berkeley: University of California Press, 1991.

Layton, Bentley. *The Gnostic Scriptures*. Garden City, NY: Doubleday, 1987.

Lee, John A. L. *A History of New Testament Lexicography*. Studies in Biblical Greek 8. Berlin: Lang, 2003.

Lefkowitz, Mary R., and Maureen B. Fant. *Women's Life in Greece and Rome. A Source Book in Translation*. 3rd ed. Baltimore: Johns Hopkins University Press, 2005.

Lewis, Naphtali. *Papyrus in Classical Antiquity*. Oxford: Clarendon, 1974.

Liddell, H. G., R. Scott, and H. S. Jones, compilers. *A Greek-English Lexicon*. 9th ed., with revised supplement. Oxford: Clarendon, 1996.

Llewelyn, Stephen R., and R. A. Kearnsley, editors. *New Documents Illustrating Early Christianity*. Vol. 7, *A Review of the Greek Inscriptions and Papyri Published in 1982–83*. The Ancient History Documentary Research Centre of Macquire University, North Hyde, New South Wales, 1994.

———, editors. *New Documents Illustrating Early Christianity*. Vol. 9, *A Review of the Greek Inscriptions and Papyri published in 1986–87*. The Ancient History Documentary Research Centre of Macquarie University. Grand Rapids: Eerdmans, 2002.

Logos Bible Study Software. Logos Research Systems. Online: http://www.logos.com/.

Lucas, F. L. *Tragedy in Relation to Aristotle's "Poetics."* 2nd, rev. ed. New York: Macmillan, 1958.

Luck, Georg, translator and annotator. *Arcana Mundi: Magic and the Occult in the Greek and Roman Worlds; A Collection of Ancient Texts*. 2nd ed. Baltimore: Johns Hopkins University Press, 2006.

Marcos, Natalio Fernández. *The Septuagint in Context*. Translated by Wilfred G. E. Watson. Leiden: Brill, 2000.

Marlowe, Michael D., editor. "Bible Research Internet Resources for Students of Scripture." Online: http://www.bible-researcher.com/index.html/.

Martin, Ralph P., and Peter H. Davids, editors. *Dictionary of the Later New Testament and Its Development*. Downers Grove, IL: InterVarsity, 1997.

McCrum, Michael, and A. G. Woodhead, compilers. *Select Documents of the Principates of the Flavian Emperors, Including the Year of Revolution, AD 68–96*. Cambridge: Cambridge University Press, 1961.

McKim, Donald K., editor. *Dictionary of Major Biblical Interpreters*. Downers Grove, IL: IVP Academic, 2007.

McKnight, Scot. *The Synoptic Gospels: An Annotated Bibliography*. Grand Rapids: Baker Books, 2000.

McLay, R. Timothy. *The Use of the Septuagint in New Testament Research*. Grand Rapids: Eerdmans, 2003.

Meltzer, Edmund S., editor. *Letters from Ancient Egypt*. Translated by Edward F. Wente. Writings from the Ancient World 1. Atlanta: Scholars, 1990.

Merriam-Webster's Collegiate Dictionary. 11th ed. Springfield, MA: Merriam-Webster, 2003.

Metzger, Bruce M. *A Textual Commentary on the Greek New Testament*. 2nd ed. Stuttgart: Deutsche Bibelgesellschaft, 1994.

Meyer, Mervin W., editor. *The Ancient Mysteries: A Sourcebook; Sacred Texts of the Mystery Religions of the Ancient Mediterranean World*. 1987. Philadelphia: University of Pennsylvania Press, 1999.

Moule, C. F. D. *An Idiom Book of New Testament Greek*. 2nd ed. Cambridge: Cambridge University Press, 1971.

Moulton, James Hope. *Prolegomena*. 1st ed. A Grammar of New Testament Greek 1. 3rd ed. Edinburgh: T. & T. Clark, 1906.

———. *Prolegomena*. 3rd ed. A Grammar of New Testament Greek 1. Edinburgh: T. & T. Clark, 1908.

Moulton, James Hope, and George Milligan. *The Vocabulary of the Greek Testament*. 1930. Grand Rapids: Eerdmans, 1980.

Moulton, William F., et al., editors. *A Concordance to the Greek New Testament*, edited by I. Howard Marshall. 6th rev. ed. T. & T. Clark, 2002.

Nestle, Eberhard, et al., editors. *Novum Testamentum Graece*. 27th ed. Stuttgart: Bibelgesellschaft, 1993.

NET Bible. *A New English Translation*. 1st ed. Spokane, WA: Biblical Studies Press, 2001. Online: http://www.bible.org/.

Neusner, Jacob, translator. *The Babylonian Talmud: A Translation and Commentary*. 22 vols. Peabody, MA: Hendrickson, 2005.

———, translator. *The Mishnah: A New Translation*. New Haven: Yale University Press, 1988.

Neusner, Jacob, et al., editors. *The Encyclopedia of Judaism*. 4 vols. 2nd ed. Leiden: Brill, 2005.

Neusner, Jacob, and William Scott, editors. *Dictionary of Judaism in the Biblical Period: 450 BCE to 600 CE*. 2 vols. New York: Macmillan, 1996.

Nickelsberg, George W. E., and Michael E. Stone, compilers. *Faith and Piety in Early Judaism: Texts and Documents*. Philadelphia: Fortress, 1983.

Oates, Whitney Jennings, and Eugene O'Neill, editors. *The Complete Greek Drama*. 2 vols. New York: Random House, 1938.

Palmer, Michael. "A Comprehensive Bibliography of Hellenistic Greek Linguistics." Online: http://www.greek-language.com/Palmer-bibiography.html.

Parry, Donald W., and Emanuel Tov, editors. *The Dead Sea Scrolls Reader*. 6 vols. Leiden: Brill, 2004–2005.

Perrin, Bernadette, translator. *Plutarch's Lives,* with an English Translation by Bernadette Perrin.

Vol. 7, *Demosthenes and Cicero. Alexander and Caesar*. 11 vols. Cambridge: Harvard University Press, 1914–1926.

Pietersma, Albert, and Benjamin G. Wright, editors. *A New English Translation of the Septuagint*. New York: Oxford University Press, 2007.

Pilch, John J. *The Cultural Dictionary of the Bible*. Collegeville, MN: Liturgical, 1999.

Pliny the Younger. *Letters*. Translated by William Melmoth. 2 vols. LCL. Cambridge: Harvard University Press, 1915.

Porter, Stanely E., editor. *Dictionary of Biblical Criticism and Interpretation*. London: Routledge, 2007.

Rahlfs, Alfred, editor. *Septuaginta: id est vetus testamentum graece juxta LXX interpretes*. 1935. Revised by Robert Hanhart. 2 vols. in one. Stuttgart: Deutsche Bibelgesellschaft, 2006.

Ramminger, J., creator. *Thesaurus Linguae Latinae*. English version created by Nigel Holmes. Bayerische Akademie. Manfred Flieger, Sec. See online http://www.thesaurus.badw.de/english/index.htm

Rice, David G., and John E. Stambaugh. *Sources for the Study of the Greek Religion*. SSGR 14. Corrected ed. Atlanta: SBL, 2009.

Richardson, Cyril C., editor. *Early Christian Fathers*. LCC 1. New York: Macmillan, 1970.

Robinson, James M., editor. *The Nag Hammadi Library*. Translated by members of the Coptic Gnostic Library Project of the Institute for Antiquity and Christianity. Rev. ed. New York: HarperCollins, 1990.

Robinson, James M., et al., editors. *The Critical Edition of Q: Synopsis, Including the Gospels of Matthew and Luke, Mark and Thomas, with English, German and French Translations of Q and Thomas*. Hermeneia Supplements. Minneapolis: Fortress, 2000.

———, et al., editors. *The Sayings Gospel Q in Greek and English*. Minneapolis: Fortress, 2001.

Robinson, O. F. *The Sources of Roman Law. Problems and Methods for Ancient Historians*. Approaching the Ancient World. London: Routledge, 1997.

Romm, James S., editor. *The Landmark Arrian: The Campaigns of Alexander*. Series editor, Robert B. Strassler. A new translation by Pamela Mensch. Introduction by Paul Cartledge. New York: Random House, 2010.

Roth, Cecil, et al., editors. *Encyclopedia Judaica*. 16 vols. Jerusalem: Keter, 1971–1972.

Rousseau, John J., and Rami Arav, *Jesus and His World: An Archaeological and Cultural Dictionary*. Minneapolis: Fortress, 1995.

Sakenfeld, Katharine Doob, general editor, et al. *The New Interpreter's Dictionary of the Bible*. 5 vols. Nashville: Abingdon, 2006–2009.

Schaps, David. *Handbook for Classical Research*. New York: Routledge, 2010.

Schiffman, Lawrence H., and James C. VanderKam, editors. *Encyclopedia of the Dead Sea Scrolls*. 2 vols. New York: Oxford University Press, 2000.

Schneemelcher, Wilhelm, editor. *New Testament Apocrypha*. Rev. ed. 2 vols. English translation edited by Robert McL. Wilson. London: James Clarke, 1991.

Scholer, David M. *A Basic Bibliographic Guide for New Testament Exegesis*. 2nd ed. Grand Rapids: Eerdmans, 1973.

Seland, Torrey, editor. "Resource Pages for Biblical Studies." Online: http://www.torreys.org/bible/biblia02.html/.

Smallwood, E. Mary, compiler. *Documents Illustrating the Principates of Nerva, Trajan, and Hadrian*. Cambridge: Cambridge University Press, 1966.

Smith, Mahlon H. Synoptic Gospels Primer. See online http://virtualreligion.net/primer/index.html#index.

Sollers, Philippe, and Jean-Edem Hallier, editors. *Tel Quel* [literary journal]. Issues 1–94. Paris: Seuil, 1960–1982.

Sontag, Susan, editor. *A Barthes Reader*. New York: Hill & Wang, 1982.

Sophocles. *The Three Theban Plays: "Antigone," "Oedipus the King," and "Oedipus at Colonus."* Translated by Robert Fagles. New York: Viking, 1982.

Soulen, Richard N., and R. Kendall Soulen, *Handbook of Biblical Criticism*. 3rd ed. Louisville: Westminster John Knox, 2001.

Spicq, Ceslas. *Theological Lexicon of the New Testament*. Translated and edited by James D. Ernest. 3 vols. Peabody, MA: Hendrickson, 1994.

Stanton, Elizabeth Cady. *The Woman's Bible: A Classic Feminist Perspective*. New York: Mineola, NY: Dover, 2002.

State University of New York at Albany. *Guide to Resources in Rabbinic Literature*. Online: http://library.albany.edu/subject/guides/Guide_to_Resources_in_Rabbinic_Literature.html/.

Stegemann, Ekkehard W., and Wolfgang Stegemann. *The Jesus Movement: A Social History of Its First Century*. Translated by O. C. Dean Jr. Minneapolis: Fortress, 1999.

Stoneman, Richard, and Richard Wallace, editors. *Classical Wall Maps*. New York: Routledge, 1989–91.

Strack, Herman L., and Paul Billerbeck. *Kommentar zum Neuen Testament aus Talmud und Midrasch*. 6 vols. Munich: Beck, 1922–28.

Swanson, Reuben J. *The Horizontal Line Synopsis of the Gospels*. Dillsboro, NC: Western North Carolina Press, 1975.

Talbert, Richard J. A., editor, in collaboration with Roger S. Bagnall et al. *The Barrington Atlas of the Greek and Roman World*. Princeton: Princeton University Press, 2000.

Tate, W. Randolph. *Interpreting the Bible: A Handbook of Terms and Methods*. Peabody, MA: Hendrickson, 2006.

Taylor, Bernard A., et al. *Analytical Lexicon to the Septuagint*. Exp. ed. Peabody, MA: Hendrickson, 2009.

Tenney, Merrill C., general editor. *The Zondervan Pictorial Encyclopedia of the Bible*. 5 vols. Grand Rapids: Zondervan, 1975.

Tertullian. *De baptismo liber. Homily on Baptism*. Text edited with an introduction, translation, and commentary by Ernest Evans. London: SPCK, 1964.

Thayer, Joseph Henry, translator and editor. *Thayer's Greek-English Lexicon of the New Testament*. Wheaton, IL: Evangel, 1974.

Throckmorton, Burton H., Jr. *Gospel Parallels: A Comparison of the Synoptic Gospels*. 5th ed. Nashville: Nelson, 1992.

Turner, Nigel. *Style*. A Grammar of New Testament Greek 4, by James Hope Moulton. Edinburgh: T. & T. Clark, 1976.

———. *Syntax*. A Grammar of New Testament Greek 3, by James Hope Moulton. Edinburgh: T. & T. Clark, 1963.

University of California–Irvine. *Thesaurus Linguae Graecae: A Digital Library of Greek Literature*. Web site. Online: http://www.tlg.uci.edu/

Van Voorst, Robert E. *Jesus outside the New Testament: An Introduction to the Ancient Evidence*. Studying the Historical Jesus. Grand Rapids: Eerdmans, 2000.

Vermes, Geza, translator and editor. *The Complete Dead Sea Scrolls in English*. New York: Allen Lane/Penguin, 1997.

Wardman, Alan. *Plutarch's Lives*. Berkeley: University of California Press, 1974.

Ware, James P., *Synopsis of the Pauline Letters in Greek and English*. Grand Rapids: Baker, 2010.

Whiston, William, translator. *The Complete Works of Josephus: Complete and Unabridged*. New Updated Edition of 1736 translation. Peabody, MA: Hendrickson, 1987.

Wilson, Walter T., editor. *Pauline Parallels: A Comprehensive Guide*. Louisville: Westminster John Knox, 2009.

Wise, Michael D., et al. *The Dead Sea Scrolls: A New Translation*. San Francisco: HarperSanFrancisco, 1996.

Wright, Robert B., editor. *The Songs of Solomon: A Critical Edition of the Greek Text*. Jewish and Christian Texts in Contexts and Related Studies 1. New York: T. & T. Clark, 2007.

Ziefle, Helmut. *Modern Theological German: A Reader and Dictionary*. Grand Rapids: Baker, 1997.

COMMENTARIES ON THE NEW TESTAMENT

Aune, David E. *Revelation 1–5*. WBC 52A. Nashville: Nelson, 1997.

———. *Revelation 6–16*. WBC 52B. Nashville: Nelson, 1998.

———. *Revelation 17–22*. WBC 52C. Nashville: Nelson, 1998.

Barrett, C. K. *The Gospel according to St. John: An Introduction with Commentary and notes on the Greek Text*. 2nd ed. London: SPCK, 1978.

Bassler, Jouette M. *1 Timothy, 2 Timothy, Titus*. ANTC. Nashville: Abingdon, 1996.

Bauckham, Richard. *Jude, 2 Peter*. WBC 50. Waco, TX: Word, 1983.

Beale, Gregory K. *The Book of Revelation*. NIGTC. Grand Rapids: Eerdmans, 1999.

Beale, Gregory K., and D. A. Carson, editors. *Commentary on the New Testament Use of the Old Testament*. Grand Rapids: Baker Academic, 2007.

Beasley-Murray, G. R., editor. *The Book of Revelation*. NCB. London: Oliphants, 1974.

Betz, Hans Dieter. *Galatians: A Commentary on Paul's Letter to the Churches in Galatia*. Hermeneia. Philadelphia: Fortress, 1975.

Bird, Michael F. *Colossians and Philemon*. NCCS. Eugene, OR: Cascade Books, 2009.

Bock, Darrell L. *Acts*. Baker Exegetical Commentary on the New Tstament. Grand Rapids: Baker Academic, 2007.

Bockmuehl, Markus. *The Epistle to the Philippians*. BNTC 11. Peabody, MA: Hendrickson, 1998.

Boring, M. Eugene. *1 Peter*. ANTC. Nashville: Abingdon, 1999.

———. *Revelation*. IBC. Louisville: John Knox, 1989.

Bovon, François. *Luke 1: A Commentary on the Gospel of Luke 1:1—9:50*. Translated by Christine M. Thomas. Hermeneia. Minneapolis: Fortress, 2002.

Brown, Raymond E. *The Epistles of John*. AB 30. Garden City, NY: Doubleday, 1982.

———. *The Gospel according to John: Introduction, Translation and Notes*. 2 vols. AB 29, 29A. Garden City, NY: Doubleday, 1966–1970.

———, et al., editors. *The New Jerome Biblical Commentary*. Englewood Cliffs, NJ: Prentice Hall, 1990.

Bruce, F. F. *The Book of the Acts*. Rev. ed. NICNT. Grand Rapids: Eerdmans, 1988.

———. *Epistle to the Galatians: A Commentary on the Greek Text*. NIGTC. Grand Rapids: Eerdmans, 1982.

Buchanan, George Wesley. *To the Hebrews*. AB 36. Garden City, NY: Doubleday, 1972.

Caird, G. B. *A Commentary on the Revelation of St. John the Divine*. HNTC. New York: Harper & Row, 1966.

Carson, D. A. *The Gospel according to John*. The Pillar New Testament Commentary. Leicester, UK: Inter-Varsity, 1991.

Chance, J. Bradley. *Acts*. Smyth and Helwys Bible Commentary. Macon, GA: Smyth & Helwys, 2007.

Charles, R. H. *A Critical and Exegetical Commentary on the Revelation of St. John*. 2 vols. ICC. Edinburgh: T. & T. Clark, 1920.

Ciampa, Roy E., and Brian S. Rosner. *The First Letter to the Corinthians*. PNTC. Grand Rapids: Eerdmans, 2010.

Collins, Adela Yarbro. *Mark: A Commentary*. Hermeneia. Minneapolis: Fortress, 2007.

Collins, Raymond F. *1 and 2 Timothy and Titus*. NTL. Louisville: Westminster John Knox, 2002.

Conzelmann, Hans. *1 Corinthians*. Translated by James W. Leitch. Hermeneia. Philadelphia: Fortress, 1975.

Cousar, Charles B. *Reading Galatians, Philippians, and 1 Thessalonians: A Literary and Theological Commentary*. Reading the New Testament Series. Macon, GA: Smyth & Helwys, 2001.

Danker, Frederick W. *Jesus and the New Age, according to St. Luke*. St. Louis, MO: Clayton, 1972.

Davies, W. D., and Dale C. Allison Jr. *A Critical and Exegetical Commentary on the Gospel according to Saint Matthew*. 3 vols. ICC. Edinburgh: T. & T. Clark, 1997.

Dibelius, Martin, and Hans Conzelmann. *The Pastoral Epistles*. Translated by Philip Buttolph and Adela Yarbro. Hermeneia. Philadelphia: Fortress, 1972.

Dibelius, Martin, and Heinrich Greeven. *James*. Hermeneia. Translated by Michael A. Williams. Philadelphia: Fortress, 1976.

Donelson, Lewis R. *Colossians, Ephesians, 1 and 2 Timothy, and Titus*. Westminster Bible Companion. Louisville: Westminster John Knox, 1996.

Elliott, John H. *1 Peter: A New Translation with Introduction and Commentary*. AB 37B. New York: Doubleday, 2001.

Evans, Craig A. *Mark 8:27—16:20*. WBC 34B; Nashville: Nelson, 2001.

Farrer, Austin. *The Revelation of St. John the Divine: A Commentary on the English Text*. Oxford: Clarendon, 1964.

Ford, J. Massyngberde. *Revelation*. AB 38. Garden City, NY: Doubleday, 1975.

France, R. T. *The Gospel of Mark*. NIGTC. Grand Rapids: Eerdmans, 2002.

Gaventa, Beverly Roberts. *The Acts of the Apostles*. ANTC. Nashville: Abingdon Press, 2003.

Green, Gene L., *The Letters to the Thessalonians*. Pillar New Testament Commentary. Grand Rapids: Eerdmans, 2002.

Green, Joel B. *The Gospel of Luke*. NICNT. Grand Rapids: Eerdmans, 1997.

Guelich, Robert A. *Mark 1—8:26*. WBC 34A. Dallas, TX: Word, 1989.

Haenchen, Ernst. *The Acts of the Apostles*. Translated by Bernard Noble et al. Philadelphia: Westminster, 1971.

Harrington, Wilfrid J. *Revelation*. SP 16. Collegeville, MN: Liturgical, 1993.

Hartin, Patrick J. *James*. SP 14. Collegeville, MN: Liturgical Press, 2004.

Hultgren, Arland J. *Paul's Letter to the Romans: A Commentary*. Grand Rapids: Eerdmans, 2011.

Johnson, Luke T. *Acts of the Apostles*. SP 5. Collegeville, MN: Liturgical, 1992.

———. *Luke*. SP 3. Collegeville: Liturgical, 1991.

Keener, Craig S. *A Commentary on the Gospel of Matthew*. Grand Rapids: Eerdmans, 1999.

———. *The Gospel of John: A Commentary*. 2 vols. Peabody, MA: Hendrickson, 2003.

Koester, Craig R. *Hebrews: A New Translation with Introduction and Commentary*. AB 36. New York: Doubleday, 2001.

Köstenberger, Andreas J. *John*. Baker Exegetical Commentary on the New Testament. Grand Rapids: Baker Academic, 2004.

Kraftchick, Steven J. *Jude, 2 Peter*. ANTC. Nashville: Abingdon, 2002.

Kruse, Colin G. *The Letters of John*. Pillar New Testament Commentary. Grand Rapids: Eerdmans, 2000.

Kysar, Robert. *The Fourth Evangelist and His Gospel: An Examination of Contemporary Scholarship*. Minneapolis: Augsburg, 1975.

Lane, William L. *Commentary on the Gospel of Mark*. NICNT. Grand Rapids: Eerdmans, 1974.

Lohse, Eduard. *Colossians and Philemon*. Translated by William R. Poehlmann and Robert J. Karris. Hermeneia. Philadelphia: Fortress, 1971.

MacDonald, Margaret Y. *Colossians and Ephesians*. SP 17. Collegeville, MN: Liturgical, 2000.

Malina, Bruce J., and John J. Pilch. *Social-Science Commentary on the Book of Acts*. Minneapolis: Fortress, 2008.

———. *Social-Science Commentary on the Book of Revelation*. Minneapolis: Fortress, 2000.

———. *Social-Science Commentary on the Letters of Paul*. Minneapolis: Fortress, 2006.

Malina, Bruce J., and Richard L. Rohrbaugh. *Social Science Commentary on the Synoptic Gospels*. 2nd ed. Minneapolis: Fortress, 2003.

Marcus, Joel. *Mark 1–8: A New Translation with Introduction and Commentary*. AB 27. New York: Doubleday, 2000.

Marshall, I. Howard. *The Gospel of Luke: A Commentary on the Greek Text*. NIGTC. Grand Rapids: Eerdmans, 1978.

Marshall, I. Howard, with Philip H. Towner. *A Critical and Exegetical Commentary on the Pastoral Epistles*. ICC. Edinburgh: T. & T. Clark, 1999.

Martyn, J. Louis. *Galatians: A New Translation with Introduction and Commentary*. AB 33A. New York: Doubleday, 1997.

McKnight, Scot. *The Letter of James*. NICNT. Grand Rapids: Eerdmans, 2011.

Michaels, J. Ramsey. *The Gospel of John*. NICNT. Grand Rapids: Eerdmans, 2010.

Moloney, Francis J. *The Gospel of John*. SP 4. Rev. ed. Collegeville, MN: Liturgical, 2005.

Moo, Douglas J. *The Epistle to the Romans.* NICNT. Grand Rapids: Eerdmans, 1996.

———. *The Letter of James.* Pillar New Testament Commentary. Grand Rapids: Eerdmans, 2000.

Mounce, Robert H. *The Book of Revelation.* NICNT 17. Grand Rapids: Eerdmans, 1977.

Nolland, John. *Luke 1—9:20.* WBC 35A. Dallas: Word, 1989

———. *Matthew.* NIGTC. Grand Rapids: Eerdmans, 2005.

O'Brien, Peter T. *The Letter to the Hebrews.* Pillar New Testament Commentary. Grand Rapids: Eerdmans, 2010.

Osiek, Carolyn. *The Shepherd of Hermas: A Commentary.* Hermeneia. Minneapolis: Fortress, 1999.

Parsons, Mikeal C. *Acts.* Paideia. Grand Rapids: Baker Academic, 2008.

Pervo, Richard I. *Acts: A Commentary.* Hermeneia. Minneapolis: Fortress, 2008.

Peterson, David G. *The Acts of the Apostles.* Pillar New Testament Commentary. Grand Rapids: Eerdmans, 2009.

Pokorný, Petr. *Colossians: A Commentary.* Translated by Siegfried S. Schatzmann. Peabody, MA: Hendrickson, 1991.

Reese, Ruth Ann. *2 Peter and Jude.* Two Horizons New Testament Commentary. Grand Rapids: Eerdmans, 2007.

Richard, Earl J. *First and Second Thessalonians.* SP 11. Collegeville, MN: Liturgical, 1995.

———. *Reading 1 Peter, Jude, and 2 Peter: A Literary and Theological Commentary.* Reding the New Testament Series. Macon, GA: Smyth and Helwys, 2000.

Schnackenburg, Rudolf. *The Gospel according to St. John.* Vol. 1. Translated by Kevin Smyth. Edited by J. Massingberde Ford and Kevin Smyth. Herder's Theological Library. New York: Herder & Herder, 1968.

———. *The Gospel according to St. John.* Vol. 2. New York: Seabury, 1980.

———. *The Gospel according to St. John.* Vol. 3. New York: Crossroad, 1982.

Selwyn, Edward Gordon. *The First Epistle of St. Peter.* London: Macmillan, 1946.

Smith, D. Moody. *First, Second, and Third John.* IBC. Louisville: John Knox, 1991.

Stock, Augustine. *Call to Discipleship: A Literary Study of Mark's Gospel.* Good News Studies 1. Wilmington, DE: Glazier, 1982.

Sumney, Jerry L. *Colossians: A Commentary.* NTL. Louisville: Westminster John Knox, 2008.

Swete, H. B. *The Apocalypse of St. John.* London: Macmillan, 1907.

Talbert, Charles H. *The Apocalypse: A Reading of the Revelation of John.* Louisville: Westminster John Knox, 1994.

———. *Ephesians and Colossians.* Paideia. Grand Rapids: Baker Academic, 2007.

———. *Reading Acts: A Literary and Theological Commentary on the Acts of the Apostles.* Rev. ed. Reading the New Testament Series. Macon, GA: Smyth & Helwys, 2005.

———. *Reading Corinthians: A Literary and Theological Commentary on 1 and 2 Corinthians.* Rev. ed. Reading the New Testament Series. Macon, GA: Smyth & Helwys, 2002.

———. *Reading Luke: A Literary and Theological Commentary.* Rev. ed. Reading the New Testament Series. Macon, GA: Smyth & Helwys, 2005.

Thiselton, Anthony C. *The First Epistle to the Corinthians.* NIGTC. Grand Rapids: Eerdmans, 2000.

Tiede, David L. *Luke.* Augsburg Commentary on the New Testament. Minneapolis: Fortress, 1988.

Torrey, Charles Cutler. *The Apocalypse of John.* New Haven: Yale University Press, 1958.

van der Waal, C. *Openbaring van Jezus Christus. Inleiding en Vertaling.* Groningen: de Vuubaak, 1971.

von Wahlde, Urban C. *The Gospel and Letters of John.* 3 vols. ECC. Grand Rapids: Eerdmans, 2010–11.

Williams, Sam K. *Galatians.* ANTC. Nashville: Abingdon, 1997.

Witherington, Ben, III. *The Acts of the Apostles: A Socio-Rhetorical Commentary.* Grand Rapids: Eerdmans, 1997.

———. *Grace in Galatia: A Commentary on St. Paul's Letter to the Galatians.* Grand Rapids: Eerdmans, 1998.

———. *Letters and Homilies for Jewish Christians: A Socio-Rhetorical Commentary on Hebrews, James and Jude.* Downers Grove, IL: IVP Academic, 2007.

ESSAYS, MONOGRAPHS, AND RELATED WORKS

Adam, A. K. M., editor. *Postmodern Interpretations of the Bible: A Reader.* St. Louis: Chalice, 2001.

———. *What Is Postmodern Biblical Criticism?* GBS. Minneapolis: Fortress, 1995

Adrados, Francisco Rodríguez. *A History of the Greek Language: From its Origins to the Present.* Translated by Francisca Rojas del Canto. Leiden: Brill, 2005.

Aland, Kurt, and Barbara Aland. *The Text of the New Testament: An Introduction to the Critical Editions and to the Theory and Practice of Modern Textual Criticism.* Translated by Erroll F. Rhodes. 2nd ed. Grand Rapids: Eerdmans, 1989.

Alexander, Loveday C. A. "Acts and Ancient Intellectual Biography." In *The Book of Acts in Its Ancient Literary Setting*, edited by Bruce W, Winter and Andrew D. Clarke, 31–64. The Book of Acts in Its First-Century Setting 1. Grand Rapids: Eerdmans, 1993.

———. *Acts in Its Ancient Literary Context: A Classicist Looks at the Acts of the Apostles.* Early Christianity in Context. Library of New Testament Studies 289. London: T. & T. Clark, 2005.

———, editor. *Images of Empire.* JSOTSup 122. Sheffield: JSOT Press, 1991.

———. *The Preface to Luke's Gospel: Literary Convention and Social Context in Luke 1:1–4 and Acts 1:1.* SNTSMS 78. Cambridge: Cambridge University Press, 1993.

Alexander, Philip S. "The Parting of the Ways from the Perspective of Rabbinic Judaism." In *Jews and Christians: The Parting of the Ways, AD 70 to 135*, edited by James D. G. Dunn, 1–25. WUNT 66. Tübingen: Mohr/Siebeck, 1992.

Algra, Keimpe, et al., editors. *Cambridge History of Hellenistic Philosophy.* Cambridge: Cambridge University Press, 1999.

Allison, Dale C. "The Historian's Jesus and the Church." In *Seeking the Identity of Jesus: A Pilgrimage*, edited by Beverly Roberts Gaventa and Richard B. Hays, 79–95. Grand Rapids: Eerdmans, 2009.

———. *The Historical Christ and the Theological Jesus.* Grand Rapids: Eerdmans, 2009.

———. *Jesus of Nazareth: Millenarian Prophet.* Minneapolis: Fortress, 1998.

———. "The Pauline Epistles and the Synoptic Gospels: The Pattern of the Parallels." *NTS* 28 (1982) 1–32.

———. *Scriptural Allusions in the New Testament: Light from the Dead Sea Scrolls.* The Dead Sea Scrolls and Christian Origins Library 5. North Richland Hills, TX: BIBAL, 2000.

———. "Was There a 'Lukan Community'?" *IBS* 10 (1988) 62–70.

Alter, Robert. *The Art of Biblical Narrative.* New York: Basic, 1981.

Anderson, Bernhard W. "God, OT View of." In *IDB* 2:427–28.

Arnold, Clinton E. *The Colossian Syncretism: The Interface between Christianity and Folk Belief at Colossae.* WUNT 2/77 Tübingen: Mohr/Siebeck, 1995.

Attridge, Harold W. *The Interpretation of Biblical History in the "Antiquiates Judaicae" of Flavius Josephus.* Harvard Dissertations in Religion 7. Missoula, MT: Scholars, 1976.

Auerbach, Eric. *Mimesis: The Representation of Reality in Western Literature.* Translated by Willard R. Task. 50th anniversary ed. Princeton: Princeton University Press, 2003.

Aulen, Gustav. *Jesus in Contemporary Historical Research.* Translated by Ingalill H. Hjelm. Philadelphia: Fortress, 1976.

Aune, David E. "The Apocalypse of John and the Problem of Genre." *Semeia* 36 (1986) 65–96.

———. *Apocalypticism, Prophecy, and Magic in Early Christianity: Collected Essays.* Grand Rapids: Baker Academic, 2008.

———. *Greco-Roman Literature and the New Testament.* SBLSBS 21. Atlanta: Scholars, 1988

———. "Magic in Early Christianity." In *ANRW* II.23.2 (1980) 1507–57.

———. *Prophecy in Early Christianity and the Ancient Mediterranean World.* Grand Rapids: Eerdmans, 1983.

———, editor. *Studies in New Testament and Early Christian Literature: Essays in Honor of Allen P. Wilkgren.* NovTSup 33. Leiden: Brill, 1972.

Austin, M. M. *The Hellenistic World from Alexander to the Roman Conquest: A Selection of Ancient Sources in Translation.* 2nd ed. Cambridge: Cambridge University Press, 2006.

Avi-Yonah, Michael, and Zvi Baras, editors. *Society and Religion in the Second Temple Period.* World History of the Jewish People: Ancient Times, 1st ser. 8. Jerusalem: Jewish History Publications, 1977.

Bailey, James L., and Lyle D. Vander Broek. *Literary Forms in the New Testament.* Louisville, Westminster John Knox, 1992.

Bailey, John A. "Who Wrote II Thessalonians?" *NTS* 25 (1979) 131–45.

Bailey, Kenneth E. "Informed Controlled Oral Tradition and the Synoptic Gospels." *Themelios* 20 (1995) 4–11.

———. *Jacob and the Prodigal: How Jesus Retold Israel's Story*. Downers Grove, IL: InterVarsity, 2003.

———. *Poet and Peasant; and, Through Peasant Eyes: A Literary-Cultural Approach to the Parables in Luke*. Combined ed. Grand Rapids: Eerdmans, 1983.

Baird, William. *The History of New Testament Research*. Vol.1, *From Deism to Tübingen*. Minneapolis: Fortress, 1992.

———. *The History of New Testament Research*. Vol. 2, *From Jonathan Edwards to Rudolf Bultmann*. Minneapolis: Fortress, 2003.

Balch, David L. *Let Wives Be Submissive: The Domestic Code in 1 Peter*. SBLMS 26. Chico,: Scholars, 1981.

Balch, David L., and Carolyn Osiek, editors. *Early Christian Families in Context: An Interdisciplinary Dialogue*. Religion, Marriage, and Family. Grand Rapids: Erdmans, 2003.

Balsdon, J. P. V. D. "The Principates of Tiberius and Gaius." In *ANRW* II.2 (1975) 86–94.

Balthasar, Hans Urs von. *Theo-Drama: Theological Dramatic Theory*. Vol. 1, *Prolegomena*. Translated by Graham Harrison. San Francisco: Ignatius, 1988.

———. *Theo-Drama: Theological Dramatic Theory*. Vol. 2, *The Dramatis Personae: Man in God*. Translated by Graham Harrison. San Francisco: Ignatius, 1990.

———. *Theo-Drama: Theological Dramatic Theory*. Vol. 3, *The Dramatis Personae: The Person in Christ*. Translated by Graham Harrison. San Francisco: Ignatius, 1992.

———. *Theo-Drama: Theological Dramatic Theory*. Vol. 4, *The Action*. Translated by Graham Harrison. San Francisco: Ignatius, 1994.

Baltzer, Klaus. *Die Biographie der Propheten*. Neukirchen-Vluyn : Neukirchener, 1975.

Bammel, Ernst, and C. F. D. Moule, editors. *Jesus and the Politics of His Day*. Cambridge: Cambridge University Press, 1984.

Barker, Kenneth L., editor. *The NIV: The Making of a Contemporary Translation*. Grand Rapids: Academie, 1986.

Bar-Kochva, Bezalel. *The Image of the Jews in Greek Literature: The Hellenistic Period*. Hellenistic Culture and Society 51. Berkeley: University of California Press, 2009.

Barr, David L. "The Apocalypse of John in the Light of Modern Narrative Theory." In *1900th Anniversary of St. John's Apokalypse: Proceedings of the International and Interdisciplinary Symposium*, 259–71 Athens: Holy Monastery of St. John, 1999.

———. *Tales of the End: A Narrative Commentary on the Book of Revelation*. The Storytellers Bible 1. Santa Rosa, CA: Polebridge, 1998.

Barr, David L, and Wentling, Judith L. "The Conventions of Classical Biography and the Genre of Luke-Acts: A Preliminary Study" pp. 63–88 in Charles H. Talbert, ed. *Luke-Acts: New Perspectives from the Society of Biblical Literature Seminar*. New York: Crossroad, 1984.

Barr, James. "Abba Isn't Daddy." *JTS* 39 (1988) 28–47.

———. *Biblical Words for Time*. 2nd, rev. ed. Studies in Biblical Theology, 1st ser. 33. Naperville, IL: Allenson, 1969.

Bartchy, S. Scott. "*MALLON CHRESAI: First Century Slavery and the Interpretation of 1 Corinthians 7:21*. SBLDS 11. Missoula, MT: Scholars Press, 1973, 1985. Repr. *First-Century Slavery and the Interpretation of 1 Corinthians 7:21*. Eugene, OR: Wipf & Stock, 2003.

Barthes, Roland. *The Pleasures of the Text*. Translated by Richard Miller. New York: Hill & Wang, 1975.

Bartlett, John R., editor. *Jews in the Hellenistic and Roman Cities*. London: Routledge, 2002.

———. *Jews in the Hellenistic World*. Cambridge Commentaries on Writings of the Jewish and Christian World 1, part 1. Cambridge: Cambridge University Press, 1985.

Barton, John. *The Oracles of God: Perceptions of Ancient Prophecy in Israel after the Exile*. New York: Oxford University Press, 1988.

———. *The Oracles of God: Perceptions of Ancient Prophecy in Israel after the Exile*. New ed. Oxford: Oxford University Press, 2007.

Barton, Stephen C. "Can We Identify the Gospel Audiences?" In *The Gospels for All Christians: Rethinking the Gospel Audiences*, edited by Richard Bauckham, 173–94. Grand Rapids: Eerdmans, 1998 .

———. "The Communal Dimensions of Earliest Christianity." *JTS* 43 (1992) 399–427.

Bauckham, Richard, editor. *The Book of Acts in Its Palestinian Setting*. The Book of Acts in Its First-Century Setting 4. Grand Rapids: Eerdmans, 1995.

———. *The Climax of Prophecy: Studies on the Book of Revelation*. Edinburgh: T. & T. Clark, 1993.

———, editor. *The Gospels for All Christians: Rethinking the Gospel Audiences*. Grand Rapids: Eerdmans, 1998.

———. "James and the Jerusalem Community." In *Jewish Believers in Jesus: The Early Centuries*, edited by Oskar Skarsaune and Reidar Hvalvik, 55–95. Peabody, MA: Hendrickson, 2007.

———. *Jesus and the Eyewitnesses: The Gospels as Eyewitness Testimony*. Grand Rapids: Eerdmans, 2006.

———. *The Testimony of the Beloved Disciple: Narrative, History, and Theology in the Gospel of John*. Grand Rapids: Baker Academic, 2007.

———. *The Theology of the Book of Revelation*. New Testament Theology. Cambridge: Cambridge University Press, 1993.

Bauer, David R. "Chiasm." In *NIDB*, 1:587–88.

Bauer, Walter. *Orthodoxy and Heresy in Earliest Christianity*. Translated by a team from the Philadelphia Seminar on Christian Origins. Edited by Robert A. Kraft and Gerhard Krodel. Philadelphia: Fortress, 1971.

———. *Rechtgläubigkeit and Ketzerei im ältesten Christentum*. 1934. BHT 10. Tübingen: Mohr/Siebeck, 1964.

Baumgarten, Albert I. *The Flourishing of Jewish Sects in the Maccabean Era: An Interpretation*. JSJSup 55. Leiden: Brill, 1997.

Baur, Ferdinand Christian. *The Church History of the First Three Centuries*. 2 vols. Translated by Allan Menzies. 3rd ed. Theological Translation Fund Library 16 and 20. Edinburgh: Williams & Norgate, 1878–1879.

Beale, G. K. "The Influence of Daniel upon the Structure and Theology of John's Apocalypse." *JETS* 27 (1984) 413–23.

———. *The Use of Daniel in Jewish Apocalyptic and in the Revelation of St. John*. Lanham, MD: University Press of America, 1984.

———. "The Use of the Old Testament in Revelation." In *It Is Written: Scripture Citing Scripture; Essays in Honor of Barnabas Lindars, SSF*, edited by D. A. Carson and H. G. M. Williamson, 318–36. Cambridge: Cambridge University Press, 1988.

Beardslee, William A. *Literary Criticism of the New Testament*. GBS. Philadelphia: Fortress, 1970.

Beasley-Murray, G. R. *Baptism in the New Testament*. 1962. Grand Rapids: Eerdmans, 1973.

Beck, Roger. *A Brief History of Ancient Astrology*. Brief Histories of the Ancient World. Malden, MA: Blackwell, 2007.

———. *The Religion of the Mithras Cult in the Roman Empire: Mysteries of the Unconquered Sun*. Oxford: Oxford University Press, 2006.

Becker, Jürgen, editor. *Christian Beginnings: Word and Community from Jesus to Post-Apostolic Times*. Translated by Annemarie S. Kidder and Reinhard Krauss. Louisville: Westminster John Knox, 1993.

———. *Jesus of Nazareth*. Translated by James E. Crouch. New York: de Gruyter, 1998.

Bell, Albert. *A Guide to the New Testament World*. Scottdale, PA: Herald, 1994.

Ben-Dov, Meir. "Temple of Herod." In *IDBSup*, 870–72

Ben-Sasson, Hayim H., ed. *A History of the Jewish People*. Cambridge: Harvard University Press, 1976

Berger, Klaus, "Hellenistische Gattungen im Neuen Testament." In *ANRW* II.25.2 (1984) 1231–45.

Berger, Peter L., and Thomas Luckmann. *The Social Construction of Reality: A Treatise in the Sociology of Knowledge*. Garden City, NY: Doubleday, 1966.

Bevan, Edwyn. "Hellenistic Popular Philosophy." In *The Hellenistic Age: Aspects of Hellenistic Civilization*, edited by J. B. Bury et al., 79–107. Cambridge: Cambridge University Press, 1925.

Bickerman, E. J. *The God of the Maccabees: Studies on the Meaning and Origin of the Maccabean Revolt*. Studies in Judaism in Late Antiquity 32. Leiden: Brill, 1979.

Bilezikian, Gilbert G. "The Gospel of Mark and Greek Tragedy." *Gordon Review* 5 (1959) 79–86.

———. *The Liberated Gospel: A Comparison of the Gospel of Mark and Greek Tragedy*. Baker Biblical Monograph. Grand Rapids: Baker, 1977.

Billows, Richard A. *Julius Caesar: The Colossus of Rome*. New York: Routledge, 2008.

Black, C. Clifton. "Rhetorical Criticism." Pages 166–88 in Joel Green, ed., *Hearing the New Testament*. 2nd ed. Grand Rapids: Eerdmans, 2010.

Black, David Alan. *New Testament Textual Criticism: A Concise Guide*. Grand Rapids: Baker, 1994.

———, editor. *Rethinking New Testament Textual Criticism*. New Testament Studies. Grand Rapids: Baker Academic, 2002.

Black, David Alan, and David R. Beck, editors. *Rethinking the Synoptic Problem*. Grand Rapids: Baker Academic, 2001.

Black, Matthew. *An Aramaic Approach to the Gospels and Acts.* 3rd ed. Peabody, MA: Hendrickson, 1998.

Blenkinsopp, Joseph. "The Age of Exile." In *The Biblical World,* edited by John Barton, 1:416–39. London: Routledge, 2002.

———. *Judaism, the First Phase: The Place of Ezra and Nehemiah in the Origins of Judaism.* Grand Rapids: Eerdmans, 2009.

Blevins, James L. "Genre of Revelation." *RevExp* 77 (1980) 393–408.

Blomberg, Craig L. *The Historical Reliability of the Gospels.* 2nd ed. Downers Grove, IL: InterVarsity Academic, 2007.

———. *Interpreting the Parables.* Downers Grove, IL: InterVarsity, 1990.

Bloom, Harold, editor. *The Revelation of St. John the Divine.* Modern Critical Interpretations. New York: Chelsea House, 1988.

Blount, Brian K. *Cultural Interpretation: Reorienting New Testament Criticism.* Minneapolis: Fortress, 1995.

Bluhm, Heinz Siegfried. *Martin Luther, Creative Translator.* St. Louis: Concorida, 1965.

———. "Martin Luther as Creative Bible Translator." *AUSS* 22 (1984) 35–44.

Bock, Darrell L. *Studying the Historical Jesus: A Guide to Sources and Methods.* Grand Rapids: Baker Academic, 2002.

Bockmuehl, Markus N. A., editor. *The Cambridge Companion to Jesus.* Cambridge Companions to Religion. Cambridge: Cambridge University Press, 2001.

———. *Jewish Law in Gentile Churches: Halakhah and the Beginning of Christian Public Ethics.* Edinburgh: T. & T. Clark, 2000.

———. *This Jesus: Martyr, Lord, Messiah.* Edinburgh: T. & T. Clark, 1994.

Bockmuehl, Markus N. A., and Donald A. Hagner, editors. *The Written Gospel.* Cambridge: Cambridge University Press, 2005.

Boman, Thorleif. *Hebrew Thought Compared with Greek.* The Library of History and Doctrine. Philadelphia: Westminster, 1960.

Bonhoeffer, Dietrich. *Discipleship.* Translated by Martin Kuske and Ilse Tödt. Edited by Geffrey B. Kelly and John D. Godsey. Dietrich Bonhoeffer Works 4. Minneapolis: Fortress, 2000.

———. *Life Together; Prayerbook of the Bible.* Translated by Daniel W. Bloesch and James H. Burtness. Edited by Geffrey B. Kelly. Dietrich Bonhoeffer Works 5. Minneapolis: Fortress, 1996.

Booth, Wayne C. *The Rhetoric of Fiction.* Chicago: University of Chicago Press, 1961.

Borg, Marcus J. *Conflict, Holiness and Politics in the Teaching of Jesus.* Studies in the Bible and early Christianity 5. New York: Mellen, 1984.

———. "The Currency of the Term 'Zealot.'" *JTS* 22 (1971) 504–12.

———. *Jesus, the New Vision: The Spirit, Culture, and the Life of Discipleship.* San Francisco: Harper & Row, 1987.

———. *Meeting Jesus Again for the First Time: The Historical Jesus and the Heart of Contemporary Faith.* San Francisco: HarperSanFrancisco, 1994.

———. "A Temperate Case for an Non-Eschatological Jesus." *Forum* 2,3 (1986) 83–103.

Bornkamm, Gunther. *Jesus of Nazareth.* Translated by Irene and Fraser McLuskey with James M. Robinson. New York: Harper, 1960.

——— et al. *Tradition and Interpretation in Matthew.* Translated by Percy Scott. NTL. Philadelphia: Westminster, 1963.

Borsch, Frederick H. *Many Things in Parables: Extravagant Stories of New Community.* Philadelphia: Fortress, 1988.

Botha, P. J. J. "The Historical Domitian—Illustrating Some Problems of Historiography." *Neot* 23 (1989) 45–59.

Bousset, Wilhelm. *Kyrios Christos: A History of the Belief in Christ from the Beginnings of Christianity to Irenaeus.* Translated by John Steely. Nashville: Abingdon, 1970.

Bovon, François. *New Testament Traditions and Apocryphal Narratives.* Translated by Jane Haapiseva-Hunter. PTMS 36. Allison Park, PA: Pickwick Publications, 1995.

———. *Studies in Early Christianity.* WUNT 161. Tübingen: Mohr/Siebeck, 2003.

———. *Studies in Early Christianity.* Grand Rapids: Baker Academic, 2005.

Bowman, John Wick. *The First Christian Drama: The Book of Revelation.* Philadelphia: Westminster, 1955.

———. "Revelation, Book of." In *IDB* 4:58–70.

———. "Revelation: Its Dramatic Structure." *Int* 9 (1955) 436–53.

———. *Which Jesus?* Philadelphia: Westminster, 1970.

Boyarin, Daniel. "The *Ioudaioi* in John and the Pre-History of Judaism." In *Pauline Conversations in Context: Essays in Honour of Calvin J. Roetzel.* edited by Janice Capel Anderson, et al., 216–39. JSNTSup 221. Sheffield: Sheffield Academic, 2002.

———. *A Radical Jew: Paul and the Politics of Identity*. Contraversions 1. Berkeley: University of California Press, 1994.

Bradley, Keith. *Slavery and Society at Rome*. Key Themes in Ancient History. Cambridge: Cambridge University Press, 1994.

Brakke, David. "Canon Formation and Social Conflict in Fourth-Century Egypt: Athanasius of Alexandria's Thirty-Ninth Festal Letter." *HTR* 87 (1994) 395–419.

Brant, Jo-Ann A. *Dialogue and Drama: Elements of Greek Tragedy in the Fourth Gospel*. Peabody, MA: Hendrickson, 2004.

Braun, Herbert. *Jesus of Nazareth. The Man and His Time*. Translated by Everett R. Kalin. Philadelphia: Fortress, 1979.

Braxton, Brad Ronnell. *No Longer Slaves: Galatians and the African American Experience*. Collegeville, MN: Liturgical, 2002.

Breck, John. *The Shape of Biblical Language: Chiasmus in the Scriptures and Beyond*. Crestwood, NY: St. Vladimir's Seminary Press, 1994.

Brewer, R. R. "Influence of Greek Drama on Apocalypse of John." *ATR* 18 (1936) 74–92.

Bright, John. *A History of Israel*. 4th ed. Westminster Aids to the Study of the Scriptures. Louisville: Westminster John Knox, 2000.

Brodie, Thomas L. *The Quest for the Origin of John's Gospel: A Source-Oriented Approach*. New York: Oxford University Press, 1993.

Brooke, George J. *The Dead Scrolls and the New Testament*. Minneapolis: Fortress, 2005.

Brown, John Pairman. *Ancient Israel and Ancient Greece: Religion, Politics, and Culture*. Minneapolis: Fortress, 2003.

Brown, Raymond E. *The Community of the Beloved Disciple*. New York: Paulist, 1979.

———. *An Introduction to the New Testament*. ABRL. New York: Doubleday, 1997.

———. "Not Jewish Christianity and Gentile Christianity but Types of Jewish/Gentile Christianity." *CBQ* 45 (1983) 74–79.

Brown, Raymond E., and John P. Meier, *Antioch and Rome: New Testament Cradles of Catholic Christianity*. New York: Paulist, 1983.

Bruce, F. F. *The English Bible: A History of Translations from the Earliest English Versions to the New English Bible*. New York: Oxford University Press, 1970.

———. "The History of New Testament Study." In *New Testament Interpretation: Essays on Principles and Methods*, edited by I. Howard Marshall, 21–59. Grand Rapids: Eerdmans, 1977.

———. "Transmission and Translation of the Bible." In *The Expositor's Bible Commentary*, edited by Frank E. Gaebelein, 1:39–57. Grand Rapids: Zondervan, 1979.

Buechler, Adolf. *Types of Jewish-Palestinian Piety from 70 BCE to 70 CE*. Jews' College Publications 8. London: Oxford University Press, 1922.

Bultmann, Rudolf. *Die Geschichte der synoptischen Tradition*. FRLANT 12. Göttingen: Vandenhoeck & Ruprecht, 1921.

———. *The History of the Synoptic Tradition*. Translated by John Marsh. New York: Harper & Row, 1963.

———. *The History of the Synoptic Tradition*. Translated by John Marsh. Rev. ed. New York: Harper & Row, 1976.

———. *The History of the Synoptic Tradition*. Translated by John Marsh. Rev. ed. Peabody, MA: Hendrickson, 1994.

———. *Jesus and the Word*. Translated by Louise Pettibone Smith and Ermine Huntress Lantero. Student's ed. New York: Scribner, 1958.

———. *Primitive Christianity in Its Contemporary Setting*. Translated by R. H. Fuller. London: Thames & Hudson, 1956.

Burch, Ernest W. "Tragic Action in the Second Gospel." *JR* 11 (1931) 346–58.

Burns, Jasper. *Great Women of Imperial Rome: Mothers and Wives of the Caesars*. London: Routledge, 2007.

Burridge, Richard A. *Four Gospels, One Jesus? A Symbolic Reading*. Grand Rapids: Eerdmans, 1994.

———. *Imitating Jesus: An Inclusive Approach to New Testament Ethics*. Grand Rapids: Eerdmans, 2007.

———. *What Are the Gospels?: A Comparison with Graeco-Roman Biography*. SNTSMS 70. Cambridge University Press, 1992.

———. *What Are the Gospels? A Comparison with Graeco-Roman Biography*. 2nd rev. ed. Grand Rapids: Eerdmans, 2004.

Burtchaell, James Tunstead. *From Synagogue to Church: Public Services and Offices of the Earliest Christian Communities*. Cambridge: Cambridge University Press, 1992.

Buss, Martin J. *Biblical Form Criticism in Its Context*. JSOTSup 274. Sheffield: Sheffield Academic, 1999.

Cadbury, Henry J. "The Greek and Jewish Traditions of Writing History." In *The*

Beginnings of Christianity, Part 1, edited by F. J. Foakes-Jackson and Kirsopp Lake, 7–29. Acts of the Apostles 2. Grand Rapids: Baker, 1979.

———. *The Making of Luke-Acts*. 1927. Reprinted, London: SPCK, 1968.

Caird, G. B. *The Language and Imagery of the Bible*. Philadelphia: Westminster, 1980.

Campbell, Constantine R. *Basics of Verbal Aspect in Biblical Greek*. Grand Rapids: Zondervan, 2008.

Campbell, Joseph. *The Hero with a Thousand Faces*. 2nd ed. Bollingen Series 47. Princeton: Princeton University Press, 1968.

Campenhausen, Hans von. *The Formation of the Christian Bible*. Translated by J. A. Baker. Philadelphia: Fortress, 1972.

Canfora, Luciano. *The Vanished Library*. Hellenistic Culture and Society 7. Berkeley: University of California Press, 1990.

Cannon, George E. *The Use of Traditional Materials in Colossians: Their Significance for the Problems of Authenticity*. Macon, GA: Mercer University Press, 1983.

Cansdale, Lena. *Qumran and the Essenes: A Re-evaluation of the Evidence*. TSAJ 60. Tübingen: Mohr/Siebeck, 1997.

Capes, David. B., et al., editors. *Israel's God and Rebecca's Children: Christology and Community in Early Judaism and Christianity*. Waco, TX: Baylor University Press, 2008.

Carey, Greg. *Ultimate Things: An Introduction to Jewish and Christian Apocalyptic Literature*. St. Louis, MO: Chalice, 2005.

Carney, Elizabeth. *Olympias: Mother of Alexander the Great*. Women of the Ancient World. New York: Routledge, 2006.

Carroll, John T. *Response to the End of History: Eschatology and Situation in Luke-Acts*. SBLDS 92. Atlanta: Scholars, 1988.

———, editor. *The Return of Jesus in Early Christianity*. Peabody, MA: Hendrickson, 2000.

Carter, Warren. *Households and Discipleship: A Study of Matthew 19–20*. JSNTSup 103. Sheffield: JSOT, 1994.

———. *John: Storyteller, Interpreter, Evangelist*. Peabody, MA: Hendrickson, 2006.

Casey, Maurice. *An Aramaic Approach to Q: Sources for the Gospels of Matthew and Luke*. SNTSMS 122. Cambridge: Cambridge University Press, 2002.

Casson, Lionel. *Everyday Life in Ancient Rome*. Rev. and expanded ed. Baltimore: Johns Hopkins University Press, 1999.

———. *Libraries in the Ancient World*. New Haven: Yale University Press, 2001.

Chance, J. Bradley. *Jerusalem, the Temple, and the New Age in Luke-Acts*. Macon, GA: Mercer University Press, 1988.

Charlesworth, James H. "The Concept of the Messiah in the Pseudepigrapha." In *ANRW* II.19.1 (1979) 188–218.

———. "From Messianology to Christology." In *The Messiah*, 3–35.

———. "A History of Pseudepigrapha Research: The Re-Emerging Importance of the Pseudepigrapha." In *ANRW* II.19.1 (1979) 54–88.

———, editor. *Jesus and the Dead Sea Scrolls*. New York: Doubleday, 1992.

———, editor. *The Messiah: Developments in Earliest Judaism and Christianity*. Minneapolis: Fortress, 1992.

Charlesworth, James H., et al., editors. *Qumran-Messianism: Studies in the Messianic Expectations in the Dead Sea Scrolls*. Tübingen: Mohr/Siebeck, 1998.

Charlesworth, James H., and Peter Pokorný, editors. *Jesus Research: An International Perspective*. Princeton-Prague Symposia Series on the Historical Jesus 1. Grand Rapids: Eerdmans, 2009.

Charlesworth, M. P. *The Roman Empire*. New York: Oxford University Press, 1967.

Chatman, Seymour. *Story and Discourse: Narrative Structure in Fiction and Film*. Ithaca, NY: Cornell University Press, 1978.

Chilton, Bruce D. *God in Strength: Jesus' Announcement of the Kingdom*. 1979. Reprinted, Sheffield, UK: JSOT Press, 1987.

———, editor. *The Kingdom of God in the Teaching of Jesus*. IRT 5. Minneapolis: Fortress, 1984.

———. "The Kingdom of God in Recent Discussion." In *Studying the Historical Jesus: Evaluations of the State of Current Research*, edited by Bruce Chilton and Craig A. Evans, 255–80. NTTS 19. Leiden: Brill, 1994.

———. *Rabbi Jesus: An Intimate Biography*. New York: Doubleday, 2000.

———. "Regnum Dei Deus Est." In *The Historical Jesus in Recent Research*, edited by James D. G. Dunn and Scot McKnight, 115–22. Sources for Biblical and Theological Study. Winona Lake, IN: Eisenbrauns, 2005.

Chilton, Bruce D., and Craig A. Evans, editors. *Authenticating the Activities of Jesus.* NTTS 28.2 Leiden: Brill, 1999.

———. *Studying the Historical Jesus: Evaluations of the State of Current Research.* NTTS 19. Leiden: Brill 1994.

Chilton, Bruce D., and Jacob Neusner. *Judaism in the New Testament: Practices and Beliefs.* London: Routledge, 1995.

Christidis, A.-F., editor. *A History of Ancient Greek: From the Beginnings to Late Antiquity.* Cambridge: Cambridge University Press, 2007.

Clark, Gordon H. *Selections from Hellenistic Philosophy.* New York: Crofts, 1940.

Clifford, Catherin E., translator. *"One Teacher": Doctrinal Authority in the Church,* by Le Groupe des Dombes. Grand Rapids: Eerdmans, 2010.

Clinton, Kevin. *Myth and Cult: The Iconography of the Eleusinian Mysteries.* Stockholm: Paul Astroms, 1992.

Cohen, Shaye J. D. *From the Maccabees to the Mishnah.* LEC 7. Louisville: Westminster John Knox, 1987.

———. "The Significance of Yavneh: Pharisees, Rabbis, and the End of Jewish Sectarianism." *HUCA* 55 (1984) 27–53.

Cohick, Lynn H. *Women in the World of the Earliest Christians: Illuminating Ancient Ways of Life.* Grand Rapids: Baker Academic, 2009.

Coleman, Kathleen M. "The Emperor Domitian and Literature." In *ANRW* II.32.5 (1986) 3087–115.

Coleman, Roger. *New Light and Truth: The Making of the Revised English Bible.* Oxford: Oxford University Press, 1989.

Collins, Adela Yarbro. *The Combat Myth in the Book of Revelation.* Harvard Dissertations in Religion 7. Missoula: Scholars, 1976.

———. *Cosmology and Eschatology in Jewish and Christian Apocalypticism.* JSJSup 50. Leiden: Brill, 1996.

———. *Crisis and Catharsis: The Power of the Apocalypse.* Philadelphia: Westminster, 1984.

———. "Introduction: Early Christian Apocalypticism." *Semeia* 36 (1986) 1–11.

———. "Numerical Symbolism in Jewish and Early Christian Apocalyptic Literature." In *ANRW* II.21.2 (1984) 1221–87.

Collins, John J. *The Apocalyptic Imagination: An Introduction to Jewish Apocalyptic Literature.* 2nd ed. Grand Rapids: Eerdmans, 1998.

———. *Between Athens and Jerusalem: Jewish Identity in the Hellenistic Diaspora.* 2nd ed.

Biblical Resource Series. Grand Rapids: Eerdmans, 2000.

———. *Beyond the Qumran Community: The Sectarian Movement of the Dead Sea Scrolls.* Grand Rapids: Eerdmans, 2010.

———. *Daniel: With an Introduction to Apocalyptic Literature.* Forms of Old Testament Literature 20. Grand Rapids: Eerdmans, 1984.

———. "An Essene Messiah? Comments on Israel Knohl, *The Messiah before Jesus.*" In *Christian Beginnings and the Dead Sea Scrolls,* edited by John J. Collins and Craig A. Evans, 37–44. Acadia Studies in Bible and Theology. Grand Rapids: Baker Academic, 2006.

———. *Jewish Cult and Hellenistic Culture: Essays on the Jewish Encounter with Hellenism and Roman Rule.* JSJSup 100. Leiden: Brill, 2005.

———. *The Origins of Apocalypticism in Judaism and Christianity.* The Encyclopedia of Apocalypticism 1. New York: Continuum, 1998.

———. *The Scepter and the Star: The Messiahs of the Dead Sea Scrolls and Other Ancient Literature.* ABRL. New York: Doubleday, 1995.

Collins, John J., and Michael A. Fishbane, editors. *Death, Ecstasy, and Other Worldly Journeys.* Albany: SUNY Press, 1995.

Collins, John J., and Gregory E. Sterling, editors. *Hellenism in the Land of Israel.* Christianity and Judaism in Antiquity 13. Notre Dame: University of Notre Dame Press, 2001.

Collins, Raymond F. *Letters That Paul Did Not Write: The Letter to the Hebrews and the Pauline Pseudepigrapha.* Good News Studies 28. Wilmington, DE: Glazier, 1988.

Colpe, Carsten. "The Oldest Jewish Christian Community." In *Christian Beginnings: Word and Community from Jesus to Post-Apostolic Times,* edited by Jürgen Becker, 75–102. Translated by Annemarie S. Kidder and Reinhard Krauss. Louisville: Westminster John Knox, 1993.

Colwell, E. C. "Greek Language." In *IDB* 2:479–82.

Comfort, Philip. *Encountering the Manuscripts: An Introduction to New Testament Paleography and Textual Criticism.* Nashville: Broadman & Holman, 2005.

———. *The Essential Guide to Bible Versions.* Wheaton, IL: Tyndale, 2000

Comfort, Philip, and David P. Barrett, editors. *The Complete Text of the Earliest New Testament Manuscripts.* Grand Rapids: Baker, 1999.

Connick, C. M. "The Dramatic Character of the Fourth Gospel." *JBL* 67 (1948) 159–69.

Conzelmann, Hans. *Jesus.* Translated by J. Raymond Lord. Edited by John Reumann. Philadelphia: Fortress, 1973.

———. *The Theology of St. Luke.* Translated by Geoffrey Buswell. 1961. Reprinted, Philadelphia: Fortress, 1982.

Cornell, T. J. *The Beginnings of Rome: Italy and Rome from the Bronze Age to the Punic Wars (c. 1000–264 BC).* Routledge History of the Ancient World. London: Routledge, 1995.

Court, John M. *Revelation.* Sheffield: JSOT, 1994.

Cox, Patricia. *Biography in Late Antiquity: A Quest for the Holy Man.* The Transformation of the Classical Heritage 5. Berkeley: University of California Press, 1983.

Cox, Roger L. "Tragedy and the Gospel Narratives." In *The Bible in Its Literary Milieu: Contemporary Essays,* edited by Vincent L. Tollers and John Maier, 298–317. Grand Rapids: Eerdmans, 1979.

Cramer, Frederick Henry. *Astrology in Roman Law and Politics.* 1954. Reprinted, Chicago: Ares, 1996.

Croce, Benedetto. *Aesthetics as Science of Expression and General Linguistics.* Translated by Douglas Ainslie. London: Macmillan, 1922.

Crook, Zeba A. "Methods and Models in New Testament Interpretation: A Critical Engagement with Louise Lawrence's Literary Ethnography." *RelSRev* 32 (2006) 87–97.

———. *Reconceptualising Conversion: Patronage, Loyalty, and Conversion in the Religions of the Ancient Mediterranean.* BZNW 130. Berlin: de Gruyter, 2004.

———. "Structure versus Agency in Studies of the Biblical Social World: Engaging with Louise Lawrence." *JSNT* 29 (2007) 251–75.

Crosby, Michael H. *House of Disciples: Church, Economics, and Justice in Matthew.* 1988. Reprinted, Eugene, OR: Wipf & Stock, 2004.

Cross, Frank L. *1 Peter: A Paschal Liturgy.* London: Mowbray, 1954.

Cross, Frank Moore. *The Ancient Library of Qumran and Modern Biblical Studies.* Haskell Lectures 1956–1957. Grand Rapids: Baker, 1980.

Crossan, John Dominic. *The Historical Jesus: The Life of a Mediterranean Jewish Peasant.* San Francisco: HarperSanFrancisco, 1991.

———. *In Parables: The Challenge of the Historical Jesus.* New York: Harper & Row, 1973.

———. "Parable and Example in the Teaching of Jesus." *NTS* 18 (1971/72) 285–307.

———. *Sayings Parallels: A Workbook for the Jesus Tradition.* 1986. Reprinted, Eugene, OR: Wipf & Stock, 2008.

Crossan, John Dominic, and Jonathan L. Reed. *In Search of Paul: How Jesus' Apostle Opposed Rome's Empire with God's Kingdom: A New Vision of Paul's Words and World.* San Francisco: HarperSanFrancisco, 2004.

Crump, David Michel. *Jesus the Intercessor: Prayer and Christology in Luke-Acts.* WUNT 2/49. Tübingen: Mohr/Siebeck, 1992.

Culler, Jonathan D. *Structuralist Poetics: Structuralism, Linguistics, and the Study of Literature.* Ithaca, NY: Cornell University Press, 1975.

Culpepper, R. Alan. *The Anatomy of the Fourth Gospel: A Study in Literary Design.* FF. Philadelphia: Fortress, 1983.

———. *The Johannine School: An Examination of the Johannine-School Hypothesis Based on the Investigation of the Nature of Ancient Schools.* SBLDS 26. Missoula: Scholars, 1975.

Dahl, Nils Alstrup. "The Concept of Baptism in Ephesians." In *Studies in Ephesians: Introductory Questions, Text- and Edition-Critical Issues, Interpretation of Texts and Themes,* edited by David Hellholm et al., 413–39. WUNT 1/131. Tübingen: Mohr/Siebeck, 200.

———. "The Story of Abraham in Luke-Acts." In *Studies in Luke-Acts: Essays Presented in Honor of Paul Schubert,* edited by Leander E. Keck and Louis Martyn, 139–58. Nashville: Abingdon, 1966.

Daniélou, Jean. *Gospel Message and Hellenistic Culture.* Translated, edited, and with a postscript by John Austin Baker. The History of Early Christian Doctrine before the Council of Nicaea 2. London: Darton, Longman & Todd, 1973.

———. *The Origins of Latin Christianity.* The History of Early Christian Doctrine before the Council of Nicaea 3. Translated by David Smith and John A. Baker. Edited and with a postscript by John A. Baker. London: Darton, Longman & Todd, 1977.

———. *The Theology of Jewish Christianity.* Translated and edited by John A. Baker. The History of Early Christian Doctrine before the Council of Nicaea 1. London: Darton, Longman & Todd, 1977.

Darnell, D. R., and D. A. Fiensy. "Hellenistic Synagogal Prayers (Second to Third Century A.D.)." Pages 671–97 in *OTP*. Vol. 2.

Daube, David. *Ancient Jewish Law: Three Inaugural Lectures.* Leiden: Brill, 1981.

Davies, W. D. *Introduction to Pharisaism.* FBBS 16. Philadelphia: Fortress, 1967.

———. *Paul and Rabbinic Judaism: Some Rabbinic Elements in Pauline Theology.* 4th ed. Philadelphia: Fortress, 1980.

Declercq, Georges. *Anno Domini: The Origins of the Christian Era.* BEEC. Turnhout: Brepols, 2000.

de Jonge, H. J. "Sonship, Wisdom, Infancy." *NTS* 24 (1978) 317–54.

De La Torre, Miguel A. *Reading the Bible from the Margins.* Maryknoll, NY: Orbis, 2002.

De Regt, L. J. "Bible Translation Theory." In *NIDB*, 1:452–53.

Desjardins, Michel. "The Portrayal of the Dissidents in 2 Peter and Jude: Does It Tell Us More about the 'Godly' than the 'Ungodly'?" *JSNT* 30 (1987) 89–102.

Devereux, George. "Achilles' Suicide in the Iliad." *Helios* 6:2 (1978–79): 3–15.

Dibelius, Martin. *The Book of Acts: Form, Style, and Theology.* Edited by K. C. Hanson. Fortress Classics in Biblical Studies. Minneapolis: Fortress, 2004.

———. *Die Formgeschichte des Evangeliums.* Tübingen: Mohr/Siebeck, 1919.

———. *From Tradition to Gospel.* Translated by Bertram Lee Woolf. Scribner Library. New York: Scribner, 1965.

———. *Studies in the Acts of the Apostles.* Edited by Heinrich Greeven. Translated by Mary Ling. London: SCM, 1956.

Diefenbach, Manfred. *Die Komposition des Lukasevangeliums unter Berucksichtigung antiker Rhetorikelemente.* Frankfurter theologische Studien 43. Frankfurt: Knecht, 1993.

Dillon, John. *The Middle Platonists, 80 BC to AD 220.* Ithaca: Cornell University Press, 1977.

DiTommaso, Lorenzo. "Apocalypses and Apocalyticism in Antiquity (Part I)." *CBR* 5 (2007) 235–86.

———. "Apocalypses and Apocalypticism in Antiquity (Part II)." *CBR* 5 (2007) 367–432.

Dochhorn, Jan. "Paulus und die polyglotte Schriftgelehrsamkeit seiner Zeit." *ZNW* 98 (2007) 189–212.

Dodd, C. H. *The Apostolic Preaching and Its Developments.* New York: Harper & Row, 1964.

———. "The Fall of Jerusalem and the 'Abomination of Desolation.'" *JRS* 37 (1947) 47–54.

———. "Introduction to the New Testament." In *New English Bible with Apocrypha.* New York: Oxford University Press, 1970.

———. *The Parables of the Kingdom.* London: Nisbet, 1935.

Dodds, E. R. *The Greeks and the Irrational.* Sather Classical Lectures 25. Berkeley: University of California Press, 1951.

———. *Pagan and Christian in an Age of Anxiety.* The Wiles Lectures 1962–63. London: Cambridge University Press, 1965.

Domeris, W. R. "The Johannine Drama." *JTSA* 42 (1983) 29–35.

Donahue, John R. *The Gospel in Parable: Metaphor, Narrative, and Theology in the Synoptic Gospels.* Philadelphia: Fortress, 1988.

———. "The Quest for the Community of Mark's Gospel." In *The Four Gospels 1992: Festschrift Frans Neirynck,* edited by F. Van Segbroek, et al., 1:817–38. 3 vols. BETL 100. Leuven: Leuven University Press, 1992.

———. "Redaction Criticism: Has the *Hauptstrasse* Become a *Sackgasse*?" In *The New Literary Criticism and the New Testament,* edited by Elizabeth Struthers Malbon and Edgar V. McKnight, 27–57. JSNTSup 109. Sheffield: Sheffield Academic, 1994.

Donelson, Lewis R. *Pseudepigraphy and Ethical Argument in the Pastoral Epistles.* HUT 22. Tübingen: Mohr/Siebeck, 1986.

Donelson, T. L. "Parallels: Use, Misuse and Limitations." *EvQ* 55 (1983) 193–210.

Donfried, Karl P. "Chronology." In *ABD* 1:1012–16.

———. *The Romans Debate.* Rev. and exp. ed. Peabody, MA: Hendrickson, 2001.

Dormeyer, Detlev. *Evangelium als literarische und theologische Gattung.* EdF 263. Darmstadt: Wissenschaftliche Buchgesellschaft, 1989

Dormeyer, Detlev, and Herbert Frankemölle. "Evangelium als literarischer und als theologischer Begriff." In *ANRW* II.25.2 (1984) 1541–704.

Doty, W. G. "The Concept of Genre in Literary Analysis." In *SBL 1972 Proceedings,* edited by L. C. McGaughy, 2:413–48. 2 vols. Missoula, MT: Society of Biblical Literature, 1972.

———. *Letters in Primitive Christianity.* GBS. Philadelphia: Fortress, 1973.

Douglas, Mary. *Purity and Danger. An Analysis of the Concepts of Pollution and Taboo.* 1966. Reprinted, London: Routledge, 1988.

Downing, F. Gerald. "The Ambiguity of the Pharisee and the Toll Collector (Luke 8:1–14) in the Greco-Roman World of Late Antiquity." *CBQ* 54 (1992) 80–92.

———. *Cynics and Christian Origins.* Edinburgh: T. & T. Clark, 1992.

Dubrow, Heather. *Genre.* The Critical Idiom 42. New York: Methuen, 1982.

Duke, Paul D. *Irony in the Fourth Gospel.* Atlanta: John Knox, 1985.

Dungan, David L. *A History of the Synoptic Problem: The Canon, the Text, and the Interpretation of the Gospels.* ABRL. New York: Doubleday, 1999.

———. "Mark—The Abridgement of Matthew and Luke." In *Jesus and Man's Hope,* edited by Donald G. Miller, 1:51–97. 2 vols. Pittsburgh: Pickwick, 1970.

———. "The New Testament Canon in Recent Study." *Int* 29 (1975) 339–51.

Dunn, James D. G. *Beginning from Jerusalem.* Christianity in the Making 2. Grand Rapids: Eerdmans, 2009.

———. *Jesus Remembered.* Christianity in the Making 1. Grand Rapids: Eerdmans, 2003.

———. "Jesus Tradition and Paul." In *Studying the Historical Jesus: Evaluations of the State of Current Research,* edited by Bruce Chilton and Craig A. Evans, 151–78. NTTS 19. Leiden: Brill 1994.

———. *Jews and Christians: The Parting of the Ways, AD 70 to 135.* WUNT 66. Tübingen: Mohr/Siebeck, 1992.

———. *The New Perspective on Paul: Collected Essays.* WUNT 185. Tübingen: Mohr/Siebeck, 2005.

———. *The New Perspective on Paul: Collected Essays.* Rev. ed. Grand Rapids: Eerdmans, 2008.

———. *The Theology of Paul's Letter to the Galatians.* New Testament Theology. Cambridge: Cambridge University Press, 1993.

———. *The Theology of Paul the Apostle.* Grand Rapids: Eerdmans, 1998.

———. *Unity and Diversity in the New Testament.* 2nd ed. London: SCM, 1990.

Dupont-Sommer, A. *The Essene Writings from Qumran.* Translated by Geza Vernes. Cleveland: World, 1962.

Eban, Abba. *My People: The Story of the Jews.* New York: Berhman, 1984.

Eddy, Paul Rhodes, and Gregory A. Boyd. *The Jesus Legend: A Case for the Historical Reliability of the Synoptic Jesus Tradition.* Grand Rapids: Baker Academic, 2007.

Edwards, James R. *The Hebrew Gospel and the Development of the Synoptic Tradition.* Grand Rapids: Eerdmans, 2009.

Ehrman, Bart D. *The Orthodox Corruption of Scripture: The Effect of Early Christological Controversies on the Text of the New Testament.* New York: Oxford University Press, 1993.

Ehrman, Bart D., and Michael W. Holmes. *The Text of the New Testament in Contemporary Research: Essays on the Status Quaestionis.* Studies and Documents 46. Grand Rapids: Eerdmans, 1995.

Elliott, John H. "A Catholic Gospel: Reflections on 'Early Catholicism' in the NT." *CBQ* 31 (1969) 213–23.

———. *A Home for the Homeless: A Sociological Exegesis of 1 Peter, Its Situation and Strategy.* 1981. Reprinted, Eugene, OR: Wipf & Stock, 2005.

———. "Jesus the Israelite Was Neither a 'Jew' Nor a 'Christian': On Correcting a Misleading Nomenclature." *JSHJ* 5 (2007) 119–52.

———. *What Is Social-Scientific Criticism?* GBS. Minneapolis: Fortress, 1993.

Elliott, Keith, and Ian Moir. *Manuscripts and the Text of the New Testament: An Introduction for English Readers.* Edinburgh: T. & T. Clark, 1995.

Elliott, Neil. *The Arrogance of Nations: Reading Romans in the Shadow of the Empire.* Paul in Critical Contexts. Minneapolis: Fortress, 2008.

———. *Liberating Paul: The Justice of God and the Politics of the Apostle.* The Bible and Liberation. Maryknoll, NY: Orbis, 1994.

———. *Liberating Paul: The Justice of God and the Politics of the Apostle.* Minneapolis: Fortress, 2005.

Ellis, E. Earle. *The Old Testament in Early Christianity: Canon and Interpretation in the Light of Modern Research.* WUNT 54. Tübingen: Mohr, 1991.

———. *Paul's Use of the Old Testament.* 1957. Grand Rapids: Baker, 1981.

———. *The Old Testament in Early Christianity: Canon and Interpretation in the Light of Modern Research.* Grand Rapids: Baker, 1992.

Elwell, Walter A., and Robert W. Yarbrough, editors. *Readings from the First-Century World: Primary Sources for New Testament*

Study. Encountering Biblical Studies. Grand Rapids: Baker, 1998.

Epp, E. J. "Issues in New Testament Textual Criticism: Moving from the Nineteenth to the Twenty-first Century." In *Rethinking New Testament Textual Criticism*, edited by David Alan Black, 17–76. New Testament Studies. Grand Rapids: Baker Academic, 2002.

Esler, Philip F. "Community and Gospel in Early Christianity: A Response to Richard Bauckham's *Gospels for All Christians*." *SJT* 51 (1998) 235–48.

———. *Community and Gospel in Luke-Acts: The Social and Political Motivations of Lucan Theology*. SNTSMS 57. Cambridge: Cambridge University Press, 1987.

———. *The First Christians in Their Social Worlds: Social-Scientific Approahces to New Testament Interpretation*. London: Routledge, 1994.

———, editor. *Modeling Early Christianity: Social Scientific Studies of the New Testament in Its Context*. London: Routledge, 1995.

Evans, Craig. *Fabricating Jesus: How Modern Scholars Distort the Gospels*. Downers Grove, IL: IVP Books, 2006.

———. "Inaugurating the Kingdom of God and Defeating the Kingdom of Satan." *BBR* 15 (2005) 49–75.

———. "Introduction: An Aramaic Approach Thirty Years Later." In *An Aramaic Approach to the Gospels and Acts*, by Matthew Black. 3rd ed. Peabody, MA: Hendrickson, 1998.

———. "Judaism, Post–AD 70." In *Dictionary of the Later New Testament and Its Development*, edited by Ralph P. Martin and Peter H. Davids, 604–11. Downers Grove, IL: InterVarsity, 1997.

——— "The Third Quest of the Historical Jesus: A Bibliographical Essay." *CSR* 28 (1999) 532–43.

Eve, Eric. *The Jewish Context of Jesus' Miracles*. JSNTSup 231. Sheffield, UK: Sheffield Academic 2002.

Farmer, William R. *Maccabees, Zealots, and Josephus*. New York: Columbia University Press, 1956.

———. "Modern Developments of Griesbach's Hypothesis." *NTS* 23 (1976–77) 275–95.

———. *The Synoptic Problem: A Critical Analysis*. Dillsboro, NC: Western North Carolina, 1978.

Farmer, William R., and Denis M. Farkasfalvy. *The Formation of the New Testament Canon: An Ecumenical Approach*. Theological Inquiries. New York: Paulist, 1983.

Fee, Gordon D. *New Testament Exegesis, A Handbook for Students and Pastors*. 3rd ed. Louisville: Westminster John Knox, 2002.

———. "The Textual Criticism of the New Testament." In *Biblical Criticism: Historical, Literary and Textual*, by R. K. Harrison, et al., 127–55. Contemporary Evangelical Perspectives. Grand Rapids: Zondervan, 1978.

———. "The Use of Greek Fathers for New Testament Textual Criticism." In *The Text of the New Testament in Contemporary Research: Essays on the Status Quaestionis*, edited by Bart D. Ehrman and Michael W. Holmes, 191–207. Studies and Documents 46. Grand Rapids: Eerdmans, 1994.

———. and Mark L. Strauss, *How To Choose a Translation for All That Its Worth*. Grand Rapids: Zondervan, 2007.

Felder, Cain Hope, editor. *Stony the Road We Tread: African American Biblical Interpretation*. Minneapolis: Fortress, 1991.

Feldman, Louis H. "Diaspora Synagogues." In *Sacred Realm: The Emergence of the Synagogue in the Ancient World*, edited by Steven Fine, 48–66. Oxford: Oxford University Press, 1996.

———. and Gohei Hata, editors. *Josephus, Judaism, and Christianity*. Detroit: Wayne State University Press, 1987.

Ferguson, Everett. *Backgrounds of Early Christianity*. 3rd ed. Grand Rapids: Eerdmans, 2003.

———. *Baptism in the Early Church: History, Theology, and Liturgy in the First Five Centuries*. Grand Rapids: Eerdmans, 2009.

Ferguson, John. *The Religions of the Roman Empire*. Ithaca, NY: Cornell University Press, 1970.

ffrench, Patrick, and Roland-François Lack, editors. *The Tel Quel Reader*. London: Routledge, 1998.

Finegan, Jack. *Encountering New Testament Manuscripts: A Working Introduction to Textual Criticism*. Grand Rapids: Eerdmans, 1974.

———. *Handbook of Biblical Chronology: Principles of Time Reckoning in the Ancient World and Problems of Chronology in the Bible*. 2nd ed. rev. & expanded. Peabody, MA: Hendrickson, 1998.

Finkelstein, Louis. *The Pharisees: The Sociological Background of Their Faith*. 2 vols. 3rd ed. Philadelphia: Jewish Publication Society, 1963.

Finlan, Stephen. *The Apostle Paul and the Pauline Tradition.* Collegeville, MN: Liturgical Press, 2008.

Fishbane, Michael. *Biblical Interpretation in Ancient Israel.* Oxford: Clarendon, 1985.

Fitzmyer, Joseph A. "The Aramaic Language and the Study of the New Testament." *JBL* 99 (1980) 1–21.

———. *The Interpretation of Scripture: In Defense of the Historical-Critical Method.* New York: Paulist, 2008.

———. "The Languages of Palestine in the First Century AD." *CBQ* 32 (1970) 501–31.

———. "The Priority of Mark and the 'Q' Source in Luke." In *Jesus and Man's Hope*, edited by Donald G. Miller, 1:131–70. 2 vols. Pittsburgh. Pickwick, 1970.

———. *A Wandering Aramean: Collected Aramaic Essays.* Missoula: Scholars, 1979.

Flanagan, N. "The Gospel of John as Drama." *The Bible Today* 14 (1981) 264–70.

Fleddermann, Harry T. *Q: A Reconstruction and Commentary.* Biblical Tools and Studies 1. Leuven: Peeters, 2005.

Flusser, David. *Jesus.* Translated by R. Walls. New York: Herder & Herder, 1969.

———. *Judaism of the Second Temple Period,* Vol. 2, *The Jewish Sages and Their Literature.* Grand Rapids: Eerdmans, 2009.

———. *Judaism of the Second Temple Period.* Vol. 1, *Qumran and Apocalypticism.* Translated by Azzan Yadin. Grand Rapids: Eerdmans., 2007.

———. and R. Steven Notley. *The Sage from Galilee: Rediscovering Jesus' Genius.* Grand Rapids: Eerdmans, 2007.

Foucault, Michel. *Language, Counter-Memory, and Practice Selected Essays and Interviews.* Edited by Donald F. Bouchard. Ithaca: Cornell University Press, 1977.

Fowler, Robert M. *Let the Reader Understand: Reader Response Criticism and the Gospel of Mark.* Minneapolis: Fortress, 1991.

France, R. T. *Divine Government: God's Kingship in the Gospel of Mark.* London: SPCK, 1990.

Francis, Fred O., and Wayne A. Meeks, translators and editors. *Conflict at Colossae: A Problem in the Interpretation of Early Christianity, Illustrated by Selected Modern Studies.* Rev. ed. SBLSBS 4. Missoula: Scholars, 1975.

Frede, Dorothea, and Brad Inwood, editors. *Language and Learning: Philosophy of Language in the Hellenistic Age.* Cambridge: Cambridge University Press, 2005.

Frederickson, Paula. *From Jesus to the Christ: The Origins of the New Testament Images of Jesus.* New Haven: Yale University Press, 1988.

Freedman, David Noel. "The Canon of the Old Testament." In *IDBSup*, 130–36.

Frey, Jörg, et al. *Pseudepigraphie und Verfassserfiktion in frühchristlichen Briefen.* Tübingen: Mohr/Siebeck, 2009.

Freyne, Sean. *Galilee, Jesus and the Gospels: Literary Approaches and Historical Investigations.* Dublin: Gill & Macmillan, 1988.

Frye, Northrop. *Anatomy of Criticism: Four Essays.* Princeton: Princeton University Press, 1957.

Fuller, Reginald H. *Interpreting the Miracles.* Philadelphia: Westminster, 1963.

Funk, Robert. *Language, Hermeneutic and Word of God: The Problem of Language in the New Testament and Contemporary Theology.* New York: Harper & Row, 1966.

———. *Parables and Presence.* Philadelphia: Fortress, 1982.

Gabba, Emilio. "True History and False History in Classical Antiquity." *JRS* 71 (1981) 50–62.

Gadamer, Hans-Georg. *Truth and Method.* Translated by Joel Weinsheimer and Donald G. Marshall. 2nd rev. ed. New York: Continuum, 1994.

Garcia Martinez, Florentino. *Qumran and Apocalyptic: Studies on the Aramaic Texts from Qumran.* STDJ 9. Leiden: Brill, 1992.

———, editor. *Wisdom and Apocalypticism in the Dead Sea Scrolls and in the Biblical Tradition.* BETL 168. Leuven: Peeters, 2003.

Garnsey, Peter, and Richard Saller. *The Early Principate.* Greece and Rome: New Surveys in the Classics 15. Clarendon, 1982.

Gaster, Theodore H. *The Dead-Sea Scriptures.* Rev. ed. Garden City, NY: Anchor, 1976.

Gaventa, Beverly Roberts and Richard B. Hays, editors. *Seeking the Identity of Jesus: A Pilgrimage.* Grand Rapids: Eerdmans, 2009.

Geertz, Clifford. *The Interpretation of Cultures: Selected Essays.* New York: Basic Books, 1973.

Genette, Gerard. *Narrative Discourse: An Essay in Method.* Translated by Jane E. Lewin. Ithaca, NY: Cornell University Press, 1980.

Georgi, Dieter. *The Opponents of Paul in 2 Corinthians: A Study of Religious Propaganda in Late Antiquity.* Translated by Harold Attridge, Isabel Best, et al. Philadelphia: Fortress, 1985.

Gerhardsson, Birger. *Memory and Manuscript: Oral Tradition and Written Transmission in Rabbinic Judaism and Early Christianity*

with Tradition and Transmission in Early
Christianity. Translated by Eric Sharpe. 2nd
ed. BRS. Grand Rapids: Eerdmans, 1998.

Gerhart, Mary. "Generic Studies." *JAAR* 45 (1977)
309–25.

Gerhart, Mary, and James G. Williams. *Genre,
Narrativity, and Theology.* Semeia 43. Atlanta:
Scholars, 1988.

Gero, Stephen. "With Walter Bauer on the Tigris:
Encratite Orthodoxy and Libertine Heresy
in Syro-Mesopotmian Christianity." Pages
287–307 in Charles W. Hedrick and Robert
Hodgson, *Nag Hammadi, Gnosticism,
and Early Christianity.* Peabody, MA:
Hendrickson, 1986.

Gill, David W. J., and Conrad Gempf, editors. *The
Book of Acts in Its Graeco-Roman Setting.* The
Book of Acts in Its First-Century Setting 2.
Grand Rapids: Eerdmans, 1994.

Godwin, Joscelyn. *Mystery Religions in the Ancient
World.* London: Thames and Hudson, 1981.

Goguel, Maurice. *Jesus and the Origins of
Christianity,* Vol. 1, *Prolegomena to the Life of
Jesus.* Translated by Olive Wyon. New York:
Harper & Row, 1960.

Goldin, Judah. *The Fathers According to Rabbi
Nathan.* Yale Judaica Series. New Haven: Yale
University Press, 1955.

Goldsworthy, Adrian. *The Fall of Carthage: The
Punic Wars 261–146 BC.* Cassell Military
Paperbacks. New York: Cassell, 2007.

Goodacre, Mark. *The Case against Q: Studies in
Markan Priority and the Synoptic Problem.*
Harrisburg, PA: Trinity, 2002.

———. *The Synoptic Problem: A Way through
the Maze.* Understanding the Bible and Its
World. London: T. & T. Clark, 2001.

Goodman, Martin. "Diaspora Reactions to the
Destruction of the Temple." In *Jews and
Christians: The Parting of the Ways, AD 70
to 135,* edited by James D. G. Dunn, 21–38.
Grand Rapids: Eerdmans, 1999.

———. *The Roman World 44 BC—AD 180.* New
York: Routledge, 1997.

———. *The Ruling Class of Judea: The Origins of
the Jewish Revolt against Rome.* Cambridge:
Cambridge University Press, 1987.

Gorman, Michael J. *Apostle of the Crucified Lord:
A Theological Introduction to Paul and His
Letters.* Grand Rapids: Eerdmans, 2004.

———. *Elements of Biblical Exegesis: A Basic Guide
for Students and Ministers.* Peabody, MA:
Hendrickson, 2001.

———. *Reading Paul.* Eugene, OR: Cascade
Books, 2008.

Gottwald, Norman K. "Poetry, Hebrew." In *IDB*
3:830–35.

Gowler, David B. *What Are They Saying about the
Parables?* New York: Paulist, 2000.

Grabbe, Lester. *A History of the Jews and Judaism
in the Second Temple Period.* 2 vols. London:
T. & T. Clark, 2004–2008.

———. "The Jews and Hellenization: Hengel
and His Critics." In *Second Temple Studies
III: Studies in Politics, Class, and Material
Culture,* edited by Philip R. Davies and John
M. Halligan, 51–66. JSOTSup 340. Sheffield:
Sheffield Academic, 2002.

Grant, Frederick C. *Ancient Roman Religion.* New
York: Macmillan; Indianapolis, IN: Bobbs-
Merrill, 1957.

Grant, Michael. *The Ancient Historians.* New York:
Scribner, 1970.

———. *The Founders of the Western World: A
History of Greece and Rome.* New York:
Scribner, 1991.

———. *Herod the Great.* London: Weidenfeld &
Nicolson, 1971.

———. *The World of Rome.* The World Histories
of Civilization. Cleveland: World, 1960.

Grant, Robert M. *Gods and the One God.*
Edited by Wayne Meeks. LEC. Louisville:
Westminster John Knox, 1986.

Green, Joel B., editor. *Hearing the New Testament:
Strategies for Interpretation.* 2nd ed. Grand
Rapids: Eerdmans, 2010.

Green, Joel B., et al., editors. *Dictionary of
Jesus and the Gospels.* Downers Grove, IL:
InterVarsity, 1992.

Green, W. S. "Palestinian Holy Men: Charismatic
Leadership and Rabbinic Tradition." In
ANRW II.19.2 (1979) 611–37.

Greenlee, J. Harold. *Introduction to New Testament
Textual Criticism.* Rev. ed. Peabody, MA:
Hendrickson, 1995.

———. "Text and Manuscripts of the New
Testament." In *ZPE* 5:697–707

———. *The Text of the New Testament: From
Manuscript to Modern Edition.* Peabody, MA:
Hendrickson, 2008.

Guelich, Robert. "The Gospel Genre." In *The
Gospel and the Gospels,* edited by Peter
Stuhlmacher, 181–219. Grand Rapids:
Eerdmans, 1991.

Gundry, Robert H. "Recent Investigations into the
Literary 'Gospel.'" Pages 97–114 in Richard
N. Longenecker and Merrill C. Tenney, ed.,
New Dimensions in New Testament Study.
Grand Rapids: Zondervan, 1974.

Gunkel, Hermann H. *Ausgewahlte Psalmen.* 4th ed. Göttingen: Vandenhoeck & Ruprecht, 1917.

———. *Genesis: Translated and Interpreted.* Translated by Mark E. Biddle. Mercer Library of Biblical Studies. Macon, GA: Mercer University Press, 1997.

Gunther, J. J. *St. Paul's Opponents and Their Background: A Study of Apocalyptic and Jewish Sectarian Teachings.* Leiden: Brill, 1973.

Guthrie, Donald. *New Testament Introduction.* 4th rev. ed. Downers Grove, IL: InterVarsity, 1990.

Hadas, Moses. *Hellenistic Culture: Fusion and Diffusion.* New York: Columbia University Press, 1959.

———. *Imperial Rome.* Great Ages of Man. Alexandria, VA: Time-Life, 1979.

Hadas, Moses, and Morton Smith. *Heroes and Gods: Spiritual Biographies in Antiquity.* Religious Perspectives 13. New York: Harper & Row, 1965.

Hahneman, G. M. T. *The Muratorian Fragment and the Development of the Canon.* Oxford: Oxford University Press, 1992.

———. "The Muratorian Fragment and the Origins of the New Testament Canon." In *The Canon Debate,* edited by Lee Martin McDonald and James A. Sanders, 401–15. Peabody, MA: Hendrickson, 2002.

Häkkinen, Sakari. "Ebionites." In *A Companion to Second-Century Christian 'Heretics,'* edited by Antti Marjanen and Petri Luomanen, 241–78. Leiden: Brill, 2008.

Hanson, K. C., and Douglas E. Oakman, *Palestine in the Time of Jesus.* 2nd ed. Minneapolis: Fortress, 2008.

Hanson, Paul D. "Apocalypse, Genre." In *IDBSup,* 27–28.

———. "Apocalypticism." In *IDBSup,* 28–34.

———. *The Dawn of Apocalyptic: The Historical and Sociological Roots of Jewish Apocalyptic Eschatology.* Rev. ed. Philadelphia: Fortress, 1979.

———. "Jewish Apocalyptic against its Near Eastern Environment." *RB* 78 (1971) 32–58.

Haran, M. "Priests and Priesthood." In *Encyclopedia Judaica* 13:1069–88

Harding, Mark. *What Are they Saying about the Pastoral Epistles?* Mahwah, NJ: Paulist, 2001.

———, and Alanna Nobbs, editors. *The Content and Setting of the Gospel Tradition.* Grand Rapids: Eerdmans, 2010.

Harnack, Karl Gustav Adolf von. *History of Dogma.* Translated by Neil Buchanan. 7 vols. New York: Dover, 1961.

———. *The Mission and Expansion of Christianity in the First Three Centuries,* vol. 1. Translated by James Moffatt. 1908. New York: Harper & Row, 1962. Online http://www.ccel.org/ccel/harnack/mission.i.html/.

———. *What Is Christianity?* 1957. Translated by Thomas Bailey Saunders. Fortress Texts in Modern Theology. Philadelphia: Fortress, 1986.

Harrington, Daniel J. *Interpreting the New Testament.* Michael Glazier, 1979. Collegeville, MN: Liturgical Press, 1990.

Harrison, R. K., et al. *Textual Criticism: Historical, Literary and Textual.* Grand Rapids: Zondervan, 1978.

Hayes, John H., and Carl R. Holladay. *Biblical Exegesis: A Beginner's Handbook.* Louisville: Westminster John Knox, 1987.

Hayes, John H., and J. Maxwell Miller, editors. *Israelite and Judean History.* OTL. Philadelphia: Westminster, 1977.

Hays, Richard B. *The Conversion of Imagination: Paul as Interpreter of Israel's Scripture.* Grand Rapids: Eerdmans, 2005.

———. "The Corrected Jesus." *First Things* 43 (May 1994) 41–48.

———. *Echoes of Scripture in the Letters of Paul.* New Haven: Yale, 1989.

———. *The Faith of Jesus Christ: The Narratuve Substructure of Galatians 3:1—4:11.* 2nd ed. Biblical Resource Series. Grand Rapids: Eerdmans, 2002.

Heckel, Waldemar. *Who's Who in the Age of Alexander the Great: Prosopography of Alexander's Empire.* Malden, MA: Blackwell, 2006.

Hedrick, Charles W. "Kingdom Sayings and Parables of Jesus in *Ap. Jas.*" *NTS* 29 (1982) 1–24.

———. *Many Things in Parables: Jesus and His Modern Critics.* Louisville: Westminster John Knox, 2004

———. "Narrative Asides in the Gospel of John." In *1900th Anniversary of St. John's Apocalypse: Proceedings of the International and Interdisciplinary Symposium,* 651–53. Athens: Holy Monastery of St. John, 1999.

———. *Parables as Poetic Fictions: The Creative Voice of Jesus.* 1994. Eugene, OR: Wipf & Stock Publishers, 2005.

———. "Paul's Conversion/Call." *JBL* 100 (1981) 415–32.

Hedrick, Charles W., and Robert Hodgson Jr., editors. *Nag Hammadi, Gnosticism, and Early Christianity*. 1986. Reprinted, Eugene, OR: Wipf & Stock, 2005.

Hedrick, Charles W., Jr. *Ancient History: Monuments and Documents*. Malden, MA: Blackwell, 2006.

Hellholm, D. "The Problem of Apocalyptic Genre and the Apocalypse of John." *Semeia* 36 (1986) 11–64.

Hemer, Colin J. *The Book of Acts in the Setting of Hellenistic History*. Edited by Conrad H. Gemf. WUNT 49. Tübingen: Mohr/Siebeck, 1989.

———. "Euraquilo and Melito." *JTS* 26 (1975) 100–111.

———. *The Letters to the Seven Churches of Asia in Their Local Setting*. Biblical Resource Series. 1986. New ed. with foreword by David E. Aune. Grand Rapids: Eerdmans, 2001.

———. "Towards a New Moulton and Milligan." *NovT* 24 (1982) 91–123.

Hengel, Martin. *Acts and the History of Earliest Christianity*. Translated by John Bowden. Philadelphia: Fortress, 1979.

———. *Between Jesus and Paul: Studies in the Earliest History of Christianity*. Translated by John Bowden. Philadelphia: Fortress, 1983.

———. *The Four Gospels and the One Gospel of Jesus Christ*. Translated by John Bowden. Harrisburg, PA: Trinity, 2000.

———. *Judaism and Hellenism: Studies in Their Encounter in Palestine during the Early Hellenistic Period*. Translated by John Bowden. 2 vols. Philadelphia: Fortress, 1974.

———. *The Septuagint as Christian Scripture: Its Prehistory and the Problem of Its Canon*. Translated by Mark E. Biddle. Grand Rapids: Baker, 2004.

———. *Was Jesus a Revolutionist?* Translated by William Klassen. FBBS 28. Philadelphia: Fortress, 1971.

———. *The Zealots: Investigations into the Jewish Freedmen Movement in the Period from Herod I until 70 AD*. Edinburgh: T. & T. Clark, 1989.

Hens-Piazza, Gina. *The New Historicism*. GBS. Minneapolis: Fortress, 2002.

Herrmann, Siegfried. *A History of Israel in Old Testament Times*. Translated by John Bowden. Philadelphia: Fortress, 1975.

Hicks, Robert D. *Stoic and Epicurean*. New York: Russell & Russell, 1962.

Hill, Craig C. *Hellenists and Hebrews: Reappraising Division within the Earliest Church*. Minneapolis: Fortress, 1992.

Hill, C. E. "The Debate over the Muratorian Fragment and the Development of the Canon." *WTJ* 57 (1995) 437–52.

Hill, David. "On the Evidence of the Creative Role of Christian Prophets." *NTS* 20 (1971–1974) 261–74.

———. "Prophecy and Prophets in the Revelation of St. John." *NTS* 18 (1971–72) 401–18.

Hirsch, Eric Donald, Jr. *Validity in Interpretation*. New Haven: Yale University Press, 1967.

Hock, Ronald F. *The Social Context of Paul's Ministry: Tentmaking and Apostleship*. Philadelphia: Fortress, 1980.

Hoehner, Harold W. *Chronological Aspects of the Life of Christ*. Grand Rapids: Zondervan, 1978.

———. *Herod Antipas*. SNTSMS 17. Cambridge: Cambridge University Press, 1972.

Hogan, Karina Martin. "Pseudepigraphy and the Periodization of History in Jewish Apocalypses." In *Pseudepigraphie und Verfasserfiktion in frühchristlichen Briefen*. Edited by Jörg Frey, Jens Herzer, Martina Janßen and Clare K. Rothschild. WUNT 246. Tübingen: Mohr Siebeck, 2009.

Hogeterp, Albert L. A. *Expectations of the End: A Comparative Traditio-Historical Study of Eschatological, Apocalytic and Messianic Ideas in the Dead Sea Scrolls and the New Testament*. Edited by by Florentino Garcia Martinez, et al. STDJ 83. Leiden: Brill, 2009.

Holladay, Carl R. *Theios Aner in Hellenistic Judaism: A Critique of the Use of This Category in New Testament Christology*. SBLDS 40. Missoula, MT: Scholars, 1977.

Holmberg, Bengt. *Paul and Power: The Structure of Authority in the Primitive Church as Reflected in the Pauline Epistles*. 1980. Reprinted, Eugene, OR: Wipf & Stock, 2004.

———. *Sociology and the New Testament: An Appraisal*. Minneapolis: Fortress, 1990.

Holmen, Tom. *Handbook for the Study of the Historical Jesus*. Leiden: Brill, 2010.

Hooker, Morna D. *The Signs of a Prophet: The Prophetic Actions of Jesus*. London: SCM, 1997.

Hope, Valerie M. *Death in Ancient Rome: A Sourcebook*. Routledge Sourcebooks for the Ancient World. London: Routledge, 2007.

Hopkins, Keith. *Conquerors and Slaves*. Sociological Studies in Roman History 1. Cambridge: Cambridge University Press, 1978.

Horrell, David, editor. *Social-Scientific Approaches to the New Testament*. Edinburgh: T. & T. Clark, 1999.

Horrocks, Geoffrey. *Greek: A History of the Language and Its Speakers*. London: Longmans, 1997.

Horsley, G. H. R. "The Fiction of Jewish Greek." In *New Documents Illustrating Early Christianity: Linguistic Essays*, 1–40. New South Wales: Macquarie University, 1989.

Horsley, G. H. R., and John A. L. Lee. "A Lexicon of the New Testament with Documentary Parallels: Some Interim Entries, 1." *Filologia Neotestamentaria* 10 (1997) 55–84.

———. "A Lexicon of the New Testament with Documentary Parallels: Some Interim Entries, 2." *Filologia Neotestamentaria* 11 (1998) 57–84.

Horsley, Richard A. "Ancient Jewish Banditry and the Revolt against Rome, AD 66–70." *CBQ* 43 (1981) 409–32.

———, editor. *Christian Origins*. A People's History of Christianity 1. Minneapolis: Fortress, 2005.

———. "Early Christian Movements: Jesus Movements and the Renewal of Israel." *HTS/TS* 62 (2004) 1201–25.

———. *Jesus and Empire: The Kingdom of God and the New World Disorder*. Minneapolis: Fortress, 2003.

———. *Jesus and the Spiral of Violence: Popular Jewish Resistance in Roman Palestine*. Minneapolis: Fortress, 1993.

———, editor. *Paul and Empire: Religion and Power in Roman Imperial Society*. Harrisburg, PA: Trinity, 1997.

———. *Paul and the Roman Imperial Order*. Harrisburg, PA: Trinity, 2004.

———. "Popular Messianic Movements around the Time of Jesus." *CBQ* 46 (1984) 471–93.

Huggins, R. V. "Matthean Posteriority." In *The Synoptic Problem and Q: Selected Studies from Novum Testamentum*, compiled by David E. Orton, 204–25. Brill's Readers in Biblical Studies 4. Leiden: Brill, 1999.

Hultgren, Arland. *The Parables of Jesus. A Commentary*. The Bible in its World. Grand Rapids: Eerdmans, 2000.

Hultgren, Stephen. *From the Damascus Covenant to the Covenant of the Community: Literary, Historical, and Theological Studies in the Dead Sea Scrolls*. STDJ 66. Leiden: Brill, 2007.

———. *Narrative Elements in the Double Tradition: A Study of Their Place within the Framework of the Gospel Narrative*. BZNW 113. Berlin: de Gruyter, 2002.

Hurtado, Larry W. *The Earliest Christian Artifacts: Manuscripts and Christian Origins*. Grand Rapids: Eerdmans, 2006.

———. *Lord Jesus Christ: Devotion to Jesus in Earliest Christianity*. Grand Rapids: Eerdmans, 2003.

———. *One God, One Lord: Early Christian Devotion and Ancient Jewish Monotheism*. Minneapolis: Fortress, 1988.

———. "Pre–70 CE Jewish Opposition to Christ-Devotion." *JTS* 50 (1999) 31–58.

Jacob, Irene, and Walter Jacob, editors. *The Healing Past: Pharmaceuticals in the Biblical and Rabbinic Worlds*. Studies in Ancient Medicine 7. Leiden: Brill, 1993.

Jagersma, Henk. *A History of Israel from Alexander the Great to Bar Kochba*. Translated by John Bowden. Philadelphia: Fortress, 1986.

Jaubert, Annie. *The Date of the Last Supper*. Translated by Issac Rafferty. New York: Alba House, 1965.

Jeremias, Joachim. *The Eucharistic Words of Jesus*. Translated by Norman Perrin. Philadelphia: Fortress, 1966.

———. *Die Gleichnisse Jesu*. Zurich: Zwingli, 1947.

———. *New Testament Theology: The Proclamation of Jesus*. Vol. 1. Translated by John Bowden. New York: Scribner, 1971.

———. *The Parables of Jesus*. Translated by S. H. Hooke. 2nd rev ed. New York: Scribner, 1972.

———. *The Problem of the Historical Jesus*. Translated by Norman Perrin. Philadelphia: Fortress, 1964.

Jervel, Jacob. *The Theology of Acts of the Apostles*. New Testament Theology. Cambridge: Cambridge University Press, 1966.

———. *The Unknown Paul: Essays on Luke-Acts and Early Christian History*. Minneapolis: Augsburg, 1984.

Jewett, Robert. *A Chronology of Paul's Life*. Philadelphia: Fortress, 1979.

———. *The Thessalonian Correspondence*. Philadelphia: Fortress, 1988.

Johnson, Luke Timothy. *Among the Gentiles: Greco-Roman Religion and Christianity*. Anchor Yale Bible Reference. New Haven: Yale University Press, 2009.

———. "John and Thomas in Context: An Exercise in Canonical Criticism." In *The Word Leaps the Gap: Essays on Scripture and Theology in Honor of Richard B. Hays*, edited by J. Ross Wagner, et al., 281–309. Grand Rapids: Eerdmans, 2008.

———. *The Real Jesus: The Misguided Quest for the Historical Jesus and the Truth of the Traditional Gospels*. San Francisco: HarperSanFrancisco, 1996.

———. *The Writings of the New Testament: An Interpretation*. Rev. ed. Minneapolis: Fortress, 1999.

Jonas, Hans. *The Gnostic Religion: The Message of the Alien God and the Beginnings of Christianity*. 2nd, enlarged ed. Boston: Beacon, 1963.

Jones, A. H. M. *The Herods of Judaea*. Oxford: Clarendon, 1967.

———. *Studies in Roman Government and Law*. Oxford: Blackwell, 1960.

Jones, Brian W. *The Emperor Domitian* . New York: Routledge, 1992.

———. *The Emperor Titus*. London: Croom Helm, 1984.

Jones, Peter Rhea. *Studying the Parables of Jesus*. Macon, GA: Smyth & Helwys, 1999.

Joubert, Stephan J., *Paul as Benefactor: Reciprocity, Strategy, and Theological Reflection in Paul's Collection*. WUNT 2/124. Tübingen: Mohr/Siebeck, 2000.

Jülicher, Adolf. *Die Gleichnisreden Jesu*. 2 vols. 1888–1899. Darmstadt: Wissenschaftliche Buchgesellschaft, 1963.

Kaiser, Otto, and Werner Georg Kümmel. *Exegetical Method: A Student's Handbook*. Translated with an introduction by Eugene V. N. Goetchius. Rev. ed. New York: Seabury, 1981.

Kalin, Everett. "The Canon of Origen." *CurTM* 17 (1990) 274–82.

———. "The Inspired Community." *Concordia Theological Monthly* 42 (1971) 541–49.

———. "The New Testament Canon of Eusebius." In *The Canon Debate*, edited by Lee Martin McDonald and James A. Sanders, 381–404. Peabody, MA: Hendrickson, 2002.

———. "Re-Examining the New Testament Canon History: 1. The Canon of Origen." *CurTM* 17 (1990) 271–82.

Kaminsky, Joel S. *Yet I Loved Jacob: Reclaiming the Biblical Concept of Election*. Nashville: Abingdon, 2007.

Kamm, Antony. *Julius Caesar: A Life*. London: Routledge, 2006.

———. *The Romans: An Introduction*. 2nd ed. New York: Routledge, 2008.

Kampen, John. *Hasideans and the Origin of Pharisaism*. SBLCSC. Atlanta: SBL, 1989.

Käsemann, Ernst. E. "Blind Alleys in the 'Jesus of History' Controversy." In *New Testament Questions of Today*, 21–65. Translated by W. J. Montague. Philadelphia: Fortress, 1979.

———. "The New Testament Canon and the Unity of the Church." In *Essays on New Testament Themes*, 101–7. Translated by W. J. Montague. Philadelphia: Fortress, 1982.

———. "Paul and Early Catholicism." In *New Testament Questions of Today*, 231–51. Translated by W. J. Montague. Philadelphia: Fortress, 1979.

———. *Perspectives on Paul*. Translated by Margaret Kohl. Philadelphia: Fortress, 1971

Katz, Steven T. "Issues in the Separation of Judaism and Christianity after 70 C.E.: A Reconsideration." *JBL* 103 (1984) 41–76.

Kaufmann, Yehezkel. *The Religion of Israel: From Its Beginnings to the Babylonian Exile*. Translated and abridged by Moshe Greenberg. Chicago: University of Chicago Press, 1960.

Keck, Leander E., and Louis Martyn, editors. *Studies in Luke-Acts: Essays Presented in Honor of Paul Schubert*. Nashville: Abingdon, 1966.

Kee, Howard Clark. *The Beginnings of Christianity: An Introduction to the New Testament*. New York: T. & T. Clark, 2005.

———. *Knowing the Truth: A Sociological Approach to New Testament Interpretation*. Minneapolis: Fortress, 1989.

———. *Medicine, Miracle, and Magic in New Testament Times*. SNTMS 55. Cambridge: Cambridge University Press, 1986.

———. *Miracle in the Early Christian World: A Study in Sociohistorical Method*. New Haven: Yale University Press, 1983.

———. and F. W. Young, *Understanding the New Testament*. Englewood Cliffs, NJ: Prentice Hall, 1957.

Keener, Craig, *The Historical Jesus of the Gospels*. Grand Rapids: Eerdmans, 2009.

Kelber, Werner H. "Redaction Criticism: On the Nature and Exposition of the Gospels." *PRSt* 6 (1979) 1–16.

Keller, Ernst, and Marie-Luise Keller. *Miracles in Dispute: A Continuing Debate*. Translated by Margaret Kohl. London: SCM, 1968.

Kennedy, George A. *New Testament Interpretation through Rhetorical Criticism*. Chapel Hill: University of North Carolina Press, 1984.

Kiley, Mark. *Colossians as Pseudepigraphy*. Biblical Seminar. Sheffield: JSOT Press, 1986.

Kim, Seyoon. *Christ and Caesar: The Gospel and the Roman Empire in the Writings of Paul and Luke*. Grand Rapids: Eerdmans, 2008.

———. *Paul and the New Perspective: Second Thoughts on the Origins of Paul's Gospel.* Grand Rapids: Eerdmans, 2004.

Kimelman, Reuven. "*Birkat-Ha-Minim* and the Lack for Evidence for an Anti-Christian Jewish Prayer in Antiquity." In *Aspects of Judaism in the Graeco-Roman Period*, edited by E. P. Sanders and A. I. Baumgarten, 221–44. Jewish and Christian Self-Definition 2. Philadelphia: Fortress, 1980.

King, Karen L. *What Is Gnosticism?* Cambridge: Belknap, 2003.

Kirchschläger, Walter. "Beobachtungen zur Struktur der lukanischen Vorgeschichten Lk 1–2." *Bibliothèque liturgique* 57 (1984) 244–51.

Kirschenbaum, Aaron. *Sons, Slaves, and Freedmen in Roman Commerce.* Jerusalem: Magnes, 1987.

Klausner, Joseph. *Jesus of Nazareth: His Life, Times, and Teaching.* Translated by Herbert Danby. 1925. Reprinted, Boston: Beacon, 1964.

Klein, Ralph W. *Israel in Exile: A Theological Interpretation.* OBT 6. Philadelphia: Fortress, 1979.

Kloppenborg, John. *Q, the Earliest Gospel: An Introduction to the Original Stories and Sayings of Jesus.* Louisville: Westminster John Knox, 2008.

———. *Excavating Q: The History and Setting of the Sayings Gospel.* Minneapolis: Fortress, 2000.

———. "The Sayings Gospel Q and the Quest of the Historical Jesus." *HTR* 89 (1996) 301–44.

Knierem, Rolf. "Old Testament Form Criticism Reconsidered" *Occasional Papers No. 6.* Claremont: Institute for Antiquity and Christianity. Originally published in *Int* 27 (1973) 431–67.

Knohl, Israel. *The Messiah before Jesus: The Suffering Servant of the Dead Sea Scrolls.* Translated by David Meisel. The S. Mark Taper Foundation Imprint in Jewish Studies. Berkeley: University of California Press, 2000.

Knox, John. *Chapters in a Life of Paul.* New York: Abingdon-Cokesbury, 1950.

Koch, Klaus. *The Rediscovery of Apocalyptic: A Polemical Work on a Neglected Area of Biblical Studies and Its Damaging Effects on Theology and Philosophy.* Studies in Biblical Theology, 2nd ser. 22. Naperville, IL: Allenson, 1972.

Koester, Craig. "The Origin and Significance of the Flight to Pella Tradition." *CBQ* 51 (1989) 91–106.

Koester, Helmut. *Ancient Christian Gospels: Their History and Development.* Philadelphia: Trinity, 1990.

———. *From Jesus to the Gospels: Interpreting the New Testament in Its Context.* Minneapolis: Fortress, 2007.

———. *Introduction to the New Testament.* Vol. 2, *History and Literature of Early Christianity.* 2nd ed. New York: de Gruyter, 2000.

———. *Introduction to the New Testament.* Vol. 1, *History, Literature, and Religion of the Hellenistic Age.* 2nd ed. New York: de Gruyter, 2002.

Kohlenberger, John R., III. *Words about the Word. A Guide to Choosing and Using your Bible.* Regency Reference Library. Grand Rapids: Zondervan, 1987.

Kokkinos, Nikos. *The Herodian Dynasty: Origins, Role in Society, and Eclipse.* Sheffield: Sheffield Academic, 1998.

Köstenberger, Andreas J. *A Theology of John's Gospel and Letters: The Word, the Christ, the Son of God.* Biblical Theology of the New Testament Series. Grand Rapids: Zondervan, 2009.

Kraft, Robert. "The Development of the Concept of 'Orthodoxy' in Early Christianity." *Current Issues in Biblical and Patristic Interpretation*, edited by Gerald Hawthorne, 47–56. Grand Rapids: Eerdmans, 1975.

Krentz, Edgar. *The Historical-Critical Method.* GBS NT. Philadelphia: Fortress, 1975.

Kubo, Sakae, and Walter F. Specht. *So Many Versions?* Rev. ed. Grand Rapids: Zondervan, 1983.

Kümmel, Werner Georg. *Introduction to the New Testament.* Rev. ed. Translated by Howard Clark Kee. Nashville; Abingdon, 1975.

———. *The New Testament: The History of the Investigation of Its Problems.* Translated by S. McLean Gilmour and Howard Clark Kee. Nashville: Abingdon, 1972.

Kurz, William S. "Hellenistic Jewish Narratives." In *Jesus and the Heritage of Israel: Luke's Narrative Claim upon Israel's Legacy*, edited by David P. Moessner, 147–70. Harrisburg, PA: Trinity, 1999.

———. *Reading Luke-Acts: Dynamics of Biblical Narrative.* Louisville: Westminster John Knox, 1993.

Kysar, Robert. "The Gospel of John in Current Research." *RelStRev* 9 (1983) 315–16.

Lampe, G. W. H. "The Evidence in the New Testament for Early Creeds, Catechisms and Liturgy." *ExpT* 71 (1960) 351–63.

Lampe, Peter. *From Paul to Valentinus: Christians at Rome in the First Two Centuries.* Translated by Michael Steinhauser. Edited by Marshall D. Johnson. Minneapolis: Fortress, 2003.

Lawrence, Louise Joy. *An Ethnography of the Gospel of Matthew: A Critical Assessment of the Use of the Honour and Shame Model in New Testament Studies.* WUNT 2/165. Tübingen: Mohr/Siebeck, 2003.

———. "'For Truly, I Tell You, They Have Received Their Reward' (Matt 6:2): Investigating Honor Precedence and Honor Virture." *CBQ* 64 (2002) 681–702.

———. "Structure, Agency and Ideology: A Response to Zeba Crook." *JSNT* 29 (2007) 271–86.

Le Donne, Anthony. *Historical Jesus: What Can we Know and How Can We Know It?* Grand Rapids: Eerdmans, 2011.

Lee, E. Kenneth. "The Drama of the Fourth Gospel." *ExpT* 65 (1953–54) 173–76.

Leiman, Shnayer Z. *The Canonization of Hebrew Scripture: The Talmudic and Midrashic Evidence.* Transactions—The Connecticut Academy of Arts and Sciences 47. Hamden, CT: Archon, 1976.

Levenson, Jon D. *The Death and Resurrection of the Beloved Son: The Transformation of Child Sacrifice in Judaism and Christianity.* New Haven: Yale University Press, 1993.

———. *Resurrection and the Restoration of Israel: The Ultimate Victory of the God of Life.* New Haven: Yale University Press, 2006.

———. *Sinai and Zion: An Entry into the Jewish Bible.* San Francsico: Harper & Row, 1985.

Levick, Barbara. *Claudius.* New Haven: Yale, 1990.

———. *Tiberius the Politician.* Rev. ed. London: Routledge, 2005.

Levine, Amy-Jill, editor. *A Feminist Companion to Matthew.* Cleveland: Pilgrim, 2001.

Levine, Amy-Jill, editor, with Marianne Blickenstaff. *A Feminist Companion to the Acts of the Apostles.* Cleveland: Pilgrim, 2004.

———. *A Feminist Companion to the Deutero-Pauline Epistles.* Feminist Companion to the New Testament and Early Christian Writings 7. London: T. & T. Clark, 2003.

Levine, Amy-Jill, et al., editors. *The Historical Jesus in Context.* Princeton Readings in Religions. Princeton: Princeton University Press, 2006.

Levine, Lee I. *The Ancient Synagogue: The First Thousand Years.* New Haven: Yale University Press, 2000.

Levinskaya, I. A. *The Book of Acts in Its Diaspora Setting.* The Book of Acts in Its First-Century Setting 5. Grand Rapids: Eerdmans, 1996.

Lewis, C. S. *The Allegory of Love: A Study in Medieval Tradition.* London. Oxford University Press, 1936, 1938.

———. *God in the Dock: Essays on Theology and Ethics.* 1970. Grand Rapids: Eerdmans, 1994.

Lewis, Jack P. *The English Bible from KJV to NIV.* 2nd ed. Grand Rapids: Baker, 1991.

———. "What Do We Mean by Jabneh?" *JBR* 32 (1964) 121–32.

Linnemann, Eta. *Is There a Synoptic Problem? Rethinking the Literary Dependence of the First Three Gospels.* Translated by Robert. W. Yarbrough. Grand Rapids: Baker, 1992.

Logan, Alastair H. B. *Gnostic Truth and Christian Heresy: A Study in the History of Gnosticism.* Edinburgh: T. & T. Clark, 1996.

Lohfink, Gerhard. *The Bible, Now I Get It!: A Form Criticism Handbook.* Garden City, NY: Doubleday, 1979.

———. *The Conversion of St. Paul: Narrative and History in Acts.* Herald Scriptural Library. Chicago: Franciscan Herald, 1976.

Longenecker, Bruce W., and Kelly D. Liebengood. *Engaging Economics: New Testament Scenarios and Early Christian Reception.* Grand Rapids: Eerdmans, 2009.

Longenecker, Richard N. *Biblical Exegesis in the Apostolic Period.* 2nd ed. Grand Rapids: Eerdmans, 1999.

———, editor. *The Challenge of Jesus' Parables.* McMaster New Testament Studies. Grand Rapids: Eerdmans, 2000.

Longenecker, Richard N., and Merrill C. Tenney. *New Dimensions in New Testament Study.* Grand Rapids: Zondervan, 1974.

Longstaff, Thomas R. W. *Evidence of Conflation in Mark? A Study in the Synoptic Problem.* SBLDS 28. Missoula: Scholars, 1977.

Louw, J. P. "New Testament Greek: Present State of the Art" *Neot* 24:2 (1990) 151–72.

Lucas, F. L. *Tragedy in Relation to Aristotle's "Poetics."* 2nd rev. ed. London: Hogarth, 1957.

Lüdemann, Gerd. *Heretics: The Other Side of Early Christianity.* Translated by John Bowden. Louisville: Westminster John Knox, 1996.

———. *Opposition to Paul in Jewish Christianity.* Translated by M. Eugene Boring. Minneapolis: Fortress, 1989.

———. *Paul, Apostle to the Gentiles: Studies in Chronology.* Translated by F. Stanley Jones. Philadelphia: Fortress, 1984.

Lupieri, Edmondo. *The Mandaeans: The Last Gnostics*. Translated by Charles Hindley. ITSORS. Grand Rapids: Eerdmans, 2002.

Maccoby, Hyam. *Early Rabbinic Writings*. CCWJCW 3. Cambridge: Cambridge University Press, 1988.

MacCullough, Diarmaid. *Christianity: The First Three Thousand Years*. New York: Viking, 2009.

MacDonald, Dennis R., editor. *Does the New Testament Imitate Homer?: Four Cases from Acts of the Apostles*. New Haven: Yale University Press, 2003.

———. *The Homeric Epics and the Gospel of Mark*. New Haven: Yale University Press, 2000.

———, editor. *Mimesis and Intertextuality in Antiquity and Christianity*. Studies in Antiquity and Christianity. Harrisburg, PA: Trinity, 2001.

MacDonald, Margaret Y. *The Pauline Churches: A Socio-Historical Study of Institutionalization in the Pauline and Deutero-Pauline Writings*. SNTSMS 60. Cambridge: Cambridge University Press, 1988.

Machen, J. Gresham. *The Origin of Paul's Religion*. 1925. Reprinted, Grand Rapids: Eerdmans, 1978.

Mack, Burton. "The Kingdom that Didn't Come: A Social History of the Q Tradents." *SBLSP* 28 (1988) 601–35.

———. *The Lost Gospel: The Book of Q and Christian Origins*. San Francisco: HarperCollins, 1993.

Maier, Paul L. "Sejanus, Pilate, and the Date of the Crucifixion." *CH* 37 (March, 1968) 1–13.

Malbon, Elizabeth Struthers, and Edgar V. McKnight, editors. *The New Literary Criticism and the New Testament*. JSNTSup 109. Sheffield, UK: Sheffield Academic, 1994.

Malherbe, Abraham J. *The Cynic Epistles: A Study Edition*. SBLSBS 12. Missoula: Scholars, 1977.

———. "*Me Genoito* in the Diatribe and Paul." *HTR* 73 (1980) 231–40.

———. *Moral Exhortation: A Greco-Roman Sourcebook*. LEC. Philadelphia: Westminster, 1986.

Malina, Bruce J. "Christ and Time: Swiss or Mediterranean?" *CBQ* 51 (1989) 1–31.

———. "Jesus as Charismatic Leader?" *BTB* 14 (1984) 51–62.

Malkin, Irad. "*Networks* and the Emergence of Greek Identity." In *Mediterranean Paradigms and Classical Antiquity*, edited by Irad Malkin, 51–74. New York: Routledge, 2005.

Mandel, Oscar. *A Definition of Tragedy*. New York: New York University Press, 1961.

Manson, T. W. *The Sayings of Jesus*. 1957. Reprinted, Grand Rapids: Eerdmans, 1979.

Mantel, Hugo. "The Development of the Oral Law During the Second Temple Period," in M. Avi-Yonah and Z. Baras, eds. *World History of the Jewish People 8: Society and Religion in the Second Temple Period* (Jerusalem: Massada, 1977) 41–64, 325–37; "Torah Scholarship," 314–80 and "Life and Law," 464–87 in Schurer and Vermes, *History 2*.

———. "Sanhedrin." In *IDBSup*, 784–86.

Marcus, Joel. "Jewish Christianity." In *The Cambridge History of Christianity: Volume 1 Origins to Constantine*, edited by Margaret M. Mitchell and Frances M. Young, 81–102. Cambridge: Cambridge University Press, 2006.

Marjanen, Antti, and Petri Luomanen, editors. *A Companion to Second-Century Christian 'Heretics.'* Leiden: Brill, 2008.

Marrou, H. I. *A History of Education in Antiquity*. Translated by George Lamb. 1956. Reprinted, Madison: University of Wisconsin Press, 1982.

Marshall, I. Howard. "'Early Catholicism' in the New Testament." In *New Dimension in New Testament Study*, edited by Richard N. Longnecker and Merrill C. Tenney, 211–31. Grand Rapids: Zondervan, 1974.

———. "Editor's Foreword." In *New Testament Interpretation: Essays on Principles and Methods*, edited by I. Howard Marshall, 1–9. 1977. Rev. ed. Carlisle, UK: Paternoster, 1979. Online: http://www.biblicalstudies.org.uk/book_nt-interpretation.html/.

———. *I Believe in the Historical Jesus*. Grand Rapids: Eerdmans, 1977.

———, editor. *New Testament Interpretation: Essays on Principles and Methods*. Grand Rapids: Eerdmans, 1977.

———. "Palestinian and Hellenistic Christianity." *NTS* 19 (1971–73) 271–87.

Martin, Dale B. *The Corinthian Body*. New Haven: Yale University Press, 1995.

Martin, Ralph P. *Carmen Christi, Philippians 2:1–11*. Rev. ed. Grand Rapids. Eerdmans, 1983

Martin, Troy, W. *By Philosophy and Empty Deceit: Colossians as Response to a Cynic Critique*. JSNTSup 118. Sheffield, UK: Sheffield Academic Press, 1996.

Martyn, J. Louis. *The Gospel of John: Essays for Interpreters*. New York: Paulist, 1978.

———. *History and Theology in the Fourth Gospel.* 3rd ed. NTL. Louisville: Westminster John Knox, 2003.

Marxsen, Willi. *Mark the Evangelist: Studies on the Redaction History of the Gospel.* Translated by James Boyce et al. Nashville: Abingdon, 1969.

Mason, Steve. *Flavius Josephus on the Pharisees: A Composition-Critical Study.* Studia Post-Biblica 39. Leiden: Brill, 1991.

———. "Jews, Judaeans, Judaizing, Judaism: Problems of Categorization in Ancient History." *JSJ* 38 (2007) 451–512.

———. *Josephus and the New Testament.* Peabody, MA: Hendrickson, 1992.

May, G. "Marcion in Contemporary Views: Results and Open Questions." *SecCent* 6 (1987–1988) 129–52.

Mazzaferri, Frederick David. *The Genre of the Book of Revelation from a Source-Critical Perspective.* Berlin: Walter de Gruyter, 1989.

McArthur, Harvey K., editor. *In Search of the Historical Jesus.* Scribner Source Books in Religion. New York: Scribner, 1969.

McCall, Marsh, Jr. *Ancient Rhetorical Theories of Simile and Comparison.* LCM. Cambridge: Harvard University Press, 1969.

McCarthy, Dennis J. *Old Testament Covenant: A Survey of the Current Opinions.* Translated and adapted by Dennis J. McCarthy. Growing Points in Theology. Oxford: Blackwell, 1972.

———. *Treaty and Covenant: A Study in Form in the Ancient Oriental Documents and in the Old Testament.* New ed. AnBib 21. Rome: Biblical Institute, 1978.

McDonald, Lee Martin. "Canon of the New Testament." In *NIDB*, 1:536–47.

McDonald, Lee Martin, and James A. Sanders, editors. *The Canon Debate.* Peabody, MA: Hendrickson, 2002.

McFague, Sallie. *Speaking in Parables: A Study in Metaphor and Theology.* Philadelphia: Fortress, 1975.

McGinn, Bernard J., et al., editors. *The Continuum History of Apocalypticism.* New York: Continuum, 2003.

McKnight, Edgar V. *What Is Form Criticism?* GBS. Philadelphia: Fortress, 1969.

McKnight, Edgar V., and Elizabeth S. Malbon, editors. *The New Literary Criticism and the New Testament.* Valley Forge, PA: Trinity, 1994.

McKnight, Scot, and Grant R. Osborne, editors. *The Face of New Testament Studies: A Survey of Recent Research.* Grand Rapids: Baker Academic, 2004.

Mealy, J. Webb. "After the Thousand Years: Resurrection and Judgment in Revelation 20." Sheffield: JSOT Press, 1992.

Meeks, Wayne. *The First Urban Christians: The Social World of the Apostle Paul.* 2nd ed. New Haven: Yale University Press, 1983.

———. "A Hermeneutics of Social Embodiment." *HTR* 79 (1986) 171–86.

———. *The Writings of St. Paul: Annotated Texts, Reception and Criticism.* Edited by Wayne A. Meeks and John T. Fitzgerald. 2nd ed. Norton Critical Edition. New York: Norton, 2007.

Meier, John P. *A Marginal Jew: Rethinking the Historical Jesus.* 4 vols. New York: Doubleday, 1991–2009.

———. *A Marginal Jew: Rethinking the Historical Jesus.* Vol. 1, *The Roots of the Problem and the Person.* New York: Doubleday, 1991.

———. *A Marginal Jew: Rethinking the Historical Jesus.* Vol. 2, *Mentor, Message, and Miracles.* New York: Doubleday, 1994.

———. *A Marginal Jew: Rethinking the Historical Jesus.* Vol. 3, *Companions and Competitors.* New York: Doubleday, 2001.

———. *A Marginal Jew: Rethinking the Historical Jesus.* Vol. 4, *Law and Love.* New York: Doubleday, 2009.

Mendenhall, George E. "Covenant Forms in Israelite Tradition." In *The Biblical Archaeologist Reader, Volume 3*, edited by Edward F. Campbell Jr. and David Noel Freedman, 25–53. Garden City, NY: Anchor, 1970.

Merlan, Philip. *From Platonism to Neoplatonism.* 2nd ed. The Hague: Nijhoff, 1960.

Metzger, Bruce M. *The Bible in Translation: Ancient and English Versions.* Grand Rapids: Baker, 2001.

———. *The Canon of the New Testament: Its Origins, Development, and Significance.* Oxford: Clarendon, 1987.

———. "The Language of the New Testament." In *IB* 7:43–59.

———. "Literary Forgeries and Canonical Pseudepigrapha." *JBL* 91 (1972) 1–24.

———. "RSV Bible." *Duke Divinity Review* 44 (1979) 70–87.

Metzger, Bruce M., and Bart D. Ehrman. *The Text of the New Testament: Its Transmission, Corruption, and Restoration.* 4th ed. New York: Oxford University Press, 2005.

Metzger, Bruce M., et al. *The Making of the New Revised Standard Version of the Bible.* Grand Rapids: Eerdmans, 1991.

Meyers, Eric M. "Synagogue, Architecture." In *IDBSup*, 842–44.

Michaels, J. Ramsey. *Interpreting the Book of Revelation*. Guides to New Testament Exegesis 7. Grand Rapids: Baker, 1992.

Millar, Fergus. "The Background of the Maccabean Revolution: Reflections on Martin Hengel's *Judaism and Hellenism*." *JJS* 29 (1978) 1–21.

———. *The Emperor in the Roman World (31 BC—AD 337)*. 2nd ed. Ithaca: Cornell University Press, 1992.

Miller, Donald G., editor. *Jesus and Man's Hope*. 2 vols. Pittsburgh: Pickwick Publications, 1970.

Miller, Merrill P. "Midrash." In *IDBSup*, 593–97.

Miller, Robert J. *The Jesus Seminar and Its Critics*. Santa Rosa: Polebridge, 1999.

Minear, Paul S. "Luke's Use of the Birth Stories." In *Studies in Luke-Acts: Essays Presented in Honor of Paul Schubert*, edited by Leander E. Keck and J. Louis Martyn, 111–30. Nashville: Abingdon, 1966.

Moessner, David P., editor. *Jesus and the Heritage of Israel: Luke's Narrative Claim upon Israel's Legacy*. Luke the Interpreter of Israel 1. Harrisburg, PA: Trinity, 1999.

Moffatt, James. *An Introduction to the Literature of the New Testament*. The International Theological Library. 3rd and rev. ed. Edinburgh: T. & T. Clark, 1918.

Momigliano, Arnaldo. *Essays in Ancient and Modern Historiography*. Blackwell's Classical Studies. Oxford: Blackwell, 1977.

Moore, Stephen D. *Literary Criticism and the Gospels: The Theoretical Challenge*. New Haven: Yale University Press, 1989.

———. *Poststructuralism and the New Testament: Derrida and Foucault at the Foot of the Cross*. Minneapolis: Fortress, 1994.

Morgan, Gwyn. *69 AD: The Year of Four Emperors*. Oxford: Oxford University Press, 2006.

Morgan, Robert. *The Nature of New Testament Theology: The Contributions of William Wrede and Adolf Schlatter*. SBT. Second Series 25. Naperville, IL: Alec R. Allenson, 1973.

Mosshammer, Alden A. *Easter Computus and the Origins of the Christian Era*. Oxford: Oxford University Press, 2008.

Moule, C. F. D. *The Birth of the New Testament*. 3rd ed. HNTC. New York: Harper & Row, 1982.

Mousourakis, George. *A Legal History of Rome*. London: Routledge, 2007.

Moxnes, Halvor. "Social Context of Luke's Community." *Int* 48 (1994) 371–89

Moyise, Steve. *The Old Testament in the Book of Revelation*. JSNTSup 115 Sheffield, UK: Academic, 1995.

Mozley, J. F. *William Tyndale*. London: SPCK, 1937.

Mussies, Gerard. "The Use of Hebrew and Aramaic in the Greek New Testament." *NTS* 30 (1984) 411–32.

Nagy, Gregory. *The Best of the Achaeans: Concepts of the Hero in Archaic Greek Poetry*. Rev. ed. Baltimore: Johns Hopkins University Press, 1999.

Nanos, Mark D., editor. *The Galatians Debate: Contemporary Issues in Rhetorical and Historical Interpretation*. Peabody, MA: Hendrickson, 2002.

———. *The Mystery of Romans. The Jewish Context of Paul's Letter*. Minneapolis: Fortress, 1996.

Neill, Stephen, and Tom Wright, *The Interpretation of the New Testament, 1861–1961*. 2nd ed. Oxford: Oxford University Press, 1988.

Neilsen, Flemming, A. J. *The Tragedy in History: Herodotus and the Deuteronomistic History*. JSOTSup 251. Sheffield, UK: Sheffield Academic, 1997.

Neirynck, Frans. *The Minor Agreements of Matthew and Luke against Mark with a Cumulative List*. BETL 37. Leuven: Leuven University Press, 1974.

Neufeld, Vernon H. *The Earliest Christian Confessions*. NTTS 5. Leiden: Brill, 1963.

Neusner, Jacob. "Destruction of the Second Temple." *Judaica* 21 (1972) 313–27.

———. *Early Rabbinic Judaism: Historical Studies in Religion, Literature, and Art*. Studies in Judaism in Late Antiquity. Leiden: Brill, 1975.

———. "The Formation of Rabbinic Judaism: Yavneh (Jamnia) from AD 71–100." In *ANRW* II.19.2 (1979) 1–42.

———. *The Four Stages of Rabbinic Judaism*. London: Routledge, 1999.

———. *Introduction to Rabbinic Literature*. New York: Doubleday, 1994.

———. "Judaism in a Time of Crisis: Four Responses to the Destruction of the Second Temple." *Judaism* 21 (1972) 311–27.

———. *Method and Meaning in Ancient Judaism*. Brown Judaic Studies 10. Missoula, MT: Scholars, 1979.

———. *Rabbinic Judaism: The Documentary History of Its Formative Age, 71–600 C.E.* Bethesda, MD: CDL, 1994.

———. *Rabbinic Literature: An Essential Guide*. Abingdon Essential Guides. Nashville: Abingdon, 2005.

———. *The Rabbinic Traditions about the Pharisees before 70*. 3 vols. South Florida Studies in the History of Judaism 202–204. Atlanta: Scholars, 1999.

Neville, D. J. *Arguments from Order in Synoptic Source Criticism: A History and Critique*. New Gospel Studies 7. Leuven: Peeters, 1994.

Newman, Barclay M., et al. *Creating and Crafting the Contemporary English Version: A New Approach to Bible Translation*. New York: American Bible Society, 1996.

Neyrey, Jerome H., *Give God the Glory: Ancient Prayer and Worship in Cultural Perspective*. Grand Rapids: Eerdmans, 2007.

———. *The Gospel of John in Cultural and Rhetorical Perspective*. Grand Rapids: Eerdmans, 2009.

———. *Paul, in Other Words: A Cultural Reading of His Letters*. Louiville: Westminster John Knox, 1990.

———, editor. *The Social World of Luke-Acts: Models for Interpretation*. Peabody, MA: Hendrickson, 1991.

Nickelsburg, George W. *Ancient Judaism and Christian Origins: Diversity, Continuity, and Transformation*. Minneapolis: Fortress, 2003.

———. *Jewish Literature between the Bible and the Mishnah: A Historical and Literary Introduction*. 2nd ed. Minneapolis: Fortress, 2005.

Nickle, Keith Fullerton. *The Collection: A Study in Paul's Strategy*. Studies in Biblical Theology 48. Naperville, IL: Allenson, 1966.

Nida, Eugene A. *Good News for Everyone: How to Use the Good News Bible (Today's English Version)*. Waco, TX: Word, 1977.

Nida, Eugene A., and Charles R. Taber, *The Theory and Practice of Translation*. Helps for Translators 8. Leiden: Brill, 1969.

Niebuhr, Barthold Georg. *Lectures on the History of Rome*. Translated by Leonhard Schmitz et al. 3 vols. 2nd ed. London: Taylor, Walton, & Maberly, 1841–1850. Online: http://www.archive.org/details/niebuhrslectureso1niebiala/.

Nock, Arthur Darby. *Conversion*. Oxford: Clarendon, 1933.

———. *Early Gentile Christianity and Its Hellenistic Background*. Harper Torchbooks. Cloister Library. New York: Harper & Row, 1964.

Norden, Eduard. *Agnostos Theos: Untersuchungen zur Formengeschichte religiöser Rede*. Leipzig: Teubner, 1913.

Nutton, Vivian. *Ancient Medicine*. Series of Antiquity. London: Routledge, 2004.

Ong, Walter J. "A Dialectic of Aural and Objective Correlatives." In *20th Century Literary Criticism: A Reader*, edited by David Lodge, 491–508. London: Longman, 1972.

———. *Orality and Literacy: The Technologizing of the Word*. New Accents. London: Routledge, 2002.

———. "A Writer's Audience Is Always a Fiction." In *Interfaces of the Word: Studies in the Evolution of Consciousness and Culture*, by Walter J. Ong, 51–81. Ithaca, NY: Cornell University Press, 1977.

Orton, David E., compiler. *The Synoptic Problem and Q: Selected Studies from Novum Testamentum*. Brill's Readers in Biblical Studies 4. Leiden: Brill, 1999.

Osborne, Grant. "Genre Criticism—Sensus Literalis." *Trinity Journal* 4:2 (1983) 1–27.

———. "Recent Trends in the Study of Apocalyptic." In *The Face of New Testament Studies. A Survey of Recent Research*, edited by Scot McKnight and Grant Osborne, 471–504. Grand Rapids: Baker Academic, 2004.

Osiek, Carolyn. *What Are They Saying about the Social Setting of the New Testament?* Rev. ed. New York: Paulist, 1992.

Osiek, Carolyn, and David L. Balch. *Families in the New Testament World: Household and House Churches*. The Family, Religion, and Culture. Louisville: John Knox, 1997.

O'Toole, Robert F. *Luke's Presentation of Jesus: A Christology*. SB 25. Rome: Biblical Institute Press, 2004.

———. *The Unity of Luke's Theology: An Analysis of Luke-Acts*. Good News Studies 9. Wilmington, DE: Glazier, 1984.

Overman, J. Andrew. "Who Were the First Urban Christians? Urbanization in Galilee in the First Century." *SBLSP* 27 (1988) 161–68.

Paget, James Carleton. "The Definition of the Terms *Jewish Christian* and *Jewish Christianity* in the History of Research." In *Jewish Believers in Jesus: The Early Centuries*, edited by Oskar Skarsaune and Reidar Hvalvik, 21–52. Peabody, MA: Hendrickson, 2007.

Palmer, Frederic. *The Drama of the Apocalypse in Relation to the Literary and Political Circumstances of Its Time*. New York: Macmillan, 1903.

Palmer, Leonard Robert. *The Greek Language*. 1980. Norman: University of Oklahoma Press, 1996.

Parker, D. C. *The Living Text of the Gospels*. Cambridge: Cambridge University Press, 1997.

Parsons, Mikeal C. *Body and Character in Luke and Acts: The Subversion of Physiognomy In Early Christianity*. Grand Rapids: Baker Academic, 2006.

———. *Luke: Storyteller, Interpreter, Evangelist*. Peabody, MA: Hendrickson, 2007.

Patte, Daniel. *Paul's Faith and the Power of the Gospel: A Structural Introduction to the Pauline Letters*. Philadelphia: Fortress, 1984.

Patterson, Stephen J. "Paul and the Jesus Tradition: It Is Time for Another Look." *HTR* 84 (1991) 21–41.

Pearson, Birger A. *Ancient Gnosticism: Traditions and Literature*. Minneapolis: Fortress, 2007.

———. "Basilides the Gnostic." In *A Companion to Second-Century Christian "Heretics,"* edited by Antii Marjanen and Petri Luomanen, 1–31. Supplements to Vigilae Christianae 76. Leiden: Brill, 2008.

———. "Exposé of the Jesus Seminar." *Di* 37:1 (1998) 21–35.

———. "1 Thes 2:11–16: A Deutero-Pauline Interpolation" *HTR* 64 (1971) 71–94.

———. "The Gospel according to the Jesus Seminar." *Religion* 25 (1995) 311–338

Perkins, Pheme. "Gnosticism." In *NIDB*, 2:581–84 (2007).

———. *Gnosticism and the New Testament*. Minneapolis: Fortress, 1993.

———. *Introduction to the Synoptic Gospels*. Grand Rapids: Eerdmans, 2007.

Perowne, Stewart. *The Later Herods: The Political Background of the New Testament*. New York: Abingdon, 1959.

———. *The Life and Times of Herod the Great*. New York: Abingdon, 1956.

Perrin, Norman. *Jesus and the Language of the Kingdom: Symbol and Metaphor in New Testament Interpretation*. Philadelphia: Fortress, 1976.

———. *The Kingdom of God in the Teaching of Jesus*. NTL. Philadelphia: Westminster, 1963.

———. *Rediscovering the Teaching of Jesus*. New York: Harper & Row, 1976.

———. *What Is Redaction Criticism?* GBS. Philadelphia: Fortress, 1969.

Perrin, Norman, and Dennis Duling. *The New Testament: An Introduction: Proclamation and Parenesis, Myth and History*. 2nd ed. New York: Harcourt Brace Jovanovich, 1982.

Pervo, Richard I. *Dating Acts between the Evangelists and the Apologists*. Santa Rosa, CA: Polebridge, 2006.

Peterson, W. L. *Tatian's Diatessaron: Its Creation, Dissemination, Significance and History in Scholarship*. Supplements to Vigilae Christianae 25. Leiden: Brill, 1994.

Petropoulos, J. C. B., editor. *Greek Magic: Ancient, Medieval and Modern*. Routledge Monographs in Classical Studies. London: Routledge, 2008.

Pilch, John J. *Healing in the New Testament: Insights from Medical and Mediterranean Anthropology*. Minneapolis: Fortress, 2000.

———, editor. *Social-Scientific Models for Interpreting the Bible: Essays by the Context Group in Honor of Bruce J. Malina*. Biblical Interpretation Series 53. Leiden: Brill, 2001.

———. *What Are They Saying about the Book of Revelation?* A Deus Book. New York: Paulist, 1978.

Pitt-Rivers, Julian. *The Fate of Shechem; Or, The Politics of Sex*. Cambridge Studies in Social Anthropology 19. Cambridge: Cambridge University Press, 1977.

———. "Honour and Social Status." In *Honour and Shame: The Values of Mediterranean Society*, edited by J. G. Péristiany, 11–77. Chicago: University of Chicago Press, 1966.

Pollard, Justin, and Howard Reid. *The Rise and Fall of Alexandria: The Birthplace of the Modern Mind*. New York: Viking, 2006.

Pomykala, Kenneth E. *The Davidic Dynasty Tradition in Early Judaism: Its History and Significance for Messianism*. SBLEJL 7. Atlanta: Scholars, 1995.

Porter, Stanley E., editor. *The Criteria for Authenticity in Historical-Jesus Research: Previous Discussions and New Proposals*. JSNTSup 91. Sheffield, UK: Sheffield Academic, 2000.

———. "Greek Grammar and Syntax." In *The Face of New Testament Studies: A Survey of Recent Research*, edited by Scot McKnight and Grant R. Osborne, 76–103. Grand Rapids: Baker Academic, 2004.

———, editor. *Handbook of Classical Rhetoric in the Hellenistic Period, 330 BC—AD 400*. Leiden: Brill, 1997.

———, editor, *Handbook to Exegesis of the New Testament*. NTTS 25. Leiden: Brill, 1997.

———, editor. *Hearing the Old Testament in the New Testament*. Grand Rapids: Eerdmans, 2006.

———, editor. *The Language of the New Testament: Classic Essays*. JSNTSup 60. Sheffield: JSOT Press, 1991.

———. "The Parable of the Unjust Steward (Luke 16:1–13): Irony *Is* the Key." In *The Bible in Three Dimensions: Essays in Celebration of Forty Years of Biblical Studies at the University of Sheffield*, edited by David J. A. Clines, et al., 121–53. Sheffield, UK: JSOT Press, 1990.

———. *Paul and His Opponents*. Pauline Studies 2. Leiden: Brill, 2005.

———. *The Paul of Acts: Essays in Literary Criticism, Rhetoric, and Theology*. WUNT 115. Tübingen: Mohr/Siebeck, 1999.

Porter, Stanley E., and Jacqueline C. R. de Roo, editors. *The Concept of the Covenant in the Second Temple Period*. JSJSup 71. Leiden: Brill, 2003.

Porter, Stanley E., and Dennis L. Stamps, editors. *Rhetorical Criticism and the Bible*. JSNTSup 195. London: Sheffield Academic, 2002.

Portier-Young, Anathea E. *Apocalypse Against Empire: Theologies of Resistance in Early Judaism*. Grand Rapids: Eerdmans, 2011.

Powell, Mark Allen. *Jesus as a Figure in History: How Modern Historians View the Man from Galilee*. Louisville: Westminster John Knox, 1998.

———. *What Is Narrative Criticism?* GBS. Minneapolis: Fortress, 1990.

Price, Roberto Salinas. *Homeric Whispers: Intimations of Orthodoxy in the "Iliad" and the "Odyssey."* San Antonio: Scylax, 2006.

———. *Homer's Blind Audience: An Essay on the Iliad's Geographical Prerequisites for the Site of Ilios*. Mexico: Casa Huicalco, 1980.

Puskas, Charles B. *The Conclusion of Luke-Acts: The Significance of Acts 28:11–31*. Eugene, OR: Pickwick Publications, 2009.

———. *The Letters of Paul: An Introduction*. Collegeville, MN: Liturgical, 1993.

———, and David Crump. *An Introduction to the Gospels and Acts*. Grand Rapids: Eerdmans, 2008.

Raisanen, Heikki, *Paul and the Law*. 2nd ed. WUNT 29. Tübingen: Mohr/Siebeck, 1987.

Ranke, Leopold von. *Geschichten der romanischen und germanischen Völker von 1494 bis 1535*. Leipzig: Reimer, 1824.

Rapske, Brian. *The Book of Acts and Paul in Roman Custody*. The Book of Acts in Its First-Century Setting 3. Grand Rapids: Eerdmans, 1994.

Ray, V. "The Formal vs. the Dynamic Equivalent Principle in NT Translation." *ResQ* 25.1 (1982) 41–56.

Reasoner, Mark. *Romans in Full Circle: A History of Interpretation*. Louisville: Westminster John Knox, 2005.

Reddish, Mitchell G., editor. *Apocalyptic Literature: A Reader*. Peabody, MA: Hendrickson, 1995.

Reicke, Bo Ivar. *The New Testament Era: The World of the Bible from 500 BC to AD 100*. Translated by David E. Green. Philadelphia: Fortress, 1974.

———. *The Roots of the Synoptic Gospels*. Philadelphia: Fortress, 1986.

———. "Synoptic Prophecies on the Destruction of Jerusalem." In *Studies in New Testament and Early Christian Literature: Essays in Honor of Allen P. Wilkgren*, edited by David E. Aune, 121–34. NovTSup 33. Leiden: Brill, 1972.

Reinhold, Gotthard G. G., editor. *The Number Seven in the Ancient Near East: Studies on the Numerical Symbolism in the Bible and Its Ancient Near Eastern Environment; Die Zahl Sieben im Alten Orient: Studien zur Zahlensymbolik in der Bibel und ihrer altorientalischen Umwelt*. Berlin: Lang, 2008.

Reitzenstein, Richard. *Hellenistic Mystery-Religions: Their Basic Ideas and Significance*. Translated by John Steely. PittTMS 15. Pittsburgh: Pickwick Publications, 1978.

Reumann, John H. *Four Centuries of the English Bible*. Philadelphia: Muhlenberg, 1961.

———. *Jesus in the Church's Gospels: Modern Scholarship and the Earliest Sources*. Philadelphia: Fortress, 1968.

Rhoads, David M. *Israel in Revolution, 1–74 C.E.: A Political History Based on the Writings of Josephus*. Philadelphia: Fortress, 1976.

Richards, E. Randolph. *Paul and First-Century Letter Writing: Secretaries, Composition, and Collection*. Downers Grove, IL: InterVarsity, 2004.

Richardson, Peter. *Herod: King of the Jews and Friend of the Romans*. Minneapolis: Fortress, 1999.

Riches, John K. "The Synoptic Evangelists and Their Communities." In *Christian Beginnings: Word and Community from Jesus to Post-Apostolic Times*, edited by Jürgen Becker, 211–42. Translated by Annemarie S. Kidder and Reinhard Krauss. Louisville: Westminster John Knox, 1993.

Richlin, Amy. *The Garden of Priapus: Sexuality and Aggression in Roman Humor*. New Haven: Yale University Press, 1983.

Richmond, L. "The Temples of Apollo and Divus Augustus on Roman Coins." In *Essays and Studies Presented to William Ridgeway*, edited by E. C. Quiggin, 191–212. Cambridge University Press, 1913.

Riesenfeld, Harald, *The Gospel Tradition and Its Beginnings: A Study in the Limits of Formgeschichte.* Translated by Margaret Rowley. London: Mowbray, 1957.

———, editor. *The Gospel Tradition and Its Beginnings: A Study in the Limits of Formgeschichte.* Translated by Margaret Rowley and Robert Kraft. 2nd ed. London: Mowbray, 1961.

Riesner, Rainer. *Paul's Early Period: Chronology, Mission Strategy, Theology.* Translated by Doug Stott. Grand Rapids: Eerdmans, 1998.

Riley, Gregory J. "'I Was Thought to Be What I Am Not': Docetic Jesus and the Johannine Tradition." *Occasional Papers Number 31.* The Institute for Antiquity and Christianity, The Claremont Graduate University, 1994.

———. *One Jesus, Many Christs: How Jesus Inspired Not One True Christianity, But Many.* 1997. Reprinted, Minneapolis: Fortress, 2000.

———. *Resurrection Reconsidered: Thomas and John in Controversy.* Minneapolis: Fortress, 1995.

———. *The River of God: A New History of Christian Origins.* New York: HarperCollins, 2003.

Rist, J. M. *Stoic Philosophy.* Cambridge: Cambridge University Press, 1969.

Rist, Martin. "Pseudepigraphy and the Early Christians." In *Studies in New Testament and Early Christian Literature: Essays in Honor of Allen P. Wilkgren,* edited by David Aune, 1–24. NovTSup 33. Leiden: Brill 1972.

Robbins, C. Michael. *The Testing of Jesus in Q.* Studies in Biblical Literature 108. Berlin: Lang, 2007.

Robbins, Vernon K. *Exploring the Texture of Texts: A Guide to Socio-Rhetorical Interpretation.* Valley Forge, PA: Trinity, 1996.

———. *The Invention of Christian Discourse.* Rhetoric of Religious Antiquity Series 1. Blandford Forum, UK: Deo, 2009.

———. *Jesus the Teacher: A Socio-Rhetorical Interpretation of Mark.* Minneapolis: Fortress, 1992.

———. *New Boundaries in Old Territory: Form and Social Rhetoric in Mark.* Emory Studies in Early Christianity 3. New York: Lang, 1994.

———. "The Social Location of the Implied Author of Luke-Acts." In *The Social World of Luke-Acts,* edited by Jerome H. Neyrey, 305–32. Peabody, MA: Hendrickson, 1991.

Roberts, J. H. "Dynamic Equivalence in Bible Translation." *Neot* 8 (1974) 1–20.

Roberts, J. J. M. "The Old Testament Contribution to Messianic Expectations." In *The Messiah: Developments in Earliest Judaism and Christianity,* edited by James H. Charlesworth, 31–51. Minneapolis: Fortress, 1992.

Robinson, James M. *A New Quest of the Historical Jesus.* Studies in Biblical Theology 25. Naperville, IL: Allenson, 1959.

———. "The Q Trajectory: Between John and Matthew via Jesus." In *The Future of Early Christianity: Essays in Honor of Helmut Koester,* edited by Birger A. Pearson, 178–89. Minneapolis: Fortress, 1991.

———. "The Real Jesus of the Sayings Gospel Q." *PSB* 18.2 (1997) 131–51.

Robinson, James M., and Helmut Koester. *Trajectories through Early Christianity.* Philadelphia: Fortress, 1971.

Robinson, J. A. T. *Redating the New Testament.* Philadelphia: Westminster, 1976.

Robinson, Maurice A. "The Case for Byzantine Priority." In *Rethinking New Testament Textual Criticism,* edited by David Alan Black, 125–40. New Testament Studies. Grand Rapids: Baker Academic, 2002.

Robinson, T. A. *The Bauer Thesis Examined: The Geography of Heresy in the Early Christian Church.* SBEC 11. Lewiston, NY: Mellen, 1988.

Roetzel, Calvin J. *The Letters of Paul: Conversations in Context.* 5th ed. Louisville: Westminster John Knox, 2009.

———. *Paul: The Man and the Myth.* Minneapolis: Fortress, 1999.

Rogers, Robert. *A Pyschoanalytic Study of the Double in Literature.* Detroit: Wayne State University Press, 1970.

Rohde, Joachim. *Rediscovering the Teaching of the Evangelists.* Translated by D. Barton. NTL. Philadelphia: Westminster, 1968.

Roisman, Joseph, editor. *Brill's Companion to Alexander the Great.* Classical Tradition. Leiden: Brill, 2002.

Roller, Duane W. *The Building Program of Herod the Great.* Berkeley: University of California Press, 1998.

Roukema, Reimer. *Gnosis and Faith in Early Christianity: An Introduction to Gnosticism.* Translated by John Bowden. Harrisburg, PA: Trinity, 1999.

Royse, James R. "Scribal Tendencies in the Transmission of the Test of the New Testament." In *The Text of the New Testament in Contemporary Research: Essays on the*

Status Quaestionis, edited by Bart D. Ehrman and Michael W. Holmes, 231–52. SD 46. Grand Rapids: Eerdmans, 1995.

Rudolph, Kurt. *Gnosis: The Nature and History of Gnosticism*. Translated by R. McL. Wilson. San Francisco: Harper & Row, 1983.

Ruiz, Jean-Pierre. *Ezekiel in the Apocalypse: The Transformation of Prophetic Language in Revelation 16,11—19,10*. European University Studies, Series 23: Theology 376. Frankfurt: Lang, 1989.

Russell, D. S., editor. "Apocalyptic Literature." Special issue, *CBQ* 39:3 (1977).

———. *Divine Disclosure: An Introduction to Jewish Apcoalyptic*. Minneapolis: Fortress, 1992.

———. *The Method and Message of Jewish Apocalyptic, 200 BC—AD 100*. OTL. Philadelphia: Westminster, 1964.

Russell, Letty M., editor. *Feminist Interpretation of the Bible*. Philadelphia: Westminster, 1985.

Ryle, H. S., and M. R. James, *Psalmoi Solomōntos: Psalms of the Pharisees*. Cambridge: Cambridge University Press, 1891.

Safrai, Shmuel. "Synagogue." In *The Jewish People in the First Century: Historical Geography, Political History, Social, Cultural, and Religious Life and Institutions*, edited by S. Safrai and M. Stern, 2:908–44. CRINT 1/2. Assen: Van Gorcum, 1974–1976.

Safrai, Shmuel, and Menachem Stern, editors. *The Jewish People in the First Century: Historical Geography, Political History, Social, Cultural, and Religious Life and Institutions*. 2 vols. CRINT 1. Assen: Van Gorcum, 1976.

Safrai, Shemuel, and Peter J. Tomson, editors. *The Literature of the Sages*, Vol. 1, *Oral Tora, Halakha, Mishna, Tosefta, Talmud, External Tractates*. CRINT 2: The Literature of the Jewish People in the Period of the Second Temple and the Talmud 3. Assen: Van Gorcum, 1987.

Safrai, Ze'ev. *The Economy of Roman Palestine*. London: Routledge, 1994.

Sampley, J. Paul, and Gerhard Krodel, editors. *The Deutero-Pauline Letters: Ephesians, Colossians, 2 Thessalonians, 1–2 Timothy, Titus*. Rev. ed. Proclamation Commentaries. Minneapolis: Fortress, 1993.

Sanders, E. P. *The Historical Figure of Jesus*. London: Penguin, 1995.

———. *Jesus and Judaism*. Philadelphia: Fortress, 1985.

———. *Jewish Law from Jesus to the Mishnah: Five Studies*. London: SCM, 1990.

———. *Judaism: Practice and Belief, 63 BCE—66 CE*. Philadelphia: Trinity, 1992.

———. *Paul, the Law, and the Jewish People*. Philadelphia: Fortress, 1983.

———. *Paul and Palestinian Judaism: A Comparison of Patterns of Religions*. London: SCM, 1977.

———. *Paul: A Very Short Introduction*. Very Short Introductions 42. Oxford: Oxford University Press, 2001.

Sanders, E. P., and A. I. Baumgarten, editors. *Jewish and Christian Self-Definition*. Vol. 2, *Aspects of Judaism in the Graeco-Roman Period*. London: SCM, 1981.

Sanders, J. A. "Dispersion." In *IDB* 1:854–56.

———. "Torah." In *IDBSup*, 909–11.

Sanders, Jack T. *New Testament Christological Hymns*. SNTSMS 15. Cambridge: Cambridge University Press, 1971.

———. *Schismatics, Sectarians, Dissidents, Deviants: The First One Hundred Years of Jewish-Christian Relations*. Valley Forge, PA: Trinity, 1993.

Sandmel, Samuel. *Herod: Profile of a Tyrant*. Philadelphia: Lippincott, 1967.

———. *Judaism and Christian Beginnings*. New York: Oxford University Press, 1978.

———. "Parallelomania." *JBL* 81 (1962) 1–13.

Sandy, D. Brent. *Plowshares and Pruning Hooks: Rethinking the Language of Biblical Prophecy and Apocalyptic*. Downers Grove, IL: InterVarsity, 2002.

Schiffman, Lawrence H. "At the Crossroads: Tannaitic Perspectives on the Jewish-Christian Schism." In *Aspects of Judaism in the Graeco-Roman Period*, edited by E. P. Sanders and A. I. Baumgarten, 111–56. Jewish and Christian Self-Definition 2. Philadelphia: Fortress, 1980.

———. *From Text to Tradition: A History of Second Temple and Rabbinic Judaism*. Hoboken, NJ: Ktav, 1991.

———. "Priests." In *HBD*, 821–23.

———. *Qumran and Jerusalem: Studies in the Dead Sea Scrolls and the History of Judaism*. Edited by Peter W. Flint, et al. Studies in the Dead Sea Scrolls and Related Literature. Grand Rapids: Eerdmans, 2010.

———. *Reclaiming the Dead Sea Scrolls*. Philadelphia: Jewish Publication Society, 1994.

———. *Texts and Traditions: A Source Reader for the Study of Second Temple and Rabbinic Judaism*. Hoboken, NJ: Ktav, 1998.

———. *Who Was a Jew? Rabbinic and Halakhic Perspectives on the Jewish–Christian Schism*. Hoboken, NJ: Ktav, 1985.

Schlueter, Carol J. *Filling Up the Measure: Polemical Hyperbole in 1 Thess 2:11–16*. JSNTSup 98. Sheffield, UK: JSOT Press, 1994.

Schmidt, Daryl D. "1 Thessalonians 2:11–16: Linguistic Evidence for an Interpolation." *JBL* 102 (1983) 261–79.

———. "The Historiography of Acts: Deuteronomistic or Hellenistic?" *SBLSP* 24 (1985) 417–27.

Schmidt, Karl Ludwig. *Der Rahmen der Geschichte Jesu*. Berlin: Trowizsch, 1919.

———. *The Place of the Gospels in the General History of Literature*. Translated by Bryon R. McCane with introduction by John Riches. Columbia: University of South Carolina Press, 2002.

Schmithals, Walter. *The Apocalyptic Movement: Introduction and Interpretation*. Translated by J. Steely. Nashville: Abingdon, 1975.

———. *Gnosticism in Corinth: An Investigation of the Letters to the Corinthians*. Translated by J. Steely. Nashville: Abingdon, 1971.

———. *The Theology of the First Christians*. Translated by O. C. Dean Jr. Louisville: Westminster John Knox, 1997.

Schneiders, Sandra M. *The Revelatory Text: Interpreting the New Testament as Sacred Scripture*. San Francisco: HarperSanFrancisco, 1991.

Schnelle, Udo. *The Apostle Paul: His Life and Theology*. Translated by M. Eugene Boring. Grand Rapids: Baker Academic, 2005.

———. *The History and Theology of the New Testament Writings*. Translated by M. Eugene Boring. Minneapolis: Fortress, 1998.

———. *Theology of the New Testament*. Translated by M. Eugene Boring. Grand Rapids: Baker Academic, 2009.

Schoedel, William R. *Ignatius of Antioch*. Hermeneia. Philadelphia: Fortress, 1985.

Schoeps, Hans Joachim. *Jewish Christianity: Factional Disputes in the Early Church*. Translated by Douglas R. A. Hare. Philadelphia: Fortress, 1969.

Scholer, David M., editor. *Social Distinctives of the Christians in the First Century: Pivotal Essays by E. A. Judge*. Peabody, MA: Hendrickson, 2007.

Scholtissek, Klaus. "The Johannine Gospel in Recent Research." In *The Face of New Testament Studies: A Survey of Recent Research*, edited by Scot McKnight and Grant R. Osborne, 441–72. Grand Rapids: Baker Academic, 2004.

Schottroff, Luise. *Envisioning the Reign of God through Parables*. Translated by Linda M. Maloney. Minneapolis: Fortress, 2006.

Schroeder, David. "Exhortation in the NT." In *IDBSup*, 303–4.

———. "Paranesis." In *IDBSup*, 643.

Schürer, Emil. *The History of the Jewish People in the Age of Jesus Christ (175 BC—AD 135)*. Revised and edited by Geza Vermes, et al. 3 vols. Edinburgh: T. & T. Clark, 1981–87.

Schüssler Fiorenza, Elizabeth. "Apokalypsis and Propheteia: The Book of Revelation in the Context of Early Christian Prophecy." In *L'Apocalypse johannique et l' Apocalyptic dans le Nouveau Testament*, edited by J. Lambrecht, 101–28. Leuven: Leuven University Press, 1980.

———. *The Book of Revelation: Justice and Judgment*. Philadelphia: Fortress, 1985.

———. "Composition and Structure of the Book of Revelation." *CBQ* 39 (1977) 344–66.

———. "The Followers of the Lamb: Visionary Rhetoric and Social-Political Situation." *Semeia* 36 (1986) 121–46.

Schweitzer, Albert. *The Mystery of the Kingdom of God: The Secret of Jesus' Messiahship and Passion*. Translated by Walter Lowrie from 1901 Ger. ed. New York: Schocken. 1984.

———. *The Quest for the Historical Jesus*. First complete edition by John Bowden. Translated by William Montgomery, Susan Cupitt et al. Fortress Classics in Biblical Studies. Minneapolis: Fortress, 2001.

Schweizer, Eduard. *Church Order in the New Testament*. Translated by Frank Clarke. Studies in Biblical Theology 32. Naperville, IL: Allenson, 1961.

———. "Concerning the Speeches in Acts." In *Studies in Luke-Acts: Essays Presented in Honor of Paul Schubert*, edited by Leander E. Keck and Louis Martyn, 208–16. Nashville: Abingdon, 1966.

Scullard, H. H. *From the Gracchi to Nero: A History of Rome 133 BC to AD 68*. 5th ed. London: Routledge, 1982.

Seager, Robin. *Tiberius*. 2nd ed. Blackwell Ancient Lives. Malden, MA: Blackwell, 2005.

Segal, Alan F. "Heavenly Ascent in Hellenistic Judaism, Early Christianity and Their Environment." In *ANRW* II.23.2 (1980) 1333–94.

Segovia, Fernando F., and Mary Ann Tolbert. *Reading from this Place*. Vol. 1, *Social*

Location and Biblical Interpretation in the United States. Minneapolis: Fortress, 1995.

Sellars, John. *Stoicism*. Ancient Philosophies 1. Berkeley: University of California Press, 2006.

Shanks, Hershel, editor. *Christianity and Rabbinic Judaism: A Parallel History of Their Origins and Early Development*. Washington DC: Biblical Archaeology Society, 1992.

Sheeley, Steven M., and Robert M. Nash Jr. *The Bible in English Translation: An Essential Guide*. Abingdon Essential Guides. Nashville: Abingdon, 1997.

Sherk, Robert K. *The Roman Empire: Augustus to Hadrian*. Translated Documents of Greece and Rome 6. Cambridge: Cambridge University Press, 1988.

Sherwin-White, A. N. *Roman Foreign Policy in the East, 168 BC to AD 1*. Norman: University of Oklahoma Press, 1984.

———. *Roman Society and Roman Law in the New Testament*. 1963. The Sarum Lectures. Grand Rapids: Baker, 1978.

Shipley, Graham. *The Greek World after Alexander 321–30 BC*. New York: Routledge, 2000.

Shires, Henry M. *Finding the Old Testament in the New*. Philadelphia: Westminster, 1974.

Shorey, Paul. *Platonism, Ancient and Modern*. Berkeley University of California Press, 1938.

Shotter, David. *Augustus Caesar*. 2nd ed. Lancaster Pamphlets in Ancient History. London: Routledge, 2005.

———. *Nero*. 2nd ed. Lancaster Pamphlets in Ancient History. London: Routledge, 2005.

Shuler, Philip L. *A Genre for the Gospels: The Biographical Character of Matthew*. Philadelphia: Fortress, 1982.

Silva, Moisés. *Biblical Words and Their Meaning*. Rev. and expanded ed. Grand Rapids: Zondervan, 1994.

———. "Modern Critical Editions and Apparatuses of the Greek New Testament." In *The Text of the New Testament in Contemporary Research: Essays on the Status Quaestionis*, edited by Bart D. Ehrman and Michael W. Holmes, 283–96. SD 46. Grand Rapids: Eerdmans, 1994.

Sim, David C. "The Gospels for All Christians? A Response to Richard Bauckham." *JSNT* 84 (2001) 1–27.

Simon, Marcel. *Jewish Sects at the Time of Jesus*. Translated by James H. Farley. Philadelphia: Fortress, 1967.

Simpson, R. T. "The Major Agreements of Matthew and Luke against Mark." *NTS* 12 (1965–66) 273–84.

Simpson, William Wynn. *Jewish Prayer and Worship: An Introduction for Christians*. London: SCM, 1965.

Skarsaune, Oskar, and Reidar Hvalvik, editors. *Jewish Believers in Jesus: The Early Centuries*. Peabody, MA: Hendrickson, 2007.

Smith, D. Moody. *The Fourth Gospel in Four Dimensions: Judaism and Jesus, the Gospels and Scripture*. Columbia, SC: University of South Carolina Press, 2008.

———. *John among the Gospels: The Relationship in Twentieth-Century Research*. Minneapolis: Fortress, 1992.

Smith, James. *The Voyage and Shipwreck of St. Paul, with Dissertations on the Life and Writings of St. Luke, and the Ships and Navigation of the Ancients*. 4th ed., rev. and cor. by Walter E. Smith. London, Longmans, Green, 1880.

Smith, Mark S. *The Early History of God: Yahweh and the Other Deities in Ancient Israel*. San Francisco: Harper & Row, 1990.

Snodgrass, Klyne R. *Stories with Intent: A Comprehensive Guide to the Parables of Jesus*. Grand Rapids: Eerdmans, 2008.

Soards, Marion L. *The Speeches in Acts: Their Content, Context, and Concerns*. Louisville: Westminster John Knox, 1994.

Song, Changwon. *Reading Romans as Diatribe*. Studies in Biblical Literature 59. New York: Lang, 2004.

Sonne, Isaiah. "Synagogue." In *IDB* 4:480–84.

Southern, Pat. *Domitian: Tragic Tyrant*. London: Routledge, 1997.

Spinks, Leroy C. "A Critical Examination of John Wick Bowman's Proposed Structure of the Revelation." *EvQ* 50 (1978) 211–22.

Spivey, Robert A., and D. Moody Smith. *Anatomy of the New Testament*. New York: Macmillan, 1969.

Squires, John T. *The Plan of God in Luke-Acts*. SNTSMS 76. Cambridge: Cambridge University Press, 1993.

Staley, Jeffrey Lloyd. *The Print's First Kiss: A Rhetorical Investigation of the Implied Reader in the Fourth Gospel*. SBLDS 82. Atlanta: Scholars, 1988.

Stanton, Graham. *Jesus of Nazareth in New Testament Preaching*. SNTSMS 27. London: Cambridge University Press, 1974.

Stark, Rodney. *The Rise of Christianity: A Sociologist Reconsiders History*. Princeton: Princeton University Press, 1996.

Stark, Rodney, and William Sims Bainbridge. *The Future of Religion: Secularization, Revival, and Cult Formation*. Berkeley: University of California Press, 1985.

Stegemann, Hartmut. *The Library of Qumran: On the Essenes, Qumran, John the Baptist, and Jesus*. Grand Rapids: Eerdmans, 1998.

Stegemann, Wolfgang, et al., editors. *The Social Setting of Jesus and the Gospels*. Minneapolis: Fortress, 2002.

Stegner, William R. "The Ancient Jewish Synagogue Homily." In *Greco-Roman Literature and the New Testament*, edited by David E. Aune, 51–69. SBLSBS 21. Atlanta: Scholars, 1988.

———. "Midrash." *JSNT* 22 (1984) 37–52.

———. "Rom 9:1–29—Midrash." *JSNT* 22 (1984) 31–52.

Stein, Robert H. *Gospels and Tradition: Studies on Redaction Criticism of the Synoptic Gospels*. Grand Rapids: Baker, 1991.

———. *Jesus the Messiah: A Survey of the Life of Christ*. Downers Grove, IL: InterVarsity, 1996.

———. "What Is *Redaktions-geschichte*?" *JBL* 83 (1969) 45–56.

Stendahl, Krister. *Paul among Jews and Gentiles, and Other Essays*. Philadelphia: Fortress, 1976.

Sterling, Gregory E. *Historiography and Self-Definition. Josephus, Luke-Acts and Apologetic Historiography*. NovTSup 64. Leiden: Brill, 1992.

Stern, M. "Zealots." In *Encyclopedia Judaica Yearbook*, 135–52. Jerusalem: Encyclopedia Judaica, 1973.

Sternberg, Meir. *The Poetics of Biblical Narrative: Ideological Literature and the Drama of Reading*. Bloomington: Indiana University Press, 1987.

Stevenson, G. H. *Roman Provincial Administration till the Age of the Antonines*. Oxford: Blackwell, 1939.

Still, Todd, and David Horrell. *After "The First Urban Christians": The Socio-Historical Study of Pauline Christianity Twenty-five Years Later*. London: T. & T. Clark, 2009.

Stinespring, William F. "Temple, Jerusalem." In *IDB* 4:534–60

Stirewalt, M. Luther, Jr. *Paul, the Letter Writer*. Grand Rapids: Eerdmans, 2003.

Stock, Augustine. *Call to Discipleship: A Literary Study of Mark's Gospel*. Good News Studies 1. Wilimington, DE: Glazier, 1982.

Stöger, Alois. "Spiritualität der lukanischen Kindheitsgeschichte." *Geist und Leben* 36 (1963) 404–17.

Stone, Jerry H. "Gospel of Mark and *Oedipus the King*: Two Tragic Visions." *Soundings* 67 (1984) 55–69.

Storkey, Alan. *Jesus and Politics: Confronting the Powers*. Grand Rapids: Baker Academic, 2005.

Stowers, Stanley K. *The Diatribe and Paul's Letter to the Romans*. SBLDS 57. Chico: Scholars, 1981.

Strack, H. L., and G. Stemberger. *Introduction to the Talmud and Midrash*. Translated by Markus Bockmuehl. 2nd emended and updated edition. Edinburgh: T. & T, Clark, 1996.

Strand, K. A. "Review of L. L. Thompson, *The Book of Revelation. Apocalypse and Empire*." *AUSS* 29 (1991) 181–90.

———. "Some Modalities of Symbolic Usage in Revelation 18." *AUSS* 24 (1986) 31–46.

Streeter, Burnett Hillman. *The Four Gospels: A Study of Origins, The Manuscript Traditions, Sources, Authorship, and Dates*. London: Macmillan, 1924.

Strelka, Joseph, editor. *Theories of Literary Genre*. University Park, PA: Pennsylvania State University Press, 1978.

Stuckenbruck, Loren. "An Approach to the New Testament through Aramaic Sources: The Recent Methodological Debate." *JSP* 8 (1991) 1–29.

Styler, G. M. "The Priority of Mark." In *The Birth of the New Testament*, edited by C. F. D. Moule, 223–32. *3rd ed. New York: Harper & Row, 1982.*

Sumney, Jerry L. *Identifying Paul's Opponents*. JSNTSup 40. Sheffield: JSOT Press, 1990.

———. "Those Who 'Pass Judgement': The Identity of the Opponents in Colossians." *Biblica 74 (1993) 361–88.*

Sundberg, Albert C. "Bible Canon and the Christian Doctrine of Inspiration." *Int* 29 (1975) 352–71.

———. "Canon Muratori: A Fourth-Century List." *HTR* 66 (1973) 1–41.

———. "The Making of the New Testament Canon." In *The Interpreter's One-Volume Commentary on the Bible*, edited by Charles M. Laymon, 216–24. Nashville: Abingdon, 1971.

———. "The 'Old Testament': A Christian Canon." *CBQ* 30 (1968) 143–55.

Sweeney, Marvin A., and Ehud Ben Zvi, editors. *The Changing Face of Form Criticism for the Twenty-first Century.* Grand Rapids: Eerdmans, 2003.

Talbert, Charles H. "The Concept of Immortals in Mediterranean Antiquity." *JBL* 94 (1975) 419–36.

———. "Prophecies of Future Greatness: The Contribution of Greco-Roman Biographies to an Understanding of Luke 1:5—4:15." In *The Divine Helmsman: Studies on God's Control of Human Events*, edited by James L. Crenshaw and Samuel Sandmel, 129–140. New York: Ktav, 1980.

———. *Literary Patterns, Theological Themes and the Genre of Luke-Acts.* SBLMS 20. Cambridge: Society of Biblical Literature, distributed by Scholars, 1974.

———. *Luke-Acts: New Perspectives from the Society of Biblical Literature Seminar.* New York: Crossroad, 1984.

———. "Prophecy and Fulfillment in Lukan Theology." In *Luke-Acts: New Perspectives from the Society of Biblical Literature Seminar*, edited by Charles H. Talbert, 91–103. New York: Crossroad, 1984.

———. *Reading the Sermon on the Mount: Character Formation and Decision Making in Matthew 1–7.* 2004. Grand Rapids: Baker Academic, 2006.

———. *What Is a Gospel? The Genre of the Canonical Gospels.* Philadelphia: Fortress, 1977.

Tarn, W. W. *Alexander the Great.* Boston: Beacon, 1956.

Tarn, W. W., and G. T. Griffith. *Hellenistic Civilization.* 3rd rev. ed. London: Arnold, 1952.

Tatum, W. Barnes. "The Epoch of Israel: Luke I–II and the Theological Plan of Luke-Acts." *NTS* 10 (1963–64) 184–95.

Taylor, Bernard A., et al., editors. *Biblical Greek Language and Lexicography: Essays in Honor of Frederick W. Danker.* Grand Rapids: Eerdmans, 2004.

Taylor, Vincent. *The Formation of the Gospel Tradition.* London: Macmillan, 1933.

———. *The Formation of the Gospel Tradition.* 2nd ed. London: Macmillan, 1935.

———. "The Origin of the Markan Passion-Sayings." *NTS* 1 (1955) 151–67.

Theissen, Gerd. *The Gospels in Context: Social and Political History in the Synoptic Tradition.* Translated by Linda M. Maloney. Minneapolis: Fortress, 1991.

———. *The Miracle Stories of the Early Christian Tradition.* Translated by Francis McDonagh. Edited by Jon Riches. Philadelphia: Fortress, 1983.

———. *The Religion of the Earliest Churches: Creating a Symbolic World.* Translated by John Bowden. Minneapolis: Fortress, 1999.

———. *The Shadow of the Galilean: The Quest of the Historical Jesus in Narrative Form.* Translated by John Bowden. Minneapolis: Fortress, 1987.

———. *The Social Setting of Pauline Christianity.* Translated by John Bowden. Philadelphia: Fortress, 1982.

———. *Sociology of Early Palestinian Christianity.* Translated by John Bowden. Philadelphia: Fortress, 1978.

Theissen, Gerd, and Annette Merz . *The Historical Jesus: A Comprehensive Guide.* Translated by John Bowden. Minneapolis: Fortress, 1998.

Thiering, Barbara. *Jesus and the Riddle of the Dead Sea Scrolls: Unlocking the Secrets of His Life Story.* San Francisco: HarperSanFrancisco, 1992.

Thiselton, Anthony C. *Hermeneutics: An Introduction.* Grand Rapids: Eerdmans, 2009.

———. *Thiselton on Hermeneutics: Collected Works with New Essays.* Grand Rapids: Eerdmans, 2006.

Thomas, Robert L. *Three Views on the Origins of the Synoptic Gospels.* Grand Rapids: Kregel, 2002.

Thompson, Leonard L. *The Book of Revelation: Apocalypse and Empire.* New York: Oxford University Press, 1990.

———. "A Sociological Analysis of Tribulation in the Apocalypse of John." *Semeia* 36 (1986) 141–74.

Tiede, David L. *The Charismatic Figure as Miracle Worker.* SBLDS 1. Missoula: Scholars, 1972.

———. "'Fighting against God': Luke's Interpretation of Jewish Rejection of the Messiah Jesus." In *Anti-Semitism and Early Christianity: Issues of Polemic and Faith*. edited by Craig A. Evans and Donald Hagner, 101–12. Minneapolis: Fortress, 1993.

Todorov, Tzvetan, *The Fantastic: A Structural Approach to a Literary Genre.* Translated by Richard Howard. CWRU Translations. Cleveland: Press of Case Western Reserve University, 1973.

Tolbert, Mary Ann, editor. *The Bible and Feminist Hermeneutics.* Semeia 28. Chico, CA: Scholars, 1983.

———. *Perspectives on the Parables: An Approach to Multiple Interpretation.* Philadelphia: Fortress, 1979.

Torrey, Charles Cutler. *Documents of the Primitive Church.* New York: Harper, 1941.

———. *The Four Gospels: A New Translation.* New York: Harper, 1933.

Toynbee, J. M. C. *Death and Burial in the Roman World.* Aspects of Greek and Roman Life. Ithaca: Cornell University Press, 1971.

Travis, Stephen H. "Form Criticism." In *New Testament Interpretation,* edited by I. Howard Marshall, 153–64. Grand Rapids: Eerdmans, 1977.

Trobisch, David. *Die Entstehung der Paulusbriefsammlung: Studien zu den Augfängen christlicher Publizistik.* NTOA 10. Frieburg/Schweiz: Universitätverlag 1989.

———. *The First Edition of the New Testament.* Oxford: Oxford University Press, 2000.

———. *Paul's Letter Collection: Tracing the Origins.* Minneapolis: Fortress, 1994.

Trocmé, Etienne. *The Childhood of Christianity.* Translated by John Bowden. London: SCM, 1997.

Troeltsch, Ernest. *The Social Teaching of the Christian Churches.* Translated by Olive Wyon. 2 vols. 1933. Library of Theological Ethics. Louisville: Westminster John Knox, 1992.

Tuckett, Christopher M. *Reading the New Testament: Methods of Interpretation.* Minneapolis: Fortress, 1987.

Twelftree, Graham H. *In the Name of Jesus: Exorcism among Early Christians.* Grand Rapids: Baker Academic, 2007.

———. *Jesus the Miracle Worker: A Historical and Theological Study.* Downers Grove, IL: InterVarsity, 1999.

Ulansey, David. *The Origins of the Mithraic Mysteries: Cosmology and Salvation in the Ancient World.* New York: Oxford University Press, 1989.

Vaganay, Leon, and Christian-Bernard Amphoux. *An Introduction to New Testament Textual Criticism.* Translated by Jenny Heimerdinger. 2nd ed. Cambridge: Cambridge University Press, 1991.

Vallée, Gerard. *A Study in Anti-Gnostic Polemics: Iraneaus, Hippolytus, and Epiphanius.* Studies in Christianity and Judaism 1. Waterloo, ON: Wilfrid Laureier University Press, 1981.

VanderKam, James C. *The Dead Sea Scrolls Today.* 2nd ed. Grand Rapids: Eerdmans, 2010.

———. *From Joshua to Caiaphas: High Priests after the Exile.* Minneapolis: Fortress, 2004.

Vanhoye, Albert. "L'Utilisation du livre d'Ézéchiel dans L'Apocalypse." *Biblica* 43 (1962): 436–76.

Van Nortwick, Thomas. *Somewhere I Have Never Travelled: The Second Self and the Hero's Journey in Ancient Epic.* New York: Oxford University Press, 1992.

Van Seters, John. *In Search of History: Historiography in the Ancient World.* New Haven: Yale University Press, 1983.

Verheyden, Joseph, editor. *The Unity of Luke-Acts.* BETL 142. Leuven: Leuven University Press, 1999.

Vermaseren, M. J. *Cybele and Attis: The Myth and the Cult.* London: Thames & Hudson, 1977.

Vermes, Geza. *The Dead Sea Scrolls: Qumran in Perspective.* Rev. ed. Philadelphia: Fortress, 1981.

———. "Hanani Ben Dosi, Part 1." *JJS* 23 (1972) 21–50.

———. "Hanina Ben Dosi, Part 2." JJS 24 (1973) 51–64.

———. *An Introduction to the Complete Dead Sea Scrolls.* Minneapolis: Fortress, 1999.

———. *Jesus and the World of Judaism.* Philadelphia: Fortress, 1984.

———. *Jesus in His Jewish Context.* Minneapolis: Fortress, 2003.

———. *Jesus the Jew: A Historian's Reading of the Gospels.* London: Collins, 1973. Philadelphia: Fortress, 1981.

———. *The Religion of Jesus the Jew.* Minneapolis: Fortress, 1993.

Verner, David C. *The Household of God: The Social World of the Pastoral Epistles* SBLDS 71. Chico, CA: Scholars, 1983.

Via, Dan O. Foreword to *What Is Form Criticism,* by Edgar V. McKnight, v–viii. GBS. Philadelphia: Forttress, 1969.

———. *Kerygma and Comedy in the New Testament:A Structuralist Approach to Hermenteutic.* Philadelphia: Fortress, 1975.

———. *What Is New Testament Theology?* GBS. Minneapolis: Fortress, 2002.

Viviano, Pauline A. "Source Criticism." In *To Each Its Own Meaning: An Introduction to Biblical Criticisms and Their Application,* edited by Steven L. McKenzie and Stephen R. Haynes, 31–57. Revised and expanded. Louisville: Westminster John Knox, 1999.

Voelz, James. "The Language of the New Testament." In *ANRW* II.25.2 (1984) 891–977.

Votaw, Clyde Weber. *The Gospels and Contemporary Biographies in the Greco-Roman World*. FBBS 27. Philadelphia: Fortress, 1970.

Wagner, J. Ross, et al., editors. *The Word Leaps the Gap: Essays on Scripture and Theology in Honor of Richard B. Hays*. Grand Rapids: Eerdmans, 2008.

Wallace, Daniel B. "The Majority Text Theory: History, Methods, and Critique." In *The Text of the New Testament in Contemporary Research: Essays on the Status Quaestionis*, edited by Bart D. Ehrman and Michael W. Holmes, 297–321. SD 46. Grand Rapids: Eerdmans, 1994.

Wasserstein, Abraham, and David J. Wasserstein. *The Legend of the Septuagint. From Classical Antiquity to Today*. New York: Cambridge University Press, 2006.

Watson, Duane F. *Invention, Arrangement, and Style: Rhetorical Criticism of Jude and 2 Peter*. SBLDS 104. Atlanta: Scholars, 1988.

Weber, Max. *Economy and Society: An Outline of Interpretative Sociology*. Edited by Guenther Roth and Claus Wittich. 2 vols. Berkeley: University of California Press, 1978.

———. *From Max Weber: Essays in Sociology*. Edited, with an introduction by H. H. Gerth and C. Wright Mills with a new preface by Bryan S. Turner. Routledge Classics in Sociology. Milton Park, UK: Routledge, 2009.

Wedderburn, Alexander J. M. *A History of the First Christians*. London: T. & T. Clark, 2005.

Weeden, Theodore J. *Mark—Traditions in Conflict*. Philadelphia: Fortress, 1971.

Weima, Jeffrey A. D. *Neglected Endings: The Significance of the Pauline Letter Closings*. JSNTSup 101. Sheffield: JSOT Press, 1994.

Weingreen, Jacob et al. "Interpretation, History of." In *IDBSup*, 436–49.

Weiss, H. F. "Pharisaios." In *TDNT* 9:1–48.

Wenham, David. "Source Criticism." In *New Testament Interpretation*, edited by I. Howard Marshall, 139–52. Rev. ed. Grand Rapids: Eerdmans, 1979.

Wenham, David, and Craig Blomberg, editors. *Gospel Perspectives: The Miracles of Jesus*. 1986. Reprinted, Eugene, OR: Wipf & Stock, 2003.

Wenham, John. *Redating Matthew, Mark and Luke: A Fresh Assault on the Synoptic Problem*. Downers Grove, IL: InterVarsity, 1992.

Westerholm, Stephen. *Perspectives Old and New on Paul: The "Lutheran" Paul and His Critics*. Grand Rapids: Eerdmans, 2004.

White, John L. *The Form and Function of the Body of the Greek Letter: A Study of the Letter-Body in the Non-Literary Papyri and in Paul the Apostle*. SBLDS 2. Missoula, MT: SBL, 1972.

———. *Light from Ancient Letters*. FF. Philadelphia: Fortress, 1986.

White, L. Michael. *From Jesus to Christianity: How Four Generations of Visionaries and Storytellers Created the New Testament and Christian Faith*. New York: HarperCollins, 2004.

White, William. "Greek Language." In *ZPE* 2: 826–34.

Wiedemann, Thomas. *Greek and Roman Slavery*. 1981. New York: Routledge, 1989.

Wilkinson, Sam. *Caligula*. Lancaster Pamphlets in Ancient History. London: Routledge, 2005.

Williams, Bernard. *Shame and Necessity*. Sather Classical Lectures 57. Berkeley: University of California Press, 1993.

Williams, David J. *Paul's Metaphors: Their Context and Character*. Peabody, MA: Hendrickson, 1999.

Williams, M[argaret]. H. "The Expulsion of the Jews from Rome in AD 19." *Latomus* 48 (1989) 761–84.

Williams, Michael Allen. *Rethinking Gnosticism: An Argument for Dismantling a Dubious Category*. Princeton: Princeton University Press, 1996.

Willis, Wendell, editor. *The Kingdom of God in 20th-Century Interpretation*. Peabody, MA: Hendrickson, 1987.

Wilson, Mark. *Charts on the Book of Revelation*. Kregel Charts of the Bible and Theology. Grand Rapids: Kregel, 2007.

Wilson, Marvin R. *Our Father Abraham: Jewish Roots of the Christian Faith*. Grand Rapids: Eerdmans, 1989.

Wilson, R. McL. *Gnosis and the New Testament*. Philadelphia: Fortress, 1968.

Winter, Bruce W., and Andrew D. Clarke, editors. *The Book of Acts in Its Ancient Literary Setting*. The Book of Acts in Its First-Century Setting 1. Grand Rapids: Eerdmans, 1993.

Wire, Antoinette Clark. *The Corinthian Women Prophets: A Reconstruction through Paul's Rhetoric*. Reprinted, Eugene, OR: Wipf & Stock, 2003.

Wisse, Frederick. "The Epistle of Jude in the History of Heresiology." In *Essays on the Nag Hammadi Texts in Honor of Alexander Böhlig*, edited by Martin Krause, 131–43. NHS 3. Leiden: Brill, 1972.

———. "Historical Method and the Johannine Community." *Arc* 20 (1992) 31–42.

Witherington, Ben, III. *The Jesus Quest: The Third Search for the Jew of Nazareth.* Downers Grove, IL: InterVarsity, 1995.

———. *Jesus the Sage: The Pilgrimage of Wisdom.* Minneapolis: Fortress, 1994.

———. *John's Wisdom: A Commentary on the Fourth Gospel.* Louisville: Westminster John Knox, 1995.

———. *New Testament Rhetoric: An Introductory Guide to the Art of Persuasion in and of the New Testament.* Eugene, OR: Cascade Books, 2009.

Wright, N. T. *The Climax of the Covenant: Christ and the Law in Pauline Theology.* Minneapolis: Fortress, 1991.

———. *Jesus and the Victory of God.* Christian Origins and the Question of God 2. Minneapolis: Fortress, 1996.

———. *The New Testament and the People of God.* Christian Origins and the Question of God 1. Minneapolis: Fortress, 1992.

———. *Paul in Fresh Perspective.* Minneapolis: Fortress, 2005.

———. *The Resurrection of the Son of God.* Christian Origins and the Question of God 3. Minneapolis: Fortress, 2003.

Wuellner, Wilhelm. "Hermeneutics and Rhetorics: From Truth and Method to Truth and Power." Special issue. *Scriptura* 3 (1989) 1–54.

———. "Where Is Rhetorical Criticism Taking Us?" *CBQ* 49 (1987) 448–63.

Yadin, Yigael. *Bar-Kokhba: The Rediscovery of the Legendary Hero of the Second Jewish Revolt against Rome.* New York: Random House, 1971.

———. *Masada: Herod's Fortress and the Zealots' Last Stand.* Translated by Moshe Pearlman. Jerusalem: Steimatzky, 1984.

Yamaunchi, Edwin M. *Pre-Christian Gnosticism: A Survey of the Proposed Evidences.* 2nd ed. Twin Books Series. Grand Rapids: Baker, 1983.

Yeo, Khiok-khng, *What Has Jerusalem To Do with Beijing? Biblical Interpretation from a Chinese Perspective.* Harrisburg, PA: Trinity, 1998.

Ysebaert, J. *Greek Baptismal Terminology: Its Origins and Early Development.* Nijmegen: Dekker & Van de Vegt, 1962.

Zadok, Ran. *The Earliest Diaspora: Israelites and Judeans in Pre-Hellenistic Mesopotamia.* Tel Aviv: Tel Aviv University Diaspora Research Institute, 2002.

Zahn, Theodor. *Introduction to the New Testament.* Translated by John M. Trout, William A. Mather, et al. 3 vols. 1909. Minneapolis: Klock & Klock, 1977.

Zoch, Paul A. *Ancient Rome: An Introductory History.* Norman: University of Oklahoma Press, 1998.

Zuntz, Gunther. *The Text of the Epistles: A Disquisition upon the Corpus Paulinum.* The Schweich Lectures of the British Academy, 1946. Oxford: Oxford University Press, 1953.

Index of Ancient Texts

Acts

246

Index of Modern Authors

Ackroyd, Peter R., 28n3, 28n5, 29n8, 65n3, 260n9, 267n25, 268n28

Adam, A. K. M., 102n39

Adrados, Francisco Rodriguez, 54n2

Aland, Barbara, 63nn1–2, 65n4, 66n7, 67nn8–9, 67nn10–11, 68n12, 69nn14–15, 70n19, 71nn20–21, 72, 73, 74n27, 277n18, 278

Aland, Kurt, 63nn1–2, 65n4, 66n7, 67nn8–9, 67nn10–11, 68n12, 69nn14–15, 70n19, 71nn20–21, 72, 73, 74n27, 277n18, 278

Alexander, Loveday C. A., 24n46, 108n12, 109n13, 221n41, 246n7

Alexander, P. S., 218n31

Algra, Keimpe, 246n7

Allison, Dale C., 170n3, 171n5, 172n6, 174n16, 177n24, 219n36

Alter, Robert, 101n38

Amphoux, Christian-Bernard, 63n2, 68n12, 69n14, 69nn16–17, 70n18

Anderson, Bernhard W., 38n48

Arav, Rami, 34n28, 39n54, 43n67, 171n5

Archer, Gleason L., 85n8

Arnim, Hans Friedrich August von, 23n44

Arnold, Clinton E., 230n6

Athanassakis, Apostolos, 113n21

Attridge, Harold W., 106n8

Aulen, Gustav, 171n5

Aune, David E., 15n28, 47n75, 107n10, 108nn11–12, 111n15, 111n17, 113n21, 114n23, 120n35, 123n45, 137n6, 141n9, 142n10, 145nn4–5, 146n8, 147n12, 150n21, 151n25, 211n17, 252n13

Austin, M. M., 4nn3–4, 6n5, 13n23

Avi-Yonah, Michael, 47n77

Bagnall, Roger S., 93n23

Bailey, James L., 97n33, 111n17

Bailey, John A., 222n42

Bailey, Kenneth E., 78n1

Baird, William, 84n7

Balch, David L., 97n33, 229n3, 253n14

Balsdon, J. P. V. D., 9n18

Balthasar, Hans Urs von, 123n45

Baltzer, Klaus, 113n21

Bammel, Ernst, 183n3

Baras, Zvi, 47n77

Barker, Kenneth L., 279n25

Bar-Kochva, Bezalel, 6n8, 25n47

Barnstone, Willis, 19n39

Barr, David L., 113n21, 115n28, 151n22

Barr, James, 107n9, 191n17